The Other Husserl

STUDIES IN CONTINENTAL THOUGHT

John Sallis, general editor

The Other Husserl

The Horizons of Transcendental Phenomenology

Donn Welton

Indiana University Press

Bloomington and Indianapolis

This book is a publication of

Indiana University Press
601 North Morton Street
Bloomington, IN 47404-3797 USA

http://www.indiana.edu/~iupress

Telephone orders 800-842-6796
Fax orders 812-855-7931
Orders by e-mail iuporder@indiana.edu

The paper used in this publication meets the minimum requirements of American National Standard for Information Sciences—Permanence of Paper for Printed Library Materials, ANSI Z39.48-1984.

Manufactured in the United States of America

Library of Congress Cataloging-in-Publication Data

Welton, Donn.
The other Husserl : the horizons of transcendental phenomenology / Donn Welton.
p. cm.
Includes bibliographical references and index.
ISBN 0-253-33795-X (cl : alk. paper)
1. Husserl, Edmund, 1859–1938. 2. Phenomenology. I. Title.

B3279.H94 .W453 2000
193—dc21

00-038906

1 2 3 4 5 05 04 03 02 01 00

For
Joan Griffin Welton
and
Curtis Columbia Welton

Those who are wise shall shine
Like the brightness of the firmament,
And those who turn many to righteousness
Like the stars forever and ever

—Daniel 12:3

Contents

Part 3. Constructions: Toward a Phenomenological Theory of Contexts

Acknowledgments

I AM ESPECIALLY grateful to two, shears in hand, who spent long hours assisting with the revisions and editing of this gangling vine of a book. Both Lanei Rodemeyer and Gina Zavota showed exceptional understanding of the project and unusual patience with the difficulties of my text as they sought to prune its ever spreading branches into fruitful form. I can only hope that the final outcome merits their hard labor. Ms. Zavota went yet a second mile by undertaking the reading and correcting of the proofs of this volume, for which I am greatly in debt to her. Julia Jansen and Steve Michelman offered valuable assistance as well, and for this I am most appreciative. There is no doubt that the final preparation of this volume would not have been possible without the extraordinary ability and hard labor of Melanie Richter-Bernburg, manuscript editor at Indiana University Press; for this I thank her.

I have learned much not only about the thought of Husserl but also about the task of philosophy from colleagues in Germany, especially Klaus Held, Manfred Frank, and Martin Lang. Klaus Held was also most helpful in discussing the design of this project in its early stages. There are colleagues at Stony Brook as well who have contributed to the formation of this book, such as David Allison, Kenneth Baynes, Edward Casey, Jeffrey Edwards, Don Ihde, and Mary Rawlinson.

The Husserl Archives in Leuven, Belgium, under the direction of Rudolf Bernet, has graciously granted the right to cite several of Husserl's manuscripts. I especially appreciate the help of Berndt Gossens, a co-worker in the Archives, in supplying the most up-to-date transcriptions of the manuscript materials I cite in chapters 5 and 6, for providing valuable background information on them and for checking my accuracy. Sebastian Luft, another co-worker, has also extended me gracious assistance on a number of occasions, for which I am most grateful. I also thank Dan Zahavi, who read parts of the manuscript in draft and offered valuable criticisms.

Work on this particular project began during a research year at the University of Tübingen and concluded during a sabbatical at Oxford University. My thanks to Klaus Hartman, now deceased, and Rom Harré for their help in making the necessary arrangements. In addition to the Husserl Archives at

Leuven, I also thank the Husserl Archives at the University of Köln, under the stewardship of Dieter Lohman, and at the University of Freiburg, where I was assisted by Sabina Mödersheim, for providing access to manuscript materials.

I have long been puzzled by acknowledgments that begin with apologies to one's wife and kin for time spent away from the hearth. Had I chosen to neglect them, the book might have been finished in half the time but, I imagine, would have been half as good. Instead, it begins with appreciation for the encouragement offered by Radina, Spencer, Kendra, Lianne, and José all the more as it came from ones who stand tall and who have taught me more than I have them.

List of Abbreviated Titles

WORKS BY EDMUND HUSSERL

Whenever available, references to both the original German text and the English translation will be given. If the translation is cited as "after [English title]" or "after Eng. trans.," the wording of the English translation is being directly quoted. The phrase "[English title] modified" or "Eng. trans. modified" means that the English text is being reproduced but with certain changes or corrections. Citations of the German text accompanied by either "[English title]" or "Eng. trans." without qualification mean that the translation belongs to the author and the English text is given for the sake of reference.

Analysen zur passiven Synthesis	*Analysen zur passiven Synthesis: Aus Vorlesungs- und Forschungsmanuskripten 1918–1926.* Edited by Margot Fleischer. *Husserliana,* Vol. 11. The Hague: Martinus Nijhoff, 1966.
Aufsätze und Vorträge (1911–1921)	*Aufsätze und Vorträge (1911–1921).* Edited by Thomas Nenon and Hans Rainer Sepp. *Husserliana,* Vol. 25. Dordrecht: Martinus Nijhoff, 1987.
Aufsätze und Vorträge (1922–1937)	*Aufsätze und Vorträge (1922–1937).* Edited by Thomas Nenon and Hans Rainer Sepp. *Husserliana,* Vol. 27. Dordrecht: Kluwer Academic Publishers, 1989.
Bedeutungslehre	*Vorlesungen über Bedeutungslehre: Sommersemester 1908.* Edited by Ursula Panzer. *Husserliana,* Vol. 26. Dordrecht: Martinus Nijhoff, 1987.
Briefwechsel	*Briefwechsel.* Edited by Karl Schuhmann in connection with Elisabeth Schuhmann. *Husserliana Doku-*

	mente, Vol. 3. Dordrecht: Kluwer Academic Publishers, 1994.
Cartesianische Meditationen	*Cartesianische Meditationen und Pariser Vorträge.* Edited by Stephen Strasser. *Husserliana,* Vol. 1. The Hague: Martinus Nijhoff, 1963.
Cartesianische Meditationen; Eng. trans.	*Cartesian Meditations: An Introduction to Phenomenology.* Translated by Dorion Cairns. The Hague: Martinus Nijhoff, 1960.
Ding und Raum	*Ding und Raum: Vorlesungen 1907.* Edited by Ulrich Claesges. *Husserliana,* Vol. 16. The Hague: Martinus Nijhoff, 1974.
Die Idee der Phänomenologie	*Die Idee der Phänomenologie: Fünf Vorlesungen.* 2nd ed. Edited by Walter Biemel. *Husserliana,* Vol. 2. The Hague: Martinus Nijhoff, 1958.
Einleitung in die Logik	*Einleitung in die Logik und Erkenntnistheorie: Vorlesungen 1906/1907.* Edited by Ulrich Melle. *Husserliana,* Vol. 24. The Hague: Martinus Nijhoff, 1984.
Erfahrung und Urteil	*Erfahrung und Urteil: Untersuchungen zur Genealogie der Logik.* Edited by L. Landgrebe. Prague: Academia-Verlag, 1938; Hamburg: Claasen, 1954.
Erfahrung und Urteil; Eng. trans.	*Experience and Judgment: Investigations in a Genealogy of Logic.* Translated by James Churchill and Karl Ameriks. Evanston, Ill.: Northwestern University Press, 1973.
Erste Philosophie I	*Erste Philosophie (1923/24).* Part 1: *Kritische Ideengeschichte.* Edited by Rudolf Boehm. *Husserliana,* Vol. 7. The Hague: Martinus Nijhoff, 1956.
Erste Philosophie II	*Erste Philosophie (1923/24).* Part 2: *Theorie der phänomenologischen Reduktion.* Edited by Rudolf Boehm. *Husserliana,* Vol. 8. The Hague: Martinus Nijhoff, 1959.

Formale und transzendentale Logik	*Formale und transzendentale Logik: Versuch einer Kritik der logischen Vernunft.* Edited by Paul Janssen. *Husserliana,* Vol. 17. The Hague: Martinus Nijhoff, 1974.
Formale und transzendentale Logik; Eng. trans.	*Formal and Transcendental Logic.* Translated by Dorion Cairns. The Hague: Martinus Nijhoff, 1969.
Ideen I	*Ideen zu einer reinen Phänomenologie und phänomenologischen Philosophie.* Vol. 1: *Allgemeine Einführung in die reine Phänomenologie. Jahrbuch für Philosophie und phänomenologische Forschung,* Vol. 1. Halle a.d. Saale: Max Niemeyer, 1913. Pp. 1–323.
Ideen I; Eng. trans.	*Ideas Pertaining to a Pure Phenomenology and to a Phenomenological Philosophy.* Book 1: *General Introduction to a Pure Phenomenology.* Translated by F. Kersten. *Collected Works,* Vol. 2. The Hague: Martinus Nijhoff, 1983.
Ideen I (Hua)	*Ideen zu einer reinen Phänomenologie und phänomenologischen Philosophie.* Vol. 1: *Allgemeine Einführung in die reine Phänomenologie.* Edited by Karl Schuhmann. *Husserliana,* Vol. 3/a. The Hague: Martinus Nijhoff, 1976.
Ideen II	*Ideen zu einer reinen Phänomenologie und phänomenologischen Philosophie.* Vol. 2: *Phänomenologische Untersuchungen zur Konstitution.* Edited by Marly Biemel. *Husserliana,* Vol. 4. The Hague: Martinus Nijhoff, 1952.
Ideen II; Eng. trans.	*Ideas Pertaining to a Pure Phenomenology and to a Phenomenological Philosophy.* Book 2: *Studies in the Phenomenology of Constitution.* Translated by Richard Rojcewicz and André Schuwer. *Collected Works,* Vol. 3. Dordrecht: Kluwer Academic Publishers, 1989.
Ideen III	*Ideen zu einer reinen Phänomenologie und phänomenologischen Philosophie.* Vol. 3: *Die Phänomenologie*

	und die Fundamente der Wissenschaften. Edited by Marly Biemel. *Husserliana,* Vol. 5. The Hague: Martinus Nijhoff, 1952.
Ideen III; Eng. trans.	*Ideas Pertaining to a Pure Phenomenology and to a Phenomenological Philosophy.* Book 3: *Phenomenology and the Foundations of the Sciences.* Translated by Ted Klein and William Pohl. *Collected Works,* Vol. 1. The Hague: Martinus Nijhoff, 1980.
Intersubjektivität I	*Zur Phänomenologie der Intersubjektivität. Erster Teil: 1905–1920.* Edited by Iso Kern. *Husserliana,* Vol. 13. The Hague: Martinus Nijhoff, 1973.
Intersubjektivität II	*Zur Phänomenologie der Intersubjektivität. Zweiter Teil: 1921–1928.* Edited by Iso Kern. *Husserliana,* Vol. 14. The Hague: Martinus Nijhoff, 1973.
Intersubjektivität III	*Zur Phänomenologie der Intersubjektivität. Dritter Teil: 1929–1935.* Edited by Iso Kern. *Husserliana,* Vol. 15. The Hague: Martinus Nijhoff, 1973.
Krisis	*Die Krisis der europäischen Wissenschaften und die transzendentale Phänomenologie: Eine Einleitung in die phänomenologische Philosophie.* Edited by Walter Biemel. *Husserliana,* Vol. 6. The Hague: Martinus Nijhoff, 1954.
Krisis; Eng. trans.	*The Crisis of European Sciences and Transcendental Phenomenology: An Introduction to Phenomenological Philosophy.* Translated by David Carr. Evanston, Ill.: Northwestern University Press, 1970.
Logische Untersuchungen (1st ed.)	*Logische Untersuchungen.* [1st ed.] 2 vols. Halle a.d. Saale: Max Niemeyer, 1900 and 1901.
Logische Untersuchungen	*Logische Untersuchungen.* 2nd rev. ed. 2 Vols. Halle a.d. Saale: Max Niemeyer, 1913 and 1921.

Logische Untersuchungen; Eng. trans.	*Logical Investigations.* Translated by J. N. Findlay. 2 vols. New York: Humanities Press, 1970.
Phänomenologische Psychologie	*Phänomenologische Psychologie: Vorlesungen Sommersemester 1925.* Edited by Walter Biemel. *Husserliana,* Vol. 9. The Hague: Martinus Nijhoff, 1968.
Phänomenologische Psychologie; Eng. trans.	*Phenomenological Psychology: Lectures, Summer Semester, 1925.* Translated by John Scanlon. The Hague: Martinus Nijhoff, 1977.
Philosophie der Arithmetik	*Philosophie der Arithmetik: Mit ergänzenden Texten (1890–1901).* Edited by Lothar Eley. *Husserliana,* Vol. 12. The Hague: Martinus Nijhoff, 1970.
Shorter Works	*Husserl: Shorter Works.* Edited by Peter McCormick and Frederick Elliston. Notre Dame, Ind.: University of Notre Dame Press, 1981.
Zeitbewusstsein	*Zur Phänomenologie des inneren Zeitbewusstseins (1893–1917).* Edited by Rudolf Boehm. *Husserliana,* Vol. 10. The Hague: Martinus Nijhoff, 1966.
Zeitbewusstsein; Eng. trans.	*On the Phenomenology of the Consciousness of Internal Time (1893–1917).* Translated by John Brough. *Collected Works,* Vol. 4. Dordrecht: Kluwer Academic Publishers, 1991.

WORKS BY OTHERS

Conversations	Cairns, Dorion. *Conversations with Husserl and Fink.* Edited by Richard Zaner. *Phaenomenologica,* Vol. 66. The Hague: Martinus Nijhoff, 1976.
Prolegomena	Heidegger, Martin. *Prolegomena zur Geschichte des Zeitbegriffs.* Frankfurt am Main: Vittorio Klostermann, 1979.

Prolegomena; Eng. trans.	Heidegger, Martin. *History of the Concept of Time.* Translated by Theodore Kisiel. Bloomington: Indiana University Press, 1985.
Sein und Zeit	Heidegger, Martin. *Sein und Zeit* [1928]. Tübingen: Max Niemeyer, 1967.
Sein und Zeit; Eng. trans.	Heidegger, Martin. *Being and Time.* Translated by John Macquarrie and Edward Robinson. New York: Harper and Row, 1962.

The Other Husserl

Introduction
Thinking about Husserl

From what rests on the surface [*dem Oberflächlichen*] one is led into the depths.
—Husserl (1936)[1]

I am in a much worse situation than you because the greatest part of my work is stuck in my manuscripts. I almost curse my inability to bring my works [*mich*] to an end and that first quite late, partly only now, the universal, systematic thoughts have come to me, which, though demanded by my previous, particular investigations, now also compel me to rework them all. Everything is in the stage of recrystallization! Perhaps I am working, with all the humanly possible expenditure of energy, only for my posthumous works.
—Husserl to Natorp (1922)[2]

A. READINGS OF HUSSERL

What could be further apart than the agendas and the goals of analytic philosophy and deconstructive thinking? While both take their bearings from a certain privileging of language, they have divergent interests, approaches and results. And even if we recognize that today neither possess anything like a canonical methodology, the styles of analysis are so radically different that even with good will they *could* not share anything in common. It comes, therefore, as no small surprise that in reading the recent interpretations of Husserl by these two schools we find a striking convergence between their representations of his phenomenological program. No doubt they have different ends in view, and we should not confuse the highly qualified appropriation of Husserl by analytically inclined interpreters with the disenfranchisement of both his theory and his method by deconstructive thinkers. But as we read deeper the general representations of Husserl with which they both work are close enough to fit together into what I call the standard picture. This work provides an alternative to the standard picture. It is an effort to portray the "other" Husserl.

My account of the various interpretations of Husserl will be restricted here to an appendix,[3] and, as the work gets under way, to some of the notes.

(The reader interested in a more detailed account of the secondary literature might turn to the appendix after finishing this paragraph.) This book is an attempt to understand the full scope of Husserl's method by dealing with his ceaseless formulations and reformulations of the phenomenological project, a task made even more complex for us because we want to move beneath a surface reading of his various theories into their inner logic, their internal motivations, their own intentional structure. If I allow this study to be drawn into a detailed confrontation with the literature on Husserl, I fear that, given its sheer mass and proliferation of distinctions, we will spend our day plodding along paths with overgrown hedges, unable to survey the entire landscape as a whole. Still, there is yet another reason, more cogent, for restricting my direct discussion of the standard picture to this appendix and, with only a few exceptions, barring it from the body of this study. This volume is an effort to reconstruct not a part or a certain strain of Husserl's phenomenology but the method as a whole. And it does so in terms of oppositions and contrasts that are, for the most part, missing from or displaced in the standard picture. My quarrel ultimately is not with details but with shared frameworks, not with particular strands but with whole tapestries. Or, to move closer to the interpretative flaw generally at work, my disagreement is not with analyses of sections of the tapestry but with the confusion of certain sections with their backing and, as a consequence, with the corresponding lack of a proper understanding of how those parts are held together by the whole. It will never do just to pull certain threads and substitute ones of a different color. Rather, my reconstruction must attempt to reweave the whole, step by step, in the hope of discovering a strength, a range, a depth, even a system not yet envisioned. Yet a third reason for this way of proceeding follows from the second: in my analysis I am interested not only in getting Husserl right, in the accuracy of my reconstruction, but also in getting philosophy right, in the viability of what will amount to a significant expansion of what is normally meant by transcendental phenomenology. Since the standard picture, I believe, gives us at best a truncated version of the scope of phenomenological method, we will have to cut new ground in our efforts to understand not only its inner logic (Part 1) but also its plausibility (Part 2) and its promise (Part 3).

This study, then, aims to provide not so much a refutation as an alternative to the standard portrait of Husserl. To do so, we must take Husserl "whole cloth," a task incredibly difficult with a thinker as complex and prolific as Husserl. My reading is necessarily schematic. While I touch on some of the more specialized issues, I do so only to deal with the larger and more basic question of Husserl's phenomenological method. It will not do to show that he changed a particular aspect of his theory, that he enlarged his notion of time or changed his concept of evidence, for example, for we are concerned with the architectonic, not particular doctrines. My strategy will be to argue that Husserl's Cartesian formulation of his method is a first rather than a final formulation and that he moves beyond its confines when he comes to expand his method through a *systematic* distinction between "static" and "genetic" phenomenological analysis. I will attempt to show that the difference between static and genetic phenomenology gives this "other" Husserl methodological resources that both his followers and his critics think are excluded in principle.[4]

At the same time, this will be a *philosophical* reading that is concerned with the question of the power and the viability of the project of transcendental phenomenology. If we catch a glimpse of the true scope and range of Husserl's method, we also begin to see gaps and tensions. Our account of its contours (Part 1) will blend into immanent critique (Part 2) as we also attempt to find, in his many working manuscripts and in his restless writings of the 1920s and 1930s, the sense in which Husserl became his own "other."

The goal of this study is to raise the account of Husserl's phenomenological method, both its scope and its limits, to a new level and, in so doing, make viable a certain appropriation of it that draws upon its special strengths. It is more than an argument about Husserl interpretation, for my hope is that a proper reconstruction of his phenomenological method may provide *Leitfaden* guiding us beyond some of our present uncertainties. With the development of a genetic method and, thereby, a systematic phenomenology, and with the introduction of his all-important notion of horizons, Husserl becomes the first transcendental philosopher to directly confront the question of *contexts.* After using this notion to reframe the notion of the world and after sorting out the relationship between Husserl and Heidegger on this issue, we will turn to the implications of this notion for the theory of meaning (Part 3).

Fortunately, our approach can draw from the work of several thinkers who have worked extensively on both Husserl's published and unpublished materials and who have challenged what I am calling the standard picture on certain crucial points. The first groundbreaking study opening new insight on the question of method was Ludwig Landgrebe's "Husserl's Departure from Cartesianism,"[5] which was a detailed analysis appearing in 1962 of *Erste Philosophie,* the then recently published lectures of Husserl on foundational questions of method, which he gave in 1923 and 1924. This was followed by yet other important studies, which continue to be neglected by the proponents of the standard picture, that investigated certain aspects of Husserl's thought in the light of his later texts, such as Klaus Held's study of temporality,[6] Elmar Holenstein's treatment of association,[7] Paul Janssen's and David Carr's accounts of history,[8] Vásquez Hoyos's investigation into teleology,[9] and Guido de Almeida's discussion of the theory of perception.[10] John Drummond raises important questions about Husserl's notion of intentionality and, through this, about his foundationalist program.[11] While not focusing on the issue of genetic analysis per se, Robert Sokolowski also has given us lucid analyses of several features of Husserl's method, such as eidetic insight, eidetic variation, and the role of his methodological solipsism. These studies are rich and attuned to what Husserl himself took to be central issues.[12]

These thinkers, however, tended to handle the question of method only in connection with the issues they were investigating. To my knowledge only four insightful studies, published since Landgrebe's article, confronted the question of method directly beyond the limits of the standard picture, but three of them are introductory. The fuller study is by Antonio Aguirre.[13] Introductory analyses are offered by David Carr,[14] a more recent account by Klaus Held,[15] and the most recent by Rudolf Bernet, Iso Kern, and Eduard Marbach.[16] Each is lucid, and the reader will find several points in my discussion acknowledging its debt to them. But apart from the fact that this will be the first study in English devoted entirely to reconstructing Husserl's method as a whole, this account will differ from theirs in that it forces the issue of systematicity, argues for a distinction between constitutive and genetic analysis, and challenges the coherence of Husserl's analysis. One new, important work that genuinely breaks new ground and that can be understood as complementary to my analysis, taking off from where the first part of my study concludes, is the lucid study recently published by Anthony Steinbock.[17] In addition, there are very important historically focused studies by Iso Kern,[18] and an exceptionally detailed and helpful chronicle by Karl Schuhmann[19]—both of which will be used extensively at certain critical junctures—that now allow us to accurately trace the course of thinking in Husserl's manuscripts between 1910 and 1936. Dorion Cairns's discussions with Husserl are especially suggestive for the years 1931 and 1932.[20] Finally, Eugen Fink's reworking of the *Cartesian Meditations* and the masterful studies of the relationship between Fink and Husserl by Ronald Bruzina prove invaluable in placing Husserl's program as a whole.[21]

B. THE QUESTION OF TEXTS

We should, of course, give the published works a central place in any interpretation of Husserl but, at the same time, weigh them as Husserl himself did. Let me use certain difficulties with Husserl's published *corpus* as a way of introducing the reading I want to propose. If we take the *Logical Investigations* (1900–1901),[22] *Ideas I* (1913),[23] and *Formal and Transcendental Logic* (1929)[24] as Husserl's primary published works, it is noteworthy that there are huge time gaps between them, especially the last two, and that each of these volumes provides us with another "introduction" to phenomenology. Each sets as its goal a general typography of subjectivity but understood as "logical reason."[25] In view of this, it is not surprising that the basic methodological framework for these studies is what Husserl calls "static phenomenology." We will find in the coming chapters, however, that "beneath" these publications—but often within them, especially the last two—Husserl worked extensively on genetic issues in his manuscripts. The forerunners of his genetic analyses are his wide-ranging lectures on space and time (between 1905 and 1910),[26] written before the publication of *Ideas I*. These studies are complemented and deepened by manuscript studies written after *Ideas I* as well (between 1918 and 1920).[27] It can also be shown that the lectures and working manuscripts now collected as *Analysis of Passive Synthesis* (written between 1918 and 1926), Husserl's first sustained attempt at a genetic account of perception and a genealogy of logic, originally were placed in the "Preparatory Considerations" of *Formal and Transcendental Logic*.[28] Husserl assumed that these studies could be taken for granted and excluded them from any consideration in that work, which focused its analysis on the structure of logic. Only in the appendices did he return to genetic issues. We have already mentioned lectures in *Erste Philosophie*, given in 1925, that involve extensive reflections on method. Interestingly, Husserl never published the *Cartesian Meditations* in German, only in a French translation (1931), as we will discuss at length in chapters 5 and 6, for he set his own extensive revisions of that text aside and left further work on them to Fink[29] in order to devote time to those manuscripts now known as *The Crisis*. Whatever the difficulties, whatever the complications, we are *driven* to these manuscripts if we ever hope to capture the whole range of Husserl's phenomenology.

In addition to the fact that Husserl designed all three works as introductions, there is a thick story to be told about each. *Ideas I* was written in a flurry of intense labor, lasting only a few months.[30] He comes to view it as a stepping stone. In a letter to Roman Ingarden in 1921 Husserl says that he regrets that Ingarden had not come to Freiburg at a later date than he did[31] in order to participate in the

> four intensive lecture semesters. Then you would have fully viewed my horizons. Indeed, I have come so much further. Even though I would not overthrow *Ideas I* (only many particular analyses that remain behind [the level of] my manuscripts), I have still taken the systematic much further and purified much in all principle matters [*in allen Prinzipiellen*].[32]

In referring to his lecture courses of this period he is clearly referring to his lectures on transcendental logic, first given in the Winter Semester of 1920/21 and partially published in *Analysis of Passive Synthesis*, a text that will be of central importance to our reconstruction of his method. We will introduce it in chapter 2. In any case, these comments, supported by others cited in chapters 2, 5, and 6 of this study, are enough to warn us against the attempt by analytic commentators to turn *Ideas I* into the definitive statement of Husserl's method.

Something similar needs to be said, parenthetically, about the *Phenomenology of the Consciousness of Internal Time,* published in 1928, a text central to Derrida's critique of Husserl's philosophy of presence. While it is a topical study and does not directly deal with method, it is also an early text, derived almost entirely from lecture manuscripts composed between 1905 and 1910. It came into being as the result of the editorial work of Edith Stein in 1917 and Martin Heidegger in 1926.[33] Bernet has done a masterful job of discussing the textual difficulties with the edition, showing that (1) the use of the notion of *Urimpression* in Part 1 is already corrected and transcended by texts from 1910 that should have been integrated into the published version, and (2) that the texts underwent a definite evolution in their formulation of the problem as a whole between 1893 and 1917 that is not reflected by the published edition.[34] In addition, the crucial studies known as the Bernauer manuscripts on time, which Husserl marked for publication, are yet to be published. Finally, Husserl himself was rather unhappy with both Heidegger's editing and his introduction. Cairns, on the basis of personal conversation, reports on Husserl's attitude toward them as follows:

> The difficulty of seeing the place of the earlier time-lectures in the whole system is the chief source of Husserl's dissatisfaction with their publication at the time with Heidegger's insufficient introduction.[35]

> Husserl sorry the time lectures were published as they were. If Fink had been here then, they would have worked them together with the later time lectures.[36]

Formal and Transcendental Logic (1929) was written in a mere two or three months. Husserl began in either November or December of 1928 and finished the following January.[37] Perhaps the need to prepare what we now call his Paris lectures, a pair of double lectures that he gave at the Sorbonne on February 23 and 25, 1929, kept him from looking back at the *Logic* and beginning the process of revision that usually insured that the text being revised would become buried and never make it into print. But a better explanation is that this was satisfactory as another introductory text and, in addition, employed certain ideas—such as the notions of critique, interest, and intersubjectivity—that are central to his mature thought. In fact, it is surprising how little attention has been given to this work by analytic, deconstructive, and critical theory interpreters.

One way of seeing these published works is to treat them as slices out of

Husserl's ongoing labors that either had the unusual fortune of coming together and then being whisked off to the publisher before he began reconceptualizing them or that he decided were satisfactory for introductory purposes. If that is the case, we cannot draw a firm line between the published and the unpublished materials, though we will clearly want to attend to the variable quality of the manuscripts.

The Paris lectures given in 1929, however, did not share the same good fortune as the *Logic.* Though he had decided to publish them and had produced a highly expanded and changed version for translation into French, which appeared as his *Méditations cartésiennes* in 1931, he quickly became unhappy with that version and started further revisions. As we will see in chapters 5 and 6, the result was that the *Cartesian Meditations* were never released in German, which means that what we now have bearing the title *Cartesianische Meditationen* is precisely the text that Husserl decided not to publish, even though he did not hesitate to recommend the French version for beginners.

Still, the strongest justification for turning to the manuscripts is found in Husserl's own expressed view of them. The sixteen years between the publication of *Ideas I* (1913) and *Formal and Transcendental Logic* (1929) were Husserl's most productive, and the amount that he wrote in that period is hardly comprehensible. But it all remained in manuscript form. Not to attend to these texts, the most important of which are carefully worked out lectures that cost him exceptional energy and as much time as his published works, sometimes more, only condemns us to ignorance of Husserl's most fruitful period of research. At the same time, however, it was also a period of immense frustration. Time and again, Husserl drew up publication plans, about which we will speak later in this work. Yet each plan fell by the wayside as new problems drew his attention away from those to which he had already devoted hundreds of pages of writing. It seems that only the rapid writing and subsequent publication of *Formal and Transcendental Logic* (1929), itself prompted by Landgrebe's editorial work on Husserl's countless manuscripts on logic and what finally became *Experience and Judgment* (1938), broke the cycle. But it came to print the year after Husserl retired from his professorship at Freiburg. Husserl comments on the extreme difficulty of these years in a letter to Alexander Pfänder in 1931:

> In the attempt to correct the drafts, quickly recognized as inadequate, to the second and third part of my *Ideas* (from the Fall of 1912) and to configure the horizons of problems open there in a much more differentiated and concrete fashion, I become caught up in new, highly comprehensive investigations (phenomenology of the person and of personalities of higher order, culture, the human surrounding world in general, transcendental phenome-

> nology of "empathy" and theory of transcendental intersubjectivity, "transcendental aesthetic" as phenomenology of the world purely as world of experience, time and individuations, phenomenology of association as theory of the constitutive achievements of passivity, phenomenology of the logos, phenomenological problematic of "metaphysics," etc.). These investigations persisted through the Freiburg years [1916–1928], which were full of labor, the manuscripts growing to a measure that could scarcely be managed. Time and again the concern grew as to whether I, at my age, could bring all this entrusted to me to a conclusion. The labor, full of ardor, led to ever new repercussions and ever new depressions. Finally, there remains a general, depressed basic mood, a dangerously sunken self-trust.[38]

No doubt his rigorous standards and relentless probing were combined with the fact that he was a pioneer cutting new paths in terribly unfamiliar terrain. Together they kept his work in a constant state of reformulation, forcing him ever to return to another beginning. He lived and even suffered under this, as we can also see in a letter to Natorp from 1922, the period when he was at work on a systematic phenomenology:

> I am in a much worse situation than you because the greatest part of my work is stuck in my manuscripts. I almost curse my inability to bring my works [*mich*] to an end and that first quite late, partly only now, the universal, systematic thoughts have come to me, which, though demanded by my previous, particular investigations, now also compel me to rework them all. Everything is in the stage of recrystallization! Perhaps I am working, with all the humanly possible expenditure of energy, only for my posthumous works.[39]

Any question as to whether a proper interpretation of Husserl's method can do without the manuscript materials, rarely consulted in the standard interpretation, is settled by Husserl's letter to Adolphe Grimme written in 1931: "Indeed, the largest and, as I actually believe, most important part of my life's work still lies in my manuscripts, scarcely manageable because of their range."[40]

Though we are still awaiting the publication of Husserl's Bernauer manuscripts on time and a critical edition of the lectures he gave in London in 1922, the appearance in the last decade of several new volumes in Husserl's collected works has made available important texts from the fertile period between 1918 and 1930. But what is especially important for our analysis and what helps us place the manuscripts on which he labored during the period is the fact that his correspondence has just been published in ten volumes.[41] We will use it extensively in our reconstruction of the way genetic analysis was situated in Husserl's plans for a comprehensive "systematic phenomenology."

Among those scholars who do recognize the centrality of the manuscripts, some have been tempted to see the difference between Husserl's static and genetic analyses as a contrast between the early and the late Husserl. No doubt the difference between static and genetic analysis was not clearly articulated in Husserl's first writings. Often there are strands or traces that employ the difference, but only incompletely, always with a certain mixture. But, as we just indicated, each of the themes that the genetic analysis of the 1920s brings to light refers back to yet earlier manuscripts. Husserl, for example, excluded any consideration of the question of temporality in *Ideas I* not because such studies did not exist but because his static method is a synchronic, structural account and, thus, rests upon a suspension of any consideration of temporal constitution. Our approach in this work will be to understand certain distinctions and exclusions in the earlier work as place holders for the studies that Husserl had already begun to draft and that he extends or undertakes in the 1920s, to understand these new texts not as reversals but as uncovering a depth, constantly being transformed, supporting that ground or field upon which Husserl labored in his published works.

At the same time, the goal before us to is to understand Husserl's development not chronologically but systematically, or, if you will, to understand the chronology in terms of the developing systematicity of his method.[42] As we will discover, this is no small task. Simply to compile an analysis of relevant texts in sequence will not do, for as Dummett reminds us, "the history of ideas is full of developments that cannot be explained by historical enquiries of the usual sort."[43] We must engage in a form of what the later Husserl himself began to think of as "depth history." For it requires us to dismantle, layer by layer, the various levels of Husserl's account, using the one controlling image he was so fond of, that of stratification, as the working picture of how his own thought was put together. Often the strata are fused or mixed together, as is true of most geological layers that undergo periodic upheaval or are exposed to the surface and the elements. But sometimes we can uncover stretches when they are clearly separated and can see the differences. Yet all of this is further complicated by the fact that this was a process of sedimentation in reverse, not one that built "up" from earlier to later but one that built "down" from later to earlier. Accordingly, our reconstruction, to be appropriate, must engage in a form not of *Aufbauen,* as though Husserl's own philosophical development moved from an unchanged foundation to a secure edifice resting on it, but of *Abbauen,* of progressively uncovering the underlying strata on which that foundation itself rests, of searching for the ground of the foundation, if you will. If we take this approach, then the introduction of genetic phenomenology, I will suggest, represents neither an abandonment of Husserl's static framework nor a patchwork that attempts to cover tears in the original fabric, but a systematic and deeper analysis of that very foundation upon which his "introductory," static analyses rest. If I am correct, we will find a certain scope to Husserl's phenomenological method to which analytic interpreters are blind and a certain depth to his transcendental analysis that deconstructive thinkers believe impossible. And we will find a method whose range and vitality we are only beginning to comprehend.

PART ONE

Contours: The Emergence of Husserl's Systematic Phenomenology

Husserl in St. Märgen, 1921. Courtesy of Husserl-Archief te Leuven.

1

The Phenomenological Turn

I can do no other than honestly say (assuming that I am not already confused through superficially acquired theories): I now see things, these things here, they themselves; I do not see images of them, nor mere signs. Obviously I can also be deceived. But on what basis does it prove to be deception? On the basis of a reliable seeing, tested time and again, that is a seeing of real things themselves [*Sachen selbst*]. To say that all seeing is a deception negates the sense of talking about deception.

—Husserl (1922/23)[1]

External perception is a standing pretension to accomplish something that it, according to its own essence, is not in a position to achieve. Thus, to a certain extent, it harbors an essential contradiction.

—Husserl (early 1920s)[2]

When Husserl asked me if I had any questions I brought up the question of how convincing a *motivation* to the performance of the phenomenological epoché can be *before* that epoché itself and the development of phenomenology itself, with its insight into the nature of evidence.

Husserl replied by developing certain considerations which can occupy us in the natural attitude: I am in the world, the world appears to me in a multitude of experiences and other acts, and what the world *is* for me is always a world which is valid [*geltend*] in my own subjectivity.

—Cairns (1931)[3]

A. PERCEPTUAL LACK

What gives rise to phenomenological analysis is an unsettling wonder in the presence of things, which themselves come to us through certain modes or manners that are not themselves objects.

In the late afternoon we enter the courtyard of a small farm nested in the Swabian Alb. The scent of cows and horses, centuries old it seems, envelops us. The frame house, barn, and tool sheds, with their crumbling plaster walls laced with beams, surround an old iron water pump that seems to mark the center of the earth. The pump catches our attention, for this is what we are seeking.

"There's the old water pump I told you about," our friend cries out, greatly relieved. The side facing us is a mixture of dark brown, red, rust, and age. As we slowly walk around it the dark brown is lost momentarily beneath a green moss, only then to blend back to brown and red on the side that now faces the sun. The beads of water clinging to the spout assure us that with a few cranks of the handle this silent monument will suddenly spring to life, quenching the thirst that always follows a day in the fields.

The object, we might say, has many "looks," many "profiles," yet they are all profiles of the same object. Normally we attend only to the pump and, with the tired farmer, to the water that it graciously provides for us. In our preoccupation with the object, the profiles, while seen, are "unthematic" and our attention moves beyond them to the object itself. It requires a certain distancing from our needs and a certain reflection upon the way in which the thing is present to us to realize expressly that this object, like all others, is always manifest in a certain way, always given in and through its particular profiles. The side facing us, while not the object, is the side *of* the pump. The profiles, we might say, are not the object but the way in which the object is present.

No doubt we can reorganize the event and turn the side facing us into a thing to which we attend and, further, about which we speak. The side of the pump with its moss may be exactly what we are looking for. Perhaps we have learned to take our bearing from this. Thus there is always the possibility that the side of the thing would become the thing upon which we focus. Yet even here that side, now the "thematic" object, is also present in and through certain profiles or aspects necessarily "unthematic": its spongy texture, moist surface, and musty smell, while not in focus, form the manner or ways in which the side of the thing is given. Interestingly, the reverse is equally possible, and what was first an object can become the manner in which something else is manifest: as we first entered the archway the pump itself was but one of the profiles in and through which the courtyard was present. The operative difference between profile and object, then, obtains even when sides become things and things become sides.[4] Since all objects of experience are given in and through profiles, all objects are given "perspectivally." This suggests we have a difference in which our relationship to things is itself constitutive.

Things, however, are not just given perspectivally but also typically, or rather are given typically in and through their perspectivity. The water pump we find in the courtyard is not completely alien to us nor is it just a buzzing confusion of impressions and sensations. Had we never seen this particular water pump, there would be little difficulty in recognizing it for what it is. Even if we did not, there would still be some typical determination exhibited by the object and its profiles, enabling us to distinguish *this* object from *that* one over there. In the interplay of object and profiles, things unfold their typical manners of presence. They appear *as* this type of object and not that, as things of one sort in contrast to another. Since types are exhibited in the interplay of profile and object, they, too, suggest that a connection to the perceiver is constitutive. When I see the pump as rusty, its shape as beautiful, its water as desired, its arm as a handle, these determinations appear as "part" of the object but in such a way that my relationship to it is directly implied. The typical way in which the object appears to us, as well as the transition from profile to profile, carry, in their wake, the realization that they are dependent upon the activities of walking around the object, of coming close or backing off, of seeing it, of simply enjoying the object, or of attempting to use it.

Because the profiles are unthematic in the course of our ordinary experience of objects, their relationship to objects is quite naturally "forgotten." This obtains not only for ordinary experience, where we are occupied with the things of our immediate concerns, but also for philosophical theories that level the difference between profile and object or acknowledge it without recourse to a notion of perspectivity. Frege's groundbreaking treatment of concepts or logical predicates as functions can be understood as the latter, as an effort to do justice to the difference between objects and profiles but without invoking the relationship to the subject as a constitutive aspect of its clarification. In Frege's theory a logical predicate term (his concept-word) does give us the determination of the object. This determination he calls the manner of givenness of the object, setting it in contrast to the object itself, named by the logical subject term (his proper name). But this effort to contrast the object and its manner of givenness fails in the final analysis because while predicates (concepts) are clearly different from objects, they logically determine objects only by establishing correlations between the object named by the logical subject and objects of yet another set (the extension of the concept). The distinction between object and profile is reduced to a relation between objects in different sets and thus lost.[5]

Phenomenological analysis builds upon differences in phenomena. The interplay of identity and difference displayed by appearances and their situated and perspectival composition calls for an account in which the one to whom the object appears is a basic factor in the description. This is achieved by a change in our interest or focus: in contrast to the "straightforward attitude," in which we are directed toward and fully occupied with the objects of our everyday concerns, a "reflection" upon the perceiver is introduced that attends to those silent or invisible achievements and those recurring patterns involved in an object being apprehended in this and not that way. With this the "forgetting" of subjectivity is overturned.

Given the fact that in perception our attention is normally focused on the whole object itself, when we inspect the perceptual object carefully we are surprised to discover that only one of its profiles is actually or directly present to us. Much of what we perceive is, by contrast, co-present, co-given, co-intended. Even more surprising is the fact that what is directly present is also shot through with absence and can itself undergo further perceptual investigation. Perception, Husserl tells us, is "according to its own sense a direct grasping of the object itself [*Selbsterfassung*]." Yet

> it is no less, according to its own sense, pre-grasping [*vorgreifend*]—the pregrasp is concerned with the co-intended—and radically so: even in the content of the directly grasped in a given moment of perception there lie moments of the pre-grasp. Basically, nothing in the perceived is purely and adequately perceived.[6]

What is present necessarily includes what is absent, i.e., there is no pure presence. Even "if we consider perception abstractly, by itself," Husserl emphasizes some ten years later,

> we find its intentional accomplishment to be presentation, making something present: the object gives itself as "there," originally there, present. But in this presence, as that of an extended and enduring object, lies a continuity of what I am still conscious of, what has flowed away and is no longer intuited at all, a continuity of "retentions"—and, in the other direction, a continuity of "protentions."[7]

The relationship between profiles and objects we have been describing is itself unintelligible without recourse to two correlative but interdependent moments of the experience in which objects are manifest. On the one hand, there are typically different "achievements" (*Leistungen*) or "acts" (*Akte*) that attend the appearing object and, within these acts, an interplay of perception and apperception, of grasping and fore-grasping, of retention and protention. On the other hand, the object manifest in and through its profiles displays a certain invariant pattern or a reidentifiable "determination," what Husserl calls a "sense" (*Sinn*).[8] Later I will argue that the sense is what organizes the profiles internally into a coherent series of presentations of the object. Thus the interplay of profile and object that gives a thing its particular presence is explained phenomenologically by recourse to the "correlation" of achievement and sense. This correlation, manifest only in reflection, constitutes the *manifest* structure of what Husserl will call intentionality.

The determinations of perceptual objects are affected not only by the internal relationship between profiles but also by the "background" or what Husserl discovered as the "horizon" situating the object. If one of our fellow hikers finds a fire in the horse barn, not only is a new chain of associations suddenly brought into play as we scramble for pails and buckets and frantically draw water but the pump itself is immediately alive with additional features quite removed from our initial perception of it. New experiences with new senses are in play. Even when we have objects other than the water pump in focus, this changed background enriches the presence of the pump and, thereby, introduces further determinations of the object.

An act is not itself a thing related to the water pump but an achievement accounting for the appearing of the water pump. It exists as an object only in and for the act of reflection. As it functions it belongs to a different domain, for it subsists as a condition of the presence of objects, not as an object. At the same time objects cannot be divorced from an internal relation to the acts in and through which they achieve presence. Characterizing acts in this way overcomes that opposition between objectivism and subjectivism, cut, as it is, from a single piece of cloth, controlling philosophical discourse up to Kant and recurring with surprising frequency today. Siding with Frege, Husserl agrees that existing objects, whether fish, facts, or finite numbers, are independent of our mental images or pictures as well as the vicissitudes of our personal and political life. Departing from Frege, he argues that the articulated presence of such independent and transcendent objects can be clarified only by describing both the mode or manner in which they are present and the structure of those achievements in which they are so exhibited. There is a genuinely new conception of mental acts in play here, one not altogether easy to grasp. On the one hand, acts do not belong to a closed interior realm available only to introspection. Rather, they have their being by virtue of their relationship to that which transcends them. On the other hand, the determinations of "the given" can be fully clarified only by seeing them in relation to certain acts that contribute to their configuration. It is neither the subject nor the object but the relationship that is primary. In Husserl's account, objectivity is taken as an essential correlate of human achievements. At the same time subjectivity is introduced not to dissolve or to replicate internally but rather to ground and secure objectivity. We will circle back on these provisional descriptions in the next couple of chapters.

Let us return to our experience of the water pump before the stable caught fire and continue our description. In viewing the pump, each side I see sets up anticipations of the sides not yet seen. The hidden side thus becomes "intended." On the basis of our present and past experience, we expect the backside will also be rust brown with red specks. As we walk around the pump this intention is then "fulfilled." Even though we can describe what the act intends apart from its fulfillment, the fulfillment, we may even say, is the goal of the act. And, in a way that sometimes surprises us, it immediately sets up new anticipations of its own in view of yet other fulfillments. Even if our intention is "disappointed" and we find the backside to be mossy green, not rust brown, there is still a fulfillment of one of the open possibilities latent in our initial perception, even as it immediately corrects our first anticipation. This fulfillment, too, sets up further anticipations of the determinations of the pump, which, for their part, draw our perceptions along a course not of their own choosing. Acts of perception are not simple events. They not only exhibit this interplay of intending and fulfilling but also are organized in such a way that they actively reach toward fulfillment. In Husserl's theory, intentional acts have both a fixed correlative and a dynamic actional structure resulting from their being drawn toward ever richer experiences of that which never fully shows itself.

B. BROKEN SPEECH

Reality, as understood by phenomenology, is not a seamless fabric without flaws. It contains its own possibilities of illusion, strife, dissonance. It exists, as Merleau-Ponty says, somewhere, in the interrogative mode, possessing its own ineluctable gaps and fissures, stumbling stones and pitfalls, shadows and shades, startles and surprises. It is never simply received but always grasped, the movement of *fassen* being always nested in *erfassen* or *auffassen;* never just registered but always reached, the movement toward it is necessary for it to come to us. As Husserl recognized especially in his late thought, unity is never read directly from things but is a dynamic achievement in the face of a presence that can never be divorced from absence, of a revealing that is simultaneously a concealing.

Because a number of studies have criticized Husserl for privileging visual perception and overgeneralizing its features, we should emphasize that his first entrance to phenomenological analysis, found in his groundbreaking *Logical Investigations* (1900–1901), was not through a study of visible objects but invisible speech. If we combine his analysis there with later studies undertaken in his 1908 lectures on theory of meaning[9] and in *Formal and Transcendental Logic* (1929), we can discover grounds for the phenomenological turn that do not rely on acts of vision and the notion of appearance.

In our narrative above there are a number of reports about the shape, the parts, and the colors of a water pump situated in the middle of a courtyard. Notice that the reports refer or at least purport to refer. They also convey information about the pump even though it is not now present to us. You, the reader, have never seen the pump. In fact, it might not even exist. If presented with an example, though, you would be able to say, within limits, whether it "fits" the object as described. This immediately suggests that in a theory of assertions about empirical objects, recourse to something more than an associative link or a truth-conditional connection between physical signs and physical objects is required if we are to understand the information borne by linguistic strings.

In the course of conversation our attention is usually fixed on the referent being described, not on the information being disseminated or even on the one communicating. Much as profiles are unthematic in our straightforward perceptual involvement with the pump, so our reports about the pump are themselves transparent; they are effaced, so to speak, under the weight of the facts they bring to expression. Usually some disturbance in the course of our experience or some breakdown in communication must occur before we focus upon the reports themselves. Maybe the pump is not where I said it was. Perhaps you know that I am colorblind and thus treat some of my report as unreliable. Or you might even be a linguist or cultural anthropologist, not a thirsty hiker, and have no interest at all in the pump or its clear water but exclusively in the different semantic or symbolic fields surrounding our descriptions of it.

When disruptions of this kind enter, speech itself and what it conveys become thematic. The normal flow of discourse is inhibited as we no longer "naively" believe the facts reported. A certain type of reflection sets in. To stay with our case of assertions, we frame the report our friend first offered as a claim. We shift our attention to the proposition that the speaker was making in the "broken" act of reporting, and query its truth or falsity, whether it fits the facts or not.[10] This engenders a crucial distinction between the *meaning* or content of the report, i.e., the fact as intended or proposed, and the *referent*, the existing objects and facts that would make the proposal true. Since a proposition can be well formed and meaningful even when false, a definition of propositional content cannot be achieved by identifying it with sets of objects and/or facts, though clearly its content must give us a way of deciding between different candidates. In fact, there is little difficulty in contrasting the content "expressed" by two conflicting proposals even when neither refers.

Encountering this difference between meaning and referent moves us to consider certain achievements of the speaking subject and to note a basic alteration in his or her attitude as constitutive. When our friend first points out the water pump to us we are not preoccupied with questions of truth and falsity. Her utterances fit into that celebration in words that give such afternoon walks their spirit and life. The joy of finding the water pump provokes her descriptions. They function not to represent but to present. We accept the facts as reported and begin to look for our tin cups. All of us share the same "posture" or "attitude" (*Einstellung*) toward what is being reported, an attitude that Husserl calls "belief." The facts as reported are accepted as givens. But this can quickly change. Discord in either the reports themselves or the manifest facts can set in. Belief turns to disbelief, confidence in the reports to bewilderment. It is not a water pump at all but a benzene tank for farm equipment. The report is no longer accepted but reframed as her belief, her shaky proposal. The disruptions in our "naive" involvement with reported fact, then, bring about not only the thematization of reports as propositions but also an awareness of the attitudes or acts supporting this difference.

The reflection upon reports and their thematization as propositions calls for an account that incorporates a description of speech-acts as one of its constitutive conditions. Notice that the acts themselves need not be referred to or given expression in the propositional content. In direct speech they silently attend, only themselves coming to our awareness when things go awry. But they are nevertheless constitutive. "Broken" speech, then, refocuses our attention away from the reported world to the correlation between claims and the attending speech-acts, between the content of meaningful signs and subjectivity.

Husserl attempts to capture the way contents and acts become thematic in communication by contrasting the "expressive" and the "indicating" operations of signs. In the First Investigation he dwells on intersubjective discourse only long enough to isolate the former and to show us how we can dispense with the latter. In making this contrast he offers us a crucial insight about normal discourse that supplements our present analysis.

When our friend makes her report about the pump, we are immediately directed to it and its cool water. But the report may not, to our surprise, fit our experience. We are thereby thrown back upon what she is saying, on what she is claiming. We turn, in Husserl's terminology, from the referents to the meaning of the string, and to the proposition that the string "expresses" (*ausdrucken*). If we speak of referents as "real" objects in space and time, then meanings can be called "ideal" in the sense that spatial and temporal coordinates are not essential to their existence, and in the sense that they can be described without identifying them with real objects or sets of real objects. Of course, with Husserl's interest in logic and the foundations of truth, this is precisely the quarry he is seeking.

At the same time he notices that speech sets much more to flight. In addition to expressing, signs also "indicate" (*anzeigen*) or "intimate" (*kundgeben*). Although her joy or attitude of belief is not referred to by what our friend says, and though it is not found when we reflect upon its expressed literal content, the string, much like smoke signals fire, *points* the listener to the attitude that enframes and the acts that frame the assertion. On the one hand, construing her report as a claim is possible because we take her act as one of proposing or maintaining a claim, not issuing a command, asking a question, or beginning a prayer. On the other hand, we detect *within* her act of proposing two nested activities of referring and predicating, of pointing to or identifying a referent and then "determining" it in predicates. Significantly, it is possible to have a number of different act-modalities or what Husserl calls "thetic qualities" with the same activities of referring and predicating and the same propositional content as their core. Over half a century later Austin and Searle came to call these two noetic levels the illocutionary and the locutionary force of the assertion.[11] The phenomenon of indication, always interwoven with that of expressing in communicative discourse, brings us before the speaker's acts and thus we have a second bridge to phenomenological analysis.[12]

The two bridges we have built thus far have carried us into an analysis of acts. The first uses the difference between strings and assertions as its starting point and invokes an analysis of attitudes to clarify that contrast. The second augments this by dealing directly with signs in communication and tracks down a difference between what they express and what they indicate. A third bridge, which we can only sketch, begins with an interesting feature of propositional content itself. It is possible to have differences in the references and thus the truth-conditions of a given proposition even if we have the same illocutionary and locutionary force in correlation to the same literal meaning. Something more is needed in our account if we are to do justice to this feature of speech. Imagine the disastrous consequences, for example, if a hair stylist confused "wash" in the context of "dirty clothes," "detergent," and "washing machine" with the same word in the context of "shampoo," "hair," and "pamper." We are not dealing here with a literal meaning and a metaphorical meaning, as we would be if we said, "Our hair stylist took a wash at the race track" or "His words of encouragement washed away my cares." Rather, we have the same literal meaning in place but different truth-conditions by virtue of the word's relationship to different *contexts* that are not an explicit feature or part of its expressed content. This third bridge, then, transports us beyond a particular correlation of act and meaning into its implicit context.

At this point, our way into phenomenological analysis through speech rejoins the path we initially took through perception. Background, we will say in the third part of this study, is the field of senses in terms of which the sense of the object is situated; context is the field of meanings in terms of which the meaning of a given segment of speech is placed. They are, in principle, latent and not manifest moments constitutive of the relationship between acts and objects. As we will see, the analysis of the interrelationship between background and context provides the key to the *depth* structure of intentionality in Husserl's phenomenology.

C. PHENOMENA

Our approach to objects calls for an interpretation that takes their relationship to the subject, and to the context in which they are situated, as constitutive of their actual or potential being. To understand objects in this way is to comprehend them as *phenomena,* not as appearances that we would place in opposition to reality, as Kant's difference between the phenomenal and the noumenal requires, but as a reality that appears. Everything that can be named or thought exists potentially for us. Its in-itself is internally tied to its for-us. Philosophically, approaching things as phenomena requires us to return to their presence, to the original way in which they are given, and to overturn those theoretical accounts that have come to confuse higher-order scientific or philosophical constructions and models with their primary being. The tall water pump as we first encounter it is not a bare particular serving as a logical substrate for concepts such as "steel," "rusty," and "water," nor is the water dropping from its spout first manifest as a mathematized entity, as a sphere with uniform surface tensions having every point equidistant from a fixed center point. Rather the pump and the cool water it offers us are alive with significance that must be understood in irreducibly experiential terms, in terms of *quality*. In the final analysis this is why phenomenology sees itself as a *descriptive* discipline.[13] While quality cannot be explained or prescribed according to rules, it can be clarified by attending to the differentiated structure exhibited by phenomena. This structure is fourfold:[14]

1. All objects are determinate objects, which is to say that as phenomena they come forth *as* something. The *as-structure* is not the result of an act of interpretation subsequent to the appearing of objects but rather is that "fold" in phenomena that allows them to appear. In Husserl and Heidegger's language this fold is called the *sense* of the object. Husserl speaks of it as the "What" of the phenomenon,[15] constitutive of its presence before the onset of the work of interpretation. Heidegger works with this same contrast between the object and its sense but restricts the "What" to a property drawn from, and thus attached to, the object as present-at-hand. This property is thus a modification of the original sense structure of things found in the context of our pretheoretical involvement with them.[16]

2. The sense is determinative of the articulated presence of phenomena. But significance requires that there be one *for* whom the object has meaning. The *for-structure* is not added to the as-structure but rather is the condition of its being. The "What" of the object is internally tied to the "How" of its appearing which, for its part, owes its being to the modalities of the for-structure.[17]

3. Phenomena appearing as determinate for us do so in a certain clearing that allows them to come forth. They come to light in an open dimension where they show themselves. Involvement in a context is that which sets them free to come forth as what they are for us.[18] This dimension is not itself an appearing phenomenon but that in which all appearing takes place. As such it constitutes the *in-structure* of phenomena.

4. The one *for* whom phenomena appear is the one *to* whom they are given. They appear to us in a clearing, which entails that they appear *from* a dimension that is not cleared, from what remains hidden, from the darkness circumscribing each clearing. In each new clearing, in each new approach, it ever withdraws. The *from-structure* arises with the in-structure yet lies in a

dimension that itself can never be brought into view in the same way as the in-structure.

The breakthrough achieved in Husserl's phenomenology was to discover the essential interrelationship between the as- and the for-structure. Its genius, however, was to then connect the as-structure and for-structure to the in-structure. The sense of the object, which constitutes its determinate presence, is not only the manner in which the object is thematized in corresponding acts of apprehension; it is also internally related to an unthematized *web* of senses. Senses are not themselves ideas located in either the world of things (Realism) or the world of the mind (Conceptualism). Rather, the web of senses is made up of multiple ways of experientially assimilating relevant objects in contexts. This web articulates the in-structure; as such it is called *horizon.* The horizon of all horizons is the *world.* The seminal insight of Husserl's phenomenology, contrary to the standard picture, was not that it offered us an analysis of consciousness but that it saw that an analysis of consciousness simultaneously brings forth and is impossible apart from an analysis of the world.

The horizon is both *ground* (*Boden*) and *end* (*Telos*). It is ground in that particular sense-determinations of an object depend upon the horizon for their specificity and, perhaps, generation. The horizon is an *end* in that experience effects a unification of perspectives or profiles in view of a sense that always exceeds what is given. When the structural description of horizon as nexus of implicated senses is expanded by a genetic account, phenomenological method becomes both an archeology and a teleology of meaning. It is this dimension of Husserl's thought, as we will see in the coming chapters, that is the key to the full scope of his philosophical method.

The from-structure, however, is left underdetermined by Husserl. He accepts a moment of hiddenness, but only for what he calls "the natural attitude." Just as the natural attitude cannot characterize subjectivity as transcendental, so its characterizations of the world reduce it to an entity. Thus the worldhood of the world is hidden or concealed. It is overcome, however, in the phenomenological attitude. What is hidden is made transparent, what is itself dark is brought to light. Heidegger differs from Husserl not in that he believes that we have a pre-acquaintance with the world as horizon in the natural attitude but in that he suggests that the hiddenness constitutive of the from-structure also remains for the philosophical attitude. Reflection is not able to overcome the darkness. The world not as disclosive site but as concealing darkness protects us philosophically from falling back into objectivism.[19] If the darkness of the world is overcome, if it comes to light in a philosophical reflection, the world as world must become *present.* But anything that becomes present, with the exception of consciousness itself, is a *Gegenständlichkeit* according to Husserl, i.e., it must become phenomenon. If the world becomes reified, the horizonal character of the world is lost.[20] While Husserl will never make the mistake of treating the world as a thing or a set of things, the suppression of the from-structure does leave us with the possibility that Husserl overdetermines the in-structure and thereby limits the notion of horizon to unthematic but thematizable fields, an issue that will occupy us in the third part of this work.

These remarks return us to, as they deepen, our starting point in this chapter: phenomenological analysis arises as an unsettling wonder, revealing the fourfold structure of phenomena.

2

Descriptive Eidetics

> You can understand now why the *Logical Investigations,* this work directed toward the psychic, could also be designated as descriptive psychology. In fact, the sole purpose which they intended and had to intend was the establishing of an inner viewing which discloses the lived experiences of thinking hidden from the thinker, and an essential description pertaining to these pure data of lived experience that moved within a pure inner viewing. But on the other hand, in order to characterize the novel peculiarity of method, the name *phenomenology* was chosen. In fact, a novel method of dealing with the psychic emerged here. . . . The task was new, the attempt to go back radically and consistently from the respective categories of objectivities and ask about the modes of consciousness determinately belonging to them. . . .
>
> —Husserl (1925)[1]

> It is difficult. The most difficult matter of philosophy in general is the phenomenological reduction, to penetrate and to exercise it with understanding.
>
> —Husserl to Ingarden (1931)[2]

A. INTERROGATIONS

If it is the disruptions in seeing and speaking that encourage the phenomenological turn, it is the attempt to capture what one finds in these disruptions that commits phenomenology to a descriptive method.

We must wait until the chapter after next to deal with Husserl's notion of the transcendental, but even his concept of phenomenological interrogation stands in striking contrast to Kant's. In the *Critique of Pure Reason*[3] Kant attempts to discover the a priori conditions of our experience of reality through a procedure in which, first, the Newtonian formulation of the composition of objective nature is viewed as definitive but as yet philosophically unfounded; second, the conditions of its being are approached in terms of the conditions of its being known; and, finally, a single set of necessary, a priori categories and corresponding principles of pure understanding, without which phenomena would lack coherent structure, are inferred on the basis of the way objects are experienced or understood. These categories and principles are constitutive or regulative of objective reality.[4] The "deductive" structure of the derivation of the categories is hypothetical, as it proceeds by inferring from any given natural complex to its necessary conditions. Its method is constructivistic, relying upon the use of transcendental arguments, in contrast to anything like inductive generalizations or the rationalist versions of direct, intuitive insight. The outcome of Kant's inquiry was to give us not only a clear set of principles that accounts for the constitution of phenomena, but also a philosophical critique of alternative theories that finally supports the Newtonian model as the best picture of the physical universe.

By the time of *Ideas I* (1913) Husserl came to believe that Kant was certainly correct in grounding the genuine meaning of the accomplishments that produce the positive sciences in a subjective, transcendental sphere.[5] But the *Crisis* (1936) accuses Kant of subverting reality by replacing the way the world is normally experienced with a certain mathematized construction, a higher order "objectification," thereby covering over the rich diversity and depth of its being. Rather than discovering the world that science necessarily has in play as the context of all its activity, Kant gets caught in the same mistake as the positive sciences by presupposing and then forgetting its presence.[6] The objects of physics, Husserl contends, must be understood as the result of specific transformations applied to the way in which we normally experience things. Consequently, Kant's inquiry into that subjectivity on the basis of which we have objective reality was bound to go amiss; it asks about the conditions of a construction based on the world, never reaching beyond that construction to the world itself, never entering the "vast depths of the Cartesian fundamental investigation," and never penetrating to a clear understanding of "the subjectivity functioning as primal source."[7] In contrast to the Kantian manner of posing questions and his "mythically constructively inferring method," Husserl turns

> to a thoroughly intuitively disclosing method, intuitive in its point of departure and in everything it discloses—even though the concept of intuitiveness may have to undergo a considerable expansion in comparison to the Kantian one, and indeed even though intuition, here, may lose its usual sense altogether through a new attitude, taking on only the general sense of original self-exhibition, but precisely only within the new sphere of being.[8]

This motif, while not yet enhanced by the notion of the life-world, is already at work in the *Ideas I* of 1913, where Husserl attempts a rehabilitation of the world of "belief." There he chooses not to denigrate the realm of everyday intentions and achievements but to dwell in it, unfold its structure, and then see its connection to higher orders of understanding. But this contrast between the world of unencumbered experience and the world as modeled through acts of understanding necessitates a deeper clarification of the notion of description. Using the history of philosophy in general and, in particular, using Kant to introduce it is not sufficient precisely because that history is also a higher order constellation, spawned by the conflicts of the philosophers. Are there roots to description commensurate with the world it brings to disclosure?

A perceptual object is often distant, half hidden, in very poor lighting. Many times we cannot tell exactly what it is. It solicits our interest, arrests our gaze. By approaching closer, by walking around the object and optimizing our view, or perhaps by picking it up and holding it up to the light, the determinations of the object multiply and we become increasingly familiar with the object in its singular existence. As we manipulate the object we are only marginally aware of our actions, only tacitly acquainted with our own perceptual capabilities. The thematic focus of our acts is entirely upon the object and its properties. In fact, the clearer the object becomes, the sharper its contours, the better defined its features, the less likely we are to reflect upon its modes of givenness, with their attending difficulties, and upon our acts of perception as they overcome obstacles along the way, as we often do when things go awry. In uninterrupted experience there is a natural tendency toward a certain "objectivation" in which the connection between acts and appearances becomes not lost but "forgotten," literally over-looked. Indeed, the philosophical tendency toward objectivism, toward treating all regions of being as consisting of object-type entities bearing properties, finds its experiential roots in this forgetfulness. But either a heightened sense of curiosity or, more often, a breach in our usual involvement with things, shifts our attention to their as-structure and its tie to the for-structure. At first the reflection is just a way of enhancing our dealings with things, of clearing up a perceptual or practical muddle. But puzzlement can turn to wonder as we begin our journey.

The recovery of subjectivity requires not just an extension of our interests into "subjective phenomena," for they too can be objectivated, but also a total redirection of our normal or basic thematic focus combined with great care not to prejudice the outcome. In particular we should not assume that what we uncover can be captured only by an objectivating mode of analysis such as pervades both the sciences and the inherited categories of philosophical discourse. In fact, Husserl himself struggled with this throughout his long career. In principle Husserl's break with objectivism takes place once he has the transcendental reduction in hand. In practice, however, he succeeds in overcoming only the objectivism of the natural sciences, his dismantling of philosophical categories being only partial and coming only gradually. In contrast to objectivism this is a type of reflection that, in breaking with our preoccupation with objects, finds traces of our pre-reflective, tacit awareness of subjectivity and then uses them to reverse the direction of our interests. It begins by leaving open the mode of description that is appropriate for this domain, insisting only that our discourse meet certain requirements of grammar, that we attend to what we see, and that we let what is exhibited control our account. Because such description also involves a break with our normalized modes of approaching and viewing things, *Ideas I* calls it the "phenomenological attitude" (*Einstellung*) and places it in opposition to the "natural attitude."[9]

Or perhaps we are dealing not with a distant or underdetermined object but with vague and cloudy ideas. We have difficulty communicating because we do not know what our speech partners, or even we ourselves, are trying to say. We begin to analyze, striving for exactness in terms, more precision in our claims. We introduce concepts that allow better contrasts, sharper distinctions, and then collaboration. Initially our focus is entirely on the concepts, their syntactic combinations, and the objects or properties to which they refer. We undertake a process of "clarification" (*Klärung*) that attempts to dissolve confusion by isolating tokens or prototypes of the concepts in play. We define by pointing to certain objects, now placed in the best light and perceived from the best vantage point. Yet here, too, the tendency to objectivation prevails and we naturally think of concepts as themselves a special kind of object, not real but ideal, that have other objects, real or ideal, as their extensions. But usually the process of clarification is much too limited to provide the needed analysis. Concepts must be understood not just in terms of their extension but also in terms of their relationship to each other. The procedure of "explication" (*Verdeutlichung*), which "plays itself out within the sphere of thought alone,"[10] is a process of understanding concepts through concepts.[11] Once again it is possible for philosophical thought to reduce the understanding of concepts to a logic of equivalent classes; but in concrete speech the process of explication always "turns back" upon both the speaker, the intentions and beliefs of the speaker that cannot be so objectified, and contexts, which exceed notions analytically entailed by the concept under consideration. Here we attempt to account for the content of a concept by the process of its formation and by what the speaker meant in his or her statements. This reflection is possible because in discourse our sentences express an intentional content, positioned in semantic fields, as they indicate a whole chain of intentional activities responsible for their construction. The interrogation of concepts, already operative in ordinary life, is a bridge to phenomenological reflection that breaks with our usual treatment of them as self-subsisting things and thinks of them in terms of what Husserl comes to call their "constitution."

Phenomenological inquiry, then, extends a type of interrogation already at play in everyday life but overthrows the tendency toward objectivism found there. While the phenomenological turn and mode of inquiry arises from a certain wonder already found in ordinary experience, phenomenological descriptions also involve a radical break with certain normalized modes framing both everyday discourse and philosophical analysis.

B. SURFACE AND DEPTH

In this first attempt to formulate his program, Husserl relied entirely on the interdependency of the as- and for-structures to provide him with an irreducible field whose composition and dynamics would be the subject matter of his phenomenology.

Reporting is admittedly quite different from perception. We have seen, however, that the analysis of each uncovers a correlation between acts or activities, on the one side, and certain determining senses or meanings, on the other. This also holds true for other types of experience. A cold winter day sends our imagination to distant lands, and we picture ourselves on a Spanish coast walking down a sunlit beach, the crystal blue water lapping at our feet. This is not an act of perception, for the scene we fantasize has diminished intensities in color saturation, instability in manifest image, and lacks depth. We might even want to speak of an altered relationship between profiles and objects in the case of mental pictures. Yet mental pictures are imbued with significance analogous to perceptual experience. We therefore find in imagination, as in perception, a correlation between the act and the senses of the manifest profile/object.

This correlation, Husserl believes, holds for all types of experience. In *Ideas I* he came to speak of the acts, or cognitive activities, ingredient in all experience as the *noesis;* the sense or meaning, in its various forms, he calls the *noema.*[12] But as of now we have neither the method nor the framework that would allow us to introduce these notions systematically. I, therefore, emphasize only that the correlation of the "form" of act and meaning makes up the basic scheme of a phenomenological description of intentionality. This is not to say that the act is *directed toward* the meaning, an imprecise way of speaking that has caused significant confusion. The act is always directed toward its intentional object or its referent. Rather it is to say that the correlation accounts for or clarifies the directedness of certain classes of mental events toward objects. We will explore Husserl's first formulation of the relationship of act and meaning in the *Logical Investigations* toward the end of this chapter and into the next. We will discover that this first attempt failed to do justice to the "noematic" features of intentionality and, accordingly, incorporates a different understanding of the "correlational a priori" of all experience than what we find in *The Idea of Phenomenology* (1907), *Ideas I,* and beyond.[13] For reasons that can only be explained when we look at the notion of reflection more carefully, Husserl often speaks of the objects of our acts as "transcendent" and our experiences of the objects as "immanent." If we accept this formulation we must say that the correlational a priori gives us not the form of immanence but the form of intentionality, i.e., immanence in its necessary relationship to transcendence.

Husserl introduced his account of intentionality by adding contrasts far more revolutionary than the first readers of the *Investigations* understood. In addition to the connection between act and content, the interdependency of the as- and for-structures can be fully described only by recourse to *intending* acts in which the object is *taken* as having a particular determination, and *fulfilling* acts that *give* the object in its determinacy. The latter provides a first approximation of what Husserl means by *evidence;* the coincidence of the object as given in fulfilling acts with the object as intended secures the validity of our claims. While Husserl first treats intending and fulfilling acts synchronically, it is not difficult to see how the structural correlation of immanence and transcendence becomes a dynamic interdependence once time is introduced into the account; the tendency of intending acts toward fulfillment imbues intentional acts with transcendence and, thereby, their teleological organization. With this dynamic interdependence, conscious life becomes understood as a field in which particular acts are situated.

These ideas give us a minimal or first topology of intentionality that employs two axes: the correlation between act and sense (or meaning) cuts across the difference between intending and fulfillment. These dyads, giving us the surface organization of the phenomenological field, are complemented by yet another that gives it verticality.

Fulfillment always places before us much more than we explicitly intended. This means that at each stage not only our intentions are confirmed, as we seek evidence, but also our experience of things is enriched. Fulfillment provides individual intentions with a "surplus" over and above their primary focus and, thus, with a context. They usually appear with determinations not previously thematic and often give rise to combinations not initially anticipated. Experience and experienced objects are "built up" in this way; simple objects become complex and complex objects always point back to prior acts and objects contributing to their present configuration. Various relations of "founding" and "founded" are nested in each object. It is even possible for discontinuity to enter, for a perception to "explode,"[14] or for entire frameworks to shift, as when what we took to be an inanimate rock suddenly moves and we discover a frog, or when that frog turns into a prince. And when these shifts take place, our previous experiences of the object's profiles are recast or reorganized by the new meaning of the whole. Profiles are dependent upon each other and upon the sense of the whole for their configuration. In turn, the whole has its meaning by virtue of the relationship between its "parts" as well as our previous experiences of other wholes. Objects gain determinacy through the dynamic interplay of intention and fulfillment; they consist of multiple relations of founding and founded that give them and, thereby, conscious life their richness.

If the connection between act and sense, and the interplay of intending and fulfillment, give us the field of this first phenomenology, then the underlying strata laid down over the course of previous experiences, as well as the meanings or senses implied by what is presently experienced, establish its *depth.* It is the task of this first phenomenology to trace identity and difference, presence and absence, coincidence and excess, founding and founded, surface and depth as they play themselves out across the correlation of noesis and noema.[15]

The difference between surface and depth allows us to return to the notion of description and to see why Husserl never offers us a table of categories, as does Kant. Kant's goal is to discover the one single set of syntheses, which he attains through the forms of judgment, in terms of which our experience of reality and thereby appearing reality itself is possible. Husserl, however, always tethers his reflections upon subjectivity to the self-givenness of objects, to "radically and consistently go[ing] back from the respective categories of objectivities and ask[ing] about the modes of consciousness determinately belonging to them."[16] Husserl, too, has a universal accomplishing subjectivity, as the next chapter will show. But, as Habermas points out, "this produces an *open* horizon of possible objects that admits of a manifold of different types of objectivities that can be grasped only descriptively."[17] This open subjectivity is bound to the specificity of the fields whose horizons it provides. Horizons, though constitutive, are themselves transformed by the course of ongoing experience. Description is the method that does justice to the facticity of the transcendental in Husserl.

The analysis that we are looking at in this chapter, however, is clearly pre-transcendental; we have only introduced the correlational a priori, anticipating distinctions to come. We have not in any way secured the applicability of the general correlation of act and meaning to the various regions of existence, nor have we understood the sense in which it grounds those regions.

C. DISPLACEMENTS

Following Husserl, I want to think of the method we are now sketching as his "first" phenomenology. But what does this mean and how are we to place this in relation to the whole of Husserl's reflections on the nature of philosophical method?

In 1921, Husserl devoted some eight handwritten pages to an analysis that he entitled "Static and Genetic Phenomenological Methods."[18] This text, to which we will return time and again in this study, is important not only because of the clarity Husserl achieved at a time when he made several attempts to understand the systematic scope of his phenomenological method (as we will study in detail in chapters 5 and 8) but also because of its hesitations, its turns and reversals. In places the analysis overwhelms itself, for in it we find not just a contrast between static and genetic analysis that, as soon as it is introduced, is destabilized by the insertion of a third type between them; we also discover a puzzling opposition between description and explanation.[19] Even the issue of the various "ways" into phenomenological analysis crowds in. We do not find this text completely coherent. But it is one of those rare passages when Husserl attempts to define his own operative terms and, thus, it is exceptionally fruitful.

Like sparks leaping from metal on a rapidly moving stone, the key concepts in Husserl's analysis fly quickly from his pen. In a note he distinguishes between not two but *three* different kinds or levels of phenomenological analysis:

> Phenomenology:
> 1) Universal phenomenology of the general structures of consciousness
> 2) Constitutive phenomenology
> 3) Phenomenology of genesis[20]

Husserl then immediately contrasts a "descriptive" or "static" phenomenology to an "explanatory phenomenology" (*beschreibende* vs. *erklärende Phänomenologie*).[21] At first Husserl thinks of "constitutive phenomenology" as belonging to static or descriptive phenomenology. "With these descriptions, the constitutive ones, there is no questioning after an explanatory genesis."[22] And we know that there is an even broader use of the notion of constitutive phenomenology as a synonym for his phenomenological method as a whole, as in a letter to Boyce Gibson in 1932: "I am of absolute certainty that constitutive phenomenology and it alone has future."[23] But in a few pages constitutive analysis seems much more like a bridge between static and genetic accounts. At the beginning constitutive phenomenology treats the "interconnections" of those items first introduced whole cloth in a static account. But, later, there is

> another "constitutive" phenomenology, that of the genesis, [which] follows the history, the necessary history of this objectification and, thereby, the history of the object itself.[24]

With this the border between static or descriptive and genetic or explanatory phenomenology seems to fade, for Husserl thinks that constitutive analysis somehow belongs to both.

So far we have but a string of names. It seems, however, that we are not only beyond the first phenomenology we are just beginning to introduce here, but also beyond his earlier framework. Yet we do not understand its import, nor do we see how these new reflections upon method reach back into the phenomenological studies of the *Investigations* and his first comprehensive introduction to transcendental phenomenology in *Ideas I*, and realign the method of static analysis operative throughout both works. These issues will occupy us for the next several chapters. But first we must secure a place from which our account can begin.

We find a phrase from our 1921 text that interprets the whole of *Ideas I* for Husserl; static analysis is a "universal phenomenology of the general structures of consciousness."[25] He adds that it is a

> phenomenology of the possibly essential forms in pure consciousness, however they have come about, and their teleological order in the domain of possible reason under the titles "object" and "sense."[26]

Of course, there is nothing in our account thus far that could enable us to understand what Husserl might mean by "pure" consciousness. There are, however, two suggestive facts: first, Husserl refers to the program of tracing the general structures of consciousness as a "first ordering"[27] of phenomenology; and second, he schematizes the structure of intentionality in terms of the three interdependent moments of the ego-cogito-cogitatum. For reasons I will attempt to explain, I want to call this first phenomenology "categorial phenomenology." In fact, I will be forcing a distinction that Husserl recognizes, but does not develop, by suggesting that it comes to us in two complementary installments. We find its first rigorous introduction in the *Logical Investigations* (1900–1901) with a number of later works fleshing out a systematic account of its pure logic (Third Investigation) and pure grammar (Fourth Investigation) that provided the guiding threads to its phenomenological analysis. In that work Husserl's task was controlled by an epistemology of cognition, and its goal was to secure our knowledge of the ideal laws governing our "presentations" and "judgments." The second installment, which we will discuss in chapters 5 to 7, comes as Husserl moves away from the "descriptive psychology" of the *Investigations* into a *transcendental* phenomenology in *Ideas I* (1913) and treats phenomena in terms not of their cognition but of their constitution, a notion quite scarce in the *Investigations*.[28] In this second stage, categorial phenomenology becomes philosophy proper. I will suggest that the key to categorial phenomenology is that it is built upon, as it restricts itself to, the relationship between the as- and for-structures.

D. PHENOMENOLOGICAL REFLECTION

Thus far we have spoken of phenomenology only in terms of its inception and the structures that it opens to analysis. Understanding its *procedure* requires a new step. Using a term that seems to turn philosophy into its opposite, Husserl speaks of phenomenology as "description."[29] Having explored the internal motivation for taking the phenomenological turn, and having introduced a rough sketch of the notion of description, we must now settle into a much more rigorous analysis of the connection between reflection and description. We will then introduce, step by step, several notions central to Husserl's categorial phenomenology.

We quickly recognize that, at one level, Husserl's talk of phenomenology as descriptive is heuristic. It does little more than provide him with a rallying point in his war against the constructivism of the Neo-Kantians, the reductionism of the Empiricist schools, and the speculative proclivities of the Idealists. Husserl is convinced that, in each of these approaches, theory overwhelms things and finds in them only its own constructions. But to speak of philosophy as descriptive also reinstates what philosophy had come to suspect, even to despise, namely, the realm of common experience. Such a characterization insists that the structures and dynamics of everyday experience be understood as having an integrity of their own that must be incorporated into any adequate philosophical account of truth. They should not be understood as the antithesis to truth, or as a type of cognition tenuously situated between knowledge and ignorance, to be denigrated, as in both Plato and Bacon, to being an idol of the cave or the marketplace. At another level Husserl believes there is not just a prejudice to overcome but also a methodological mistake that needs to be avoided. The specification of phenomenology as descriptive is also directed to the methods of the sciences; philosophy can adopt neither the explanatory constructions of the natural sciences nor the interpretative accounts of the social and cultural sciences if one of its tasks is to provide a "grounding" of these sciences. To do so would be a category mistake of the worst order, one that the entirety of Husserl's phenomenology was designed to avoid. By valorizing one of the empirical methods and thus making it the basis of all the others, phenomenology would fall prey to the mistake of grounding the whole upon one of its parts, itself in need of grounding. Interestingly, it is precisely the task of securing the sciences, not that of rejecting them, that demands a method and a field different from theirs. Lastly, phenomenology is descriptive in the sense that it wants to neutralize its own presence and to allow the fields it reveals to exhibit their contours. The call to description is simultaneously a call to rigor, to requiring our concepts and ideas not so much to symbolize the visible but to render it, to present things as they are presented to us. Describing is a labor of tracing, of snaring in the medium of ideas what is otherwise in constant flight, not of sculpting, of giving shape to a reality that otherwise lacks it. Accordingly, Husserl insists that fields of experience be articulated only in terms appropriate to the way things are given. Their essences, as a result, are not "exact" or mathematical but "essentially inexact" or, better, "morphological" precisely because they have imprecise, often fluid borders that can only be roughly drawn and because there is no algorithm that completely and exhaustively delimits their extension.[30] And though inexact essences higher on the scale of generality are "strict," even they lack a finite set of rules that would allow us to generate each member of the set. They resist pure operational reductions for the simple reason that they have semantic content.[31]

But does description, one could object, really set phenomenology off from the natural and human sciences? They not only explain or interpret; they also describe and classify. Some sciences, such as botany, anatomy and phonology, are dominantly classificatory. A second objection follows from the nature of phenomenological descriptions themselves: if they do not employ exact concepts and if both their extensions and the properties of their referents cannot be sufficiently determined by rules, then we have an element of undecidability in all descriptions. The concept underdetermines, and this introduces an inescapable element of interpretation that is not itself exclusively controlled by the particular field of experience under description. As we will see later, this second issue carries phenomenology beyond its first formulation. It is possible, however, to give a provisional answer to the first problem from within Husserl's static account.

Husserl wisely resists the temptation to force a distinction between two languages, one scientific, the other phenomenological. The crucial difference between the descriptions of the sciences and those of phenomenology can be seen as a difference in logical grammars. It is a difference clarified by a trait of categorial phenomenology already anticipated in our account of its inception; all descriptions take place under a "reflection." As we live "straightforwardly" toward the things in our world, we turn our attention back upon this relationship itself and thus refocus our interest, often following a guiding thread provided by a disrupted perception or broken speech. The fascination with things is broken as we concentrate upon the tie between ourselves and the countless ways objects of our world are manifest. In the phenomenological reflection, as we saw, not only is the implicit difference between profile and object made explicit, the acts giving rise to that difference are also uncovered. This means that the grammar of its descriptions is different from those in the sciences: under the reflection the hidden but operative *correlation* of acts and meanings becomes not only the *field* of the analysis but also the *scheme* of its descriptions. Often Husserl calls the freeing of this field for description the "phenomenological reduction," but we will restrict this name to Husserl's transcendental account.[32] Let us simply say for now that this is the field opened by the phenomenological reflection.

Had we only the reflection, however, phenomenology would be no more than a chronicle or a list of items in a field. We can even speculate that we might not have any descriptions at all, only markers ordering the sequence or positions of phenomena. As we describe, though, we attend to the variant and invariant features of our object. The reflection upon experience involves a double look, one that takes an individual object as it is and then revalues both it and our experience of it as a sample, an instance. For example, my experience of the pump is a fact, a single dated event that took place in a particular location. Yet our interest as philosophers is not in biography, even less in personal psychology. As we reflect, we take both the act and the object as illustrations or instances of a certain type of act-object interconnection, in this case perception. Those features that prove to hold for all perceptions of a certain type of object are said to compose its "essence." Thus we must say that phenomenology gives us a description not of the fact but of the essence of intentional experiences, i.e., a description of the facticity of particular act-object connections in terms of their essential possibility. The goal of the phenomenological reflection, then, is a thematization of the essence of intentionality. In Husserl's language the phenomenological reflection must undergo an *eidetic reduction.*

E. EIDETIC REDUCTION

In order to understand the way in which the phenomenological reflection is supplemented by an eidetic reduction, we must deal with Husserl's theory of essences in general. While all phenomenology involves both, they should not be considered identical for the simple reason that the empirical sciences employ, or at least rely upon, eidetic analysis, but as practiced they do not use phenomenological reflection. To be sure, there is a second-order phenomenological account of these sciences that requires both, but as positive disciplines they focus entirely upon the production of coherent theories about the essence of certain facts. Or, to touch upon one of the more difficult and underdeveloped sides of Husserl's theory, the phenomenological account of the empirical sciences proceeds by the use of what Husserl calls regional or material ontologies. These ontologies, all involving eidetic analysis, are then construed as fields of *cognition* under the phenomenological reflection of the *Logical Investigations* (1900–1901). Eventually, once we move to the expansion of the notion of phenomenological reflection by that of the phenomenological *reduction* in *Ideas I* (1913), they are understood as fields of *constitution.* But as disciplines that initially stand on their own, the sciences employ eidetic analysis and are not phenomenological. It is only when we attempt to understand their domains not as fields of existing facts but as fields of our cognition of existing facts that a phenomenological reflection first comes into play.

One of the interesting outcomes of this contrast is that in principle we can have a phenomenological reflection that is not eidetic. The result would be a chronicle of individual experiences, a rather dull sequential autobiography or biography. More importantly, we can have an eidetic reduction that is not yet phenomenological, which would give us both empirical systems of classification and empirical schemes of explanation, mostly causal, if we restrict our analysis to the working sciences of the day. Should we move to the level of material ontology we could provide a rational account of the particular domains in which each discipline labors. While such ontologies from within the natural attitude are not phenomenology, understanding their domains as fields of cognition calls forth phenomenological description.

To do justice to the difference between eidetic and phenomenological analysis, we must run with Husserl's notion of essences for several pages, discuss their different types, see what areas he did attempt to cover with them, and then return in a later section to the question of how this is related to his phenomenological account of the subject.

We have stressed the difference between facts, be they psychological or physical, and essences. But Husserl is convinced that essences are objects and not just general names of sets of things. Compared to objects belonging to the real world, however, "the essence (eidos) is an object of a different order."[33] But what can this mean? Is this a return to the metaphysical difficulties of Platonism?

The first point supporting the treatment of essences as objects is semantic. If we define "object" simply as what can function as the topic or "subject of a true (categorial, affirmative) sentence,"[34] then "object" (*Gegenstand*) is much broader in scope than "thing" (*Ding*) or even "fact" (*Tatsache, Sachverhalt*). Anything to which we can refer is an object, including essences. Husserl understands the way in which language controls this account:

> Indeed, I have not invented this general concept of the object but only restored the one required by all purely logical sentences and, at the same time, pointed out that it is in principle indispensable. . . .[35]

This point is followed by a second. In a given domain, the rules determining inclusion in and exclusion from a particular essence can be specified and can hold true regardless of the number of objects with which we are acquainted or even if there are no objects at all in its extension.[36] If essences cannot be reduced to names that stand for groupings of perceptions or things, then they must be "given" in a way different from real things or actual facts. In keeping with Husserl's theory of intentionality, they must themselves be objects manifested by a different kind of act. Husserl calls it *eidetic intuition.*

> The essence (eidos) is a new kind of object. Just as the given of an individual intuition of [perceptual] experience is an individual object, so the given of eidetic intuition is a pure essence.
>
> Here we are not presented with a mere external analogy but radical commonality. Eidetic seeing is precisely intuition, just as an eidetic object is precisely an object. The generalization of the correlative concepts "intuition" and "object," belonging, as they do, together, is not an arbitrary idea but convincingly required by the nature of the matter.[37]

Since essences can be presented in higher order acts of eidetic insight analogous to the way perceptual objects are presented in acts of sensuous intuition, Husserl claims, essences must be thought of as ideal *singulars;* i.e., their names refer to intensional entities that are not reducible to their extensions.[38] Husserl is careful to distinguish them from the acts and the semantic content of acts (what he sometimes calls "concepts")[39] that allow them to be so presented:

> Each species . . . presupposes a meaning in which it is presented and this meaning is itself again a species. But the meaning in which an object is thought and its object, the species itself, are not one and the same. . . . Thus the universality [i.e., the species] *that* we think does not resolve itself into the universality of the meanings *in which* we think of it.[40]

These distinctions call for further clarification, all the more so since the interplay of profile and object deemed essential to phenomena seems to break down in the case of essences, and since the reason we gave for handling essences as objects might just as well be construed as a semantic account of why we tend to falsely objectivate them and endow them with misplaced concreteness. If we are to have ontologies we must provide an account of essences themselves. In our treatment we must see if we can account for their difference from real objects and for their place in Husserl's topology of the different realms of existence. Having just stressed the difference between the use of essential analyses of various regions without the phenomenological reflection and a phenomenological description of those regions construed as fields of cognition, the task before us in the next chapter is to provide a phenomenological account of kinds of essences that applies to all regional ontologies.

3

Categorial Phenomenology and Ontology

> The ideality of what is specific is . . . the complete opposite of reality [*Realität*] or individuality.
>
> —Husserl (1901)[1]

> This world is historically changing in its particular styles but [is] invariant in its invariant structures of generality.
>
> —Husserl (ca. 1936)[2]

A. FROM PERCEPTUAL TYPES TO EMPIRICAL ESSENCES[3]

The distinctions among types, empirical essences and pure essences, Husserl believes, are constantly employed by various sciences but are not adequately analyzed by them or, as they stay within their limits as objectivating disciplines, are clarified by them only extensionally—what we might understand today as a truth-functional approach. Interestingly, Husserl argues not against the possibility or even the fruitfulness of this type of analysis but against its reductionism. The phenomenological turn is designed to undercut such reductionism by providing a story about essences that describes the cognitive conditions under which they are apprehended as ideal singulars. The concept of eidetic intuition, which carried heavy burdens in the *Logical Investigations*, was gradually expanded by later, more sophisticated studies, ones that emphasized the conceptual processes involved in the formation and apprehension of essences. The image of eidetic intuition gave way to eidetic variation beginning around the time of *Ideas I* (1913). We introduce it here because, contrary to some views, it is very much a part of the working method of static analysis.[4]

Returning to our water pump, we discover that its features are not randomly presented but have a certain order and a relationship to each other and, beyond this, to other kinds of things. The object was presented *as* rusty, green, speckled with red. These are *typical* features of the pump and perhaps of others like it. Rust, green, and red are determinations that we co-apprehend as we apprehend the tall object as a pump. Notice that we can go a step further and focus not just upon the pump but also specifically on the rusty, red side of the pump facing us and then upon the rust and red themselves. This last step requires us to loosen our first perceptual bond with the object and concentrate on rust and red for their own sake. With these features in focus we can, so to speak, let the object go as we explore them. Normally we do this by, first, imagining contrasts and differences, say, between red and green, rust and galvanized; second, supplying a name and then descriptions that do not simply use the predicates *red* and *rusty* but mention the concepts "red" and "rust"; third, describing them in relation to other concepts; and, finally, adding confirmation to these proposed specifications as we return to our first object or other samples like it. In this way we come to apprehend an idea that could apply to a number of different things; we do not apprehend a thing, a rusty, red side, or even the rust and the red of the side in their typical presence, but rust and red themselves. In Husserl's terms, we gain insight into universals.

Notice what happens to the object with which we began. The noetic difference between focusing on the individual, as in perception, and explicitly attending to its species, as in the case of eidetic intuition, changes the way in which the pump is present to us. No doubt, the same real object is in front of us, but the acts and the presentation are completely different. In the case of perception, the object serves as

> the presentative basis for an act intending the individual, i.e., for an act in which we apply ourselves to what is appearing and intend this thing or this feature, this part of the thing. In the second case it is the presentative basis for an act intending and apprehending a species, i.e., while the thing appears, or rather the feature in the thing, we do not intend this objec [illegible] feature, this here and now; rather we intend its *content*, its "idea"; we mean not this red moment in the house but *the red* [as such].[5]

This shift accounts for the strict categorial difference between real objects and their universals. But notice that the act of eidetic intuition in play here is such that we are thematizing a universal that applies only to real objects. In its difference from the object, the universal still maintains a relationship to existing objects. Universals, themselves ideal and not real objects, are *empirical* essences. By this Husserl means that our characterizations of essences are necessarily provisional, open to further experience that solidifies or modifies our initial conceptions. But this should not mislead us into viewing empirical ideation as empirical induction or into reducing eidetic insight to a process that points to features shared by several sample objects as we fix them with a general name. Such a process would not give us a universal, because it only collects real features under a label and because it does not cover *all* but only *some* real instances, namely, the ones compared. Without this change in quantification, without this fundamental shift from *some* to *all,* universals would be reducible to collections of "scattered manifolds,"[6] concepts to names of sets of particulars. The all, never gleaned from induction, is what distinguishes the world of essences from the world of facts. At the same time Husserl realizes that the *all* is limited. While our descriptions of "red" or "rust" are universal statements, the quantifier "all" has "an empirical extension,"[7] which entails that the future course of experience determines not just the application but also the content of the eidos. The essence is "open" and capable of being corrected, or even canceled, by what comes to us in experience. In Husserl's words, its "all" is "an all in time."[8] For this reason Husserl speaks of universals as *contingent* essences.[9]

But beyond their contingent character there is also an unavoidable vagueness or inexactness that results from the fact that such universals are drawn directly from the "vague Gestalt types" and the "fluid" things of perceptual experience. Husserl explains himself in this way:

> Phenomenology drops *only the individuation* [of the samples]; but the whole essential content, in the fullness of its concretion, it elevates into eidetic consciousness and takes it as an ideally identical essence which, like any other essence, could be singularized not only *hic et nunc* but also in countless examples. One sees at once that there can be no thought of an [exact] conceptual, terminological *fixing* of this or any other such fluid *concretum*, and that the same holds with respect to each of its immediate and no less fluid parts and abstract moments.[10]

And this finds its counterpart in our language:

> The most perfect geometry and the most perfect practical mastery . . . cannot enable the descriptive natural scientist to express (in exact geometrical concepts) what he expresses in such a simple, understandable, and completely appropriate manner by the words "notches," "scalloped," "lens-shaped," and "umbelliform," and the like—all of them concepts which are *essentially, rather than accidentally, inexact* and *consequently* also non-mathematical.[11]

Empirical essences are not only contingent but, as a result of the vagueness and fluidity of the configurations they raise to an eidetic level, they are also *morphological.*

This characterization will affect the theory of pure essences—the notion Husserl sets in contrast to empirical universals—as well as our understanding of phenomenology itself, inasmuch as it is an a priori discipline that, paradoxically, belongs to that class of sciences condemned to work with inexact, morphological concepts.[12] Because of this influence, it is crucial to see that empirical universals are found at different levels with varying degrees of generality and that even those that belong to higher levels never completely lose their morphological character and, thus, are not describable in exact (i.e., mathematical) terms. But even if they cannot be articulated by exact ideas, they still can be rendered with rigor.

> But though there can be no speaking of an unambiguous determination of *eidetic singularities* in our sphere of description, the situation is quite otherwise in the case of essences belonging to *higher levels of specificity.* These are accessible to rigid differentiation, to an identification that holds through change [*identifizierende Durchhaltung*], and to strict conceptual formulation and, likewise, to an analysis into component essences. In their case, accordingly, the tasks of a comprehensive scientific description can be meaningfully imposed.[13]

When we move beyond the basic to higher levels, especially those that subsume the lower, we are able to fix the generic essence of a certain domain in "strict" (but not exact) concepts.[14]

Perhaps the best way to understand the difference between perceptual individuals and empirical essences is to trace the differences in unity and plurality, identity and difference as they are played out in the perception, and then apprehension, of empirical essences. This will enable us to see the somewhat stark notion of eidetic intuition as a placeholder for what is a rather complex *process* involved in our comprehension of essences. The account that follows must, given the scope of the method now in play, treat this process only in terms of its structural features rather than in terms of any possible temporal or historical dimensions.

Perception always involves the activity of detecting a multiplicity of sides and phases, in and through which it perceives the object as something persisting as the same. We experience the object as "the identical thing which alters and sometimes does not alter, which lasts and endures on throughout the flow of the multiplicity."[15] But in this case the unity in play is not a universal but an individual, a real object; furthermore, the profiles are not variants but perspectives. Strictly speaking, real objects do not undergo variation [*Variation*] though they might be constantly undergoing alteration [*Veränderung*].[16] Identity here would only be that of a self-same individual object in contrast to changing profiles. The process of empirical ideation, by contrast, is really a process of "bound" eidetic variation[17] that builds upon perception in three steps. (a) We begin with a particular object and treat it as a sample or model that can be compared to others that are *similar to* or *like* it. This first level preserves that moment of difference in the internal determinacy of what is manifest, for without it we would not have the possibility of contrast so essential to similarity. (b) Our interest is not in collecting further objects, as though we were searching for more apples to put in our basket, but rather in attending to that which makes them the *same.* As we keep the objects or determinations in mind as a multiplicity, we attend "in the sequence of their appearance to *overlapping coincidence* and thereby pass into a *synthetic unity* in which they all appear as variations of one another."[18] In this continual coincidence we discover "the 'what' or the content that remains necessarily invariable in the coincidence."[19] Difference slackens its internal tie to what is present and is only required to preserve the link between the invariant and its variations. (3) Finally, there is a moment of "identifying what agrees over against the differences."[20] And here difference is simply "what has not joined the unity of agreement."[21] In this third step we move not just from similarity to sameness but also from sameness to identity. We thereby gain the universal whose *scope* includes all its instances but whose *content* is restricted, limited to the samples we have compared or imagined. Much as all empirical predications are "occasional," which Husserl realized by the time he published the second edition of his first five logical investigations (1913),[22] so all empirical essences are contextual, which means that such universals are not only contingent, limited to an empirical application, but also a posteriori, having a content determined by that application.

B. FROM EMPIRICAL TO PURE ESSENCES

To arrive at a priori essences, Husserl suggests, we must effect a transformation of empirical into pure ideation, and, correspondingly, of empirical into pure essences. He envisions this as a shift from the existing world to "a world of absolutely pure possibilities,"[23] from viewing the content of essences in relation to the actual objects and features to viewing it in relation to possible objects and features. The individuals we consider are taken not as *selected samples* for which we find a shared trait but optional or *arbitrary examples* for which we could substitute any possible object that belongs to this group. No longer is the essence a universal bound to a finite set of variants, it is an eidos that applies to "an 'openly infinite' multiplicity,"[24] i.e., any *possible* member of the set. "The remarkable and extremely important consciousness of the 'and so on, at will' belongs essentially to each multiplicity of variation."[25] The extension of the eidos is one of "free possibilities,"[26] its "all" is "not an all in time."[27]

These first distinctions are much in need of further clarification, for there are a number of problems that immediately present themselves. If the process of intuiting pure essences seems to presuppose that we have isolated empirical universals, then either (a) a pure essence is simply a rearticulation of the content of the empirical universal with only the tie to real objects suspended, such that the essence retains the morphological character of the empirical essence, or (b) pure essences are gained by moving to a higher degree of generality and, accordingly, are different in content from empirical essences. Perhaps pure essences arise as we focus on the identity that persists across various empirical universals but not individuals. Under certain circumstances the variants would be morphological but the pure essence would not. Of course, this would mean that ideation of pure essences would involve not only a severing of any internal tie to the empirical but also a further process of generalization.

Husserl views *red* as both an empirical and a pure essence,[28] however, and seems to think that the elimination of contingency is the only condition necessary to move from the first alternative to the second. This would mean both that at least some pure essences are morphological and that it must be possible to combine the notion of morphological and a priori. When we move up the scale of generality we do gain precision, or what Husserl thinks of as strictness (still in contrast to the exactness of mathematics),[29] but even here it seems that essences retain their morphological character. This must mean that the precision comes intensionally by spelling out the coherent relation that one essence has to others, not extensionally by a conventional stipulation of what counts as an instance.

All this leads to two crucial questions: (a) what precisely is the relationship between an empirical and a pure essence, and (b) how can morphological essences with unclear borders, and inexact contents, be viewed as a priori?

To understand the difference between empirical and pure essences, we must attend to a complication that Husserl introduces into his account. We have already seen that universals give us "something identical"[30] to this red here and that red there. Adding new instances does not change this:

> We may gain for this red here and that red there something identical to both and a universal. But only a universal of just this and that red. We do not gain the pure red taken universally as eidos [i.e., as pure essence]. Of course by bringing into play a third or several reds whenever they are presented we can recognize that the universal of the two is identically the same as the universal of the many. But in doing so we gain always only common characters and universalities that are tied to empirical extensions.[31]

Were the issue simply that contingent universals link essences to actual objects, we would need only distinguish them from possible objects to have a tidy contrast. But Husserl extends empirical universals to include "real possibility." The actual objects we use as samples have a horizon, which means that we can envision any number of similar objects that will be given later on. The extension even of empirical universals, much to our surprise, is "an infinitely open one."[32] He explains:

> When it is a question of the realities of the infinite pregiven world, we can imagine *an arbitrary number of particulars capable of being given later on*, which likewise includes this empirical universal as a *real possibility*. The extension is then an infinitely open one, and still the unity of the empirically acquired species and the higher genus is a "contingent" one.[33]

Thus the difference between empirical and pure is not that the extension of the first is limited to actual objects while the second extends to possible objects, as we might believe from the discussion in *Phenomenological Psychology.* In *Experience and Judgment* Husserl tries to put the pieces together for us:

> [Pure] concepts do not circumscribe an extension that, as it were, is open merely *after the event,* but beforehand, *a priori.* This envelopment beforehand signifies that they must be capable of *prescribing rules to all empirical particulars.* With empirical concepts, infinity of extension implies only that I can imagine an arbitrary number of like particulars without it actually being evident whether, in the progress of actual experience, this presumptively posited "again and again" might perhaps undergo a cancellation, whether this being able to continue might one day actually reach a limit. With pure concepts, on the other hand, this infinity of actually being-able-to-continue is *given with evidence,* precisely because *before* all experience, these concepts prescribe rules for its later course and, consequently, rule out a sudden change, a cancellation.[34]

And he adds this warning:

> It is necessary to point out that even totally free variation is not enough to actually give us the universal as pure. . . . If we practice variation freely but cling secretly to the fact that, e.g., these must be arbitrary sounds *in the world,* heard or able to be heard by men on earth, then we certainly have an essential universal as an *eidos* but one *related to our world of fact* and bound to this universal fact. It is a secret bond in that, for understandable reasons, it is imperceptible to us.[35]

The reason an empirical concept has an open extension but is nevertheless contingent is "because the member acting as the point of departure for the comparison was contingent, given in actual experience."[36] Let's call this a process of empirical ideation, which we will now contrast to pure ideation proper. In order to achieve pure ideation, as we have seen, the tie not just to real objects but to the real or empirical *world* must be severed, for this removes the contingency that attaches to empirical universals. This requires that we not only break the connection to actual and possible objects but also suspend what *Experience and Judgment* calls "empirical horizons."[37] There are three keys to achieving pure essences: first, we exchange bound for free variation; second, the extension of the essence must be kept infinitely open; and, third, we place the essence in relation to possible instead of to actual objects (whether present or absent), thereby *exchanging the actual world for the possible.* The object no longer *specifies* the essences but the reverse holds; i.e., the object becomes an *instance.* This has the result of placing the essence in relation to other types of essences and of allowing us to speak of the way they may or may not form a coherent region of being.

There is an important and interesting question as to whether Husserl has a notion of a "worldbound" or a "transworld" a priori, to echo a contrast found in Plantinga and Mohanty.[38] Is Husserl exchanging the actual world for possible worlds, or is he making a distinction between the actual world viewed as factual (including both what is really absent and present) and the actual world viewed as possible?

Ideas I draws an important distinction that seems to exclude the first option by recognizing the logical possibility of a world beside "our world" but arguing that such a notion leads to "countersense." Logically there is no analytic or formal contradiction found in the hypothesis of a second world. But the argument that any world in addition to ours must be one that we could experience, or in some way apprehend, forces us to conclude that there is only one world, assuming it is properly described. He puts it this way:

> If we ask about the essential conditions of its validity, about the manner of demonstration required by its sense, or if we ask about the manner of demonstration in general that is determined in principle through the thesis of a transcendent [world]—however we may legitimately generalize its essence—then we recognize that it, of necessity, would have to be *experiencable,* not merely for an ego understood as an empty logical possibility but for my *actual ego* as the discoverable unity of my interconnections of experience.[39]

Husserl certainly does recognize that from an "eidetic" point of view we can treat "the real world" as a particular case of "manifold possible worlds." But the latter are intelligible only as the "correlates" of the "idea of an experiencing consciousness with more or less ordered interconnections of experience."[40] The requirement that a possible world be in principle one that we can actually experience means that the existence of a world besides the one with which we are acquainted is impossible, keeping in mind that world functions here not as an *object* of experiences but as the *condition* of the objects of experience, i.e., of there being different types of regions.

On this issue I would follow Mohanty, who is inclined to view the a priori as worldbound.[41] The fact that we have a serious problem with transworld identity (the individual in one world being the same as an individual in another world), and even with transworld possibility—keeping the law of excluded middle in one world and excluding it in another entails that there is no identical notion of possibility in both worlds—suggests that trying to clarify Husserl's notion of the a priori by recourse to possible worlds would only invite confusion. To explain Husserl's position further, Mohanty argues that saying that an actual object need not be actual and could be a mere possibility does not mean that the same object can be in many possible worlds. What Husserl does in suspending "empirical horizons," then, is move to a world of pure possibility, not to possible worlds. I have attempted to capture this by saying that we shift from a sample (actual individual) to an example (possible individual) when we apprehend pure essences, i.e., the essence specifies the parameters of what the individual is rather than the reverse. Furthermore, Husserl's talk of multiple horizons does not mean that there are many possible worlds as much as it means that there are many possible formations or complexes of significance in play in the world in which we live; i.e., the notion of horizon might be just the *historical* specification of the one world viewed as possibility. We will return to this issue in chapter 13. For now, we must draw out one implication of this discussion for eidetic analysis.

Notice that if the eidetic reduction can take place apart from the phenomenological reduction, and eidetic disciplines can move beyond empirical generalities to a priori structures, then we must recognize that even *within* what Husserl will call the natural attitude there is a certain sense in which we put the existing world into "suspension":

> As the firmest and most universal of all our habitualities, the world is valid and remains in its actual validity for us, no matter what interests we may pursue; like all interests, those involving eidetic cognition are also related to it. With every exercise of imagination—like the one which we have already considered, set in motion by the supposition of possible particulars, chosen arbitrarily and falling under a concept attained empirically, and so also with every imaginative variation involving the intention of seeing ideas—the world is co-posited; every fact and every *eidos* remains related to the factual world, belonging to this world. Because of its universality, we, of course, do not notice in the natural attitude this hidden positing of the world and this bond to being.
>
> Only if we become conscious of this bond, *putting it consciously out of play,* and so also free this broadest surrounding horizon of variants from all connection to experiential validity, do we achieve perfect purity. Then we find ourselves, so to speak, in a pure world of imagination, a *world of absolutely pure possibility.*[42]

If *all* connections to the existing world, to what is actual as well as what is absent are severed, this affects more than the question of contingency. It would also eliminate any empirical connection between speakers and referents as determinative of the content of pure essences, leaving us only with possible speakers and what can be called semantic referents, i.e., possible objects whose determinations are fixed entirely by the conceptual content of the essence. Since the referents are not samples of the essence (thus binding its content) but purely arbitrary examples, it must be the content that binds the referents, not the other way around. This means that the question of whether a particular trait is *necessary* and not just whether it always has and always will occur, can be settled only by recourse to the relationship between pure essences. In this way we can account for a possible difference not just in modality of the extension of the essence (actual vs. possible) but also in the content itself. The difference, however, is *not* the level of generality.

While Husserl did not resolve this problem, I think we can clarify it by contrasting the way that identity and difference operate in empirical and pure ideation. Empirical ideation actually builds upon a recognition of similarity (or likeness) and contrast already at play "passively" in perception. The unity that it articulates is actually "preconstituted in the passive coincidence of likeness" that we find in perceptual recognition.[43] But in reflecting upon the perceptual type in play, we focus on the *red* of the thing appearing redly, and it is comprehended not as a *likeness* of appearing moments but as an *identity* that unites them. Difference is understood as those determinations of appearance that do not enter into such a coincidence. And this introduces a crucial change at the level of grammar: "The judgment *S is p* in which *p* designates the *individual moment* in the individual object *S* is completely different from the judgment *S is p* in which *p* designates the *universal*. . . ."[44]

But in the case of pure ideation what is special to *red* cannot be discerned by relating it to the factual world (physical or psychological). While our understanding of the pure eidos always presupposes our apprehension of the corresponding universal and its relationship to other universals, its content must be determined only by the ties of necessity that obtain between those empirical universals. Its rules articulate, then, not a generally observable grouping of facts but a relationship between (empirical) essences, e.g., what must be true for there to be red *in opposition to* blue, green, etc. This would be to speak about "red" not as it "subsumes" existing moments of objects but as it "subordinates" and is subordinated by related concepts and as it figures in a genealogy of color concepts.[45] We articulate not identity in opposition to factual differences but identity in its essential difference. Thus *red* can be a *pure* essence (we need not move to color or a higher genus to get this), but only if tied to another essence (e.g., blue, green, white), and only if its *content* is determined by that relationship. It can be a priori if we can give a rule or rules that hold for any *red* object in relation to blue, green, and white ones that we can imagine and thus for all its possible examples in the world. The pure essence *red* proves to be that without which a red object "cannot be intuitively imagined as such."[46] While *red* retains its morphological character when we look at samples, as some blend into others, the relationship between the color universals themselves is such that they cover all actual and possible cases of color. The rule(s) defining that relationship are strict though they are not algorithms. There is no imprecision or vagueness at that level.

It is, of course, tempting to argue that these essences must also be *exact.* Husserl comes close to this when, in Section 89 of *Experience and Judgment,* he draws a strict parallel between pure color theory and geometry and suggests that neither of them presupposes existing samples or even the real world. In making this comparison he distinguishes the kind of necessity that can be attributed to pure essences themselves. Mathematics has eidetic laws that are necessary and universal in the strict sense, admitting of no possible exceptions. Furthermore, mathematical notions have "an exactly circumscribed multiplicity of variations" that is determined "a priori."[47] But Husserl also points to important differences. Mathematics operates by "deductive intuition" and "necessary inference," procedures denied to other domains of pure essential intuition in general and to phenomenology in particular. In short, not only is ideation (of empirical universals) different from the idealization involved in our "intuition" of pure essences, but this idealization can also be set in contrast to the formalization necessary for mathematics. To put this in terms that Husserl employs in *Formal and Transcendental Logic*, the ontology of colors is a material and not a formal ontology. We will use this hesitation on Husserl's part to return to the second question raised above, the question of how we can have pure essences that are a priori yet not exact.

In the process of free variation, *Experience and Judgment* tells us, we discover "a necessary structure" and thereby "necessary laws which determine what must necessarily belong to an object in order that it can be an object of this kind."[48] From the context we realize that it is the Kantian notion of necessity that is in play here: whereas mathematical essences give both necessary and sufficient conditions for their extensions, pure essences that are morphological can give only necessary, not sufficient, conditions for an X to be an object of this particular kind. Every member of the extension must comply with the conditions of the possibility of objects of their kind. But these conditions, unlike those of mathematics, are such that they are not sufficient to generate all the manifest determinations of such items. By contrast, the objects of mathematics are "definite manifolds" that are "exhaustively defined" by their essences. The rules "completely and unambiguously" determine the "totality of all possible formations belonging to the province."[49]

But even with this distinction between exact and strict, it still seems odd that Husserl would connect pure essences and a priori truths to a procedure that describes their apprehension, suggesting that a connection to *our understanding* of a priori truths and pure essences is essential to their being. Is this not to confuse the ideal with the real, to confuse the ideal being of pure ontological laws with the real being of our images and representations of such laws, robbing the former of their ideality? Is this not to confuse truths known independently of experience with those that rely entirely on experience, to somehow build an element of contingency into that of necessity?

Any view that takes the a priori as a kind of truth—and Husserl, with Frege, does emphasize the relationship between concepts as the locus of such truths—still has to include a fundamental epistemic person-proposition relation.[50] In order to avoid begging the question of what is meant by "independent of experience," this person-proposition relation must be true to the fact that any person who thinks about a priori propositions does so amidst a constant stream of other kinds of experience and against a background of diverse perceptual and conceptual objects. The claim that *p* is known independently of experience presupposes that a person has *enough experience* to discover or come to know that the proposition is true solely on the basis of further ratiocination. Horowitz, whose analysis is especially helpful here, has introduced into her explication of "knowing independently of experience" a contingency factor making it possible: "*a* can know *p* independently of experience if and only if in the very world in which *a* exists, *p* is true, and *a* has the concepts in *p*, *a* has enough experience to know *p*."[51] It is this factor that Husserl's account preserves. His connections between perception, empirical and pure ideation, combined with his notion of horizon, build a background of experience into the theory sufficient for a person to come to know a priori truths as qualitatively different from an empirical object or fact.

At the same time, the inclusion of the subject-proposition relation, so fundamental to phenomenology, alleviates a problem that haunts possible worlds theories. Husserl, if we are correct, was careful enough to contrast the world viewed as factual and the same world viewed as possible, and to define the a priori in terms of the latter, not in terms of possible worlds. The move to the world as possible was designed to secure the qualification that all pure ideation be independent of experience. But if we have possible worlds (plural) in play, then there is nothing to exclude a radical "epistemological type" qualification from entering, once the tie to experience is severed.[52] It is possible that God and humans know two different classes of truths, both of which are independent of experience. They might be different types of knowers with only some shared concepts. This introduces a relativizing of truths, not to individuals within a single type or single epistemological paradigm but to different types or paradigms. We can extend this beyond the case of God and humans to cases between humans:

> What is perhaps of more interest, it is possible to accommodate views according to which (i) different groups of people can know different classes of truths independently of experience, and (ii) it is literally impossible for people in one of these groups to acquire some of the concepts available to people in another of these groups (e.g., Americans/Tibetans, twentieth-century Europeans/fourteenth-century Europeans . . .).[53]

This does not undermine the possibility of a priori truth, as Horowitz suggests, for it need only be known by *some* member of *some* type. But with possible worlds theory we accommodate type diversity at the expense of relativism. By contrast, Husserl would argue that there would be a way of legitimizing one a priori concept in contrast to another and a way of adjudicating between different systems of a priori truths.

Because Husserl distinguished the factual world and that world viewed as possible rather than the actual world and possible worlds, he has, in principle, a control on an epistemological type qualification. Different groups of people knowing different classes of truths independently of experience may find a site of adjudication in the fact that these truths are related to one world as possible. At the same time this will allow Husserl to do justice to the fact that there can be different conceptual cores for different regions. I will return to these issues in chapter 11.

We will have to see how Husserl's theory of the life-world attempts to handle the relativism of epistemological types. It is a threat that haunted him even more in his later writings as he progressively expanded the scope of his phenomenology.

C. REGIONS

To the distinction between "empirical" and "pure" Husserl adds several others. We can only give a few indications. One of the essential properties of the color red is that it can appear only by being the color *of* something, only as spatially extended. While sounds seem to require only temporal spans, reds without surfaces are unthinkable. To capture this Husserl calls *red* an "abstract essence" or, shorter, an "abstractum."[54] Abstracta are "dependent moments," requiring items from a different category for their subsistence. Water pumps have no such dependency. "Water pump," by way of contrast, is a "concrete essence" or "whole" presupposing neither abstracta nor other wholes for their existence. Thus Husserl labels such essences "concreta."[55]

From this point in the account, the transition to a basic or fundamental eidos, what Husserl calls a "region," is a fairly simple matter. We submit the results of eidetic intuition to new variations. *Red* and *water pump* are understood as specifications of the genus *color* and *pump,* which are variants of *material moment* and *extended thing,* both of which are essential specifications of the region *physical object.* There is not one canonical path for several are possible. But we continue with one path until we reach a point that does not allow for the process of free variation. "The highest universals are obtained by variation of ideas."[56] In the logic of parts and wholes, which Husserl develops in the Third Investigation, the ontological relationship between pure essences can be set in contrast to the classificatory and explanatory schemes employed in the empirical sciences. A region, while it is the most general of the essences in a given domain, cannot be reached by inductive generalization; such a generalization would reduce the region to an empirical universal, to a notion as it might function in one of the empirical sciences, not in ontology. At the same time a region is the highest "synthetic unity" of a concretum (not an abstractum), and it includes its subordinate differences or species as possibilities.[57] We can speak of the essence as a "regional category," for it prescribes in a priori fashion the necessary condition or "rule" of any object being a member of this region or, phenomenologically expressed, any object appearing as an object of this basic kind. Along with Kant, Husserl thinks of such rules as a priori synthetic truths.[58]

The focus of our account thus far has been upon the relationship between types of essences, a study crucial for any systematic theory of the various domains of objects and our cognition of such domains. This study was formal in the sense that it was the nature of empirical and pure essences themselves, not differences of content, that held our interest. The differences between empirical and pure essences required us to reflect upon the various procedures or achievements by means of which each is comprehended. The gaps in, and the instability of, the relationship between different kinds of "objects," ranging from the lowest level of perception to those essences delimiting the realm of pure possibility, brought the "subject" to the fore. Husserl's descriptive method gives him the strategy by means of which he can approach and explicate the various regions according to their special content. Regional essences are, of course, pure, but in the description of each region as a whole, we move from an empirical base through shared structures to certain necessary features. A region, then, consists of a certain "*Stufenbau.*"[59] We can study the various rules that govern the "objective" relationships between elements within a step as well as those between levels. At each step, however, we are describing complexes that "appear," that are experienced or comprehended. The effort to do justice to this feature brings in phenomenological accounts of both the forms of the essences in play and their particular content, which means that it isolates those structural differences that set one region off from others in terms of its fundamentally different modes of presence.

The path we have followed in this chapter has been one that begins with phenomena and then moves "upward" to empirical and pure essences, locating regional ontologies among the latter. But there is another path that Husserl takes: a path from the top down, from the somewhat self-contained study of pure logic to its relationship to cognition. In fact, this is the working method of the *Logical Investigations* (1900–1901), which is then developed in *Formal and Transcendental Logic* (1929). There he considerably expands and develops his earlier drafts in the *Prolegomena* to his *Logical Investigations* and in the Third and Fourth Investigations,[60] speaking of pure logic as consisting of two correlative disciplines: formal ontology, which accounts for the most general conditions and forms of any object whatsoever that can be referred to in scientific discourse; and formal apophantics, which handles the conditions and forms of that discourse as well formed and meaningful.[61] Each discipline is further subdivided while remaining roughly parallel to the other:

Formal Apophantics (Formal categories of meaning)	Formal Ontology (Formal categories of objects)
1. "Pure grammar" or "pure syntax"[62]	1. Pure formal categories of any object whatsoever[65]
2. "Logic of consequences," i.e., of "non-contradiction"[63]	2. [Analytico-formal concept of possibility]
3. "Logic of possible truths"[64]	3. "Analytico-formal concept of actuality"[66]

I will have to refer the reader to other discussions of his pure logic[67] and restrict myself to tracing only one connection important for our analysis. Husserl goes on to expand the scope of this logic by suggesting that the three disciplines above provide us the "pure forms of all significational formations" and the pure forms of object formations "that as a matter of a priori possibility can occur *within* a science."[68] But in order to have both a genuine logic and a rich science we must account for "systems of judgments in their entirety,"[69] i.e., must cover different possible sciences. While Husserl's terminology is not as consistent as we would like, the introduction of this new discipline requires a distinction between idealization, which is the type of eidetic variation that is involved in our cognition of ontologies, and formalization, which does justice to the inherently mathematical character of the theory of multiplicities. When we move to this level of analysis, two additional disciplines are required:

4. "Formal theory of theory forms" or "theory of possible forms of theories"[70]	4. "Formal theory of multiplicity [Mannigfaltigkeit]"[71]

Where do material ontologies fit into this account? The shift from formal to material ontology occurs when we move from a consideration of multiplicity as a whole to a determinate manifold, from the totality of regions to one region in its particularity. Husserl places regional ontologies in contrast to formal ontology, an analytic a priori discipline, in this way:

> On the one side stand *material* essences; and in a certain sense they are the "essences proper." But on the other side there stands something that is indeed eidetic but that, nevertheless, differs in its fundamental essence: a mere *essence-form,* which is indeed an essence but completely *"empty,"* an essence that, *in the manner pertaining to an empty form, fits all possible essences;* it is an essence which, with its formal universality, has all material universalities, even the highest of them, under it and prescribes *laws* for them by virtue of the formal truths pertaining to its formal universality. There-

> fore the so-called *"formal region"* is, after all, not something co-ordinate with the material regions (the regions simpliciter); *properly it is not a region but the empty form of any region whatever;* all the regions, with all their materially filled eidetic particularizations stand, not alongside it, but *under* it—though only formally. This subordination of the material to the formal is shown by the circumstance that *formal ontology contains the forms of all ontologies* (*scl.* all ontologies "proper," all "material ontologies") and *prescribes* for material ontologies a formal structure common to them all. . . .[72]

Bernet has suggested that regional ontologies are much like what Kant describes as rational sciences. He explains:

> Unlike formal ontology, the material ontologies are oriented not toward the formal concept "object-as-such" but rather toward the concept of a region of objective being. In traditional terminology, mental and corporeal being are regions of being. The material ontologies related to these regions are then nothing other than *psychologia rationalis* (rational psychology) and rational physics as related to *natura formaliter spectata* (nature regarded formally). "Rational" sciences are distinguished from empirical sciences. While the latter observe, classify, and seek to grasp the laws governing matters of fact, the former explore the essential determination of the region of being underlying these matters of fact.[73]

As a priori disciplines, material ontologies give us "objective" laws that regulate all the items that fall within a particular domain. But ontological regions must be understood as regions of actual or possible *cognition,* not as regions of being in opposition to such cognition. The being of objects of a particular domain can be thought not just *as* given but *in* their givenness, i.e., in terms of their mode or manner of comprehension. The theory of regions necessarily involves comprehension and then judgments, which, in turn, confront us with the question of securing their validity. We can see, then, that the internal connection between ontology and apophantics is what can provide us with a bridge to issues of meaning and, thereby, to the question of intentionality. Husserl does not speak of a material apophantics, but it would arise when (a) we take a critical interest that shifts our attention from objects given to the givenness of objects in a region, (b) we attend to the sense in which such givenness can be understood as the reference of judgments whose meaning specifies the mode or manner in which an object is intended, and (c) we inquire about the different logical grammars that regulate our cognition of materially distinct regions. The effort to come to grips with the interplay between regions, cognition, and grammar eventually builds the bridge to a transcendental logic in which formal logic, or what Husserl sometimes calls "analytic logic," finds its foundations in transcendental subjectivity. We should understand, then, that the analysis of pure essences opens the gate to a host of disciplines that form the core of Husserl's "rational sciences" and his philosophy of science. If we place this analysis alongside the account we gave above of the different types of essences and their respective modes of cognition, the relationship between phenomenology and ontology involves a study of these domains:

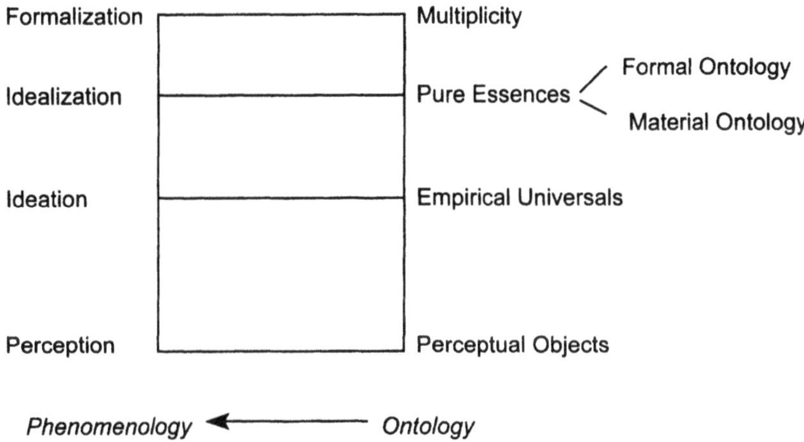

Fig. 3.1. Phenomenology and Ontology

We can now understand the sense in which the ontologies proposed by Husserl require a phenomenological account. The essences articulating the differences between regions are grounded in the fundamental, possible *modes of givenness* of those regions. Yet there is, at least for the account we have developed thus far, a co-dependence: if phenomenology provides ontology with an account of how the domains and its theory can be secured, then ontology gives phenomenology its substance, for the different regions of beings both provoke and guide our analysis into the various categories of act-meaning correlations. "The task was new, the attempt to go back radically and consistently from the respective categories of objectivities and ask about the modes of consciousness determinately belonging to them. . . . "[74] This interdependence, as well as the characterization of these correlations as the field of necessary conditions, has invited us to call this first phenomenology categorial phenomenology. In an effort to capture the sense in which this phenomenology is guided by an eidetic analysis of different regions and by the need to discover foundations for logic, and in an effort to situate his program in terms of Kant's contrast between the Aesthetic and the Analytic in his first *Critique,* Husserl refers to it as "analytic phenomenology."[75]

As this would take us down a long and difficult path, one that runs tangentially to our present course, we cannot enter here into the actual content of Husserl's regional ontologies. We have belabored the differences between types of essences and the interplay of phenomenology and ontology (before the reduction proper) because these have a direct bearing on the systematic nature of phenomenological method. But the account of regions themselves is really an application of that method. Thus we introduce them only in a general way, using the following chart with a few references from *Ideas II* in the hope that it will provide the reader with a sense of the range of Husserl's regional studies. Regional ontologies were developed in *Ideas II* with the transcendental reduction of *Ideas I* in full view. There is little doubt that for Husserl the full notion of constitution can be uncovered only after the transcendental turn, which we have yet to introduce. But the fact that regional ontologies could be situated in the pre-transcendental framework of the *Logical Investigations,*[76] and the fact that Husserl himself viewed his account of formal logic per se in *Formal and Transcendental Logic* as continuous with that earlier analysis[77] allows us to introduce regions at this stage.

In *Ideas II* Husserl proposes a fundamental distinction among the regions of physical nature, psychophysical life, and culture, the realm he calls "spirit." Significantly, Husserl does not view the essences of the different regional ontologies as hierarchically related, nor is there a linear, unidirectional ordering between the regions. Rather, different regions are much more like overlapping families with various ties of founding and founded between the categories constitutive of them. On the one hand, regions provide the grounds for all positive sciences or disciplines; on the other, each region is itself provided with a phenomenological clarification in terms of the type of noetic-noematic correlation in play. Roughly put, regional and formal ontologies, understood as internally tied to apophantics, give us the systematic form of Husserl's philosophy of science that his introduction of static phenomenology is designed to support and clarify. Table 3.1 is restricted to Husserl's own labels and is designed to give the reader only a rough idea of the range of his categorial phenomenology.

D. SUBJECTIVITY

In our account so far, the domain of mental acts and intentional contents is a dimension not directly analyzed but *implicated* by the configuration of phenomena (chapter 1) and the different types of essences (this chapter). Through their structure we are led to an awareness of the structure of this domain and the need to bring it explicitly into focus, i.e., without reflecting upon this domain we fathom neither the manifest presence of things and signs nor the fundamental differences between various eidetic levels. But how is intentionality itself to be studied?

Table 3.1. The Range of Categorial Phenomenology

The Phenomenological Attitude		Regional Ontology	Regional Field	Natural Attitude	Empirical Sciences
Act Types	**Fields of Sense**[78]				
Objectivating	Perceptual	Material things	Nature I[79]	(Theoretical)[80]	Physics[81]
Desiring[82]	Want and needs	Objects of need			
			Nature	**Naturalistic (Scientific)**[86]	**Natural Sciences**[83]
Affective valuing[84]	Felt values[85]	Objects of felt values			
Action[87]	Utility[88]	Objects of use	Nature II		
Motility	Kinesthetic	Lived body	Animal nature		Physiological psychology[89]
Empathy	Personal psychological	Soul		(Psychological)	
					Personal psychology[90]
Communicative interaction	Social psychological	Person[91]	[Human nature]	**Personalistic**	
			Spirit		
Social experience[92]	Social and political	Social persons and collectives[93]			History[94]
					Human Sciences[95]
Artistic	Cultural	Cultural objects	Culture		

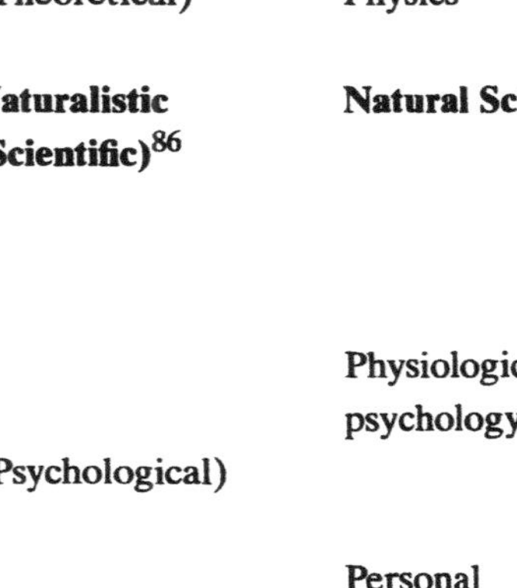

Husserl's phenomenology of "subjectivity" was designed to be not only a rigorous but also a general, structural analysis. He would have little interest in the peculiarities of how Kendra and Lianne go about perceiving corn flakes or intuiting essences as they have breakfast. The only recourse open to Husserl thus far is simply to turn his method of essential analysis upon mental life and directly subject cognition itself to eidetic description. To put it rigorously, we have *employed* a phenomenological reflection through providing a phenomenological account of the *operative* terms that allow for an eidetic analysis of various types of objects. We have yet to apply that analysis directly to the special subject matter, to that otherwise invisible "phenomenon" opened by the phenomenological reflection itself, the subject. Until this occurs, phenomenology can be no more than autobiography, a personal preface to logic. Not being itself the subject matter of analysis, it cannot serve in a "scientific" account of the cognitive conditions of ontology.

If we turn to a few elements of Husserl's notion of evidence, we can capture the reason why an account of mental acts must be more than a private, introspective affair. As we have seen, all knowledge based on perception is presumptive, provisional, fallible, undergoing constant change. This is rooted in the fact that all real objects and facts are given perspectivally and thus that there is a certain excess hidden from our gaze, an abiding indeterminacy that is inescapable. As a result, our apprehension of empirical universals is always "inadequate" in the sense that their content is always open to revision. We might say that their presence is analogous to the way objects are always given through profiles. In the case of pure essences or categories, however, this interplay of profile and object is missing. Not only do they themselves lack spatial and temporal existence but also in the move to pure possibility, the connection to empirical existence has been suspended. Pure essences have no backsides, no depth, and no "surplus" that is not comprehended. Thus they are always "adequately" given. This *phenomenological* difference between inadequate and adequate intuition is transformed into an *epistemological* difference by what Husserl calls the "principle of principles" of all phenomenology:

> . . . each originary presentative intuition is a legitimating source of cognition, everything offering itself to us in 'intuition' originally . . . is simply to be received as what it gives itself, yet only within the limits in which it gives itself.[96]

Since in their originary presentation empirical essences are given as morphological, and thus as possessing a certain indeterminacy, while pure essences are precise and adequately given, they have differential truth values. As we saw, empirical essences never lose their imprecise borders, and their rules are always open to change and correction. By contrast, pure essences function in such a way that they give the a priori "synthetic" structural conditions for an object belonging to a particular region (material ontology) or the a priori "analytic" structural conditions that govern both our discourse about objects and all objects in general (formal ontology).[97] In that such structures regulate objects, not the reverse, Husserl is convinced that our intuition of them is not inductive. Once they meet certain coherency conditions, our intuitions of them constitute certain and secure knowledge.

At this stage in our analysis, Husserl's assertions that phenomenology is rigorous and its claims true can mean no more than the claims that cognition itself has an essence and that it can be adequately intuited. We see now why Husserl thinks of phenomenological analysis as being not only reflective but also eidetic. Only what is "eidetically grasped in pure intuition" within the reflection can become "an extensive source of absolute knowledge."[98] Because of the difference in the presentations of facts and essences, Husserl is convinced that only under the eidetic reduction is phenomenology able to secure its hypotheses with unshakable evidence and thus lay claim to becoming "strict science."

The phenomenological reflection and the eidetic reduction can be understood as the operative axes that allow Husserl to treat ontological regions as fields of cognition and simultaneously to control the account of the connection between act and meaning. If we take seriously Husserl's claim that the task of his first phenomenological studies consisted of the "attempt to go back radically and consistently from the respective categories of objectivities and ask about the modes of consciousness determinately belonging to them,"[99] and if we integrate this into the difference between eidetic reduction and phenomenological reflection, then we gain purchase on the scope of Husserl's categorial phenomenology.

We are now able to confront several problems that arise when we turn with Husserl to a direct analysis of subjectivity, having first discovered several things: (a) the motives for phenomenological reflection in our experiential and discursive engagement with things; (b) the sense in which phenomenological descriptions are eidetic and, correspondingly, directed toward essences whose ideal being brings them into the realm of what can be directly grasped with certainty; and (c) that Husserl wants to preserve an internal connection between those essences and the acts in and through which they are apprehended.

We have argued that in reflecting upon our experience of things, be they sunlit beaches or broken promises, we discover a structural connection between the act and the sense in and through which the object has its determinate presence. But what precisely is the relationship between this greater structure and the particular experiences we undergo? Not only do things have a significance that can be shared by other things, their significance also transcends the particular perceiver or speaker as others see the same object or use

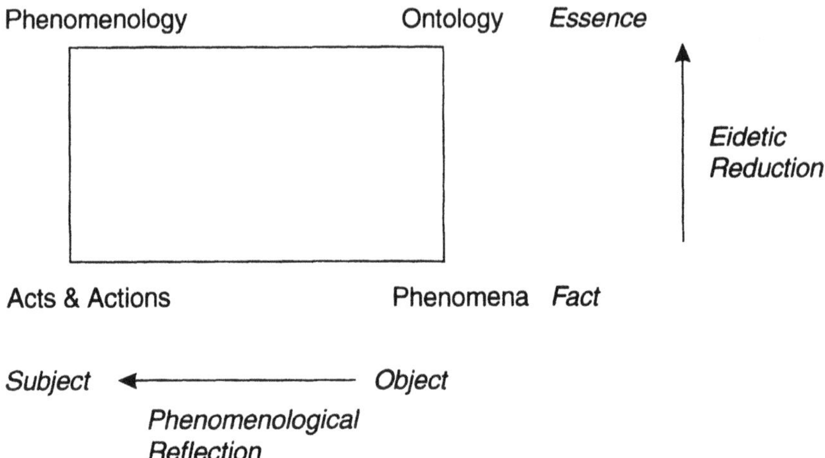

Fig. 3.2. The Axes of Categorial Phenomenology

the same concepts when describing it. In what sense, then, is this significance related to my individual acts?

Our introduction of essences presents even nastier questions for two reasons. On the one hand, Husserl has argued that there are certain achievements that are constitutive of essences and, in particular, of the difference between types, empirical universals, and pure essences. On the other hand, only a moment's reflection will tell us that ideal entities, by their very definition and their difference from the real, do not require my acts in order to exist. Pure essences are a priori and thus lack any necessary tie to the real for their existence. If they are not known *as* independent of our mental acts, themselves quite real, they cease to be ideal objects. Finding them is a matter of discovery, not invention. The equations for a body's rate of fall, for example, present me with a rule that holds true whether I have thought it or not, whether I believe it or not. "What I mean by the sentence in question or (when I hear it) grasp as its meaning, is the same thing, whether I think and exist or not, and whether or not there are *any* thinking persons and acts."[100] In fact, the order of dependency seems to be the reverse: it is that rule "outside of me" that I must comprehend if I can be said to understand gravity. Certainly, this line of thinking goes, a subject need not construct this rule in order for gravity to exist. Perhaps Husserl has not really shown the dependence of the as-structure on the for-structure but, at best, he has shown only the reverse, only the way our cognition or comprehension of phenomena must be put together, only the way in which the as-structure grounds the for-structure. We can see then that the notion of presence, when connected to the question of the for-structure, actually conceals a double ambiguity that we must now sort out: presence can mean given to me or given through me, constituted for me or constituted by me.

Husserl's first detailed response to these issues, which we find in the *Logical Investigations*, respected the requirements of realism to the extent that it distinguished the laws accounting for the essential structures of objects (his logic of parts and whole) from those accounting for our judgments (his pure logico-grammatical laws) about objects; yet it was faithful to Kant's insight that objects are not possessed of a being in opposition to understanding but have their being only as *possible* objects of cognition. His concerns in that work are predominately epistemological, and the function of its phenomenology is to ground and thereby to secure the validity of pure logic. The *Investigations* concentrated on the differences between types of evidence, ranging from the inadequate and "presumptive" givenness of sensuous perception to the adequate and direct givenness of categorial intuition, in order to show how logic belongs to the latter. It then focused upon the difference between inadequate, sensuous perception and adequate inner perception, in order to show how we can secure our judgments related to logical categories and laws. As a result, the questions as to how one places pure essences or pure logical laws in relation to concrete acts of understanding, and as to how one situates the semantic content by which objects are intended and given, were answered by handling both in an analogous fashion.

Husserl's account of the relationship between essences and mental life places three ideas in relation to each other: (a) neither individuals nor essences should ever be confused with the meaning in and through which they are presented; (b) the intuition of a logical law is not essential to the being of that law; and (c) ideal laws, however, can regulate acts of thinking. Let me deal with these in order.

1. The difference between an essence and the manner in which it is given, itself dependent upon the intentional acts, is roughly the difference between referent and meaning. One should never confuse the number 4 and the way it is presented, e.g., the second even number in the number series. Since meaning is also ideal, Husserl adds: "The universality *that* we think of does not . . . resolve itself into the universality of the meanings *in which* we think of it."[101]

2. The analysis that we undertook in the earlier part of this chapter attempted to show how we come to essences by "ascending" from the level of perception to that of ideation and idealization. In the language of the *Investigations*, we move from sensuous intuition to categorial intuition. And we saw that, in *Experience and Judgment*, this image of a fixed event is replaced by a notion of process, of eidetic variation. The process, however, does not "create" the logical laws any more than perception creates real objects. At this point in our analysis we can say only that essences are viewed under the aspect of our

cognition of them, that the process is necessary for the comprehension, but not for the being, of ideal laws. Husserl puts it this way:

> The capacity to comprehend ideationally the universal in the singular, to comprehend intuitively [*schauend*] the concept in the empirical presentation, and to be assured of the identity of our conceptual intentions in repeated presentation, is presupposed by the possibility of cognition. Just as, in the act of ideation, we intuitively apprehend a concept—as the single species, whose unity over against factual instances, or instances thought of as matters of fact, we lay hold of insightfully—so we can also gain the evidence of the logical laws, which relate to concepts formed in this or that manner. . . . Wherever acts of conceptual presentation are carried out, we encounter concepts: our presentations have their "contents," their ideal meanings, which we can take possession of abstractively, in ideational abstraction, and this means that we have given generally the possibility of the *application* of logical laws. The *validity* of these laws is, however, absolutely unrestricted; it does not depend on us or anyone else being able to perform conceptual presentations, or to sustain or repeat such presentations in the consciousness that they have the identical intention.[102]

3. It is not Husserl's argument with the psychologistic theories of his day but with the anti-psychologistic formalists, his philosophical kin, that tells us the most about how he characterizes the relationship between logic's laws (which he considered not only unconditional but purely theoretical) and human thought. His approach revolves around the thesis that "every theoretical statement . . . permits of a normative transformation"[103] or, to put it in terms of whole disciplines, "pure logic is that first and most essential foundation of methodological logic,"[104] methodological logic being understood as the working, applied method of the sciences. While basic laws of logic are not in themselves rules of mental acts of thinking, and while they do not, as theoretical, directly regulate the working methods and practice of science, they necessarily become normative of the "specifically human art of thinking"[105] if one wants to think coherently. In addition, they become regulative of historically circumscribed scientific methods and techniques of knowing, if science lays claim to objective, coherent theory and to truth.[106] While the theoretical discipline of logic has no "concern with mental facts," Husserl says, logical terms and laws once transformed do serve as "general names for psychical experiences and dispositions."[107] Such names as "presentation," "concept," "judgment," "syllogism," "proof," "theory," "necessity," etc., can "stand for class-concepts of mental states such as belong to psychology."[108] Such laws, then, are psychological only after being transformed; once transformed they are related to individual, mental events or acts as concept is to extension or, since Husserl thinks of such laws as essences, as a species is to its instances.

The analysis of signification and of what the *Investigations* generally calls "meaning-bestowing acts" is of necessity more complicated, for the idealities we are considering seem to have their being only as expressed by mental acts. The First Investigation is careful to tether meaning to what is in principle expressible in signs. Generally following Brentano's distinction between two irreducibly different types of acts, presentations (*Vorstellungen*) and judgments (*Urteile*), Husserl thinks of the first as what is brought to expression by the use of names (proper and common) and the second by the use of a certain class of sentences. Presentations can exist without judgments, but all judgments point back to at least one presentation on which they are based. In the case of linguistically articulated judgments, Husserl treats their meaning as a constitutive element of our cognitive relationship to the world; in using them, the speaker purports to refer *to* a referent in and *through* the meaning (itself an ideal significational unity, a thought) expressed by the signs. Correspondingly, understanding the meaning of an assertion is to grasp the (semantic) referent as the speaker intends it.[109]

But how is meaning, ideal in nature, to be connected to acts of judging if we assume that these are psychological factual events? Husserl expands upon this provisional account in the Fifth Investigation by distinguishing between the quality and the matter of an act (Section 20), a contrast that has become almost commonplace due to the work of Austin and Searle.[110] Presenting, asserting, questioning and wishing are acts with different qualities that can all have the same content, e.g., "there are intelligent beings on Mars." The opposite case, an act with the same quality having different contents, is also possible, e.g., I can judge not only that there are intelligent beings on Mars but also that they like bagels and that bagels are even heavier there than they are in New York. But just what do we mean by content here? If the content is a state-of-affairs or an intentional object, then it is an object toward which the act is directed; it "transcends" the act and is not "part" of it, Husserl suggests. This is, in fact, the case in fulfilling acts. But acts need not be fulfilled to be intentional and to have significance. In fact, our Martians with their bagels do not exist at all. What, then, does content mean? Husserl claims that by content he means not the object intended but "being related to an object" or, better, "the manner [*Weise*] of objective relation."[111] This would mean that differences in content would be differences exhibited in how *the act itself* is related to the object, i.e., pointing to or "presenting" this and not that object in the case of names, "judging" about this and not that state-of-affairs in the case of sentences.[112] The matter or content, then, is that which gives the act reference to an object "*in the precise way in which it is intended.*" It determines "not only *that* it grasps the object but also *as* what it grasps it."[113] The matter of the act is specified by the sense or meaning "animated" or lived through in the act of apprehension.[114]

What makes this untidy, however, is that the Fifth Investigation also clearly speaks of the matter of the act as both its sense and yet as a *part* of the act: "quality and matter count for us . . . as the wholly essential, and so never to be dispensed with, constituents [*Bestandstücke*] of an act."[115] More directly, "content in the sense of 'matter' is a component of the concrete act-experience [*Komponente des konkreten Akterlebnisses*]."[116] Quality and content are said to form the "intentional essence" of the act. Since this covers all acts of cognition, Husserl further tailors this notion for speech-acts alone by speaking of it as having a "semantic essence [*bedeutungsmäßige Wesen*]." The term essence, however, points us in the right direction. He adds the clarification for which we are looking: "The ideational abstraction of this essence yields 'meaning' in our ideal sense."[117] This settles the issue as to what Husserl means by "component." It means component of the essence of the act, not of the act itself. What shows this is that you and I can have different "presentations" of Greenland's icy wastes in the sense of numerically and psychologically different mental images or acts, but we can have the same "content" and "presentation" in the sense of sharing the same *manner of being directed* to the object, of intending it according to the same *meaning*. Husserl explains:

> Talk about the same presentation, judgment, etc., points to no individual sameness of acts, as if my consciousness were in some way conjoined with someone else's. It also means no relation of perfect likeness, of indiscernibility as regards inner constituents [*innere Konstituentien*], as if the one act merely duplicated the other. We have the same presentation of a thing, when we have presentations in which the thing is not merely presented, but presented as exactly the same; following our previous treatment we may add "presented with the same apprehensional sense" or "based on the same matter."[118]

This leads us to Husserl's own formulation of how ideal senses or meanings are to be related to acts.

> The genuine identity that we here assert is none other than the *identity of the species*. As a species, and only as a species, can it, as ideal unity, span the dispersed multiplicity of individual singulars. . . . The multiple singulars of the ideally one meaning are, naturally, the corresponding acts [second edition: act moments] of intending, the meaning-intention. The meaning is related to the actual acts of intending (the logical presentation to the act of presentation, the logical judgment to the act of judgment, the logical conclusion to the act of concluding) just as redness *in specie* is related to the slips of paper lying here all "having" the same redness. In addition to other constituting moments (extension, form, and such like) each strip has its individual redness, i.e., its individual instance [*Einzelfall*] of this color-species, though it itself exists neither in these strips nor anywhere else in all the world, and particularly not "in our thought" in so far as the latter is part of the domain of real being, of the sphere of temporality.

> Meanings form, we can say further, a class of *concepts* in the sense of *"universal objects."*[119]

But just what is the instance, the individual case that we correlate to meaning? On the one hand, we can say that it is the concrete act as a whole with its quality and matter. On the other hand, Husserl understands the matter as the particular manner in which an individual act intends or takes its object. The act might have "other constitutive moments," but it is the manner of its relatedness that is the individual feature that serves as the instance of the meaning. This must be what Husserl has in mind when he says:

> We conceive of meanings as ideal unities. . . . A certain moment in the concrete act of intending corresponds to the meaning. The essential character of this act consists in this moment, i.e., it necessarily belongs to each concrete act in which this same meaning is "realized."[120]

This means that Husserl views the essence of intentional acts as consisting of an a priori *connection* between act and sense (ideal). We do not yet have an a priori *correlation* of act and sense. Let me briefly expand on this thought by noting a significant advantage of his early approach and then two corrections that Husserl introduces later.

Distinguishing between the essence (as species) and instance of the act, Husserl's intentional characterization of acts makes no ontological commitments as to how the instance is put together neurophysiologically. "The ideality of what is specific is . . . the complete opposite of reality [*Realität*] or individuality."[121] To assume that it does is to confuse an essential "macro-feature" of acts as a whole (its intentional or semantical essence) with its real "micro-features," analogous to confusing the moisture of water with the lattice structure of water molecules.[122] Just as water can be wet without any of its molecules being wet, so acts can "have" meaning without any of their underlying "real" components being that meaning. What is "really in" the act does not arise because Husserl leaves open the question of the material composition (in principle, even the empirical psychological composition) of the instances. The meaning or signification as "semantic essence" is individuated in a real act or a series of real acts, but it does not exist as ideal "in" the particular psychological event.

> The psychological stock [*Bestand*] here involved is well-known to be vastly manifold, varying greatly from one individual to the next, and for the same individual from one moment to another, even in respect to "one and the same" word.[123]
>
> . . . it is, therefore, understandable that our unified experience of the meaningfully functioning expression should, from case to case, reveal considerable psychological differences even while its meaning remains strictly the same.[124]

The only requirement here is that, however its physical or psychological "stuff" or "stock" is constructed as a "real" event, the act *as a whole* exhibits a differentiated manner of presenting or intending the object. This preserves, Husserl believes, both the ideality of meaning and the reality of psychological acts. Of course, we will see directly that this is immediately rendered problematic by Husserl's own description of his analysis as a piece of "descriptive psychology,"[125] an issue not really sorted out until he places psychology in clear opposition to transcendental phenomenology. But the fact that Husserl distinguishes the structural features of the act from the act as a fact means that his early theory is much closer to what we find in *Ideas I* than what is usually assumed. If there is a difficulty with the specifics of the early theory, Husserl realizes, it has to do with how meaning itself was characterized.

Husserl attempts to *assimilate* the signification constitutive of speech-acts or, more broadly, of all intentional acts, into the notion of essence. This results in his characterization of the relationship between meaning and acts as a *connection* between individual and species. If acts were treated as real psychological events, then locating meaning in them would both threaten their ideality and clearly undermine his whole critique of psychologism. Husserl combines this concern with an argument that meaning must be a species in order to account for its ideality, and that its ideality is necessary to account for (a) the repetition of signs with the same intentional content in different acts, (b) the presence of conceptual import from signs even in the absence of reference, and (c) the sharing of that same import by different speakers or hearers. But this analysis probably confuses *being ideal* with *being a species,* and then confuses acts of signification *having* an essence (which they do, no matter how the "ideality" of their meaning is characterized) with signification (as ideal) *being* an essence. This is initially corrected by Husserl's transcendental turn, which first stabilizes his effort to remove the features of acts as described from the realm of the real. The turn, then, secures its descriptions as ones that isolate structural features or moments that are necessary conditions of real acts. Further, connection comes through understanding such structural features as organized in such a way that we have a *correlation* of act-qualities with the meanings in and through which objects are intended. Both are *parts* (technically, interdependent moments) of the transcendental structure of the act. In this revised account, which we find emerging in the period between the *Investigations* and *Ideas I,* the signifying acts themselves are no longer instances of ideal meanings for the simple reason that the signifying component is now viewed as part of their (transcendental) structure. As a result, the a priori connection of act and meaning becomes a correlational a priori of noesis and noema. This change is supported by another that occurs between *Ideas I* and *Formal and Transcendental Logic,* in which Husserl reformulates his understanding of the ideal of meaning in terms of a certain rule governing the use of signs or, to express its phenomenological counterpart, a certain ability we have to use signs to refer to objects "again and again" (*immer wieder*). Meaning is not an essence, not an ideal entity to which we refer or which we employ to represent something other than itself, but rather is what one could call a *scheme* of signification. Intentions can be repeated as well as shared by others. They are not atemporal but transtemporal, not so much ideal as "irreal."[126] We will return to this again in chapter 7.

This leads us to a final set of problems that arises when we notice a certain circularity in play. Phenomenology, designed to give a grounding to essences as they function in cognition, necessarily uses essences to know the nature of subjectivity. This has the result of transforming the grounding discipline into one of the regions known and thus calls into question its foundational status. In fact, there is an important difference between an ontological and an epistemological (and then phenomenological) notion of foundation in play that Husserl seems to overlook.[127]

As we have suggested, it is possible to undertake an eidetic analysis of different regions of objects without explicitly reflecting upon the cognizing subject. In principle it is also possible to undertake a reflective study of mental life that recognizes its fundamental difference from objects of nature but still preserves its status as a region. But this seems to reintroduce a new threat of psychologism. Initially Husserl did not see this difficulty, because for him the phenomenological reflection simultaneously included an eidetic reduction, and thus he thought the differences in essences between the subjective and the objective sufficient to support his contrast between the fields of phenomenology and ontology. He did not fully realize that, according to the force of the distinctions in play, the phenomenological description of the mental would be identical to what would be produced through an essential analysis of the region of the psyche, i.e., through a regional ontology of psychological life.

Husserl came to see, in other words, that the special content of his first phenomenology, whose role it was to provide an epistemological grounding of the various disciplines, might itself be construed as a regional discipline. After the *Investigations* he realized that its phenomenology, even as it stood over against the empirical psychology of his day, could legitimately be reframed as a phenomenological psychology. Indeed, the first edition even referred to it as a "descriptive psychology."[128] While the *Investigations* avoided the typical empiricist forms of psychologism, it nevertheless might have fallen prey, Husserl worries, to taking one of the limited regions in need of grounding (psychology) for the ground itself, a category mistake not within or between regions but, even worse, between the regions and their ground.[129] As this issue will be considered at length later,[130] we only emphasize again the fact that the phenomenology we are presently using to clarify regional ontologies is one that had not been submitted to what *Ideas I* would come to call the transcendental reduction. Though this early phenomenology involved a phenomenological reflection, in the final analysis it would belong to what Husserl would call the natural attitude. Perhaps we should say that this phenomenology has not yet escaped the natural attitude, to the extent that Husserl believed that this attitude would enframe the discipline of psychology. Even though we will give a rigorous description of the connection itself, there is, at this point, no way of justifying the general applicability of a correlational approach to all regions of being. As a result this phenomenology remains a well-motivated strategy but not yet a self-grounded method.

E. CONSTRAINTS

Husserl's phenomenology called philosophy from its preoccupation with speculation and argumentation back to an uncluttered consideration of the field of experience basic to human understanding. Using his further reflections in the 1920s on this first approach, we may say that categorial phenomenology actually imposes a twofold restriction upon the analysis of the field of experience. First, we are limited to a general classificatory analysis of types of mental acts and experiences that would belong to a theory of knowledge. One way of understanding the scope of this first program is historically. Roughly, the method of categorial phenomenology was embraced and employed by the Munich school of phenomenology, a group of thinkers that took their inspiration from the phenomenology of Husserl's *Logical Investigations* and rejected the transcendental turn of *Ideas I.*[131] Secondly, the very notion of eidetic intuition, even as expanded by an account of the process of variation, is a mode of analysis that takes temporally different samples only according to their manifest determinations and describes them using the dyads of similar and contrasting, identity and difference, form and materials. As a result, intentional acts undergo a structural rather than a processional analysis. This first approach tends to stylize acts as achievements that work with fixed meanings within established contexts. Their labor, as it were, is one of selection, of choice, of comparison and contrast, and of providing decisive confirmation. Acts are not studies as actions, even less as interactions, as dynamic, productive, and pregnant. They are events, not processes. With an orientation toward what can be gleaned by pure idealization, they exhibit only synchronic, not diachronic, features.

We might even say, to echo the text of 1921, that Husserl comes to read this first phenomenology as a limited project, caught up in a labor of conceptual "sorting" (*Scheidung*), of mastering phenomena through "categories," and of describing the various "types" of act-meaning-object correlations and their systematic "order" with respect to each other.[132] Its goal is to provide a typology of acts in relation to varying fields of objects and, finally, to the various a priori disciplines forming our regional and formal ontologies.

Thus in this first account the life of the subject is schematized not in terms of its cognitive development, even less of its loves and labors, but rather in terms of its immediate acts of cognition, what it believes and what it knows. The analysis always reaches for structural conditions; therefore, the dynamic process involved in the generation of such acts of cognition is systematically disregarded. The result is that conscious life is viewed as a correlational, intentional structure, precisely that kind of structure that can be unfolded by an analysis of the necessary conditions of knowledge.

4

The Transcendental in Transcendence

What is actually perceived, what is more or less clearly co-present and determined . . . , is partially permeated, partially enveloped by an horizon, itself dimly conscious, of indeterminate reality.

—Husserl (1913)[1]

The first breakthrough of this universal a priori of correlation between experienced object and manners of givenness (which occurred during work on my *Logical Investigations* around 1898) affected me so deeply that my whole subsequent life-work has been dominated by the task of systematically elaborating on this correlational a priori.

—Husserl (1936)[2]

A. FROM PHENOMENOLOGY TO PHILOSOPHY

The analysis undertaken thus far employs a descriptive approach that treats things and kinds of things in relation to acts of cognition. The account of the structural differences between various act-object clusters simultaneously shows which types are irreducible to each other and which are simple or more basic than higher order or more complex types. The approach is phenomenological because the typological differences between objects given to us in our "straightforward" engagement with them is interpreted through a "reflective" analysis that describes the types of acts and patterns of significance subtending their presence. It seems, though, that the general applicability of this scheme of description is limited, for up to this point in our analysis we can claim of intentionality only that it is a general structure that accounts for the cognitive relationship between the as- and for-structure. Even so, this theory, whose contours we have only sketched, is powerful and innovative. Its proper analysis could easily occupy us for the rest of this book. For some of Husserl's contemporaries it sufficed as the working method they employed throughout their philosophical careers; categorial phenomenology and the method of eidetic insight and description were all the basic tools needed by some of

Husserl's closest associates, the Munich school, to launch rich philosophical investigations of their own.

As his thinking progressed, Husserl came not to reject their efforts but rather to view these studies as limited undertakings because of their foreshortening of the question of method. But then the latter was everything to him. He writes in a letter to Ingarden in 1918:

> Even Pfänder's phenomenology is, in fact, something essentially different from mine. Because the problem of constitution never fully surfaces he, who is otherwise basically reliable and solid, lands in a dogmatic metaphysics. Already Geiger is only 1/4 phenomenology.[3]

All that his reflective descriptions provided, Husserl came to believe, was an introduction, a "first ordering,"[4] a few preliminary steps requiring many more if phenomenology were to become a foundational discipline. This can be put more forcefully: the categorial phenomenology of the *Investigations* is more of a prolegomena to philosophy than philosophy itself. Husserl realized between the *Logical Investigations* (1900–1901) and *Ideas I* (1913) that, while his investigations certainly supplied seminal studies into the phenomenological bases of a theory of logic and cognition, his method lacked the scope and universality required to make it genuinely philosophical. It had neither broken free of providing a "critique of knowledge"[5] nor entered the courts of philosophy. We find two structural paradoxes that kept his phenomenology outside philosophy's gates:

1. We have stressed that regional categories are not of a single order or family. Rules of contrasting regions may be different in content as well as in type. We can look for certain conditions that apply to all regions, as we saw in the last chapter, but this requires us to "empty out" their content as we move to the level of "any object whatsoever" and submit them to a formal analysis. Husserl accepts the formalist strategy of bringing the rules constitutive of different regions under the domain of other rules, more general or universal in scope, and eventually under formal mathematics, but then argues that, in order to uncover true grounds, such regional and formal rules must become "clues" to a transverse account that ties them to what we have called the correlational a priori. As a supplement and then as grounds for the formal model, Husserl provides an analysis of cognitive achievements, incapable of being reduced to formal rules, that accounts for factors essential to the structure of knowledge. Furthermore, since it is the correlational a priori that accounts for the ordering of different regions, it cannot be one of the regions, and thus is not derived by moving to yet a higher node of generality in the trees of species and genus relations. But this leads to a problem that can be formulated via the concept of intuition: even if we grant that essential analysis may be a method

suitable for dealing with particular regions, it is clearly an open question as to whether this analysis is capable of comprehending the general structure of subjectivity holding for *all* regions since, by definition, its structure is different from that of the regions. The backside of this criticism runs as follows: in assuming that consciousness has an essence that can be intuited (and then described in terms of the notion of an intentional a priori), we necessarily assume that consciousness can become an object (*Gegenstand*). But to the extent that it is an object, it ceases to be capable of providing the ground for any object whatsoever. Our account in the last chapter relied upon the notion of an intentional a priori, but we still do not have the methodological resources to account for its "position" as a grounding structure and thus do not have a very precise analysis of its role in Husserl's theory.

This problem is akin to another in the same family. The analysis of empirical and pure essences was introduced in order to clarify the structure of various regional ontologies, including the region of the psyche. It allowed us to accomplish two things *within* regional studies: to differentiate between empirical generalizations or "contingent" essences and a priori categories, and to specify the necessary conditions of all objects in the region, and thereby define the scope and essential features of the region. The phenomenological analysis of the underlying structure of intentionality then functioned to ground the analysis of empirical and pure essences by providing a scheme in terms of which regions of being could be understood as regions of cognition. But a difficulty arises in the type of essence that articulates the structure of intentionality itself. Our first characterization worked with the idea that the essence of intentionality is not exact but morphological; i.e., it is not a rule that generates its set by an exhaustive specification or "exact determination"[6] of the features of its members, but rather it is a structure shared by existing acts having diverse features and thus apprehended only in "descriptive concepts."[7] If its structure were given as an empirical essence, however, then intentionality would be only a product of generalization and thus no more than a probable, general feature. Because it would lack necessity and universality, it could not serve as a foundational structure. Thus Husserl rightly denies that the intuition of acts and their thematization as intentional depends upon induction.[8] He also argues that at a certain level of generality, descriptive concepts are no longer "vague" but "strict"[9] and "pure." While particular correlations can be apprehended in terms of their possibility and thus as pure essences (in the region of psychology), the single structure said to subtend *all* regions (and this must include psychology) cannot be given in a pure essence, as described thus far, for the following reason: this structure is not a region or a regional category, it is not the highest category over all regions, and it is not the formal condition of a single region or of the totality of regions. Rather, it belongs to another order, transversely situated, accounting for a certain coincidence between the edifice of knowledge and the order of being. To contrast the straightforward attitude with the reflective, and to say that reflection is sufficient to transform what is not an object into an object, either begs the question or simply avoids the issue of whether one should apply "object-like" analyses to intentionality. Categorial phenomenology, therefore, seems to employ the notion of intentionality as basic, without being able to clarify or justify either the sense in which that which is no object is an object, or that special discourse required for its thematization. In short, we have not given adequate justification for applying the resources of essential analysis to what in principle is neither a region nor the form of all regions, not an object but the condition of all objecthood.

This line of criticism is very close to what Thomas Seebohm has defined as "the paradox of subjectivity" that attends a phenomenology whose method is limited to the reflective, eidetic method of the *Investigations*, to "a mundane" or world-bound reflection. Seebohm calls it mundane phenomenology; Husserl himself labels it empirical phenomenology:[10]

> The universal form of this "paradox of subjectivity" runs as follows: every reflection that analyzes the activities in which the subject both knows what is and tries to determine the justifiable validity claims of such a knowing must consider the world or sum total of beings known as the correlate of the knowing subject. However, in such a mundane reflection the being of the knowing subject can only be understood as "being in the world." Hence, the knowing of the world *is* also in the world. Since every being in the world is what it is only as determined by its environment or its place in the world, this is the case as well with the subject's "knowing of the world." Thus, if one raises the question of the "being" of the subject in the mundane attitude, the consequence of the most general answer is relativism. This relativism destroys the very possibility of the claims for universal validity, which is at least assumed to be a possibility at the beginning of every epistemological reflection.[11]

2. In formulating the task and content of philosophy, Plato and especially Aristotle argued that it is, first and foremost, not a science of beings but a science of the being of beings, not about the many things that are but about "the whole of being as such."[12] Things, of course, have their to-be in being this or that. While their determinate presence engages our interest and diverse types of cognition, there is, implicit in our apprehension of "what" a thing is, an acquaintance with its "is." Yet "to be" is not another determination of the thing nor is it a most general concept including all determinations. Aristotle insisted that "to be" belongs to a different order. "This science is not the same as any of the particular sciences."[13] The generality of being is not that of a genus, does not cover the highest region of things according to a species and genus classification.[14] In relation to such classificatory trees we can, following medie-

val thinkers, characterize being itself as "transcendental," for neither can it be comprehended as a being nor does it belong to the field of those concepts that specify or are themselves specified by beings.

Husserl's name for that totality which includes all that is without itself being a being reads "world."[15] It is striking that the opening pages of *Ideas I,* a work that attempts, above all else, to transform "pure phenomenology" into "a phenomenological philosophy," as the title reminds us, begin with this notion: "The world is the totality of objects of possible experience . . . "[16] Yet if the world is not an object, not even in Husserl's broad sense, its comprehension cannot be explained in terms of the apprehension of an object, whether real or ideal. This distinction enables us to formulate a counterpart to the paradox about the nature of subjectivity just discussed. A gap in method becomes visible, for to the extent that eidetic intuition is suitable for constructing regional and formal ontologies, it is highly inappropriate for the task of apprehending what in principle is never objectively present, never a *Gegenständlichkeit.* The features of the world as a "whole" will not be those of regions *within* the world, of its "parts," nor can they be the features of the set of all objects if the notion of world is a grounding and not a formal notion. Let me call this the paradox of objectivity.

In fact there is a double problem here. Not only is the world different from what one gains through an ontological analysis, it is also different from what can be gleaned from concentrating on the interconnection between the quality and the matter of acts. Neither the in- nor the from-structure can ever be comprehended by those forms of cognition appropriate to the as-structure. For phenomenology to become *philosophy,* then, it must not only deliver a science of regions within the world but also give us an account of how our knowledge of the world itself is possible. In addition, it must provide not just a phenomenology of the interdependency of the as- and for-structures but also a phenomenology of the in-structure in a way that does not confuse it with the first.[17]

If wonder at the fact that objects are given in and through profiles leads naturally to phenomenological reflection, then the emergence of these two paradoxes pushes that phenomenology beyond itself into philosophy. The paradoxes introduce a motivation for the development of phenomenology into a transcendental register coming from the requirements of philosophy itself. The paradox that cognition can be conceptualized as the basis for the givenness of all phenomena only if it is one of the things that appears, and the paradox that the totality of beings can be comprehended only as a being entail that mundane phenomenology is incoherent.

In fact, another issue that stirred Husserl runs even deeper than internal consistency, as important as such consistency must be for a logician attempting to undergird logic with proper footings. When Husserl first introduced phenomenology in the *Investigations,* he set it in opposition to psychologism, the program of reducing logical laws to psychological laws. Such a theory denied the universal and necessary character of logic precisely because "psychological 'laws' are for us 'empirical laws,' approximate generalities of coexistence and succession, relating to matters of fact which may in one case be thus, in another case otherwise."[18] His own characterization, in the first edition, of his phenomenological study of logic as "descriptive psychology,"[19] though it stunned Frege and created confusions that Husserl regretted, was not so much a betrayal of Husserl's initial critique as an unfortunate choice of terms. From the outset his phenomenology operated with both a type of description and a notion of mental life fundamentally different from those current in the empiricist psychological theories of his day. In addition Husserl was convinced that his "laws" of mental life have validity independent of what we glean by empirical generalization. What proved much more threatening was Husserl's growing realization that there is a third discipline, "phenomenological psychology," one which he himself brought into being,[20] and one which is neither empiricist psychology nor phenomenological philosophy proper. What surprised him was that its scope is such that act-meaning connections, such as those studied in the last chapter, fall under its domain. But since phenomenological psychology is a regional discipline, Husserl had a new threat of psychologism coming from within phenomenology itself. Thus while the *Investigations* as a whole was designed as a response to psychologism and thereby to relativism, Husserl realized that in refuting the first he had only opened up a much more serious form of the second. Isolating the most powerful motive for Husserl's own development, we can say that he realized that these two paradoxes, which constitute the underlying tensions of all the various types of relativism he criticized (psychologism, anthropologism, naturalism, historicism), are inescapable structural features of categorial phenomenology itself. Because relativism leads to skepticism, phenomenology would become yet another symptom of the groundlessness of thought rather than a response to it. The notion of motivation here should not be understood in psychological terms. Skepticism functions transcendentally, creating the "classical situation" for the beginning of true philosophy: "ideally it is clear that the idea of an absolute and radically grounded science must draw [*schöpfen*] its meaning from such a situation lest it inevitably land only in epistemological naiveté."[21] Faced with an outcome opposite its design, transcendental phenomenology must become a discipline that allows us to get at the heart of relativism from the side of philosophical method.

I will return to the question of relativism through the issue of psychologism in chapter 10 and thus will delay its discussion until that time. In this chapter I will deal with the paradox of the world and allow its clarification to open up an account of the first problem. At the same time, there is a second task at hand in this chapter. I want to take one step back from Husserl's texts and allow the ideas we have developed in the last three chapters to flow on their own. While Husserl's formulation of his transcendental method in *The Idea of Phenomenology*[22] and *Ideas I* was bound up with the requirements of his Cartesian way, I will be following my hunch in this chapter that there is a notion of what he called the phenomenological reduction that is central to the project of static phenomenology but is somewhat independent of certain specific features of its Cartesian formulation in those two works. The next chapter, however, will turn to them in some detail and situate their Cartesian approach in relation to what we discover here. Focusing on the issue of the world, set in contrast for the moment to the concept of subjectivity, allows us to do this.

B. THE WORLD IN TRANSCENDENCE

In first describing the phenomenological turn we saw that objects of experience rely upon, as they also reveal, an acquaintance with the perceptual and conceptual capabilities of the experiencing subject. Using this acquaintance as our guiding clue, we were able to draw cognitive acts into the account. The experience of objects, however, discloses much more, for these same objects open upon and implicate an acquaintance with the world. In seeing, hearing, or touching things at hand, Husserl argues in the opening sections of the "Basic Phenomenological Considerations" of *Ideas I,* we simultaneously co-apprehend the world itself. How are we to understand this?

Notice that our experience of a thing is such that it does not apprehend isolated or discrete items requiring special acts, comparing them with other items, equally discrete, and then combining them into wholes. Rather, a thing appears in the shifting and relative interplay of profile and object. If we "break down" the experience and view the object "abstractively," we realize that, in our perception of the object as a whole, we experience more than what we find in each of its perspectives. We find that the object given "transcends" the actual profiles and, in the shift from one to the other, its determinate presence is neither exhausted nor fully given in any one of them. In the same way, the object "itself" presents and makes present something more than we find "in itself." In our opening example, the pump as a whole is itself but a "profile" of the courtyard, the farm, perhaps the surrounding hills. In being directed toward the pump we are co-directed beyond it. In every act of fulfillment giving us the water pump, new anticipations arise that point to the environment in which the pump is situated and then even beyond that to ever wider fields. Even when our intentions are disappointed and our initial expectations dashed, when things we thought existed dissolve into illusions, a basic trust in the existence of the world perdures. Ongoing experience may cancel our "particular belief" in the existence of the object, but it does so only on the basis of an abiding confidence or "general belief" in the existence of the world. It is this belief which gives to intentional acts both their direction and their teleological organization and which even augments the "forgetting" of subjectivity that is constitutive of its transcendence.

This "pointing" of objects beyond themselves to the world is made possible by the fact that backgrounds contribute to and thus are internally tied to the determinations exhibited by objects. For example, in a production entitled "Multiples" performed by the Berlin Tanzfabrik, there are dance movements set in three different scenes to contrasting voices, costumes, and stage settings, each with what we take to be a different solo dancer. Various slides are projected on the wall with lyrics ranging from nonsensical dada phonemes to black street poetry. Several identical dance movements are repeated, but their changed sequential relations to each other as well as their new settings make it difficult to recognize them from one scene to the next. Only during the curtain call at the end of the piece do we realize that it was not three different dancers but a single one that performed the three solos. Here the background, usually unnoticed because of the familiarity of our settings, overwhelmed the figure, bringing the individuality, the "face" of the dancer, into subjection. Interestingly, the recognition of the single dancer brings with it not only a correction of our earlier experience but also an awareness of the usually invisible interplay between object and environment.

Thus, even before the incisions of philosophy, we are acquainted with objects as objects-in-the-world and thereby with the world. Husserl tells us in *Ideas I:*

> In this way I find myself in waking consciousness—all the time, without being able to change it—in relation to one and the same world perduring throughout changes in the composition of its contents. It is continually "at hand" for me, and I myself am a member of it. Thereby, this world is not there for me simply as a world of mere things but, in the same immediacy, as a world of values, a world of goods, a practical world. I find the things before me equipped not only with material properties but also with value traits, such as beautiful and hideous, pleasing and displeasing, agreeable and disagreeable, etc. Immediately things stand there as objects of use, the "table" with its "books," the "drinking glass," the "vase," the "piano," etc. These values and practical traits belong constitutively to the "at hand" objects as such, regardless of whether or not I am occupied with them and the objects.[23]

Borrowing a term that Husserl uses starting in the early 1920s,[24] we call this world the *pregiven* world. We do this for two reasons: first, in order not to prejudge whether it is identical to what Husserl speaks of later as the lifeworld, an issue we will take up in chapter 13; and second, in order to set it in contrast to two transcendental *characterizations* of that world, one ontological and the other phenomenological. We are directly, if only tacitly, acquainted with the pregiven world but not originally as an *object* of knowledge, whether scientific or philosophical. In perceiving an object, I simultaneously receive its background. To do justice to the fact that the world (*Welt*) as a whole is always manifest in and through the particular world (*Umwelt*)—be it an economic or an aesthetic world, a factory or a home, etc.—we must not confuse the *pregiven world* (whole) with a *co-given environment* (part) in which not only particular objects, but also my individual relationship to these objects, is situated. In a text from 1925, Husserl explains it in this way:

> . . . we must say that not only single world-realities are experienced, but also from the start, the world is experienced. Though an especially attending and grasping perception may hold simply for this house here, still, we have the house in a broader perceptual field; the surrounding street, the garden are also partially in this field, and even are actually seen. But, in that respect the world has no end; every field of seeing and looking has an open outer horizon, which can not be separated from that experience. To it belong, with regard to consciousness, the possible continuations of experience in which visual field lines up with visual field, actual field of experience with field of experience; and they combine in unities of experience in such a way that it is proper to say that one and the same world is continually experienced, but only this or that single province of it is experienced in particular and "actually." But we can go further, always look about us anew, and so on *in infinitum*. . . .
>
> In this way we have described [*umschrieben*] the only original, genuine concept of the *natural world-experience* or of the *experienced world*. . . .[25]

Husserl is phenomenologically uncovering the world as present *in* or *to* the natural attitude, i.e., the world as *pregiven*. But it is not yet a proper *transcendental phenomenological* characterization. If we call the "experienced world" horizon, as Husserl does here, then we must not confuse it, co-given within "natural world-experience," with the full transcendental characterization of that horizon. The latter has not yet been achieved.

Perhaps we should dwell on this point. It is crucial to see that the world is co-given in everyday experience without itself being explicitly thematic. The account we are now offering is phenomenological in the sense that we rely upon modes of givenness and a certain basic framework of intentional experience in our explication of the way the world functions for natural experience. But as co-given it is itself in need of deeper clarification. What we have is a *disclosure* of the presence of the world as horizon in its fundamental difference from phenomena, found in the course of everyday experience, but we do not yet have a transcendental phenomenological *characterization* of the world as horizon. The first is co-given in "straightforward" experience; the second is "given" only under what we will shortly call the phenomenological reduction. To relate them directly, we might say that the notions of a pregiven world in general, and an environment in particular, are necessary to do justice to the fact that all perceptual objects are figures within or against a ground, while the transcendental notion of horizon proper attends to the difference or "limit" between figure and ground that provides things with their determinate presence.

This description of the framework constitutive of our everyday awareness actually builds upon that notion of intentionality described in the last chapter. "Straightforward" acts tethered to objects or facts are subtended by a "basic form of all 'actual' life"[26] in which I am related through and beyond them to the world itself. Thus the tie between act and object is itself enframed by a more encompassing relation between an interrelated cluster of acts and the world.[27] This deeper enframing is called the "natural" attitude in *Ideas I*.[28]

> Natural cognition begins with experience and remains *within* experience. In that . . . attitude that we are calling the "natural" attitude the total horizon of possible research can be designated with one word: it is the world.[29]

> The natural world . . . is always and immediately there for me as long as I live naturally in and toward it. As long as this is the case I am "positioned naturally."[30]

The fact that the world is "always and immediately there for me" should not be confused with the idea that it is there as referent. In contrast to objects in the world, the world itself is "posited" not explicitly in a single act but implicitly throughout all "straightforward" acts of referring. Each attempt to comprehend it as an object causes it to recede, which is to say that even in the various ways of speaking within the natural attitude about the world as a whole, the world has withdrawn. To put it in terms of the theory of judgments, the world is the correlate not of a "particular thesis," articulated or sorted by a predicate, but of a "general thesis" maintained and assumed by the "is" of all assertions.[31] This difference is reflected in Husserl's logical grammar, for he refused, unlike Frege, to dismantle the *is* of *S is p* and transform it into either a component of the predicate term (function) or the assertive force external to the content of what is asserted.[32] The "is" operates at a fundamentally different level than either the *S* or the *p*. To set it in relation to the notion of phenomena, the world is not one of the "givens," the natural attitude is tacitly acquainted with its existence in such a way that it is ever "pregiven." When the phenomenological reflection proper is introduced, this phenomenal difference will be based on a transcendental difference; the world's transcendence can never be overtaken by any referential act within the natural attitude precisely because it is constitutive of that attitude.

In order to sort out the terms and to set up contrasts with what will follow in the next two sections, let me suggest this rough depiction of the distinctions we have drawn here.

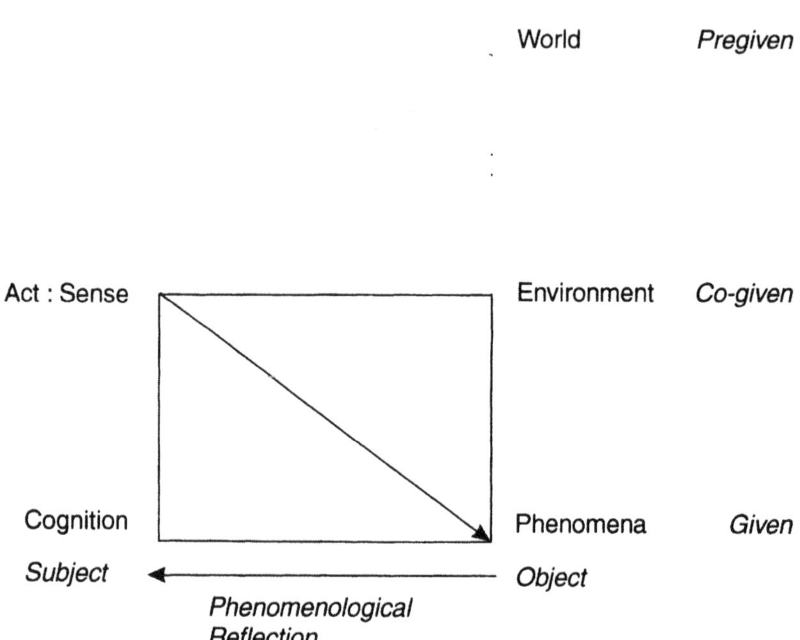

Fig. 4.1. The Pregiven World and Its Disclosure

The pregivenness and transcendence of the world is operative not just for the realm of uncritical, everyday experience, what Plato designated the sphere of opinion or belief (*pistis, doxa*), but beneath the projects of scientific inquiry as well, Plato's realm of reasoning (*dianoia*).[33] The phrase "natural attitude" is hardly a term of denigration; instead it describes that inescapable framework or encompassing "interest" constitutive of our involvement with things, even when we submit them to scientific investigation. It not only covers our posture as "average" citizens, buying bread for breakfast, rushing for the subway, reading the sports page, but also circumscribes the labors of all "positive"[34] sciences, for example, when one citizen as a biologist tests her cultures for traces of nitrates or another, as a psychologist, interprets the symptoms of a client as signs of a multiple personality disorder. Even in those sciences that conceptualize whole environments, whether ecological, economic, or cultural, the underlying relation to the pregiven world is constitutive yet not properly grasped. No doubt such notions as biosphere, agricultural balance, or auditory culture can serve as "indexes" of the world. But in each of their straightforward characterizations of the world from within the natural attitude, the world withdraws.

In provocative fashion, Husserl extends this thesis to the efforts of philosophy, to Plato's domain of understanding proper (*noesis*). All scientific, as well as most philosophical, theories of the world are enframed *within* the natural attitude. This means that not only are they blind to subjectivity, at least as he comes to analyze it, but also, in their very attempts to comprehend the totality of what is, they operate with a covert belief in the world, not attending to it in its proper being. Empiricism and rationalism or, in logic, psychologism and formalism, are ever recurring alternatives that must result from this double "forgetting." Consequently, the world is implicitly or explicitly characterized as a positive entity. In a few places, however, Husserl does recognize that some of the better theories (especially those of Descartes, Kant, and Dilthey) introduce tears in the seamless closure of the natural attitude. While they never really "penetrate" the world in its proper being, they do offer, consistent with the limits and method of their analysis, their own theories of being as a whole that are forerunners of the phenomenological account.[35] This requires us, then, to think further about the relationship between a positive and a phenomenological characterization of world.

C. WORLD AS TOTALITY AND WORLD AS HORIZON

We have suggested that (a) our everyday acquaintance with things and places involves a preacquaintance with the world, but (b) in all our various ways of apprehending things, the world is never one of the things directly experienced. It situates all cognition without itself being properly comprehended by cognition. We saw that Husserl gathers all such experience and understanding under the heading of natural cognition; its framework he labels the natural attitude. To say that all natural cognition takes place within the natural attitude is to say that it is made possible by a pervasive, tacit belief in the existence of that which cannot be grasped as an object. Even for those scientific disciplines that are concerned with environments, the world is not thematized in its proper being. For this a radical overturning of the natural by the phenomenological attitude is required.

But Husserl's rejection of a positive characterization of the world as philosophically adequate can easily obscure a far more interesting fact: not only does he allow for its ontological characterization, he even gives it a systematic place within the scope of his phenomenology. In fact, it is precisely this integration that provides the working goal of categorial phenomenology.

The issue centers on the nature and status of an ontology of the world in Husserl's phenomenology. What is at play here is two different philosophical *characterizations* of the pregiven world, both of which, as I will now suggest, are transcendental; and what we are concerned with is their interconnection.[36] One is ontological and the other phenomenological. We should begin by noting again Husserl's attitude toward ontology.

Husserl is interested not in a dismissal but in a rehabilitation or "reform"[37] of ontology, the outline of which we treated in the last chapter. At the same time a formal analysis of the world that infers it as a necessary condition of the existence of interconnected facts can become the guiding thread, leading to a proper phenomenological theory of the world. Though he sometimes runs the two characterizations together, attributing the same or similar features to both, Husserl clearly has the ontological and the phenomenological descriptions of world differentiated at the level of his system as a whole.[38] In fact, the *Abbau* of the ontological notion that belongs to the first parts of both *Ideas I* and *Formal and Transcendental Logic* becomes the point of access to the phenomenological concept presented in their second parts. Since this difference, found well before the notion of world is expanded by that of life-world, is also the key to his characterization of subjectivity, we must be more explicit as to how Husserl approaches an ontological characterization of the world and integrates it into his own system.

"Natural cognition begins with experience and remains *within* experience,"[39] we quoted above. All its researches, actual and possible, are sciences of the world. Yet no one science deals with the world itself but only with certain ensembles of facts and/or objects within the world. These sciences must be treated as regions of the world if we are to account for the scope and interrelatedness of natural knowledge. Approaching the world "naturally" entails a certain way of describing the world philosophically. In other words, the inference to the world as a whole takes place in two steps: the semantic analysis of propositions being true is set in relation to ontological or causal analyses of the condition of there being facts (or objects); and an analysis of a given set of facts is contrasted to an analysis of the condition of the possibility of facts as a whole, thus introducing the possibility of distinguishing between regional ontologies and the universal analysis of the world itself. Husserl accepts the thesis that we cannot understand the interconnection between facts in a science, and then between sciences, without assuming the existence of the world as a whole, and of certain conditions that must hold for any object whatsoever. The world, whose existence must be assumed if we are to assure the possibility of a rational connection between regions, is inferred on the basis of theoretical arguments as a *totality.* In the words of the opening lines of *Ideas I:*

> The world is the total [*Gesamtinbegriff*] of the objects of possible experience and experiential cognition, of objects that are cognizable in appropriate theoretical thought on the basis of actual experience.[40]

In the language of semantics, the world is the totality of the referents of actually and possibly true propositions; in terms that hold for all the natural sciences, the world is the totality of all entities causally connected. In both the philosophical and the natural scientific versions, the procedure that is followed uses eidetic variation to move from objects and facts to an ontological or material *condition,* without which they could not be interrelated objects of cognition. This approach views the world not as a collection of individuals with features reducible to the combinatory properties of its extension but as an existing totality, as an "idea"[41] necessary to account for the being of facts and/or objects. If correctly constructed, the ontological characterization of the world becomes the guiding thread for a phenomenological account.

To bring this issue into focus in a way that Husserl rarely does, it is possible to argue for a *transcendental characterization* of the world that avoids the mistake of treating it as positive and yet keeps it *within* the confines of an ontological account and, thus, the natural attitude.[42] This is best understood by turning to the early Wittgenstein, a philosopher never discussed or even read by Husserl, as far as we know.[43] The *Tractatus*[44] offers a characterization of the world based on the fundamental difference between an item in the world and the world itself. The world, Wittgenstein argues, is the "totality" of facts or of subsisting states-of-affairs.[45] It is not a totality of objects, though objects are drawn into the account as elements whose relation to one another is determined in our logical depiction of facts.[46] Additionally, the world is not a "sum" or set of facts, for then the notion would be reduced to its extension; there would be nothing but the facts themselves. Rather, over and above the sum of the facts the world is "the whole of reality"[47] with its own "form"[48] and "limits."[49] Treating the world as the totality of states-of-affairs provides Wittgenstein with that ontological assumption needed for a philosophical characterization of the discourse of truth: just as names cannot occur in isolation but must have a meaning in the context of a proposition, and just as propositions have a logical form that is "exhibited"[50] in them, so objects exist only in connection with each other in states-of-affairs, and states-of-affairs in an internal relationship that forms the totality of the world.[51] This "mirroring" of logic and ontology allows Wittgenstein to argue that (a) scientific language as a whole "describes" the totality of subsisting states-of-affairs,[52] (b) the essence of the proposition (its propositional form) gives the essence of both language and the world,[53] and (c) the limits of language are also the limits of the world.[54]

Wittgenstein, then, clearly uses the notion of totality as essential to a philosophical clarification of the world. However, he draws a powerful conclusion that comes from the recognition that his analysis, being transcendental, cannot itself belong to the world. The sum of true sentences for Wittgenstein coincides with the total content (actual and possible) of the positive sciences.[55] Since philosophy is not about facts within the world but about the world itself, it is not one of the positive sciences and thus does not belong to that order determined by the true and false sentences of the language. Strictly speaking, Wittgenstein tells us, it is "transcendental."[56] He speculates that, were the world as a whole to be apprehended, it would require an intuition *sub specie aeternitatis.* The absence of such an intuition, as well as his rejection of anything like the fundamental shift in frameworks effected by the phenomenological reduction, which we will trace in the next section, leaves Wittgenstein with recourse only to the nonconceptual: "The feeling of the world as a limited whole is the mystical."[57] As such it cannot be given expression in language that is meaningful, for its descriptions would be neither true nor false. It could never be a referent because it lacks reference and, in principle, cannot be depicted in the language of the sciences. As not only the world, but also the entire content of philosophy, is transcendental, Wittgenstein's conclusion is as consistent as it is austere: "One must be silent about that of which one cannot speak."[58] "The proper method of philosophy would actually be: to say nothing."[59]

Husserl is convinced that phenomenology can fill the silence with more than song. He would not reject Wittgenstein's claim that the world can be treated as a totality, for, in a way that is surprisingly close to him, Husserl has a certain "mirroring" between the levels of formal apophantics and formal ontology.[60] And for both of these systems, *mathesis universalis* would be the language that allows one to describe the form of their interrelationship. Husserl would also recognize that there is a decisive advancement made by Wittgenstein over other theories of the world, those which transcend a first "naiveté" that treats the world as an object only to be caught in a second that treats the world as positive. For in placing the world at a transcendental level, Wittgenstein also dismantles the positivity of the world. Husserl's response would be that the negativity of silence to which Wittgenstein is driven is precisely the logical outcome of a theory of the world designed to stabilize the hegemony of scientific discourse, one which suddenly recognizes that its own descriptions do not belong to that discourse or to one of the domains of the objective sciences. The hegemony of scientific discourse can be broken only by finding a point of reference outside its entire framework and by understanding its grammar and its world as the result of transformations that can be clarified phenomenologically. But to demonstrate this we must return to a phenomenological characterization of world.

We saw that all objects have a certain background that is itself integral to our experience of them. In our experience of the interrelated traits of an object, especially in cases where our intentions are disappointed or corrected, our perceptions bring with them not only a tacit acquaintance with the world but also a "general" or "nonthetic" belief in its *existence.* To understand the way in which particular experiences of objects deliver a belief in the existence of the world is to recognize our point of entry into a phenomenological dismantling of a positive conception of the world.[61] This link needs to be pursued.

Every object perceived consists of a certain "core" of what is actually presented and a manifold of profiles not in focus but co-present and in this sense co-given. It is, of course, possible to take what is only anticipated and seek its fulfillment in actual perceptions. I can walk around the pump, and thereby the anticipated profile, perhaps vague and not fully specified, is fleshed out and determined. It is also possible to move from my perception of the pump to that of the courtyard and eventually to the field dimly "indicated" by the pump when it occupied my initial perception. Each experience unfolds a number of possibilities of experiencing new profiles or objects that are not totally random but, as Husserl often says, anticipated according to a "prescribed style." I am free to move in this direction or that, to investigate the backside or to turn my attention to the courtyard. While the course of my further experience is not precisely specified, the sense or meanings determining my present perception limit its possibilities. The fact that the side or object actually in focus gives rise to such anticipations indicates that I am acquainted with a cluster of possibilities.

At this point, though, the analysis can easily go astray. Neither the courtyard, nor the farm, nor even the wider surroundings should be identified as the world, for each can easily become an *object* of new acts of reference.[62] Each would still be positive. By contrast, the world in which all things have their determinate presence is not itself a thing nor does it have the character of a determinate referent. We also cannot reduce it to a particular environment outside the focus of a given act of perception. By incorporating a reflection upon the intentional relationship between acts and objects into its account, phenomenology allows us to understand the world as neither a whole of interrelated facts, nor a totality referred to in interrelated intentional acts. Rather, the world is that *nexus* disclosed in the movement from pump to courtyard to farm to environment. It is that web of significance, that *Verweisungszusammenhang,* or nexus of referential implications, which each intentional connection of act and object has as its necessary ground. To capture this in a word, *Ideas I* introduces the term "horizon":

> The world, consciously "at hand" for me in my waking moments, cannot be exhausted by that co-presence—whether it be intuitively clear or in the dark, distinct or indistinct—surrounding the actual field of perception. Rather its fixed order of being is such [*in einer festen Seinsordnung*] that it extends into the unlimited [*Unbegrenzte*]. What is actually perceived, what is more or less clearly co-present and determined . . . , is partially permeated, partially enveloped by an horizon, itself dimly conscious, of indeterminate reality. . . . [What surrounds the field of perception] is indeterminate [i.e., consists of anticipated senses with certain possibilities of fulfillment left open] and endless, i.e., the horizon, shrouded and impossible to fully determine, is necessarily there.[63]

Attempting to escape the "*philosophical* absolutizing of the world" either into irreducible reality standing over against consciousness (realism) or into a reality constructed by consciousness (subjective idealism), Husserl argues in

Ideas I that "the world itself has its whole being as a certain 'sense' which presupposes absolute consciousness, as field of the bestowal of sense."[64] This fundamental notion to all of Husserl's phenomenology is unchanged in his last work, the *Crisis:*

> the world as it is for us becomes understandable as a structure of meaning formed out of elementary intentionalities. The being of these intentionalities themselves is nothing but one sense-formation [*Sinnbildung*] operating together with another, "constituting" new sense [*Sinn*] through synthesis.[65]

As nexus of sense the world can be understood initially as a horizon of possible determinability attending the things of experience. In the case of perceptual objects, their perspectival character involves an openness and indeterminacy inviting further experience. That which is anticipated is not random thought; rather it involves a

> determinableness which has a rigorously prescribed style. It forebodes [*deutet vor*] possible perceptual multiplicities which, continually merging into one another, join together to make up the unity of one perception in which the continuously enduring thing displays ever new (or, retrogressing, the old) sides in ever new series of adumbrations.[66]

Much later Husserl puts the same point in this way:

> This sense, the *cogitatum qua cogitatum,* can never be presented as a finished given. It *comes to clarity* first only through this explication of the horizon and the horizons continually and newly awakened. The predelineation itself is always incomplete, but in its *lack of determinacy* [we find] a *structure of determinableness.* For example, the cube leaves much open in respect to the unseen sides, but it is nevertheless already *apprehended* in advance [*im voraus*] as cube, and then in distinguishing qualities [*Sonderheit*] such as colored, rough, etc., whereby each of these determinations continually leaves open further determining qualities [*Besonderheiten*].[67]

In addition there is a noetic counterpart to this understanding of the horizon:

> Here there is always at play in these possibilities an *I can* and an *I do,* respectively, *I can do other than I am doing.* . . . The horizons are predelineated potentialities.[68]
>
> Each lived experience has a changing *horizon* with the alternation of its nexus of consciousness and with the alteration of the phases of its own stream—potentialities of consciousness belonging to an intentional horizon of referential implications related to itself [*Horizont der Verweisung auf ihm selbst*]. For example, there belongs to each outer perception a referential implication [that moves] from the *actually perceived* side of the perceptual object to the *co-intended,* not yet perceived but only expected side, a side at first not intuited but anticipated and empty. . . . [The act possesses] a constant *protention* that has a new sense with each phase of the perception.[69]

The world as horizon is *transcendental,* inasmuch as it makes possible the determinate presence of beings but is itself never identifiable as a being. As *phenomenologically* characterized, the horizon belongs to the order of meaning and supplies the ground of intentionality. Characterizing the world as horizon allows us to avoid the fatal mistake undergirding the natural attitude, that of framing the question about the "to be" of the world as about an entity, a being.

D. FROM REFLECTION TO REDUCTION

The phenomenological concept of the world as horizon, to which we will return in greater detail in chapters 13 to 15, describes the world as it operates *in the natural attitude.* It is a characterization of the world in its pregivenness. As such it is the inescapable context of all activities of human life, be they the ordinary labors of the worker or the extraordinary undertakings of science. There is the added complication of a philosophical approach to the world as a whole that characterizes it as an existent of a higher order, as a totality. This notion is a transcendental concept inasmuch as, in the better theories, it is not derived by a generalization over beings but rather is the condition of their "to be" and thus their interconnection. But the characterization of the world as totality does not thematize the world as it is *constitutive of the natural attitude.* Rather, it necessarily presupposes that world in attempting to formulate certain logical (Husserl) or grammatical (Wittgenstein) conditions obtaining for all objects of cognition. Husserl uses this point to argue that the ontological conception of the world as totality is derivative and that it must be supplemented, if not supplanted, by a conception of the world as horizon. But in order to establish this we must be able to raise the notion of horizon to the level of theory, to transform our acquaintance with the world from within the world to a comprehension of the world "as a whole," and guarantee that we will not fall back into treating it "objectivistically." The noematics of the difference between world as totality and world as horizon calls for a noetics of how we can bring that difference into focus.

Husserl wants to deal with this issue by finding a methodological tool that will enable him to isolate, and then put out of play, the one underlying character binding together all the regions of the world and, as a consequence, all positive characterizations of it. Whether scientific or philosophical, "natural" accounts of the world are framed by a belief in this global dimension. Such a belief undergirds the prevalence and power of the "straightforward" attitude. Phenomenological analysis, if it is to escape the natural attitude, must effect a shift equally general in scope, a change not at the level of acts but at the level of the attitude supporting the positivity of the world.

The decisive breakthrough came when Husserl realized that the method of immanent reflection alone, the approach of the *Logical Investigations*, would be inadequate to achieve this: "however carefully it may observe and analyze, however truly it may be directed toward my pure psychical life, toward the pure inwardness of my soul, bare reflection remains *natural, psychological reflection* as long as it is without such a method."[70]

The activity of apprehending an object as intentional involves a moment of transcendence that carries us not just beyond the profiles to the object as a whole but also beyond the determinacy of the whole to its "being there," its existence. Being itself "is not a real predicate,"[71] is never itself one of the determinations and is certainly not one of the objects perceived. But though never apprehended, it is ever delivered in all determinate experience. Though it is never thematic in our straightforward apprehension of things, it is the "to be" of all objects as objects, all facts as facts *in* the world; in attaining fulfillment, being is obtained. Husserl reasons that if we can find a way of reflecting upon our belief in existence as a whole, we can encompass *all that is* without assuming that we can say or know in advance *what it is*, or even that the whole of what is admits of conceptual closure.

These ideas refer us back to studies that Husserl undertook in his *Logical Investigations* on the question of being and the special role that the term "is" plays in propositions. Husserl's theses that all speech acts have a semantic essence consisting of quality and matter, that different act-qualities can have a single matter, that judgments are based on presentations, and, further, that all true judgments are ratified in corresponding fulfilling acts, allow him to argue that statements of fact and their confirmation in experience are basic. All the diverse forms of cognition have "objectifying acts" at their base,[72] acts which can be expressed by statements having the core form *S is p*.[73] Husserl is careful to say that in the act of fulfillment we can have nested intuitive acts of presenting the referents of *S* or *p*, which are individuals (either a *concretum* or *abstractum*), but the *is* that binds the referents of the *S* and the *p*, and which is at play in *all* matters of fact, cannot be so comprehended. "The objective correlates of categorial forms are not 'real' moments."[74] While we can "sensuously intuit" or perceive what is meant by the element "gold" and the color "yellow," we do not see in the same way the gold-*being*-yellow.[75] Because of its difference from sensuous objects, this peculiar feature requires recourse to a different form of apprehension appropriate to it. The *Investigations* call it categorial intuition. It comprehends not an object but what is constitutive of objecthood, not a fact but what is constitutive of facticity itself. It apprehends that which fulfills the "general thesis" at play in all particular theses. In experiencing objects or facts *as* they exist, all objectifying acts apprehend them *in* their existence.

To understand this important step in Husserl's theory, we must emphasize that a tacit belief in existence undergirds not just the objects we attend to but also the various regions we comprehend and the world we thematize, both scientifically and ontologically. In our experience of things and, then, in our scientific and philosophical discussions of them, existence is ever delivered to us. The key to encompassing and then disengaging positivity as a whole, then, is somehow to suspend that one underlying belief or, correspondingly, those characteristics that make it possible in all of its diverse forms. Husserl's way of expressing it is to say that the natural attitude as a whole must be "put out of play." We no longer "go along" with the normal course of living toward things, no longer "play along" with the belief in existence, a belief operative in and thus constitutive both of all particular acts fixed on their referents and of the world that is co-given in and with each given. We "suspend" or "hold in abeyance" this unthematized yet global belief and this has the result of shifting our attention to an analysis of what, if anything, remains. To put it noematically, existence is "bracketed." The "neutralization" of the natural attitude Husserl calls *epoché*.[76]

This moment of exclusion is combined with a moment of reversal and inclusion in Husserl's transcendental account; in opposition to the "straightforward" or natural attitude, always absorbed in its particular tasks and concerns and, thus, only aware of the world partially and at its margins, the phenomenological attitude makes our life as a whole its theme. This requires an "unnatural," perhaps violent reversal of the normal direction of our thought. In other words, the *reflexive* but tacit acquaintance we have with intentional life and, through it, with the world is made into a topic of explicit *reflection* and then of a methodological *purification* that, in putting out of play that condition necessary for both the subject and the world to appear as "objects," as beings, gives us access to them in their being. The suspension of the thesis of existence, constitutive of its transcendence, has the effect of bringing the world as a whole within the scope of what can be mastered in and through direct "immanent" descriptions. It also fundamentally alters the level at which the notion of the world is to be determined; it displaces the notion of world from the order of referents—of things, facts, events, environments—and resituates it in the order of meaning—of significance, of the fundamental bond between intentional life and referents. Thus as soon as the natural attitude is replaced by the phenomenological attitude we find a fundamental change in the way the world is described. It is brought to light not as (a) a causal nexus, as in natural scientific explanations, or (b) a sociopolitical environment, as in social scientific accounts, or (c) as historical world, as in the chronicles of history, or (d) a universe or circumscribable All of unlimited beings, as in some formal and transcendental accounts. Rather, it is understood as a "unity of sense," as that unbound matrix of significance constitutive of the determinate presence of objects in the world and of the variety of worlds set in brackets. The "to be" of the world itself, then, is characterized not in terms of existence but in terms of significance: "The world itself has its entire being as a certain 'sense.'"[77] To put it more accurately, it is that *nexus of significance* in terms of which all things have their determinate presence for subjects intentionally related to them.

The combination of these two moments of exclusion and inclusion form what Husserl famously calls the phenomenological reduction. Since its function is to give us the field of phenomenological investigations as a whole, we can say that it constitutes *the* method of transcendental phenomenology.

Perhaps, now, we can grasp the deeper sense behind Husserl's idea that existence is suspended by the phenomenological epoché. The bracketing of the thesis of existence allows us to reflect upon the structure of intentionality, which we gain through phenomenological reflection. It also allows us to break open the natural concept of the world, for without the assumption of existence we cannot meaningfully speak about an existing whole of beings, and without that there can be no totality. The "absolute" world of the natural attitude becomes "relative." The phenomenological procedures of bracketing and reflection, then, effect a shift to a position from which the world is envisioned as the nexus of meaning, and thus as necessarily connected with subjectivity. If, with Husserl, we speak of the reduction as withholding any positing of transcendence, the cognitive counterpart to the notion of existence, and thereby as opening the "absolute" givenness of immanence, it is only to discover the transcendental in the process of making phenomena in their transcendence possible.

We see, then, that there are striking differences between the ontological and phenomenological characterizations of world. Though both might be "transcendental," the first takes world as a totality of facts, the second as the interconnected web of significance. The first belongs to the order of referents, the second to the order of meaning. Also, the positive account of world requires that it have closure while the phenomenological account speaks of horizon as open and unbound. Finally, there is a striking contrast between the type of unity required for the coherence of science and that required for the integrity of experience. Wittgenstein, in his *Tractatus*, is convinced that the world is not directly mirrored or exhibited in the discourse of science; he thus hypothetically justifies the treatment of the world as totality by the need to ground the unity of the sciences as a single finite system of truths. In contrast, the world for Husserl is exhibited *across* various fields of experience, including those that are neither linguistic nor scientific, and it functions, in principle, to account for their unity by recourse to the experiential interrelation and divergence of paradigmatically different regions.

We now have the key to the transformation of Husserl's phenomenology into a transcendental register. It is not the discovery, groundbreaking as it was, of the relation of the as- to the for-structure, but the discovery that the interconnection between the as-structure and the for-structure is itself dependent upon the in-structure, that initiates the move to transcendental analysis. In its course, the as- and for-structures are reframed as transcendental. The introduction of this level of analysis is what changes phenomenology into philosophy.

E. TRANSCENDENTAL SUBJECTIVITY

Generally overlooked in discussions of the reduction in *Ideas I,* a work which barely manages to weave its diverse strands into a whole, is that the analysis of the world is given an ontological (Section 1) and a "natural" (Sections 27–30) characterization before Husserl sets off in pursuit of the notion of subjectivity (beginning with Section 31). We have unpacked the concept of the world, if only in a preliminary way,[78] in the hope that this will give us a point of access to the notion of subjectivity that is not overwhelmed by Husserl's Cartesian notion of evidence. The characterization of the world as nexus of significance deepens the intentional connection between objects of cognition and cognition itself for Husserl's theory. As nexus of significance, the world opens for us a field of experiential possibilities. But this means that we are acquainted with these possibilities as ones that we have at our disposal.[79] The horizon as a field of *possibilities* entails subjectivity as a field of *potentialities:*

> Ingredient in these possibilities we find in play an *I can* and an *I do,* respectively, *I am capable of doing other than I do. . . .* The horizons are prescribed potentialities. We can also say that one can interrogate each horizon according to what lies in it, explicate it [and] *disclose* the actual potentialities of the life of consciousness.[80]

In principle this is the deeper connection between acts and meaning that Husserl needed to transform his initial theory of intentionality; if the world is a nexus of sense, then we necessarily have an internal tie between objects and the systems of cognitive production and interaction in, for, or through which things have their significance. If the world has its entire being as significance, then subjectivity as "the field of sense-bestowal"[81] is already entailed. Thus world as the nexus of sense entails a correlative notion of subjectivity, not just particular "sense-bestowing acts" but also an interrelated whole of capabilities, habitualities, and modes of interaction in terms of which things acquire their lived qualities. Determinate objects are situated not only in a *nexus* of possible determinations but also in a *field* of possible actions and interactions of concrete subjects. It is precisely this mutual implication of possibilities and potentialities, of nexus and field, to which the notion of horizon leads us, that introduces subjectivity as the locus of cognitive achievements.

Great care is needed here. The mode of presentation in *The Idea of Phenomenology* and *Ideas I* made it look as if the reduction consisted of bracketing what is transcendent to human consciousness in order to turn to it as a realm of immanence. We will see in the next chapter that Husserl's Cartesian treatment of subjectivity as a "remainder" after the bracketing of the world not only encourages but also requires this interpretation. But in fact the existence placed between brackets applies not only to transcendent but also to immanent being. What is suspended, then, is not just the existence of the world but also the factual being of a subject in an existing environment.[82] What the analysis yields are not statements about factual conditions of cognition but statements about the transcendental conditions of the possibility of cognition.

Shifting his analysis to a transcendental level finally allowed Husserl to distinguish acts as real events from acts understood in terms of a transcendental structure (thus in terms of a notion of synthesis internally connected to meaning), and then to view acts and meaning as two components of a single (transcendental) structure rather than treating acts as instantiations of structures (meanings) belonging to another level (species) and realm (ideal), as he did in the *Logical Investigations.* As a result, the a priori *connection* between act and meaning was understood as an a priori *correlation.* In the lectures now called *The Idea of Phenomenology* (from 1907), he describes it this way:

> Naturally not only the individual acts come into consideration here but also their complexes, their interconnections of agreement and disagreement, and the teleologies that emerge within them. These complexes are not conglomerates but . . . unities of cognition which, as cognitive unities, also have their unity as objective correlates.[83]

This point is also emphasized in lectures from 1906/07: "It is the task of *transcendental phenomenology* (or transcendental philosophy) to make clear the interconnections between true being and knowing and thus, in general, to research the correlations between act, meaning, and object."[84] Phenomenology gained a rich field, which it could submit to analysis, due to three events: (a) the shift from a "descriptive psychological" to a transcendental phenomenological account, (b) the corresponding transformation of the a priori connection between act and meaning into an a priori correlation of act and meaning, and (c) the recognition not only of the variegated interconnections between various acts and complexes of objects but also between larger systems of achievements and webs of significance. Husserl calls this field the field of *constitution* and its analysis *constitutive analysis.* The introduction of the notion of constitution simultaneously deepens the notion of categorial phenomenology and carries us beyond its provisional formulations. We will take this up in chapter 7.

This analysis would suggest two tiers to a transcendental phenomenological account. The specific correlations between act and meaning, or what Husserl also calls ego-cogito-cogitatum, are subtended by a general correlation of subjectivity and world. The bracketing of existence has a double application to the first tier, that of the act-meaning correlation: with the suspension of contingency, it yields intentionality as a *pure* structure that is not mixed by the material constraints essential to regional analysis, while with its severance from the realm of beings, it secures intentionality as a *transcendental* structure that applies to all regions of analysis. The notion of horizon is situated in a second tier, i.e., as the nexus of significance and possible cognitive achievements upon which a particular correlation of act and meaning in the first tier depends. The transcendental movement to phenomenological analysis arises when the "regional" correlations between acts and meanings undergo an analysis that places them within the "universal" correlations of (a) the "capabilities" or "capacities" of interacting subjects, and (b) frameworks of possible determinations. To put it another way, the correlation of act and meaning has the reciprocation of subjectivity and world as its ground. Gaining subjectivity and world through the transcendental reduction secures the correlation of act and meaning as a transcendental structure. Husserl calls this correlation the noetic-noematic structure.

This can be charted in two ways. The first takes its guiding clue from everyday life and "pretheoretical," concrete environments while the second "moves back" from theoretical experience and the world as defined by ontology. Static analysis is capable of understanding the structural difference between the two. The account of how one moves from the first to the second in a given historical environment, however, requires a genetic account.

By starting with intentionality, we avoid the two classical errors mentioned above: the world is neither identified with nor reduced to subjectivity, as in idealism; and subjectivity is neither identified with nor derived from world, as in empiricism. World and subjectivity are co-originary and irreducible. The horizon transcendentally interpreted is the field of their reciprocation, a field dyadically distributed.

This transcendental account builds upon the results of the categorial phenomenology of the *Investigations.* The suggestion that subjectivity and world are co-originary is a logical extension of the treatment of acts and significance as correlative, as irreducible features of all particular acts of cognition. In the next chapter, however, we will see that, for special reasons, Husserl submitted these first results of his transcendental account to further interpretation in *Ideas I.* In particular, Husserl attempted to understand transcendental subjectivity by the notion of pure consciousness and to treat the phenomenological

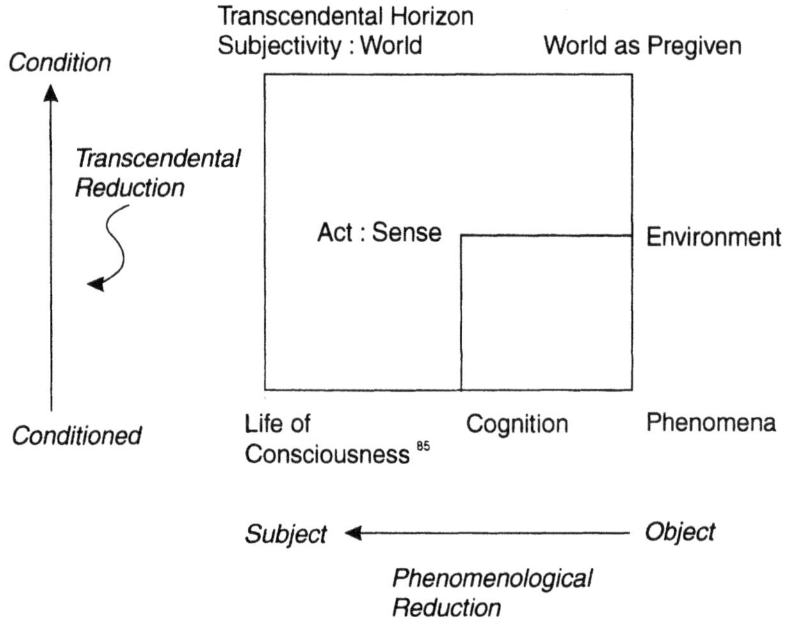

Fig. 4.2. The Pregiven World and Transcendental Phenomenology

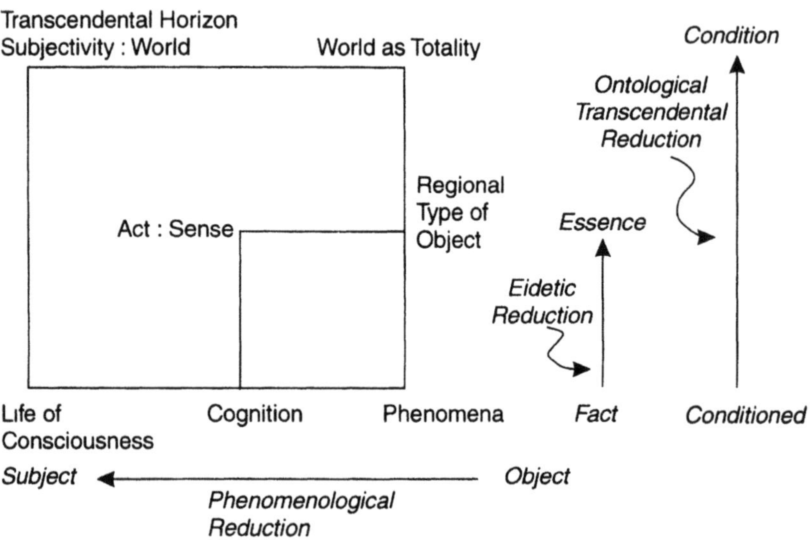

Fig. 4.3. The World as Totality and Transcendental Phenomenology

reduction as an *exclusion* of the world. This had the result of introducing more than an *asymmetry* into their relationship; it also created an *ontological division* between ego and world and then an *ontological priority* of the ego over the world.

This chapter has been concerned with providing a typology of Husserl's "static" transcendental analysis, one that I think plausible, before the special requirements of his Cartesian account are taken on board. But at that we still have not raised the question of its legitimacy or its justification. For this we must wait until chapter 11.

5

Cartesian Enclosures

> In that book [*Ideas I*] eidetic phenomenology is restricted to the domain of strictly eidetic "description," i.e., to the domain of immediately intuitable [*einsichtiger*], essential structures of transcendental subjectivity. For this domain already comprises in itself a systematically [self]closed infinity of essential characteristics. . . . Indeed, even the descriptive sphere is restricted to a level readily accessible; thus the problematic of the temporalization of the immanent temporal sphere remains excluded.
>
> —Husserl (1931)[1]

> . . . descriptive a priori phenomenology (visible in *Ideas* [I] in its actual workings) as directly cultivating the transcendental soil, is in itself "first philosophy," the philosophy of the beginning.
>
> —Husserl (1931)[2]

HUSSERL'S DESCRIPTIVE PHENOMENOLOGY became philosophy by enlarging its *scope* and redefining its *method.* Taking its first discovery of an internal relation between acts and phenomena and placing it within a larger correlational tie between subjectivity and world expanded its scope. Its method was thoroughly revised through the notion of the phenomenological reduction, now given the task of encompassing "the whole of being" and thereby securing the transcendental status of what it discovers as grounding structures.

In the last chapter our account of the movement within categorial phenomenology, from its initial development in the *Investigations* to transcendental method proper in *Ideas I,* introduced two things: a notion of the correlational a priori that treats subjectivity and world as equiprimordial moments, and a theory of the phenomenological reduction that leaves open the question of the "various ways, all equally possible" into transcendental analysis. In short, chapter 4 used the question of the being of beings to introduce the concept of the world and then to understand subjectivity as a co-originary correlative feature of what is meant by horizon. But our analysis is still incomplete, for we skirted Husserl's explicit formulations in *Ideas I.*

Our account in the last chapter was simplified by disregarding two strands that *Ideas I* wove into its analysis. In a way that echoes the methodological privileging of the monologue, as the First Investigation did in attempting to get at the signification of speech-acts, Husserl uses the sphere of individual experience as the point of access to a transcendental account. As a result subjectivity is characterized as *consciousness*. In *Ideas I* static phenomenology becomes essentially a descriptive discipline that treats not just the structure of consciousness but also consciousness itself as transcendental and thus as the universal ground of all phenomena. This characterization has the result of configuring the analysis of intentionality, so central to static analysis, in a particular way (Section B). This first strand, however, is interwoven with a second in *Ideas I*, a specific framing of the phenomenological reduction by the requirements of a strong notion of intuitive evidence. If it was Kant who taught Husserl that his phenomenology could become philosophy only if it became transcendental and uncovered the difference between regional fields and their ground, it was Descartes who taught him that the scope of his phenomenology could become secure only by a radical, reflective type of evidence that simultaneously covered the totality of that ground. We will attempt to isolate the features of a static analysis once submitted to a Cartesian formulation (Section A). Unfortunately, Husserl did not realize at first the extent to which the Kantian and the Cartesian approaches are in tension with each other. As his thought progressed, he became increasingly aware of the limitations of what he came to call his Cartesian way into transcendental analysis. I will save my own critique of this program until chapter 10. Here I will trace Husserl's own reflections upon its limits, suggesting that while he did "depart" from Cartesianism, to echo Landgrebe's well chosen term,[3] he never abandoned it (Section C). I will then ask why his *Cartesian Meditations*, a later work that has dominated the standard picture of Husserl, was never published by Husserl in German, looking in particular at his relationship to Heidegger in this connection and then whether this text does not refute the thesis that Husserl departed from his earlier Cartesian formulation of the reduction (Section D). In the next chapter we will discuss the alternatives he suggests to the Cartesian way and suggest that beneath their various formulations, we find a common approach that can be called the Kantian way.

A. CARTESIAN AFFINITIES

Before turning our attention to the evidence for securing the correlational a priori as the founding structure of phenomenology, we must begin with the question of why Husserl even needs such a ground. What function would it serve? In particular, why is it necessary in order to provide foundations for regional disciplines?

Husserl is concerned with finding a ground not for the existence of the world, as if he were a subjective idealist, but for our cognition of the world or, to put it noematically, for the world as cognized. This program is framed by the older philosophical question of what things can be known directly on the basis of themselves and what things can be known only on the basis of something else. That which is known on the basis of itself requires nothing outside itself in order to be known and thus can be known beyond any doubt. That which is known through itself is roughly what is meant by the Latin predicate "evident."[4] According to Descartes and Leibniz, only self-consciousness can be described as immediately and directly known and thus as evident, i.e., self-evident. Knowing consciousness does not come through the mediation of yet something else. The peculiar nature of such immediate knowledge is that it guarantees the existence of that which is known. As Husserl was fond of saying, in this realm to be is to be perceived.[5]

But why do we need such self-evidence? Of what value is this piece of direct knowledge? What function does it serve in relation to the sciences? In systems that view knowledge as deductive in nature, it secures them against falling into an infinite regress. Summarizing Heinrich Jacobi on this topic, Manfred Frank puts it this way:

> Derivations require that *from which* they are derived. And they are related to their ground as what is conditioned to their condition. All conclusions, deductions, arguments are at play in the realm of conditioned consciousness, i.e., of consciousness that is not unconditionally conscious of its in-itself (out of its own means). Thus all cognition that we acquire upon the path of rational derivations from grounds is mediated. . . . But, Jacobi suggests, the ideas of the conditioned and the unconditioned "are indivisibly linked with one another, and that in such a way that the idea of the conditioned presupposes the idea of the unconditioned and can only be given with *the latter.*"[6]

Husserl accepts this basic distinction between the ground and the grounded, the unconditional and the conditioned as well as the indispensable link between them. But since he views neither cognition in general nor science in particular as exclusively deductive enterprises, the function of this ground cannot be to avoid an infinite regress in the chain of deduction:

> But perhaps *a new idea of the grounding of knowledge,* namely as transcendental grounding, is opened with the Cartesian discovery of the transcendental ego. Indeed, in place of wanting to assess the *ego cogito* as an apodictically evident premise for conclusions ostensibly leading to a transcendental subjectivity, we direct our attention to the fact that the phenomenological epoché frees up (to me, the meditating philosopher) an infinite realm of being of a new kind, as a sphere of a new kind of transcendental experience.[7]

If self-consciousness functions to avoid an infinite regress, then it is in the chain of experiences; the *ego cogito* accounts for the unity of experiences (even if it be reduced to nothing but its sequence in time, a unity of before and after) and thereby the framing of regions of being as spheres of *constitution.* The immediacy and evidence Husserl wants is Cartesian, but we will see that the way the *ego cogito* functions as ground is Kantian.

Any discussion of Husserl's appropriation of Cartesianism should begin by identifying the leading ideas of Descartes that most engaged him.

1. Descartes, at least in his *Meditations,*[8] took up the project of providing a secure and unshakeable foundation for knowledge. Over against the flux of human opinion and beliefs, as well as the uncertainties of natural knowledge, Descartes sought an absolute body of truth as well as an indubitable starting point that would allow him to secure that body. The quest for secure evidence and foundations animates the entire Cartesian approach.

2. Because of the uncertainty of natural knowledge and because of the contingency of factual experience, we can never find a ground for our knowledge of the natural world in that world itself. Apart from the fact that we are repeatedly confronted with errors, not only in our interpretation of things but also in our perceptions, all empirical cognition depends upon something other than itself for its content and its confirmation. The response that we can factor this out by recourse to inductive generalization and statistical analysis will not do for Descartes or Husserl since this, at best, provides us with only probable, never certain, knowledge. Furthermore, there is in principle, Descartes argues, the possibility that the entire world is but a thin fabric of delusions, woven at the hands of a deceiving spirit. Descartes sees only one possibility that will prevent these difficulties from leading to a permanent and pervasive *skepticism.* If we can find at least one cognitive *fact* whose presence simultaneously guarantees its existence, it will provide us with a frame on which we could weave the fabric of secure truth. Having shown that natural or outer experience will never provide such a fact, Descartes finds it in the realm of *inner experience.* Since all acts of natural experience are simultaneously acts in which I am aware of the event of experiencing, and since this awareness persists even when the object experienced is an illusion and would continue to persist should it turn out that the entire world is only a delusion, I can at least be sure that the process of thinking itself is occurring and, thus, that at least this one cognitive fact exists. My reflective intuition of the "I am thinking" provides indubitable evidence, for in this case there is a coincidence between its "being perceived" and its "being," securing its existence, and manifesting itself as unmediated and unconditioned, securing its position as *arché.*

3. This difference between two types of experience, outer and inner, and two fields, the external and the internal world, rests for Descartes on a metaphysical dualism of two kinds of substances, *res extensa* and *res cogitans.* Only a world extended in time and space could be a world of illusions and delusions

precisely because only such a world consists of objects and events whose perception neither encompasses the whole perceived nor secures its existence. The treatment of the *cogito* as a qualitatively different substance and thus as lacking such coordinates guaranteed that its intuition would be without remainder.

From the time of his early publications, Husserl clearly rejected the dualism of *res extensa* and *res cogitans,* viewing it as a speculative construction. Not only is such a dualism contradicted by the conception of intentionality but it is not even required to distinguish "physical" and "psychic phenomena." He argued in the *Logical Investigations* that

> the *character of the evidence* already delivers to us a *descriptive feature* that distinguishes [outer] and [inner] perceptions. All presuppositions about metaphysical realities are empty. It is a character that is either given or missing with the perceptual experience and this alone determines the division.[9]

Still, other references in the *Logical Investigations* indicate that, at that time, Husserl had not seriously engaged Descartes's ideas in an effort to define philosophical method. This did take place between the *Investigations* and *Ideas I*[10] with the result that, while Husserl rejected the third, he warmly embraced the first two aspects of Descartes's theory. The third, however, is not that easy to extricate from the first two, and so we find a certain dualism, ontological in nature, haunting Husserl's formulation of the reduction in *Ideas I.*

The long-standing philosophical contrast between opinion or belief and knowledge is reaffirmed in Husserl not by a rejection of perception as irrelevant for knowledge, but by a suspension of all our accepted judgments about the nature of things, whether ordinary or scientific, in order to turn to "the things themselves" and the project of constructing a theoretical map of the world that is faithful to their structure. The first, general sense Husserl gives his notion of the reduction is polemical: no construction of reality, from the more pedestrian to the most penetrating, can be assumed at the outset as true and privileged. All must be weighed, secured, and integrated before being accepted as valid.

Husserl, though, uses Descartes to cast the reduction into a particular form. He does not rest with the notions of reflection and eidetic analysis, those notions forming the core of the phenomenological reduction in our account thus far. Rather, they are *supplemented* by a procedure that takes the very realm Descartes treated as dubitable and sets it, as a whole, out of play. Not only particular objects and facts but also the world as their totality are in question. Husserl suspends the *one* feature of the world encompassing *all* the others in such a way that the latter remain phenomena capable of undergoing eidetic and constitutive analyses. As we saw, he sets the *existence* of the world in brackets. But then, having accepted the Cartesian difference between inner, immediate and outer, mediate experience, he suggests that something remains. What we find as a *residue* that can be directly and immediately intuited, are mental acts, the *cogito.* Of course, the theory of intentionality treats this *cogito* only in relation to a *cogitatum,* and Husserl emphasizes this critical difference from Descartes. But the residue is identified as the domain of immanence.

Had Husserl understood this residue as merely the product of his epistemology here, as was the tendency in his first clear formulation of the reduction in his 1907 lectures "The Idea of Phenomenology," he would have distinguished only between two types of descriptions or interpretative frameworks, with arguments for the legitimacy of the transcendental in contrast to the scientific. But he adds an *ontological* opposition to this epistemological difference, which is clearly a decisive step beyond the static analysis that we have described thus far. In *Ideas I,* he introduces the thesis that pure transcendental knowledge, which is about the pure essential structures of subjectivity in their internal relation to each other, depends upon the discovery of a sphere of *being* as a *whole* from which all contingency has been eliminated:

> Since the reader already knows that the interest governing these meditations concerns a new eidetics, he will at first expect that, more particularly, the world as matter of fact is excluded but not the *world as Eidos,* not any other sphere of essences. Indeed, the exclusion of the world actually does not signify the exclusion of the world of, e.g., the number series or arithmetic as relating to it.
>
> Nevertheless we shall not take this path; it does not lead toward our goal[,] which we can also characterize as *the acquisition of a new region of being never before delimited in its own peculiarity*—a region which, like any other genuine region, is a region of *individual being.*[11]

The elimination of contingency results, Husserl believes, from the discovery of a realm of being in which we do not have the interplay of profile and object, and the "surplus" of presence over what is given, for it is this feature that determines cognition as provisional, presumptive, and corrigible. The phenomenal difference between immanence and transcendence is transposed into an ontological difference between absolute being and phenomenal being[12] that then accounts for the epistemological difference between the indubitable and the dubitable.[13] Pure cognition is not perspectival and dependent upon the ongoing course of experience but rather, once the appropriate position (*Einstellung*) is established, it is able to completely enclose consciousness in a single act of comprehension. The transcendental is understood not in terms of eidetic categories and principles but as itself a *res,* "a region of being." Furthermore, the "to be" of consciousness can be adequately intuited by its "to be perceived," a residue without remainder.

The idea that consciousness is a being without residue controls the Cartesian formulation of the reduction. Husserl strengthens this with yet another thesis:

> while the being of consciousness . . . would indeed be necessarily modified by an annihilation of the world of physical things[,] its own existence would not be modified. . . . Consequently no real being, no being which is presented and legitimated in consciousness by appearances, is necessary to the being of consciousness itself (in the broadest sense, the stream of mental processes).[14]

If we suspend the thesis of existence that defines the being of the world, treat consciousness as what abides, and take it as an item whose intuition guarantees its *absolute* being, then we necessarily have a *subordination* of the world to consciousness. Husserl recognizes the force of this conclusion and describes it in this way:

> In so far as their respective senses are concerned, a veritable abyss yawns between consciousness and reality. Here, an adumbrated being, not capable of ever becoming given absolutely, merely accidental and relative; there, a necessary and absolute being, essentially incapable of becoming given by virtue of adumbration and appearance.[15]

The result of the reduction is a difference between the "absolute being" of consciousness and the "relative being" of the world.

The Cartesian formulation of the reduction, then, begins with the suspension of our "general" belief in existence as a way of disrupting our "fascination" with or "absorption" in the realm of phenomena as a whole, in order then to articulate its structure and, thereby, the internal tie between their constitution and cognitive life. It then introduces the bracketing of the world, understood as a sphere of being, an ontic quasi-region, in order to discover a *second* sphere of *being* that is left over, that remains. Husserl requires the latter because he wants to treat subjectivity not as "an empty logical possibility" but as "actual,"[16] and because he believes that it avoids the regressive, hypothetical approach to the transcendental taken by Kant and the Neo-Kantians. The first will always be part of the phenomenological reduction and is found when Husserl attempts other formulations of the reduction in his later thought. But the second is special to his Cartesian way. There are other features as well.

Against the background of this second ontological condition, we saw that the suspension of the thesis of existence, necessary for the discovery of essences as pure, is interpreted not just as a bracketing of our belief in the factical world[17] but also as an imaginative "annihilation" (*Vernichtung*) of the world itself, i.e., of the sphere of being whose existence transcends its being perceived. But this entails that the residue of consciousness is a closed or self-contained sphere of interior or inner being. Reflecting back on *Ideas I* in 1931,

Husserl characterized the transcendental subjectivity open to analysis in that work as "an infinite, self-enclosed, absolutely autonomous realm."[18] Given this closure, our inner experience or intuition can secure its own existence (*Dasein*)[19] precisely because what is intuited is given *adequately,* which means transparently, without the interplay of profile and object, and *apodictically,* beyond doubt since its perception guarantees its existence, itself different in kind from that existence which the epoché sets out of play.

The convergence of the notion of a self-enclosed realm with that of intuitive givenness leads Husserl to a specific characterization of the notion of transcendental subjectivity. That which both has "actual being" and is adequately present to me after the reduction is *the stream of consciousness.* Since the sphere opened through phenomenological reflection has the quality of immediate presence, consciousness is necessarily characterized as *my* consciousness and as an *immanent* sphere. The effect of this is not to use the notion of consciousness as a point of access to transcendental subjectivity but to reduce that subjectivity to consciousness: "The transcendental reduction binds me to the stream of my pure conscious experiences and to the unities constituted through the actualities and potentialities of such experiences."[20]

The identification of subjectivity as consciousness requires that the structure of intentionality be interpreted as within the sphere of immanence, that it find all structural differences or oppositions "in the innerlyness [*Innerlichkeit*] of consciousness."[21] By bracketing the existence of the world, the Cartesian reduction effected a transvaluation of objects into unities of appearances whose being and being-thus-and-so must be accounted for without invoking the existence of the world, i.e., from the side of their appearance *to* conscious acts that terminate in them. As a consequence, an object can be treated within the reduction only as an *X* or an *object-pole*[22] whose sense functions to unite its appearances into its orderly presentation. "If we take this sense fully, with its intuitive plenia, then there results a determinate and very important concept of *appearances.*"[23] The Cartesian reduction also effects a transvaluation of concrete persons into egos whose being must be accounted for strictly in terms of the stream of conscious experiences. Since the experiences themselves are what we actually undergo, the ego itself can enter the account only in terms of its function of unifying a series of acts related to appearances. As such it is a *subject-pole.*[24] Consciousness is situated between subject- and object-pole. Accordingly the "immanent" structure of intentionality as articulated by the Cartesian reduction is as follows:[25]

ego-pole < mental acts : senses > object-pole

While Husserl argues that the structure of consciousness opened to view is essentially intentional and thus tied to transcendence, the fact that this is a piece of inner analysis and the fact that it is achieved by a suspension of our belief in the world have the effect of subordinating the world to consciousness and thus treating it as derivative, as a realm of relative being in contrast to absolute being. The Cartesian way, in short, undercuts the equiprimordiality of subjectivity and world. Let me pursue this idea in some detail.

B. STATIC ANALYSIS AND EGOLOGY

Perhaps we can find a deeper reason for this characterization of the subject and the world in *Ideas I.* Let me suggest that, first, the restriction of subjectivity to a stream of consciousness manifest to a transcendental reflection is the result of a necessary objectivating transformation built into the procedure of the reduction. To put it critically, this restriction is the result of Husserl underestimating the extent to which what *Ideas II* calls the "theoretical attitude" persists after and prevails through the transcendental reduction. Second, this results in the *asymmetry* in the relationship between subjectivity and world being transformed into a necessary *subordination* of world to subject. Let me elaborate on these two issues for they tell us much about the limits of the static analysis of *Ideas I.*

1. As we have seen, phenomenological reflection makes explicit the interplay of profile and object operative throughout perceptual experience: each object is given in and through a multiplicity of its profiles. To capture this distinction, *Ideas I* relies on the term "appearance," using it critically to capture the contrast between "appearing X" and "X appearing as a," not metaphysically to introduce a difference between phenomena and noumena. Husserl employs it in his efforts to secure the neutrality of his descriptions and to bring them under the governance of "the things themselves." It seems, however, to impose an unexpected restriction of its own on the analysis.

The clue to the framework giving rise to the transcendental analysis of *Ideas I* is actually found in the opening sections to *Ideas II.* There Husserl expressly calls the interest of "the observing and thinking subject" engaged in the process of cognitive assessment—whether it be that of physics or art criticism—the "doxic-theoretic" attitude;[26] and he contrasts it to our living in an uncritical perceptual, axiological, or practical attitude.[27] The theoretical attitude effects a modification of our relationship to whatever objects might be at hand in order to undertake a critical analysis of these objects. Noetically, "experiencing this" and "knowing how" are recast as "knowing that." Noematically, things enjoyed and things-to-hand are framed as items known. I do not simply play with the round ball; I judge that it is a globe and not a cube. I do not just enjoy the color array of a Klee painting; I describe the use of counterpositioning in its composition. In each case we can say that our interest in theory has the effect of "objectivating," to use Husserl's term, of lifting the object out of our unreflective appropriations of it and modifying it into a topic of analysis. The object is distanced, retained only as an item seen, thought, or judged by a thinking subject.

Initially Husserl was convinced that the theoretical attitude was one among the other "natural" attitudes and thus suspended by the phenomenological reduction. In such a scheme there would be little risk of confusing it with the phenomenological attitude, as it would be one among others submitted to constitutive analysis. But the phenomenological attitude of *Ideas I*, it seems, employs the same procedures as the theoretical attitude of *Ideas II*, i.e., a neutralization of our involvement with things, a corresponding attending to objects as phenomena, and then a reflection upon the thinking subject. Looking at it after the reduction, phenomenology is, above all else, a theoretical enterprise. If we employ a contrast between *attitude* and *interest*, then perhaps we can say that the suspension of the natural attitude still takes place within a certain interest, that of constructing truthful theory. Even if we grant the neutralization of the natural attitude (which should include the theoretical attitude among others) we have not thereby secured the neutralization of the *interest* (a theoretical attitude) driving the first. This problem is especially acute for the Cartesian way because it does not argue for a progressive dismantling of the natural attitude or use an appropriate notion of critique to carry us back to the transcendental standpoint. Instead it relies on a single methodological device (the disengagement of the belief in existence) to suspend the power of the natural attitude as a whole and to transport us to a field of analysis free of all interests. The fact that the problem of skepticism is what motivates the introduction of the reduction, and the fact that the reduction necessarily relies on certain operative concepts (conditioned and unconditioned, mediate and immediate, adequate and inadequate, etc.) that "exceed" what the phenomena themselves present, are sure indications that Husserl's reduction remains enframed by a theoretical attitude. This immediately raises the possibility that this attitude, untouched by the reduction, might unknowingly introduce transformations of its own that affect the *outcome* of analysis within the transcendental attitude.

This coincidence of interest and the theoretical attitude should not be used to argue that Husserl cannot distinguish the natural from the phenomenological attitude. Rather, it shows that, since he used a Cartesian version of the reduction to distinguish them, his phenomenological analysis replicates certain operative features and notions internal to the "unreduced" theoretical attitude. The interest in theory, and the epistemic approach that his Cartesian approach involves, control the descriptions and thus bring with them a tacit assumption that subjectivity should be treated as a "thinking and observing subject." In turn, this view of subjectivity shapes the outcome of Husserl's analysis within the reduction.

The reduction as a theoretical undertaking establishes a certain clearing in which objects give themselves as *appearances* to and for us. The reflection does not merely find what is there; as intentional, it exercises functions of its own that set the course of analysis. As appearances, objects are necessarily objects of experience. The experience of objects is irreducibly *my* experience; i.e., as appearances objects belong to the sphere of what is mine. The reduction and its "annihilation" of the world guarantee that the world can be included only to the extent that it can be approached from the side of my stream of consciousness. This means that I can know it only in and through appearances. In the broadest sense, I am acquainted with the world only as *my* world. Having it as my world entails an "I" to whom the world belongs in the sense that there is an ego to whom the world appears. This ego is not a part of the world, does not itself "appear" in the world. If we count the items in the world, the "I" will not be one of them precisely because it is the condition of our having a world in which things can appear. Significantly, the converse does not hold true: I cannot argue from the fact that I am acquainted with *my* ego apart from the world to the idea that the world is not part of the ego or to the thesis that the world (as appearance) does not depend upon the ego. Wittgenstein drew out the logical consequences of this asymmetry: "the subject does not belong to the world but rather is a limit of the world."[28] Husserl's version of this point reads: the "'I am' is the irreducible, intentional ground for my world."[29]

The introduction of the ego and its treatment as transcendental in *Ideas I* is a decisive step beyond Husserl's earlier analysis: "In the *Logical Investigations* I proposed a skepticism on the question of the pure ego that I could no longer hold to in the progress of my [further] studies."[30] Clearly the *Investigations* already have the notion of acts or experiences. They also speak of the subject in terms of a certain psychological condition of theoretical knowledge: "it is a priori evident that thinking subjects in general . . . must be competent to carry out the kinds of acts in which theoretical knowledge is realized."[31] But what the *Investigations* do not have and what is needed in *Ideas I* is a notion of the ego that is equivalent to neither the psychological subject nor one of its experiences: "we never stumble upon the pure ego as one experience among other experiences."[32] Since the ego is "something identical throughout all actual and possible changes in experience" it cannot be understood as a "piece" or moment of such experiences.[33] In his efforts to clarify his analysis as transcendental, Husserl appropriates the Kantian formulation as his own: "The 'I think' must be able to accompany all my (re)presentations."[34]

The second book of *Ideas*, however, goes on to broaden this description beyond Kant. The ego is

> that which, in acts of perception, is directed to what is perceived, in acts of knowing to what is known, in acts of phantasy to what is phantasized . . . ; in each act-achievement there lies a ray of directedness that I can only describe as taking its point of departure in the "I," which, evidently, thereby remains

> numerically identical and undivided while it lives in these manifold acts, takes part spontaneously in them, and goes in ever new rays through them toward what is objective in their sense. To speak more precisely, the pure I is related to objects in very different modes, according to the kind of act-achievement.[35]

The expression Husserl uses to describe the intimate and close tie between the ego and its acts is "function." The term is Kant's, but its interpretation is not.[36] He says:

> In the acts . . . the pure ego exercises its pure "functions" and thus we would like to designate the acts themselves, in an extended sense, as functions. Thereby, the pure ego can, on the one hand, be distinguished from the acts as the ego functioning in them and which, through them, is related to objects; on the other hand, the ego is to be distinguished only abstractively [*sic*]. Abstractive in so far as the ego cannot be thought of as something separable from these experiences, from its "life," just as, conversely, these experiences cannot be thought of except as a medium of the life of the ego.[37]

This chain of ideas leads us to what Husserl understands as the irreducible ground disclosed by transcendental phenomenology:

> Insofar as every cogito requires a cogitatum and this stands in relation to the pure ego through the achievements of its acts, we find a remarkable polarity in every act: on the one side, the I-pole; on the other, the object as counterpole.[38]

The correlation of acts and meanings here is based not on the correlation of subjectivity and world, for between them *Ideas I* sees only an "abyss of meaning."[39] Consistent with the scope of categorial phenomenology and what can be extracted from the sphere of "mineness," however, this correlation is based on the *polarity* of ego and object. In confining analysis to the stream of consciousness, the world is lost; i.e., it can be integrated only as phenomena or, better, as their projected limit, as the totality of the objects of cognition. What Husserl did not realize was that the full scope of transcendental subjectivity is also lost, i.e., it is comprehensible only as ego, as the identical subject that functions in all acts. The object, "a totally different kind of unity" than the ego,[40] has a unity that is attested to in the "coincidence" of the acts related to it.[41] This analysis in *Ideas II* rejoins that in *Ideas I* as Husserl quotes Kant again, but with a change: "The pure ego must be able to accompany all my (re)presentations."[42]

The question we raised about the way in which a theoretical attitude "preforms" the approach Husserl takes is one he himself raised in lectures given during the Winter Semester of 1922/23, lectures directly concerned with the Cartesian way. We will look at this course, "Introduction to Philosophy," in detail in the next chapter, but for now we lift out the one line of thought concerned with this problem and indicate how Husserl attempts to handle it.

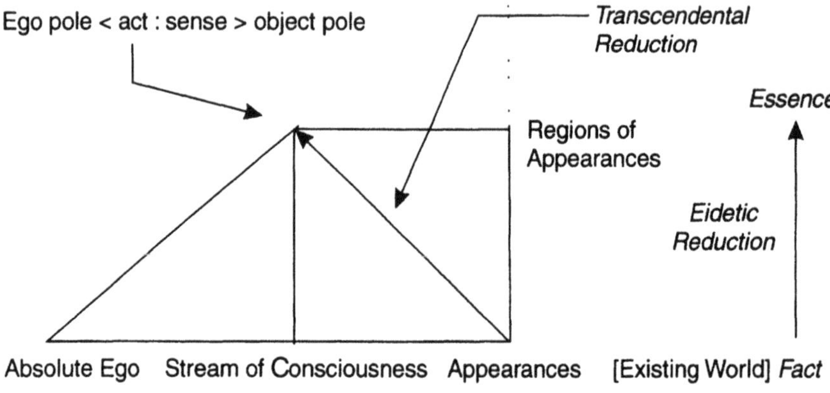

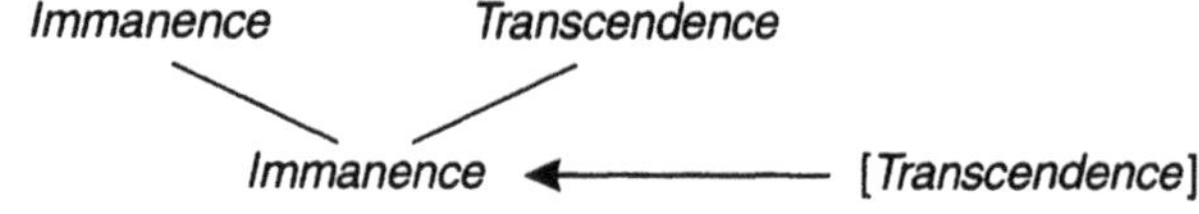

Fig. 5.1. Transcendental Phenomenology under the Cartesian Reduction

At the beginning of this lecture course, Husserl worries that the interest in truth and reason that established the field from which transcendental phenomenology analyzes subjectivity results in a much too restrictive notion of subjectivity, one that treats it only as *Erkenntnissubjektivität*, the subject of cognitive acts alone.[43] The problem is obvious: "Cognition is one function of life. But the life of the ego, one will say, is not only cognizing life."[44] This leads to a notion that anticipates Wittgenstein's emphasis upon "forms of life" by two decades:

> But in other forms of life there is a striving directed toward other things, to the beautiful, to what is commercially usable, and such like. The subject in action produces works of truth such as theories, it produces works of beautiful art, it works upon commercial goods. . . . "[45]

Sensing that this will put a strain on his efforts to treat the noetic-noematic structure of cognition as the basic form of areas that are not themselves fields of cognition, Husserl attempts to contain them by looking to the rational interests or norms that might be at play in these domains. Thus he says:

> Had we earlier—in the narrower region of reason, that of cognition—required that subjectivity—here as cognizing—be made in pure reflection into a universal theme, and that, indeed, before all questions about evidence and non-evidence, reason and non-reason, so the same must also hold true for the total theory of reason. Thus what is required is the universal study of the full and entire subjectivity to the extent that it in some way stands under possible norms of reason. First in the higher levels of research it must thematize what is specific to reason itself and all types of reason and that according to the sides of the activities specific to reason as well as according to the sides of the constructions of reason (theories, works of art, etc.). Therewith we would have a much more comprehensive philosophy that, if we grasp it as a science of the ultimate and principal universals, shows itself related to the idea of humanity in general and the idea of an authentic, human culture in general.[46]

Here Husserl begins to see how much the theoretical interest controls his original account and recognizes the need for a broader basis. He isolates one of the limits of the Cartesian approach of *Ideas I*, which then carries him beyond its identification of the transcendental sphere with the egological into a rearticulation of that sphere as intersubjective. In this text he puts this point in the following way:

> Because subjectivity is essentially communal subjectivity or living in communal form, because the individual life is only a thread in the weave of a universal, all-encompassing communal life, then this science [i.e., the universal, philosophical theory of reason][47] is related at the outset to universal, communal subjectivity and universal communal life.[48]

We will return to these issues in the next chapter and chapter 12.

2. The Cartesian reduction of subjectivity to the ego, we want to emphasize, carries in its wake a certain restriction on what can serve as the "uncircumventable" (*unhintergehbar*) foundational structure of transcendental analysis. Since the ego is understood as a synthesizing pole, its proper correlate is not world but object. "I-act-object belong essentially together; in this idea they cannot be separated."[49] As in Kant the ego comes into play as the condition of the possibility of our having coherent cognition of objects. But Husserl's analysis in *Ideas I* overdetermines the *asymmetry* between "I" and "object" by blending this with a Cartesian ontological difference between "absolute" and "relative being." The world is thereby treated as "*a merely intentional being*, such that it has the merely secondary relative sense of being *for* a consciousness."[50] As a result, the difference between ego and world becomes understood as an *ontological priority* of the ego over the world and thereby as an ontological reduction of world to the sphere of "immanence," to the domain of the subject.[51]

If we claim that the transcendental analysis of subjectivity as ego loses the alterity of world in *Ideas I,* we must also say that those passages in *Ideas II* that do justice to the nature of the world as horizon achieve this only by inserting the concept of transcendental ego into a broader notion of subjectivity. This is achieved, however, at the cost of methodological consistency. When we view the "I" as a "person," we recover a richer connection to the world. There is also reciprocity in their relationship: on the one hand, I am a "constitutive part of the real environment;"[52] on the other, the person as a "free I"[53] reigns over his/her environment. In yet another text, printed as an appendix to *Ideas II* and written about 1917, the gathering of the world into this account completely displaces the egological perspective in two steps: (a) "This living subject is the subject of actual life;"[54] and (b) life entails world:

> To his own life there necessarily belongs an intuitive life-horizon, to him as a human life there belongs a horizon of things, which are not merely [physical] bodies but, instead, objects of value, goods, etc. . . . [55]

Thus we have a correlation not between ego and object (as poles) but between "subjectivity" or the "subject of life," and "horizon" or "life-world."[56] The difficulty with this later account, however, is that we have clearly left the plane of what can be called transcendental analysis, especially when compared to the method of *Ideas I;* from the perspective of *Ideas II,* the treatment of the subject as person is a *regional* study. We have subjectivity but not transcendental subjectivity. Only as empirical double, only as object in the world, is an enhanced notion of the subject and its relationship to an enriched notion of the world restored. It will not take Husserl long, however, to attempt to integrate this richer account into his transcendental analysis.

The breakthrough to the notion of world as horizon, then, is something gained by Husserl's transcendental turn. But the treatment of the subject is still limited in its scope, limited by the fact that this account fused the theoretical attitude and its reliance upon the cognizing subject with the phenomenological notion of subjectivity. This fusion clarifies the underlying tensions resulting from the limited scope of Husserl's static analysis. To the extent that subjectivity is defined as ego, it is transcendental but at the expense of losing the world as its equiprimordial correlate; to the extent that it introduces an enlarged notion of subjectivity as the correlate of world, it ceases to be transcendental, both in that it becomes object and in that its analysis becomes regional. Yet the characterization of subjectivity as ego, analogous to Kant's transcendental unity of apperception, is not an accidental but a necessary feature of any account that treats, first, the subject as a "logically thinking subject,"[57] i.e., the subject in terms of its acts of knowledge, and, second, objects as appearances, i.e., the "in itself" as "for me." Systematically seen, the polarity of ego and object and the priority of ego over object are consequences of these two steps.

While these features are a necessary part of Husserl's Cartesian account, few have realized that this is not the only way Husserl frames a foundational, *static* analysis of intentionality and of the relationship between subjectivity and world. In the published work, we see this with striking clarity, as *Formal and Transcendental Logic* takes the analysis we just outlined in *Ideas II* and transposes it to a transcendental register. Before we move to the next section, we can look briefly at how Husserl attempts to account for the notion of world as a whole on the basis of his phenomenological conception of horizon. The world envisioned as a whole has the "sense" of being a "universe" and of being "transcendent." "The pregivenness of the world as indubitably existing universum (as universum and not unconnected heap) is the foundation for judgments for all positive sciences."[58] This sense refers us back to subjectivity and "the manifold of real and possible achievements" in which the "idea" of the world as a whole is "prescribed."[59] Yet one of the senses that the world as universe of being has "for me" is that it is there "for others:" "the world . . . has in its own sense as objective world the *categorial form* of 'being ever a true world' not only for me but for everyone."[60] "The situated modes of the givenness of the world are such for real and possible praxis, my own and those of the community."[61] Thus we are carried beyond the sphere of what is *mine* into "a community of experience" and praxis correlative to the world as universe.[62] The world as totality, as "objective," presupposes a notion not of subjectivity but of "sense-constituting intersubjectivity."[63]

It seems that Cartesian analysis is turned inside out: not only is the subject reinscribed into the world but also the notion of subjectivity is displaced by that of intersubjectivity. But here, again, we must wait, for the structural tensions between the notions of horizon and totality are worked out only in Husserl's genetic account; the world *being* a totality, it will be suggested, is understood in terms of its *becoming* a whole.

C. THE LIMITS OF THE CARTESIAN WAY

This formulation of Husserl's Cartesian program is enough to raise the question of whether Husserl ever departed from Cartesianism, to echo the title of Ludwig Landgrebe's famous essay,[64] or whether he remained, unrepentant, a Cartesian to his last day, as Manfred Sommer wants to argue.[65] Considerable care must be taken in the formulation of the issue. It should be clear by now that this question is quite different from that of whether or not Husserl ever abandoned static phenomenology. The latter he never did. Nor should we reduce the issue to whether, having given a Cartesian formulation to his static program in *The Idea of Phenomenology* and *Ideas I* and having set his genetic phenomenology in contrast to a static analysis, he did not attempt in later texts, such as the *Cartesian Meditations*, to regather his new studies under a Cartesian reflection. For it seems that he did this as well, though we will see in the next section that the story is much more interesting precisely because each new attempt brought new failures to light. Rather, the question for us now is whether he held to all three features, unmodified, of the Cartesian program we sketched in Section A.

Husserl never relinquished the search for a fixed and firm basis for knowledge. If anything, it was precisely this unremitting quest for a secure foundation that drove him into ever deeper analyses. Because he did not envision his method as simply procedural but as reductive, as providing an analysis of complexity in terms of constitutive clusters that were not just hypothetical deductive constructs but also allowed of intuitive confirmation, he remained a Cartesian. Like Descartes he spent his philosophical career designing and redesigning, then building and rebuilding both the foundation of philosophy and the edifice erected upon it. Whatever the changes in the content of the theory, the ideal of a rational and unified account of the domains of being endures.

Yet this sense of Cartesianism is relatively weak, almost uninteresting, and says little about its distinctive elements, which we sketched above, and gives us little insight into why Husserl himself became increasingly concerned with the limits of this program. In this section I want to sketch five considerations central to this question, which point to certain tensions in Husserl's original fusion of phenomenological philosophy with Cartesian analysis. Increasingly Husserl came to see that the Cartesian way, narrowly construed, was able to account for neither the scope nor the depth of the transcendental. His repeated attempts to utilize this way, although he increasingly sensed its restrictions, led to an attempt at expanding it from within. This effort reached its culmination in the *Cartesian Meditations,* a work that Husserl finally abandoned in order to take up work on the *Crisis* (1934–1937). I will save an analysis of that work until the next section in order to concentrate on Husserl's own reflections upon the Cartesian way in other works. What, precisely, are the limits he came to recognize?

1. The first consideration has to do with a restriction imposed by the Cartesian *reduction* as a whole. Since a bracketing of the world brings this reduction into play, we are left with a type of apprehension that does not move *through* the world. As a result the ego we gain is "empty." In the *Crisis* Husserl puts it thus:

> I note in passing that the much shorter way to the transcendental epoché in my *Ideas* . . . which I call the "Cartesian way" (since it is thought of as being attained merely by reflectively engrossing oneself in the Cartesian epoché of the *Meditations* while critically purifying it of Descartes' prejudices and confusions), has a great shortcoming: while it leads to the transcendental ego in one leap, as it were, it brings this ego into view as apparently empty

of content, since there can be no preparatory explication; so one is at a loss, at first, to know what has been gained by it, much less how, starting with this, a completely new sort of fundamental science, decisive for philosophy, has been attained.[66]

2. This is tied to a second issue: because it reduces the world to no more than its presence to consciousness, Cartesian reflection always begins with "finished" apperceptions and then looks for essential structures. Since we are restricted to what is displayed to the reflective gaze, any levels that are "beneath" that surface remain concealed. *Phenomenological Psychology* has an especially lucid passage on the limits of *phenomenological reflection* as a type of inner experience. What Husserl says there of his *Investigations* is even truer of *Ideas I:*

> Of particular importance, but noticed only very late, is the fact that reflective, so-called "internal" experience has very many levels and depth-dimensions and is exceedingly difficult to put into practice whenever one strives to go beyond the most superficial level. Indeed, at first one had no inkling at all of the depths and mediacies. One did not see that internal experience is not a simple reflection which would lead without further ado to the concreteness of the respective interiorities, but that the concrete admitted of being grasped as a theme only in many levels of reflection, that internal experience is a process of disclosure to be effected in every new reflection. The demand for pure and systematically progressing description ... [is] a great field of difficult work. ...[67]

3. Problems with the nature of reflection have a direct bearing on the sense in which the world is transcendent. Does the Cartesian reduction simply thematize the world or does it introduce a crucial transformation of its being? Profiles bespeak the relationality of objects and acts. They are the way in and through which existing objects are given, which for their part are never exhausted in any single profile. The possibility of further perspectives on the same object, never spent in any one of them, is what phenomenologically exhibits the transcendence of the existing object and thereby the transcendence of the world. Transcendence accounts for both the situatedness of objects given to acts of consciousness and the relational character of these acts. But characterizing the reduction as a bracketing of existence results in the reframing of Husserl's notion of *situated* transcendence as a notion of *subjective* transcendence.[68] Once consciousness is interpreted as a sphere of absolute being different in kind from that of the mundane world, then consciousness can be related to an object only if that object is pulled into it. Transcendence belongs to immanence, not the reverse. Phenomenology, as Husserl himself decided to call it, becomes idealism.

Husserl worried that his language of exclusion, particularly in *Ideas I,* could lead to the idea that the world is lost, i.e., reduced to subjective phenomenon, or to the idea that subjectivity does not belong to the realm of what does exist. In commenting on the sentence " . . . our goal . . . which we can also characterize as the acquisition of a new region of being never before delimited in its own peculiarity," Husserl adds this marginal note in his own copy of *Ideas I:*

> Is the worldly All not the All of whatever exists? Is there any sense to ask for that which "remains"? As a matter of fact, the expression is objectionable because, having been taken from the world of sensuous reality, it carries with it the thought of doing away with one part of a whole, one part of a real context. The question may, however, still have a legitimate sense when stated in the form: What can still be posited as being if the worldly All, the All of reality, remains parenthesized.[69]

In fact, the "Epilogue" written for the first English translation of *Ideas I* and published in 1931 realizes that the talk of "annihilating" the world makes it difficult to see that the goal of phenomenology is in fact to clarify the world:

> Above all: phenomenological idealism does not deny the actual existence of the real world (in the first place, that means nature), as if it maintained that the world were mere semblance [*Schein*], to which natural thinking and the positive science would be subject, though unwittingly. Its sole task and accomplishment is to clarify the sense of this world, precisely the sense in which everyone accepts it—and rightly so—as actually existing. That the world exists, that it is given as existing universe in uninterrupted experience that is constantly fusing into universal concordance, is entirely beyond doubt. But it is quite another matter to understand this indubitability which sustains life and positive science and to clarify the ground of its legitimacy.[70]

4. The uncertainty as to the status of the world after the Cartesian reduction creates a similar uncertainty in the status of subjectivity. As a consequence of the former, we find certain difficulties surrounding the identification of transcendental subjectivity as the stream of consciousness.

What put Husserl's account into a bind, as he increasingly came to realize in the 1920s, was that he had already made a place for a psychological description of subjectivity *before* the bracketing of the natural attitude, and that such a reflection treated it as a stream of consciousness. While what he called phenomenological psychology was clearly a reflective discipline concerned with the essential structures of consciousness, it was a "positive" science and thus did not involve the transcendental reduction. But since the transcendental reflection must take such a result as a "phenomenon" to be explained in terms of the constitutive activities of transcendental subjectivity, why did he assume that transcendental subjectivity itself would also be a stream of experience? His answer was that phenomenological psychology and transcendental phenomenology have the same content. But this only created a second problem;

having assumed that the consciousness that is the object of a psychological reflection has the same content and the same quality of evidence as the subjectivity I reflect upon within the reduction, being also adequately given, Husserl effected a curious splitting of the ego into two parts, one mundane and the other transcendental, but without a single feature that is descriptively different. Could it be that the identification of subjectivity as consciousness is a *necessary* result of relying upon inner experience within the reduction?

In another manuscript from around 1924,[71] Husserl fastened on to the misleading metaphor of "residuum" and repeated the point we just made concerning the loss of the world. He says:

> The clarification of the theme "transcendental subjectivity" and of the new appearing perceptions here, which, once put into action systematically, produce the new ontic ground, has many more difficulties than I initially thought. (1) First of all, it is better to avoid the talk of a phenomenological "residuum" as well as "putting the world out of play." It easily misleads one to the view that the world drops out of what can be thematized phenomenologically and, instead, only "subjective" acts, modes of appearances, etc., related to the world would be themes. . . . [72]

He then introduced a line of thought that frees his notion of a transcendental sphere of experience from that of consciousness:

> But in yet another respect we must be especially attentive and keep at bay dangerous prejudices. First of all, it could appear as obvious that the subjectivity gained through the reduction as "residuum" were my own "pure" subjectivity, [so to speak, my private ego][73]. . . .
>
> I begin with the fact that first of all I in the [course of my] natural life exercise a natural reflection and thereby apperceive myself as a human person. I [then] consider this as phenomenologist: the validity of this apperception falls under the reduction and the person purely as such, as pure consciousness, itself belongs to what counts as my *transcendental sphere of experience*. . . . Originally I emphasized too much in this reduction the stream of consciousness, as if the reduction treated this.
>
> In any case this was my initial view in the introduction of the phenomenological reduction in 1907. In this resided an error in principle, though one none too easy to see through. It was transcended by the "extension" of the phenomenological reduction to monadic intersubjectivity in the lectures of Fall, 1910.[74] Already at that time I explained: it could appear that the reduction to the "stream of experience" would yield a new kind of solipsism. But this difficulty is solved when we make it clear that the reduction does not, first of all, simply lead to the *actual* stream of consciousness (and its ego-pole), but, as I put it in 1910, that each experienced thing—and so the entire world, as ever valid in streaming experience (first as nature)—is an "index" for an infinite manifold of *possible* experiences.[75]

As this text continues, it becomes clear that this approach has the advantage of allowing Husserl to bring together his notion of transcendental subjectivity with that of horizon, of what is intentionally *implicit,* which by definition goes beyond that which can be directly experienced. The reduction at play in this text clearly outstrips its Cartesian formulation and comes close to reversing the asymmetry between consciousness and world.

When Husserl wrote his "Epilogue" to *Ideas I* some twenty years later, he looked back on the first characterization of transcendental subjectivity in *Ideas I;* he did not find there a self-enclosed "realm" of "being." He wrote of an "open and infinite *field* of pure phenomenological givens,"[76] as we will emphasize in the next chapter. Only the "structure" or the "essence" is "self-enclosed and self-coherent."[77] This led to a formulation that one cannot find in the Cartesian account of *Ideas I:*

> . . . it has been shown that "transcendental subjectivity," as what is given in transcendental experience for the one engaged at the moment in self-reflection, means not only "I as transcendental Ego-self," taken concretely in the life of my own transcendental consciousness, but, in addition, also refers to the co-subjects that present themselves as transcendental in my transcendental life, in the transcendental we-community which is co-presented. Transcendental intersubjectivity is thus the one in which the real world is constituted as objective, as being for "everybody." This is where the real world gets its sense. . . .[78]

It may be this formulation introduced a transformation of the way Husserl proposed in *Ideas I,* turning it into the way through phenomenological psychology, which, for its part, does restrict itself to the domain of consciousness. If so, this transformed way becomes subsumed under the way through the positive sciences, I will argue shortly, and we are no longer in the Cartesian way.

5. As a result of the restricted view of the world (point 3) and of the untenable identification of (pure) consciousness with transcendental subjectivity (point 4), the Cartesian way has difficulty maintaining a difference between the world as the totality of the objects and facts of cognition and my representation of it.

If we take the world given to us as the "true world," then we must see it as a whole given not once for all but through a process of ongoing confirmations and corrections. Accordingly, the world, as an "idea prescribed in the very process of its validation," is an intersubjective world. But such is not the world given in the Cartesian reduction, for with the recourse to the sphere of what is immediately mine other minds are excluded, i.e., treated as phenomena. As Husserl worked out the implications of this line of thought in a text from about 1924, he realizes the following:

> As long as I do not get a hold of the *full universality* of transcendental subjectivity, i.e., as *inter*-subjectivity, in transcendental experience and thought, and recognize therein the *world as the correlate of this intersubjectivity* . . . with other words, as long as I have not transcendentally explicated transcendental subjectivity in its full scope as living in the condition of humanity or natural worldliness (and discovered only as human society in the world) and transcendentally understood myself and my We, there remains the *tension* [*Spannung*] *between [my] (re)presentation of the world*—the merely individual and subjective, human (re)presentation of the worldly—*and the world itself*. . . . Only after I have chosen the ultimate transcendental standpoint and, from that point, have circumscribed the infinity of transcendental all-subjectivity in its totality, *does this tension disappear, does the difference between (re)presentation and reality disappear.*[79]

The opposition between my (subjective) representation and the world, he realized, appears as "an unbridgeable opposition" when one begins with the individual ego. "If we remain in the [Cartesian] *epoché* how are we ever to move beyond [our] representations of the world?"[80]

Unfortunately, his own answer to this question in this text was entirely *ad hominem* and he did little more than deride those who were unusually "anxious" and shied away from the "doubtless necessity" of suspending our belief in the world.[81] What little he did say is irrelevant because he did not respond from within the Cartesian framework, but only appealed to the difference between transcendental and ordinary analysis and to the universality of transcendental subjectivity.[82] Husserl attempted to handle this later by a special form of presentation that is appropriate to the other as other subjectivity, i.e., by the notion of empathy.[83] Whatever problem we will find with it, recourse to empathy only affirms the point we are after, namely, that the characterization of transcendental subjectivity in terms of intersubjectivity outstrips both the notion of consciousness serving as a base for the Cartesian reduction of *Ideas I* and that work's restriction of the world to the sphere of immanence.

D. HEIDEGGER AND HUSSERL'S "MEDITATIONS"

Do these hesitations and difficulties that Husserl himself came to recognize mean that he abandoned the Cartesianism of *Ideas I*? Or do they rather isolate certain problems that he would have to treat in the course of strengthening that approach? They are serious issues, not minor imperfections, but it may be that the full depth of their critical import did not become clear to Husserl until he actually attempted to rework his Cartesian analysis into a final, coherent formulation. The existence of the *Cartesian Meditations,* a late work published close to twenty years (1931) after *Ideas I* and at least five years after Husserl's most intense labor on the alternative ways into the reduction (roughly 1923–1925),[84] has been taken by most as sufficient proof that the program of phenomenology is thoroughly Cartesian and remained so throughout the long course of Husserl's development after 1906 or 1907. The underlying assumption guiding this interpretation of the *Cartesian Meditations* is that, while it extends the analysis of *Ideas I* in the direction of a theory of intersubjectivity, it is perfectly at one with that work in its understanding of method. Whatever other paths Husserl entertained, there is a consensus that the Cartesian way is the purest statement of his phenomenology.

In our last section, however, we became convinced that the issue is not quite so simple. We must be careful, first of all, not to think that Husserl introduced the Cartesian way between 1906 and 1913, attempted to frame alternatives between 1923 and 1925, only to return to the former in 1929. The question of an alternative method, as shown by his text on static and genetic method and his lectures on genetic logic, both collected in *Analysen zur passiven Synthesis,* reaches back to 1921 and then extends through his last work, the *Crisis.* On the one hand, the Cartesian way does persist. Even during the period in the 1920s when his alternative ways received much direct attention, Husserl did not hesitate to continue developing his Cartesian path and even presented it in lectures in both London (1922) and Paris (1929) as a primer for those first coming to grips with his thought. The existence of the *Cartesian Meditations,* and the fact that he recommended its French translation to readers as late as 1933 even as he began developing the text of the *Crisis,* also convinces us that it was never overthrown. On the other hand, the consideration of alternative ways to the reduction cannot be construed as an interlude during which Husserl tried and finally abandoned their use. The presence of *Formal and Transcendental Logic,* the proofs of which he finished correcting just as he began working on the Paris lectures, clearly establishes that. Indeed, when we look back we can see that Husserl's earlier *Investigations,* and even some of the later sections of *Ideas I* (read in conjunction with *Ideas II*), can be understood, *de facto* if not *de jure,* as moving down one of his alternative paths. Even more suggestive is his lecture course from the Winter Semester of 1910/11, "Grundprobleme der Phänomenologie," where Husserl already attempted to move from the "natural concept of the world" to a transcendental phenomenology.[85] Whatever else we say about the various ways to the reduction, we must begin with the recognition that they coexist, side by side, throughout most of Husserl's philosophical journey.

I hope, however, to press beyond even this way of putting the issue by looking at Husserl's *Meditations* in terms of both its history and its content. The working assumption of the standard view is not only that *Ideas I* and the *Meditations* are cut from the same bolt, but also that their materials have been tailored to produce identical suits, the second being somewhat larger to accommodate the intervening years of growth. But if it turns out that the *Meditations*, even as it stands, shows certain alterations in its pattern, and that Husserl's decision not to present it to the German public was due to serious flaws he discovered in it, then we might have new insight into Husserl's "departure" from Cartesianism.

We must pause to note that we have also identified a deeper issue: the crucial question for us as we strive to understand phenomenology systematically is not whether the Cartesian formulation of static analysis is wedded to the Cartesian way, as it obviously must be, but whether the program of static analysis as a whole is wedded to the Cartesian way. Framing the question like this then allows us to ask precise questions about the history of the *Cartesian Meditations* and how Husserl himself came to view that work. We will do this in the context of a discussion of the role that Heidegger might have played in Husserl's later works. In the next chapter we will go on to ask whether the *Meditations* might not itself introduce significant transformations of the Cartesian way of *Ideas I*, a question rarely if ever put to this text by proponents of the standard picture.

The story surrounding Husserl's "Cartesian Meditations"—I will now use quotes when referring to the project that Husserl gave to his translators in 1929 and then continued to work on up to about 1933, and italic to refer to the text we now have printed[86]—is one with countless twists and turns, and ultimately one of deep frustration. Fortunately, we have fine instructions on how to navigate the labyrinth from Iso Kern, Karl Schuhmann and, most recently, Ronald Bruzina.[87] We mentioned in the Introduction that Husserl held two pairs of lectures at the Sorbonne (February 23 and 25, 1929) titled "Introduction into Transcendental Phenomenology."[88] Immediately afterwards he began revising these lectures extensively, working mostly on the problem of intersubjectivity, in order to produce a text that could then be translated into French. He not only revised the original text, which became the four individual meditations, but also expanded it with a fifth meditation on the issue of intersubjectivity. When he laid down his pen on April 7, 1929, the day before his seventieth birthday, he thought the work was complete. But the day after the celebrations he became troubled by its inadequacies and spent the next four weeks revising it. The small book was finished about the middle of May, and the French translation, bearing the title *Méditations cartésiennes*, appeared in 1931. There is no doubt that Husserl was initially happy with the outcome and even thought that a German version of this work would finally set his method on solid ground. On May 26 he wrote Roman Ingarden:

> With full steam I had to work until the 7th of April to finish the expansion of the Paris lectures. Unfortunately, I found afterwards [i.e., after his birthday] that this finished product would hardly be satisfactory because I—in order to avoid difficult accounts and not to overstep too much the style (the

> "Sommaire") of the Paris lectures—had to leave gaps in the presentation of the proof. This affected the theory of intersubjectivity (respectively, monadology and transcendental idealism of phenomenology). I decided to make the work *whole* and gave a complete construction of the transcendental theory of the experience of the alien [*Fremderfahrung*]. In this way a complete construction of new "Cartesian Meditations" (so the present title) came about. . . . I view this as my main text and will let it appear soon with Niemeyer.[89]

But the fact is that Husserl himself never published the *Cartesian Meditations* in German. Why was it withheld from publication? Surely this is a most surprising fate for a book that he considered his "main text."

There has been much speculation as to the relationship between Husserl and Heidegger. Views range from the thesis that Heidegger's *Being and Time* (1928) produced a fundamental change in Husserl's philosophical perspective, precipitating the introduction of the notion of the life-world that we find in the *Crisis,* to the opposite view that Husserl remained so insular and was so absorbed in his own line of thought that his growing disagreement with Heidegger was, at most, a source of disappointment, not redirection. Clearly the first approach is misguided for, as we will see in chapter 13, Husserl had introduced the notion of the life-world into his writings in the early 1920s and had devoted several studies to it well before he had Heidegger's *Being and Time* in hand. The second claim is not accurate either, for reasons that will become apparent in the story we are telling about the "Cartesian Meditations."

Heidegger had completed his Habilitation in 1915 and found himself mixing military service with efforts to continue his academic work at Freiburg as a *Privatdozent* (a position awarded with the Habilitation but without salary) in 1916, the year Husserl first moved to Freiburg from Göttingen. While Heidegger certainly knew of Husserl and his work, the *Investigations* being a book he thoroughly studied in 1909 and *Ideas I* a book that cost him his summer holidays in 1914,[90] it seems that Husserl, his senior by thirty years, had not met Heidegger.[91] Due to a heart ailment, Heidegger's military service kept him in Freiburg working for the Postal Control Office and lecturing for the Winter Semester of 1916/17 on "Basic Problems in Logic." Naturally this allowed for ongoing contact and exchanges.

It may have been Natorp's request for information on Heidegger that caused Husserl to pay attention to the young scholar. A post had opened up at Marburg and Natorp wanted to know whether Heidegger should be considered. Though Husserl responded in 1917 in somewhat neutral terms, not having had him as a student and not knowing him that well, the letter was favorable to Heidegger; eventually he was short-listed. By the Winter Semester of

1917/18, however, Husserl and Heidegger became "sufficiently close . . . to discuss philosophy on a personal basis."[92]

After the war, with the country in shambles, Husserl doggedly persisted in applying to the ministry of higher education in Karlsruhe to have a permanent special post created for Heidegger in the Philosophy Department. Husserl was unhappy with Heidegger's tenuous position as what we would call a temporary or adjunct instructor, and he used the force of his pen to try to better it. We know that Heidegger became involved in the editing work for the *Jahrbuch,* and Husserl mentioned to Ingarden in July of 1920 that he might set Heidegger to work on a piece that was due to appear.[93] Husserl also took pains to assist him in other ways. After receiving seven thousand marks from the Canadian Winthrop Bell in the summer of 1920 for research purposes, Husserl wrote that he had not yet decided how to spend the gift but that

> *stante pede,* so to speak, I have first presented 1000 Marks to our excellent [*trefflich*] Heidegger, who is as poor as a church mouse and is now most fortunate and able to procure for himself several important primary sources in the philosophy of religion.[94]

Eventually Husserl's persistence with Karlsruhe paid off and, beginning in the Winter Semester of 1920/21, Heidegger was given a permanent post as *Assistant,* a post equivalent to what we might call a regular lecturer. It should not be confused with the position of being one of Husserl's working assistants, of which there were only three: Edith Stein, who came with him from Göttingen; Ludwig Landgrebe; and Eugen Fink. Heidegger also taught a lecture course in the Phenomenology of Religion[95] and worked with Husserl, leading a number of study groups[96] in that semester.

Husserl was also instrumental in helping Heidegger, after serious delays caused by Heidegger's lack of publications, to finally secure a position at Marburg, which he assumed in the Winter Semester of 1923/24. For a second time he exchanged letters with Natorp, but this time gave Heidegger the highest praise and an unequivocal endorsement for the post.[97] Heidegger did not take to Marburg, finding the atmosphere "stuffy" and "stifling"[98] and the professors, with the exception of Rudolf Bultmann, uninteresting. The relationship with Husserl continued as Heidegger, escaping that "foggy hole,"[99] spent semester breaks and vacations in his mountain hut in Todnauberg, not far from Freiburg, often passing through Freiburg on his way there. Sometimes Heidegger stayed in Husserl's home, where both he and his wife were always welcome. In particular, he attended birthday celebrations for Husserl (April 8). In fact, it was at such an occasion in 1926 that Heidegger publicly dedicated his forthcoming *Being and Time* to Husserl. That work appeared in the spring of 1927.

During Heidegger's tenure at Marburg, Nicholi Hartmann's chair became vacant and Heidegger applied for the position. For yet a third time Husserl wrote Marburg on his behalf, telling his correspondent Ernst Jaensch that Heidegger was to be preferred to any person they might have had in mind for the post. He continued: "In my eyes Heidegger is without a doubt the most important figure among the rising generation." He added, almost prophetically, "unless some singularly unhappy stroke of irrational chance or fate intervenes to prevent it, he is predestined to be a philosopher of great stature, a leader far beyond the confusions and frailties of the present age."[100] The appointment was delayed due to departmental politics and holdups created by the central ministry in Berlin. By the time he was offered the post two years later in October of 1927, Heidegger knew that he was on his way to Freiburg as Husserl's successor.

Husserl, it seems, was a man of delayed reactions. Not only did he wait almost two years (1923–1924) after his lectures in London (1922) to engage classic British Empiricism,[101] choosing instead to rehearse Descartes to his English audience,[102] he also did not fully come to grips with the crucial differences between Heidegger's and his own thought until the summer of 1929, three years after Heidegger presented him with the dedication of *Being and Time* on April 8, 1926. He did have concerns earlier, and he even arranged a special meeting to discuss matters. Husserl's wife, who often did correspondence for him, wrote Heidegger on December 30, 1927:

> My husband would like you to arrange your return trip [from Todnauberg to Marburg] so that you can devote a whole day for a scientific [*wissenschaftlich*] discussion over your book [*Being and Time*]. He has occupied himself the whole vacation exclusively with its study and finds it necessary to let himself be instructed with you[103] about much that does not want to become entirely clear to him.[104]

Heidegger did visit Husserl a few days later, on January 8, 1928. While we do not have a direct account of the outcome of their discussions, I believe there is a reference to it in a letter he wrote to Pfänder in 1931. Reflecting back on the course of his relationship with Heidegger, Husserl said:

> Of course, as *Being and Time* appeared in 1927, I was alienated by the new style of language and thought. At first I trusted his post-publication clarification: he is one who advances my research.[105] I derived the impression of an exceptional, though not clarified intellectual energy, and honestly took pains to penetrate and accept it. In the face of theories whose access was so difficult for my type of thinking, I did not want to come to grips with the fact that in them the methods of my phenomenological research and [its] scientific rigor [*Wissenschaftlichkeit*] in general are abandoned. Somehow the blame rests with me and with Heidegger only so far as he leaped much too quickly into problems of a higher stage. He himself steadily denied that

> he is abandoning my transcendental phenomenology and directed me to his future second volume [of *Being and Time*]. Because of my weak sense of self-confidence at that time I preferred to doubt myself and my ability to follow, understand and evaluate alien motives of thought.[106]

Even the failed attempt over several months in 1927 and 1928 to write an article together for the *Encyclopaedia Britannica,* the drafts of which clearly show how differently the two thinkers were approaching the very definition of phenomenology,[107] was not sufficient to awaken Husserl to how difficult it would be to find a common path. Kern suggests that "he attributed these tensions between him and Heidegger to the lack of shared philosophical discussions (Heidegger had taught in Marburg since 1924)[108] and hoped to achieve oneness, long wished and felt, through a deeper exchange of thought."[109] But it is also clear from this letter and others that Husserl's inability to bring his own work to published form deeply shook his confidence in himself. It was not so much with the editorial side of this problem that Husserl needed help. Heidegger did do one final, cursory editing job on Husserl's *Phenomenology of the Consciousness of Internal Time* (1928);[110] but Landgrebe, who had already been at work since 1923 pulling together his mass of manuscripts into coherent presentations, was joined by Fink in 1928. Rather, his need was for "the best" of the new generation to carry the banner of phenomenology into the future. Heidegger was one of the few who thought of himself as developing phenomenology in a transcendental register. If Cairns's report is accurate, then according to Husserl's own words, he often said to Heidegger: "You and I are *die Phänomenologie.*"[111] Husserl's letter to Pfänder also mentions a certain psychological dimension to his relationship with Heidegger. It speaks of him following the younger Heidegger's career at Marburg as if it were his own and intimates that he was disarmed by Heidegger's effusive "geniality."[112] In any case, Husserl strongly supported Heidegger as his successor at Freiburg. He even did an additional lecture course beyond his retirement in the Summer Semester of 1928, as Heidegger could not take up his post until the Winter Semester of 1928/29. At the time of Husserl's seventieth birthday on April 8, 1929, the very day after Husserl had finished a draft of the "Cartesian Meditations" and only a day or two before he began further revisions of the Fifth Meditation (the whole project being sent off to the French translators on May 17), the relationship between the two philosophers was still intact.[113]

By the end of that very summer, however, matters were quite different. With the *Cartesian Meditations* off to the translators and *Formal and Transcendental Logic* printed at the end of June, Husserl devoted the next two months to a thorough reading of Heidegger's work. If we take seriously Malvine Husserl's statement that Edmund spent "the whole vacation [Christmas of 1927] exclusively with its study," we have to say that he gave himself to a second detailed reading of his younger friend's book. This time, however, it seems that he studied not only *Being and Time* but also *Kant and the Problem of Metaphysics* and perhaps even *The Essence of Reasons.*[114] On July 24, 1929, Heidegger held his inaugural address, "What Is Metaphysics?"[115] which Husserl attended. During this most official of public academic events, Heidegger, standing as Husserl's successor, challenged his approach in terms close enough to Husserl that he would have to understand the difference. It may have been this address that most surprised Husserl and finally galvanized a clear understanding of their differences.[116] Though the lecture did not mention Husserl once, there are at least three things about its content that lend weight to this interpretation.

1. Heidegger plays upon the difference between the positivity of the sciences and what they, claiming exclusive access to the truth, would be forced to understand as the reference of any discourse that exceeds this positivity. They conclude that such discourse is about "nothing" and its subject matter is "nothingness." Heidegger uses this difference, itself an "ontic" version of his ontological difference between Being and beings, to argue that nothingness is the sole object of metaphysics. In his interpretation he introduces Dasein, his replacement for Husserl's notion of transcendental subjectivity, only to the extent that it provides a disclosure of nothingness. The lecture has no place for the notion of intentionality as the fundamental structure that allows us to keep positivity as a transcendent correlate of subjectivity. In effect, Heidegger is taking up the question of the totality of beings and thus is working within the same scope as Husserl's Cartesian way. But he does so without the notion of reduction. The reversal is effected by attending to the "not" of our discourse and to the phenomenon of negation more generally, and then by seeking their ground in the notion of the Nothing. "Is there not negation and the Not only because there is the Nothing? . . . The nothing is more originary than the not and the negation."[117] The similarity to and this crucial difference from Husserl come to expression in this way: "The nothing is the negation of the totality [*Allheit*] of beings [*Seiende*]."[118] The negation of the totality leads neither to another being nor to a second sphere in which such a being, the stream of consciousness, would be located, but to "sheer not-being."

2. This is coupled with the insight that such a procedure does not require us to assume that we can actually *grasp* the whole of being (*Seiende*). Heidegger challenges the idea that the totality of being must itself be "given" so that it can then fall under a negation, as it would have to for *Ideas I,* in which Husserl's explanation of the reduction calls for the imaginative *Vernichtung* of the whole. How then do we frame the notion of such a whole? While we cannot grasp it absolutely through an act of reason, we nevertheless find ourselves "in the middle of beings [*Seiende*] as a whole."[119] The disclosure of this whole in its proper Being as nothing comes through the mediation of anxiety (*Angst*), a notion familiar to us from *Being and Time.* This means that it is

known not by an objectivating act, as Husserl's notion of a phenomenological reflection would suggest, but through *"die Befindlichkeit der Stimmung,"* through the type of situated affectivity that attends moods.[120]

3. This notion of nothingness creates a sheer division between the domain of *beings* and the domain that belongs to phenomenology, without assuming that we have a domain of *being* that is comparable to that of beings, as we find in the Cartesian way. But at the same time, this leaves what Husserl would only think of as a frightening gap between the productive achievements of science and their ground. In place of epistemological ties between intentionality and the construction of regional ontologies, which function as critical accounts of the various domains of the natural sciences, Heidegger introduced a vague appeal to a metaphysics of nothingness. "Scientific Dasein is possible only if in advance it holds itself out into the nothing. It first understands itself for what it is only when it does not give up the nothing."[121] Heidegger's connection is much too tenuous for Husserl, and we can see why he thinks the whole analysis is lacking in scientific rigor.[122]

This is how Husserl himself described the situation in the letter to Pfänder a year and a half later:

> Immediately after the publication of my last book [i.e., *Formal and Transcendental Logic*] I devoted two months to the study of *Being and Time* as well as the newer writings in order to come to a sober and final position on the Heideggerian philosophy. I came to the distressing result that I cannot do anything with this Heideggerian profundity, with its ingenious unscientific rigor [*Unwissenschaftlichkeit*]; that Heidegger's open and concealed critique [of my phenomenology] rests upon crude misunderstandings; that he is caught up in the construction of a system of philosophy of precisely that type that I have constantly reckoned as the task of my life to make impossible once and for all.[123] Everyone else had already seen this for some time, only I not. I have not concealed my findings from Heidegger.[124]

In the very next text that Husserl wrote, an "Epilogue" composed in September and October of 1929 that was to be printed as the preface to the English translation of *Ideas I* (1931) by Boyce Gibson, and in several related manuscripts connected to his rereading of *Ideas I,* he emphasized two crucial points that go to the core of what he thought Heidegger misunderstood. The first is the nature of the phenomenological reduction and the second, perhaps a consequence of the first, is the failure of philosophers to distinguish a pure psychology[125] or a pure anthropology[126]—the framework of *Being and Time,* Husserl believed—from transcendental phenomenology. The "Epilogue" emphasized the idea of philosophy as "sober work, to be conducted in the spirit of the most radical scientific rigor [*Wissenschaftlichkeit*]."[127] But at best this is a manifesto. Husserl would have to respond to Heidegger by spelling out a rigorous and detailed alternative to Heidegger's approach.

With the "Epilogue" finished sometime in October 1929, Husserl took up the "Cartesian Meditations" again, with the goal of getting it ready for publication in German. One would think that because a complete German text had already been sent to Levinas and Pilfer for the French translation, only a few additions would be needed. This must have been Husserl's view originally because *Formal and Transcendental Logic,* which was written (November 1928 to January 1929) just before he composed the Paris lectures (January and early February 1929), the printer's proofs of which must have been corrected in early 1929, announced that the "Meditations" were to be published that fall.[128] But the volleys from Heidegger were still ringing in his ears, and he was not about to launch a rowboat into contested waters. The "Epilogue" itself tells us something rather astonishing, showing us that Husserl was forced to do more than make a few corrections to the "Meditations." After informing the reader that further work by the author could be found in his *Formal and Transcendental Logic,* he first refers to the forthcoming French translation of the "Cartesian Meditations," which "gives in mere foundational lines a short introduction into phenomenological philosophy," then announces a German edition to appear shortly, and finally adds the surprising words that it will contain

> as additional matter a second Introduction, in which the clarification of the idea of a personal (on the lines of a mental science) and natural anthropology and psychology . . . is undertaken as an initial problem.[129]

The issue of a "natural anthropology" is code for precisely the problem he finds with *Being and Time.* In other words, he realized that, at best, the version of the "Meditations" he sent to the French translators (the *Meditations* that we accept today) was only a "short introduction" and would not provide an adequate response to Heidegger. He envisioned writing a second introduction that would address the challenge posed by his work and, perhaps, even rewriting the "Meditations" in a form that would be much more appropriate to a German audience. The quote also intimates that he was thinking of characterizing the phenomenological reduction as mediated by a critique of a regional discipline, in this case "the idea of a personal and natural anthropology." A letter dated December 2, 1929, to Ingarden, cited by Kern as well,[130] shows that Husserl's decision not to publish the translated version of the "Meditations," and to significantly revise it, was due to his reaction to Heidegger:

> The thorough study of Heidegger? I came to the result that I cannot fit the work [i.e., *Being and Time*][131] into the framework of my phenomenology, unfortunately, but in addition that I must fully and completely reject it as to its method and also in the essentials of its content. All the more do I set

> great store by the fully developed German edition of the "Cartesian Meditations" forming my systematic "main work."[132]

His point about the method and content of Heidegger's work was also central in a letter to Hicks three months later. Referring to Gilbert Ryle's critical review of *Being and Time,*[133] he said that he

> knows this diligent review in which he [Ryle] also speaks about my phenomenology, but he has not grasped its full sense and range. Since Heidegger in no way follows my method and does nothing more than build further my descriptive and intentional psychology drafted in my "Ideas" [*Ideas I*], not a single word of the objections directed against him apply to me.[134]

Husserl returned often in his later work to the problem of psychologism, netting with it the related fallacy of anthropologism, because he believed its analysis would provide the key to a critique of Heidegger. But we are after a different issue here. He told Ingarden that it would be the reconstructed and fully worked out version [*Ausgestaltung*] of the "Meditations," and not the undeveloped version (i.e., not the *Meditations* we presently have in print) that would form his *Hauptwerk.* At the same time he blended this with talk of a *systematic* work. But where do we find this new text? What became of his resolve to provide a fully revised version of the "Meditations?"

He immediately put his hands to the task and, as Kern documents so well,[135] combined his 1928 Amsterdam Lecture,[136] itself concerned with the relationship between psychology and transcendental phenomenology, with other texts on this theme and then set about writing additional studies. He also turned to other materials on the question of intersubjectivity and temporal constitution. We even have a short "foreword" to this "second introduction."[137] His efforts were interrupted between November 1929 and the beginning of February 1930 because, among other reasons, Landgrebe worked with him on ordering a number of his manuscripts on logic with a view toward what became *Experience and Judgment.* He got caught up in this project only to realize subsequently that it would take much too long and that he should not put off "the German revisions of the *Cartesian Mediations,*" for it would be "the main work [*Hauptwerk*] of my life." In this letter, written to Ingarden on March 19, 1930, he continues by saying that the "small French text" could not simply be transferred to the present German situation, itself made critical by a "faddish swing to a philosophy of 'existence,'" and an "abandonment of 'philosophy as rigorous science,'" obviously a reference to Heidegger. This calls for a

> much broader exposition and further development, up to the highest 'metaphysical' problematic. I am working with excellent powers and the most extreme concentration; I will not be finished with the book before autumn.[138]

With all of his energy directed at reworking the "Meditations" and finally providing a response to Heidegger, he suddenly changed his plan and discontinued any direct work on the "Meditations" for about a year. In its place Husserl returned to the idea of a great systematic work, the project that occupied him in 1920 or 1921. Why this shift in direction? Kern suggests that Husserl was stung by the analysis of the relationship between his and Heidegger's phenomenology in a series of articles that Georg Misch wrote and even dedicated to Husserl.[139] Coming from someone sympathetic, they pointed Husserl to the need for a much fuller account of the reduction than what had been published. Extensive discussions with Fink also resulted in first his own and then a subsequent draft by Fink for a "System of Phenomenological Philosophy," dated August 13, 1930.[140] In any case Husserl turned his attention to the systematic work and to a large manuscript by Fink, a draft of its opening section delivered to Husserl November 1930.[141] In December 1930, he wrote Pfänder: "In place of a German edition [of the "Cartesian Meditations"] I am thinking in the next year of publishing a larger work that is appropriate for the German public."[142] Georg Misch had received a similar report the previous month: "The book, in preparation for ten years, now really coming into being, will hopefully produce, as a whole systematic construction, fullest clarity."[143] Husserl wrote drafts for this large systematic work in 1930 and 1931; we must wait until chapter 8 to discuss them. He worked intensely on the project until April 1931, when he was interrupted by a commitment from which he could not escape. Between April and June he drafted and then gave the lecture "Phenomenology and Anthropology"[144] in Frankfurt am Main, Berlin, and Halle a.d. Saale, returning to Freiburg exhausted.[145]

Though Husserl was hard at work on this larger systematic project, he still hoped to publish the "Meditations" (and even his 1917–1918 Bernauer manuscripts on time!) in the *Jahrbuch*. He indicated his designs in a letter to Ingarden dated February 16, 1931:

> I am working furiously. Unfortunately the new work will not be ready for *Jahrbuch* XI, despite the breathless efforts of the whole last year, which, thank God, have brought a great deal of internal clarity and self-corroboration, but as well demanded a lot of refashioning, more precise defining, etc. I am putting into the *Jahrbuch* the Cartesian Meditations (expanded by Fink and if need be by myself) and the Bernau manuscripts on time, which Fink by himself has already made into a unified text (and a rather comprehensive one).[146]

As Bruzina shows, Husserl faced a dilemma:

> On the one hand, what was really needed, and what his own rich investigations really led to, was something broader in conception than the Meditations, but to bring that something—embodied in the systematic plan Fink

> had worked out for him—to satisfactory completion was an enormous task. There were serious grounds for doubt that it could actually be done, given the demands it would make upon him, especially in view of his age—he was now in his seventy-second year—and the illnesses he seemed too often to fall prey to. On the other hand, the Cartesian Meditations were basically finished, and thus were far closer to readiness for publication. But if they were to be brought up to the level and comprehensiveness of Husserl's new realizations, they would need extensive reworking; and the effort at reworking them in turn would reveal the basic limitations under which the overall conception of the Meditations suffered.[147]

Husserl's solution was to divide the labors, with Fink carrying the burden of the revisions of the "Meditations" and Husserl providing ongoing discussions and critical analysis of Fink's materials.

Husserl's hope that the "Meditations" would be published soon continued for another few years. Ingarden's critical remarks on the "French Meditations" must have arrived in May, as there is a letter from Malvine Husserl, dated May 15, 1931, thanking him for them and updating him: "The German edition is in any case to be expanded and enlarged by two meditations. Dr. Fink is working on them together with my husband."[148] The next *Jahrbuch* would publish the German version of the *Méditations cartésiennes*, Husserl told Cairns in July.[149] During that same summer Husserl also told Cairns that he had made three attempts at an "introduction," mentioning the London lectures of 1922, the Paris lectures of 1929, and the "German Meditations," which was underway.[150] A few days later he admitted that, as an introduction, the "French Meditations" (just published a few months before) gave an "unsatisfactory result." Cairns noted, "He hopes, however, that the *German Meditations* will be more successful."[151] But his labor on it in about August lasted only a short time. By the end of October or the beginning of November 1931, at the latest, he left the project with Fink.[152] In its place returned the systematic work, on which he labored with all vigor until February 1932, after which time even his interest in the "systematic work" gave way to work on his *Nachlaß* as a whole (May 1932 to August 1934). He also glanced occasionally at the "Meditations." On January 7, 1932, he wrote Boyce Gibson: "I have again taken up the intention, abandoned for a time, to work out the *Méditations* in German (abandoned for the sake of a comprehensive systematic work, on which I am working)."[153] We find some additional work devoted to the "Meditations" in February 1932, but Husserl told Cairns in May that he had given up the idea of a short introduction to phenomenology, which it was to have provided. In this conversation Husserl also indicated some uncertainty about the outcome of Fink's reworking of the "Meditations":

> Husserl took care particularly to emphasize the importance of the phenomenological reduction. Apparently with the *Meditations* in mind, Husserl

> said he had given up the idea of a short introduction to phenomenology, by which he meant a short exposition of the phenomenological reduction. Concerning Fink's *Ausarbeitung* <working out, development> of the *Meditations* Husserl said—Fink was absent—that he would study it through, but the book would be '*ganz anders*' <quite different>.[154]

Husserl did critically engage Fink's suggestions for revising the five Meditations, delivered in the summer of 1932, and Fink's now famous Sixth Meditation, delivered in installments between August and October 1932. But by this point the project had becomes Fink's, as he moved with Husserl's material in creative directions of his own, becoming less of an assistant and more of a co-author, even setting the direction of the project.[155] Husserl seemed to return to and study Fink's work in the summer of 1933 and winter of 1933/34. But I would suggest that, when Husserl spoke in a letter to Ingarden on August 19, 1932, of a hoped for "replacement" for the "Meditations . . . whose old form is not appropriate for the German public,"[156] it was his final judgment on the version that we now have. Even five years after that fateful summer of 1929 there was still no adequate response to Heidegger in the form of either a new, revised "Meditations" or a systematic work that Husserl could publish. By the summer of 1934 and until his final illness in August 1937, he was fully engaged in the project that would become the *Crisis.*[157]

6

Transcendental Disclosures

When we proceed, philosophizing with Kant, not by starting from his beginning and moving forward in his paths but by inquiring back into what was thus taken for granted (that of which Kantian thinking, like everyone's thinking, makes use as unquestioned and available), when we become conscious of it as "presuppositions" and accord these their own universal and theoretical interest, then there opens up to us, to our growing astonishment, an infinity of ever new phenomena belonging to a new dimension, coming to light only through consistent penetration into the meaning- and validity-implications of what was thus taken for granted. . . .

—Husserl (1936)[1]

In the reflections to which I have devoted myself these many years, I have pursued various ways, all equally possible, aimed at bringing forth, in an absolutely transparent and compelling fashion, precisely that motivation that presses [us] beyond the natural positivity of life and science and requires as necessary the conversion to the transcendental [attitude], the phenomenological reduction.

—Husserl (1931)[2]

This transcendental *egology* is the first phenomenology in itself; it is consciously "solipsistic" but proves, in general, to be the fundamental area of phenomenology that extends so much further and spans all philosophy that can be truly called such.

—Husserl (1930)[3]

The whole of transcendental egology is preliminary [*vor-läufige*] phenomenology. . . . Egology is an *abstraction,* but a necessary and not merely possible abstraction.

—Eugen Fink (1928–1929)[4]

THE NEED TO RESPOND to the philosophical currents in Germany, we suggested, pushed Husserl beyond his plan to publish the "Cartesian Meditations" and into the project of a larger systematic work. If we put to the side the other projects on which Husserl was working, as we suggested in the last chapter, Husserl's own labors on the "Meditations" and his "Systematic Work" have roughly this sequence:

1. Paris lectures and their revision into the "French Meditations," January 1929 to May 1929;
2. revision of "French Meditations" into a possible "German Meditations," October 1929 to March 1930;
3. turn to a "Systematic Work," summer 1930 to February 1932.

The span between 1929 and 1932, however, was not the first or even the most fruitful period in which Husserl attempted to construct a "larger systematic work." We will look at this in some detail in the next chapter and discover that Husserl's first attempt at a systematic work arose just when Husserl was developing the difference between static and genetic phenomenology. For now, we turn our attention to yet another surprise: the "French Meditations" was not the first time after *Ideas I* (1913) that Husserl attempted to construct a work expressly designed to be a set of Cartesian meditations, nor was it the first time that such a project was placed in relation to a projected systematic work. As mentioned in the last chapter, Husserl stated to Cairns that the London lectures of 1922 were the first of three attempts at providing an "introduction" to his philosophy.[5] The four lectures Husserl gave in June of that year bear the general title "Phenomenological Method and Phenomenological Philosophy."[6] In them, he attempts to provide his English audience, including no less than G. E. Moore and C. K. Ogden, among others, with a clear explanation of the Cartesian way into his phenomenological philosophy. The preparation for these lectures, which began in the spring of 1922, displaced a full year's work on "a large systematic work,"[7] reversing the sequence of 1930 but not its outcome. Anticipating the fate of the "French Meditations," Husserl substantially reviewed the London lectures during the summer and fall of 1922 in the hope that they could then be published. They were never put to print, but at least the revised version did serve as the lecture course, "Introduction to Philosophy,"[8] that Husserl gave in the Winter Semester of 1922/23. We find this sequence, then, in 1922:

1. preparation for a "large Systematic Work," spring 1921 to spring 1922;
2. preparation and delivery of London lectures, spring 1922 to June 1922;
3. revision of London lectures and presentation of a lecture course "Introduction to Philosophy," Winter Semester 1922/23.

The revisions that Husserl made to the London lectures consist mostly of two large interventions in the original text.[9] These revisions cluster around the same three sets of issues as his revisions to the 1929 "French Meditations." They modify and qualify the original materials in such a way that while the old is not destroyed, it is certainly destabilized and transformed. In particular, the revisions allow us to see the context *behind* the Cartesian way and lend support to our suggestion that it is primarily an introduction or, as he put it, a "guiding principle [*hodegetisches Prinzip*],"[10] a first step leading one into phenomenological method as a whole. We will use the lecture course "Introduction to Philosophy" in conjunction with Husserl's post-"French Meditations" comments to isolate the three crucial issues coming from within Husserl's own thinking that moved him beyond the "French Meditations" and, finally, beyond the Cartesian way.

A. POST-CARTESIAN MEDITATIONS

In looking for signs of Husserl's own concerns over the Cartesian way, I will examine primarily the "French Meditations"—as in the last chapter, this term refers to the German text from the summer of 1929 and its corresponding French translation, which appeared in 1931—and blend in materials from the 1922/23 lecture course when they illuminate the issues we find. Given the fact that Husserl had thought critically about the question of the Cartesian way in these and other texts during the 1920s, we will find indications of changes in the 1929 text itself (see the discussion of "The Question of the Way into the Reduction" below). We will then focus on Husserl's own reflections in several manuscripts upon two central notions in the "French Meditations" (printed as *Husserliana,* Vol. 1, and translated by Cairns into English). Husserl made some of these reflections before publishing the "French Meditations" (see the discussion of "Evidence and the Ego" below) and others on the way to what he hoped would be the "German Meditations," a project, as we have seen, that he never completed (see the discussion of "From Subjectivity to Intersubjectivity" below). We will treat both the anomaly that the theory of adequate perception did not change between *Ideas I* and the *Meditations* (see "Evidence and the Ego") and a surprising development that causes us to rethink what is required for a transcendental ground, thereby rendering the question of adequate evidence moot ("From Subjectivity to Intersubjectivity").

1. The Question of the Way into the Reduction

Husserl opens the First Meditation with an approach that is identical to that of *Ideas I:* "Thus we begin anew, each for and in himself, with the decision of a radically beginning philosopher to set out of play all of our convictions counting as valid for us until now and, among them as well, all our sciences."[11] In fact the existing sciences, be they material or mathematical, cannot even be used as a model or "example" of the foundational science which we seek. But then Husserl diverges from this position. Whereas no science can be taken as valid, there is a certain "universal idea" of science governing the factually given sciences. This idea we are allowed to take as a "presumption" and to then cull from it at least two crucial features: the difference between "immediate" and "mediate" judgments, gaining thereby the difference between supposition and presupposition; and the difference between a presumptive claim and a fulfilled or ratified claim, gaining thereby the notion of evidence.[12] Ingarden, responding directly to Husserl's text, protests that this will not do; because we are still taking our cue from factually existing sciences, we have not yet established a justification for such an idea.[13] Putting this issue to the side for the moment, Ingarden's remarks confirm that Husserl begins with a suspension of the different sciences at the same time that he sees a general normative ideal operative in those sciences.

This was not his explicit starting point in *Ideas I.* Instead, he effected, on the basis of "our complete freedom,"[14] a total and "radical alteration"[15] of the natural attitude in order to gain the phenomenological attitude. Furthermore, he applied the classical Cartesian distinction between the dubitability of the external world and the indubitability of inner perception in order to distinguish the being of the world from the being of consciousness. There is no appeal to mediating ideas gleaned from the general form of science; Husserl relies only upon the qualitative differences found within experience itself. But by the time the *Meditations* makes a contrast between the evidence of the world (not apodictic) and the *ego cogito* (apodictic),[16] Husserl has already preloaded a concept of grounding and evidence into his account.

We can find confirmation for this in one of Cairns's discussions with Husserl. Cairns had been given Fink's draft of his revision of Husserl's First Meditation. He studied and then discussed it with Husserl in May 1932. He reports that Husserl "would avoid beginning as Fink does in the *Entwurf* <draft> with the idea of philosophy." What Husserl expressly defends is "a motivation under the guidance of the ideal of sciences, as we find it phenomenologically, [i.e.,] the ideal of factual scientific inquiry." He rejects Cairns's own suggestion of beginning with "the ideal of *radikal* <radical> knowledge," i.e., "a motivation independent of cultural situation and universal."[17] If Husserl will not open with the essence of philosophy (Fink) or the ideal of radical knowledge (Cairns), but instead insists on beginning with the ideal of scientific inquiry as it exists, then he is beyond the beginning formulation of the Cartesian way.

If we look at the London lectures, and then at the additional text that Husserl wrote as a new introduction to its materials in his lecture course for Winter Semester 1922/23, we find him dealing with these issues with exceptional rigor. The London lectures provide us with roughly the same approach as the First Meditation, but with greater precision. The new introduction, however, presses beyond the parameters of the earlier texts and gives us one of the first versions of his way through a critique of the positive sciences, as will be noted in the next section. This intervention indicates both the sense in which the Cartesian way is not itself self-sufficient and the sense in which the different ways require and call each other forth. I begin with his opening to the London lectures and then the introduction he placed in front of that text in his lecture course "Introduction to Philosophy."

In the course of introducing the Cartesian way in his London lectures, Husserl himself presents a key problem: in asking where "I" can begin searching for a starting point that is "to be justified absolutely"[18] and that is "a necessary foundation,"[19] he realizes that he must first ask "what type of completeness do I actually intend and require for my future acts of cognition under the title 'absolute justification.'"[20] However, before I have a ground for knowledge I have to be able to say what counts as justification. Husserl attempts to solve the problem as he does in the *Meditations,* by suggesting that he can take from past knowledge "exemplary materials for the clarification of this ideal"[21] but that he take them as "pure possibility"[22] and "merely construct from them concepts"[23] that he then comprehends. From this process he derives his notion of intuition; cognizing judgments by nature aim at

> a seeing or insight of such a kind that the believed is not just believed but itself seen or seen into, itself apprehended, itself grasped. Such a belief, directed at "evident" givens, is itself called an evident or evidently grounded belief.[24]

The problem is that this notion of evidence is not a product of the Cartesian reflection but instead acts as its catalyst. Structurally, this is a notion that is gleaned by variation from the natural attitude. In this text, unlike in the First Meditation, Husserl recognizes that he must clarify the notion of justification "before everything else,"[25] before effecting the Cartesian reduction.

Of course, once he captures this notion of intuitive insight, the Cartesian way seems secured. Husserl adds to it the idea of "complete evidence"[26] which he identifies as "an adequate seeing or seeing into,"[27] in which "the believed object is itself grasped"[28] and nothing remains "by way of an anticipating intention."[29] He then applies this idea to the objects of inner experience, deriving from them a field of facts: "Only the pure lived experience as fact, that which remains uncontested even if I assume that there is no world, is the apodictic, the transcendental 'phenomenon' of phenomenology."[30] "For," he adds, "the non-being of the world does not touch the being of this pure experience."[31]

But, as we have seen, in the lecture course of 1922/23, Husserl adds some thirty-nine manuscript pages *before* the original introduction, thereby questioning his point of entry. The London lectures themselves only hint, at the very beginning, that there are various paths: "There are different ways into phenomenology. I want to choose for these lectures the most basic."[32] I will examine this additional introduction for two reasons: it shows us the way in which Husserl must rely upon a non-Cartesian point of access to the Cartesian way—even though he still claims that it is "mere foreplay and does not belong to the play itself, which now should begin in earnest"[33]—and because it provides us with an insightful early (1922) text which treats the way through a critique of the positive sciences.

Beginning with a contrast between the regional disciplines of the positive sciences and the universal discipline of philosophy, we can make a first approximation as to the content of this philosophy by thinking of it as responding to the "needs" of the sciences:

> Philosophy is related to the whole of the world in its full universality and to the whole of being [*Seiende*] as such, in a sense to be extended randomly, and thus it is related back thereby to all sciences. Philosophy treats problems all of which pertain to the sciences in a very serious manner, fulfills or attempts to fulfill [the theoretical] needs that all the sciences and in all levels of their generality do not fulfill, but which are very much alive in them.[34]

In this manuscript that clearly sketches the way through the positive sciences some twelve years before the *Crisis*, Husserl explains that these needs arise when science

> turns its gaze backwards, namely to the deepest foundations, to the basic concepts and principles, [and becomes concerned] not about technics but the practice of its methodology. Something similar occurs when it is a matter of moving beyond mathematically technical [questions] and of making intelligible the deepest meaning and the limits of the legitimacy of the entire mathematical project.[35]

He then gives an impressive list of examples. First, in mathematics we find problems of (a) the continuum, (b) set theory (leading to philosophical problems such as the construction of mathematical concepts), (c) the relation of mathematical insight to the ideal objects it produces, and (d) the meaning of validity. Next, in physics we have problems of (a) understanding the nature of causality, (b) using geometrical concepts, (c) comprehending the natures of space and time, and (d) the origin and meaning of relativity. The human sciences also use foundational concepts that require clarification. Finally, as regards science in general, he mentions methodological problems such as the exclusion of "secondary" qualities and teleological explanations. Husserl finds the *motive* for his philosophical turn in the lack of harmony among the basic concepts of the sciences:

> When the positive researcher is in [the middle of] his work—thus in a concrete and factually oriented attitude [as he] observes, experiments and theorizes—so he gains to a large extent theorems and theories that have their rationality in themselves, convincing by virtue of their necessary validity,

> each one understanding the facts with the same attitude and, beyond that, proving themselves true in experience. Still, the foundational concepts, the conceptually basic materials from which all further concepts and thus all theorems of a science derive their meaning, have, on the one hand, an originary, clear self-intelligibility to them, but nevertheless, on the other hand, a puzzling indeterminacy and fluctuation of meaning. This is displayed when indeterminacies and even contradictions result when one, freely applying universal propositions, intuited as evident, decides to let their consequences unfold, [thereby] showing that their foundation is unclear.[36]

This allows Husserl to find an internal connection between the foundational "puzzles and riddles" of the sciences and philosophy:

> For all these [foundational] concepts, it is the case that they are at the same time obvious in themselves and [yet] full of riddles. Thus they are no longer permitted to play the role of being pregiven and taken for granted in the sciences. . . . [A new science is required,] devoted to making what is taken for granted into a problem. Indeed, it is not too much to say that everything that is taken for granted for the natural man (and also the scientist dwelling in the natural attitude) shows itself in reflection as arrested in the deepest riddles. It is paradoxical but true if one labels philosophy as precisely the science of what is taken as obvious in itself.[37]

With this mandate Husserl builds his transition to transcendental phenomenological analysis:

> What is shown by all of this is that the treatment of these philosophical issues is not just a matter of simple reflections that are to be attached separately to the individual, positive sciences. It requires much more. Under the direction of those broader groups of concepts that form the *common good* of all sciences, it requires a *universal theory of science,* which treats in general all problems inseparably bound up with the idea of science as science. That must hold true in two correlative directions that we can juxtapose as the knowing subjectivity and the known objectivity, the last itself being further divisible, so that we can also speak of *three correlative directions* [of its analysis]: (1) the direction toward *scientific [acts of] knowing;* (2) the direction toward the *significational contents* necessarily framed in knowing (thus concepts and propositions and, respectively, truth); and finally (3) the direction toward the *objectivities* being determined through this significational content (i.e., being determined in truth in correct knowledge). Only when the theory of science researches the correlative [a priori], thus what indivisibly belongs together in its correlation, only when it holds in view the[se] reciprocal, essential features, only then can it become a philosophical discipline, a truly foundational science, a science of ultimate clarification.[38]

This process of moving through "the positivity" of the sciences and thereby "pressing to a higher position from which to raise questions" is a process of "critique,"[39] which Husserl describes as "die höchste Selbstbesinnung der Erkenntnis," a phrase that practically defies translation.[40] The notions of critique and *Besinnung* begin to play an increasingly important role as he recognizes the need to supplement the Cartesian way. In 1922, Husserl still took the Cartesian way as the "most basic of all philosophical methods,"[41] but he became increasingly attuned to the difficulties of that way.

Both the opening sections of the 1922/23 lecture course "Introduction to Philosophy" and the 1929 "French Meditations" rely upon a certain supplement that they then attempt to marginalize. Still, this way through the sciences lacks the specificity and thereby the necessity that Husserl later adds in the *Crisis.* There the reflection upon the sciences, which opens his path to phenomenology, is not just upon certain conceptual problems in the sciences or a general guiding ideal found in different sciences but also upon an *historically developed* idea that governs the rise of modern science. The element of time becomes integrated into the analysis. This is precisely why the *Crisis* begins not with a "presumptive" idea of science in general but instead with its famous analysis of Galileo.[42] Husserl's realization in the *Crisis,* though, that the Cartesian way does not provide a concrete explication of the way up from the natural world to the transcendental phenomenological attitude[43] may already have been at work in these opening pages of both the 1922/23 lecture course and the *Meditations.*

2. Evidence and the Ego

We now have the opportunity to recover a notion central to Husserl, one that our analysis up until this point has, perhaps surprisingly, kept in its margins. To be sure, our discussions of eidetic variation in chapter 2, and of Husserl's affinities with Descartes in the opening section of this chapter, touched upon his concept of evidence. In the first discussion we were largely concerned with the issue of how essences are generated and distributed and not so much with a consideration of validity. The second drew parallels with Descartes's search for sure epistemological grounds for theory. But now we must confront the concept of evidence directly, at least as it applies to the transcendental sphere.[44] We will approach it by asking if there are differences in Husserl's treatment of evidence in *Ideas I,* in the *Meditations,* and then in the working texts for the "German Meditations." I will sketch a central feature of the doctrine of evidence, the *ego cogito cogitatum,* and then see how it is used to secure the grounding structure of all static analysis.

The notion of evidence is roughly equivalent to the notion of presence or of self-givenness. As we saw in the first chapter, there is a difference between our anticipations of a coming object or fact and the arrival of that object or fact. The object as "meant" becomes the object as "given." This does not mean that Husserl relies on a simple notion of atomic elements or observation statements to carry his notion of truth. Evidence is not the same as *Geltung,* as validity or justification. *Geltung* is a richer and much more complex notion, one that corresponds in Husserl's texts to the project of securing of truth. "The evidence we have must also *justify* itself to us as evidence."[45] But it does mean that, in the context of this larger project, the features and then gradients of givenness exercise a decisive role. There is a difference not only between "merely intended" and "given" but also, among the givens, between objects perceived, imagined, recollected, etc. In Husserl's theory the "bodily" presence of the perceived object has a certain priority: it is the paradigmatic type of presence that gives us our most basic type of evidence.

What is crucial for this theory, however, is the fact that the given does not have to be "adequately" given to count as evidence. Husserl clearly argues that "original evidence" can be either "adequate" or "inadequate." The salient feature seems to be its directness or immediacy, in contrast to things or ideas that are given indirectly or by the mediation of something else (e.g., the abstractable elements of a complex, the conclusion of an argument).[46] In the case of adequate evidence, however, there is a complete coincidence between the senses in which the object is intended and the senses in which it is given. There is no "surplus," nothing in the intention itself that goes unfulfilled. If evidence is adequate, Husserl says, it is "in principle no longer capable of 'being strengthened' or of 'being weakened,' thus *without gradients of weight.*"[47] In fact an object's being "adequately" given excludes "its being otherwise."[48] In the case of inadequate evidence, fulfillment involves only a partial coincidence between the senses constituting the intention and those ingredient in the fulfilling act. My description of the pump as red can never be adequately fulfilled, because the pump as perceived has countless other qualities that "exceed" the content of the claim and because the meanings of the terms "red" and "pump" are never exhausted by this one object, no matter how typical it might be. If something is inadequately given, the further course of experience may "cancel" previous perceptions of profiles and even "explode" the cognition as a whole.[49] In fact, no object of "outer" experience is ever given fully or all at once. This is due to the difference between objects and their profiles. Not all profiles of the object are given as is the side directly facing us. There are profiles whose presence is secured only by anticipation, profiles that are not actually manifest but are co-given with what is actually present. To cast it in terms of the theory of sense, there are protended qualities of the object that form part of our experience of it, but they lack any direct intuitive fulfillment. All transcendent objects, Husserl tells us, are inadequately given.

Husserl believes, however, that in the case of transcendent objects the notion of adequacy can be recaptured at a higher level: "In principle there corresponds to each 'truly existing' object the idea of a possible consciousness in which the object itself is given originally and thereby is adequately grasped completely."[50] Corresponding to each category of objects with "a universal essence that in principle is to be brought to adequate givenness,"[51] we have a category of apprehension that "prescribes a rule for the way an object standing under it according to its sense and mode of givenness would be brought to adequate, originary givenness. . . . "[52] What is adequately given, then, is not the object but its idea, its "idea in the Kantian sense," as Husserl puts it.[53] As such an idea it can be intuited under the reduction by a higher order act involving categorial intuition and thus certain idealizations. But the underlying intuitions on which it is based are always inadequate.

The concept of apodicticity in *Ideas I* seems tethered to that of adequacy and to "insight into an essence or essential relations."[54] Husserl does recognize, however, that it can be applied to our experience of transcendent things in those cases where we recognize "the necessity of the being-so of a posited individual."[55] In the opening pages of *Ideas I* he says:

> the consciousness (closer, a judgment-consciousness) of a necessity in which a predicatively formed state-of-affairs is conscious as a particular case of an eidetic universality is called *apodictic,* the judgment itself, the proposition, an *apodictic* (also apodictically "necessary") *consequence* of the universal to which it is related.[56]

Apodicticity carries the idea that a certain complex is necessary and indubitable in the sense that we cannot imagine it not existing. In a loose sense we can say that the notion of adequacy applies to what is given while the notion of apodicticity qualifies a possible type of relationship that might hold between such givens. With Husserl's rigorous rejection of the notion that evidence is a type of feeling,[57] we can see why both terms are central to his account of evidence. These distinctions now allow us to identify the special status *Ideas I* attributes to the evidence that obtains for consciousness. I will examine the way the notion of evidence leads Husserl to his Cartesian characterization of consciousness in *Ideas I.* I will also refer to his London lectures of 1922 because they reinforce the notion of evidence found in *Ideas I.*

a. As I am undergoing an experience, as I am "living in the cogito," I do not have it "actually conscious as an intentional object," Husserl asserts.[58] I can make it such by a "reflective turn of the gaze" and grasp it "in the form of a new *cogitatio,* directed to it in the manner of a sheer apprehension, a perceptual apprehension."[59] In "transcendent perception" the object perceived is not itself internal to the act of perceiving it. But in acts directed immanently toward lived-experiences (*Erlebnisse*), their intentional objects "belong to the same stream of experience as they themselves." Here "consciousness and its object form an individual unity produced purely through experiences."[60]

b. The immanent perception of experiences "is a sheer viewing of something which[61] is (or can become) perceptually given as absolute,"[62] and this means that it is not given as something that achieves its identity through different modes of appearances, different adumbrations. In the case of transcendent perception, Husserl says that

> the thing seen remains a mixture of what is properly seen and what is not seen. Thus it always remains open that <in the> course of further perceiving it might turn out that the seen is not as it ostensibly was seen or, indeed, that it does not exist at all, that the seen dissolves into an illusion or a dream.[63]

In the case of immanent perception what I think about the perceived object may be mistaken, but what I intuit is "absolutely there with its qualities."[64] *The Idea of Phenomenology* speaks of what is intuited as a "sphere of absolute givenness."[65] "It is given as a being, as a this-there/here; to doubt its being makes no sense whatsoever."[66] Husserl then adds the notion of evidence that controls the whole of his Cartesian account:

> This being-given, which excludes any meaningful doubt and is a sheer, immediate viewing and grasping of the intended objectivity itself as it is, forms the pregnant concept of evidence understood as immediate evidence.[67]

c. Having introduced the notion of absolute givenness, Husserl must ask what allows things given in immanent perception to be so given. Because there is no difference between object and profiles and because each experience, or at least a "core" of each lived-experience, is given as what it is without remainder, we have to conclude that lived-experiences are *adequately* given. This thesis was already established in the *Logical Investigations:*

> Every perception is characterized by the intention of grasping its object as present, and *in propria persona.* To this intention perception corresponds with complete perfection, achieves *adequacy,* if the object in it is itself actually present, and in the strictest sense present *in propria persona,* is exhaustively apprehended as that which it is, and is therefore itself internal to [*reell*] our perceiving of it. It is accordingly clear, and evident from the mere essence of perception, that adequate perception can only be "inner" perception, that it can only be trained upon experiences simultaneously given, and belonging to a single experience with itself. This holds, precisely stated, only for experiences in the purely phenomenological sense.[68]

In *Ideas I* this adequacy is what accounts for apodicticity: because experiences are given without sides, without profiles, they are absolutely "*undurchstreichbar*" as Husserl adds in the margin of one of his copies.[69] In the London lectures we have the same argument: if something is adequately given then "all the moments" of the intention or the judgment are "completely fulfilled."[70] We cannot be mistaken about their existence. If I grasp in reflection my lived-experience, I have grasped an absolute Itself whose existence in principle cannot be negated.[71] This is precisely how he discusses adequate givenness in the London lectures: "while something is adequately given it cannot be negated or doubted. We can also characterize this with the words: what is adequately evident is given in apodictic certainty."[72]

d. There is a special type of necessity that obtains for the apprehension of mental life in contrast to real objects. The positing of anything physical is "contingent" in the sense that there is always the possibility that the further course of experience will introduce perceptions that cannot be united harmoniously with what has gone before. The earlier experience becomes transformed and sometimes completely negated; its object can always turn out not to exist at all. Only indirectly, by exhibiting a law that is necessary, can we attribute necessity to natural objects or facts. The apple is necessarily either green or non-green because this state of affairs is regulated by an eidetic necessity, the law of excluded middle. By contrast, the apprehension of a mental event or process is "empirically necessary,"[73] not because it is a particular case (itself contingent) subsumed under an eidetic law, but because it is an individual that cannot fail to exist. Any mental event that is present *must* exist. The possibility of a future negation is excluded by the very nature of the experience. The very being of the experience guarantees its existence. Thus Husserl claims that it has "the necessity of a *fact,* and is called so because an eidetic law is involved *in* the fact and, indeed, in this case, involved in the *existence* of the fact as fact."[74]

e. In the *Investigations* Husserl assumes that any lived-experience given in immanent perception will be adequately given as a whole. By the time of *Ideas I,* after devoting a full lecture course to an analysis of the internal consciousness of time in 1905, he has modified his view as he realizes that not all of a lived-experience can be so given:

> A lived-experience . . . is never perceived completely; it cannot be grasped adequately in its full unity. Essentially it is a flow; directing our reflective regard to it, we can swim along after it always starting from the Now-point, while the spans behind us are lost to our perception. We have a consciousness of what is immediately flowing away [from us] only in the form of a retention, or else in the form of a recollection that looks back. Finally, my whole stream of experience is a unity of lived-experience which, of essential necessity, cannot be apprehended completely in a perceiving that "swims along with it." But *this* incompleteness or "imperfection," belonging to the essence of the perception of a lived-experience, is in principle different from what we find in the essence of "transcendent" perception, of perception through adumbrations, through something like appearance.[75]

The lack of what is found in transcendent perception, adumbrations, and appearances through profiles, does not itself guarantee adequacy in immanent perception. The problem comes by attending not only to our recollections of past lived-experiences, which necessarily belong to the same stream of current experiences and yet are absent, but also to retention, the form of the Now that though still actual, is sliding into the past. This leaves us with only a "core" of the actual for which we can claim any direct and immediate givenness. Husserl explains: "Lived experiences are essentially such that a regard of insightful perception can be directed, quite immediately, to each actual and living experience as an originary present."[76] What is missing from the actual present, from what is adequately given, however, Husserl attempts to load into the reflection itself. He continues:

> This takes place in the form of a *"reflection,"* which has the remarkable feature that it in principle characterizes what is grasped in it perceptually not only as something that is now and that endures while being regarded perceptually, but as something that *already existed,* even *before* this gaze was turned to it.[77]

This recovery of the whole at the level of reflection allows Husserl to argue both that we only have a core of lived-experience, the actual Now, which is adequately given, and that in grasping it we can still infer the whole of our conscious life as existing beyond doubt. Notice how he moves from one to the other:

> . . . though my stream of experience be not grasped in [its] wide[r] scope, be unknown according to those areas of the stream that have already run off and that are yet future, nevertheless so far as I direct my gaze to the flowing life in its actual present and take it purely as it itself is and grasp myself thereby as the pure subject of this life . . . then I can say directly and necessarily: *I am,* this life is, I live: cogito.
>
> There belongs to each stream of experience and ego as such the possibility in principle of gaining this evidence.[78]
>
> . . . *my* consciousness in general is originally and absolutely given not only with respect to its essence but also with respect to its existence.[79]

The stream as a whole is *apodictically* but not adequately given. But this is possible only because there is a core anchoring the evidence that is both adequately and apodictically given, the Now. Will this, though, be enough to secure the existence of that grounding structure upon which all static analysis depends? Does not the evidence as applied to consciousness necessarily depend upon the role of memory? In an addition (from 1929) to a personal copy of *Ideas I,* Husserl writes:

> It may be that identifiability and therewith a being-able-to-go-back-again [i.e., memory] belong to the being of the lived-experience; it may be that the absoluteness of states [*Beständen*] of recollection and [their] apodictic im-

port is presupposed, above all if I am to speak of my life, my stream of experience, my identical I-being in their proper essential purity. . . .[80]

f. As it stands, then, we have secured only the existence, and not the scope, of consciousness, which serves as the basis of Husserl's analysis. For this we need not just the experience in the Now but also the "endless unity" of the whole stream of experience, a "form necessarily spanning all the experiences of a pure I."[81] Setting aside his attempt, just mentioned, to encompass its scope by immanent perception itself, Husserl shrewdly attempts to bring together the crucial fact that much, if not most, of what composes this stream is not present, with the thesis that it as a whole can be rendered present through a higher-order form of intuition. While adequate intuition will "never" suffice to cover the "*whole* nexus" of experience, we have a different type of intuition of the "limitlessness of progressing on"[82] that finds adequacy at another level:

> In the continuous progression from apprehension to apprehension we also apprehend . . . in a certain sense the *stream of experience as a unity.* We do not apprehend it as we do a single experience but in the manner of an *idea in the Kantian sense.* It is not something posited or affirmed by chance but an absolutely indubitable given—in a correspondingly broader sense of the word givenness. This indubitably, although also grounded upon intuition, has an entirely different source from what exists for the being of lived-experiences, as they come to pure givenness in immanent perception. It is the special character of the ideation which apprehends a Kantian "idea" that it does not thereby lose the clear insight because the adequate determination of its content—here the stream of experience—is unattainable.[83]

The recovery of the adequate givenness of the ego and its experiences at the level of the eidos is also found in the London lectures:

> Instead of actualities, let us consider egological possibilities. . . . What we gain as the primary [science] is not a factual science of my ego and its *cogitationes* as it is factically, but rather an eidetic science. To be more precise, as primary we gain for systematic, eidetic description an endless field of essential features—immediately, adequately open to view and objectively specifiable—of a transcendental subjectivity in general, of its possible consciousness, of its possible intentional achievements.[84]

The problem that this poses, however, is that we come very close to assimilating the process of intuiting the essence of the stream of consciousness with the process of intuiting the essence of anything, including that of transcendent objects, thereby losing any difference between the two realms. We will come back to this problem in chapter 10, but for now we want to return to the *Cartesian Meditations.*

When we compare this developed theory of immanent perception with what Husserl proposes in the *Meditations,* we find roughly the same theory as

Ideas I. There are certain shifts in emphasis, however, that we find in the *Meditations.* He is quick to decouple adequacy and apodicticity: "Adequation and apodicticity need not go hand in hand."[85] In addition, the notion of apodicticity is less settled. On the one hand, we have the older emphasis upon its efficacy: "Should they be inadequate, they must at least have a recognizable apodictic content, an ontic content by virtue of which apodicticity is secured once for all as absolutely firm."[86] On the other hand, the fact that inadequacy is now in play entails that evidence at the level of original evidence is not "once for all absolutely firm." In fact, Husserl recognizes the frailty of his original notion and admits that while such evidence excludes doubt, it can still be doubted, i.e., what appears as certain in this Now might appear as doubtful tomorrow.[87] As a result he adds a new requirement for evidence to be apodictic: it must be able to withstand "critical reflection,"[88] which means that it must be situated within a larger set of valid claims that can provide it with justification. There is no *Evidenz* without a broader scheme of *Geltung.*

As a consequence, the *Meditations* shifts the burden away from the adequately given to the originally given. In only one place does Husserl echo his position in *Ideas I:* a "core," if only a core, is "adequately experienced," and that is

> the living self-present, which expresses the grammatical sense of the proposition *ego cogito,* while there extends beyond that only an indeterminately general, presumptive horizon, comprising what is not actually experienced but necessarily co-intended.[89]

The horizon refers to the past that is no longer actual. But at the same time he stresses that the epoché gives "the entire stream of my experiential life" and that this is *originally* given: "And, at that, it is continually there *for me,* continually conscious perceptually as[90] a field of the present in the most original originality [*ursprüngliche Originalität*]."[91] Even though he still distinguishes what "transpires in the living present" from the larger field that composes consciousness, his reduction to the "sphere of ownness" in the Fifth Meditation allows him to access both the actualities and the potentialities of the stream of experience.[92]

The reluctance to let go of the notion of adequacy is not surprising from the point of view of the overall needs of a Cartesian approach; without at least a core of conscious life adequately given, we lose any binding phenomenological distinction between the quality of evidence for immanent and that for transcendent perception. If this distinction is lost, the evidence of the *ego cogito* also becomes "presumptive," i.e., dependent upon other evidence and thus not independently confirmable. Only at the level of the idea, of the essence, could the *ego cogito cogitatum* regain indubitability, but even there we could not demonstrate that it is the ground upon which the rest of truth depends. Husserl, however, had thought through this notion with considerable lucidity during the 1920s. In the "Introduction to Philosophy" lecture course of 1922/23, Husserl recognizes that even if the living present were to be given adequately, its grounding structure, the whole stream of experiences, would not be gained. For this one must rely upon memory, which immediately raises the question of its reliability, its "apodicticity." Thus he says:

> If memory is no longer a source of apodictic certainty for my past *cogitationes*, then I can no longer speak of my endless stream of life, of my past ego and my past intentional experiences. . . . I have only the momentary *ego cogito* while it is present, and that only as long as my reflective gaze is directed toward it. . . . If the *ego cogito* has flowed off . . . I can remember something about it but, even if I am absolutely sure of the current memory as a present experience, I cannot be sure of what I remembered.[93]

In this text he does not withdraw from the devastating implications of this for his program:

> I would not be able to speak of the endless stream of life, of my life spanning an endless past and an endless future, of phenomenological time as an actual form of actual life, etc. I am restricted, so it appears, to the absolutely sterile "I am": I perceive, now while I perceive; I think, namely while I now think; I feel, and that only while I feel, etc. While such occur I can view them in reflection and construct fully useless propositions; they do not yield permanent truth . . . but only a fruitless, fleeting fit to [*Anpassung an*] a fleeting life in the present.[94]

Even if we grant adequacy to the Now, it proves to be much less than what Husserl needs. He must also rely on memory. In principle memory cannot yield adequate evidence; in practice there are no guarantees that it as an act will give us apodictic evidence.[95]

With these issues pressing Husserl's original account, it is not surprising that Husserl begins to speak not just of an intuition but also of a *critique* of immanent perception. When we look again at the portion of his 1922/23 lectures that supplements the London lectures, we find that he re-emphasizes the close interconnection between adequacy and apodicticity: "apodicticity is the back side of adequation, the intended is itself given immediately and without any anticipation whose confirmation still remains in question."[96] He begins, however, to speak of the object of immanent perception in terms of *degrees* of optimal presentations and confesses that, even within its framework, an adequately given phenomenon is an *abstraction.* This foreshadows a crucial difference, which we will discuss in the next section, between what is originally given and what is purely and primordially given. The latter might be adequately present but is, in itself, an abstraction from what is original. This passage is one of the most provocative from the 1922/23 lecture course:

> But we must now recognize that original self-apprehension has a necessary structure and has in itself again gradualities without which it is not even conceivable. Precisely here, in the critique of immanent perception, is the first place to learn this. . . . Thereby the respective, actual Now has the advantage of being a *highest* and *most complete* phase of self-givenness. Only in it is the tone, as the tone-moment in question, grasped in absolute selfness according to its being and being-so, itself contained, in a certain sense, immanently in what is grasped. Nevertheless, that is only an abstract way of speaking; actually, it is only meaningful to speak of being and being-so because this tone-phase is a functioning phase in a synthesis of streaming-away. The tone is the unity that gives itself as single and identifiable [only] in the streaming synthesis of the continual intentionality of what itself appears by degrees, of what is completely unthinkable without [such] graduality. . . . And, indeed, when I hear a melody the melody heard in absolute originality is not the tone now sounding and enduring but rather the melody, the perceptual unity forming itself thus and so, forming in the passage through the form of the Now but also the forms of the past and the form of the open future. . . . [97]

If we look at how Husserl came to understand time and even at the way the *Meditations* treats space, it is all the more surprising that the notion of adequacy still resonates in his analysis. The Here cannot be understood simply as a point but only in opposition and contrast to a There. Each belongs to "my primordial sphere," yet each is experienced only in contrast to the other.[98] Without the There, necessarily beyond anything that admits of adequate experience, there is no Here.

Husserl came to realize that not just "outer" but also "inner" objects are gradually given, as evidenced in Cairns's records from this period. In reaction to *Ideas I* and the thesis that lived-experiences, *Erlebnisse,* have no profiles, Husserl says: "*Erlebnisse* are, through passive intentionality (retentionality) constituted *in a sense* through *Abschattungen* <adumbrations>."[99] We find this in another conversation with Cairns:

> Husserl observed that omitting considerations of the *Zeitbewusstsein* <time consciousness> in *Ideen [I]* had been dangerous and that when one took into consideration the temporal modalization of acts one had indeed something like *Abschattung,* an identity throughout a multiplicity of disparate moments.[100]

Indeed, the central anomaly of *Ideas I* is that despite the suspension of the question of time and the resulting commitment to a form of synchronic analysis, Husserl nevertheless understood presence in terms of an adequately given present. Though he omitted time-consciousness, he still needed a temporal marker for lived-experience in order to assure its immediacy. Directly treating time-consciousness might have enabled Husserl to realize this in *Ideas I.* But had he done so, then the concept of adequacy would have been relativized, at the very least; for as soon as his earlier theory of an *Urimpression,* a datum constituting the Now, was modified by his notion of the *living Now,*[101] which it was even before *Ideas I,* then the Now becomes not a point but a *field* of the present, necessarily shot through with retentions and protentions. The adequate givenness of consciousness, like the givenness of transcendent objects, would have become an "idea in the Kantian sense," something not actually realized but only anticipated in and through our reflection upon it. I will wait until chapter 10 before further exploring the relationship between the concept of time and evidence.

These reflections are sufficient, however, to isolate the main tension in the notion of evidence supporting the Cartesian way. To the extent that such evidence is said to be *adequate* and *self-justifying,* it yields only a core of a lived-experience that in some abstract sense is only immediately Now. But this result is *insufficient* to supply and then secure the grounding structure required for a transcendental phenomenology with a Cartesian notion of evidence, i.e., the stream of consciousness as a whole. Conversely, to the extent that a phenomenological intuition is *sufficient* to supply and secure that structure, it is necessarily *inadequate* and thus not *self-evident.* It becomes sufficient and thereby *apodictic* only through *supplementation* with arguments, through *critique.* Lacking immediate self-evidence, then, phenomenological intuition requires bridging arguments in order to provide justification. The use of the *hypothetical,* thus, becomes an inescapable feature of such evidence. We have an element of *construction* in play; precisely what Husserl finds objectionable in Kant becomes apparent in his own work.

3. From Subjectivity to Intersubjectivity[102]

Did Husserl simply pass over these issues in his analysis of the reduction? Was he blind to the internal tensions in his text? And is there any relationship between these questions and the reason Husserl finally dropped his plan to publish a second "Meditations"? The materials he drafted after he sent the "French Meditations" to the translators in June of 1929 in preparation to write a proper "German Meditations" provide us with some answers. These same manuscripts also address the tension that underlies the problems we reviewed concerning adequate evidence.

A remarkable text, written in October or November 1929,[103] as he plunged into his first reworking of the *Meditations,* addresses the notion of bracketing, one of the most serious issues with the Cartesian reduction. Husserl worried that it would not be possible to "think away" other egos without abandoning the world as it is, i.e., the world as it appears in the reduction. Under the epoché in both *Ideas I* and the *Meditations,* I can "take away" the other without factoring out myself, Husserl says; the ego in its original temporality is an "unchangeable necessity"[104] that remains. This is a familiar thesis. However, Husserl immediately adds:

> But that needs to be thought through again: with the transformation of all my contemporaries into appearances [*Schein*], the remaining world cannot remain unchanged—above all not I, myself. . . . As a further consequence, I (that is, I myself) am fundamentally changed. . . . [105]

This idea is also found in another text from this period:

> . . . I am positioned as equal in relation to every other as constituting co-bearer of the world. As I myself, so also is every other necessary for the existence of the world—the very same world that is for me real and objective. I cannot think away any without giving up this world. No determinate other subject and, by implication, no indeterminate other, anticipated in the open horizon-sense, is to be thought away.[106]

Husserl drives home the implications of this for the full "objectivity" of the world within the reduction:

> Let us think of a stepwise constitution of the objective world. "So long" as no other is constituted in my primordial sphere—assuming that this would even be conceivable—my primordial world would be a mere "construction" of my primordial *ego*. But as I experience an *alter ego* as another human, and that in a proper if only presumptive validity, I have posited a primordial world of the other human as a construction of *his* (transcendental) *ego*. At the same time, it is evident that there is an identity where his primordial world and mine overlap, and that this identity grows through reciprocally bringing the remaining excess on one and then the other side to mutual validity, so that, in general, a common world and then also a shared cultural world is constituted.[107]

This points to a confusion inherent in the original understanding of world in the Cartesian reduction. On the one hand, the being of the world was "thought away" and reduced to the co-referential correlate of a *solus ipse* and its constituting achievements; the world preserves its transcendence but not its status as an "objective" world. On the other hand, none of its objective content was to be lost, only placed in relation to the subject. In these texts, however, Husserl realized that the bracketing of the world, as required by his Cartesian program, would alter the way in which the ego would appear and be thematized. In response, he attempts to drive a wedge between the "primordial" and the "original" world: "The solipsistically reduced world is not to be confused with the primordial world, nor the solipsistic reduction with the primordial reduction," he argues.[108] After the primordial reduction what remains is only my stream of experiences and the experiences that my own ego undergoes. This reduction necessarily excludes the other as belonging in any sense to the sphere of subjectivity: "All my experiences of empathy belong to the primordial sphere but not the other . . . experienced therein. So also with all determinations of intersubjective culture."[109] Only under this condition could we ever have something like an *adequate* givenness to a lived experience. By contrast, the solipsistic reduction simply thematizes an ego in general in relation to a world. This style of the reduction comes to carry the burden of his transcendental phenomenology. In the case of this reduction, the ongoing course of experience, which includes such experiences as empathy and achieving agreement, is so configured that "the solipsistic world gains the sense of an intersubjective world."[110] In another text, written during these same months, he gives us a clue as to how they are internally connected: the beings that are exhibited to the ego within the solipsistic reduction have not only an "inner" horizon but also an "outer" horizon, one which opens upon yet other beings vitally connected to the first. "This type of sense-openness of the constitution in horizons is now the basis for higher formations of sense through intersubjectivity."[111] Ultimately, this even reverses the priority of solipsistic and shared world: "In the course of its experiential life the solipsistic world is disclosed to the ego . . . as a *restricted presentation* of an intersubjective world."[112] Husserl realizes that this has direct implications for the essential determinations of the ego found after the reduction: "There belongs to the essence of the ego finding itself as *solus* that it can find itself as *socius* with fellows in the course of its further living."[113]

Setting the primordial reduction in contrast to the solipsistic, I would suggest, is the solution to a problem that Husserl had already worked through to some extent in the "French Meditations." If one begins with "pure egology," as any methodological solipsism must, it appears that a "transcendental solipsism"[114] is inevitable. He argues that this solipsism is only a "philosophically lower level" that must be "limited in respect to its method" if intersubjectivity is to come into play as a "founded, higher level."[115] If the methodological solipsism that Husserl employs in the *Cartesian Meditations* consists of not a primordial but an original reduction, then there is an internal link between the egological and the intersubjective reduction. Furthermore, the distinction between the primordial and the solipsistic reduction provides new insight into how the Fifth Meditation is to be understood and the sense in which Husserl moved beyond his own Cartesianism. The analysis of intersubjectivity in the Fifth Meditation is an *explication* of that sphere of subjectivity provisionally opened in the First and Second Meditation, not a supplement that goes beyond it and thereby leaves it intact.[116] Husserl joins the primordial and the solipsistic by suggesting that the primordial ego is "a level of my concrete ego."[117] This means, however, that the primordial is derived only by abstraction and is not primary as far as this method is concerned. Once we take the solipsistic in place of the primordial reduction as our starting point, we have a notion of the correlation of ego and world that preserves the notion of horizon. It, thereby, also preserves an internal connection between this notion and the correlation of intersubjectivity and (shared) world, which serves as the richest ground of all phenomenological schemes of constitution and explanation. This also solves, in principle, the problem we suggested earlier regarding the insufficient yield from an adequately intuited primal present. This difficulty is displaced by a rich notion of a transcendental sphere that is *provisionally* egological and then later "explicated" as intersubjective. Husserl's recurring use of the term "monad" in place of pure ego in the *Meditations* already signals this change within his static method. While the notion of adequacy is certainly required for a primordial reduction, for the solipsistic reduction it need not be and, indeed, cannot be invoked; the evidence securing transcendental subjectivity need be only apodictic for this first, provisional phenomenology.

What helped Husserl see the internal connection between the solipsistic reduction and intersubjectivity in these manuscripts on the *Meditations* was his introduction of a perspective, completely missing from the Fifth Meditation, which for its part remains static and constitutive.[118]

> In pursing the possibilities contained in a solipsistic ego, respectively, in a solipsistic world we can think of a genesis as genesis of a solipsistic ego to a person of a human world and the solipsistic world to an intersubjective, human world coming out of it.[119]

We will have to save this line of thought, however, until later chapters on genetic analysis.

Husserl moved yet further away from the necessity of beginning with adequate presence, as he was still tempted to do in the *Meditations*, in another text written in March 1930. This text specifically refers to the Second Meditation and questions its starting point. He realized that the course of the reduction is shaped by the world put in brackets, i.e., by the way it is initially characterized. There are therefore two possibilities. On the one hand, the reduced world can mean the world of *my* experience, thus requiring me to come to other egos indirectly. Once I have validated their existence I can speak of the world of our shared experience.[120] On the other hand, I can start with the world ("in its ontological structure") at the outset as intersubjective and as related to *our* shared experience. Husserl argued that the latter would require a different set of parameters for the concept of temporality: "then we have an immanent, common time of the We—we-present, we-past, we-future."[121] In fact, he entertained the idea of moving from the second to the first[122] and, in effect, reversing the order of the Fifth and the Second Meditations. But he stopped short of this, recognizing that either way is possible. Still, the distinction between the two, he adds,

> is important for the doctrine of the phenomenological reduction. Starting from intersubjectivity one can establish an intersubjective reduction in that

> one brackets the world existing in itself and executes the reduction upon the universum of all that is intersubjective, which includes in itself all individual subjects. The second step: reduction to intersubjectively, ultimately constituting life, the intersubjective "stream of experience," the communalization of all that is egological.[123]

Husserl also admits that, in principle, either way could be taken in another text specifically addressed to the First Meditation and the course of the reduction there:

> "Reduction to transcendental subjectivity"; that proves to be ambiguous. The subjectivity posited in the epoché can be understood as "my monadic own," the monadic own subjectivity of the phenomenologizing ego, or[124] as the transcendental intersubjectivity enclosing that subjectivity in itself.
>
> If one understands under subjectivity the primordially [= originally] concrete ego, the I-pole as pole of his actual and possible acts, concretely one with them—thus as pole of his experiences and of what is inseparable from them—then we have as a parallel concept concrete intersubjectivity as the All of the primordially concrete egos. . . . [125]

This allows Husserl to distinguish between the transcendental reduction as opening an *ego* with its stream of consciousness and its mental achievements and such a reduction as opening a transcendental *sphere* or *field* of analysis that must then be filled in according to other considerations. The first was Husserl's initial model, but the second is what his analysis requires once he understands transcendental subjectivity as intersubjectivity.

These reflections devoted to the limits of the Cartesian way were written after the *Meditations* was published in the version that we now have as the *Cartesianische Meditationen.* Surprisingly, Husserl had already raised most of these issues surrounding the role of intersubjectivity some eight years earlier, with considerable lucidity, as he reworked his London lectures into his 1922/23 lecture course "Introduction to Philosophy." This material is important not only because it crystallizes a line of thought that goes as far back as Husserl's 1910/11 lecture course "Basic Problems of Phenomenology"[126] and forms his first direct confrontation after *Ideas I* with a developed formulation of the Cartesian way (as given in the London lectures), but also because it helps to place the "French Meditations" in the same rhetorical context as the London lectures. It also strengthens our argument that the London lectures should be understood as a first introduction for the uninformed and, perhaps, the unconverted. Since this material is not published and not known to scholars, I will let it unfold as Husserl wrote it.

Husserl undertakes a rather detailed account of empathy (*Einfühlung*), an act or cluster of acts that allows us to experience the other as a subject, an account which emphasizes the difference in temporal structures between empathy and immanent perception:

> Empathy, looked at according to its essential features, is a form of presentification; in this respect it is similar to memory and anticipation. But with differences. Recollection opens upon [the] past, that is, my past, and, viewed from a transcendental perspective, my transcendental past, my past *cogito*. Likewise originary anticipation upon the future. Empathy, however, opens upon the present, but not upon mine but an alien present and, going through it, upon an alien past and future. To be sure, my self-perception opens upon my present [acts of] experiencing. However, properly speaking I cannot perceive the [acts of] experiencing of the alien but only co-perceive them improperly through empathy.[127]

This leads to an interesting theory as to how the act of empathy is itself constructed:

> Here, the recourse to consciousness, the reflection in this presentification, leads to a real and hypothetically possible perception having this content: had I touched in that way, then I would perceive this and that tactually; had I turned the gaze differently in a particular way, then I would now have this and that image; had I placed myself on this and that location, then my appearances would be these and those, etc.[128]

In short, a system of shared coordinates emerges. Properly constructed, the perception of the other leads to an expansion of what is given in the reduction, a necessary insertion of my subjectivity into intersubjectivity. Notice that in this text empathy gives me not only the other subjectivity as a "whole" but also an "interconnection" between my subjectivity and that of the other at the transcendental level:

> If we utilize the experience of empathy, built upon the physical experience of the alien body, not as the basis of an objective judgment about the alien human as a member of a [human] world, but rather apply it phenomenologically, then it expands the nexus, closed in itself, of my actual and possibly motivated experiences (my present, past, and expectant, future experiences) into a second nexus of this type, namely into a whole, second subjectivity. Through the play of gestures, etc., only individual nexes of experience [of the alien] come to be particularly experienced, but they are then surrounded by an indeterminate horizon of experiences that cannot be known further. Finally, we have an entire subject that, as a whole, was already indicated in a general and indeterminate way through the total style of the lived-body. In precisely the way that my own pure egological nexus of experience, with its actual and for me possible experiences, is [also] a nexus given to [transcendent] experience—and this givenness yields a natural, naive basis justifying judgments—so is the interconnection between my whole transcendental life and that of the other given as a nexus of [transcendent] experience and can be transcendentally judged [as] empirical.[129]

With my experience and that of the other forming a single nexus, Husserl recognizes the radical implications that this has for a notion of the present:

> Even so through empathy, a presentifying mode of experience, an *alien experiential present* reaches out into my experiential present. And if I "switch off" the objective world and, thereby, also my fellow man as an objective reality, there still remains the transcendental nexus of my stream of consciousness with his stream of consciousness, which is itself transcendentally experienced in interconnection with mine.[130]

Even though "transcendental-social subjectivity is not given to me as originally as is my ego,"[131] this line of thought allows Husserl to expressly reject the restriction of the transcendental sphere to the egological:

> The system of empathetic presentification, which corresponds to and is superimposed upon the inwardly projected system of perceptions and possibilities of perception of the alien lived-body, is a system of transcendentally pure [transcendent] experiences belonging to the type "presentifications." Thus, it would be false to say that the transcendental reduction reduces me to my own inner being and inner life, to my own transcendental subjectivity. The reduction reduces me, wherever I have in my [transcendent] experience of alien subjectivity this and that or any number of other egos, to a, so to speak, many headed transcendental subjectivity that spans with its own All these alter egos with all of their life, with all of their appearances and intentional correlates.[132]

With this, any appeal to adequacy as what secures the transcendental sphere is destroyed, both because in principle the consciousness of the other is not directly given and because, while I do posit an All of subjects as "a universal nexus,"[133] what "I actually have in my field of empathy [are] only a few alter egos [with] an open horizon of ever new, really possible acts of empathy that would yield for me yet other alter egos."[134] Husserl then makes the next logical move, claiming that there belongs to this nexus

> a transcendental-social time as the most universal time in which all the times of the individual egos coincide, and in which all streams of consciousness of the individual egos are united to a bound, transcendental-social stream of consciousness.[135]

However problematic this appeal to a trans-individual, social stream of consciousness and to a transcendental social time may be, the result is not an invalidation but a restriction of the analysis first presented in the London lectures. There is a certain *epistemic* priority of my ego over the other because of the directness and richness of what is given in my reflection and because the justification of the existence of the other (at the transcendental level) takes my ego as its point of departure. But the explication of the transcendental sphere as an intersubjective nexus resulting from the transcendental reduction entails that intersubjectivity has a *foundational* priority or is at least *co-foundational* with subjectivity in the sense both that subjectivity is the proper correlate of the world as a whole and that the reciprocation of world, subjectivity, and intersubjectivity is the most basic or grounding structure. In this text Husserl recognizes a significant difference between the order of knowing and the order of being.

With the difference between the primordial and the original reduction, and the corresponding loss of adequacy as a criterion of the ego's givenness, the Cartesian way loses the privilege it enjoyed on the basis of a difference in being between ego and the other, between ego and the world. With the subjective "sphere of being" robbed of its quasi-ontological status, the remaining asymmetry of ego and world or ego and other is not sufficient to secure the solipsistic ego as the irreducible and *unhintergehbarer* ground of phenomenological method. Husserl greatly restricts the privilege and even necessity of the Cartesian way, it seems, immediately after giving the London lectures and sending the "French Meditations" to the translators. He recognizes that, contrary to the path of knowing, the way of being accords equal privilege to the intersubjective world and intersubjective life and that one could even reverse the course of the "French Meditations." Indeed, this alternate way is the approach that Husserl, armed with a concept of history, finally takes in the *Crisis.*

In summary, Husserl's indecision as to the best "way" into his *Meditations* (point 1) is more than a question as to what the First Meditation should look like. There is a deeper problem resulting from a change in the notion of evidence appropriate to the transcendental ego (point 2), which then leads to a fundamentally different conception of the way in which intersubjectivity is related to the analysis of evidence (point 3). In particular, because there is no longer a fruitful connection between adequate evidence and the whole stream of consciousness (point 2), Husserl must distinguish between a "primordial" and an "egological" reduction. As a result, he defines subjectivity not as a private sphere that leads to the other's consciousness only by transgression, but only as provisionally "my own." In itself it is intersubjective in nature, as explained in the (new) Fifth Meditation. The asymmetry of ego and other is preserved, but they belong not to two different spheres of being, as the first formulations of the Cartesian way demanded, but to a single field linked through the notion of horizon. These changes in the notion of the Cartesian way are what finally enable Husserl to secure the equioriginality of subjectivity, intersubjectivity, and world, a notion required by his later thought.

Although these reflections transform Husserl's Cartesian way beyond its earlier configuration, they do not thereby put an end to it. There are at least three reasons for this. The first is heuristic. It was a "short introduction" that Husserl could recommend, quite suitable for the French but certainly not for the Germans "in the situation now" with its "modish swing to a philosophy of existence."[136] A second, more compelling reason is theoretical. Once he purifies the static method by replacing the ontological notion of spheres of "being" with an epistemological notion of fields of analysis and a phenomenological notion of spheres of constitution, he has a form of solipsism that is free of ontological commitments and is genuinely "methodological." To be more precise, Husserl can finally overcome the way the epistemological requirement of adequacy itself gives rise to a metaphysical construction of the subject. For the "given" is no longer the type of entity that must be able to present itself without remainder, transparently, immediately. The notion of subjectivity is finally freed from the notion of consciousness as a self-enclosed, individual stream. The final reason is systematic. Ever so gradually, the task of a phenomenology of consciousness is overtaken and mostly subsumed by the way through intentional psychology. While the latter is different in principle, moving from a "science" to its transcendental grounds, Husserl becomes convinced that the full content of his analysis of consciousness under the Cartesian epoché could be found in intentional psychology. This introduced the problem of transcendental psychologism, as I will argue in chapter 10. It also meant that the Cartesian way is to be expanded and transformed into "the direct way," a notion that we will turn to in the next section.

B. THE WAYS TO TRANSCENDENTAL ANALYSIS

We have seen in the course of this chapter that Husserl himself challenged his first formulations of the Cartesian way, which relied upon the tenuous epistemological notions of immediacy, adequacy, and transparency. In their wake, these formulations treated subjectivity as a closed sphere of being, of mineness, and of presence—an ontologically untenable position. The issue ultimately was not the individual problems inherent in each of these notions, but that, because of the problems, they collectively delivered neither the full scope nor the genuine depth of the transcendental. These early formulations could go no further than the *ego cogito cogitatum,* and even that they interpreted in terms of a certain immediacy to the *cogito* that threatened to transform the *cogitatum* and its attending world into a representation.

There is yet another way of understanding what is behind the Cartesian way. Husserl uses his expansive version of logic as a guide for his first formulations of the Cartesian way, although the reduction was to exclude it in principle. He looks to this logic, found in both the *Logical Investigations* (Third and Fourth Investigations) and *Ideas I* (Part 1), as he makes the phenomenological turn. Stabilized by the opposition between essence and fact, logic and its sub-disciplines are ideal constructions; they must be described in terms of "ideal" modes of cognition that could be achieved by anyone "in general." The analysis of perception secured the contrast between the real and the ideal and showed how the real can be rendered in the ideal. Because the theoretical attitude undergirds this project, any given subject matter could be traced back only to the essence of its cognition. The ego is mine but its structure belongs to cognition itself. Furthermore, while the object is an appearance in my stream of consciousness, its transcendence entails that it would appear in this way to any consciousness. It was possible for Husserl to restrict the scope of the transcendental to the *ego cogito cogitatum* and marginalize issues like intersubjectivity and the "pretheoretical" world because it was not the practice of science but the theory of science, not the rhetoric of interacting participants but the propositions of detached thinkers, not the mixed history of the lives of thinkers but the products of their research for which he had to account. Theory was understood as just theory and not as a set of cognitive practices, with internal ties to what exceeds the view of the individual acting or failing to act in accordance with the requirements of "the things themselves."

By contrast, we have seen that Husserl's further reflections in various texts during the 1920s, and especially those designed to lead to a revision of the *Cartesian Meditations*, carried him beyond his first formulations into an expanded version of the Cartesian way. We have yet to understand in our analysis, however, how a modified Cartesian way could contribute to transcendental analysis as a whole. We gain this understanding most clearly if we think of the revised Cartesian way as Husserl's *direct* way into transcendental analysis, setting it in contrast to his indirect ways.[137] The latter lead us through mediating fields of analysis, where critique, as we are calling it, invites a transition to a transcendental account. The direct way, however, starts not from the question of positivity but from the problem of negativity, from that which confronts positivity as its complete opposite. This direct way begins, then, not in a certain field of set materials but in the lack of any sure starting point. Its interlocutor is neither the reductionist scientist nor the "objectivist" philosopher but instead is the skeptic, who is already situated at the level of what is transcendental discourse. This way is required in order to answer skepticism in a manner that avoids begging the question. Just as the skeptic, in his or her opening gambit, does not ask about one thing in particular but about everything at once, so the direct way, unconcerned about the broadest and most general differences among individuals, moves back from and calls into question the whole of beings.

An even deeper function for the modified Cartesian way is discovered by examining its internal tie to the indirect ways. Husserl realized that in moving to the transcendental "in one leap" the results of the Cartesian way appear "empty of content."[138] He also realized, however belatedly, that the Cartesian way in general, and the *Meditations* in particular, could never be anything more than introductory. They are introductory in a double sense: they supply the beginner with his/her first overview and, more importantly, provide the indirect ways with their *preliminary* transcendental scheme of understanding. The Cartesian way effects a piece of adduction, to use Peirce's famous term, that yields a provisional frame of reference and a sense of direction to the more or less inductive movement of the indirect ways. In doing so, it opens a field of analysis that can be filled out and even modified. At the same time the direct way is dependent upon these ways and thus loses self-sufficiency. Perhaps it is not even correct to label this a "way," for it does not operate alongside others but creates the framework within which they function as types of transcendental analysis.

In what follows I will touch upon the different "indirect" paths that Husserl mentions, having labored on the Cartesian way up to this point and having sketched aspects of the way through the positive sciences. In contrast with the Cartesian way, we will place these indirect ways under the label of the Kantian way. Husserl himself does not use this term; but the analysis he gives in his expanded version of a 1924 lecture to the Kant Society, "Kant and the Idea of Transcendental Philosophy," allows us to introduce it.[139] In general, any indirect way requires an appropriate mediating discipline from which it questions back to its condition of possibility. Just as Kant, in first *Critique,* uses the logical features of judgment in general as his "clue" to the pure transcendental concepts of understanding, which he calls categories,[140] so Husserl "questions back" from a certain positive or ontological discipline to its transcendental constitution. At first he mentions a surprising variety of mediating disciplines. I want to suggest, however, that no matter how many paths Husserl mentions, there are basically only two general directions they can follow. Let me briefly describe each of the *ways* in terms of these two general *approaches.*

1. The Approach through Intentional Psychology[141]

It did not take Husserl long to realize that his tidy contrast in the *Investigations* between empirical psychology and phenomenology would not be able to instigate the radical transformation of the discipline of psychology that he envisioned. The fact that he called his first phenomenology a "descriptive psychology" in the first edition indicated that contrast among empirical psychology (and even here a distinction could be made between the impoverished psychology of the empiricists, which he rejected, and proper, subsidiary statistical psychology), phenomenological psychology, and pure phenomenology was needed. Recognizing this need, however, drew Husserl into repeated attempts to clarify how the latter two differed. While Husserl wanted to argue that transcendental phenomenology was not psychology, he also saw that, in fact, all of the *Investigations* could be construed as part of phenomenological psychology. As we have pointed out, this motivated both his introduction of the reduction and the transposition of phenomenology proper into a transcendental register. His solution was to treat a phenomenological psychology of the subject as a transitional discipline, as one of the ways to a pure phenomenology of the transcendental ego. How could Husserl show that there is, in fact, a different attitude in play? Husserl had three options; he would have to find a contrast in the *content* of the two disciplines, in the kind of *reflection* through which they are known, or in the quality or kind of *evidence* accompanying them. The last would be close to impossible if both were "pure" disciplines, as he claims. Given both the fact that only one stream of consciousness is disclosed and that we rely in both cases upon a form of immanent reflection, the quality of evidence should be the same. Husserl relied upon a combination of his first two options when he approached these difficulties in *First Philosophy*:[142] the difference in the kind of reflection in these two disciplines led to a difference in their content. In *First Philosophy* he claims that the way through intentional psychology supplements the Cartesian way "so that the *ego cogito* does not remain an empty word";[143] there would therefore have to be a contrast in content of the transcendental ego over the psychological ego, not the reverse, to carry the distinction.

In *First Philosophy,* lectures that Husserl gave in 1923 and 1924, he attempted to understand how there is a difference in the type of reflection. He initially fell back on the thesis that psychology, even as an analysis of pure consciousness, operates within the natural attitude like any other positive science. He explains it thus:

> The epoché that I [as psychologist] exercise . . . leaves untouched the natural ontic validity of all acts. . . . I have the goal of winning the act-experiences of the actual act-subject as pure experiences, and that according to their pure experiential characteristics. But that does not mean that I, the psychologist, automatically would want to set out of play my own position of belief vis-à-vis the perceived as such (e.g., posited things, values, etc.). I want to and, in fact, do set it out of play only relatively, in relation to my goal. . . . I have thus not simply and absolutely inhibited my position [i.e., the natural attitude] to the real being of the intentional object of the actual acts.[144]

How can we shift from a pure psychological analysis to "viewing transcendental pure life?"[145] Husserl understood this question as asking which "transformation and heightening of the method" of analysis is required "to unharness the epoché and extend it to *absolute universality.*"[146] His solution in these lectures was to suggest that the epoché "extends beyond" the acts first disclosed in a psychological mode of analysis and covers not only their objects but also the "intentional implications"[147] which lie behind actual phenomena open to psychological analysis. In short, the epoché accounts for the "background."[148] He relied on his theory of horizons and seemed convinced that only a transcendental epoché could include such horizons. The resulting universality provides us with our ego as a whole and more: "In truth we stand in the singleness of an endless nexus of life, in the endlessness of one's own and intersubjective, historical life."[149]

In a critical text that Husserl added to this course of lectures, however, he grapples with the difficulty with this thesis:

> Against this approach one can object: when I as psychologist want to bring to light the pure soulish interconnection for myself and each other, that which composes what is purely soulish in its entirety for me—and I do indeed want the pure soul in general—I must carry out a universal phenomenological reduction.... All individual reductions to individual acts move within a universal and, at the outset, all-encompassing [psychological] reduction, and result in individual pure acts [being treated as] moments of a pure soul as a whole.[150]

Psychology is not only individual but also "universal." The contrast between an individual soul and the whole intersubjective interconnection of souls will never be sufficient to establish a difference between psychological and transcendental phenomenological analysis.

In chapter 10, we will consider how Husserl addressed this difference and follow out the critical implications of this line of thought. Whatever the outcome of our study there, we can now see that Husserl thought that a phenomenological psychology of the ego, including its achievements, was a discipline in its own right as well as a transitional step on the way to a full transcendental phenomenology. This approach to the transcendental moves through a positive study of the subject *per se,* not of a certain field of objects.

2. The Approach through Ontological Critique

Under the approach through ontological critique, we include such diverse paths as the ways through a critique of logic,[151] through a critique of the positive sciences,[152] and through an ontology of the world.[153] These culminate in the path that dominates the *Crisis,* the way through the life-world. In each case we have various "objective" and "transcendent" domains, be they real or ideal, that provide our guiding thread. If we think the approach through intentional psychology moves from the psychological to the transcendental subject, then the approach through ontological critique "is opposite to that suggested by the Cartesian approach."[154] At times Husserl saw affinities with Kant's regressive procedure. On the negative side the ontological approach dismantles the prejudice of objectivism, as Husserl finally called it in the *Crisis,*[155] the metatheoretical assumption that the world is itself a being and that all beings can be disclosed through a discourse appropriate to objects and their interrelationship. On the positive side, what we are calling his Kantian way takes various kinds of "totalities" or "wholes" as "an *index* or *guide-line* for inquiring back into the multiplicities of manners of appearing and their intentional structures."[156] The scope of these disciplines provides clues to the scope of transcendental phenomenological analysis. Because the Kantian way works through a "critique" of the given, it is not necessary to suspend our belief in the existence of the world, as in the Cartesian way, in order to initiate the phenomenological turn. Rather, there are certain gaps, disturbances, reversals, conundrums in phenomena, brought to light in the course of experience or engaged critique, that provoke the turn. Nor is it necessary to treat subjectivity as a self-contained sphere of being. The movement is from *cogitatum* with its horizons to *cogito* and then to the various "forms of life" of engaged subjects.

Husserl works with these ideas in "Kant and the Idea of Transcendental Philosophy," a rarely discussed text that I would call his "Kantian Meditations," all the more important because it begins with the same level of generality as the Cartesian way. There his characterization of the transcendental for the most part breaks out of its Cartesian parameters, though there is one section where he falls back into his older description. We can see the special features of his way through critical interrogation or *Besinnung* of the world, made all the more interesting because the concept of the life-world is not yet employed and because these reflections come from precisely the period in which Husserl is attempting to clarify the difference between static and genetic method. We will follow his line of thought as the path he traces in this text serves as a paradigm for the way through ontological critique.

Husserl began with the critical observation that, though the world is "the totality of realities,"[157] our experience is always "incomplete," i.e., "we grasp only fragments of the world and even these only one side at a time, and the sides, again, never in ultimately valid adequacy."[158] This is not just a factual limitation: "An actually complete experience is impossible; for in principle there is no limit set to a progression."[159] This incompleteness, however, does not mean that the world remains beyond experience. Through experience we become "acquainted" with it and its "real *Dasein*."[160] It is certified or testified by harmonious experience; i.e., in the course of harmonious experience taken as a whole, there is an indubitable acquaintance with the existing world itself.[161] In other words, the acquaintance we have with the world is an implicit and necessary feature of all explicit and focal acts related to particular objects. This entails that, in cognition related or directed toward the world, there is a "harmony" between the world itself and the acts and structures of cognition. This harmony is *presupposed* by all positive sciences without their being able to study or justify it. "All positive questions move within the framework of the world's unquestionable pre-givenness in living experience. . . . "[162]

It is the task of phenomenology to put the world in question, and it does so not by skeptically "decomposing"[163] it but by first accepting its "being in itself" and its status as "pregiven"[164] and then asking how it is to be understood, how this *sense* of the world "takes shape subjectively or intersubjectively in our own cognitive achievement."[165] Thus, the absolute transcendence of the world is not denied but sustained—"the being-in-itself of the world is an indubitable fact"[166]—in the turn to its constitution in our cognitive achievements. At the same time this turn allows us to understand its being-in-itself as a *presupposition* that lacks grounding. Thus Husserl adds:

> There can be only *one* method of really answering all such questions and of obtaining a real understanding of the relationships between cognized being and cognizing consciousness. One must study cognizing life itself in its own achievements of essence . . . and observe how consciousness in itself and according to its essential type constitutes and bears in itself objective sense and how it constitutes in itself "true" sense, in order then to find in itself the thus constituted sense as existing "in itself," as true being and truth "in itself."[167]

There is another feature of this way through the world that distinguishes it from the Cartesian way of *Ideas I:* a separation between "pure subjective and intersubjective consciousness" and my own stream of experience or my own consciousness.[168] The restriction to the sphere of ownness and to the soliloquy is seen as problematic and, perhaps, not sufficient in scope to account for its correlate, the world as a whole. As he puts it:

> . . . one must pay careful attention to the fact that a possible transcendental subjectivity in general is not merely to be understood as a possible singular but rather also as a possible communicative subjectivity, and primarily as one such that purely according to consciousness, that is to say, through possible intersubjective acts of consciousness, it encloses together into a possible *allness* a multiplicity of individual transcendental subjects. To what extent a "solipsistic" subjectivity is at all possible in thought, outside of all community, is itself one of the transcendental problems.[169]

Thus Husserl defines his task; it is one that

> goes after subjective and intersubjective consciousness in all its actual and possible forms, particular and synthetic forms, and quite exclusively directs its gaze upon what belongs to consciousness in and for itself.[170]

He even enriches his analysis of immanence in a transcendental register by developing his notion of subjectivity into intersubjectivity, though he does fall back on speaking of the world as "in" subjectivity, confusing subjectivity as the field of transcendental analysis in general with subjectivity as the life of consciousness:

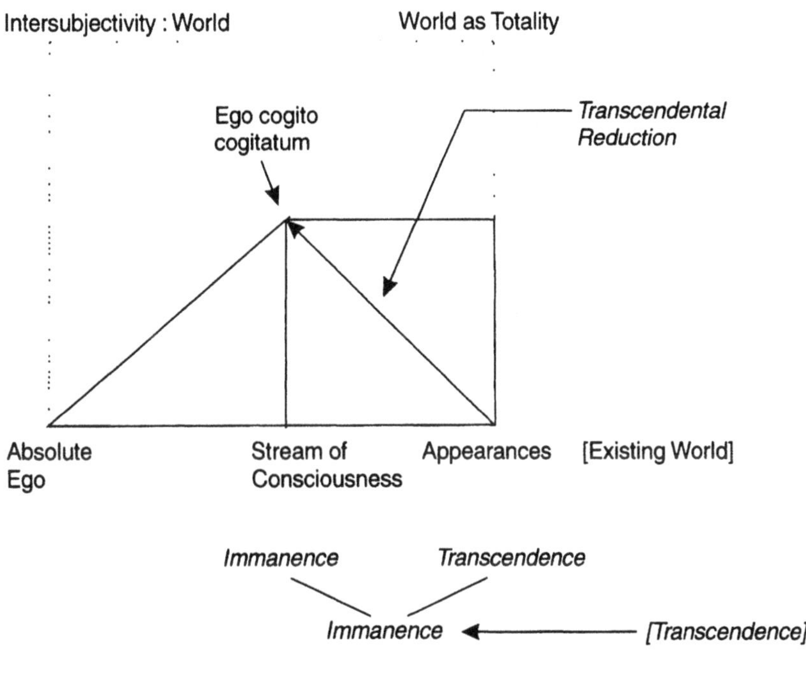

Fig. 6.1. The Cartesian Way to Transcendental Phenomenology

> The factual life of consciousness, the universal life of consciousness, in its *transcendental intersubjective immanence,* bears in itself as "phenomenon" the correlative fact of the world constituted as presentation in it.[171]

Reflecting on his methodological solipsism, Husserl understands its starting point in the individual ego as one that is provisional, as a "first restriction" of the analysis that requires supplementation by

> the widest framework of the universal community of subjects standing in possible communication with the individual ego and with one another, that is to say, in relation to "everybody whatsoever" and transcendental intersubjectivity.[172]

In chapter 3 we sketched how this approach works when logic, with its interrelated disciplines of ontology and apophantics, is taken as the guiding idea. In chapter 10 we will return to the Cartesian way and look at the issue of psychologism in a transcendental register. The way through the life-world,

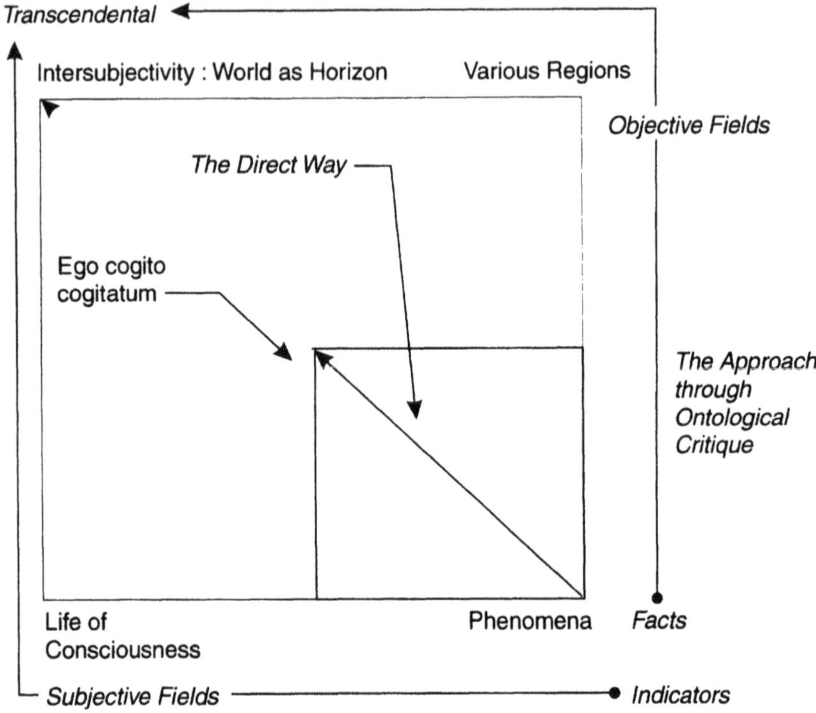

Fig. 6.2. Direct and Indirect Ways to Transcendental Phenomenology

finally, will be our exclusive theme in the last three chapters of this work, as we will find in it the most enduring sense of transcendental phenomenology.

At the risk of grossly oversimplifying the matter, let me summarize the analysis of this chapter with contrasting diagrams. The full scope of Husserl's transcendental analysis with its complementary approaches (Fig. 6.2) can be glimpsed by opposing it to the Cartesian way as outlined in *Ideas I* (Fig. 6.1).

7

From Categorial to Constitutive Phenomenology

The transcendental "absolute" which we have open to view through the reduction is, in truth, not the final [level], which is something that constitutes itself in a certain profound and completely peculiar sense and has its ultimate source in what is finally and truly absolute.

Fortunately, we can leave out of consideration the enigma of time-consciousness in our preliminary analyses without endangering their rigor.

—Husserl (1913)[1]

The independence of the being of a proposition from the accidental judgment and judging does not yet mean that the ideal-identical is a specific [i.e., belonging to the domain of species].[2] But, starting from there, the final clarification leads into the deepest constitutive problems whose relationship to the original consciousness of time is not hidden to you. For I am working not on a mere phenomenology of time[3]—one that allows itself to be separated purely for itself—but on the colossal problem of individuation, of the constitution of individual (thus "factual") being in general, and that according to its essentially basic formations. Thus it is now a matter of a . . . radical phenomenology.

—Husserl to Ingarden (1918)[4]

But the phenomenological method, though it overcomes this first naiveté of the natural attitude, only leads us first into a new naïveté, that of simple descriptive act analysis. This in turn must be overcome by progress to the deeper constitutional analysis.

Constitutional analysis is not the same as descriptive analysis. . . . Such naïveté is present also in Heidegger so far as he takes *Dasein* (human existence) as basic instead of having its constitution, its genesis parallel to the world-genesis.

—Husserl as reported by Cairns (1931)[5]

Categorial phenomenology sets as its task the construction of a typology of the correlations between kinds of acts or achievements and the different regions of objects and/or facts. Once it has described various correlations in contrast to others, constitutive phenomenology extends the program of categorial phenomenology by attending to the "thickness" of each correlation, by studying how each is implicitly related to other nested transformations or types of correlations upon which each manifest correlation depends. The notion of constitution becomes fully engaged once the theory of the horizon is integrated into the field of analysis and thus each act is understood as situated in a *field* of achievements to which it has internal ties.

In Husserl's development a gradual shift from categorial to constitutive phenomenology is found in the studies that he devoted to the question of what he calls "modalization." Dimly anticipated in the opening sections of the Fifth Investigation and touched upon in a few of his analyses in *Ideas II,* the study of modalizations came into its own with *Analysis of Passive Synthesis,* certain sections of *Formal and Transcendental Logic,* and *Experience and Judgment,* works forged mostly during the 1920s. In this chapter we will trace his constitutive analyses of perception or, more broadly, experience, on the one hand, and claiming or, more broadly, speaking, on the other. These analyses are strategically chosen; for rather than being *one* of the regions of Husserl's ontology, they account for the conditions for framing and then establishing the content of *any* region, or, to put it more accurately, they function at the level of the transcendental condition for developing truthful descriptions in any particular region. The constitutive account of speech and perception further clarifies the straightforward opposition between meaning-intending and meaning-fulfilling acts employed by categorial phenomenology; for it replaces simple reflection with a "process of disclosure,"[6] and a "static" opposition with a "dynamic" contrast, although this contrast does not yet fully integrate time and temporalization into its explanations. The horizon comes into play only as a system of meaning- or sense-implications, not as a temporally deployed scheme of constitution. For that we must wait for the turn to genetic analysis.

Because of the way modalization must be factored into our account, we are not approaching the notion of constitutive phenomenology as Husserl did in *Ideas I,* with the full force of his Cartesian approach propelling the analysis. We attempted in chapter 5 to locate the ideas that push the notion of the reduction into his Cartesian formulation. We can therefore raise the question of what static analysis would look like if we were to rescind the specific strictures of the Cartesian way. How does acquiring the difference between a Cartesian and a "Kantian" notion of the reduction, and then the difference between static and genetic analysis, free up static analysis and produce new insight into the notion of constitution?

While my account extends beyond anything that Husserl expressly argued, it is plausible to view the constitutive analysis of claims and perception, of speech and experience, as the most promising way of reformulating, in non-

Cartesian terms, Husserl's "direct way" into transcendental analysis. Three considerations support this position: (a) rather than speech and experience being each a single region in Husserl's ontology, they function as *cognitive* conditions for framing and then establishing any given region; (b) rather than being reducible to an intentional psychology of speech-acts and acts of judgment, speech and experience function as *epistemic* conditions for that discipline; and (c) the need to establish an internal link between subjectivity and intersubjectivity, itself necessary to do justice to the full scope of the correlational a priori, can be handled not only by recourse to experience, as Husserl's account of empathy attempts, but also by considering the role of communicative interaction. Together speech and experience give us *dynamic* conditions for any empirical or regional discipline.

If this approach is correct, we might have new light on the place of *Experience and Judgment* in Husserl's program. This text was one that Landgrebe began to assemble in 1924 or 1925 from manuscripts reaching back to at least 1915.[7] We saw in chapter 5 that the need for further consultation and work on this text drew Husserl's attention away from his revisions of the *Meditations* between November 1929 and the beginning of February 1930. The bulk of this text was clearly Husserl's, with some of the earlier sections, it seems, composed by Landgrebe. After long delays, caused largely by the uncertain political climate in Germany and Landgrebe's personal circumstances, the work was published in 1938, the year of Husserl's death. There are a number of hints that allow us to understand this work not only as providing key features of a genetic account of logic but also, if not by its design then by its content, as employing a non-Cartesian approach to constitutive analysis. These are the fact that (a) the analysis of modalizations dominates the work; (b) the procedure of eidetic variation becomes the working method for its constitutive descriptions, enriching the notion of intuition to the point where it is almost displaced; and (c) while the theory of modalization attempts to account for several points where the "prepredicative" (or "prelinguistic") and the "predicative" (or "linguistic") pass over into one another, time is not incorporated into the account. We have a "genealogy of logic" that is actually a constitutive account, that understands the interplay between experience and judgment as dynamic but not (yet) as temporal, an approach made plausible by the fact that the logical formations for which it accounts are themselves ideal.

In this chapter I will resume the account developed (chapters 1 to 4) before we turned to the Cartesian way (chapters 5 and 6). The characterization of the phenomenological method in the earlier chapters, I can now confess, was free of the particular requirements of Husserl's Cartesian method. However, because we restricted ourselves to the concept of world (chapter 4) and suspended any sustained discussion of the notion of constitution itself, we were only able to introduce partially the theory of the reduction. This chapter begins by making good on this shortfall.

A. THE FIELD OF CONSTITUTION

By becoming transcendental, phenomenology becomes philosophy. In chapter 4 we used the in-structure in its difference from the as- and for-structures as a way of introducing the notion of world and employed the difference between world and beings-in-the-world as the key to a characterization of world as horizon. Now we must explore the way in which the characterization of the ground of phenomenology as transcendental does much more than secure the form of its description, much more than elevate categorial phenomenology with its series of phenomenological studies into a "universal phenomenology," a general philosophical theory. The transcendental reduction moves phenomenology beyond typology and into typography. The transcendental turn transforms the correlations first uncovered by a categorial account into schemes of *constitution,* thereby securing phenomenology as both an *epistemic* account of how phenomena are known and a *structural* account of how they achieve their being as phenomena. Types of phenomena are transcendentally characterized as fields of constitution. But what does Husserl mean by "constitution"?

Husserl consistently distinguishes a theory of causality from a theory of constitution by restricting the former to an analysis of the production of and interaction between physical events, and by employing the latter to account for the composition of intentional events. A theory of constitution describes and explains phenomena-facts (PF), be they experienced objects, complexes, or events, by recourse to a set of mental facts (MF) that belong to *me* or, more generally, to an individual self that stands in the relation of constituting (C) the phenomena-facts

(MF) C (PF)

Since there are multiple mental facts for any phenomenon-fact belonging to a single type, we have:

$(MF_1, MF_2, MF_3 \ldots MF_n)$ C (PF)

When Husserl first introduced his theory in *Ideas I,* he argued that there are roughly three types of mental facts that are relevant to the description of intentionality: the mode or "quality" of the act (AQ), the sensorial complex (SC), and the significational element, what he calls in general the noematic content. Rejecting the idea that the whole (PF) is merely the result of the additive properties of the elements of the sensorial complex, Husserl incorporated an ideal, structuring element, which he called the noema (N), into his account. In addition, the act quality is not merely added to the rest of the elements but qualifies them as a whole. Employing the dyad of form and matter, he arrived at the following scheme to describe the way in which mental facts are constitutive of noncompound phenomena-facts:

AQ [N (SC)] C (PF)

There are, roughly put, two possible ways of understanding this scheme of constitution open to Husserl. The first option is to say that the phenomenon-fact is exhaustively explained by the mental facts belonging to my consciousness such that: (a) the whole (PF) is the result of the combination of the mental facts, and (b) the whole does not contain any properties that are not those of the mental facts and the relationship between them. In this case the order of explanation is from mental facts to phenomena-facts, and the analysis gives us not only necessary but also *sufficient* conditions for the existence of a phenomenon-fact. Having (MF_1, MF_2, MF_3 . . . MF_n) is all that is required to have (PF). This option, along with Husserl's first Cartesian formulations, is based on the assumption that we have a way of directly apprehending mental facts independent of their being or being approached through phenomena-facts. The second option is (a) to view the whole (PF) as a result of the combination of the mental facts *plus* a non-mental, or mental but non-factlike, feature, and (b) to treat the whole as having (some) properties that are more than the properties of the mental facts and the relationship between them. In this case the order of explanation would be from phenomena-facts to mental facts, and the analysis would give us only *necessary* conditions. The order of explanation would proceed from (PF_n) to (MF_1, MF_2, MF_3 . . . MF_n) and need not involve the claim that we have access to (MF_1, MF_2, MF_3 . . . MF_n) independently of (PF_n).

The claim that we do not have mental facts (MF) independently of phenomena-facts (PF), however, does not entail that we lack direct acquaintance with mental facts. If we did, we would fall into problems with what is called the reflection theory.[8] Rather, it means that when we reflect upon and apprehend the mental facts of which we are directly aware, we co-apprehend their correlative phenomena-facts (the thesis of intentionality), we can thematize mental facts only in correlation with phenomena-facts for which they account, and we conceive of the functions or operations (condition) of mental facts in terms of the structures of the phenomena-facts to which they give rise (conditioned).

Husserl began with the first option and continually attempted to return to it. He believed that it was required to bring all domains under the rules of reason, one of the requirements of his transcendental idealism. However,

Husserl's thesis that the noema was an ideal feature already created problems in placing it into the domain of mental facts, all the more so since the noema accounts for the organization of the whole of the phenomenon-fact that "precedes" or situates the elements of the sensorial complex and, thus, must be very different in kind. In addition, the act quality, as we stressed, is not added to the other two mental facts but qualifies them. Even so, these features are not as important as the discovery of the horizonal quality of phenomena, a non-factlike feature of mental life. All phenomena-facts are situated in *contexts* against *backgrounds* that contribute to their determinations but are not themselves facts. This discovery, as well as the difficulties attending his theory of adequate evidence, moved Husserl to adopt the second option. Even more important are yet other internal reasons having to do with a deepening of the notion of constitution and the very concept of a phenomenological method, as we will see.

Let us once again consider the manuscript "Static and Genetic Method" from 1921. In chapter 2 we suggested that the term "constitutive phenomenology" was ambiguously situated between what Husserl called a "universal phenomenology of the general structures of consciousness" and a "phenomenology of genesis." Husserl first combined a categorial account with a constitutive phenomenology as he brought them under the rubric of static phenomenology; he then set static in opposition to genetic phenomenology. He wrote:

> Each apperception has a structure according to noesis and noema. Each, according to its kind, carries out a bestowal of sense and a positing of an object in doxic modalities. It requires a particular form of analysis, which we are to carry out, to shed light on the intentionality of an apperception, to describe, according to noetic and noematic structures, from all sides, the possible types of fulfillment and the systems of possible fulfillment, whether complete or in the process of being continuously completed. With these descriptions, the constitutive ones, there is no question of an explanatory genesis.[9]

Since the question of genesis will occupy us extensively in the next two chapters, we need only emphasize the sense in which static phenomenology marshals the resources of both categorial and constitutive analyses to produce the kind of descriptions that we undertook in chapter 1. Objects of perception, categorically distinct from corresponding reports about them and from higher-order eidetic intuitions of their essences, are described as objects presented in and through their profiles. These profiles are correlated with moments of apperception and perception nested in the whole perceptual act in which the objects are experienced. An object is not just there for the subject, as a player upon the passive stage of the mind. Rather, its presentation requires certain achievements of the subject, in which its unity is "built up" from the determinations exhibited in and through the interplay of profiles and object. We saw in chapters 2 and 3 that a categorial phenomenology gives an account of objects within different regions—physical nature, the person, or culture, for example—by recourse to their meaning and to the various ways in which their presence is achieved. It also gives us a provisional ordering between the regions, though it is restricted to a comparison of the structurally different features of each. This ordering can then be complemented by a constitutive account of how one might be derived from or internally related to the other through a series of noetic-noematic modifications. Still, "there is no question of an explanatory genesis." In static analysis we have an account of structural modifications that abstracts from the crucial question of concrete development.

But as soon as Husserl distanced static phenomenology from genetic analysis in the 1921 text, he contrasted a constitutive with a categorial account *within* the program of static phenomenology. To be sure, Husserl did not always preserve this distinction in other writings.[10] But here it is deliberately introduced.[11] How are these contrasting disciplines to be understood?

Transcendental analysis not only establishes the correlativity of subjectivity and world as a *ground* securing regional analysis, it also uses that correlativity to account for its *depth*. When Husserl contrasted categorial to constitutive descriptions, he thought of them together as coordinate disciplines that move from surface to depth, thereby transforming the provisional notion of grounding structure into that of a transcendental *field*. In addition to a *horizontal* ordering by categorial phenomenology of different noetic-noematic correlations that parallel various regions, there is a *vertical* study that deals with a variety of transformations within each correlation. In such a study we move

> to a constitutive characterization, to descriptions of all the modal transformations in retentions, recollections, expectations, etc., and thereby follow a principle systematically ordering the apperceptions, one that [vertically] cuts across [*sich kreuzt*] the sorting [*Scheidung*] of apperceptions according to the most general genera of objects (regions of objects actually or possibly existing).[12]

Thus we see that a second descriptive discipline, the constitutive, cuts across the first, the categorial. Here constitution is either a setting or coming together of elements "from below" into a constellation of a different level, which allows us to speak of founding relationships, or the active combination of elements "upward" into a unity of a higher level, in which case we talk of construction or composition.[13] The vertical axis gives us the depth of each level and thereby "connects" those constellations distributed horizontally, sorting them in terms of logical relations of wholes and parts, of founding and founded.

At the risk of mixing terminology, we might say that the discovery of the notion of the horizon by transcendental phenomenology opens the vertical axis of constitution. In contrast to analyses along the horizontal axis, constitutive phenomenology treats an array of "modal transformations" that apply to a variety of different noetic-noematic correlations. It is concerned with "structures and modalities that encompass all categories of apperceptions."[14] Husserl's lectures delivered during this period explore these structures and modalities in considerable detail.[15] Transformations of the certain into the doubtful, the affirmative into the negative, the actual into the possible, all cut across the various genera of objects and acts uncovered by our first reflections. In addition to modalizations, which Husserl wanted to relate to complete act-object correlations,[16] there are syntheses within single correlations, such as temporal changes, dispersions, continuities and discontinuities, ever different but always operative in various acts and objects. Even such features as similarity and difference, proximity and distance, and unity and disseverance traverse any number of categorial orders.

Constitutive phenomenology, then, isolates the deep structures of different types or levels of experience. The *correlation* between achievement and sense, first discovered in a reflection upon the transcendent object given in and through its appearances, is reframed as a *constitutive* condition of that object in its difference from others and is thereby enlarged through an account of the various "levels" or "layers," nested in a given categorial type, that *motivate* "the achievement of transcendence."[17] Constitutive phenomenology provides an account of regions by recourse to the way they are "built up." Intentionality accounts not only for structure but also for "origins."

Husserl's effort to sketch his "systematic phenomenology,"[18] as he began calling it during this period, works with several contrasting features of categorial and constitutive analysis. The *topic* of the former is a typology or classification of the different "essential shapes"[19] of noetic-noematic correlations, while the second provides a description of the "modal modifications" that "encompass all categories of apperception," both passive and active.[20] The *starting point* for categorial analysis is the "division of apperceptions according to regions of objects," i.e., regional ontologies.[21] Constitutional analysis proper simply builds upon the results of such a classification. Gathering these two together, Husserl asked: "Is not static phenomenology precisely the phenomenology of guiding threads, the phenomenology of the constitution of leading types of objectivities . . . ?"[22] The clearest contrast can be seen in the *scheme* of analysis. Working with the difference between profile and object, categorial analysis uses the distinction between intention and fulfillment to frame its analysis. "I follow the correlation: unity of the appearing object and multiplicity of the appearances uniting in such a way that they are noetically harmonious."[23] In contrast to such horizontal studies, a vertical analysis provides us with a "typology of the interconnections in consciousness of a particular developmental level,"[24] as well as a description of "modalizations" transforming one level into another.

B. DOUBLING BACK

The movement beyond a categorial account into a full constitutive analysis allows us to return to our starting point and there characterize it in terms of its essential role in a transcendental phenomenology.

Categorial phenomenology, as it was introduced in the *Logical Investigations,* uses the correlation of act and significance in conjunction with the epistemic difference between intending and fulfilling experiences to establish its descriptions. The fact that Husserl gives us a *logic* of these correlations means that his account of them is general. But this should not make us lose sight of the fact that the correlations themselves are specific to regions and that it is the structure of the region that provides the clarification of the types of correlations present in it. The *Investigations* leaves us with a general theory of acts without an account of the unity of all acts, a theory of regions of the world without a theory of the world, and a theory of significance without a notion of horizon. While it does offer us a logic of parts and wholes, the *Investigations,* in which we find categorial phenomenology first brought to expression, has neither an egological conception of consciousness nor a notion of the world (or horizon). Furthermore, it is not a transcendental theory. Methodologically we cannot find a decisive difference between it and a descriptive psychology. As a consequence it lacks, at least in statements of its own program, the crucial notion of phenomenological constitution.[25]

With the introduction of the phenomenological reduction we acquired the "whole" of being itself, i.e., the "whole" world, which, as horizon, implicates the "whole" of subjectivity. This allowed us to secure the ground of categorial phenomenology by situating the for-structure at a transcendental level. Phenomenology thus became "a universal phenomenology."

There is a Socratic movement to this period of Husserl's thinking; for constitutive analysis, initiated in *Ideas I* but clarified only in the 1920s, returns us to categorial analysis and compels us to reinterpret our starting point. We can *double back* to its analyses. The connection between act and significance, reinterpreted transcendentally, is described as the correlation of noesis and noema. The initial understanding of this correlation through the notion of necessary conditions is expanded through a notion of constitutive conditions. Regions, in turn, arise in fields of constitution. By accounting for both the surface and the depth of various fields, the notion of constitution provides a transcendental account of transcendence.

C. THE ORIGIN OF PRESENCE

Since we have construed the horizontal axis as the one situating all regional ontologies, we could move on to a vertical account of these different regions and their structures. But this would be an analysis much too vast and complex for us to attempt here. Rather, we will introduce an account that will allow us to say something about those "structures and modalities," as just quoted, "that encompass *all* categories of apperceptions."[26]

Husserl's study of these general vertical structures and modalities concentrated on acts involved in bringing phenomena to presence, on the one hand, and different types of discourse, on the other. It then turned to the differential relationship between these two facets in the constitution of contrasting regions. Their interplay unfolds the web of *significance,* by means of which phenomenology defines the *being* of appearances.

What makes Husserl's account of perception and discourse so baffling—and what eventually makes genetic phenomenology so hard to fathom—is that we fail to grasp the fact that they must be "located" in the transcendental field of constitutive phenomenology and that they, as a result, undergo a constitutive reinterpretation over and above the first provisional descriptions of his categorial account. This confusion is no doubt due not only to the fact that we can undertake a regional ontology of each, perhaps under the disciplinary headings of phenomenological psychology and linguistics, but also to the fact that the Cartesian reflection necessarily passes over them as it thematizes the relation between "finished" formations and their conditions.

We will attempt to avoid such mistakes here. At the same time there is little doubt that Husserl's account of the deep structure of regions is quite limited. I am referring not only to the rich alternatives offered by such thinkers as Heidegger, Foucault, Derrida, Lyotard, and Habermas, but also to the fact that Husserl's treatments of language and experience are not sensitive to the different ways they are deployed in the deep structure of various regions. Husserl sensed that his analysis of perception, his paradigm case of originary experience, had to be expanded into a much broader notion in order for experience to be integrated into it. He also recognized that his phenomenology marginalized the communicative dimensions of discourse.[27] While he did expand the notion of perception and carry out several necessary studies, he did not give language the attention it requires. We do find excursions, though, that are quite suggestive. In what follows we will remain within the limits of his analysis and, perhaps, be surprised by how far they do carry us. Because the spadework on Husserl's texts has been done in an earlier work,[28] my discussion of perception and speech will not be bound to textual analysis, as were the last two chapters. Instead, I will concentrate on how the issues function in a genuinely constitutive account. This will allow me to clarify Husserl's distinctions while I extend them in ways consistent with his program as a whole.

The account of perception, to which we will now return, shows us how we move along a single vertical line of analysis and simultaneously gives us a brief analysis of a mode of experience that Husserl takes as *basic* to all vertical accounts. Husserl's account of perception is one of the most contested parts of his theory. I will attempt to place the issue on new ground by describing a certain development in his theory.

At the risk of drawing it dry, let us return to our water pump standing in the middle of the farmyard. The pump is not an object "in" the mind of the subject, nor does phenomenology place it there. Even when we are in a simple intending phase of the experience of the pump, the focus of the act is upon the transcendent object. The object in focus, no doubt, is "taken" or intended in a particular mode, which is contributed by the act. But even in this phase of intending, not yet fulfilled, the act is one of *anticipation* and thus does not terminate in its own "takes." In anticipation we are directed "through" and "beyond" the anticipatory phase, to the object being intended and, finally, to the object in the manner of its givenness. The givenness of the object constitutes the goal of the act. It is not only the intending or anticipation of the rust-colored side but also its fulfillment, the rusty side seen, that Husserl wanted to explain through his notion of intentionality.

Not all acts of fulfillment are acts of perception, however. In addition to acts of perception that terminate in objects here and now, there are acts of recollection and explicit expectation that have past and future possible objects as their fulfillment. There are also achievements of mental depicting that fill out an intention in imagination. No doubt the acts transpire, and the object-complex is given in a particular present. But unlike in perception, the objects in these cases have temporal features that fix them in the past or the future or, in the case of imagination, "over" a present. Thus, not all acts of fulfillment *present* an object but all *presentify* or *make* an object present. To capture this difference Husserl distinguishes between two different types of fulfillment, between "presentiation" (*Gegenwärtigung*) and "presentification" (*Vergegenwärtigung*). In most cases we could even speak of the latter as re-presentiating the object for, to a greater or lesser extent, such acts depend or build upon a previous act of perception. In Husserl's terminology they are "founded" upon perception.

Even within presentiation itself, however, there are differences to be made, for the water pump as perceived may be unclear, distant, shaded, or simply lost in the downpour of an afternoon shower. Only when we approach, or when the rain ceases, is our perceiving optimal, the object distinct. In optimal perceptions, neither too "far" nor too "close," objects are not "vaguely" but "originally" given. The original givenness of an object in acts of presentiation is called "intuition" (*Anschauung*).

Husserl preserves this working contrast between original presentiation and varieties of presentification, as he recognizes that there must be modes of presentation that are appropriate to different regions. The notion of intuition thereby is greatly expanded; it is the noetic counterpart of optimal experiential givenness. At the same time, Husserl argues that embodied perception provides an acquaintance with the world on which all modes of presentation rely and to which they all, in different ways, refer. It is the most basic of the different types of intuitive experience. Husserl's account of perception, therefore, gives a full account of the mode of experience underlying the region of nature and simultaneously a partial account of those regions beyond nature.

The difference between presentiation and presentification is problematic for Husserl's stricter formulations of the notion of eidetic intuition. If Husserl is to have an apodictic basis for establishing essential statements, eidetic insight must be a form of presentiation. Eidetic analysis necessarily involves comparison across time, however, which necessitates an inescapable element of presentification in essential evidence. Only later did Husserl realize that, as a consequence, all variations must include an element of "critique." But for now let us concentrate on the perception of real objects and the contrast between presentiation and presentification in order to further specify Husserl's account of the constitution of originary perception.

Originary intuition consists of fulfillment in a present. Derrida's emphasis upon the priority of the present in Husserl is correct, at least for perception and this level of analysis.[29] In fact, if the only significant contrast Husserl made had been between presentiation and presentification, much of Derrida's critique would be appropriate. Yet even here, not to mention the reformulation of these priorities in his genetic account, Husserl treats perception (*Wahrnehmung*) or presentiation as complex, as including at least an abstract difference between the "presentation" (*Präsentation*) or "sensing" (*Perzeption*) of the profile or perspective directly before us, and the "appresentation" (*Appräsentation*) or "apperception" (*Apperzeption*) of the other profiles forming the object as a whole. Though the term *Apperzeption* is rarely found in *Ideas I*,[30] when it does appear it seems to function generally as a synonym for *Wahrnehmung*. He clearly identifies them in our 1922 text: "Originary apperception is perception [*Wahrnehmung*]."[31] Still, Husserl consciously chooses the term *Apperzeption* because it emphasizes the excess, the surplus that each act of sensible apprehension carries in itself:

> Could we not define apperception in this way: a consciousness that not only has something conscious in it but, at the same time, has it conscious as [the] motivating factor for something else . . . pointing to this other as something belonging to it, motivated through it.[32]

While categorial accounts involve comparing different features and acts at different times, suggesting a structural account of what is the same and what is different, constitutive analysis presses for a further analysis of the act in terms of what causes it to apprehend more than what is explicitly given. This newer account seems to move in the order not of conceptual meaning but of aesthetic senses, not of logical entailment but of affective implications. In Husserl's constitutive descriptions, originary presence necessarily includes originary absence, soliciting that movement of transcendence whereby absence is transformed into provisional presence in such a way that absence is preserved. All perception as presentiation, thus, is laden with a "surplus" never exhausted in the now.

In the opening descriptions in chapter 1 I stressed the difference between profile and object and suggested that profiles are themselves not in focus, though they are ingredient in the manner in which the object is given. Even though we are preacquainted with them, only in acts of explicit reflection do profiles become "object-like" and thereby a topic of analysis. In addition, static phenomenology, oriented as it is to an analysis of types of knowledge and evidence, focuses only on a certain type of perception, only on *epistemic* perception. Given these two facts, it follows that Husserl began by using the traditional dyad of form and content to describe the constitution of perception. Ingarden, one of the few philosophers who could critically engage Husserl in a way that caused him to listen, wrote Husserl in 1918 about the type of experience Husserl had, as a matter of fact, described in the *Logical Investigations.* His words also apply to Husserl's descriptions in *Ideas I:*

> The problem of knowledge [*Erkenntnis*] is taken in hand where knowledge proper (the "coming to know") is already achieved and is basically concerned merely with a re-knowing [*Wiedererkennen*]. We already *have* "an idea" about the object and are concerned whether the intuitively manifest object agrees (fulfills the intention) with the idea (the significative intention). It seems to me that the analyses of the Sixth Investigation must be undergirded [*unterbaut*] by a consideration of *original* knowledge, when we first learn to "grasp conceptually" [*begreifen*] the object, when we do not yet have an idea about it and first build the "idea" and, possibly, further rebuild it and "fit" it to the object. The *origin* of the significative intention must be shown. . . . (This would also have to be carried out in view of the analysis of perception in the *Ideas [I]*!).[33]

On the one hand, the kind of perception first studied was actually a form of perceptual *recognition,* of *looking for* an X in which the determinations anticipated were propositionally or conceptually specified "in advance." On the other hand, the perceptual object was understood by contrast as an individual, "a this-there whose factual essence is a concretum,"[34] i.e., as an instance of an essence. Accordingly, Husserl's first account of perception distinguished two analytic steps: (a) the act is a form whose content is the noema; and (b) the noema is a form whose content is the intentional object. In *Ideas I* he added to this a first, provisional constitutive account: non-objective sensorial "data" (subjective, noetic content) are "animated" or interpreted by the act (noetic form) according to the sense (noematic form) and thus become the profiles or appearances of the object (objective content). This account is plausible in cases of perceptual recognition guided by explicit concepts expressible in language, where there is a high component of interpretation. When my friend asks me to bring him a large drinking cup, I set out to find an object that matches the description. What I see becomes relevant, becomes a profile, on the basis of its fit. When I do bring my friend the cup, its relevant features are just those specified in the speech-act: its profiles (content) are ordered precisely according to the meaning (form) of the description guiding my act (form).

However, Husserl's theory in *Ideas I* interpreted the content being "interpreted" by the act according to a somewhat classical notion of sense-data and tended to treat the material composition of the perceptual object as a composite of such data. As a result, it comes perilously close to phenomenalism. Furthermore, it contains an unbridgeable gap between real data and ideal meanings.[35] Husserl thus became increasingly unhappy with his initial form-content account of perception. In the 1920s he introduced a much more developed theory of perception that treated not only epistemic perception but also a more basic and extensive type of *nonepistemic* perception, finally using the resources of a constitutive phenomenology to their fullest.

Although Husserl spoke of profiles as data (present) on the basis of which acts of perception of objects (absent) are based, he conceived of data themselves as only *abstract* moments (absent) whose isolation presupposes the perception of the whole object (present). This made him realize that his notion of sense-data needed to be dismantled and reinterpreted. In one of the London lectures he put this issue clearly:

> It would turn the analysis of outer perception completely upside down if one, beginning with and [mis]led by the sense-data tradition, wanted to say: perceived [objects] are complexes of sense-data. Indeed, sense-data are in the ıle false products of a theoretical analysis in the psychological attitude. The concretely full phenomenon exactly as it is offered in immediate intuition, however, is the necessary starting point of each phenomenological description; according to our method, each claim must be drawn directly from pure intuition. In this respect it is clear that what comes first is not "I see data of sensation" but rather I see houses, trees, and so on; I hear in the distance bells, a wagon rattle, etc.[36]

In another text that stems from as early as 1918[37] Husserl recognized first that the distinction between sense and hyletic content is the result of *contrasting* perceptual intending and fulfillment, and, second, that they should not be considered two separate components that happen to be combined in an act of perception:

> The sense [in which the object as such is conscious] is not an empty but a [somehow] fully determinate sense. Rather it is, through and through, "full," fulfilled sense, covered, as it were, with the fullness of intuition. We cannot place two components next to one another, sense and its filling, in what is intuited as such. Only by contrasting empty and full sense do we gain the difference.[38]

Sense-data, then, cannot be construed as elements that are animated by a meaning-bestowing act. They are "abstract" or abstractable *dependent* moments that can be isolated only by contrasting acts of intending an object with what is given in the act of fulfillment, and then by selectively screening the latter. But if the form-content scheme will not suffice as a constitutive account of perception, how is perception to be characterized?

The profiles of the pump are related to each other in a number of different ways. When we walk about the pump, the color remains uniform as one profile "blends" into the next, and we see them as "similar" or "homogeneous." Only when we reach the backside and suddenly find mossy green, not rust speckled with red, does one side suddenly "contrast" with the others and appear as "different" or "heterogeneous." The material color of the profiles, furthermore, is connected with their textures, which, in turn, exhibit their own similarities and contrasts. These sensuous aspects of profiles, Husserl realized, cannot be treated as data whose combination creates perceptual objects. Rather they are "moments" or "dependent aspects" of wholes, and they can be viewed as isolated individuals only by selectively screening the entire perceptual object and abstractly focusing on a section of the side.

Husserl may have made his decisive breakthrough on this issue in studies on time about 1909, earlier than the writing of *Ideas I*. If this is true, it reinforces our argument that the static analysis prevalent in *Ideas I* is provisional and that Husserl had already prepared for, though not developed, what became his genetic account. In order to have something like a sense-datum as *given*, there would have to be a mode in which it could be experienced as such. It would have to be a distinct sensation with at least a temporal marker. Husserl, however, rejects the idea that we have something like a "primal sensation-consciousness" in which a particular sensation, such as a "tone-point," is itself actually present.[39] He reasons that anything that is actually present, anything having the form of Now, must presuppose *continuity*. "Primal sensation" could be no more than a "non-self-sufficient phase of originativeness." He adds: "Primal sensation is something *abstract*."[40]

Husserl's exclusion of temporal constitution in *Ideas I* delayed the impact of such ideas; only when he took up the "colossal problem of individuation," as he put it to Ingarden in 1918,[41] did the effect of these ideas become apparent. Even in *Ideas I,* however, he rejected the theory that data have any independent existence and, to use Hume's metaphor, dance on the passive and merely receptive stage of the mind. In most empiricist theories, the relationships between sense data are "blind" (a term Husserl also uses in *Ideas I*), driven by a hidden mechanism of association in which combinations of profiles and objects are independent of the acts of the mind. At least Husserl required a principle of internal organization, the noema, in *Ideas I.* However, when he took up the term "association" and even used it to mark this field of studies in the 1920s, he set it in contrast to earlier theories by describing it as "passive synthesis." The differences between blended and contrasting content are supported by what Husserl calls syntheses of homogeneity and heterogeneity, themselves dependent moments or features of syntheses of presentiation constituting perceptual wholes. Passive syntheses came to account for an inescapable *affectivity* that Husserl called the "affective power [*Kraft*] that perceptual fields exercise upon acts of perception."[42]

There are two simultaneous dismantlings of the provisional notion of sense-data used in Husserl's categorial account: the first is noematic, as sensorial phases or aspects are viewed as integral moments of surfaces and profiles; and the second is noetic, as sensorial syntheses are treated as dependent syntheses presupposing continuity and thus nested in larger acts of perception. These changes affected his characterization of the noema of perceptual acts. When we make a precise division between the meaning and the referent of speech-acts, for example, we treat the noema as that which accounts for acts of intending (i.e., the activity of referring even in the absence of referents). Perception, however, requires a certain integration of the noema into the perceptual object. If we were to think of speech-acts as triadic in structure, consisting of act, meaning (noema), and referent (fulfillment), then perception could be seen as dyadic, consisting of acts of perception in relation to perceived objects. The sense, or perceptual noema, would not be a "third item" or an "ideal content" between acts and objects but instead would be a scheme that accounted for the integration of profiles, and profiles and objects, in terms of interrelated syntheses of perception. Since perception is apperception, it is directed toward a whole that exceeds what can be isolated in a present. Perception always takes place within a "horizon" of sense, a horizon developing in the very course of ongoing perceptual experience.

This very important reframing of the classical notion of sensation is but one of the features of Husserl's developed account of perception. A second part is even more revolutionary.

When we move from the front to the sides of the water pump, we notice that, while the sides may have the same manifest quality, they have very different shapes and different positions. Profiles, in short, are also *perspectives.* As perspectives they are not accounted for "inherently" by recourse to sensorial syntheses but "relationally" by recourse to spatial syntheses. The spatial co-ordinates of perception, however, are those of experience, not those defined by algebra. Husserl carefully contrasted the lived space of perceptual objects with the uniform extension of Newtonian space. In place of a mathematized grid, Husserl described lived space delineated by experiential relations of over and under, left and right, back and fore. These specify both the basic dimensionality of lived space and the constitutive conditions under which profiles are perspectives.

The search for a ground for spatiality led Husserl not to another level of mental synthesis but rather to the *body.* The lived co-ordinates of over-under, left-right, and back-fore are themselves rooted in the basic relations of the body to its environment. The body in this account is not one of the perceived items "in" space but rather a "null" or "center" out from which, like the eye of a hurricane, space radiates.[43]

The notion of the body adds much to Husserl's first account of perception. Husserl's categorial analysis always approaches the question of perception from the side of the cognitive information, obtained by the watchful eye. This first theory gives not so much a theory of perception as a theory of perceptual concepts. But this framework can be understood in terms of corporeality. Husserl's static approach to perception, undergirded by an interest in truth, presupposes a specific bodily modality, that of the *fixed* eye in a *stationary* body; but this stationary body is a mode of the body of *action,* of the "I can." The focused gaze is one of the "capabilities" of the body perceiving. By integrating acts of perception into bodily actions in his constitutive account of perception, Husserl shows one way in which epistemic perception is a specific modification of nonepistemic perception.

There is another result, even more important, that comes from integrating perception into the body. If epistemic perception finds its correlate in the "fixed" look, then nonepistemic perception arises through the "moving" gaze. It explores as it is drawn. It approaches as it is solicited. By placing perception in relationship to the actions of the body, Husserl realized that the perceptual meanings constitutive of appearances arise in correlation with not only associative and spatial syntheses but also, more generally, with reciprocal modes of assimilation and accommodation, to adopt Piaget's terms. Perceiving is a way of taking things in hand, of grasping them; things stimulate and affect us in ways that require us to adjust to them, to approach or stand back. Husserl's integration of perception into the "I can" preserves the internal tie between perception and action, a tie that Heidegger thought Husserl had lost.

Ideas I leaves "out of consideration the enigma of time-consciousness" and, in addition, does not deal with spatiality. The recovery of both these basic forms of constitution carried Husserl beyond his first analysis into his full constitutive, and then his genetic phenomenology. We find these modalities at work in two different registers. First, in his constitutive analysis, they function as basic syntheses underlying the varieties of experiential acts. This account is then extended in his genetic analysis when Husserl discovers that the connection between different types of vertical structures is itself temporal. Second, from the point of view of the method itself, we can think of constitutive phenomenology as an explication of the "spatiality" of the transcendental field, while genetic analysis unfolds its "temporality." For the present we must stay in the first register and finish its constitutive analysis. We will deal with the genetic account and the second register in chapters 8 and 9.

We suggested earlier that originary perception could be treated as an act of presentiation clearly distinct from the presentifying acts of recollection and expectation. Our walking around the water pump and the movement from one perspective to the next, however, did not take place in the blink of an eye. Indeed, if we did not in some sense "keep" the previous phases in the present one, we would never perceive the sides as profiles *of* an object; our act could never achieve anything but an intellectual synthesis of the "parts" into the "whole." In addition to spatiality there is also an irreducible temporality to perceptual objects, even within originary perception, a temporality completely neglected by categorial phenomenology.

In our perception of the pump, the profiles just perceived are still an active part of the "Now" in which a new profile is present. The previous ones successively "fall away" from the present, but they are not yet lost to a past whose retrieval would require distinct and separate acts of recollection. *Retention* holds on to that phase of the now which is passing away. The present phase also opens upon the next profile, the coming perception; we do not require a second act of expectation that projects, dimly or clearly, the next side. Rather *protention* is that phase of the Now that is coming into presence. Though Husserl was initially tempted to see the Now as an impressional point between the two, he quickly realized that such a point, as we just saw, is but an "abstract limit." The "living present," by contrast, consists of an overlapping of retention and protention in the Now. In fact, this concatenation of temporal phases extends beyond what is actively present into what is nonactively or distantly present, perhaps the part of the day or week that leads up to my experience of the water pump or, less distinctly, the rest of the day anticipated after my drink of water. Indeed, this overlapping in the Now is what finally accounts for the possibility of recollection, which begins with retention, and expectation, which begins with protention. This interplay of protention and retention also undergirds the syntheses of association and spatiality, making this level of analysis the most basic.

Although his theory of time leads into some of Husserl's most profound studies and, as we will suggest, provides the key to his genetic account, its analysis makes its first entry at the level of constitutive analysis. Since our account thus far has used temporalization to tag a difference between static and genetic analysis, further clarification is in order.

The richness of Husserl's constitutive analyses results from viewing a phenomenon and its attending act(s) in terms of the modalizations to which they are connected. While the theory of modalization is primarily used to examine the relationship between complete act-object correlations, it is also possible to probe the underlying "passive syntheses" of a single correlation, to look for nested levels of constitution that make it possible. We move regressively, from the aesthetic qualities to the spatial configurations to the temporal deployment of the correlation. Temporalization is both discovered as its condition and analyzed *structurally*. Because it is a synthesis accounting for the temporal character of not only an object but also of the material and spatial syntheses related to that object, Husserl treats temporality as the most basic level. This will then lead to his genetic analysis, further substantiating the claim that the border between constitutive and genetic analysis is somewhat fluid. Having derived temporalization through an analysis of perception, though, we have not clarified the ways in which it functions in other modalities and accounts for our experience of order among them. In addition, we understand temporalization neither at the level of meaning and sense nor in terms of its relation to transcendental analysis. For this we must wait until we can focus on genetic analysis proper.

Husserl's constitutive account of perception in terms of interlocking associative, spatial, and temporal syntheses displaced his static characterization of perception as an interpretative apprehension (*Auffassung*) of data by meaning; it also introduced a proper notion of perceptual *sense* (*Wahrnehmungssinn*). The debate in secondary literature over Husserl's notion of the noema has centered around *Ideas I* and for the most part has not looked into his rethinking the problem of "individuation" during the 1920s. In so doing, such debate has overlooked the way in which these studies, with their displacement of the form-content account of perception, transformed the concept of the perceptual noema. In view of our account in this chapter, it seems plausible to suggest that perceptual senses are not Fregian-like ideal intensional [*sic*] entities but *schemata* that organize, as they themselves are configured by, the relationship between perceptual syntheses and perceptual fields. They are structures embodied in perceptual intentionality as a whole and account for (preconceptual) aesthetic, spatial, and temporal features that are anticipated, as they are constituted, in the course of perception.[44] They coordinate the relationship between different passive syntheses and then between those syntheses and various field properties. We find at least three nested levels in the basic correlation of acts of perceiving and perceived objects.

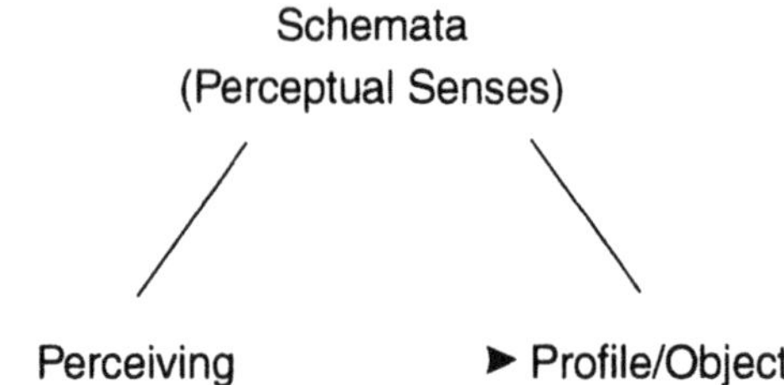

Associative Syntheses	: Aesthetic Features
Homogeneity	Blended/Similar
Heterogeneity	Contrast/Difference

Spatial Syntheses	: Spatial Field
Over/Under	Height
Left/Right	Width
Fore/Back	Depth
Close/Far	Proximity

Temporal Synthesis	: Temporal Field
Retending	Passing/Succession
Protending	Coming/Succession
Presentiation	Living Now/Simultaneity

Fig. 7.1. Dimensions of Passive Synthesis

This account of perception provides us with a sample of an analysis of the constitutive levels forming the deep structure of the region of nature. Each of the regions sketched in chapter 3 could undergo such an analysis. We selected perception not only because it received the most attention in Husserl's studies but also because it is the most basic level of experience. Husserl even claimed that

> perception and its parallel modes of intuition are the first basic configurations of consciousness that are relevant for the structure [*Aufbau*] of specifically logical consciousness. They are the first foundations in logic's building that must be explicated and understood.[45]

This account of perception, then, functions both as a prototype for analyzing the varieties of experiential givenness of different regions and as a nested and irreducible vertical level found in the constitution of all regions.

D. BESPEAKING PRESENCE

What is missing from our account above is how the move from originary to epistemic perception can be brought about. The analysis above accounts for the manifest presence of the regional field from which theory will extract an ontology of nature. But Husserl's categorial analysis of perception in terms of form and content was derivative, applicable at best to certain constrained types. He replaced it, we suggested, with a constitutive analysis of aesthetic syntheses in the 1920s. Husserl was interested, however, in the constitution not only of regional fields but also regional ontologies. In order for us to secure the latter, we have to account for the type of understanding in which they come to articulation and are secured. Both comprehension and evidence are required. Therefore, we need a clarification of how we effect the change from intention to fulfillment and, in particular, of how we move from ordinary perception to a mode of critical perception that yields confirmation. The account thus far already suggests that the epistemic perception operative within a given field takes place against a backdrop of unencumbered perception and that the ontologies we construct already presupposed a *familiarity* with the regions whose structures we attempt to describe. But what accounts for the transformation of one into the other?

Husserl offers us two fertile accounts of this change. The first remains within the course of perception itself, describing several interconnected modifications or "modalities" a perception undergoes when disrupted. For example, the disappointment or partial fulfillment of an intention produces perceptual negation and often a "retro-effective" cancellation of previous perceptual beliefs. Another example: two different perceptions of the same complex that are in conflict introduce doubt. It is resolved either by confirmation of one of the options or negation of them both.[46] The second way of creating a change, which we will pursue here because it allows us to confront the problem of language, comes with the intervention of assertions, of claims that draw us beyond our absorption in things and require us to look again.

Introducing speech at this point is also motivated by another concern. We have developed the notion of perceptual experience but, of course, experience alone does not produce knowledge. We must also clarify the derivation or origin of a conceptuality that is constitutive of different regional ontologies. Husserl framed this analysis by contrasting the "passive" syntheses of perception with the "active syntheses" of "predicative thinking." I will now focus on those modes of understanding that *give rise* to the propositional turn, to judgments that work with assertions, and thus to the discourse of regional disciplines. In an effort to capture the dynamic character of the movement between ordinary and rigorous discourse, Husserl would think of this as an account of "modalization."

There is an unexpected advantage that comes from our consideration of the origin of assertions. This account, unlike the analysis of perception, clearly cuts across different regions by virtue of the interdependence of different semantic fields and contexts. As soon as we provide a constitutive analysis of the depth of a given region in terms of transformations of discourse, we have necessarily related it to other regions.[47] For any study of "active" synthesis, as Husserl called the act of judgment, constitutive analysis slides into genetic. The difference between constitutive and genetic is not hard and fast but instead "operative," and thus we are dealing with a progressive deepening of analysis rather than with distinct steps.

Since all "active" syntheses are governed by what Searle called a principle of expressibility[48] we have another distinct advantage: being able to use differentiation within speech contexts as our point of access into an account of mental acts in general and of understanding in particular. Let me develop the case of broken speech offered in our opening chapter.[49]

From the time of Aristotle, any and all declarative sentences of the form *S is p* were assumed to express propositions and thus to be the basic carriers of truth.[50] For him and those who followed him, there was a fundamental difference between such statements and sentences used to express commands, wishes, or prayers; for the latter group cannot be true or false.[51] But as far as I know, no distinction has ever been drawn between a propositional and a nonpropositional use of the string *S is p,* nor has there been any effort to understand *S is p* in terms of certain modal transformations that might underlie it. Rather, all sentences having the surface form *S is p* have been identified as expressive of propositions. If *S is p* is then taken to be the basic form from which all other modalities are derived, two conclusions inevitably follow: (a) since *S is p* is an irreducible grammatical form, its logical content is basic to all other types of speech that employ a modalized form of *S is p;* and (b) a logical analysis of truth-conditions fixes both the meaning and the (legitimate) use of *S is p.*

Once this thesis and its corollaries are in play, the crucial semantic question then becomes how to bridge the gap between the content expressed by *S is p* and the world. With the field circumscribed in this way we are, in the last analysis, driven to one of two ways of describing truth-conditions: either the logical content is assumed to be the meaning (and not the reference) of the string, and thus its truth conditions are characterized in terms of correspondence or extensional conditions; or the logical content is treated as the reference of the string, and thus its truth conditions analyzed as coherency conditions or a calculus for determining equivalent classes. The history of semantics seems to alternate between these two ways. Breaking the cycle of these alternatives requires us to rethink the analysis of *S is p,* which Husserl's theory of modalization encourages us to do.

Imagine that we are in the process of moving into a new apartment, and you load up both our friend Apollo and me with boxes of books, instructing us to put them on the rug in the study. After we lug our burdens up the stairs we discover that there are two rugs in the room, one sort of brown and the other, maybe, beige. Not knowing where the boxes should go I return with the question, "What color is the rug on which I should put the boxes?" You answer: "The rug is beige."

Or, perhaps, I know that the boxes are to go on the beige rug but, since the electricity has not been turned on, I cannot tell whether the rug by the desk is brown or beige. I turn to Apollo, a health nut whose diet these days consists mostly of carrots and sunflower seeds, and ask him what is the color of the rug by the desk. He replies, "It is beige." I nod and put the boxes on it.

When we take them in context, neither of these utterances of the sentence *The rug is beige* has the activity of staking a truth claim as its purpose. In describing to me the color of the rug my speech partners are simply providing indicators as to where to put the box of books. I fully accept their reports and either go off in search of the beige rug or take the rug by the desk as beige without question.

Notice that our sentence *S is p* blends into the actions we are undertaking and functions to facilitate our involvement in the task at hand. The string serves to "articulate" the field of our actions and thus provide us with our bearing. But while the string allows me to discriminate, while it certainly gives me direction and particular instructions, none of us are actually "interested" in its truth or correctness. We are simply trying to get the job done with the least number of slipped discs.

We could even go on to suggest that the meaning of the string *S is p* consists of a conceptual scheme that can be described only in terms of heuristic rules of identification and determination. Here use and interactions are constitutive. The meaning is "ideal" in the sense, as Husserl came to put it, that we find it at work "time and again" (*immer wieder*), in the sense that the same rule could be in play in a different but similar situation. The meaning of *S is p* should be understood, first of all, in terms of the way it facilitates our involvement with things; the string would be overdetermined if we said that in using it we take up the predicate as an ideal, intensional entity and that our speech-act consists of sorting objects by concepts or attributing certain properties to individuals. Rather, *S is p* functions more like a tool that enhances the task at hand. Our string functions not to represent but to present, not to conceptualize but to control, not to analyze but to assimilate.

There is, of course, the reply that while our utterance of *S is p* may not be used explicitly to stake a claim, it does so implicitly. Thus, even when I tell Apollo that the rug is beige for the purpose of giving him a place to put the books, what I am also doing, perhaps "unconsciously," is uttering the truth claim that the rug is beige. I will deal with this in the next section, but here I will supply a preliminary response. It seems to me that there are three problems with this reply: (a) it may confuse a *de facto* structural account of the use of *S is p* with a *de jure* description of its correct use and then argue that the second is the condition of the first; (b) if we can show how its use as a claim results from a certain transformation of its use as a report, if we sketch certain modalizations involved in this transformation, there would not be a need for recourse to latent or unconscious intentions; and (c) it does not account for how *S is p* can be used meaningfully and successfully even when it fails to meet the truth-conditions of its use as a proposition. For example, the description would probably be "good enough" if the rug were not beige but dirty white, or if it were not a rug at all but a horse blanket. For this seems to be no more problematic than driving a nail with a pair of pliers.

If we introduce another variation, however, we can see where the question of truth enters. After being instructed to put the boxes on the beige rug, neither Apollo nor I can find such a rug in the study. We go looking for it in another room, in which case the description still functions as a report for us. If we cannot find it there either, then we might come to a point where we cease our activity altogether, turn upon the description itself, take it as the speaker's proposal, and question its correctness. When we do this, the sentence itself comes into focus, and we try to clarify just *what* it says. In reflecting we "objectify" the meaning of the string. As a result, the predicates are reframed as *concepts*, with relations to objects that are governed by truth-conditions. Seeking confirmation consists of setting concepts in relation to things, and of determining whether those concepts are lawfully applied. In addition, what the sentence expresses becomes envisioned as a *claim* or proposition by virtue of the fact that what it reports becomes enframed as a *proposed fact* that you suppose to be the case. We take what Sokolowski has called "a propositional turn."[52] A change in *Einstellung* or interest prompts it: as we attend to the fact being (re)presented by the string *S is p*, the report is taken as a truth claim. To understand a claim is to be able to articulate the truth-conditions that determine its meaning and thereby to specify its possible confirmation. Only claims can be true or false and, thus, only claims are propositions.

Turning practical language into truth talk arises not only in the absence of referents but also when there is a certain discrepancy between what we anticipate and what we find. There often comes a point where the object we perceive deviates enough from what we expected that it "disappoints" our anticipations. Maybe the only rug we find is dark blue. *Negation* sets in. Where there is a certain continuity with what we expected (for it is still a rug), what we see only "crosses out" part of the intention. "The general frame of sense is kept and fulfilled . . . [but] now something 'other' comes forth, a conflict between the intentions still living and the senses founding the new intuitions."[53]

When further thresholds are crossed, negation easily turns to *doubt.* Perhaps the only object we find on the floor is a linen tablecloth, just the kind of thing upon which we would not put dusty boxes of books. An "irresolvable conflict" arises between the claim and what we see or, should Apollo insist that this thing on the floor is really a rug, between two different "interpretations" of what is seen. While negation attends the realization that the rug can *not* be *both* beige *and* blue, doubt affects the sense of the whole as we realize that we are dealing with *either* a rug *or* a tablecloth.[54] This is precisely the point where, in the face of perception, the question of truth and falsity "sets in."[55] Husserl expressly connects the experiences of negation and doubt to *questioning.* "The passive disjunctive tension between problematic possibilities (doubt in the passive sense) motivates an active doubting, an action setting the ego into a certain splitting of the act. . . . There arises a striving for a firm decision, which produces a questioning."[56] Husserl suggests that "each possible judgment can be thought of as the content of a question."[57] It is precisely this connection with the process of questioning that both constitutes the propositional turn and keeps truth talk rooted in practice: "Questioning is a [mode of] practical action in relation to judging."[58] Since the process of questioning is what mediates the difference between saying and judging, between reporting and claiming, Husserl's genetic account of judgment gives us an internal connection between pragmatics and analytics: "All reason is simultaneously practical reason, and so also logical reason."[59]

Let me pause to prevent a possible misunderstanding. Reports and claims are not two different entities. We do not have the string *The rug is beige* and then something else. Rather, claims are reports; they are used, however, not as something ready-to-hand that facilitates our circumspective involvement with objects in a certain environment, to draw on Heidegger's categories, but as something present-at-hand connected to the epistemic activity of asserting, proposing, or maintaining.[60] Claims do not belong to everyday talk or chatter, or, rather, they carry us beyond it toward accurate representational discourse. They are governed by a reflective search for truth, not by an unreflective, shared engagement with things. It is not the difference in surface grammar but the differences in *interest,* in the way the string is taken up by the act, that generate the contrast between reports and truth claims. The change in attitude is such that we withdraw from our immediate acceptance of what is reported, ceasing to live in what *Ideas I* calls the "doxic" mode,[61] and call into question the facts expressed by the sentence, taking them as merely proposed by the speaker. The interest subtending claims is in (scientific) correctness. As soon as we place this process into an intersubjective context, we can see that framing a claim also involves an obligation to our speech partner to be responsible to the truth. In short, it is a "theoretical interest"[62] in truth that is constitutive of the field of propositions.

I want to suggest that it is not just difference in interests but also in referential function that demarcates reports from claims. If we take the simple case of two persons in communication whose sentences have the form *S is p*, then it might be possible to distinguish between *referential* and *truth conditions* and to use this distinction to secure the difference we are making between reports and claims; referential conditions make possible the successful use of *S is p* as a report, while claims are also subject to truth-conditions.

Referential conditions specified the "good enough" object or affairs-complex intended by the speaker's "different enough" use of the description *the Sp* or the sentence *S is p.* Two reports would be the same if they functioned to present the same referent the speaker intended; thus to determine if they were equivalent, the listener would have to take recourse in the object or affairs-complex the speaker intended to pick out by using *S is p* as the listener "went along" with the belief expressed therein.

The *truth conditions* are defined by the actual or possible object or affairs-complex that fits or "fulfills" the noematic content of the description *the Sp* or the sentence *S is p* uttered by the speaker and understood by the listener as such. Two sentences would express the same claim (Frege: thought; Husserl: proposition or state-of-affairs) if they were synonymous in any context (i.e., if they made the same statement) and if they had the same actual or possible object or affairs-complex as their semantic referent.

In addition to the beige rug case above, we can suggest another example where we have a divergence between referential conditions and truth-conditions. Imagine that Mr. Barnaby, a wealthy banker whose family is a hornet's nest of intrigue, is murdered. I am convinced that Cuthbert, his son-in-law, is the culprit and refer to him as Barnaby's murderer. You happen to share my belief, accept my way of describing him, and use the designator "Barnaby's murderer" to pick out the son-in-law as well. We might successfully refer to the son-in-law in this way as we gossip over the back fence. Our talk clearly sets him in contrast to other members of the family. Disturbed by certain clues uncovered in the course of his investigation, you later discover that it was not the son-in-law but his wife who plunged the deadly dagger into her father's chest. My report that Cuthbert was Barnaby's murderer no longer expresses a belief shared by you but instead is reframed as my mistaken claim. If we insist on identifying referential conditions with truth-conditions, and reports with claims, we would have to say that in our talk over the back fence the claims successfully referred, even though they were false. But by definition a false claim is one that fails to refer. In our case, the speaker did succeed in referring, even if it turned out that Cuthbert was not Barnaby's murderer. If we take such sentences as reports, however, we can see that the intentions of the speakers, as well as the semantic import of the terms, determine reference. Our "propositional turn" forces us to recognize a difference between them and allows us to raise thereby the question of truth.

E. TYPES OF MEANING

Having drawn the distinction between reports and claims as a whole, we must now do several things: first, focus on the one decisive issue for our understanding of Husserl's theory; second, attend to the question of how this issue is worked out in Husserl's development; third, make a distinction among four different possible characterizations of noematic content; and, finally, conclude with an application of these issues to a recent discussion of the thing-in-itself.

In the *Logical Investigations* (1900–1901) Husserl set occasional expressions in contrast to objective expressions; he later recognized, in the preface to the 1913 second edition, that all "empirical concepts" are "occasional." Recognizing that empirical expressions have a meaning that requires us to attend to their context and the situation in which they are uttered forced Husserl to attend to the question of the interplay of ordinary and scientific discourse. In the last section we used two examples to help make a distinction between reports and claims and to show that taking *S is p* as a claim involves a certain reflection upon our nonepistemic use of *S is p.* The difference has been generated pragmatically, i.e., in terms of how *S is p* is being used. In our account, the "interest in truth" configures *S is p* as expressive of a proposition. But now the crucial question for our purposes is whether, behind the difference between interest and referential structure, there is also a substantial difference in their noematic content.[63] This is another way of getting at the question of whether we can reduce reports to implicit claims. In attempting to understand how they are connected, we have two choices. Either

a. in using *S is p* as a report I am *implicitly* using *S is p* as a claim; the act of reflecting upon the report discovers a proposition that is already there; or

b. in using *S is p* as a report I am not implicitly using it as a claim; the act of reflecting upon *S is p* is what constructs it as a proposition.

The first option would describe the relationship between reports and claims by stressing the difference between the meaning and the reference of *S is p.* When we use *S is p* as a report we are focused upon the speaker's intentional referent. As we go about our tasks, the string functions to direct us in one way and not another. What fulfills the string may "fit" the noematic content more or less; we let the task define just how tight that fit has to be. We discover how reference is possible by reflecting upon the meaning of the string, which in this case is what Frege called the thought and what Husserl called the proposition or the intended state-of-affairs. In this reflection I discover what was "unthematic," but nevertheless already present, in our use of the report. The proposition forms the "matter" or the "noema" of the act and accounts for the act taking the object in the way that it does. Thus the theory: because using *S is p* as a report implicitly uses *S is p* as a claim, the report is made possible because its meaning is a proposition that forms the intentional content of my act of taking x as p.

The second option would attempt to account for the tie between reports and claims without treating the claim *S is p* as the condition of the possibility of the report *S is p*. There is a "straightforward" use of *S is p* in which it functions to articulate the as-structure of phenomena. As long as this is not challenged, as a result of either the speaker finding the report muddled and/or discrepancies with what appears, the report is believed or accepted, and we get on with the business at hand. The report, however, can be challenged. That challenge of, or turn upon, the report is what produces the proposition; i.e., the challenge is constitutive of *S is p*'s expressing a claim intended by the speaker. If we call the proposition the meaning of the string, then it cannot be the condition of our using *S is p* as a report for the simple reason that the proposition is produced only by reflecting upon reports. Part of reflecting upon the report being offered is asking what it means, i.e., what claim is being put forward. The noematic content undergoes a change: the working, "good enough" scheme of differentiation is replaced by concepts set in opposition to other concepts, which are used to sort objects or to attribute properties to those objects. At the same time the purpose of the reflection is to raise the question of truth in relation to the initial report. This allows us to see an internal connection: the claim becomes a *rule* that we follow if we report correctly.

What is Husserl's own position on this alternative? In texts written between the *Logical Investigations* and *Ideas I,* and in *Ideas I* itself, Husserl clearly takes the first option, thus placing him in a long line of thinkers stretching back to Aristotle. He explicitly states this in his 1908 lectures on the theory of meaning. After distinguishing between (a) the object to which an assertion refers and (b) "what is said as such" and given as an "objectivity" in reflection upon the assertion, Husserl identifies the latter as the noematic meaning of the act. What is said or thought as such is just the "object taken in the manner in which it is meant or thought."[64] Since it is both ideal and given in reflection or a "nominalization," Husserl calls the meaning a "categorial objectivity" and sometimes a "propositional [objectivity]."[65] The act of reflection does not create the propositional objectivity but discovers it as something already there:

> the categorial [is determined] as the objectivity that, so to speak, is conscious to us *implicite* and that becomes an object-about-which [we reflect] through a new positioning of the gaze, the "categorial reflection," and through a nominalization following in it.[66]

The theory of modalizations above, however, clearly shows Husserl moving in the direction of the second option, with one important qualification. Husserl always maintains the difference between the meaning and reference of a string, even when he argued for the dependence of reference upon meaning in his theory of intentionality. The difference, then, is also manifested in *a different characterization of meaning* for reports and claims, not just in their differing reference. Even though we derive claims from a reflection upon reports, we cannot view propositions as merely the meaning of reports. Does Husserl ever support this second option?

Elsewhere,[67] I have suggested that Husserl's later reflections on the question of language, and on the difference between ordinary and scientific or rigorous speech, move him beyond his first construction of meaning as an atemporal, ideal object. I suggested three reasons: (a) the analysis of modalizations shows that acts of claiming are themselves implicitly tied to other types of acts; (b) the "ideality" of meaning becomes construed in terms of a scheme of repeatability of signs in similar contexts with similar backgrounds; and (c) the intersubjective, dialogical dimensions of language determine both the manner in which meaningful strings are employed and the manner in which their meanings are constituted. To capture this difference, I labeled the meaning of reports a "conceptual scheme." Clearly this is a task for further study; we will return to the question of meaning in our final chapter once we have the notion of context in hand. For now a provisional sketch of the relationship between the two options must suffice. The key to working out a characterization of the meaning of reports that does not treat it as a proposition (Frege's thought) is to recognize that claims are already a form of reflective discourse in which the conceptual scheme of the report is itself objectified and configured as a thought or proposition or rule. If the rule regulates the sentences first used as reports it becomes a claim. In the *Crisis*, as we will see in chapter 13, understanding the difference between these two types of sentences is crucial for understanding both what Husserl called the process of "activation" or "reactivation," of requiring certain accepted reports to be submitted to analysis, and what he called "sedimentation," whereby claims settle into shared beliefs and become part of the everyday discourse of a community.[68]

When we place this difference between epistemic and nonepistemic uses of *S is p* alongside the difference we drew above, between epistemic and nonepistemic types of perception, the following distinctions in types of meaning or sense are required by constitutive phenomenology.[69] Husserl does not bring his various discussions together in this way; we are clearly going beyond both his terminology and his analysis. Hopefully the following charts will serve to map the basic differences among types of acts (chart 1), and types of meaning (chart 2), that have to be accommodated by any adequate theory of the significational component or noematic content of these kinds of intentional acts.

Speech here is restricted to the use of the grammatical unit *S is p* (and by implication, any compounds of that same form). All we can do here is designate the terms that a full account would set in contrast to each other and then briefly characterize them:

1. The meaning of a claim is thematized by the nominalized form of the report (*S is p* → *that S is p*) and is a proposition that (a) regulates *S is p* when used to propose a state-of-affairs, and (b) can itself be characterized by three different sets of rules: (i) apophantic rules giving certain syntactic conditions for framing well-formed claims; (ii) intensional conditions in which the content of the proposition's predicates can be rendered as concepts and then demarcated in relation to other concepts; and (iii) ontic rules that give us the truth-conditions under which *S is p* could be true and thereby could qualify as a claim.

2. If the analysis of the meaning of claims consists of a reflection upon the (logical) content of statements, then the analysis of the meaning of reports focuses upon schemes of conceiving that account for the intentional structure of reports. As a consequence, the meaning of predicates of reports is characterized not in terms of a content under truth-conditions but relationally, in terms of signs standing in paradigmatic and syntagmatic relation to the predicate as it functions to facilitate our involvement with things. The scheme of use and possible uses gives us access to the predicate's conceptual import, which for its part may be characterized as a mental model, thus involving the imagination. Reports, in short, are tools that enable us to engage the world in terms of plans of action and interaction.

3. Perceptual senses, we suggested, are the noematic components of nonepistemic, or what Husserl calls "passive," forms of perception. They are schemata that can be characterized in terms of three types of syntheses (aesthetic, spatial, and temporal) that are part of the way we assimilate what we experience as we perceptually accommodate our senses to the world.

4. Epistemic perception, by contrast with nonepistemic perception, is understood as a form of perceptual recognition guided and "invited" by the concepts employed in speech. As in the case of claims, there is a certain reflective element in play, and, for example, the similarity and difference passively apprehended in apperception itself becomes the focus of our perceptual concern. We not only see x as similar to y but we also see the similarity of x to y. We move to a perceptual explication of the type in play, usually guided by the

	Perception	Speech
Epistemic	Perceptual Recognition	Claiming
Nonepistemic	Originary Perception	Reporting

Types of Acts

	Perception	Speech
Epistemic	Perceptual Type	Propostion
Nonepistemic	Perceptual Schema	Conceptual Schema

Types of Noematic Content

Fig. 7.2. Types of Noematic Content

conceptual system that we are employing in this particular field or in view of this one task.

In departing from a straightforward exposition of Husserl, I am attempting to sort out and bring order to different aspects of his analysis. While it is hardly adequate as a developed theory of the different types of sense, my extrapolation gives us a rough picture of certain important distinctions and raises a few problems about two recent discussions concerned with the constitution of meaning and objects. Both the analytic phenomenological interpretation of the noematic object as the X bearing predicates,[70] and the closely related, recent attempt by Dieter Henrich to resurrect a notion of the thing-in-itself,[71] are the inevitable products of a certain treatment of *S is p*. Let me attempt to catch them both in a single net.

Even if we grant that F(x) reproduces the structure of *S is p* when used as a proposition, the analyses by many analytic phenomenologists and by Henrich make four assumptions, all of which are problematic in the light of our study thus far:

a. All perceiving is a form of knowing, which in turn is defined as propositional in nature.
b. The structure of *all* sentences of the form *S is p* can be given a Fregian interpretation and thus reproduced by F(x).
c. F(x) is primitive and thus mirrors the basic structure of things or, respectively, articulates the basic elements of our cognitive relationship to things.
d. All determinations of the thing are conveyed by F.

Given these four assumptions, the conclusion that x stands for the X bearing predicates (logical version) or the thing-in-itself (ontological version) is inescapable.

Husserl's response, which we can only indicate on the basis of the analysis offered above, would look something like this:

a. If one defines understanding as propositional in nature, then originary perception is not a form of understanding precisely because it is prelinguistic. Husserl would reject such a restricted notion of understanding and speak of a prepropositional acquaintance or experience that is based in perception. Its analysis, once we comprehend the nature of constitutional phenomenology, is given not in a "transcendental analytic" but a "transcendental aesthetics."[72]
b. At best F(x) gives only the form of the propositional uses of *S is p*. In fact, it may not even give that much, if we think of the "is" as based in a form of categorial synthesis irreducible to either the identifying acts associated with *S* or the acts of sorting or attributing linked to *p*, as Husserl suggested in the Sixth Investigation.[73]
c. F(x) is derived from and depends upon a transformation of our nonepistemic modes of speaking and seeing into the epistemic modes of proposing and recognition. It may be basic, but it is not primitive.
d. Perceptual objects have determinations that are phenomenologically explained by recourse not to concepts but to *types*, perceptual structures that are preconceptual in nature. They constitute the perceptual qualities of things. In fact, the determinations of an object given in perception must themselves undergo a process of "objectification" before they become the properties of a thing picked out by F.

If Husserl's analysis is correct, if the difference between using *S is p* as a report and as a truth claim can be clarified by a theory of modalizations and different interests, then we have a rather precise way of relating a phenomenological *grammatical analysis* to a *logical analysis* of both the meaning and the reference of sentences, and of relating linguistics to logic. This would be quite valuable, for the confusion of these two levels is one of the most pernicious and perduring of philosophical errors.

These results, then, show us what a constitutive account of assertions or claims that integrates perception might look like. Such an account would rest on underlying levels of (a) reports, which use rough and ready conceptual schemata to organize their registrations of facts, (b) negations, in which passive syntheses of perception create conflicts with what is anticipated on the basis of reports, (c) doubts, which transform the thetic attitude of belief into puzzlement, (d) questioning, in which we thematize predicates as concepts or as functions in the logical sense and consider their applicability, and (e) obligations to our speech partner to tell the truth. These strata form the vertical axis of constitution. While we have given a description that is especially appropriate to the region of physical objects and facts, it also serves as a model for a transcendental constitutive account of other regions. In the case of persons and social and cultural formations, the account of experience becomes much more complex, as does the way language configures and represents experience.

The striking result of this analysis, I would suggest, is that it enables us to see how the interplay of (ordinary) language and (nonepistemic) perception that is constitutive of a regional field is internally tied to the dialectic of assertions and confirmation that produce our regional ontologies. In the final analysis, this is what makes our ontologies phenomenological and gives them their roots in the world.

8

The Turn to Genetic Analysis

> For more than a decade I have already overcome the stage of static Platonism and have framed the idea of transcendental genesis as the main theme of phenomenology.
>
> —Husserl to Natorp (1918)[1]

> To trace [the order of] constitution is not to trace the [order of] genesis, which is, precisely, the genesis of constitution, itself actuated as genesis in a monad.
>
> —Husserl (1921)[2]

> This year was a time of great interpretative reflections [*Besinnungen*]. I thought through yet a final time [*sic*] the principle, basic ideas and lines of direction of phenomenology.
>
> —Husserl to Grimme (1922)[3]

> Of particular importance, but noticed only very late [in the historical development of the analysis of internal experience], is the fact that reflective, so-called "internal," experience has very many levels and depth-dimensions and is exceedingly difficult to put into practice whenever one strives to go beyond the most superficial level. Indeed, at first one had no inkling at all of the depths and mediacies. One did not see that internal experience is not a simple reflection which would lead without further ado to the concreteness of the respective interiorities, but that the concrete admitted of being grasped as a theme only in many levels of reflection, that internal experience is a process of disclosure to be effected in ever new reflection.
>
> —Husserl (1925)[4]

A. BRIDGING STATIC AND GENETIC ANALYSIS

The effect of our account of Husserl's Cartesian way was to differentiate between static analysis and the Cartesian formulation of it and simultaneously to reopen the question of how to contrast static and genetic phenomenology once beyond that formulation. Discovering the limits of the Cartesian way does not in itself justify the introduction of a genetic account. At first it requires only a non-Cartesian formulation of static analysis, which we have already sketched in chapters 2 through 4 and 7. This undertaking changes Husserl's focus from a grounding transcendental *structure,* absolute subjectivity, to a transcendental *field,* co-coordinated by horizontal and vertical axes, in which constitutive descriptions move. Since these two axes cover both surface and depth of the phenomenological field, they seem exhaustive. This claim is further substantiated by the surprising fact that our constitutive analysis of perception has already invoked the notions of retention and protention, recollection and expectation. According to Husserl's theory, the analysis of temporality brings us to the most basic "form," the deepest "absolute"[5] beyond which there is nothing further to explore.

This issue dovetails with a second. The claim that Husserl has a systematic phenomenology raises a serious challenge: to account for the radical diversity and heterogeneity of that which is covered by the term genetic phenomenology. Husserl applies this label to areas so different from one another that we are perplexed as to how they could ever be placed under a single category and why he even attempts to do so. In the early 1920s Husserl wrote that genetic analysis gives an account of "the ethical form of life as an a priori and essential formation of possible human life," and even "the idea of true humanity and its method of giving shape to itself."[6] But it also deals with "the constitutive physiological processes and the way in which they condition the unity of a physical world with a counterposed lived body."[7] Genetic phenomenology somehow bridges two extremes of (a) macrocosmic analyses of ethical and cultural contributions to our present understanding and experience of the world, even including the entire history of scientific and philosophical thought in a series of articles Husserl wrote from 1922 to 1924[8] and then again in the *Crisis;* and (b) detailed microcosmic accounts of precultural, structural components of our most rudimentary perceptions and the way in which they yield a shared experience of nature. We might well wonder whether genetic analysis simply designates all the issues left out of consideration, for either contingent or principled reasons, by static phenomenology. While consistently standing in opposition to static theory then, genetic analysis itself may lack any systemic tie between its diverse topics. If Husserl was merely sweeping together the remainders left by static phenomenology, it would be futile to seek a unifying principle to such studies, and, as a consequence, to argue that Husserl actually has a systematic phenomenology.

In this chapter, I will continue the account begun in the last chapter and then locate, as precisely as possible, the issues which motivated Husserl's development of genetic phenomenology. In our examination of Husserl's method we have already found a certain mode of analysis and a trajectory that Husserl himself, it seems, did not fully grasp until he began to elaborate upon his notion of "horizon." This will guide us into the internal connection between the diverse aspects of Husserl's theory.

Husserl's engagement with Frege's theory, we tend to forget, means that the *Logical Investigations* were as concerned with the limits of an objectivist or formalist as it was with a critique of a psychologistic theory of meaning. Frege argued that both predicate terms, what he called "concept-words," and, at another level, propositions, have an intension that can be set in contrast to their extension. Yet his formalist *specification* of their content and of the difference between their meaning and reference is exhausted by an account of truth-conditions.[9] It does not require recourse either to the acts or achievements supporting propositional content, or to an experiential account of the way in which propositions are "saturated" or confirmed. Frege systematically blocked any effort to supplement his theory with intentional descriptions. With this restriction, referents could be described only as givens explicable in and through the terms used to refer to or sort them, i.e., either as objects named by the subject term or as instances that fall under the predicate term.

Husserl's approach to these issues, we saw in the last chapter, was to drive a wedge between conditions of meaning and conditions of truth and to treat propositions as the correlates of epistemically vested speech-acts. Already in his *Logical Investigations* he saw that more than a *categorial* analysis of those conditions essential to the construction or fulfillment of meaningful claims was needed; an account of the *dynamic* interplay between the activities of framing claims and of then achieving experiential confirmation was also required.[10] Because the "content" of the two does not coincide, confirmation constantly gives rise to expansion and further elaboration, which, in turn, calls for additional evidence.

In the *Logical Investigations* Husserl was content to let this structural interplay of proposing and confirming define his notion of horizon. It stood, roughly, for the background of preconscious content, both propositional and experiential, that supported ongoing intentions and that is implicit or unthematic in a given fulfillment. To be sure, this was a vast improvement over Frege, for it included a rich account of both propositional acts and experiential objects. Yet even here the idea that fulfillment involved a coincidence between intentional content (characterized as an abstract logical entity) and intuitively presented content, together with the idea that the background was understood as the prethematic content logically or semantically entailed by a particular fulfillment, meant that noematic content in general was leveled and modeled after propositional content. In addition, the content fulfilling the intention was treated mainly in terms of its identity or "coincidence" (*Deckung*) with the intended content. Husserl had found the key contrast he needed between the conceptual content of propositional acts and the determinate content of experiential acts; he fixed it terminologically as a difference between meaning (*Bedeutung*) and sense (*Sinn*).[11] But his restriction of the *characterization* of this contrast to the sphere of well-formed and, then, confirmed judgments tended to compress the scopes of both, to collapse the features that distinguished them, and thus to limit his notion of horizon to something like a semantic field of paradigmatic substitutions.

In the 1920s Husserl came to view his first phenomenology, initially proposed in his *Logical Investigations* and then transposed into a transcendental register in *Ideas I,* as adequate for placing the foundations of logic beyond the alternatives of psychologism and formalism, although still in need of an expanded account. By design, the whole question of temporality, and, consequently, of transformation and development had been suspended.[12] In an effort to expand his account Husserl returned at this time to the issues with which he began in the First Investigation, in particular to perceptual experience and speech. Looking at further developments in his theory of perception and language will give us access to the systemic tie between static and genetic analysis.

In order to properly situate Husserl's first detailed genetic account of perception, and thereby genetic analysis in general (found in the manuscripts now collected in *Analysen zur passiven Synthesis*), we need first to place these texts in relation to a striking development in Husserl's own thought after *Ideas I.* Originally Husserl projected three volumes to his *Ideas Pertaining to a Pure Phenomenology and Phenomenological Philosophy.* The first was published in 1913, but the second remained in manuscript form and the third progressed no further than sketches. In 1924 and 1925, Landgrebe revised the original editing that Edith Stein had done on these manuscripts; but even then, as Landgrebe reports it, Husserl viewed them only as "materials."[13] No doubt the war, the loss of one son, the serious wounding of another (twice), and the difficult times afterwards all contributed to Husserl's decision to set this project aside; but it was his desire to press further in his understanding of the phenomenological method that was decisive. In 1921 he began preparing what he called a "large systematic work," a project that superseded his original plan to finish the publication of the three volumes of *Ideas.* At the end of November 1921, he wrote Roman Ingarden: "For several months now I have been working through my much too large manuscripts and am planning a large systematic work, which, building up from below, could serve as [the] foundational work of phenomenology."[14]

This plan for a systematic work provides the framework for two of Husserl's most important and productive texts: his lectures on transcendental logic, first given in the Winter Semester of 1920/21, and what are known as the St. Margen manuscripts on time, the bulk of which were composed during the summer break of 1921 (August to the end of October). For our purposes it is the former that is of primary importance.

In another letter to Ingarden the very next month, Husserl reassured him that he would not "overthrow" *Ideas I*, even though a number of its points were not well developed and all of its principle matters needed to be "purified." "Indeed, I have come so much further," he says.[15] In this context, Husserl mentioned his lectures over four semesters but specifically had in view his lectures on transcendental logic, first given in the Winter Semester of 1920–21. The bulk of these lectures, which were given again in the Summer Semester of 1923 and the Winter Semester of 1925–26, has been printed as *Analysen zur passiven Synthesis,* the text from which we draw so much for our analysis. Husserl worked on them intensely, and their importance became clear to others as well. Pfänder, writing from Munich, knew of them;[16] and one of Pfänder's students, Phillip Schwarz, decided to begin his further studies in Freiburg early in order to hear them.[17] This material is clearly bound up with Husserl's efforts to expand the scope of his previous phenomenology and to develop a system. While planning and drafting these lectures, he wrote Bell in September of 1920: "I want to draft the Logic [lectures] in an entirely new spirit, as the most universal formal doctrine of the principles of the whole of philosophy. In its main line I am coming to a—system. . . . "[18] The lectures, he also told Ingarden that December, were "the fruit of labor over many years."[19] It seems that his belief in the importance of these lectures for his system only increased when they were repeated in the Winter Semester of 1925/26, for he wrote Mahnke during that semester that they treat "the basic fundamentals of a systematic phenomenology of world-constitution. . . . "[20]

The invitation to give the London lectures in the summer of 1922 delayed his progress on the Logic, however, since the first half of 1922 was spent largely on their preparation. Husserl then offered a lecture course, "Introduction to Philosophy,"[21] during the Winter Semester of 1922/23. In a letter to Bell in December 1922, he referred to these lectures in connection with his effort to construct a systematic method, and he was very emphatic about the issue of a proper "beginning" or point of access to a systematic method:

> It is for me the most difficult course and actually I have been working, for over a year, on the systematic course of thought that I am now bringing to lecture form—it is the same that was lectured in London in compressed form. It has become clearer time and again for me—that precisely from being bound to teaching and from the many, under different titles, attempted lectures directed toward an introduction into phenomenology—that here is where one of the largest tasks of a system of philosophy lies: the question [*Aufgabe*] of the proper beginning, the guided ascent of the knower from the step of natural conceptual naiveté to the step of the beginning of "absolutely justified science," that of "philosophy."[22]

With the lectures he gave in London just behind him, we see him blending elements of his Cartesian way into his thinking about a system of phenomenology. The letter continues:

> The production of the correct motivation, laying clear the necessity of "beginning" with the ego cogito, to give it the sense of the phenomenological reduction, of moving from transcendental consciousness and ego to the eidetic analysis of the transcendental sphere, and thereby to expand the ego, the pure I to the "I-all," taking up empathy, and so on—I am breaking my head over this, which is not for indolent people.[23]

This effort to find a proper route into his systematic phenomenology, to find an appropriate point of access, led to frustration. "Introduction to Philosophy" builds upon but adjusts the Cartesian approach of the London lectures, thereby complicating its execution. A year later, Husserl began to explore in systematic fashion alternative routes to the reduction in "First Philosophy," a lecture course held during the Winter Semester of 1923–24.[24] His concerns with a proper beginning, a point of access to transcendental analysis, deflected Husserl from his original design of constructing a systematic phenomenology. It took him another five or six years to return to it. From this, though, we can see that the concrete execution of a genetic phenomenology of perception, the focus of *Analysen zur passiven Synthesis,* was designed to be a fundamental part of his systematic approach to phenomenology.

There is a second way that we can approach the manuscripts now published as *Analysen zur passiven Synthesis.* When we place them next to later works, we discover that Husserl thought of the former as an extended introduction to *Formal and Transcendental Logic.* This work, above all others, effectively challenged his earlier neglect of the relationship between ordinary and rigorous, scientific discourse (and, we might add, the implications of this for the characterization of noematic content) in earlier accounts. Originally the bulk of what we now have as *Passive Synthesis* included the word "Urkonstitutionen" in one of its subtitles[25] and is referred to as a piece of "genetic logic" in another manuscript.[26] On the basis of textual evidence, we can see that this material actually belongs to the introductory sections of *Formal and Transcendental Logic* but was excluded from the main sections of the text.[27] From a systematic point of view, he assumed that the analysis of "passive" synthesis had already been carried out and he concentrated on issues directly concerned with formal and then transcendental logic, with "active" synthesis.

Husserl's concern in these manuscripts was to radically expand the field of studies first circumscribed by Kant's Transcendental Aesthetic.[28] In them, Husserl studied not only time and space, which he reinterpreted phenomenologically, but also certain basic structures of perceptual experience, in play "before" those that are regulated by Kant's categories and his Transcendental Logic. Even when he did turn to a logic, Husserl provided both an account of certain necessary conditions presupposed by judgments about experience, and an account of the genesis of judgments, of those structural transformations of both experience and language that constitute the level of theoretic, representational discourse. The particular issue that he explored in these lecture manuscripts, one that brought his account of perception together with the account of logic in *Formal and Transcendental Logic*, can be understood as the problems of *passive synthesis* and *perceptual modalities*. These problems amount to variations in acts and contexts that impact meaning without necessarily finding direct expression in propositional content. As we saw, this calls forth a distinct characterization not only of perceptual sense but also of the constitutive dimensions of meaning. The latter cannot be grasped through reflection upon either the truth-conditions of the logical content of truth-claims, or the meaning interpreted phenomenologically in terms of logical "meaning-bestowing" acts. Husserl's expanded account of meaning effected a certain contextualization and, thereby, traced the "genesis" of the type of speech-act and perceptual act that static analysis had privileged and understood as basic. This movement accounts for both the underlying unity and the diversity of genetic analyses.

As we sketched in the last chapter, the treatment of perception in terms of passive synthesis, the primary achievement of Husserl's lecture course, amounted to a reconsideration of his static form-content schematization of perception. Not only did he see this dyad as provisional but, more importantly, he also understood the type of perception he first set in relation to propositions—what we can now see as epistemic perceptual recognition guided by conceptual differences—as limited and as controlled by an interest in confirmation, in securing evidence. This type of perception presupposes a broader background of perceptual awareness laden with determinacy and, thus, a type of aesthetic significance that requires its own characterization. Once he framed this background not just as a "condition" of the structure of cognition but also as a motivational matrix that accounts for the *development* of cognition, he moved into a genetic account.

Analogously, propositional discourse arises from ordinary interactive talk and involves certain transformations that make speech capable of bearing the type of referential relationship to objects and facts that model-theoretic accounts claim for it. For example, when Frege speaks of the concept as the referent of the predicate term, he is correct in the sense that the determination of truth turns upon reports, focuses upon the silent meaning displayed in our use of predicates, and, as a result, treats it as an abstract idea that can be defined and then specified in terms of a rule-governed relationship to real objects and facts. The surface structure of the resulting statements may be the same as everyday sentences, but the *use* of predicates in propositions is already a way of *mentioning* and objectifying their meaning as content. In our search for objectivity and confirmation, we are as focused on the scientific or objective concepts we employ as we are on the objects or facts to which they apply. The interest in objective truth and rigorously definable ideas does not simply pick out the meaning that signs already have. Instead, it builds up, through stipulation and operational descriptions, a concept that can be granted admission to the language of science. However, these signs are already laden with meanings of their own, which is to say that meaning logically characterized is possible only against a context of linguistic meaning (with other dimensions) that will never be captured by a search for "cores" of content. Furthermore, the meaning of everyday discourse is not eternally fixed but undergoes development and change. For the later Husserl there are three bridges to the dynamic, historical interplay between ordinary language and the discourse of truth: the undergirding of claims by ordinary discourse, the ever recurring sedimentation of truth talk into ordinary life and thought, and the fact that ordinary talk is changed by the way it functions in our involvement with things.

B. VERTICAL DEPTH

In order to provide a synoptic view of the specific concerns and the scope of Husserl's genetic phenomenology, I will step back from an analysis of his texts for a moment. While keeping to the account of experience and judgment that we have employed thus far, I will consider what would be required to give a full account of meaning and, thereby, intentionality. I would suggest that an adequate account of the relationship between intentional life and phenomena along Husserlian lines would distinguish three levels. They would be found within the field of analysis opened by the vertical axis of phenomenological clarifications. Figure 8.1 is an attempt to interpret Husserl's genetic analysis as a program designed to give us access to the third level and to understand the third level's relations to the first two. I will make only a few suggestions about the internal structure of each level, treating them as Husserl would, and then describe its connection to the others.

1. A *logical* characterization of meaning views meaning as a rule-governed relationship between representations, be they logical signs or abstract mental entities, and real entities, be they objects, facts, or, in some recent versions, factual situations. Being sensitive to the diversity of discourse, a *phenomenological* characterization of assertions does not reject the possibility of formalizing the tie between signs and referents in this way. Instead, it requires a supplement that incorporates both the "logical acts" in and through which such ties are achieved and the experiential acts in and through which referents come to be observed. Observation is an *epistemic* type of perception in that its primary goal is to secure confirmation of the claim under consideration. It is guided or directed by the concepts expressed in propositions; when it sees X *as* Y, the Y is specified by a particular node in the conceptual map in play. Epistemic perception ranges from perceptual reading, where the lack of determinacy in what is experienced is settled by a certain interpretation in view of an existing body of knowledge, to perceptual re-cognition, where the observer is asked to match data to a certain conceptual template or to pick them

Discourse Types and Conditions	*Discourse Field*	*Referential Field*	*Experiential Types and Conditions*
		Level One	
Theoretic Representational Discourse	Scientific Language	Established Objects and Facts	Epistemic Perceptual Observation
		Level Two	
Communicative Interaction	Ordinary Speech	Everyday Things and Complexes	Nonepistemic Perceptual Involvement
		Level Three	
Narrative and Metaphoric Models	Context	Background	Affective and Corporeal Archetypes

Fig. 8.1

out according to a set of instructions. Epistemic perception expects a yes or no answer from things, although it does not always receive one. Here the characterization of (epistemic) perception as hermeneutic or interpretative applies without equivocation; since perceiving is organized in terms of differences that are conceptual in content. What is seen is always an instance or example of the objective fact *as* described. Furthermore, confirmation often involves the mediation of instrumentation and experimentation and a "reading" that is special to them. In these cases we might even want to speak of a "double reading," for the interpretative reading of instruments is essential to specifying the reading of phenomena as facts.

2. While the phenomenological "supplement" to a logical characterization requires the integration of (logical) acts into the account of meaning, as well as rules covering not just signs and referents but also acts, it is still not adequate to capture all the dimensions, or even a basic dimension of the meaning of discourse in general. This first level rests on others which have no direct representation in its propositional content or structure, because the protologic necessary to develop a language of propositions introduces certain

critical *exclusions* that, once effected, are then "forgotten." Setting aside the interesting question of the relationship between logical and linguistic syntactic structure, propositions undergo at least these semantic transformations that set them in contrast with ordinary language:

a. For propositions, signs are freed from four types of functions: (i) *instrumental* or *performative* functions by virtue of which they become tools to appropriate or move things (the word "brick" spoken by a master to the apprentice), (ii) *analogue* functions by virtue of which their physical properties are direct representations of what they stand for (contrasting lengths of line to different height), (iii) *indicative* functions by virtue of which they refer on the basis of a perceptual "associative" tie to an object (smoke and fire), and (iv) *intimating* functions by virtue of which they exhibit, in excess of what is directly referred to in the claim, something of the speaker's mental state or history (wishes or hopes). Only what Husserl calls their *expressive* function is preserved; i.e., they refer by virtue of a meaning, which is a conceptual, rule-governed tie between signs and referents. In short, linguistic signs are described only to the extent that they are capable of bearing an ideal meaning. With the elimination of these functions, speech-acts are necessarily construed as meaning-bearing or meaning-bestowing acts. Speech-acts are reduced to *expressive* acts.
b. Furthermore, the meaning expressed is constrained by the need to provide direct representations. Logical expressions are *objective* inasmuch as, first, *metaphorical* concepts are eliminated and replaced by a redescription of the fact or situation using *literal* meaning; second, *subjective* variations in meaning are, in principle, disassociated and then each delimited according to its ideal content; and third, *occasional* or indexical expressions, which depend upon a perception of a concrete situation for their meaning, can be replaced by those that do not. In the simultaneous suspension of poetic, praxical, and bodily dimensions of meaning, the expressive act is reduced to its role of bearing objective meaning. Expressive acts, as a consequence, are all *logical* acts.
c. Finally, the speaker is understood as one bound not to his or her culture but to the rule of reason. The meaning of expressions is not just described but also submitted to analysis and, when necessary, stipulated. If communicative interaction is considered, only the ideal community of speakers is envisioned. The telos of rigorous discourse is the construction of a language that can be freed from cultural relativity even as it is shared across cultures.

Though "forgotten," these transformations give rise in varying degrees to propositional discourse. Only within these parameters can a logical characterization of meaning—and a phenomenology built upon it—get started and have validity. When we rescind these transformations, we return to ordinary discourse and to dimensions of meaning suspended or, better, hidden by propositional structure. Doing so opens the possibility of a phenomenology basic to a *linguistic* characterization of meaning that is concerned with ordinary discourse.

3. We must wait until the last chapters of this book to develop the connection between the meaning of ordinary discourse and the context of that discourse. The analysis of perception in terms of a characterization of background will likewise be handled there. For our present purposes we need only a few ideas to set the second in contrast to the third level.

The phenomenological characterization of meaning that takes its bearings from propositional discourse treats meaning as an ideal entity, with relations of logical entailment to other ideal meanings, and then interprets meaning as an abstract, intentional structure. Meaning is understood as a self-identical content that supports its relationship to other nodes in the conceptual map and simultaneously makes reference possible. Use is a function of form or structure, i.e., it is not itself constitutive of content. By contrast, a linguistic characterization takes its bearings from ordinary language and reads structure from function. Husserl began to move in this direction but did not fully clarify the way in which the meaning of ordinary discourse should be treated. Had he done so, it would have resulted in a different characterization of meaning (and of noematic content), where meaning would be seen not as an ideal object but as a *differential structure* in which its relationship to other signs as used in a semantic field would be constitutive of "content." The meaning of a string is determined by (a) the *syntagmatic* relation that a sign has to other signs with different syntactic markers in the same string, (b) the *paradigmatic* relation that a sign with a particular syntactic marker has to other signs in a given semantic *field* that could be substituted for it, and (c) what we might call the *syntagmatic* relation that a given string has to other sentences in a given discursive *context.* An adequate characterization of meaning, therefore, requires recourse not just to rules of substitution, themselves dependent upon the structure of a given semantic field, but also to context, to the interlocking sets of tacit beliefs that are in play. Fields and contexts, neither of which are directly *expressed* but only *indicated* or implied in the string itself, undergird a well-formed string and are intrinsic to the determination of its meaning.

At this second level, there is a corresponding change, which we will also introduce into our consideration of perception. Its role in our everyday involvement with things is integrated not into a project of representing the world but into one of assimilating and accommodating ourselves to it. Experienced things are present to us primarily as correlates of our actions, as items that we use and manipulate for a variety of practical tasks. Accordingly, nonepistemic perception is involved; i.e., it is more a matter of finding our way around things, or with things, than of observation. In Part 3 we will characterize the sense of experienced things in terms of a nexus of involvement.

At the third level, by contrast, we find controlling narrative and metaphoric images giving to a text or an extended piece of discourse both meaning and logic that exceed what can be derived from a logical or direct linguistic analysis of the parts, but which establish lines of implications that control the line of thoughts. These range from specifiable semantic fields that situate the use of a term; to underlying fore-conceptions or models that control pieces of text or segments of discourse; to paradigms, more or less definable, that "frame" communication for whole communities. This forms what I will call context.

Correspondingly, at the third level, experience is understood as situated within broad aesthetic, praxical, and affective fields. These highly diverse sets of conditions range from specific aesthetic fields (e.g., colors) with schematic clusters; to contrasting types of actions situating a given act or action; to types of embodied skills and motility supporting all actions; to acquired ways of handling things, which Husserl came to call "secondary sensibility"; to "habitualities"; and, finally, to that affectivity that delivers us as a whole over to the world, which Heidegger described as *Befindlichkeit.* In contrast to the types operative in the second level, we can speak of these as archetypes. I will call this background.

The second and third levels secure the historicity of our incarnate existence and, through their internal connection to the first, of our theoretical modes of framing the world. Logical discourse *rests* on ordinary discourse in the sense that it can be understood as a transformation of culturally and historically defined ways of comprehending the world. Logical discourse *becomes* ordinary discourse, introducing its own metaphors when it becomes accepted and disseminated, becomes *sedimented* into our everyday way of envisioning things. We can also find a parallel connection on the side of experience. Experimentation and observation always *arise* out of, and are situated against, a background of practical and aesthetic experience, transforming it in ways that never quite suspend its relative and contingent character. Yet the results of certain theoretical and practical disciplines are themselves transformative of the space in which we move, the paths we walk, the work we undertake. Action organized becomes production and production recreates environments. These achievements become *sedimented* into the world and take their place as part of the background in terms of which clusters of interactions acquire their significance as wholes.

This third level, however, is not so much a member of a series as a level that is found "behind" the first two. It gives us not a third type of meaning but the context and background found "between" strings. It is not a type of discourse as such, but instead includes narrative and metaphorical models at play in both everyday and logical discourse. In addition, it does not give us another type of sense, for it is not a third kind of experience. Rather, it is the clustering of senses constitutive of actions or affections into wholes that situate and frame entire regions of what we experience.

An expansion of the vertical axis to include background and context provides a link to what Husserl envisioned with genetic analysis. We have treated regional phenomenological ontologies or, given a shift in focus, regional disciplines, as situated along a horizontal axis. Their "clarification" employs a mode of analysis that traces the various noetic and noematic structures that are constitutive of each region. By using identity and difference, comparison and contrast, static phenomenology places each region in relation to the others, noting which elements of the others are derived and which are new in each.

The *ground* of the horizontal axis is intentionality, i.e., the correlational a priori that is both uncovered and secured by transcendental reflection. Constitutive analysis clarifies this ground in terms of a vertical axis that makes it possible, thereby transforming the transcendental into a *field*. The three levels we just sketched as transcendental, as opposed to ontological, structures are found along that axis. We give a genetic account when we represent these levels as more than a deep structure "implicated" or "implied" by the surface structure, understanding them also as field conditions that allow for the concrete *transformations* of intentionality by virtue of which one region emerges from another or is itself changed. Given the way the third level is internally tied to the other two, constitutive analysis leads to a genetic phenomenology that places its structures in relation to context and background—and thereby to historical contingency and development. In the next chapter I will suggest that the "spatial" images of "strata" so essential to Husserl's static phenomenology are not displaced but, in fact, are expanded and then supplemented by "temporal" images of generation. The structural account of differences in types of intentionality is expanded by a temporal account of how those differences come to be. The world is thus reframed as a *life*-world.

Of course, this thesis is no more than a promissory note. We have much more to do before we can tender it. The notion of genetic analysis is so difficult, as we will see, because Husserl developed it only after his static method was in hand and, to some extent, after it had been overextended, covering more than its own organizing principles would allow. This difficulty is compounded by the fact that the first two levels sketched above can also be studied "regionally," clouding their role as essential features of a transcendental account.

C. THE CRITIQUE OF GENETIC PSYCHOLOGY IN HUSSERL'S EARLY WRITINGS

As is true of most of the central concepts prominent in Husserl's later phenomenology, the notions of genesis, origins, and genetic explanation underwent a long and twisted development. I find three stages, the first of which will be sketched in this section.

In his very early work Husserl thought that descriptive psychology could provide insight into the foundations of mathematics and logic, only to realize later that phenomenology was something quite different. In his first major work, the *Philosophy of Arithmetic,*[29] he attempted to answer questions about the "origin" (*Entstehung*) or "sources" (*Quellen*) of the mathematical concepts of multiplicity and of magnitude by looking to the psychological activities of collective combination and comparison.[30] In a very loose sense we could say that this work provided an account of the generation of mathematical operations, though Husserl did not use the term "genetic" in his account. Coupling on to Kant, Husserl even uses time to define the notion of mathematical operation, but then subverts Kant by viewing it as a "psychological precondition."[31] Since Husserl always moves "back" from logical or arithmetical concepts to their psychological origin, he pays virtually no attention to an account of either the method as a whole or the psychological domain, either in his Habilitation of 1887[32] or in his *Philosophy of Arithmetic* of 1891.

Husserl came to reject this psychological interpretation of arithmetic, replacing it with a phenomenological one; this development is reflected in how the notion of "genetic" is treated in the *Logical Investigations.* While these earlier studies do not directly characterize psychology as a genetic discipline the first edition of the *Logical Investigations* (1900–1901) leaves no doubt that it is. In this text, Husserl distinguished between the method of phenomenology (which he, unfortunately, also calls "descriptive psychology") and naturalistic or empirical psychology, a method that he generally labels "genetic."[33] Roughly put, phenomenology is concerned with a description of the immanent contents of the stream of consciousness as manifest in "inner perception." By contrast, empirical psychology seems to be a "genetic" discipline that provides causal explanations of the origin and development of such content. But in the first edition of the Fifth Investigation, this opposition is elaborated in a way that makes it hard to sustain. Because of the pivotal role played by this opposition in Husserl's theory, we must dwell on his analysis there for a few moments.

In the first edition, Husserl employs the concept of genetic analysis in connection with the issue of whether there is any phenomenological evidence for the existence of an ego over and above the stream of experiences. While he did not believe that there was such evidence, Husserl suggested that we turn to "adequate" inner perception in order to settle the question.[34] The "core" of evidence "in the present moment" turns out to be just the concatenation of lived-experiences themselves. But this is not all that we find:

> To this region [i.e., the life of consciousness] there also comes forth what memory presents to us as what had been present earlier in evidence, thus belonging to one's own past ego. (Evidence or evident probability of the *I was.*) Then also everything that, on empirical [*sic*] grounds, can be assumed to co-exist with what at each instant is adequately perceived, i.e., as *continuously cohering* with it in *unity.* When I say here "continuously cohering with it in unity" I mean the unity of the concrete whole whose parts are either [dependent] *moments,* mutually founding and requiring each other in their co-existence, or [independent] *pieces* that, through their own nature in their co-existence, found forms of unity, real forms that actually belong to the content of the whole as internally indwelling moments. These unities of co-existence pass continuously from moment to moment into one another, constituting a unity of change [of the stream of consciousness], which, for its part, demands the continuous persistence or, at least, continuous change of a moment essential for the unity of the whole and, thus, inseparable from it as a whole. This role is played by subjective time-consciousness. . . .[35]

What discipline handles those areas that "co-exist" with what is adequately perceived? What type of analysis gives us an account of the unity, of the whole stream of experience? After speaking of "subjective time-consciousness" as the steady duration or change essential to the unity of concrete wholes of experience, the Fifth Investigation adds, mixing phenomenological with psychological analysis, that this time-consciousness is what constitutes "the content of the I as a soulish unity, as the self-enclosed, temporally developing unity of all its 'lived-experiences.'"[36] He employs the concept of the "soul" here, a notion that he, in *Ideas II,* unequivocally identified as designating a regional discipline, such as psychology. Since Husserl also thought at the time of the first edition of the *Investigations* that an analysis of the "ego" would be an analysis of the "soul," and that the "soul" belonged to psychology, he had difficulty distinguishing a psychology of the ego from its treatment in phenomenology proper. In the Fifth Investigation he explains that the "soul" is "what determines the area of psychology as a doctrine of 'psychic' lived-experiences or 'contents of consciousness.'"[37] He then supplies this mixed characterization of psychology, which, as far as I know, includes the only other occurrence of the word "genetisch" in the *Investigations.*

> Psychology's task—descriptively—is to study the ego-experiences (or conscious contents) in their essential species and forms of combination, in order to explore—genetically—their origin and perishing, and the causal patterns and laws of their formation and transformation. For psychology conscious contents are contents of an ego, and so its task is to explore the

> real essence of the ego . . . , to explore the interweaving of psychic elements in the ego, and their subsequent development and degeneration.[38]

To the extent that Husserl moves from descriptive psychology—which, except for the reference to the ego, must have the same content as phenomenology in the first edition—into explanatory psychology, he sees that one level of description, that of the structure of conscious content, calls for and even requires yet another, that of its "origin" and "transformation." The only things that prevent this analysis from being applicable to phenomenology as a whole are a rejection in the first edition of any "Kantian" notion of a "pure ego" on phenomenological grounds, and his bald statement that all he is capable of finding is "the empirical ego,"[39] which is what naturalistic psychology covers.

In fact the paragraph quoted above, belonging to a section that Husserl dropped in its entirety from the second edition, places his opposition between phenomenology and psychology, and then between phenomenology and genetic analysis, into a double bind. On the one hand, it seems that, in *contrast* to phenomenology, psychology deals with certain aspects of conscious life that are essential to its existence as a "concrete whole," such as the unity of conscious content with the past, the function of time-consciousness as a whole, and the notion of a concrete ego. On the other hand, psychology seems incomplete without the added genetic descriptions. Husserl quickly resolves the first bind. By the time of the second edition, all of the aspects of conscious life that originally belonged to psychology have become part of phenomenology proper. But this only pushed to the margins the genetic side of the original account of those aspects.

In the first stage, then, Husserl treated genetic analysis as a component of psychological analysis,[40] which he had difficulty keeping distinct from phenomenology since he envisioned the latter as descriptive psychology. The first stage came to a conclusion when this slight tendency toward integrating genetic analysis into descriptive analysis was emphatically reversed in the period between the first edition of the *Investigations* (1900–1901) and *Ideas I* (1913). As a result of the breakthrough to transcendental method introduced in a 1907 lecture course[41] and developed in *Ideas I,* Husserl rejected his first formulations and placed the notion of phenomenological description and its elaboration through the theory of constitution squarely in opposition to all psychological accounts of mental life. The subject matter of phenomenology, as he warned his readers in the Foreword (1913) to the second edition of his *Investigations,* is not "lived-experiences or classes of lived-experiences of empirical persons" but the structure of "pure" experience.[42] The consequence of this difference for our considerations is clear: since genetic analysis always belonged to a psychological description of the development of human cognition in the *Investigations,* it too is banished from his transcendental phenomenology to, at best, a part of the regional discipline of psychology.

Husserl later realized that a difference between "empirical psychology," at least as understood by the Empiricist tradition or the newly emerging experimental psychology, and his "descriptive psychology" existed as far back as the first edition. In the section deleted from the first edition, his own version of psychology distinguished between the descriptive content and the intended object of an act of perception and the place of acts in contrast to both. These notions must become "the foundation of scientific epistemology and psychology."[43] As Husserl emphasized in lectures in 1925, what gave his psychology in the *Investigations* "an essentially different countenance"[44] from those that came before was that its "aim was a purely epistemological one."[45] It attempted to cut a path between the empiricist valorization of psychology as the method of philosophy and the Kantian rejection of psychological descriptions as epistemologically irrelevant. Still, Husserl knew that, for all its "novelty," his theory was infected with an inescapable category mistake. However much the first edition of the *Investigations* also effected "an essential transformation"[46] of the idea of descriptive psychology as it was first defined by Brentano, it was limited in scope and did not "embrace the totality of all possible objects as such and the totality of possible consciousness as such, or of possible subjectivity as such."[47] Twenty-five years later, Husserl was much clearer as to the result:

> But as long as this analysis was thought of as empirical, the objection of the anti-psychologists could not be met, as to how a theory of knowledge, a science of the a priori principles which are supposed to make intelligible the possibility of objective productions of reason could be grounded in psychology, in an empirical science. Added to this is the fact that the founding descriptive or psycho-genetic investigations remained necessarily without results, that is, they were unable to lead to an understanding of the logical and the ethical because they were incapable of penetrating to any genuine intentional analysis.[48]

There is one final hint in the *Investigations,* however, that is rather suggestive. The Sixth Investigation distinguishes a "static" from a "dynamic" description of the relationship between two qualitatively different types of acts: speech-acts and intuitive or perceptual acts. Husserl contrasts a situation where our naming or describing is an act of recognizing (*Erkennen*) what is already perceptually present (static union), with one where the act of signification (speech-act) and the act of intuition are "disjoined in time" and where the "fulfillment" of the first by the second is "dynamic," taking on a "temporal pattern."[49] We saw in the last chapter that this need not be an account of temporality or of temporal generation but can be limited to the structural differences between acts that are distinguished by temporal markers. The "intending" or "signifying" act precedes either the intuitive act fulfilling it or the "synthesis of distinction" (*Unterscheidung*) in which the intuition creates "disagreement" or "conflict" with the initial intention.[50] Time serves only to "tag" numerically different acts. But there is an indication that something more might be in play when Husserl speaks not only of "the unity of identity" or the non-identity between intended and fulfilling object,[51] but also of the phenomenon of "partial identity," in which the fulfillment "contains *more* than its fulfillment needs."[52]

D. THE EMERGENCE OF GENETIC ANALYSIS IN HUSSERL'S MIDDLE WRITINGS

With the contrast between psychology, the discipline that houses all genetic descriptions, and transcendental analysis developing into a stable opposition by the time *Ideas I* was published in 1913, it comes as no small surprise to find a 1912 manuscript consciously using the term "genetic" in conjunction with phenomenology proper. This opens a second phase in Husserl's use of the notion of genetic analysis. There are two passages in a supplemental text to *Ideas III*, the volume concerned with the relationship between phenomenology and ontology, where Husserl introduces this notion to explain his theory of constitution. The first passage employs it only as an "image" or "picture," a product of our interpretative imagination. In fact, it is used just as another way of elaborating the relations of founding and founded, of ground and grounded, and of the dependency of some levels upon others, all of which is explicated by constitutive analysis:

> One can think of the formation of levels of the constitution using the image of a genesis, by imagining experience to be carried out actually only in the givens of the lowest level alone; then that which is new in the next level comes forth, and with it new unities are constituted, etc. But this is a genesis of the same sort as is carried out in mathematics. It would be most wrongheaded to think here of psychological genesis and of a [psychological] explanation of the ideas of the world and the ego which men in the world have. We are not dealing with that at all here. We are merely depicting what kind of strata lie in the *essence* of the real givens themselves and, on the other hand, what kind of strata here are in the apprehension of these data. . . .[53]

The second passage works with the ideas in the first in order to set constitutive phenomenology over against ontology. While ontology's mode of consideration is "katastematic," taking the unities it considers "in their identity" as something "fixed," and attempting to locate their place in a given regional topography,

> the phenomenological-constitutive consideration takes the unity in the flow, namely as unity of a constitutive flow. It follows up the movements, the courses, in which such unity and every component, side, [and] real property of such unity is the correlate of identity. This consideration is in a certain measure kinetic or "genetic": a "genesis" belonging to a totally different "transcendental" world as the natural and natural scientific genesis. . . . Each unity of cognition . . . has its "history" or also, speaking correlatively, the consciousness of this real thing has its "history," its immanent teleology in the form of a regulated system of modes of manifestation and authentication essentially belonging to it, modes that can be elicited from this consciousness, drawn out by questioning it.[54]

Here the reference to a teleological ordering suggests that what controls the analysis is something more than the idea of a simple unity accidentally or randomly fashioned. Rather this is a unity achieved in coordination with that "objective sense" of the whole that is both being determined by the ongoing course of experience through the system of sense implications in play, and is determining that course, ordering each profile as its adumbration. The organization is "teleological," which in Husserl's understanding means that the principle ordering the profiles is a set of rules that determine the structural identity of the object in terms of its projected "optimal" givenness. The progression of appearances toward this optimum will take place in time. Still, temporality is not one of the principles used to explain this progression. While we detect the beginnings of a new development in this text—it seems that this reference to a genesis belonging to "a totally different 'transcendental' world" opens a possibility that Husserl had not imagined to this point—temporality *per se* does not factor in the "history" that this analysis uncovers.[55] We are still within the confines of a constitutive account, however, and have not arrived at genesis proper.

The discussion thus far allows us to sort out three features of a constitutive account that should not be confused with genetic analysis proper. At the same time, we understand these features, once isolated, as bridges to genetic phenomenology.

1. In our description of the interplay of profiles and object, profiles were treated as a manifold of appearances that are not only materially (noematically) but also temporally (noetically) differentiated as they present the whole that is given through each of its profiles. But describing perception in this way is not yet genetic analysis proper because the account is still guided by the *unity* of the object and, thus, the profiles, while abstractable, are dependent elements presupposed by that unity. The "fixed" and "finished" types of objects and their respective intentional conditions provide us with the framework for this account. The added fact that this unity is understood as teleological means that it is specified and confirmed in the progressive *approxima-*

tions of our experiences of it. In other words, there is a "dynamic" side to static accounts in which the three nested levels of associative, spatial, and temporal synthesis could be understood only as "necessary conditions" of their being an experiential object or complex of this particular type. As long as we restrict the account to structural conditions of what we take at the outset as "finished," we still have not yet arrived at its becoming proper.

2. The relationship *between* levels can be understood strictly in terms of dyads such as "basic" and "derived," "simple" and "complex," "primary" and "secondary," "founding" and "founded." For example, to treat acts of asserting a claim as dependent upon a modal transformation of reporting into questioning, or acts of categorial intuition as presupposing sensuous intuition, or acts of aesthetic judgment as presupposing perception is to understand surface levels in terms of their conditions. Since this type of dependency can be gained through a consideration of *meaning*-implications and epistemic conditions, we have not yet understood the special content of a genetic account.

3. There is a related point that directly applies to the notion of horizon itself. It factored into our constitutive account as we placed assertions, for example, in the context of certain transformations of everyday discourse that are constitutive of them yet not "thematic" or directly expressed in their propositional content. Analogously, the notion of epistemic perception has a background of perceptual acquaintance that is "forgotten" in our more focused observation of things. But we have not yet covered the sense in which everyday discourse and nonepistemic perception are themselves situated in horizons, nor have we found a connection between horizons and their development. The theory of horizons, too, is still contained by the notion of setting "conditions."

What complicates our understanding of this middle stage is the fact that, between 1905 and 1910, Husserl developed the theory of time-consciousness, to which he also alludes in the first edition of the *Investigations*, without so much as mentioning the idea of a genetic analysis.[56] Given Husserl's conviction, expressed in 1922, that "time, seen from within, is the form of intentional genesis,"[57] and even that, as he puts it about a decade later, temporality "builds itself up in a constant, passive and fully universal genesis,"[58] we are left bewildered as to how this is possible. Clearly the account of time-consciousness belongs to the "first and most basic level" of "genetic problems,"[59] as Husserl puts it in the *Cartesian Meditations*. Yet the first extensive studies on time were undertaken well before Husserl had the notion of a genetic phenomenology in hand. If time is to provide the key to the meaning of genetic analysis, how is it that we have the rudiments of his theory of time well before genetic phenomenology took shape in Husserl's thought?

The relationship between the accounts of time and of genetic method is especially complex and will occupy us in the next chapter. Here we can only attend to a provisional answer to our immediate question. We find a certain development in Husserl's understanding of the nature of temporality not just between 1905 and about 1910, as studied in Brough's and Bernet's excellent accounts,[60] but also between that period and the early twenties. As Husserl reflected upon his first descriptions, he suggested that they treated time only according to its form, and viewed its transformations only as modalizations. As a result, we have arrived at, but not entered, a genetic account. To expand on an earlier quotation:

> With these descriptions, the constitutive ones, there is no question of an explanatory genesis. Nor is there one if we move from original impressions (perceptions)—as a generally typical or generic characterization applicable to all apperceptions—to a constitutive characterization, to descriptions of all the modal transformations in retentions, recollections, expectations, etc., and thereby follow a principle systematically ordering the apperceptions, one that [vertically] cuts across the sorting of the apperceptions according to the most general genera of objects. . . . [61]

To view time as a "generic" or "typical" feature or as a "modal transformation" of apperceptions is really to treat time as no different than other modal "forms." But "the span of living retention" belonging to the "living present," Husserl realized, is neither itself a modalization nor is it, by itself, capable of being modalized.[62] But in his account, the special tie between the non-modal phases of temporality or pre-modalized objects of experience and temporality itself is not clear.

We find other hints that Husserl grew increasingly concerned with his initial analysis of time. In particular the account of the present was too abstract, as though it were a form that could be severed from its content. Thus he says: "mere form is obviously an abstraction, and thus the intentional analysis of time and its achievement is, from the outset, an abstractive one." As a consequence, the first theory of time does not give us "the necessary synthetic structures of the streaming present and the unified stream of the present somehow affecting what is specific to content."[63] Husserl exclaimed: "and so the entire theory of time-consciousness is a conceptual idealization."[64] In short, we do not yet have a theory that articulates the "concrete present" in its essential "streaming,"[65] nor have we accounted for the sense in which time is *internal* to the "difference of content."[66] In view of these self-critical remarks, it seems plausible to suggest that the account of time-consciousness was initially a piece of *constitutive* phenomenology. As we will see, the transition to genetic analysis is achieved only after Husserl takes up three crucial phenomena marginalized by static analysis: "indication," "association," and the problem of "motivation."

In breaking with the usual way this is understood, I am suggesting that the difference between static and genetic analysis cannot be construed simply as a contrast between synchronic and diachronic analysis. What we are speaking of as static or synchronic analysis also has a diachronic side to it since a constitutive account generally requires comparisons of features at T_1, T_2, and T_3. Even the notion of eidetic variation requires this. We allow temporal "form" to factor into the description of the given. These, however, are structural comparisons that do not raise the question of development and of the *transformation* of T_1 into T_2 into T_3. They are not yet an "internal" diachronic account.

In the third stage, which was underway by 1917[67] and crystallized in the 1921 text "Static and Genetic Phenomenological Method," genetic analysis proper integrated temporality into its descriptions. Even time itself is understood as the result of a genesis. We will take this up in the next chapter; now we must finish our account of how genetic analysis emerges in Husserl's texts.

Given what we have said about the complete absence of the notion of genetic analysis in *Ideas I* and its introduction into *Ideas III* only as an imaginative image, we are surprised to see it occurring with frequency in the third section of *Ideas II*.[68] To understand this, though, we must pay attention to how *Ideas II* was composed. The first draft of 1912 treated only physical nature and the question of lived body and soul, from which it then moved into the materials that we now have as *Ideas III* on philosophy of science.[69] Edith Stein's first longhand draft, about 1916, did not contain the account of the sociocultural world. It was only in her second draft of 1918 that she, drawing from a distinct manuscript that goes back to 1913, expanded the plan to include the materials that we now have as Section 3. It is clear that these materials were written or rewritten later than Sections 1 and 2. There seem to be some further revisions to the main text but the main additions that we find in Landgrebe's 1924–1925 typed copy, the third draft on which the Husserliana edition is based, are the extensive appendices, all but the first three of which relate to Section 3. This probably explains the fact that *all* the references to a "genetic" account, which Husserl began to develop between 1918 and 1921, are in Section 3 and its appendices, not in the two earlier sections, where his work on passive synthesis during the early 1920s would encourage us to look.

The sociocultural world and its various formations are the result, in Husserl's terminology, of "active" syntheses. As complexes that are social compositions, we can readily see that their existence is dependent upon active construction, upon human achievements that build "upwardly" out of pre-existing elements. Given the fact that cultural formations and values wear their development, so to speak, on their sleeves, it is much easier to see how an account of their structure would call for an additional account of their generation. Husserl's first published genetic analysis, written after he had clearly distinguished genetic from static phenomenology, was a series of articles for a Japanese periodical, three of which were published between 1923 and 1924.

They concentrated on issues of "active" constitution, not passive synthesis: "Let us attempt to develop genetically the ethical form of life as an a priori and essential formation of possible human life, i.e., of the motivation leading for essential reasons to the ethical form of life."[70] As we will discuss in chapter 12, these articles undertake a genetic study of ethical norms, cultural formations, and the notion of history itself. The notion of a genetic analysis began to bear fruit in both regional and historical studies. At the same time, Husserl used it to deepen his understanding of language and speech and of how they function in his "vertical" account of constitution, as we will explore below.

Genetic analysis, however, is applied to areas of not only "active" but also "passive" synthesis. His transcendental aesthetics of experience, developed during this period, was not only integrated into a genetic account of judgments, as we documented above, but was itself a piece of genetic analysis. We find this in several of the texts written between 1920 and 1926, now collected as *Analysen zur passiven Synthesis.* In the next chapter we turn to these studies.

9

Genetic Phenomenology

Time, seen from within, is the form of intentional genesis.

—Husserl (1922)[1]

A. PHENOMENOLOGY AS SYSTEM AND GENETIC ANALYSIS

In the last chapter we sketched how the development of a distinction between static and genetic phenomenology arose simultaneously with Husserl's efforts to construct a system of phenomenology in the early 1920s. Can we also find an internal link between the project of developing a systematic phenomenological method and genetic analysis in the later work?

Husserl drafted a plan, we saw, for a larger systematic work and began working intensely on it during 1921 and 1922. In the Winter Semester of 1920–21, Husserl held lectures with the title "Logic," which he repeated twice, in the Summer Semester of 1923 and the Winter Semester of 1925–26. What we now have as *Analysen zur passiven Synthesis* contains major portions of these lectures. I placed this text, with its effort to approach the theory of constitution from the side of perceptual modalities and temporal issues, and with his first attempt to apply his newly found genetic analysis to both perception and theory of judgment, at the center of Husserl's expansion of phenomenological method. The summer vacation between July 31 and October 26, 1921 in St. Märgen, a small town in the mountains of the Black Forest not far from Freiburg, was devoted to prodigious and productive labor on the question of time in connection with these issues. But it seems that Husserl was not able to get the plan as a whole in hand. His frustration is found in the letter to Natorp from February of 1922 that was quoted in the Introduction:

> I am in a much worse situation than you because the greatest part of my work is stuck in my manuscripts. I almost despise my inability to bring my works [*mich*] to an end and that first quite late, partly only now, the universal, systematic thoughts have come to me [*zuteil werden*], which, though demanded by my previous, particular investigations, now also compel me to

> rework them all. Everything is in the stage of recrystallization! Perhaps I am working, with all the humanly possible expenditure of energy, only for my posthumous works.[2]

While Husserl's sketches and drafts of his larger systematic work are extensive, not a single piece came to publication.[3] If Kern is correct, Husserl did not so much give up this larger systematic work as decide it was simply too much to be tackled head-on. In its place he decided to present a smaller, systematic introduction that would later allow work on related, more manageable portions.[4] Perhaps this decision was also the result of circumstances, for he was deflected from his immediate work on the larger project by an invitation to hold a series of four lectures in London, which he did in June 1922, and then the decision to deepen and prepare them for publication. His lectures, "Introduction into Philosophy," given in the Winter Semester of 1922–23, and what we now have as *Erste Philosophie,* which contains lectures presented in the Winter Semester of 1923–24, were the fruits of these labors. He wrote Ingarden in 1923 that he had decided not to publish the London lectures but was working with an assistant to prepare the version expanded by the 1922–23 lectures for the printer.[5] There is no longer any mention of his systematic project. To Johannes Dauber he writes: "I hope now in '24 to be able to open a series of publications first with an introductory text (*meditationes de prima philosophie*), then, in systematic succession, basic pieces, which in the future can continue from many sides [*allseitig*]."[6]

It seems that Husserl had abandoned the project of a systematic phenomenology after the early 1920s but suddenly revived it in the summer of 1930, when he speaks of the project in his letters and drafts a new outline of the systematic work. In order to understand this sudden turn, we need only recall the frustrations he had with his efforts to transform the "French Meditations" into a German version. Within months after he developed his own objections to the text of the *Cartesian Meditations* that he had sent for translation to France, we find him constructing new plans in the summer of 1930 for a systematic work. This project was to replace the very imperfect, though modified, Cartesian way of the *Meditations* by subsuming what was valuable in it into a larger and rather different framework. The project of a systematic phenomenology, however, was never really abandoned in the early 1920s but only eclipsed by more immediate concerns and approached piecemeal through partial studies. This is why Husserl reported to Georg Misch in November 1930 that he was engaged in writing a book on his system that had been "in preparation for ten years."[7] The next month he spoke of it to Ingarden as a work he had been "inwardly preparing for a decade and am now working out."[8]

We find two drafts for a systematic work: the first, written by Husserl, was prepared probably just before the second, constructed by Fink and submitted to Husserl August 13, 1930. Husserl, as unrealistic as ever, was planning five volumes. While we cannot enter into a full discussion of the differences between these two drafts,[9] we do want to give the full text of Husserl's own draft, as it exhibits the way the contrast between static and genetic analysis has come to control his method as a whole, and thus demonstrates that this contrast is not a side feature or afterthought, as the standard interpretation tends to treat it, but is absolutely central to his concept of philosophy. We will then draw one comparison with Fink's outline:

> Volume I: Foundational considerations toward a doctrine of egological consciousness[10] (general theory of intentionality in its essentially general forms, on all modifications).
>
> [Volume] II: Constitution of egological worldliness. Noematic and noetic theory of the constitution of spatio-temporality and spatio-temporal objectivity [*Gegenständlichkeit*] of the empirical domain [*Empirie*]. Empirical world in all steps. Lived-body, thing, I as *solus.* First of all static.
>
> [Volume] III: The *autogenesis* of the *ego* as solipsistic abstraction. The theory of passive genesis, association. The pre-constitution [*Vorkonstitution*], constitution of pre-given objects. The constitution of objects in a categorial direction. Constitution of emotions and will, person, culture—solipsistic.[11]
>
> Volume IV: The constitution of intersubjectivity and the social world. Empathy. Constitution of men. Constitution of the historical world. Intersubjective temporo-spatiality. Infinity. The idealization of exact nature (how much of this belongs under III?). Static: Men and surrounding world.
>
> Volume V: Transcendental genesis of the objective world. Transcendental genesis of man and humanities. The problems of generation. The problems of self-conservation, man in the genuine [*Echtheit*]. Humanity and destiny. The problems of teleology and God.[12]

The very simplicity of this draft, as well as its scope, gives us great insight into the fundamental terms controlling Husserl's most developed thinking about the phenomenological method.

The difference, firstly, between static and genetic analysis cuts across the contrast between solipsistic and intersubjective constitution. Empathy can be given a static description, which should finally settle the question of how we are to understand the Fifth Meditation. Significantly, it is the solipsistic approach that Husserl at this point views as an "abstraction," an indication that the burden of his notion of constitution is carried here by his notion of intersubjectivity.

Secondly, the movement from static to genetic analysis between Volumes I to III roughly parallels the movement from a "transcendental analytic" to Husserl's reformed version of a "transcendental aesthetic." Another shift from static to genetic analysis occurs between Volumes IV and V, but it seems that the conjunction of intersubjectivity and genetic analysis pushes the notion of genetic phenomenology beyond its earlier limits in the direction of what Husserl during this period calls generative phenomenology.[13] It is striking how close this draft is to the 1921 text:

"Static and Genetic Phenomenological Methods" from 1921	Sketch of a "Systematic Work," Vols. I–V from 1930
Universal phenomenology of the general structures of consciousness	I. General theory of intentionality in its essentially general forms
Constitutive phenomenology of worldliness; noematic and noetic analysis of the constitution of spatio-temporality	II. Constitution of egological theory
Phenomenology of genesis	III. Theory of passive genesis

We can also find a rough parallel between the same 1921 text and the movement from Volume IV to V in Husserl's 1930 outline:

Universal phenomenology of the general structures of consciousness	IVa. Static: Men and surrounding world
Constitutive phenomenology and the social and historical world; intersubjective spatio-temporality	IVb. The constitution of intersubjectivity
Phenomenology of the genesis of generation	V. Transcendental genesis; the problems

In order to simultaneously characterize, thirdly, the relationship between the levels of passive constitution and active constitution, on the one hand, and the levels of solipsistic and intersubjective constitution, on the other, Husserl used the terms "preconstitution" and "pregiven" in his characterization of the domain of Volume III. The notion of "preconstitution" sets his account in contrast to what is coming in Volumes IV and V, which recovers intersubjectivity. The term indicates that we are not yet at the level of concrete social constitution and the full concrete determinacy of objects of experience. The notion of "pregiven," however, looks back to Volumes I and II. It indicates not only that there is a level of what Husserl calls "autogenesis" at work before the active noetic achievement of the subject, but also that the world, as part of the subject-world correlation taken as irreducible by the transcendental reflection, itself rests upon a *pregiven* world. If so, then the solipsistic analysis of intentionality has not given us an irreducible ground. The ground is itself the product of a deeper constitution, which the scheme of monological act and ideal meaning cannot capture. For Husserl, then, "pregiven" came to mean both that there are schemes of constitution that do not follow the simple triad *ego-cogito-cogitatum* and, more importantly, that a structural phenomenological account of the *being* of phenomena must be supplemented with a genetic account of their *becoming.*

Fourthly, the introduction of the regions of "person" and "culture" in Volume III under a "solipsistic" account is puzzling until we realize that this is precisely the viewpoint of *Ideas II.* Not just the various domains of nature but also those of "spirit," fully intersubjective in their constitution, are included because they, too, are "phenomena" and thus are domains that must undergo a categorial and then a constitutional analysis. The crucial difference to the introduction of intersubjectivity in Volume IV is that there we move beyond the tentative solipsistic framing of the *process* of constitution of Volumes I to III. Intersubjectivity comes into play not as a phenomenal field being constituted but as part of the scheme of constitution itself, as the dynamic, constituting agency in and through which we have the constituted. We are no longer under a solipsistic abstraction, even though we still initiate the description of Volume IV using static analysis. The best example of Husserl effecting this shift from the egological to the intersubjective field from within his static account, we have argued, is Husserl's Fifth Meditation. We suggested in chapter 6 that it is best understood as a proper explication of the domain of what the first four Meditations meant by the ego. Having just written it, it was still very fresh in his mind as he wrote this draft. Husserl's outline noted a crucial difference as Volume IV overturns the "solipsistic abstraction" of Volumes I to III: the correlation used for intersubjective static accounts is not ego and object but "men and world."

Finally, we also find a hint that not just space but also time is to be given a static as well as genetic analysis. The static analysis of time would be a structural account of the experience of time, much as we find in his *Phenomenology of the Consciousness of Internal Time.* We will turn in the next sections to the issue of the relationship between genetic analysis and temporality.

Fink, probably on the basis of Husserl's draft and then in further consultation with him, also constructed a plan, much wider in scope than Husserl's. The draft is about five times as long, but proposed two volumes in place of Husserl's five. Only the first volume is fleshed out and richly described, the second having no more than section headings. I reproduce only the book and section titles.

First Book:
The Levels of Pure Phenomenology

Section I: About the Beginning and the Principle of Philosophy

Section II: Regressive Phenomenology

Section III: Progressive Phenomenology

Section IV: Basic Elements of Phenomenological Metaphysics

Second Book:
Ontology and Phenomenology

Section I: The Idea of Universal "Transcendental Aesthetic"

Section II: Nature and Spirit

Section III: From Pure Inner-Psychology to Transcendental Phenomenology[14]

When Husserl wrote Ingarden in December 1930, a few months after receiving Fink's proposal, he had this outline, or at least its progression of topics, in mind:

> But naturally and at my age [71] what lies on my heart is the systematic foundational work of phenomenology, which I actually have been inwardly preparing for a decade and am now working out. . . .
>
> Since the past summer, since the publication of the last book [*Formal and Transcendental Logic*], I have been in impassioned, deepened study of the first attempts, drafts, of the manifold lines of thought, of the universal problematic of transcendental phenomenology—as universal philosophy that, well constructed, spans and provides final grounding to all ontologies (all a priori sciences) and all sciences in general. . . . The first and perhaps greatest difficulty lies in radical freedom from pre-judgments [*Vorurteilslosigkeit*] and its method of phenomenological reduction. The latter—understood by none of my old students—now undergoes elucidation from many sides, there remaining no dark corner and no other alternative [*Ausweichen*]. This alone is already becoming a large section [cf. Fink's draft, Book 1, Section 1 above]. And then follows the systematics of the constitutive analysis of the "pregiven world" [Book 1, Section 2 or Volume II of original draft?], then further genetic phenomenology [Book 1, Section 3 or Volume III of original draft?], and the "metaphysical problematic," in particular in the phenomenological sense of metaphysical [Book 1, Section 4]. Then, still further, with transcendental subjectivity the absolute is directly opened up through special transcendental *experience*. . . .
>
> Bringing this to a finished state will cost enormous time; but I certainly hope to be able to publish at least a first half in the next *Yearbook* (Fall 1931). My highly gifted Fink helps valiantly; without him I would be lost.[15]

Though Husserl traces its progression in this letter, I still find a significant shift in Fink's outline that does not square with either Husserl's first draft or what he finally publishes in the *Crisis.* It revolves around Husserl's description to Ingarden of what follows Section 1. Husserl speaks of it as "the systematics of the constitutive analysis of the 'pregiven world,' then further genetic phenomenology." But Fink's draft revolves around the opposition between regressive and progressive phenomenology, an "*Abbau-Analyse*" and an "*Aufbau-Analyse.*" The strongest reason for introducing the latter, I would say, is Fink's suggestion that progressive analysis attacks the issue of "the *perfectivity* of the transcendental life,"[16] i.e., this analysis must be the discipline that will allow Husserl to deal teleologically with the issues of a true humanity and its destiny. The notion of genetic in this context is restricted to "ideal-genetic." But Fink wanted to emphasize "the 'constructive' character of progressive analysis" and, in that context, speaks of progressive analysis as "neither 'genetic' nor dependent upon 'conditions of possibility.' "[17] As a result I think, perhaps in contrast to Kern,[18] Fink *replaces* Husserl's dependence upon the opposition between static and genetic with a different contrast between regressive and progressive. The other possibility is that he subsumed the contrast between static and genetic, as it related to various modalities of passive synthesis, under regressive analysis; thought of Husserl's genetic account of active synthesis as "progressive" and "constructive"; and then looked for a much more metaphysically focused discussion to supplement the phenomenological account of the *Aufbau,* calling it "phenomenological metaphysics."[19] When we compare Husserl's with Fink's sketches for a systematic work, the former is much closer to the course that Husserl had been following for a decade.

There is yet another reason for Husserl's return to his systematic project of 1921–1922. Kern has suggested, with his usual excellent documentation, that Husserl's decision to abandon the *Meditations* project in order to take up work on his "System of Phenomenological Philosophy" was due not only to the internal difficulties he found with the argument of the *Meditations* but also with his reading, between April and October, 1930, of the first two installments of Georg Misch's "Lebensphilosophie und Phänomenologie," itself dedicated to Husserl upon the occasion of his seventieth birthday. Misch, who took over Husserl's post at Göttingen in 1917 after Husserl moved to Freiburg, had sent the first of three installments to Husserl in May or June of 1929,[20] the second coming before August and the third probably in the summer or early Fall, 1930.[21] While the work deals largely with Heidegger, Misch portrays Husserl as much too bound to intellectualism and sets Dilthey's theory of a genesis of the different categories of life in contrast to Husserl's statically conceived notion of intentionality.[22] Husserl knew that this criticism would hold true of *Ideas I,* and perhaps even *Formal and Transcendental Logic,* which Misch briefly discusses, even though it had only just appeared.[23] Husserl also knew that he was well beyond the limits of that method though, alas, nothing had been published that would give his readers any indications of this. The best the public had were a few hints buried in the second appendix to the *Logic*. Misch's distinction between static and genetic analysis would also give Husserl an external point of view on the *Meditations* and help Husserl see them as part of the problem, not the response he was seeking to Heidegger. In any case, Husserl's "System of Phenomenological Philosophy" would have to anticipate criticisms coming from Dilthey students, made all the more important because Husserl had a long-standing involvement and, in his own words to Misch, an "inner commonality" [*innere Gemeinsamkeit*] with Dilthey's work.[24] In fact, Husserl wrote Misch that he intends to show that "the 'ahistorical' Husserl *had* to take distance from history only for a time."[25] In general, we can say that reading Misch forced Husserl not so much to relate his notion of genetic phenomenology to the issue of historical development, for that we have as early as 1922,[26] but to clearly place history in relation to his overall method. Indeed, the problem of history seemed to push Husserl beyond his first outline and may account for several themes in Fink's version, especially its characterization of the world open to static phenomenological analysis as itself a pregiven world. One could even speculate that the problem of history eventually caused Husserl, once again, to abandon work on the "System" by 1934—it being, in any case, far beyond anything he could have possibly managed—and to take up what finally became the *Crisis*.

B. CONCRETE SUBJECTIVITY AND THE QUESTION OF MOTIVATION

While arguing for the simultaneous development of the concept of a system of phenomenology and of genetic analysis, we have also seen how Husserl's work in this direction came in alternating periods of intense, focused labor and long, unfruitful periods in which the sheer volume and diversity of his interests seemed to overwhelm him as he scampered from one project to the next. This tendency, found in the period surrounding his writing of the various volumes of *Ideas*, was aggravated in his later period by both his frustration at bringing to publication works he thought were only a few months from completion, and by the additional distraction of a number of invitations to give lectures in various places. The result is that his work on genetic analysis is scattered, and we are faced with the task of piecing it together. What follows is such a reconstruction, but one in which it may not be possible to draw a clean line between Husserl's thought and my appropriation of it.

Perhaps the best way to capture the internal problematic that requires transcendental phenomenology to be extended in the direction of genetic analysis is to follow Husserl as he deepens his analysis of the transcendental ego and attempts to account for its individuation and its peculiar historicity. This story, too, has several twists and turns. We begin by continuing the discussion of the *Logical Investigations* undertaken in the last chapter.

Given the prominence of the concept of the transcendental ego in *Ideas I* (1913), we are surprised to find Husserl arguing for a non-egological conception of consciousness in the first edition of the *Logical Investigations* (1900–1901). The Fifth Investigation, as we saw above, argues that attributing lived experiences to a "psychic individual or ego" is not really "a phenomenological finding."[27] Husserl is only willing to concede that the ego exists as "an empirical object." While it may be an object of scientific observation, as it is for the empirical discipline of psychology, it is not discoverable through phenomenological insight, which in the *Investigations* means "inner perception." Since Husserl's notion of an empirical ego is the forerunner of what he will later describe as the personal and, then, the concrete ego, it is important to note how he thought we could move from the empirical to the phenomenological level in the *Investigations:*

> If we cut out the ego-body [*Ichleib*] from the empirical ego and if we then restrict the purely psychic ego to its phenomenological content, the latter reduces itself to a unity of consciousness, to a real complex of lived experiences. . . . The ego is simply identical with its own interconnected unity.[28]

In other words, the suspension of the tie between the body and consciousness transforms the concrete, empirical ego into the pure stream of experience and allows it to be circumscribed by inner "adequate" perception.

As we look deeper, however, we find a second account of the ego that is somewhat at odds with his exclusion of it from the realm of phenomenology. Counterpoised to the Kantian ego, which Husserl thought had hidden metaphysical features, the first edition did propose a notion of subjectivity that is not only nonempirical, as did Kant, but also nonegological, as we just saw. Husserl also realized, however, that consciousness is anchored in the world through the various experiences in which objects are apprehended and, in particular, through the temporality of such experiences. The stream of consciousness consists of "unities that co-exist and pass continuously from moment to moment into one another, constituting a unity of change."[29] The nexus of consciousness has "the unity of a concrete whole" by virtue of "subjective time-consciousness," which secures the "form" of "continuous duration or continuous change." Interestingly, when Husserl included time in the analysis of the first edition of the *Investigations,* it had the effect of fashioning the stream into a "soulish unity," into a temporally on-going, developing unity of all its 'experiences.' "[30] Thereby, Husserl claimed, the concept of lived experience was "expanded" or enlarged into a notion that could account for the constituting of the soul and, thereby, of an ego. Thus, while the first edition lacks the notion of the ego as a "phenomenological find" and thinks of it as psychological, it does connect temporality and the stream of experience in its efforts to account for the "concrete whole" of conscious life; Husserl also suggested that this link gives us the notion of a soul, his term in the first edition for the ego in its concreteness.[31]

Having boldly announced in the first edition, after citing Natorp's description of the ego as a subjective center for all the contents of consciousness, that he is "quite unable to find this ego," Husserl adds in the second edition of 1913 a note in which he meekly confesses: "I have since managed to find it."[32] Of course he is not interested in an "ego-metaphysics," into which he thinks the Neo-Kantians fell. That same year he argued in *Ideas I* for the existence of an ego as a transcendental "pole" of the stream of consciousness, echoing an idea that he attributed to the soul in the *Investigations.* But the fact that *Ideas I* expressly omits any consideration of time-consciousness from its characterization means, given the backdrop of the *Investigations,* that there is no risk of confusing the transcendental ego with the concrete, empirical ego. This also means, however, that the notion of the "I" is formal and quite close to Kant's, no doubt a function of the fact that Kant was the one that provoked Husserl to reframe his phenomenology, in the period between the *Investigations* and *Ideas I,* as a proper transcendental method, and no doubt a function of the fact that the method of *Ideas I* is static.[33] Reflecting on his treatment of the ego in *Ideas I* over fifteen years later, Husserl admitted that "the interrogation of what specifically characterizes the ego was not yet broached in the first volume of the *Ideas.*"[34]

What immediately reopened the question of the nature of the ego is the different way of conceiving of the "I" developed in *Ideas II.* While Husserl continued to insist on an absolute difference between "pure subjectivity" or the "pure ego" and the "psychic ego" or "psychic subject,"[35] he devoted extensive studies to the latter in *Ideas II,* concentrating on the "personal I" situated in a certain environment (*Umwelt*). These studies, which "seemingly cohere very closely with Husserl's turn to a *genetic* understanding of the problem of constitution,"[36] began to impact his conception of the transcendental ego once he came to see Kant's theory as unduly formal and abstract. In his advanced theory he wanted to keep Kant's connection between the unity of the ego and the unity of the field of apperception. "As an 'I,' the 'I' has unity in virtue of the world. . . . "[37] Yet, in contrast, he presses toward a "concrete" notion of the transcendental I, and suggests that the transcendental ego, understood in terms of its development over time, is, in fact, the "standing and abiding personal ego,"[38] a connection that surprisingly echoes what we found in the *Investigations.*

This move poses a problem for Husserl. His later thought goes to great lengths not to turn this concrete ego back into a psychological subject. As he keeps his account in a transcendental register, however, the ego is characterized as possessing certain capabilities or capacities (*Vermögen* or *Vermöglichkeiten*). In addition it has acquired dispositional tendencies, or at least has the capacity to acquire dispositional tendencies, what Husserl calls habitualities (*Habitualitäten*), that result from recurring interaction with the world. Treating these as part of the account of constitution means that our concrete sensibility always has a "secondary sensibility" (*sekundäre Sinnlichkeit*), for now we must include the "history" of our experience, both individual and corporate, in the account. Finally, it means that the ego is necessarily incarnate, in possession of corporeality (*Leiblichkeit*). But how can Husserl's transcendental method incorporate these features as structures of the transcendental ego?

If static analysis gives us the "form" of the structure of intentionality, genetic analysis is an effort to articulate this structure without presupposing that its form can be finally severed from content. The initial abstraction, which sets an ego-pole in opposition to an object-pole, is taken as only provisional, largely because Husserl realized that it does not allow him to account for its "individuation." The ego must be studied not just as a pole perduring throughout the succession of intentional experiences, giving them unity, but as a concrete subject that has its own capabilities, interests, and acquired convictions. The ego is thick with what Husserl calls "individual history":

> The pure Ego of any given *cogitatio* already has absolute individuation, and the *cogitatio* itself is something absolutely individual in itself. The Ego, however, is not an empty pole but is the bearer of its habitualities, and that implies that it has its individual history.[39]

Concretely considered, the ego consists of certain capabilities of experience and tendencies to act or react that are built up over time through the actual functioning of conscious life. In a rare passage that compares a constitutive with a genetic account, Husserl speaks of the formal regularity or the formal structure of past, present, and future that "places" the particular noetic-noematic experiences with their "flowing modes of givenness." He then adds:

> But, within this form life goes on as a motivated course of particular constituting achievements with a multiplicity of particular motivations and motivational systems, which, according to the universal lawful regularities of genesis, produce a unity of the universal genesis of the ego. The ego constitutes itself for itself, so to speak, in the unity of a history. And as we said that the constitution of the ego contains all the constitutions of all the objectivities existing for it, whether these be immanent or transcendent, ideal or real, so we must now add that the constitutive systems, by virtue of which

> such and such objects and categories of objects exist for the ego, are themselves possible only within the framework of a lawfully regulated genesis. At the same time they [i.e., the constitutive systems] are bound by the universal, genetic form that makes the concrete ego (the monad) possible as a unity, as having a particular content of its being that is compossible. That a nature, a cultural world, a human world with its social forms, etc., exists for me, means that possibilities of corresponding experience exist for me, as experiences I can at any time bring into play and continue in a certain synthetic style, whether or not I am at present actually experiencing objects belonging to the region in question. It signifies, furthermore, that other modes of consciousness corresponding to them—vague intendings and the like—exist as possibilities for me, and also that these other modes of consciousness have possibilities of becoming fulfilled or disappointed by experiences of predelineated types. And this entails a firmly developed habituality, one developed and acquired by a certain genesis regulated by eidetic laws.[40]

Correspondingly, the object is not just an empty pole giving thematic focus to a present intentional act but is also thick with its own history. All our previous experiences of the object "remain attached to the object qua intentional by virtue of a *habitus*. . . . " This means that experience effects a change in the way the object is presented to us, that it has "a lasting result with regard to the object." Husserl explains:

> . . . even if the object has been given again originally, that is, perceptually, and is not just realized in memory, the new cognition has a content of sense essentially other than the preceding perceptions. The object is *pregiven* with a new content of sense; it is present to consciousness with the *horizon*—an empty horizon to be sure [i.e., not yet specified by fulfillment]—of *acquired cognitions:* the precipitation of the [previous] active bestowal of sense, of the preceding attribution of a determination, is now a component of the sense of an act of perception, even if it is not really explicated anew.[41]

Concrete objects are *sedimented* objects. Objects are originally given only against a background of being pregiven, of "secondary sensibility."

This analysis of the habitualities and capacities of the ego, along with the view of "pregiven" objects as thick with sedimentation, is Husserl's way of recovering the in-structure lost in his first static account of the ego. At the same time it opens to view the genesis that accounts for their historicity.

Husserl realizes that the only way to finally free his account from the abstract nature of a Kantian approach is to expand his notion of the ego through the idea of life, for this notion allows the "history" of intentionality to be factored into an account of the ego. This shift in emphasis also allows Husserl to discover a deeper connection between the ego and the world, and then the ego and intersubjectivity. These ideas come together with unusual lucidity in a text from 1921 or 1922:

> The "I" in the proper sense is the I-pole with the habitualities, capabilities, that accrue to it from its life and positional stances. But [even] this is an abstraction. It becomes concrete when, in addition, we take [into consideration] its entire, concrete life with its intentionality. And in that all true objectivity is a rule of reason for this intentionality—not only as actual but also as freely variable by the I (in the I-can-convince-myself, I-can-penetrate-deeper-into-the-world-in-experience)—the world also belongs to the I. . . .
>
> Just like the whole world, which is there for me, so also every other I and the I's bound together in communities belong to the concretion of my I. They belong there—as a rational or "evidently" valid idea—as the counter pole of my ego, as we showed. But they are not merely true, intentional correlates; rather they are themselves I's, absolutely existing themselves, although appresented for me only rationally. That means the following: there belongs to the concretion of my I not only an intentional rule "true being" under the title "other I" (a rule of my possible experiences in empathy) but there also belongs to the idea of true being—as of a being harmoniously appresented as yet "another" I (*alter ego*)—an I itself, in accord with the sense of empathy, an absolute being just as I am such. And on the basis of this appresentation [which gives the other as a Thou] I can—much like I, in relation to myself, find a determination of an I by an I—effect a determination of a Thou by an I; the appresented I, likewise, can decide to determine me, and I, by means of the empathy in play, must experience this determination of me as real.[42] I am determined through him as he through me. We meet in an absolute relationship; we do not meet in relation externally but rather we become one in I-acts that run out from I to Thou and Thou to I and that have their effect.[43]

With concreteness we gain an internal connection both to the world as a life-world and to the other as a Thou, as more than just my "intentional correlate," and thus to the reciprocity that characterizes the "absolute relation" of I and Thou. This account begins to carry Husserl's analysis in a direction that standard readings believe excluded by his method. Perhaps a comparison with Heidegger will make this clearer.

Husserl's reliance on subjectivity is radically different from Heidegger's explication of the *Da* of *Dasein* and his unpacking of the in-structure by recourse to spatiality, affectivity (*Befindlichkeit*), and understanding.[44] In spite of these striking differences, Husserl's way of unfolding the in-structure by thinking of subjectivity as *concrete* brings him much closer to Heidegger's approach than is usually thought. Notice that Husserl's genetic phenomenology, with a notion of concrete subjectivity in place, moves in the same two directions as Heidegger's notions of affectivity and understanding: (a) The account of affectivity does not feature the notion of moods, but it clearly has as its goal the situating of subjectivity in its world and the having of that world in a nonthetic way. Husserl's account of passive synthesis and theory of perceptual modalization are his version of how the world catches us up in a circuit of relations that are not of our own making. While the notion of moods or attunement is alien to Husserl we might even argue that Husserl expands the domain of affectivity, placing here one thing that Heidegger wants to locate in understanding (the theory of perception) and one things he avoids altogether (the body). One can almost hear him complain of Heidegger, as he did of Kant, that he does not "suspect the magnitude" of the "lower levels of experience." He could add: "What especially must not be overlooked is the constant reciprocal relation of the constituting ego and lived-body, on the one side, and real thinghood, on the other."[45] (b) The theory of active genesis, of active synthesis, of "judgment" proper, and even of the formation of "spiritual" constructions, all point back to the "active syntheses" of cognition, and to the role of understanding in the construction of the meaningfulness that places subjectivity in relationship to its world.

No doubt, these connections are worth a discussion in their own right, and one will be provided in chapter 14. For now we must connect these general points concerning the concrete ego to certain ideas that open up a genetic understanding of its intentional life.

Recall that Husserl's constitutive account introduced the notion of apperception in order to describe the transcending achievement of acts of perception. Husserl extends this notion not just to cover the concatenation of profiles through which an object is given but also to bridge the vertical structure of all intentional acts; that of which we are conscious carries with it an awareness of something more or something else, not in the sense that I deduce or induce yet another item by way of a logical inference but in that the content of my present experience "points to this other as belonging to it, as motivated through it."[46] The notion of pointing or indication accounts for the connection between the explicit content of an act and its implicit features, those "pre-constitutive" levels that are implied by its surface structure. The disclosure of these levels is the task of a developed constitutive phenomenology. But as soon as Husserl thinks of these levels not only as presupposed but also as *productive,* not only as a "condition" but also as a "source," their interrelationship articulates an order of genesis. What genetic analysis uncovers, first of all, is not yet another level along the vertical axis but the "laws" of transformation that account for the constitution of the surface structure from its depth structures. Such laws give us the "history" of consciousness:

> It is necessary to establish the universal and basic laws governing the construction of apperceptions from basic apperceptions and to systematically derive the possible formations and thus to clarify each given construct according to its origin.
>
> This "history" of consciousness (the history of all possible appercep-

> tions) is not concerned with the discovery of factual genesis for factual apperceptions . . . but rather each gestalt of apperception is an essence-gestalt and has its genesis according to essential laws. Thus there is contained in the idea of such an apperception that it is to undergo a "genetic analysis."[47]

To this Husserl adds the claim that such laws give us "the mode of the genesis in which any apperception of this type originally arises in an individual stream of consciousness."[48] But how are we to understand this? Does not a constitutive account already provide us with laws systematically ordering apperceptions?

The reframing of the scheme of implicating and implicated, used throughout constitutive analysis, as a scheme of *motivation* is what, in the final analysis, transforms the formal conception of the ego, required by static analysis, into its concrete description. Laws of constitution are recast as laws of genesis:

> The eidetic laws of compossibility (rules that govern in the fact simultaneous or successive existence and possible existence together) are laws of causality in a maximally broad sense—laws for an If and Then. Yet it is better to avoid here the expression causality, which is laden with prejudices, and to speak of *motivation* in the transcendental sphere (and in the sphere of "pure" psychology). The universe of lived experiences composing the inherent [*reell*], subsisting constituents of the transcendental ego, is a compossible universe only in the universal *unity-form of the flux,* in which all elements, flowing within it, are themselves ordered. Accordingly, this most general form of all particular forms of concrete lived experiences—and of all formations constituted [as] flowing in the flux of such experiences—is the form of motivation connecting all and governing each element in particular. We can further describe it as a *formal, lawful regularity of a universal genesis*. . . .
>
> But within this form life runs on as a motivated course of particular, constituting achievements with multiple, particular motivations and motivational systems, which, according to the universal lawful regularity of genesis, produces the unity of a universal genesis of the ego.[49]

As a first approximation we can say that this emphasis in Husserl's genetic account is not upon new strata but upon that which accounts for their developing interrelationship, not upon structural levels but relations of concrete transformation. Genetic analysis reframes constitution—the account of the "abstractable" noetic and noematic elements nested in a given experiential complex or of the active construction of higher complexes—in terms of development by describing the conditions of the concrete configuration of complexes that are deployed over time. What makes genetic analysis especially difficult to comprehend is the fact that it traces the relationship not so much between one type of act and those other types logically presupposed or entailed by its execution but rather between the development or "becoming" of an intentional act in terms of its horizon and the resulting transformation of that horizon. The horizon is envisioned not just as an implied network of significance but as a nexus of "motivation," as the reciprocal transformation of subjectivity and world that leads to, as it is affected by, the concrete deployment of acts. In short, genetic phenomenology is concerned with the becoming of the in-structure itself.

We are finally in a position to give a first answer to the diversity of topics that we raised as a problem in the opening pages of the last chapter. What ultimately holds the disparate areas of Husserl's genetic descriptions together is that each area, be it microprocesses of sensuous synthesis or macroprocesses of cultural construction, is submitted to this reframing and, thereby, related to "earlier" configurations of a particular region or different regions by virtue of *lateral* connections in the deep structure that allow for their development.

Genetic analysis overcomes what is perhaps the most serious limitation in Husserl's static concept of the ego. Recall that his analysis in his First Investigation of the indexical "I" treated it as having both a "general meaning," in which it refers to the subject, and a specific occasional meaning, in which it picks out the speaker as an individual. Husserl's turn to the monologue, the harbinger of his reliance upon static analysis under the aegis of the Cartesian way of *Ideas I,* preserves the sense in which the consciousness uncovered is an individual fact. But the indexical "I" also harbors a general meaning, and thus the disclosure of *my* consciousness could give rise to an essential description of consciousness or of subjectivity in general. The task of description involves an imagination whose task is to cast the experiences of the I into a general form and to penetrate its internal coherence and meaning. But while Husserl's analysis could account for the transition from fact to eidetic structure, it could not admit that the individuality of the ego is in some sense derived. It tended to suppress the idea, powerfully demonstrated by Hegel, that "I," which designates the subject in general, comes to refer to the individual only by means of a process of negation, of contrast and identification. The subject that is universal and that can thereby have transcendental status *becomes* an individual.[50] Husserl's static account necessarily neglected the process involved in individuation. It is only with his notion of genetic analysis that Husserl recovered this process and began to describe certain schemes of individuation—sedimentation, habitualization, discourse, home vs. alien world, etc.—constitutive of the subject becoming an individual.

We cannot begin to undertake a comprehensive account of how this would work across the various regions outlined in chapter 3; instead, we must restrict our further explication of genetic phenomenology to continuing the studies of perception and judgment already underway in previous chapters. Husserl proposes, contrary to our expectations, not only a genetic account of "passivity," of perception, but of "activity," of the active achievements of cognition.

C. THE OCCASIONALITY OF SPEECH

The constitutive analysis of judging was placed in chapter 7 in relation to the implicated activities of negating, doubting, and questioning. They are "conditions" without which we could not understand the activity of judgment itself. At the same time, the interrelated activities of doubting and questioning also "motivate" the activity of judging. This also holds true for all cognitive acts: "So is each activity motivated and we have pure genesis in the sphere of the acts as pure act-genesis in the form that I, carrying out the act, am determined by the fact that I have carried out the other acts."[51] This latent history of other acts establishes the direction and expectations of each manifest act. In a study of "active genesis," Husserl claims, we discover "the form of the motivation of my thinking, valuing, willing through what is other."[52]

If genetic analysis is to account for the becoming of the in-structure it must have a theory of meaning that preserves the internal tie to *contexts.* In the First Investigation, as is well known, Husserl severed the indicating from the expressive functions of signs in an effort to isolate the field of "objective" expressions, those capable of being combined into claims that are either true or false. The technique Husserl used to effect the separation of indication from expression was methodological solipsism: in silent discourse with myself, speech ceases to be utterances with a physical presence bringing into play its own ties both to things in the world and to other speakers whose mental life is always on the other side of what I can directly view. Because objective expressions are those whose content can be understood independent of particular speech situations and prior to an apprehension of objects that "fulfill" acts that use such expression, they eliminate the speaker's reference or any other tie to referents that might be different in kind or content from that specified by the meaning of the expression. And this allowed Husserl to treat meaning as idea and to make a clean conceptual distinction between meaning and referent. Objective expressions, accordingly, are quite different from "occasional expressions," or indexicals, whose meaning can be grasped only by attending to the context of their utterance or by allowing referents to play a decisive role in their specification. The analysis of meaning and of speech-acts that Husserl went on to propose in the *Investigations* took objective expressions as its guiding thread and excluded occasional expression from its considerations. But this move at the level of protologic configured the characterization of meaning itself: since the world of referents is a spatial and temporal world, and since we use expressions with the same meaning to refer to countless real objects in that world, Husserl drew the plausible conclusion that meanings are timeless, ideal entities. As such meanings are the essential constituents of propositions.

By contrast, genetic analysis attempts to return speech to its original contexts, which is to say that speech is returned to its essential occasionality. Husserl himself realized that an analysis of indication, pushed to the side and considered extrinsic to an account of meaning in both the *Investigations* and *Ideas I,* "already constitutes the nucleus of genetic phenomenology."[53] If propositional discourse is derived from certain transformations in both our experience and our communication with others, then a genetic account might give us a theory of how signs can *acquire* a meaning that is "ideal" and "timeless."

By the time of *Formal and Transcendental Logic* (1929), Husserl was much more attuned to various kinds of discourse and to the "interests" giving rise to them. There are sections in which he dwells on the difference between ordinary and propositional uses of declarative sentences.[54] In addition, the analysis of what he, distancing himself from his first account in the *Logical Investigations,* calls "occasional judgments" is even more suggestive, for here we have some hints of a different characterization of meaning.[55]

In an important text penned just before *Formal and Transcendental Logic,*[56] Husserl expressly contrasts "scientific statements [*wissenschaftliche Aussagen*]" with the "descriptive statements of everyday life [*die deskriptiven Aussagen des Alltags*]." These "occasional" or "situational" statements "are related to the concrete situation in which the ego, in the course of its life, has its experiential evidence . . . in terms of its practical intentions."[57] If we want to turn these statements into scientific claims, their "conceptuality [*Begrifflichkeit*]" must undergo a process of "conceptual construction [*Begriffsbildung*]." This assumes, however, that we are acquainted with "words in their meaning," for we "use" them in such a way that they "fit" experience. "Occasional judgments need not be intuitive, evident; they point to a practical situation. . . . "[58]

This implies that the theory of meaning first proposed in the *Investigations* reflected only *one* possible use of language, that constitutive of scientific discourse:

> First and foremost the logician considers language only in its ideality, as the identical grammatical word over against its real or possible realizations, as the identical grammatical sentence or sentential context.[59]

We arrive at language in its ideality only by disregarding the dimensions of speech that would be essential for an analysis of its ordinary use:

> We leave out of consideration the pointing *tendencies* belonging to words, as to all signs. . . . We also leave out of consideration other psychic experiences that are interwoven with them as, for example, those in which we turn our-

> selves to our speech partner, wanting to state our judgment to him, and so on.[60]

Given this constriction, it is clear why "here [ordinary] language comes into consideration only secondarily." Language is treated only as "an appropriate scientific language" that is "bound" to a specific "epistemic-technical goal."[61]

The realization of this limitation in the static analysis of meaning opens the way for a genetic account. Just how are we to describe these meanings that are not (logical) concepts and that are not "*vorhanden*"[62] as ideal "objects" of acts but, in some sense, are themselves presupposed by such? *Formal and Transcendental Logic* itself contains two fertile suggestions.

1. "Judgments as senses have . . . a sense-genesis."[63] At first glance the "genetic order" seems restricted to relations of consequence, to concepts entailed or implicated by the concept in play. But this notion is extended as Husserl speaks about a certain "historicality" of senses and the way in which they "level by level, point back to original sense and the noematic intentionality belonging to it."[64] And we are told that "this applies . . . not merely to syntactic implications but also the deeper-lying genesis already belonging to the [semantic] basic 'cores' and pointing back to their origination from experiences."[65]

2. What sets "occasional judgments" over against propositional claims is that they are dependent upon the *context* of their utterance for their referents. Husserl explains this by speaking of a "situational horizon" fundamentally different from what can be thematized in an explicit reflection upon statements:

> One can explicate these horizons subsequently, but the *constituting horizon-intentionality*, through which the surrounding world of everyday life is ever a *world of experience*, is always prior to the explication. It is this that *essentially determines the meaning of occasional judgments*, always far beyond what is and can be said, expressly and explicitly, in the words themselves.[66]

Whereas the "proposed object as such" is always the product of an explicit judgment and the treatment of it as meaning is always tied to an act of reflection, we are speaking of both an horizon that precedes the activity of judging and a characterization of meaning that does not glean its features from a reflection upon making a claim. As a result, a new and different characterization of meaning is required:

> [These horizons], then, are "presuppositions" that, as intentional implicates contained in constituting intentionality, continually determine the sense of the object [*gegenständlicher Sinn*] of the immediate experiential environment and which, therefore, have a totally different character than . . . the idealizing presuppositions of predicative judging discussed by us until now.[67]

In chapter 7 we raised, based upon Husserl's own reflections upon these matters, the question as to whether his general characterization of meaning as an ideal entity might be true, at best, only of propositional discourse. Whatever the inadequacies of this theory, Husserl generally speaks of the meaning of scientific discourse in these terms up to his very last writings.[68] But the fact that situational discourse is viewed not only as different but also as determining that context from which propositional discourse arises means that we have, on Husserl's own terms, reopened the question of how this more basic notion of meaning is to be characterized.

Husserl's later theory of meaning emphasizes the sense in which the "ideality" of meaning is linked not to ideal entities but to the "again and again," to repetition and schemata of repeatability, as formulated in a text from 1925:

> In the after-one-another of repetition the consciousness of unity is grounded.... The consciousness of repetition is a special [*ausgezeichnete*] form of the consciousness of identity. It is the basic, constitutive form in which identity is given. This is the basic, self-giving achievement of this consciousness.[69]

The meaning of propositional discourse, then, is not irreducible but has an identity that is produced. If the meaning of "occasional" discourse could be characterized as a *schema* that ties context, use, and content to the activity of intending in communication, as we suggested in chapter 7, then the meaning of rigorous, propositional discourse is the result of that scheme being developed into a *rule* that allows for repetition in different contexts and that connects use to truth conditions. This notion allows us to introduce the internal connection between the meaning of objective discourse and time. The ideality or trans-temporality of the meaning of truth talk becomes, once we see those transformations constitutive of it, a particular form of temporality: it is that form (repeatability) of using the same sign at different times in different contexts in relation to the same reference.

In Husserl's genetic account, meaning is given not only a temporal but also a dialogical characterization. With the priority of occasional or situational discourse in genetic analysis, the provisional starting point in the monologue is relinquished, for occasional speech is necessarily intersubjective speech that involves a process of (re)activation and sedimentation.

The turn to the monologue was designed initially as a technique of severing the expressive from the indicative functions of signs in discourse. Starting with the "solipsistic attitude" provided a provisional point of entry to a phenomenological theory of meaning. But with the Cartesian way this technique was elevated to the level of method and overdetermined by an opposition between relative and absolute being: the sphere of "ownness," once properly reduced and described, is the only realm in which evidence is both apodictic and adequate. As a consequence, communication is not a constitutive feature of the field whose articulation discloses the transcendental structures of experience. Both the categorial and constitutive accounts outlined above, interestingly enough, could be construed as studies in the sphere of ownness, for none of the descriptions require the least from an analysis of intersubjectivity or communication. Still, the Cartesian formulation of this traffics in a confusion, for it is one thing to say that we have introduced distinctions, eidetic in nature, for which the *difference* between subjectivity and intersubjectivity is not directly relevant—though this distinction could very well form the background against which our analysis takes place—and another thing to claim that since I have privileged access to a sphere of being that is uniquely my own, intersubjectivity is secondary and, eventually, must be derived from this realm. The latter keeps the question of intersubjectivity and communication in a subordinate, derivative position; the former opens the door to its analysis. In his later work Husserl himself realized that what is required is not a transcendental analysis that valorizes the difference between my ego and the other but rather one that transcends it:

> In these meditations I carry out all constructions of knowledge and, in a certain manner, [all] practical [constructions] in a solipsistic attitude. At first I have no occasion to speak of an intersubjective thought, of intersubjective confirmation and truth. . . . But as soon as community is drawn into consideration . . . then we fix, with an additional consideration, the observation that monosubjective mathematics is *eo ipso* intersubjective and, conversely, no intersubjective mathematics is possible that is not already completely grounded as monosubjective.[70]

This allows Husserl to speak of a certain methodological "abstraction" making static analysis possible and thus to recognize the priority of intersubjective communication:

> At first I thought of, to a certain extent, an egological logic, i.e., a grounding of the analytic without drawing in the problems of intersubjectivity.
>
> But this requires a careful consideration of its sense. Language is, to begin with, intersubjective and the sense of the existing world is already intersubjective from the outset. . . .
>
> After I have done as though I only wanted to gain knowledge for myself, what is required is the grounding of the intersubjective validity of the analytic first constructed *in abstraction,* i.e., it requires investigations that enlarge [upon the first].[71]

These new investigations are supplied by genetic analysis. Thus the "history" of expressive acts brings us to communicative acts and to that field of meaning which transcends my particular appropriations of it. The language that I appropriate is itself "thick" with the sedimentations not just of my past uses of it but also of a whole culture. My active speaking is always a way of reactivating what has become deposited over time. This means that over time not only the content of everyday talk but also of propositional judgments forms a "secondary passivity."[72] Furthermore, speech is designed primarily to enable us to sustain and direct our involvement in intersubjective contexts. By turning to discourse we enter that "space" upon which the ideality of propositional language is built.

The genetic analysis of speech is an account of the essential temporality and spatiality of meaning. It supplies a theory of what we are calling *context.*

D. PERCEPTUAL SITUATIONS

If the genetic analysis of language discovers context through the notion of occasionality, the genetic analysis of perception discovers *background* through the notions of association and affectivity. The leading concept of motivation led us above to an account of meaning-implication and its "deployment" across various layers and types of "active synthesis"; when applied to "passive synthesis," by contrast, it leads us to a phenomenology of "association." "The universal principle of passive genesis for the constitution of all objectivities given completely prior to the products of activity, bears the title association."[73]

The concept of association is not defined here, as it was in Husserl's earlier accounts, as a psychological principle.

> The title 'association' denotes for us a form and lawful regularity of immanent genesis that invariably belongs to consciousness in general, but not, as for the psychologists, a form of objective, psycho-physical causality. . . . We are moving within the framework of the phenomenological reduction in which all objective reality and objective causality are "bracketed."[74]

In the empiricists' accounts, association is a connection between experiences or objects of experience established not by sense but strictly by the simultaneous occurrence over time of the items linked, by proximity or contiguity. But Husserl transforms this account by discovering the element of perceptual meaning at this level of analysis. This concept of association is Husserl's way of integrating the phenomenon of indication, excluded from his static accounts, into an account of perceptual meaning and, thereby, discovering its essential tie to temporality and subjectivity. The later Husserl goes far beyond Locke and Hume, viewing association as

> a title, most comprehensive, for an intentional, essential lawfulness to the constitution of the pure ego, a realm of the "innate" a priori without which an ego as such is unthinkable. Only through the phenomenology of gene-

> sis does the ego become understandable as an infinite nexus, connected in the unity of a universal genesis, of achievements belonging together synthetically—in levels that must fit the universal, persisting form of temporality. . . .[75]

As association is woven into Husserl's account of apperception, we can say, building on what we discovered in chapter 7, that association is not just a constitutive but also a genetic principle; it accounts for the way in which profiles are "built up" into wholes over time. The sequence of profiles spans time and, thus, both retention and protention must be introduced to account for the differences between their coexistence and succession. Apperception is not just projective but "drawn" or "pulled" by the object, which means that its sense, brought into play by the retention of earlier experiences similar to this one, directs the ongoing course of experience. There is a "transfer" of sense essential to perception that accounts for the "induction" at play perceptually. This points back to experiences in which that sense was first acquired and then became habitual:

> As Hume correctly teaches, habit is not only our nurse. Rather it is the function of consciousness that shapes and constantly further shapes the world [and,] indeed, all objectivity. "Habit" is the primordial source of every bestowal of objective sense, habit as induction, though, of course, accompanied by a corresponding fulfillment, which is the constant and primordial force constitutive of existence.[76]

But we cannot stop the account here, for these notions do not yet allow us to understand the sense in which perception is always "situational" and involves a movement of extrication as much as one of projection. Recall that constitutional analysis characterized transcendence from the side of immanence. This analysis implicitly confers a particular movement to the treatment of intentionality: acts "transcend" as they are directed "outwardly" through profiles to objects. This tendency is due to more than the vantage point of a Cartesian analysis; it also arises because of the description of experience in terms of the dynamic interplay of intending and fulfillment. The account of passive synthesis, however, opens the door to other features of experience. My experience is simultaneously one of mastering and being mastered, of actions and resistance, of invading and being invaded. In the case of perception I not only act but I am acted upon, I not only effect but I am caught up in a larger realm of affectivity. My acts optimize my view of objects but only as they are drawing me to them. Not only do acts intend objects but also objects capture our acts. Often we are directed to them only because they capture us; our "ray" of intention is matched by a "counter-ray" directed from the object to us.[77] The image of a linear, projective movement to intentional acts, characteristic of the *Logical Investigations* and *Ideas I*, becomes replaced by a notion of circular intentionality. A full analysis of apperception requires an account of *affectivity* and of how "acts are motivated through . . . a genetic relation to the non-active [*ausseraktiv*] sphere."[78] The notion of affection, then, complements the analysis of association. Together they convey the sense in which perceptual intentionality consists of a circuit involving both projection and rejection, transcendence and being solicited, reaching and being drawn. And together they call for an integration of the lived-body into the account.

We must not move too quickly here. Since Husserl wants to run his version of association through the notion of passive synthesis, we have not really sprung the limits of an analysis that is restricted to consciousness. Only the notion of affection opens up yet deeper dimensions. Husserl recognizes this when he tells his listeners that with these studies he is moving into "a phenomenology of the so-called unconscious."[79] Of course, in one sense all of passive synthesis is unconscious. But it seems that integrating affectivity into his account opens another possibility, which we can get at by returning to the notion of protention.

The difficulty, which Husserl only touched upon, with his original notion of protention is that it seems to bring nothing new to the process of perception. It is not really "constitutive" since it seems reduced to reproducing and projecting what is housed in memory. "Associative expectation obviously presupposes association, which, as awakened, relates back to 'memory.'"[80] The problem is that, at best, this yields multiple "configurations" of possibilities,[81] which seems much more general than what actually takes place in perception. In perception we do not anticipate all of these possibilities but only a restricted cluster, "only one line from a multidimensional continuum of the total horizon" of "what is co-present."[82] Why is this one line intended or protended rather than another chosen? We cannot explain this just on the basis of protention as inverted retention.

In *Passive Synthesis* Husserl recognizes that protention is "the second side of the basic genetic lawfulness that rules the unity-stream constituting conscious life as temporal [*Zeit*].[83] Each impressional Now is not only linked to "an intentional horizon of the past" but also to "a protentional horizon of the future." We can explicate both horizons. But then Husserl adds: "all this is already known to us." He moved the analysis forward by questioning whether the two "empty presentations" of retention and protention (empty because the object is not present in a living Now) are "of the same type," differentiated only by their contrasting functions. He began to explore yet other differences. Protention in contrast to the "pure passivity" of retention seems to involve an element of activity in that its anticipatory structure offers "open arms" to the future.[84] In addition, protention, not retention, is what carries the "being-directed-toward" essential to "passive perception." Husserl argues that association is not simply the linking of retentions and (present) impressions but requires protention. "Only in the protentional line of originary time-consciousness does association govern."[85] Protention, then, is what engages retention, not the reverse.

There is yet another idea that Husserl explored in this regard. In a somewhat fragmentary piece he attempted to handle this problem by connecting his account of protention with that of the body:

> The line [actually protended] is the line actualized and specifically motivated through the actual course of the kinaestheses, of the subjective movement of the eyes, etc. Precisely through this motivation does it acquire the character of actual expectation. The remaining horizon is a system of potential expectations.[86]

Even this remaining horizon, through, is understood as the correlate of the "totality of kinaestheses." Husserl added:

> The kinaestheses that belong to expectation bear in themselves the consciousness of 'can-do' [*Können*], namely [the consciousness] of the staging 'can-do' and thereby, as a consequence, the 'can-do' bringing to pass the courses of appearances motivated through them.[87]

A genetic account of affectivity leads us, then, to a deepening of the notion of protention and, as a consequence, to an integration of the "moving" lived-body into the account. This is part of the background in terms of which all perception is situated. With this the contrast between association and affection becomes integrated into the corporeal movements of appropriation and accommodation, as Piaget saw so clearly.[88]

We also find a temporality to perception that is different from speech. Perceptual senses have not just that abstract temporality exhibited in their repetition in different acts at different times, much like what we find in linguistic meanings, but also a concrete temporal component, for in our anticipations of a new profile we protend not only its quality and its place but also its temporal modulations or its rhythm. Disappointment has as much to do with the tempo and timing of things as with their qualities. Since this also transfers to other cases similar to the present one, it must be part of the perceptual sense in play.

Husserl, then, integrated an account of affectivity into his genetic account of associative syntheses. The extensive analysis of association and affectivity is what finally gives us an account of the perceptual horizon that breaks with Husserl's first tendency to characterize it as he did linguistic meanings. As we will suggest in chapter 13, we now have an "aesthetic" notion of background in which senses are schemata that emerge in, as they account for, the perceptual configuration of profiles and object in relation to embodied perceptual acts. In principle, if not in Husserl's own practice, this completes the integration of background into his theory. A genetic phenomenology of perception moves us into an account of the temporality of senses, i.e., it is an analysis of those *lateral* connections between different vertical lines of constitution that we are calling *background.*

E. TEMPORALITY AND GENESIS

The usual contrasts between active and passive begin to come apart in a genetic analysis of perception and speech. Perception, viewed as passive in static analysis, in now understood in terms of multiple syntheses that are integrated through their protentions into the actions of the body, only to then find a new passivity in the phenomenon of affection. Speech, thought of as active synthesis, takes place against a passive context of an acquired language and sedimented meanings established by a community of speakers, who, for their part, stake active claims of their own.

Taking our clue from this expansion of the accounts of perception and speech, we can now pinpoint the decisive difference between static and genetic analysis. Husserl's genetic phenomenology attempts, I am suggesting, an account of the developing interplay of context and background by understanding the horizon as itself temporal. In his published works this idea comes to expression for the first time in *Formal and Transcendental Logic:*

> "Static" analysis is guided by the unity of the intended object. Thus it starts from the unclear modes of givenness and, following what is indicated by them as intentional modification, strives toward what is clear. Genetic intentional analysis [by contrast] is directed toward *the entire concrete interconnection* in which each consciousness and its intentional object as such actually stand. Then immediately there come into question the other intentional indications that belong to the *situation,* in which, for example, the one exercising the activity of judging stands. And this entails the question of the immanent unity of the temporality of life that has its "history" therein, in such a way that every single conscious experience occurring temporally has its own "history," i.e., its temporal genesis.[89]

The account of "situations" is an account of that habitual world over against which individual objects arise and of the temporality of life in terms of which particular acts have their temporal genesis. Genetic analysis is not concerned with just those vertical syntheses attending different kinds of act/object correlations, as in a constitutive account, but with that which is no act, no synthesis, with that which simultaneously contextualizes consciousness and renders each object worldly. In another text Husserl even refers to this as the "Kantian problem of the 'unconscious.'"[90] Ultimately, it is an account of that inescapable nexus without which things would have no place, no situated intelligibility, no concrete presence, and without which our actions and acts would have no temporal source, no spatial shape, no concrete effects. This is why he dared to call this analysis "explanatory" and why his account is so difficult to understand. At first it looks as if he is uncovering aspects of acts and objects not available to his first model of descriptive analysis. In fact, it is an account of the *interconnections* of acts and objects and meanings not manifest in any particular act or any set of acts studied vertically. As such we can describe the horizon as a *nexus of motivated implications.*

Given the correlative nature of Husserl's scheme of phenomenological descriptions, the analysis of the temporality of the horizon in terms of context should invoke a notion of intersubjectivity, while its study as background should find its support in an account of the body. There clearly are probes in these directions, as we indicated above. But because of an inadequate theory of intersubjectivity, which, for the most part, continued to model the presence of the other in terms of his notion of expression and not indication, and because of his restricted, even uneasy account of corporeality, the role of communicative interaction and the "disciplining" of the body, as Foucault might put it, is underplayed and Husserl depends upon the notion of conscious acts to carry the core of his theory of temporality. As he puts it in 1921, "the histories of the constitution of the object lie enclosed in the universal genesis of a monad."[91]

However limited, the crucial connection between genetic analysis and temporality is nevertheless made in Husserl. We are surprised to see how far he was able to go within these limits. We need to follow him along one final stretch of the path.

We suggested that constitutive analysis opens upon a genetic account, which means that its vertical account is the first step in a genetic analysis. This can now be understood by turning to the description of time. To speak of the transformation of a present perception into a past, or of the way in which a current experience is tied by certain laws to past apperceptions, shows how temporal analysis—falling, as it does, outside of a categorial but within a constitutive phenomenology—provides us with an understanding not only of the present act of perception but also of how this one act can follow an earlier one. What Husserl wanted to do was supplement this "form" account of necessary succession with a "content" theory of structural development or emergence. Genetic analysis is not a theory of the *being* of acts in terms of their horizontal and vertical "conditions" but of the *becoming* of acts, of their temporal development. Husserl is unusually clear on this score:

> The stream of consciousness is a stream of a standing genesis, not a mere after-one-another but rather an out-of-one-another, a becoming according to laws of necessary succession in which concrete apperceptions of different types grow out of primal apperceptions or out of apperceptive intentions of

> a primitive kind—underneath them all, the apperceptions which allow the universal apperception of a world to come about.[92]

In this way time acquires a new position. It is considered not only as one level of the act deeper than the others, as occurs in a constitutive analysis, but rather is introduced as the explanatory scheme of genetic analysis itself: "The universal and essential form of intentional genesis, to which all others are related back, is that of the constitution of immanent temporality."[93]

Husserl continually reworked the theory of time throughout his life.[94] The theory of internal time-consciousness helps solve a special difficulty Husserl has related to the nature of self-awareness. Keep in mind that consciousness under the transcendental reduction accounts for the constitution of any and all objects, which means that as constituting, as functioning, it itself is not an object. I cannot say that the awareness I have of consciousness itself results from a reflection upon it for the simple reason that rendering consciousness thematic in reflection turns it into an object (of analysis), a procedure that already assumes that I am acquainted with consciousness. Self-awareness is always on this side of the objectification produced by the act of reflection. In his effort to clarify the nature of consciousness, which is no object, and to explain how it can have a prereflective awareness of itself, Husserl spoke of it as temporalization itself. As Held explains: "I slip away from myself in each moment of my conscious life into the past but am nevertheless continually aware of myself. This basic retention is the most originary synthesis."[95] This produces a type of self-identification that is pre-objective,

> in which my primal ego is something immutably standing and remaining, and yet through the pre-objective self-distancing, it is something streaming in a lively fashion, i.e., something that can become other, over against what it was previously. Thus my ego in its deepest dimension is a living being in which "standing" and "streaming" are one.[96]

While Husserl focused upon the individual, concrete ego, his account of genesis spilled over those banks. The reciprocity we discover between the I and the Thou means that the development of the ego is necessarily bound up with its relation to others and a shared life together in community. For this reason we find Husserl's very late work moving in the direction of yet another type of analysis, called *generative* phenomenology, in which the existential parameters of life and death, home-world and alien-world, and of earth and world are used to expand his first notion of genetic analysis.[97]

This completes the scope of genetic analysis. Temporality is that final source in terms of which all development, all becoming, including that of conscious life itself, is explained. "The basic laws of genesis are the laws of originary time-consciousness."[98] I have suggested that genetic analysis accounts not only for the constitution of my concrete life but also of the horizon itself. "Time, seen from within, is the form of intentional genesis."[99]

F. SYSTEMATIC PHENOMENOLOGY

In an effort to pull the different aspects of Husserl's phenomenology into a comprehensive summary, I would like to chart the course of our deliberations in these nine chapters. I have suggested that the key to understanding genetic phenomenology is first to clarify its relationship to the project of a transcendental phenomenology as Husserl first framed it in *Ideas I,* to set that project in relationship to a reframing of the field of transcendental analysis once the results of his Cartesian way are seen as provisional and once Husserl begins to search for "origins" and then to understand how his account of eidetic structures is supplemented by a theory of transformation. Our working thesis in these nine chapters is that the sequence of disciplines that forms Husserl's systematic phenomenology is also, roughly, a series of stages through which the development of his systematic phenomenology passed.

1. The first discipline, developed in *Ideas I* and *II,* attempts to secure a transcendental ground for formal and regional ontologies. That ground is the *structure* of intentionality. Husserl thinks of regional ontologies as phenomenological studies that use eidetic methods to describe the essential structures of a given, restricted domain of beings or objects in terms of the manner they are presented in experience. He sometimes labels his method here "analytic phenomenology"; I have called it categorial phenomenology because its goal is to clarify the basic categories of beings in terms of certain structural invariants that constitute and certain rules that regulate the relationship between kinds of beings and types of experience. Regional ontologies each articulate a "part" of the "whole." The clarification of the totality itself requires recourse to what is "foundational" to all regional fields. That discipline is transcendental phenomenology proper. But in 1921 Husserl went on to restrict its scope as he describes this grounding discipline as a "universal phenomenology of the general structures of consciousness." Together with categorial phenomenology it forms the core of what he, also during this period, labeled "static" phenomenology.

The task of a static phenomenology is to *secure* that structure (intentionality) that provides the irreducible ground to the various regions, which then allows us to frame each as a sphere of constitution. The method that secures the ground of all regions in intentionality also provides each with its basic form of analysis. Since the as-structure of appearances is understood in terms of the one to whom or for whom objects and complexes are manifest, all intentional analysis is "correlational"; in accounting for the determinacy of beings, the relevant type of sense-structures (noema) is placed in relationship to the type of acts (noesis) in and through which objects or complexes are apprehended or used.

The transcendental phenomenology of *Ideas I* was limited to "the immediately intuitable, essential structures of transcendental subjectivity." Accordingly, the transcendental domain was not a field with depth. As he reflects upon *Ideas I* a decade and a half after its publication, he acknowledged that "the descriptive domain [there] is limited to its more easily accessible level." What *Ideas I* covered was "a systematically self-enclosed infinity of essential properties."[100]

The treatment of intentionality as a grounding structure with essential properties rather than a field with depth was fostered by his Cartesian formulation of the reduction in *Ideas I,* which created an ontological divide between the being of the world and the being of subjectivity. As a result the ground of the various regions of the world was secured without using a regressive analysis that would move back from their structures to their origins. Instead, we are limited to an account that gives us an irreducible, necessary, and universal structure apprehended "all at once" in a transcendental reflection, without a clear understanding of how it is internally connected to the regional ontologies we are attempting to clarify.

2. In *Ideas I,* transcendental phenomenology was taken to be constitutive phenomenology. But with the development of a genetic phenomenology Husserl came to treat constitutive analysis as different from his first "universal phenomenology of the general structures of consciousness." Through its study of the horizonal structure of experience and through its analysis of underlying modalizations and transformations that give rise to manifest structures, constitutive analysis uncovers a depth to "the sphere of being" first opened by the transcendental reduction. In contrast to a horizontal axis along which regional fields are situated, a vertical axis is opened, transforming the grounding structure of intentionality into a transcendental *field* to be explored. By adding depth it enables us to understand how the regions basic to and explicated by regional ontologies are *derived.* The difference between surface and depth establishes an *internal* connection between regional and transcendental fields.

Without using regional ontologies as our guiding thread, we will not understand the difference between the horizontal and the vertical axis of the field of constitution. Constitutive phenomenology, properly understood, does not give us yet "another" region besides the ones opened by categorial analysis but rather describes structures, belonging to the order of sense or meaning, which allow regions to become determinate fields. If the focus in categorial phenomenology is on the identity and difference of eidetic structures of a given field, the concern in constitutive phenomenology is to trace the "origin" of those structures by looking at, for example, transformations by which everyday speech becomes propositional discourse, as well as the experiences that make such transformations possible. As we saw, this involves a study of the internal ties between modalities of active synthesis and then between active and passive synthesis.

3. The account of origins in constitutive phenomenology forms a bridge to genetic analysis proper. Before dealing with their relationship we should summarize the contrast between genetic and static phenomenology more generally.

Genetic phenomenology *reframes* the results of Husserl's static account by rescinding two "abstractions" that made his first characterization of intentionality possible. First, the "pure ego," initially described as a "pole" of unity definable only in terms of the acts and actions that it serves to relate, is recast as an "abstract" structure of the "concrete ego," which has yet other transcendental features. It possesses general capabilities or capacities, whose exercise leads to the acquisition of dispositional tendencies to experience things one way rather than another, what Husserl calls "habitualities." Together they introduce a certain historicity to consciousness. Second, the world, which *Ideas I* reduced and drew into the sphere of "immanence" as a counterpole, as "something identical" posited by consciousness,[101] is reframed as a concrete world that has undergone a process of sedimentation in which past achievements have been deposited into its being. In short, the first notion of intentional consciousness is now elaborated as intentional *life;* the first notion of world is recast as *life-world.*

As a result, genetic analysis *expands* the parameters of the intentional structure first opened by static analysis. However fixed Husserl was on an egological starting point, the concrete ego itself is understood as essentially relational, as subjectivity immersed in intersubjectivity and situated in a community. In addition, the world is now elaborated both as equiprimordial with intersubjectivity and as a historically circumscribed life-world. The effect of this reframing and expansion was to internally connect the *being* of the field of intentionality with its *becoming.*

Static analysis deals neither with the "enigma" of time-consciousness nor with spatiality. The recovery of these moments, which carries us beyond Husserl's categorial analysis into his constitutive and then his genetic phenomenology, takes place in two different registers. In his constitutive analysis they are studied as "syntheses" underlying the varieties of experiential acts. And this account is extended in his genetic analysis when Husserl discovers, through a further analysis of embodied movement and protention, the internal connection between space and time. But from the point of view of the method itself, we can think of constitutive phenomenology as an explication of the "spatiality" of the transcendental field, while genetic analysis unfolds its "temporality."

This second register is brought into play by a development in phenomenological method that allows it to integrate temporally and historically configured structures into its first "formal" notion of the horizon. The depth first discovered through a constitutive account can be described not only in terms of structural but also temporal transformations. At the same time this locates the difference between constitutive and genetic phenomenology. As he puts it in a manuscript from 1921, "to trace [the order of] constitution is not to trace the [order of] genesis, which is, precisely, the genesis of constitution, itself actuated as genesis in a monad."[102] If constitutive analysis deals with vertical transformations according to schemes of implicated and implicator, of conditioned and condition, genetic analysis treats lateral transformation according to spatial and temporal schemes that account for development. Genetic phenomenology deepens the account of the *world* by adding to a constitutive account an analysis of the role of background and context in the configuration of regions of experience. It deepens the account of our *being in* the world by schematizing the *temporal* interplay of experience and discourse constitutive of the transformations within a region or between regions. Genetic analysis treats the dynamic interplay of experience and discourse as deployed over time and as part of a process, historical in nature, that accounts for the *concrete* configuration of a region.

In general we can say that genetic analysis treats the *relationship* between the regions or the transformation of a whole region into another historical form by seeing transformative structures as *temporal.* What is distinct about genetic analysis is that it accounts for various *lateral* relationships between different *vertical* lines of constitution found in the transcendental field. These lateral relations define the diachronic *interplay* of language, experience, and appearances in terms of background and context, an interplay that is at work in the deep structure of those regions covered by categorial phenomenology.

4. The acts of experience in and through which objects, fields, and even the self are presented are all characterized as syntheses by Husserl. Static analysis describes them in terms of their form and then examines the rules regulating different noetic-noematic correlations. By contrast, genetic analysis understands syntheses not just in terms of form, but also in terms of productive achievement, not just in terms of their being but also their becoming. Husserl dealt mainly with two forms of genesis, which he distinguishes as active and passive. Active genesis refers to the conscious or deliberate production of different *ideal* complexes of understanding or *real* cultural complexes from preconstituted elements or objects. Complexes of understanding may range from something like counting to advanced scientific theories. Real cultural complexes may run from a shepherd's song to Beethoven's Ninth Symphony, from a child's sketch to a composition by Paul Klee.

Since Husserl was concerned with the issue of truth, his later accounts of active genesis focused upon the transformations of meaning that allow us to effect a change from "occasional," everyday talk to something like propositional discourse. He suggested that all truth statements indicate "earlier" types of speech and then experience from which they arise. Judgments have a "genesis of meaning." They point back, level by level, to modal transformations from which they are derived, to nested or implied meanings in any one of those levels, to a context not directly expressed in their content yet constitutive of the meaning in play, and, finally, to the origination of their semantic elements from experience. This gives not only a certain "occasionality" but also a definable "historicality" to "objective" discourse.

All active synthesis, however, is interwoven with what is not spontaneously produced. The final level to which active synthesis points is passive synthesis. This level might itself be the result of previous acts of active production that have become sedimented into the world and, as a result, form a "secondary sensibility." Or it might be a level of embodied perception through which things are presented without active construction or interpretation, a level of "originary sensibility."

Husserl's account of passive synthesis moves through his constitutive to his genetic analysis. He described, as we saw, the presence of similarity and contrast played out in the relationship between profiles and objects, recurring across a number of different regional fields, and undertook a clarification of their "origin." In doing so he studied the differential interplay of associative, spatial, and temporal syntheses that account for the transfer of sense involved in our recognition of something as familiar and for the transformation of sense that arises either as a result of becoming acquainted with new features or of being disappointed in our anticipations. Transformation, however, has not only a structural but also a temporal dimension. Protention, to the extent that it directs experience and cuts a certain "line" of anticipation through the multiple possibilities thrown up by a given object, even links us to the motility of the lived-body and a certain affectivity that draws our intentions into a nexus of involvement. Ultimately all passive syntheses rest upon the interplay of retention and protention; this allowed Husserl to treat the basic laws of genesis as laws of time-consciousness.

The account of passive synthesis belongs to a discipline that Husserl, echoing but greatly expanding Kant, called transcendental aesthetics. Husserl took originary perception as his paradigm case here, which he sets in contrast to the active production of propositional claims studied by his transcendental logic. But also previous active constructions that have become sedimented and thus part of our sense of things fall under its jurisdiction as well. Transcendental aesthetics, then, covers not just perceptual senses but, with modification, the acquired and habitual meanings that also shape our concrete life-world.

This gives us yet another interesting way of understanding the difference between constitutive and genetic analysis. We can say that constitutive phenomenology schematizes the structural transformations making phenomenal fields possible according to transcendental *space*. They are framed as layers or strata beneath each field, providing it with its supporting ground. Genetic phenomenology schematizes those transformations in terms of transcendental *time*, and thus as a process of development in which the earlier gives rise to the later, and in which the later draws and gives direction to the now. Not only is the ideality of sense and meaning clarified through the notion of repeatability over time, but their transference and transformation rest upon the interlacing of retentions and protentions across a living present.

At yet a deeper and final level of genetic analysis Husserl discovers that space and time themselves are not just "forms" but are generated, on the one hand, by the interplay of position, motility, and place, and on the other, by the standing-streaming flow of the process of self-temporalization itself. Husserl's studies of the self-generation of space and time are clearly the most difficult of all his genetic studies.

5. Given these differences in levels and descriptions, we are not surprised to discover Husserl differentiating the methods of analysis appropriate to each. While not consistent in his usage, there are differences in the type of analysis that secures evidence for each kind of discipline. Roughly, there is a shift in focus from structural differences to structural transformations to, finally, temporal and historical transformations. I provide only the names Husserl gave to each, offering references in place of commentary, as I will return to the question of analysis in chapters 11, 12, and 15.

6. For methodological reasons having to do with his theory of evidence, Husserl used the single ego and its acquired world as his starting point. Some of his genetic analyses stay within these parameters. But Husserl was fully aware of the fact that subjectivity is necessarily concrete, that the other is not merely a correlate of "my" own intentional acts, but someone who affects me, and that we are always situated not only in a body but also in a world. This led him to speak of a genesis not just of my experience but of community, ethical life, culture, and religion. In his published writings this appears for the first time in a series of articles he wrote for a Japanese periodical, partially published between 1923 and 1924, which we will study in detail in chapter 12. There he traces a development through the course of history toward a certain *telos* in which rational interaction becomes normative.

Once Husserl found a way of integrating the notion of development and transformation into his phenomenological method, and once he found a way of moving from his first starting point to communal existence and the life-world, new horizons opened for his phenomenology. For this reason we find Husserl's very late work moving in the direction of yet another type of analy-

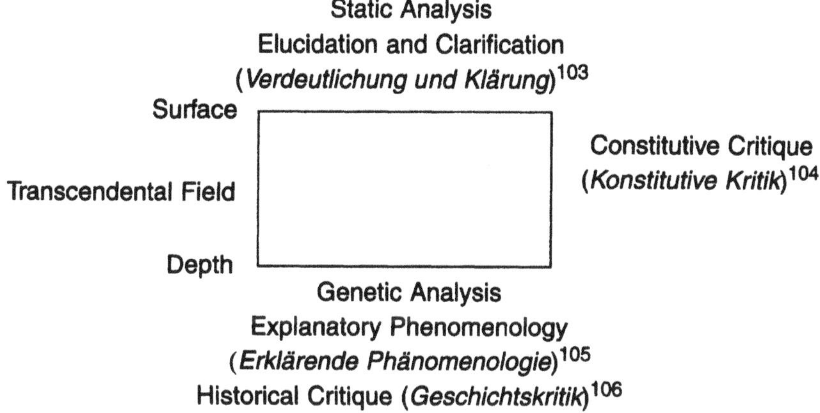

Fig. 9.1. Methods of Analysis

sis, called *generative* phenomenology, which I mentioned above. What it is that holds his genetic and generative accounts together is that temporality is understood as the final source in terms of which all development, all becoming, including that interplay of conscious life and world constitutive of our essential historicity, is explained. "Time, seen from within, is the form of intentional genesis."[107]

This clarification of the difference between categorial, constitutive, and genetic phenomenology shows us how deeply Heidegger's working method in *Sein und Zeit,* for all the striking differences in content resulting from its application, is indebted to Husserl's framework. While it does not actually attempt to carry them out, *Sein und Zeit* establishes a place for regional ontologies. Because he wants the use of "ontological" to be reserved for his transcendental account, Heidegger characterizes such regional disciplines as "ontic." With that to the side, Division I undertakes extensive *structural* descriptions of the various moments of Dasein as being-in-the-world, as well as accounts of the "origins" of the present-at-hand, on the one hand, and assertions, on the other. It clearly works with the resources of a constitutive phenomenology with one important qualification: Heidegger avoided treating any one constitutive level as absolutely basic, stressing instead the sense in which founding relations are relative and in which each level is yet another dependent "moment" of the whole structure of Dasein. Division II then attempts to reframe the results of this account in terms of *temporality,* which is precisely what Husserl's notion of genetic phenomenology calls for. However different the content of their theories, there is a surprising coincidence between the different levels of their systematic phenomenological methods. We will return to this connection in chapter 14.

With this we conclude our study of the contours of Husserl's method. Ever so much was left out of consideration and ever so many concrete analyses left undone in order to achieve breadth and to get at the heart of his concept of philosophy. But if the broad outline I have sketched is a fair representation of the scope of Husserl's phenomenology, then we do indeed have a very different Husserl than the one found in the standard interpretation. This difference, however, is itself a result of an ever deepening process of thinking in which Husserl became his own Other.

PART TWO

Critique: The Limits of Husserl's Phenomenological Method

Husserl. Ca. 1920. Courtesy of Anna-Maria Husserl.

10

Transcendental Psychologism

> . . . there is a remarkable thoroughgoing parallelism between a correctly executed phenomenological psychology and a transcendental phenomenology. To every eidetic, as well as to every empirical, constellation [*Feststellung*] on the one side, a parallel must correspond on the other side. And yet this whole theoretical content, if taken, in the natural attitude, as psychology, as a positive science relating to the pregiven world, is utterly non-philosophical; whereas the "same" content in the transcendental attitude, and consequently understood as transcendental phenomenology, is a philosophical science. Indeed, it even achieves the rank of the philosophically fundamental science, as a science that cultivates, in description, the transcendental ground, which henceforth remains the exclusive ground of all philosophical knowledge.
>
> —Husserl (1931)[1]
>
> Even transcendental psychology also is precisely psychology.
>
> —Husserl (1900)[2]

IN THE NEXT three chapters we will engage in a critique *of* and a critique *with* Husserlian analysis. For it is only by turning to critique that we can raise the issue of legitimacy.

In the first part of this study I argued that Husserl progressively overcame his Cartesian way into transcendental analysis, found in *Ideas I* (1913), by proposing a difference between static and genetic analysis and, then, between alternative paths to the reduction; next by attempting to rearticulate its basic principles in his *Cartesian Meditations* of 1929; and finally, by realizing that it was still much too limited a conception to do justice to the full scope of his method and his own concrete studies. I suggested that while Husserl departed from that way, he never truly abandoned it, if we mean by his Cartesian approach that he employed a transcendental method of reflection that always took consciousness as the irreducible, fundamental ground upon which the edifice of knowledge could be erected. If this is the case, submitting this thesis to critical analysis is a way of testing the adequacy of his method. This critique becomes all the more relevant to contemporary concerns in view of the very recent attempts in German philosophy by Dieter Henrich and Manfred Frank to rehabilitate the notion of self-consciousness.[3] The critical thesis that I will argue in this chapter is that, while a philosophical method that employs a self-sufficient reflection upon consciousness can escape garden variety empiricist versions of the fallacy of psychologism, it necessarily falls prey to that same error in another register, namely, to transcendental psychologism. I argue that this problem undercuts any efforts to legitimize the thesis that consciousness is the irreducible and uncircumventable (*unhintergehbarer*) ground of transcendental analysis. In the next chapter I will recover the sense in which the turn to consciousness, free of any theory of adequate presence, provides a guiding thread for what becomes transcendental analysis. But here my purpose is strictly critical. My critique will be attuned to certain problems involving the problem of time and the "apodicticity" of memory. We will deal with temporality both with respect to how it accounts for the unity of consciousness and how it qualifies the type of evidence we can have of that unity. I will attempt to introduce Husserl's version of involuntary memory and then argue that phenomenological method, contrary to Husserl's claims, has an inescapably constructive aspect.

With this critique of Husserl's Cartesian formulations in hand, the next chapter will provide a positive account of static transcendental method. There I will deal with the relationship between the transcendental reduction and transcendental arguments and attempt to provide an analysis of the direct way into the reduction that is not Cartesian, i.e., to supply a Husserlian version of Kant's transcendental deduction. This deduction will treat the issue of legitimization from a static perspective. The twelfth chapter will not turn to the *Crisis of European Science* (composed between 1934 and 1937), the usual source used to understand how Husserl's genetic phenomenology was applied to the question of legitimization in the context of historical and sociocultural studies. Instead, it will undertake a study of five articles partially published a decade earlier (1923 and 1924) in the Japanese periodical *Kaizo*. This is Husserl's first sustained analysis of the problem of culture using his newly developed genetic method. It will allow us both to expand the account of genetic analysis just discussed in Part 1 and to critically engage certain aspects of his theory. In particular, I will raise the issue of whether transcendental phenomenology's dependence upon the category of self-consciousness undercuts a conception of rationality and understanding that is dialogical and contextually attuned.

A. THE PROBLEM OF PSYCHOLOGISM

Psychologism, the theory that attempts to reduce all semantic and syntactic organization to the mental contents and operations of empirical subjects, poses a fundamental threat to philosophical theory by introducing a fundamental confusion into that theory, reducing any level of discourse ostensibly ranging over philosophy's various regions to one of those regions, psychology. Psychologism effects this reduction by undercutting the ideal nature of linguistic and logical constructs, which, in turn, leaves inexplicable not only the sense in which concepts and claims are trans-subjective but also the way in which their referents and their validity can usually be established without recourse to the images and associations lodged in the mind of their proponents. The reduction of predicate content to mental images or representations and the equating of syntactic formations with psychological associations or operations transform all the domains of philosophical theory into a branch of psychology and their logics into questions of subjective linkage. Rather than philosophy having a place of its own, one which would provide the ontological and epistemological grounding of the various natural and human sciences, both the method and the task of philosophy are identified with that of psychology. This equation precipitates the most pernicious of category mistakes: the single, regional science of psychology, itself in need of grounds, is taken to be the foundation of all the other positive sciences. In Husserl's lecture course "Phenomenological Psychology" (offered three times between 1925 and 1928)—a text we will examine later in this chapter—the fallacy is identified in this way:

> Psychology is itself a positive science and, as is the case with the kind of research carried out in all positive sciences, does not touch the question that applies to them all concerning the ontological meaning of its [own] region of being.[4]

The temptation has been to answer the threat of psychologism with a strict formalism, as we find in Frege and the early Wittgenstein, in which questions of interpretation are discarded in favor of questions of justification. The latter questions are, in turn, answered through a reconstructive procedure that entertains only rule-governed logical representations of a world construed as a totality of facts. For formalism, the range of human acts, actions, and interactions engaged in modeling and remodeling our all-too-human world have no more to add to our syntactic and semantic analyses than the reflected image could add to the structure of the mirror in which it dwells. According to the formalist, psychological facts, should there be such, are no different ontologically than all the other facts to which we refer in our sciences. They have no more to contribute to the foundations of the sciences than prunes or puppies.

Perhaps no philosopher has spent more ink attempting to chart a course between the alternatives of psychologism and formalism than Husserl. While there are earlier critical probes of his own psychologism in the *Philosophy of Arithmetic,* as Mohanty's historical reconstruction has shown,[5] the definitive critique of the theory as it was formulated by other philosophers began in earnest at the turn of the century with the publication of his *Prolegomena to Pure*

Logic (1900), and it continued over the course of the next thirty-five years. The way in which he handled the problem, his successes and failures, are highly relevant to current discussions, for Husserl, unlike almost any other contemporary philosopher, exhibits in the movement of his own thinking the very course of philosophy throughout this century.

The story of Husserl's early flirtation with psychologism in the *Philosophy of Arithmetic* (1891), his first efforts to press beyond these formulations, Frege's scathing attack upon him, and his subsequent refutation of psychologism in the *Prolegomena,* is well documented in Mohanty's insightful study.[6] We can also infer from the four surviving letters of the Frege-Husserl correspondence[7] that the elation Frege must have experienced in reading Husserl's critique of psychologism in the *Prolegomena* may have been dashed quickly when he went on to study the *Logical Investigations* proper, published the following year (1901), only to discover Husserl undergirding his analysis of meaning with a "descriptive psychology," as the first edition put it.[8] I will pause to recount some of the central points in this debate. I will also sketch how *Ideas I* introduces a shift in analysis designed to handle the methodological problems left unresolved by the *Investigations.* Furthermore, I want to break new ground and concentrate on the work Husserl undertook on this issue after *Ideas I,* on the lecture manuscript "Phenomenological Psychology," composed primarily between 1925 and 1928, as its content is not well known.[9] It is these last studies that allow us to see how the problem of psychologism, now recognized in a transcendental register, turns inside out not only Husserl's first approach to phenomenology but also the operative concepts ordering some of the current work on the relationship between language and mind.

B. A FIRST CRITIQUE OF PSYCHOLOGISM

In the *Prolegomena,* Husserl coordinates his critique of psychologism with a less pronounced, almost muted, attack upon formalism. His general strategy is to argue that every normative discipline, such as logic or linguistics, rests upon one or more theoretical disciplines.[10] The controversy with both psychologism and formalism concerns the nature of this theoretical discipline, psychologism proposing psychology as a basis and formalism grounding logic in a meta-logic of construction rules. Against the first, Husserl suggests that one lands in internal contradictions methodologically and false statements descriptively if psychology, an empirical, regional science, is made into a theoretical science grounding logic and/or the theory of science. Against the second, Husserl argues that propositions are essentially syntactically formed units of meaning and that an analysis of meaning is incomplete without a study of the acts, even of the interactions, in and through which meaningful signs are used to refer. The theoretical discipline that Husserl proposes is the science of phenomenology.

We, of course, will concentrate on the critique of psychology here. If we take knowledge to be a property of *acts* of judgment that have been validated through either direct or indirect evidence, and if we take truth to be a property of the *objects* of correct judgments,[11] then the key to Husserl's critique of psychologism is the thesis that logic is not reducible to laws of knowing but, rather, is concerned with relations of truth.[12] Let me attempt to distill his critique into three interrelated theses, bearing in mind the discussion of propositions offered above in chapter 7.

1. We begin with the familiar distinction between the meaning and the reference of predicate terms. While the referent is not part of our mental life, Husserl does construe the meaning as belonging to the content of the act. It is an *Inhalt* or content in a very specific way, however, for Husserl distinguishes between the *real* act of judging and the proposition, which, as an *ideal* unit, forms the content of the act.[13] Such ideal unities are complexes of meanings, and they remain identical throughout variations in the acts that appropriate them.

2. Not only must we distinguish the acts of judging from the proposition judged, even as we understand such propositions as the content of such acts, but we must also set the proposition judged in contrast to my psychological image or experiential representation (*Vorstellung*) of the proposition. The proposition is an ideal species over against the multiplicity of images and ideas that I may have of it, as well as over against the various acts in which it may be thematic.[14] This thesis can be cast in terms of temporal differences: because all psychic life is temporally determined, its acts and its images are also temporal; propositions, however, are not temporal but transtemporal and, thus, can neither be considered psychological facts nor reduced to psychic contents.[15]

3. If we confuse propositions with psychic phenomena, we will also conflate logical laws and relations with causal laws determining the course of psychic life. But even if we admit that thinking proceeds according to causal laws and that the ideal norms of logic could serve to justify the thoughts we have, it is not the case that the norms are identical with such laws.[16] There is neither correspondence nor any relationship of derivation between "A causes B" and the principles of identity, contradiction, and excluded middle.[17] In general, Husserl argues, it is impossible to derive logical laws from matters of fact, be they material or mental. Conversely, no logical law implicates a matter of fact. Moreover, it is clear that those combinations excluded by objective logical laws are not excluded from acts of thinking; this would be impossible if logical laws were causal laws.[18]

Frege would readily agree with these ideas. The problems arise when

Husserl presses for further clarification of how meanings and acts are connected, and when he pauses to characterize the method he is using. As we saw in chapter 3, in the First Investigation Husserl continues the emphasis of the *Prolegomena* and stresses the break between meanings and acts, suggesting that meaning is related to the actual acts of intending as a self-identical species is to objects that have that trait. "Meanings form, we could also say, a class of concepts in the sense of 'ideal objects.'"[19] In the Fifth Investigation, however, Husserl combines an analysis of meaning with an analysis of acts in such a way that the meaning accounts for the way in which the object is intended or determined.[20] As such, he treats meaning not just as an *Inhalt* exemplified by or instantiated in the act but as the *matter* of the act, even speaks of it as "a component of the concrete act-experience, which it may share with acts of quite different quality."[21] Since matter provides the act with a particular, characteristic intention and accounts for the way the object is determined or taken, Husserl is convinced that matter must be a component of the intentional experience itself.[22]

To say that the meaning is a component of the act is to say that it is a descriptive feature of the act itself, not just exemplified by something else in the act, perhaps an image or mental representation. Without it being a component of the act, the varieties of presentational possibilities cannot be understood. This addition to the theory creates a clear tension within Husserl's earlier analysis, however, for the first edition described act components as *reell,* as immanent or real parts of the act and thus psychological in nature.[23] To the extent that the Fifth and Sixth Investigations treat meaning as moments of acts, Husserl's emphasis on the irreality or ideality of meaning is threatened, and the specter of psychologism reappears.

C. THE TRANSCENDENTAL TURN AS A RESPONSE TO PSYCHOLOGISM

The lack of clarity as to both the matter of intentional acts and the method of analysis became evident to Husserl rather quickly. It is quite likely that Frege, once again, played a role. In a letter of 1906 he penned sharp words to Husserl:

> The logicians, it seems to me, adhere too much to language and grammar, and are too much caught up in psychology. . . . Logic, in no way, is a part of psychology. The Pythagorean theorem expresses the same thought for all men, while each person has his own representations, feelings, and resolutions that are different from those of every other person. Thoughts are not psychic structures, and thinking is not an inner producing and forming, but an apprehension of thoughts which are already objectively given.[24]

The first book of *Ideas*, published some twelve years after the *Investigations*, responds to the internal threat of psychologism by reframing two crucial points, one having to do with the analysis of acts, the other having to do with the question of method.

Husserl came to believe that his analysis in the *Investigations* was one-sided and that it stressed a typology of mental experiences, the noetic, to the detriment of that which gave those acts or experiences their determinate semantic references, what he later called the noematic. *Ideas I* emphasizes the correlational nature of acts and argues that we find two interdependent moments: the *quality*, or what we today call the "force," of the act is always tied to the manner in which the object of its concerns is taken or intended, the *Sinn* (sense) or *Bedeutung* (meaning) of the act. The reason why this is not a simple reiteration of what we find in the *Investigations*, though, is that Husserl is much clearer about the fact that this correlation of noesis and noema is not a real component of acts, as though this were an inventory of phenomenal elements open to psychological reflection, but an a priori structure that is displayed in a variety of acts.

All of this is supported, however, by a crucial distinction in method between psychological analysis, a regional discipline found among other human sciences, and transcendental phenomenological analysis, the method of philosophy proper (as we saw in chapter 4). The goal of this distinction is to drive a wedge between empirical psychology and philosophy and, Husserl feels, to undercut psychologism once and for all by stressing the different methods of these two disciplines.

In a later reflection upon Husserl's work during this period, Heidegger provided an appropriate summary of the points I just made:

> The first volume of the [*Logical Investigations*] . . . brings the refutation of psychologism in logic by showing that the doctrine of thought and knowledge cannot be based on psychology. In contrast, the second volume [of the first edition], which was published the following year and was three times as long, contains the description of the acts of consciousness essential for the constitution of knowledge. So it is a psychology after all. . . . Accordingly, Husserl falls back, with his phenomenological description of the phenomena of consciousness, into the position of psychologism, which he had just refuted. But if such a gross error cannot be attributed to Husserl's work, then what is the phenomenological description of the acts of consciousness? Wherein does what is peculiar to phenomenology consist if it is neither logic nor psychology? . . .
>
> "Pure phenomenology" is the "fundamental science" of philosophy which is characterized by that phenomenology. "Pure" means: "transcendental phenomenology." However, the "subjectivity" of the knowing, acting, and valuing subject is posited as "transcendental." Both terms, "subjec-

tivity" and "transcendental," show that "phenomenology" consciously and decidedly moved into the tradition of modern philosophy but in such a way that "transcendental subjectivity" attains a more original and universal determination through phenomenology. Phenomenology retained "experiences of consciousness" as its thematic realm, but now in the systematically planned and secured investigation of the *structure* of acts of experience together with the investigation of the objects experienced in those acts with regard to their objectivity.[25]

D. REFRAMING PSYCHOLOGY

The story just told is not new, nor is Heidegger the only one who offers such a version of Husserl's solution to psychologism. As we begin to reflect further on these matters, however, we quickly realize that this solution will not work. It depends upon an impoverished notion of psychology, one which views it as a simple, empirical discipline whose task is to provide an inventory of mental elements and operations of association, as, for example, in the theories of John Stuart Mill and Hermann Ebbinghaus. No doubt this can be contrasted quite easily with a non-introspective, reflective description of the structure of engaged acts and actions, especially if we hold in suspense the assumption of factual existence, which is necessary for any empirical discipline, and move to the level of necessary conditions. In other words, using the language of *Ideas I,* the essential difference between transcendental phenomenology and psychological analysis lies in the fact that transcendental phenomenology is a *pure* eidetic discipline which, in order to secure necessary conditions, employs a reduction or bracketing of all existence claims upon its field:

> In its purely eidetic attitude, setting all transcendent [existents] out of play, phenomenology arrives, on its own ground of pure consciousness, at this whole complex of transcendental problems in the specific sense; and it is from this that it earns the name of transcendental phenomenology.[26]

This contrast between transcendental phenomenology and empirical psychology is destabilized, however, because Husserl, developing a strand we already find in *Ideas I,* envisions a reclamation of psychology itself. He realizes that there can be a psychology which is itself phenomenological and which is different from the older empiricist project. In 1925, some thirteen years after *Ideas I,* he even suggests that such a phenomenological psychology is not only eidetic but also requires a bracketing of existence in order to arrive at a proper analysis of the psyche. Not merely a reflection upon conscious life but also a reduction of real existence is needed to lead us back to the field of phenomena proper to phenomenological psychology. As soon as Husserl argues this thesis, however, he immediately conflicts with his original idea that all regional sciences take place within the natural attitude and without brackets.

In his lecture course on phenomenological psychology, given three times between the Summer Semester of 1925 and the Summer Semester of 1928, as well as in his *Encyclopaedia Britannica* article (1927) and his Amsterdam lectures (1928),[27] Husserl not only recognized this difficulty but attempted to respond to it in various ways. I will attempt to show, however, that the *results* of these elaborations, contrary to Husserl's expressed belief, rob transcendental phenomenology not only of a *content* but even of a *method* that can be distinguished from those of phenomenological psychology. Because it is unable to recover a distinctive method and a unique scope for transcendental analysis, his Cartesian way as just formulated implodes under the weight of a problem that Husserl himself identified as transcendental psychologism.

E. THE LOSS OF A DISTINCT TRANSCENDENTAL METHOD AND CONTENT

In his lectures on phenomenological psychology, Husserl reported that he had only recently (*neuerdings*) come to distinguish between "philosophical-transcendental phenomenology" and "psychological phenomenology." Elaborating upon the latter, he suggests that it not only reflects upon consciousness but also "inhibits every perceptual positing of the object (under consideration) and of any other transcendent object."[28] What it "delivers to us is the *pure,* in itself closed domain of psychic phenomena in their concrete and total unity."[29]

How is this different from the transcendental reduction (under a Cartesian description)? At this point Husserl wavers. A pure phenomenological psychologist must "set the world out of play [*die Welt ausser Geltung setzen*]"[30] in order to gain the pure field of consciousness. But on the other hand, "I, as psychologist, . . . have the world in play [*die Welt in Geltung*] and want to stay with it as such."[31] The solution that Husserl proposes is one that takes the empirical psyche not as a field *outside* the real world, experiencing it while transcending it, but rather as a hollow *within* the totality of the world, immanent to it yet not identical with any of its parts. To paraphrase Husserl, in the psychologically pure attitude, I bracket my existence as a person, as well as the world experienced by me as simply existing, in order to uncover my pure psychic subjectivity. This is done in such a way, however, that I apperceive pure subjectivity as still being a soul, an apperception that presupposes the validity of the world. My soul, however, is not fixed in the world as a component of it, as an item that is perceived as objective and real, posited as empirically existing. Rather, my soul is perceived more like a subjective fact; it is in the world, and yet, as pure psychic inferiority, free from all suppositions of real existence.[32]

We must be careful here. Husserl's method of describing consciousness is one that sets out of play the claim of existence necessary for one to identify mental facts with physical facts, as we would find in standard materialist views. His strategy is to abstractively reflect back from our perceived world, which we take as existing, to the mental activities of the soul, a soul found only in the world but said to exist in a radically different sense. In this way, Husserl believes that he can explain how psychology, concerned with pure subjectivity, can be a regional science distinct from the region of physical being.

But even if we grant that this notion of bracketing is adequate to secure a distinction between mental and physical being and to undermine any materialist identification of the former with the latter, we still must ask how the introduction of a pure psychological reduction alongside the transcendental phenomenological reduction redefines the scope of these two disciplines and how Husserl is going to maintain their distinctness. Having redefined phenomenological psychology as he did, Husserl still believed that he could distinguish it from Cartesian phenomenology not only in terms of its *content* but also in terms of the range and efficacy of *reflection*. I want to suggest that in neither case is Husserl successful. Let me take up the issue of reflection first.

Husserl often takes the psychological ego as one of the items upon which I as transcendental ego can and do reflect: "The totality of the natural attitude with its constructs are only constitutive occurrences in transcendental subjectivity."[33] If this were Husserl's only approach, then we could establish a contrast between the psychological and transcendental reflections by suggesting that the transcendental reflection covers one item (the psychological ego) not included in a psychological reflection. A psychological reflection might open consciousness to view as a field in which all phenomena are displayed; the transcendental reflection, however, would have that field as one of the displayed phenomena. As a result, the transcendental ego could be distinguished from the psychological ego by being the ego that has the psychological ego as its theme, as its object, while the reverse would never be true. Even in the face of an obvious infinite regress, Husserl often presents this position.

In his 1925 lectures, however, Husserl argues that the psychological ego is not only able to perceive *itself* reflectively but that within this reflection I can carry out "an eidetic egological study of the necessary structures of my soul as a soul in general."[34] Because this reflection can be executed only by a bracketing of the general thesis of the natural attitude, it seems that there is no definitive contrast between phenomenological psychology and transcendental phenomenology, at least not one that can be read from the structure of the reflection itself. The difference cannot simply be stipulated but must be a feature that can be read off the different reflections.

If the difference is not in the *nature* of the reflection per se, perhaps it can be found in the range of the reflection, in the *content* reflected upon. Once again Husserl wavers, and it is difficult to find consistent theory. The working differentiations between psychology and transcendental phenomenology found in *Ideas I* no longer control Husserl's texts after 1925. Phenomenological psychology is concerned with an interpretation of the world in terms of "my" experience of it and with the various types and levels of conscious syntheses constituting that experience.[35] Transcendental analysis, however, is also concerned with an interpretation of the world as it is displayed in the sphere of my "original experience" and with the dimensions of subjectivity undergoing these experiences.[36] At one point Husserl boldly suggests that

> the universe of the certifiable givens of my original experience is identical with the universe of the certifiable givens of my pure soulish . . . experience.[37]
>
> [In the phenomenological psychological reduction] I [, on the one side,] search for forms which must occur in every monad and, on the other side, I encounter *universal, structural forms* which give unity to the monad in its entirety. The manner of proceeding here has its difficulties. *Everything* that I have handled in the transcendental attitude as phenomenological appears here on the ground of a natural attitude as *a priori, descriptive psychology* of the monadic soul.[38]

With this the dilemma is set. Phenomenological psychology is not only able to study the structure of intentionality and to interpret the correlation between consciousness and objective being in terms of noesis and noema,[39] it is also able to describe essential types of evidence,[40] the entire system of human reason, and the essential forms of possible worlds of experience.[41]

F. COMPLEMENTARITY AND IDENTITY

The momentum of his detailed studies of phenomenological psychology carries Husserl deeper into psychologism than ever before. He cannot but draw back: "the world . . . is nothing but the noematic correlate of universal [transcendental] subjectivity."[42] "My soulish subjectivity," in turn, " . . . is a component of concrete humanity and thus [a] noematically appearing [object]."[43] Cartesian analysis requires that the psychological ego become the correlate of an ego that it is not and, correspondingly, that the psychological field be set in contrast to transcendental consciousness:

> It is now evident that the apperceiving life of consciousness wherein the world . . . and human beings are constituted as real and existing . . . is not that soulish [life] which belongs to . . . the real world.[44]
>
> The transcendental ontic field is, according to the method of transcendental reduction giving us access, a [field] parallel to the phenomenological psychological field with its method of psychological reduction providing access.[45]

What we find, as a result, is a continual shifting between two ways of relating phenomenological psychology and transcendental phenomenology, and, correspondingly, the psychological and the transcendental ego. In the citation above, Husserl holds a *complementarity thesis:* transcendental phenomenology is an analysis of a set of phenomena or structures not included in the set of phenomena or structures described by psychology (or any other regional science). At other times, Husserl operates with an *identity thesis:* transcendental phenomenology ranges over the same set of phenomena or structures described by phenomenological psychology. Husserl's analysis is torn between the complementarity and identity theses. Such tension, I would argue, is necessarily ingredient in any transcendental phenomenological theory that relies upon the Cartesian strategy of directly intuiting consciousness.

The push toward one alternative or the other comes from different directions. When Husserl is absorbed in the detailed task of elaborating phenomenological psychology as pure and eidetic, he moves in the direction of the identity thesis. The range of this psychology leaves no residue, no field that transcendental phenomenology could claim as uniquely its own. Transcendental analysis is overtaken by psychological analysis. The threat this poses for the fundamental distinctions of his *Wissenschaftstheorie* as well as the specter of psychologism, however, is met only by Husserl's recourse to the complementarity thesis. Yet the complementarity thesis, by opposing the transcendental to the psychological field, portends a two-world theory, with two isomorphic spheres of "being" or "phenomena."[46] His efforts in the *Encyclopaedia Britannica* article[47] and the Amsterdam lectures[48] to rectify the "transcendental semblance [*Schein*] of a doubling [*Verdoppelung*]" of worlds and to ameliorate the "parallelism" of psychological and transcendental fields[49] could proceed only by a reaffirmation of the identity thesis. Nevertheless, Husserl makes a concession at this point which neither the structure of the reflection nor differentiations within the phenomenological field can justify:

> even if the psychological theory of knowledge is grounded, and that in full universality, it still requires the Copernican revolution in order to give this entire phenomenology and theory of reason transcendental meaning.[50]

With this one might agree. But the question remains whether a Cartesian approach, which necessarily ties reflection to a field of experience taken as actual, mental events, is able to effect such a revolution. As Husserl frankly recognized in his *Prolegomena,* "even transcendental psychology also is precisely psychology."[51]

G. MEMORY AND TRANSCENDENTAL METHOD

Perhaps our analysis should move more slowly, taking seriously Husserl's emphasis upon a Copernican revolution. Perhaps we should look not to a structural difference in content or in types of reflection as the individuating feature of a transcendental analysis, but instead to a difference established by the special task of philosophy itself, the task of providing a grounding for knowledge. This alternative would treat the transcendental reduction as an *interpretative* transformation of the same field uncovered by a pure phenomenological psychology. There would be no difference in the scope of the reflection nor in the content of the field that is present (the identity thesis). The difference would be created solely by a change in attitude,[52] which would both be constitutive of the transcendental level of analysis and allow us to treat the transcendental as the condition of the psychological (a kind of complementarity thesis).

Treating the reduction as an interpretative transformation of a field demarcated by psychology, however, would never suffice for Husserl, for in this case the field would be transcendental only because of a reduction that *created* it as such by stipulation. This would fly in the face of Husserl's claim that the transcendental field is an "absolute fact"[53] and in some sense given. It would be only relative, dependent upon the performance of the reduction not merely for its thematization but also for its *being.* In addition, the motive for taking the transcendental turn becomes incomprehensible. Since nothing within the content given or the reflective act exercised would be different from what we acquire through a pure psychology, the reasons for taking a transcendental turn could be found only in certain gaps, fissures, or conundrums that haunt the positive sciences, which is precisely what the Cartesian way cannot entertain because of its suspension of the natural world. Alternatively, such gaps could be filled by yet another positive science, psychology, because they are issues involving cognition. Thus, the motive for taking the transcendental turn would be entirely external and we could never know why one needs this level of interpretation at all.

There is yet another option open to Husserl. Treating the reduction as an interpretative transformation works only if we can go on to secure transcendental subjectivity as the absolute ground. The difference between the natural attitude constitutive of the positive sciences and the transcendental attitude itself would be established by a difference in the quality or type of *evidence.* This is possible, Husserl believes, only if the evidence we offer disavows "indirect knowledge" and meets the twin criteria of adequacy and apodicticity. This account is already familiar from our discussion in chapter 6. I now want to expand upon that discussion in order to get at what I take to be the deepest problem with the Cartesian way.

Because Husserl's attempt to maintain both the complementarity and the identity thesis entailed that transcendental subjectivity could not have novel content absent from subjectivity as described by phenomenological psychology, what must be new is the epistemological status of our claims. The transcendental ego can serve as ground because it possesses an *Erkenntnisdignität*[54] absent from consciousness analyzed psychologically. If transcendental subjectivity can be encompassed by intuition adequately and if this is accepted as evidence, then we might be able to speak of the transcendental ego as the absolute ground of the empirical ego in an epistemological sense (complementarity thesis) while preserving the ontic identity of the two (identity thesis). But can this be achieved? Do we have adequate evidence of transcendental subjectivity?

We saw in chapter 6 that Husserl argued in *Ideas I* that our immanent perception of the *ego-cogito-cogitatum* is indubitable and free of the inadequacy that burdens our perception of real, transcendent objects.[55] While *Ideas I* denies that we have an indubitable and non-presumptive apprehension of the object's "self," it does allow such an apprehension of the *Erlebnis,* the lived experience, itself. But what does this mean? What exactly is intuited?

Husserl comes to realize that he must answer these questions by recourse not just to the identity of the object of reflection (the mental process) and its appearances but also to his theory of time. He attempts to ground the absolute and immediate grasping of the *Erlebnis* in the absolute Now, in distinction to the past and future. Thus we read in the original 1912 edition of *Ideas I:*

> The mental process does not present itself, we said, [through adumbrations or profiles]. That means that the perception of a mental process is a simple viewing of something that is perceptually given as absolute and not given as something identical through modes of appearance, each of which is an adumbration. . . . A mental process of feeling is not adumbrated. If I look at it, I have something absolute; it does not have sides that present [the mental process] sometimes in one mode, sometimes in another.[56]

The corrections that Husserl made to this passage in his own copies in the later 1920s and that are included in the Husserliana edition are significant (changes italicized):

> The mental process does not present itself *as perceptually present according to its whole present content (and thus in each moment).* That means that the perception of a mental process is a simple viewing of something that *in its*

> *present, at every point in its Now* is perceptually given as absolute and not given as something identical through modes of appearance, each of which is a *one-sided* adumbration. . . . A mental process of feeling is not adumbrated.[57]

Husserl became convinced that the absolute evidence for the *ego-cogito* was confined to the primitive present. The text continues (insertions from 1929 italicized):

> If I look at it, I have *with respect to each point of its continuous present* something absolute; it does not have sides that present [the mental process] sometimes in one mode, sometimes in another.[58]

The "content" of this Now is without perspectives and adumbrations. This also means that while the reflection upon the mental process necessarily takes on the modifications of presentification, the mental process thematized in the reflection is given as absolute and originary.[59] But now Husserl realizes that his results are impoverished: at best we only have the momentary Now, the Now "at every point in its Now."

This line of thought is based on the idea that there is an originary presentiation (*Gegenwärtigung*) without any admixture of presentification (*Vergegenwärtigung*), that within this Now the *Erlebnis* is displayed in complete lucidity, and that this mental process gives itself unaffected by the noetic components of the reflection without which it could never be thematized. The problem with this solution, as we began to see in chapter 6, is that it relies upon a notion of the Now that Husserl himself comes to reject. There is in fact a development in Husserl's theory of time that makes this reliance on adequate presence untenable.

Husserl's initial descriptions of time-consciousness did speak of a primal or impressional Now. Even though it exists only as part of a continuity of retentions and protentions, the primal Now was nevertheless intuited.[60] The mental process, which was absolutely present, was given as such only in the impressional Now. In the subsequent analysis of time, however, the notion of a primal Now is replaced by the concept of the "living Now," in which presentiations of what is present always have a temporal spread or span interlaced with protentions and retentions.[61] To argue, as Husserl does in *Ideas I,* that consciousness is both displayed as lucid and given as absolute in each point of the Now runs head on into the problem recognized by the later Husserl that such an impressional Now does not exist, or rather, exists only as an abstract limit and is never experienced.

The obvious solution here is to expand the scope of what is absolutely given by turning to the living Now and suggesting that it, not the impressional Now, marks the field of experience that is present immediately and directly.

Such an enlargement would preserve the connection between original evidence and presentiation (*Gegenwärtigung*). It would allow Husserl to maintain his theory that "memorial consciousness . . . is not originarily presentative"[62] and to keep its validating power subordinate to perception: " . . . the rationality, the character of legitimacy, of memory springs from the power of perception, . . . even if perception is 'not in play.' "[63]

But what have we gained with this? I want to isolate a series of problems that arise with Husserl's turn to the living Now, but to do so I must first specify how memory is subordinate to presentiation for Husserl and then discuss a crucial second revision to the theory of time-consciousness, one that destabilizes the power of presentiation for him. I will then suggest that this revision points to a different understanding of evidence in keeping with the turn to genetic analysis.

We have repeatedly stressed the difference between acts in which an object is intended and those in which the intention is fulfilled. Any act of intending has in play a more or less determinate noematic content that may or may not be fulfilled. For both the *Logical Investigations* and *Ideas I,* the difference in value between memory and originary insight comes into play only for the mode in which an intended sense is fulfilled, not for the sense intended and seeking fulfillment.[64] Were I to ask you to bring over a bottle of good Chardonnay to complement the bluefish we are having for dinner, there is a determinate noematic content in play specifying a referent for which you might have to spend some time looking, the very same content, I might add, should I make the same request of our other guests. Clearly, without memory there would be no intention, either on your or my part. If we distinguish questions of the formation of noematic content from questions of evidence (the fulfillment of that content), we find that Husserl only accords memory its inferior status in relation to the latter. Static analysis separates the question of genesis from that of validity.

This contrast between memory and presentiation (in the case of fulfilling acts), however, is immediately strengthened by a crucial difference between recollection and retention, one of the most important finds in Husserl's analysis of time-consciousness.[65] Our experience suggests that, while we are listening to the second bar of a Brahms symphony, the first bar is indeed still retained in our present experience. It does not require a distinct act of recollection to retrieve and connect it to the present. In everything present lingers a past phase. The past, in turn, is actual in the Now as a Now that is becoming past, not as a part retrieved and returned to the Now. The Now, then, is not an impressional or punctual Now but a "living Now" in which we have an overlapping of retention and protention. Retention itself is different from recollection, *primäre Erinnerung* from *Wiedererinnerung,*[66] in that retention is not the product of a second independent act, as is recollection, but a nested synthesis that forms part of the present experiential act. Recollection, to relate the two more directly, is a second, subsequent act usually based upon an initial act of perception, which itself has retention as one of its necessary features. While there is no perception without retention, there is perception without recollection.

The difference between retention and recollection is what allowed Husserl to keep the problem of memorial reconstruction at a considerable distance from phenomenological method in *Ideas I.* Retention, due to its status of being "just now" and proximate to the newly present, loses none of its directness. It has an "absolute legitimacy" that allows Husserl to argue for the "absolute legitimacy" of our reflections upon what necessarily is "flowing away."[67] The fact that consciousness is a stream, ever in a process of change, does not undermine the possibility of reflecting upon it and grasping it without employing hypothetical inferences or reconstruction. By contrast memory, at best, has only a "relative legitimacy."[68] Memory can always be "outweighed" by fresh perceptions, by new evidence. Furthermore, when unclouded, memory consists of a simple reproduction of a previous present. This entails that memory does not make contributions of its own. The result of this distinction, Husserl believes, is to free his method of the weight of the past by giving it a point of reference in the present.

In *Ideas I* the power of the past to configure the present is kept at a distance because retentional content was thought of as "near," recollected content as "far," as distant from the Now. This whole account, however, depends upon a very restricted concept of retention. Near and far are terms that gauge the temporal distance from the Now, understood as impressional. What immediately trailed off into the past was retained; once it receded beyond a certain point, which Husserl did not attempt to measure, an act of recollection would have to be introduced to retrieve it. This allowed Husserl both to demonstrate the internal connection between the present and the past (retention) and yet to understand temporal constitution in such a way that the past, both structurally and in terms of its content, does not control the present; acts of presentiation necessarily include retentions but are independent of all presentifications.

There was a striking development in Husserl's theory of memory, however, that destabilized this balance and that has a direct bearing on our question of method. This development can be found in Husserl's now familiar lectures given between 1920 and 1926, collected as *Analysen zur passiven Synthesis;* here he introduces a type of memory that seems to fall between retention and recollection as they have been described thus far. Discussing memory's ability to reproduce its content without distortion, Husserl reaches for his usual concept of retention. "The living present . . . cannot be canceled out, doubt is not possible here. This is also true of the span of the living retentions belonging to it."[69] He continues: "We want to say expressly that each continuing retention, living yet dying away, cannot be modalized,"[70] i.e., cannot be doubted. If retention preserves what is and was present without distortion, then we have secured the primacy of the living Now and yet kept recollection, a second act, and its content, a reproduced content, distinct from retention. Husserl begins to worry, however, that retention alone will not yield what can count as evidence. In attempting to deal with this, he uncovers a feature of memory completely missing from his earlier analysis of time.[71] He lands on a notion of involuntary memory, an aspect of the work of memory different from both retention and active recollection as we just defined them. At first he attempts to blend this with his understanding of retention as "near" and thinks of involuntary memory as a type of "passive" recollection triggered by the content of the near-retention. Since this is one of the most provocative texts from the 1920s, I will cite him at length:

> I can attentively hold a tone dying away "in my grip," even grip it firmer. Here we have something of a most primitive activity. But it can also be the case that I am not at all attentive, not actively turned to it and the series of tones, and yet it exercises a particular pull [*Reiz*]. By virtue of an associative wakening [*Weckung*] it obtains the character of an intention. In this or that case, and entirely involuntarily, this pulling (this affection) possibly discharges in a recollection that appears not generally but [specifically] as the fulfillment of the intention. Notice that this recollection is essentially other than a retention and is not, perhaps, a mere enlivening of the retention in the sense of increasing its level of clarity. A clear retention, whose essence we apprehend as the step lying next to the primal impression, always remains a retention. Each retention is what it is and has its intentional mode only as attached [*an der Stelle*] to the streaming perceiving to which it belongs. [This] recollection, however, is a kind of re-perception, i.e., it is not perception at all but something constituting itself anew, a new beginning with its primal now and retentional dying away, but in the mode of reproduction. In this recollection all the retentional steps appear "again," reproductively modified. If such a recollection is linked to a retention containing such a pull, then it necessarily appears in a coincidence of sense and being with the retention. The very same tone, dying away and sunken, appears again and I live through its being once again. And even this can be repeated, again I can, voluntarily or involuntarily, reproduce the tone or an entire tone phrase or even an entire melody.[72]

In contrast to recollection, which is active and depends upon representing a previous perception, Husserl describes an involuntary memory that is directly engaged by and continuous with retention. Central to his genetic theory of noematic senses is the emergence of their identity over time. The notion of involuntary memory here is to account for their progressive constitution in a way that does not require the intervention of interpretation. It is also to account for the reappearance of the same object: involuntary memory reproduces "all the retentional steps" and thus we have the temporal conditions under which an object can appear as the very same. Notice, however, that the retention setting all this in motion is defined as what lies immediately next to the Now. If retention is thought of as near the optimal Now and recollection as further away from it, involuntary memory is directly tied to "near-memory" in contrast to the distant or "far-memory" of active recollection.[73] But if this is the case, then we have a serious problem:

> The justification of near-memory does not yet yield a clarification of the possibility of the knowledge of an immanent object as existing in itself. For here we are still bound to the series of recollections that are tied to a living retention, that take their point of departure from it, and that extract self-giving evidence from it. Only after we have justified far-memory do we have the possibility of recognizing an immanent temporal object as existing across time.[74]

This difficulty requires us to look at *Fernerinnerung* again. Following Husserl's ideas, as he works through the notion of far-memory, enables us to uncover startling results. His terminology, however, is a bit confusing. Bear with me as I attempt to reconstruct the essential steps.

Searching for another name for involuntary memory, Husserl introduces the term "empty recollection" because such memory does not arise with the construction of an explicit intention but with a stimulus or a certain association, that brings it to life spontaneously. He tell us: "empty recollection is actually no recollection but wakening, i.e., the affective pull [*Reiz*] of a retentional deposit [*Niederschlag*] emerging from the oblivion [*Versunkenheit*] of memory."[75] In another text this idea is extended:

> One should not confuse recollection proper, the conscious process of reproductively reconstruing an object . . . and what we call empty recollection.[76] *It would be better to distinguish near-retention and far-retention and to no longer call this far-retention recollection.*[77] We can make the contrast [between far-retention and recollection proper] clear when we think of a musical motif governing a further musical movement and thereby always in hand, when it repeatedly affects the ego, the ego coming back to it in rays of attention without actually reproducing it [in an act of recollection].[78]

Having distinguished involuntary memory from recollection and tied it to retention, Husserl rejects equating involuntary memory with near-memory. From this text we can see that what is distant from the Now, what lies buried in the past, can be as present through retention as what has just transpired. Moreover, it does not require a separate act of recollection for it to be operative. Involuntary memory is what links the "distant" to the "near" and opens up the retentional horizon of time-consciousness:

> . . . a retention related to a remote past, one which we, I suggest, can apprehend as nothing other than a still living continuation of a corresponding near-retention, becomes lifted out, i.e., its objective, past content can, in a single stroke, by itself affect [me] and possibly determine a turning of the gaze, of the ego, without an actual recollection coming into play.[79]

The notion of involuntary memory not only allows us to speak of a retention being related to "a remote past" that is itself a continuation of a near past but also introduces an internal connection between affectivity and the present. Not only does a near past engage a distant past but, now that far-retention is not the same as recollection proper and thus cannot be clearly separated from presentiation, it is also possible for the reverse to take place, for the past to affect me and provoke my present intentions. Our intentions can be engaged by what is not in our conscious control, what escapes our attention, what intrudes upon the present without my active recollection, what "pulls" the ego in its direction, and, most significant of all, what escapes the full view of the act of reflection.

We have traced a certain progression in Husserl's theory from the difference between retention and recollection to the extensions of the retentional horizon beyond the near to the distant past through the notion of involuntary memory and, then, to the affective character of involuntary memory. These changes give us a much richer theory of temporal consciousness. It may require an act of recollection to recall what I had for breakfast this morning but no such act when I walk into a room that I have not inhabited for a month and automatically flip on the light switch. In principle it seems that what is retained can be quite distant from the present and yet still be "actual." If so, we cannot saddle the theory of temporality with the thesis that only what is "close" to a punctual Now is present, that only what has a very short span, perhaps a few seconds, is originary. This, in essence, is the fatal mistake of Derrida's analysis of Husserl's theory of time in his *Speech and Phenomena.* The originary consists of what is actual in a broad sense, which can include matters that have receded from our attention but are kept alive by the quality of the present experience or, more broadly, the situation in which we move and have our being.

H. THE PROBLEM OF TRANSCENDENTAL EVIDENCE

In this chapter as a whole we are interested not in further elaborating Husserl's concept of time-consciousness but rather in seeing how the developments we have traced bear on the question of phenomenological method and the problem of transcendental psychologism. In situating this discussion, we should take advantage of Husserl's emendations to the theory of temporalization. Clearly, his analysis is truer to the richness and complexity of memory. It accounts for perceptual acquaintance and a certain experiential significance to things, a significance that results from their reidentification across retentions and that is not the result of our acts of interpretation or descriptions. In addition, we all have experiences quite removed from the now that linger and sometimes haunt our present. Husserl even begins to speak of the unconscious in this context and to recognize the way that the past can transform the present while still escaping our attention. The accounts of affectivity and then the whole account of how habits and dispositions are built up can find support in the theory of involuntary memory. The reciprocal interplay of consciousness and world, the understanding of intentionality as "circular," and the dynamics of active, effective ego and passive, affective life—themes that come into their own in the 1920s—all require at least this development to the theory of temporalization. These gains, however, come at a certain cost.

For a Cartesian approach the stream of consciousness is an *absolute fact*, my knowledge of it indubitable. In order for it to serve as the irreducible transcendental ground of both the significance and, thereby, the presence of all that is, at least these six features must be in play: (a) consciousness must be the type of entity that I can directly grasp in reflection as having an existence that depends upon nothing other than itself; (b) mental acts or processes (*Erlebnisse*) must be given as wholes without "profiles," without "remainder," and without features that are not transparent to reflective reflection; (c) the noematic content of the mental act must also be grasped, for without it we cannot arrive at a structural contrast between different types of intentional objects and regions; (d) I must be able to intuit not only my lived experiences as wholes but also the interrelations and connections between them as a whole; (e) this entails that consciousness must be intuited as a "stream of consciousness" as a whole; and (f) not only must I grasp it as a synchronic but also as a diachronic whole. The description of consciousness in its essential temporality presupposes that I can grasp it as a temporal whole and that I can identify it accurately in acts of recollection. Without recollection we do not have reidentification, and without reidentification we do not have a way of discovering identity and difference and, thus, speaking about the essential structure of consciousness.

I find two sets of problems that the analysis of time poses for Husserl's Cartesian formulation of the reduction. The first has to do with the *range* of the reflection, the second with the *fallibility* of memory.

We have spoken positively of Husserl's expansion of the notion of retention by his treatment of involuntary memory. Even with the notion of "far" retention, however, we do not have enough to give us the "whole" stream of experience. Husserl expressly argued, in an important manuscript from 1922 to 1923 now entitled "The Apodicticity of Recollection," that we must therefore turn to memory.[80] Memory, this text tells us, is the "entry way" to "my transcendental experiential past." He continues:

> If memory is no longer a source of apodictic certainty for my past cogitations, then I can no longer speak of my endless stream of life, of my past ego and my past intentional experiences. . . . I have only the momentary *ego cogito*[81] while it is present, and that only as long as my reflective gaze is directed toward it. . . . If the *ego cogito*[82] has flowed off . . . I can remember something about it but, even if I am absolutely certain of the current memory as a present experience, I cannot be certain of what I remember.[83]

Husserl clearly realizes the devastating implications of frailty of memory for his program:

> I may not speak at all of my endless stream of life, of my life extending itself throughout an endless past and into an endless future, of phenomenological time as an actual form of actual life, etc. I am restricted, so it appears, to the absolutely sterile "I am": I perceive, now while I am perceiving; I think, namely while I am now thinking; I feel, and that only while I am feeling, etc. While such occur I can view them in reflection and construct fully useless statements, [for] they do not yield permanent truth . . . but only a barren, fleeting articulation of [*Anpassung an*] a fleeting life in the present.[84]

Husserl comes to see that genuine evidence requires repeatability, which means recollection, precisely what he, in *Ideas I,* characterized as relative and not absolute. Thus he lands in a double bind: to the extent that he claims that absolute consciousness is directly intuited, he cannot claim that it is adequately given with indubitable evidence, which requires recollection; to the extent that he claims authentic and secure evidence for absolute consciousness, he is required to turn to the past and thus cannot maintain that it is immediately intuited. Even if we could grasp the mental process adequately within a Now, such a grasping would not yield evidence in any strong sense, for it would only be momentary. Presentification, which is not originary, must come into play if we are to reflect upon consciousness as a whole. It is Husserl himself who brings several of these ideas together in this manuscript:

> . . . evidences [of pure presentation] only have a momentary ineliminative certainty that is attached to the flow of perception and retention. But these evidences do not give us apodictic certainty of the infinite past and future of life, no certainty about the identical ego that is the subject of this infinite life and the subject of certainties which it can authenticate again and again even after the original, living certainty stemming from original perception has passed away with it. It is because of recollection that we first have the "again and again's." The possibility of facts that are in themselves [*an sich*]

> stems out of it, facts, that is, which are originally experienced in perception but which can be experienced again any number of times, can be again identified as the same and (because of this) again described and described in an identical manner and in an identical truth any number of times. Thus—and this means the same thing—there is an enduring in contrast to the momentary truth.[85]

With the loss of the momentary Now as the arena within which truth is displayed in its finality and with the recognition that all presentiation (*Gegenwärtigung*) is necessarily presentification (*Vergegenwärtigung*), Husserl attempts to reclaim the veracity of intuition by arguing for the apodicticity of recollection.[86] Although he argues strongly that conscious events are adequately given, at least within the Now, and that recollection has the power to "completely" reproduce these events—thus creating facts which are *an sich* and establishing the truth—he also concedes that complete recollection is "an upper limit."[87] "The retentional sphere which is proximate" to the Now, he urges, is apodictic.[88] Yet authentic evidence requires more than this. Recollection proper must be employed, and for this Husserl concedes that there is always a "margin of uncertainty,"[89] for, as stated in *Ideas I,* "memorial consciousness . . . is not originally presentative [*originär Gebende*].[90]

In addition to the fact that memory is not originary and that its employment to secure the evidence of transcendental subjectivity entails an element of reconstruction that undercuts Husserl's Cartesian formulation of the reduction, there is also a rather obvious fallibility to memory. Memory produces not just a change in the temporal position of an experience but also is infected with decreasing transparency and recurring distortion. If retention covers not only near but far memory, then we are faced with the problem of possible distortion, an issue that Husserl's earlier emphasis upon near memory could overlook. In "The Apodicticity of Recollection" Husserl attempts, at one point, to deny the possibility of significant deception taking place in memory.[91] He senses, however, that this position cannot be maintained and recognizes, for example, the problem of fusing distinct memories into one (*Verschmelzung*) or of blending in various features that do not belong to the original image (*Übermalung*).[92] Even when this does not occur there are inescapable gradations of clarity that attend what is recollected. Thus, what is purely present is itself tied to a past that is not transparent in the sense that it cannot be recuperated by a reflection upon what is present to consciousness. The reliance upon reflection and intuition is inadequate to overtake consciousness as a whole, which is what Husserl requires to give his phenomenology transcendental grounding.

There are important consequences that we can draw from our account of Husserl's method. The inability of the Cartesian notion of evidence to provide an irreducible starting point suggests, first of all, the need to introduce a critical procedure in place of Husserl's reliance on intuition. The necessary temporal extension of the mental processes reflected upon, the presence of displacement and condensation infecting all mental objects,[93] and the difficulty in moving from a single cluster of mental processes optimally manifest to a conception of the whole of consciousness, would all suggest that adequate reflection is a limiting ideal and not attainable through a kind of reflective intuition. To get what he needs, Husserl must introduce an element of reconstruction, the very thing that the Cartesian way was designed to overthrow.

Husserl was reluctant to give up the Cartesian way because he worried that it would throw him back into a Kantian or Neo-Kantian conception of the ego. Undercutting the possibility of an apodictic intuition of the ego while maintaining the complementary thesis entails that the only way to continue speaking of transcendental subjectivity would be to sever it from the notion of consciousness in any psychologically real sense and to emphasize its epistemological character, treating it much like Kant's transcendental unity of apperception.[94] In this case the transcendental ego would not be a descriptive given but rather a construct hypothetically inferred. We could comprehend but never apprehend it. As a logical ego it would be empty, i.e., defined only by the types of acts which it unites. Such a concept, however, gives us far less than what Husserl requires from his transcendental ego, especially once the abstractions first employed to define it are set aside and we unpack its concreteness (as we suggested in chapter 8). Accordingly, the field open to phenomenological reflection *underdetermines* the concepts that we extract from it. This means that the procedure of eidetic variation and the intuition of essences cannot proceed without the importation of theoretical motivations from outside the findings of the reduction.

These two overlapping issues—the margin of uncertainty in the heart of our intuition of the transcendental ego and the tacit working of theoretical interests that supply an interpretative element not itself produced by the reduction—introduce contingency into the core of Husserl's Cartesian undertaking. They belong to a clearly locatable fissure that will eventually become a chasm between his Cartesian way and the ways through the positive sciences and, eventually, the life-world.

At one level we could say that Husserl chose to live with the problem of transcendental psychologism rather than live without the transcendental ego. But at another we can see, as a second consequence, that Husserl himself dismantled his own reliance upon the modernist paradigm. In place of a return to Kantianism and its methodology we find a notion of constitutive critique and then genetic analysis. The consistent application of the Cartesian demand for immediate presence required Husserl to integrate recollection into his account, thereby transforming that demand into something other than itself. All self-reflection necessarily involves a critical reflection upon the past. Thus *self-reflection* becomes, in a minimal sense, *historical reflection.*[95]

I. THE TURN TO INTERSUBJECTIVITY

The problems we have located in the last section were not unknown to Husserl; rather, they grew out of the internal development of his own phenomenology. In particular we have seen that, in the 1920s, he developed a systematic distinction between static and genetic phenomenology. It is impossible to find a clean break in Husserl's texts between these two because he took his newer genetic analysis to be an enlargement of the first static account. At the same time, he clearly transformed the results of his static descriptions by taking their "irreducible" structures as placeholders for a richer, genetic analysis. For our purposes in this chapter, there are two crucial transformations that have a direct bearing on the question of transcendental psychologism.

In the lectures on philosophical psychology (from 1925 onward), Husserl acknowledges that his earlier discovery of the transcendental ego as the correlate of the world arose from the question of "how this experience of the world is structured according to its *static* intentionality [i.e., according to a static analysis of intentionality] and not *genetically.*"[96] A genetic account, as I indicated in the last chapter, would require us to see the ego itself in terms of a dynamic development. This brings the notion of the subject together with that of history:

> Genetic . . . investigation is a study of the genesis—the passive as well as the active—in which the monad unfolds and develops; in which, within the monad, the monadic ego gains its personal unity and becomes the subject of a surrounding world . . . and, thereby, in the end, the subject of a history.[97]

This feature is supplemented by a second, already indicated in chapter 6. Husserl gradually extends the reduction beyond the sphere of the *solus ipse* to encompass other subjects. At first this extension was found within a regional account. For example, in *Ideas II* he recognized that, while each subject has its own spatial orientation with its own sense of coordinates (right-left, over-under, fore-back), the constitution of an "objective space" arises only by a system of exchanges between the "here" and the "there" in which the "there" is the "here" of another subject. Objective space is grounded in the transpositioning of places. The objectivity of objects and their qualities, in turn, is established only in an intersubjective community.[98] Analogously, the objectivity of the social world, Husserl suggests, is established through a bond of "reciprocal understanding."[99] In one place in *Ideas II,* Husserl, in contrast to his procedure in the Fifth Meditation, thinks of empathy and communication as mutually contributing sources of the constitution of intersubjectivity.

> Empathy is not a mediated experience—as if the other were being experienced as a psychophysical annex to his body—but an immediate experience of the other.
>
> Something similar holds true for the experience of communication with others, of reciprocal exchange with them. If we see one another in the eyes, then subject comes into immediate contact with subject. I speak to him, he speaks to me; I command him, he obeys. Those are immediately experienced personal relationships, although in this experience of others and of communication with them certain types of presentifications are in play, and I have original, perceptual experience only of my own subjectivity. The mediateness of the expression is not the mediateness of an experiential inference [*Erfahrungsschlusse*]. We "see" the other and not merely the body of the other; he is not only bodily but mentally self-present "in his own person."[100]

Whatever the hesitations of the earlier writings, that which had been grounded previously on the ego alone becomes increasingly based on intersubjectivity, which is now treated as the "absolute ground of being," as the "sense of being" of everything existing in the world.[101] As a result, transcendental subjectivity in its most fundamental structure is understood as transcendental intersubjectivity. Though it was not developed in interesting ways, Husserl understood this new ground as a "communicative totality" of subjects.[102]

In this chapter I have argued that in order for the Cartesian way, as formulated in *Ideas I,* to succeed, a legitimate distinction between psychological subjectivity and transcendental subjectivity must be based on either (a) a contrast in their *content* or structure, or (b) a difference in the type of *reflection* through which each is known, or (c) a difference in the quality of *evidence* accompanying the reflection. The rich characterization of phenomenological psychology and the descriptions of the psychological ego that Husserl gave during the 1920s are such that there is no significant difference in content or structure from the transcendental ego. Furthermore, the reflection giving the psychological ego is also accompanied by a reduction of existence and, thus, seems to have the same structure and scope as the transcendental reflection. Finally, the developments in the theory of time mean that the kind of intuitive evidence that gave the transcendental ego its privileged position over the empirical ego is not attainable. As a consequence, we are thrown back upon uncertainty and the necessity of reconstruction. A static analysis bound to the Cartesian way, then, cannot offer a solution to the problem of transcendental psychologism. But we also saw that Husserl expands both the scope of his method through his differentiation between static and genetic analysis, and, with this, the scope of the field open to transcendental reflection. If methodological solipsism is a constitutive feature of the Cartesian reduction and its resulting concept of the ego, then the reinterpretation of transcendental subjectivity as intersubjectivity requires us to go beyond that approach. While problems of a different type might emerge, there is no longer a difficulty with transcendental psychologism. The sphere of ownness becomes a "formal indicator," to use Heidegger's language,[103] and thus reinterpreted in terms of the reciprocity of I and others. The development of a systematic phenomenology now enables us to understand how transcendental phenomenology first employs methodological solipsism as a provisional point of access to the phenomenological field and then dismantles that approach by one that is more basic and that situates the subject in relation to others. In this way, transcendental psychologism can be seen as a necessary semblance, shown to be such by a phenomenology that moves beyond its own beginning.

11

Transcendental Phenomenology and the Question of Its Legitimacy

> Because he understands inner perception in this empiricist, psychological sense and because, warned by Hume's skepticism, he fears every recourse to the psychological as an absurd perversion of the genuine problem of the understanding, Kant gets involved in his mythical concept-formation. He forbids his readers to transpose the results of his regressive procedure into intuitive concepts, forbids every attempt to carry out a progressive construction which begins with original and purely self-evident intuitions and proceeds through truly self-evident individual steps. His transcendental concepts are thus unclear in a quite peculiar way, such that for reasons of principle they can never be transposed into clarity, can never be transformed into a formation of meaning that is direct and procures self-evidence.
>
> ... This would have required a fundamentally and essentially different regressive method from that of Kant, which rests on those unquestioned assumptions: not a mythically, constructively inferring method, but a thoroughly intuitively disclosing method, intuitive in its point of departure and in everything it discloses—even though the concept of intuitiveness may have to undergo a considerable expansion in comparison to the Kantian one, and indeed even though intuition, here, may lose its usual sense altogether through a new attitude, taking on only the general sense of original self-exhibition. ...
>
> —Husserl (1934–1936)[1]

PERHAPS I CAN situate this chapter by reviewing the line of thought that leads up to the issues it attempts to address. In his efforts to develop his earlier descriptive phenomenology into philosophy proper, a project that carried him from the *Logical Investigations* of 1900–1901 to the *Ideas Pertaining to a Pure Phenomenology* of 1913, Husserl transformed his phenomenology into a transcendental theory that claimed to articulate the most general and basic structure(s) upon which the edifice of knowledge can be erected. While the distinction between the empirical and the transcendental, as well as the sense in which the transcendental clarifies objectivity in terms of subjectivity, were derived from Kant, Husserl's insistence upon employing a notion of "adequate givenness" or "direct intuition" to characterize the kind of evidence that secures the transcendental was derived from Descartes or, more accurately, from his understanding of what Descartes meant by his notion of "clear and distinct ideas." This would have puzzled Kant. In the *Prolegomena* Kant placed his own "regressive-analytic method" in contrast to a "progressive synthetic method."[2] The first treats the conditions of possibility it isolates as necessary presuppositions for what is *factually* given, i.e., for what could *possibly* be given factually. By contrast, the progressive method begins with what is given to reason "and, without basing itself on any fact at all, attempts to develop knowledge out of its original seeds."[3] Apart from how this distinction applies to Kant's own systematic philosophy, he clearly thought that Descartes employed a version of the latter method and, as a result, had no way of securing an internal connection between his mathematics, which is contributed by the understanding to our representation of reality, and reality itself. Husserl would agree with this, emphatically rejecting formalism as adequate; but then he sensed that Kant's regressive method is adrift, lacking intuitive disclosure, which ultimately means that it, too, is left with a chasm between conceptual schemes and noumenal reality and that it depends upon a notion of facticity that it uncritically assumes.

What Husserl attempted, in short, is to combine the "regressive" with the "progressive" method that Kant set in opposition to it, even as he replaced Kant's constructivism with a phenomenological procedure of description. As a result the transcendental is gained not by hypothetically inferring the necessary conditions (a set of unified categories) of the appearance of objects but by a methodologically induced reflective analysis that opens the transcendental as a field to direct intuition and that then uses procedures of eidetic variation to regressively discover different sets of transcendental conditions reigning over different regions of being. This is the "fundamentally different regressive method" that Husserl had in mind in our text above from the *Crisis*. In *Ideas I*, however, Husserl wedded his notion of intuition to a Cartesian notion of evidence, with its emphasis upon transparency and immediacy, in an effort to avoid the oblique, hypothetico-deductive method of Kant. Employing his procedure of bracketing, the transcendental was understood as a field of analysis directly given and immediately apprehended. The structure of that field was defined for Husserl by his notion of intentionality, which he also called the correlational a priori in his later writings.

Husserl's Cartesian way, as he himself came to label it, relied upon an adequate inner perception of a methodologically purified realm of transparent givens. I argued in the last chapter that this approach fails to deliver the justification necessary to secure either the status or the basic structures of transcendental analysis and that it is trapped in transcendental psychologism. If one maintains that Husserl's phenomenology is incurably Cartesian, then this argument can be used to reject his transcendental phenomenology altogether. In fact, I would argue that this result is unavoidable if we stay just with

Husserl's first published excursion into transcendental analysis in *Ideas I,* as have the vast majority of commentators, be they analytic, critical theoretical, or deconstructivist.

There are, however, alternative approaches open to phenomenology, ones that Husserl did indeed explore but never quite mastered. In fact, in the work he undertook after 1918 he developed not only alternative "paths" or "ways" into transcendental analysis but also struggled to place these in relation to a systematic difference between static and genetic method. This is why Husserl qualified the notion of intuition in the passage that forms the epigraph for this chapter, redefining it broadly as "originary self-exhibition." In turning away from a theory of adequate givenness to a notion of "original self-exhibition" he recognized that phenomenological description must incorporate what Kant called *critique* into itself. In this chapter, however, I will not trace that historical development, as it was sketched in chapter 6. Rather, I want to work in a more systematic vein and attempt to present a positive case for a "direct" way into transcendental analysis. I will do so by arguing for a modified version of transcendental phenomenological analysis in the context of Husserl's relation to Kant.

What I am looking for here is a phenomenological equivalent of Kant's famous "transcendental deduction," which he offers in his *Critique of Pure Reason,* but one that combines his *regressive* method with a *direct* way of securing the transcendental field as ground. The direct way, as I am using it, does not rely upon nor does it require a notion of adequate givenness. In place of that notion I will use transcendental arguments and thereby connect the notion of insight to that of argumentation. Because I am more interested here in the structure and viability of transcendental analysis *per se* than I am in sorting out the intricacies of Kant's text, I will rely upon several of our contemporaries to carry his banner.[4] Needless to say, I will be reaching for broad and rather general comparisons.

A. THE TRANSCENDENTAL REDUCTION AS A TRANSCENDENTAL DEDUCTION

Husserl's emphasis upon the priority of description and his fulminations against the speculative constructions of the Neo-Kantians meant that he did not pay particular attention to the peculiar language and logic of transcendental analysis. Though hardly one of his more lucid pieces of writing, Kant did append a *Methodenlehre* to the end of his first *Critique,* in which he attempted to reflect upon the form of his method as a whole. By contrast, Husserl does not allow for a reflection upon his method from outside its content, i.e., his reflection upon method articulates the way the analysis is *de-*

ployed in terms of what it *discloses*. Perhaps we can simply say that for him the analysis is the method. As a consequence, transcendental analysis cannot itself undergo a transcendental reflection. We should not underestimate the positive value of this restriction. Continuing to speak of intuition or, better, description at this level is a way of preventing conditions of possibility from having conditions of possibility, of rules requiring a rule as to how to use the rules. But there was a price to pay as well. The emphasis upon intuition meant that Husserl literally overlooked the special form of discourse and argumentation that is appropriate for transcendental analysis. In fact, Husserl did not become directly engaged by the problem of his own transcendental discourse until Fink began to push him in this direction in the very late 1920s; even then we find the better insights coming from his assistant rather than from him.[5] The issue, however, becomes all the more pressing once we deny that transcendental analysis is simply a description of transcendental structures directly and adequately intuited, and once we understand the mediating role of argumentation in articulating and establishing those structures. I want to make good on Husserl's lack by sketching a phenomenological equivalent of Kant's transcendental deduction, one that the master himself did not attempt.

An important hint as to how one can approach this comes by returning to his lectures on "Transcendental Logic" and in particular the issue of various modalizations involved in judgments leading to evidence. You will recall that this lecture course was given three times between 1920 and 1926 and is now published as *Analysen zur passiven Synthesis*. One of its most suggestive studies, which we touched upon in chapter seven,[6] connects the process of questioning to that of judgment. "Each possible judgment can be thought as content of a question."[7] Questions arise because a settled fact or field of facts becomes doubtful and, perhaps, negated. What we took for granted is transformed into a field of problematic possibilities. Questioning awakens on our part a certain dissatisfaction and then a desire to move to a resolution. "The theme of a question," Husserl says of a situation where there are only two options, "is obviously either a problematic individual whose disjunctive counterpart remains extra-thematic (as when I simply ask: is that a puppet?) or the entire problematic disjunction (as in the question: is that a puppet or a person?)."[8] Questions are teleologically organized in the sense that "the proper sense of questioning is uncovered through answering, respectively, in the answer. For with the answer there occurs a fulfillment of the striving that brings a relaxing of tension, a satisfaction."[9] By connecting the process of questioning to that of judgment and thereby to "cognition and its formations,"[10] questioning is understood as an internal part of "a logic understood as a science of cognizing and the cognized."[11] This move then allows Husserl to locate a *practical* dimension to all thought:

> ... adjudicating life, including rationally adjudicating life, is a medium for a unique wishing, striving, willing, acting, whose goal is judgments and judgments of a particular form. All reason is, at the same time, practical reason, and so also logical reason. ... Thus questioning is a practical action related to judgments.[12]

The theory that reason contains a practical dimension expands any question of the legitimacy of a priori categories. In addition to issues of logical entailment and logical coherence, as we might find in a strict formalist approach, we must also place possible alternative sets of categories in relation to the issue of their actual employment. Transcendental analysis includes an account of the *use* of categorial cores. It accounts for the conditions of knowing-that by also understanding knowing-that as a form of knowing-how.

With this larger frame of reference in view, Husserl's static "transcendental deduction" has roughly two stages. There is a first "regressive" stage concerned with the derivation of the categories themselves; it has this form:

1. Having objects of one regional type (as opposed to another) is conditioned upon there being a certain conceptual scheme that provides criteria of how one type is individuated in contrast to others, and that has certain general categorial concepts and rules that apply to all possible objects of the region.
2. A certain conceptual scheme having a core set of categories and rules can be the condition of X being an object of a certain region because that set is constitutive of X being such an object, not merely regulative of the X that is such an object.
3. A conceptual scheme having a core set of categories and rules can be constitutive of X being an object of a certain region because it is a cognitive structure known and employed in experiences of and/or activities involving those objects.

Result: The third claim—that a certain conceptual scheme, having a core set of categories and rules, is employed in experiences of and/or activities involving objects of a certain region—legitimizes the first claim, i.e., that having objects of one regional type (as opposed to another) is conditional upon there being a conceptual scheme that individuates one type of object in contrast to others and that provides general categories and rules that apply to all objects of that region.[13]

This deduction is self-referential in the sense that the conclusion makes possible the starting point of the proof,[14] that is, the fact that categories are necessarily employed in and thereby make possible our experience of objects legitimates the claim that they are necessary conditions of the possibility of such objects (of experience). The factual is the basis from which we derive the normative that is the ground of the factual.

To carry this "deduction," however, we also need an additional proof that experiences and their cognitive structure(s) are not just hypothetically inferred from their results or output, i.e., are not just the result of the one doing the descriptions taking an "intentional stance" toward the brain. To secure the whole field of analysis as transcendental, we need a proof that is "ostensive" and in this sense positive. We move, then, to the ground of the analysis just given. Like Kant, this ground will be understood as transcendental subjectivity. Unlike Kant, the issue of the *unity* of knowledge is not as important as marking the difference between "mundane" or empirical and transcendental analysis, and as finding a general structure or field that will make possible the *diversity* of types of knowledge. A "direct" approach is required if we are to establish this. Yet, if my critique of Husserl's Cartesianism is correct, it cannot be one that simply relies upon a vague notion of reflection or intuitive insight. To secure this field we must show that it exists and that it has an internal connection to all that *can* be experienced.

The second stage, establishing the existence of this field in a transcendental register, which means *in contrast* to any item existing in the world, comes in two steps, one securing the existence of a subject that experiences or knows, and the second establishing the existence of cognitive acts or achievements by that subject. To be genuinely self-evident, they must be self-reflexive and self-grounding. Each must face directly the skeptic's doubts that it or anything else exists. The "progressive" argument securing the existence of the subject is surprisingly simple:

I doubt whether x exists
X exists is true

The only possible object that could be designated by x is the I or the ego. This is a trivial result unless it is complemented by a second argument:

I doubt whether p is true
P is true

In this case, p can be replaced only by "I am thinking," Descartes's famous *ego cogito*, and perhaps certain variations directly derived from it, such as "I am undergoing experience" or "I am conscious."[15] Notice that both arguments use doubt to self-referentially secure what cannot be doubted; in this sense, the results are self-evident.

However, to employ this result properly and to connect it to the analysis establishing the existence of transcendental categories, it is necessary to sort out a mistake that both Descartes and Husserl made. We must be careful to distinguish between consciousness and the *ego cogito* proper. To get at this let me unpack the notion of experience, of the *cogito*. Now that we have its existence secured, what is its essence? There are three relational structures that characterize it:

Of-structure: All experience is necessarily an experience *of* something; each *ego cogito* is an *ego cogito cogitatum.*
As-structure: Each *cogitatum* is present *as* something.
For-structure: Each *cogitatum* is present as something only by being present *for* or *to* someone.

These structures, defining but not exhausting the notion of intentionality for us,[16] undergird and make possible the relationship between objects, conceptual schemes (categories), and experiences sketched in stage one above. They, too, must be understood as transcendental.

The reason why one should distinguish intentionality from consciousness is simply that not all consciousness-of is intentional. The pain that I am in, the euphoria that floods my being, or the depression that grips me all lack a *cogitatum.* In these cases, there is not an object that transcends the mental event. Perhaps we can say that the notion of consciousness is much broader than that of intentionality. Furthermore, one should not confuse intentional acts as a particular psychological episode with intentionality as a structure that all such acts have. This, I hope, will help us avoid a pervasive mistake we find throughout Husserl's writings. Consciousness *per se,* even as grasped in phenomenological reflection, is not transcendental.[17] There are no transcendental pains—except for the odd colleague, of course. Nor are intentional acts as mental episodes transcendental. It is only intentionality as a general structure, having these three sub-structures, that can be characterized as transcendental. If we identify this as transcendental subjectivity, then we can dispense with Husserl's notion of transcendental consciousness and, thereby, the problem of psychologism that immediately follows on its heels once transcendental proofs become ostensive. The break with psychologism is further encouraged by the fact that I do not have to rely upon intuition, in the sense of an adequate inner seeing of consciousness, to establish these ideas.

At the same time, this "direct way" into transcendental subjectivity, moving with self-reflective arguments, produces only an empty *field* of analysis. Even stage one gives us no more than the form that all specific, regional disciplines will take. It is only when we add the "regressive" step that fleshes out a given region with materials that we get content and, thereby, various families of transcendental conditions. This is the more reconstructive element that belongs to what Husserl calls the "indirect" ways to transcendental analysis. The value, and even necessity, of the "direct" way, in contrast to the "indirect" ways, is not only that it opens up the field of phenomenological analysis as a whole but also that it introduces a constraint on the nature of transcendental analysis, namely, that we can decide whether certain categories are applicable to a particular region by recourse to the issue of whether they are also necessary to our experience of the objects of that region. With the whole picture sketched, let me return to the question of categories.

In an effort to exhibit the structure of transcendental analysis, I want to employ one fairly transparent example, well known because it is one of Wittgenstein's favorites, and then introduce a second that sketches how Husserl would account for the region of material nature, that region of primary concern to Kant's first *Critique.* I will then add a few comments about the general structure of transcendental proofs.

Assuming that chess is like a region and that the pieces are like objects that belong to that region, its analysis would involve these steps:

1′. Having a, b, c, etc., as pieces is conditioned upon there being a certain conceptual scheme that provides criteria of how to individuate one in contrast to the other pieces and that has certain categorial concepts and rules that apply to all possible chess pieces.

2′. Since the core set of categories contains the rules without which a, b, c, etc., could not exist as chess pieces, that set is constitutive of a, b, c, etc., being chess pieces.

3′. The categories constitutive of a, b, c, etc., being chess pieces are categories and rules that any subject necessarily knows and employs in his experience of and/or his action involving a, b, c, etc., as chess pieces.

Result′: The fact that certain categories and rules are necessarily known and employed in any subject's experience of or involvement with a, b, c, etc., as chess pieces legitimizes those categories and rules being necessary to a, b, c, etc., being chess pieces.

A transcendental account of the region of material nature would have a similar form. Generally put, it would look like this:

1″. Having a, b, c, etc., as objects, relations, events, etc., of a physical system is conditioned upon there being a set of conceptual schemes that provides criteria of how each is individuated in contrast to the others and that has certain categories and rules that apply to all the elements of the region.

2″. Since the categories and rules specify the conditions without which a, b, c, etc., could not exist as elements of a physical system, the categories and rules are constitutive of a, b, c, etc., being such elements.

3″. The categories and rules constitutive of a, b, c, etc., being elements of a physical system are categories and rules that any subject necessarily knows and employs in his experience of and/or his action involving a, b, c, etc., as such elements.

Result″: The fact that a given set of categories and rules is necessarily known and employed in any subject's experience of or involvement with a, b, c, etc., as elements of a physical system legitimizes those categories and rules being necessary to a, b, c, etc., being such elements.

Some of the categories that Husserl explores are extension (also as it is related to mass, figure, and form), quality (warmth, weight, sound), substance, movement, and causality.[18] Their treatment, not just as conditions of the being of physical objects but as constitutive of the experience of these objects, requires that they also be described as schemata of experience, a single scheme often involving a number of different interrelated schemata.[19] With these examples in hand, let me say a few things about the structure of our deduction.

The first thing to note, of course, is that it is not a deduction. The categories and transcendental propositions themselves are not established from concepts alone but "always only indirectly through the relation of these concepts to something altogether contingent, namely, *possible experience*," Kant tells us.[20] The "deduction" in stage one itself does not move from premises to a conclusion using standard rules of derivation. Rather, each of the levels must be understood as an explication of certain features or conditions that are implicit in the previous one. This is a case of what Husserl frequently describes in his later writings as *Besinnung*. As we progress, the analysis moves in each new level to what is implicit, in the sense of being indispensable to the previous one. The subsequent steps are richer than the earlier. Taylor calls a transcendental argument a "chain of indispensability claims,"[21] for without them we cannot make sense of the objects we have understood as objects of possible experience. As a corollary of this, we must insist that these claims do not account for undergoing mental events in general but for experience in the primary sense of being experience-of an object. I may have awareness that consists of a *lack* of experience, an awareness of buzzing confusion and nothing focused, but if my awareness involves an experiential act, involves being conscious-of-something, then it will have certain conceptual cores indispensable to it.

Husserl stresses that experiences are self-evidently given in our reflection upon them. Once we move beyond a Cartesian notion of adequate givens to carry the notion of self-evident and apodictic certainty, we can understand this thesis in the following way: transcendental arguments are based on articulating a certain insight we have into our own experience and they always refer back to that experience.[22] The activity of playing chess would be voided if a player just moved pieces around at will. But also if she moved the pieces around in a way that just happens to coincide with what the rules allow. To be engaged in the activity of playing chess, one must have some grasp of the rules.[23] Analogously, one cannot be said to undergo experience were it not related to objects as significant unities, if they did not have an as-structure.

Significant unities, however, do not just happen to coincide with the rules that account for their significance. It must be the case that I, in some sense, am acquainted with the conceptual schemes and the categorial conditions that make it possible for me to have an experience of significant objects. Were we not acquainted with these conditions, we could not have the act of experiencing objects. This point is necessary to preserve the self-referential nature of the deduction. I believe that this is what Husserl should have been after when he said, "the concept of intuitiveness may have to undergo a considerable expansion in comparison to the Kantian one."[24] Categories are derived from insight into the nature of experience itself. This insight, I am arguing, is not only articulated but also mediated by indispensability claims. Only in this way can we speak of them as self-evident.

The obvious problem with all of this, however, is that, as experience of physical objects runs its course, I am not at all conscious of these conditions. In the case of chess I know what the rules are because I have learned them. Playing the game assumes that I am conscious of them and have usually accepted some formulation of them.[25] If I were conscious of the conditions of my experience of physical objects, I would be able to articulate just what they are, much as a chess player, when asked, can tell us the rules for moving pieces. But in the case of physical systems or what Husserl calls material nature, I have a perceptual engagement with the world that need not involve learning rules and that usually does not involve my being consciously aware of either the categories or the rules that are constitutive of what I experience. Even when we reflect, bringing such conditions to light involves long and arduous labor, with very little agreement as to what these conditions are. How can we then claim that I must know them in order to have experiences?

This is a serious issue; to find a possible solution we have to look beyond Husserl. In speaking about the way in which the significance of a tool becomes thematic, Heidegger looks not to its normal functioning but to situations in which there is either a breakdown or a loss of appropriateness for the task at hand.[26] Analogously, the conditions of experience may become thematic when things go awry, when doubt and negation or even disintegration enter. I may be said to know (step 3) these categories not in the sense that I can give a complete and full formulation of them or that I have learned them as I have the rules of chess. Taylor suggests that knowing them entails only that I must be able to recognize certain conditions under which my experience fails to be coherent.[27] We are acquainted with categories not in the sense that while undergoing experience I can directly formulate them, as I might the rules of a game, but in the sense that I "must be able to recognize these as conditions of failure."[28] Our ability to recognize the breakdown of our own experience entails that we are acquainted with a conceptual scheme and its attending categorial concepts. This is what we turn to in reflection, what is "self-evident," and what gives our analysis its guiding clues. As philosophers we then attempt to bring these structures to articulation.

B. CONCEPTUAL SHIFTS AND TRANSCENDENTAL ANALYSIS

The force of transcendental phenomenological analysis is to show that relative to every region of being and to the type of entities and relations that constitute a single region, one is bound to assume a certain capacity for knowledge, with attending cognitive conditions in general and a certain interplay of linguistic and experiential conditions in particular. Ontological debate becomes undecidable and ontological distinctions empty or arbitrary without reference to this ground. Husserl's analysis does not reduce the complement of ontology to linguistic interpretation alone but blends this together with the older Kantian concern with cognition itself. Ontology is referred back not just to linguistic fields, for language games themselves are unintelligible without reference to cognitive systems upon which they depend.

Where Husserl departs from Kant, however, is in his emphasis upon the plurality of categories that could be grounded by a transcendental analysis of what Kant calls pure reason.[29] Kant's first *Critique* worked to provide a plausible account of the legitimacy of certain a priori ideas (precisely those for which there is no corresponding simple impression or methodical derivation from simple impressions).[30] The set of a priori concepts he wished to establish had two features: unrestricted universality and unqualified necessity. Such concepts, along with others that are analytically entailed, *must* apply to any and *all* objects of experience. Following Rosenberg, we can call the set of concepts that must apply to all possible objects a "conceptual core."[31] Both Husserl and Kant were convinced that by delineating the conditions of our *experiencing* any object whatsoever we would find that this conceptual core also contains the conditions of the *being* of any object (capable of entering our experience). The place where Husserl and Kant depart can be located by asking whether there are only one or many core sets of categories that apply to our experience of objects.

Kant was convinced that there is a single conceptual core, that this core is invariant, and that Newton had given us the best clues as to what categories belong in it. As a consequence, the notion of an intersubjective, public object became coextensive with that of a physical object. I do not think that it is an historical accident, as Rosenberg suggests,[32] that Kant took all objects to be physical objects, for had he used the more general notion of any (fully indeterminate) X, it would not have been possible to produce anything but a purely formal analysis. Husserl might argue, as we saw in chapter 3, that this would culminate only in *mathesis universalis,* his version of formal ontology. Synthetic a priori truths arise because Kant's most general set of any possible object whatsoever had, in fact, specific "pre"-determinations, roughly those of the objects of Newtonian physics, and because that physics required certain necessary synthetic categories for its domain (causality, individual, relation, etc.). At the same time, Kant was sure that transcendental analysis would give us not one among possibly other conceptual cores but that single invariant core that holds for any objects of experience.

Except for certain shared formal and "empty" mathematical conditions, Husserl argues, in contrast to Kant, that because there are many different regions of objects and corresponding types of experience, there are many conceptual cores.[33] While the ontology of physical objects sets the scope of Kant's transcendental analysis in the first *Critique,* Husserl used different types of objects—physical, biological, psychological, social, political, and cultural—as the guiding threads for his transcendental reflections. This even allows Husserl, once he supplements his own static with a genetic analysis, to do justice to theory succession in the sciences and to recognize a plurality of object-concepts within a single domain.[34] As a consequence, there is a certain relativity of regions, language-games, and transcendental conditions. The genius of Husserl's approach lies in his showing that we have many regional ontologies, not just a single one, with families of overlapping and differing transcendental conditions, that flesh out our analysis of transcendental subjectivity. The universality of the analysis, in turn, is secured for Husserl not by recourse to a single table of categories. Rather, it is secured by arguing that, beneath the diversity of ontologies and regional conditions, there is a universal and necessary *correlation* of cognitive achievements, systems of significance, and types of objects, a correlation that forms the irreducible, necessary condition of their having different categorial structures. As we saw, this is the structure of intentionality. The diversity of categorial frameworks and even epistemological types is regulated only by the theses that they belong to a single world and that there is a shared correlational a priori employed across different regions and types.

C. TRANSCENDENTAL AESTHETICS

This difference on the issue of conceptual cores is directly related to and probably the result of the contrasting architectonics of Kant's and Husserl's respective systems. We can best approach this by noting a second crucial difference between them—one that will find, in chapter 14, a surprising counterpart in the relationship between Husserl and Heidegger—having to do with the question of what we treat today as the role of interpretation in the constitution of perception. Rosenberg argues that Kant's theory has the great strength of sorting out a conflation in Hume's theory of impressions. For Hume, impressions, themselves the irreducible elements of his system, play two rather different roles. On some occasions, an impression is treated as a particular sensation on the model of a mental image. A red triangle, for example, is thought of as "a patch of mental pigment in an iconic mental picture."[35] On other occasions, it functions like a basic knowing episode, i.e., the conviction that something is red and is rectangular. As a knowing episode, it serves as a premise from which inferences may be drawn. "The model here is judgmental; it is the mental sentence (inner speech)," Rosenberg speculates.[36] Rosenberg locates with precision how Kant sorted out this conflation, assigning the first role to sensibility, which he understood as the content or matter of experience, and the second to the understanding, which supplies the categorial forms. Experience, which for Kant is roughly what Husserl thinks of as a fulfilled perception, is something to which both moments contribute. "It is a kind of resultant vector sum of these two components."[37] This leads to Kant's antirealist view that the world gains its deep structure through the categorial forms that are contributed by the understanding. Experience as a whole, then, has these two interrelated moments: a receptive or passive side that undergoes sensations, and an active judgmental side that brings the manifold of impressions under its a priori concepts.

The basic opposition between sensibility and understanding (judgment) that organized Kant's theory is replaced in Husserl's phenomenology by the contrast between experience and judgment (understanding). The form-content dyad employed in *Ideas I,* and Husserl's conception there of noematic form animating or interpreting hyletic content, came rather close to Kant. Husserl, however, quickly grew unhappy with this analysis of perception and replaced that very provisional theory with a much more adequate account, as we saw in chapter 7. The problem of individuation, as he wrote Ingarden in 1918, had not been handled satisfactorily.[38] In essence, Husserl approached his new theory, itself framed as he was developing his genetic method, by constructing an alternative transcendental aesthetics to Kant's. While the Transcendental Aesthetics part of Kant's first *Critique* dealt only with the forms of sensible intuition (time and space), Husserl flooded that part of Kant's system with a rich account of (non-epistemic) perception as well as a genetic analysis of the interplay not only of spatial and temporal but also what he called associative syntheses, a notion that echoes Hume's concept of association even as the addition of the term "synthesis" dismantles it.[39] "Prescientific" objects, understood as the basic or, at least, one of the limiting types of experience, are located there, which means that we have "appearances" before the Transcendental Analytic section to which they were restricted in Kant. What Kant called the manifold, Husserl shows, is not formless but preformed, yet it has a type of perceptual or aesthetic significance that Kant could only think of as "preconceptual" and, therefore, "precategorial." In addition, Husserl's late work might also place there artifacts that have become "sedimented" into everyday experience. If Husserl were to put this directly to Kant, he would argue that understanding, treated as a form of active synthesis, does not work upon blind data but brings its categorial apparatus to bear on what already possesses structure and "form," i.e., that already has what Kant could only call a categorial structure. To turn this another way, the objects that we do find in Kant's Analytic, full-blown objects of science, belong to a higher order and are not experientially basic. Constitution at this higher level must be understood not as elementary but as a transformation of what is elemental.

This modification, I would argue, recovers one of the features that a Kantian needs for his or her system, once diachronic changes in categorial frameworks are taken seriously, namely, a "core" notion of the object. If the categorial system that synthesizes the manifold is understood as either temporally or historically conditioned, as the succession of theory in the natural sciences might suggest, then one conceptual core could be replaced by a different paradigm. Since Kant's theory of the experience of objects is defined by the opposition between unformed sensibility and form-giving understanding, and since it falls to understanding to provide intelligible structure, the plurality of conceptual cores entails that there cannot be a single a priori conceptual core and, thus, no univocal notion of the object. Husserl's reformulation of Kant's transcendental aesthetic opens the possibility of a constitution of something like "natural" objects of perception where Kant thought there was none, namely "before" the active engagement of scientific understanding. This assistance, however, comes at a rather high price to the efficacy and autonomy of the sciences. For at the core of our everyday experience of the world we find a type of determinacy—a certain "excess" or "surplus," gathered by our gaze and articulated "semiologically" by our involvement with things—that the sciences, and any transcendental reflection bound to their concepts, cannot comprehend, as well as a certain reference beyond the categorial apparatus of the sciences that they cannot apprehend. To Kant, this idea would sound like a violation of his difference between the phenomenal and the noumenal. Yet this realm of "pretheoretical" experience is the one in which we, for the most part, move and have our being.

D. SELF-REFLECTION AND SELF-REFERENTIALITY

There is yet a third decisive difference between Husserl and Kant, but one made possible only because they share a common approach to the question of the objective validity of transcendental knowledge. If both Kant's critical transcendental method and Husserl's transcendental phenomenological method are *self-reflective,* then their respective strategies of legitimization both rely upon *self-referentiality.*

Bubner has argued that self-referentiality characterizes and is alone relevant for Kant's transcendental argument.[40] Transcendental knowledge cannot be derived from a principle of metaphysically higher, indubitable insight. Bubner explains:

> For having such a principle at one's disposal would require the possession of a type of knowledge other than the sense-conditioned knowledge of experience which is related to objective reality and whose validity it is which requires demonstration. The knowledge which we in fact have can be legitimated at no other level than that of the facticity of knowledge.[41]

Bubner's approach finds support in Rosenberg, who treats Kant's deduction of the categories as a juridical defense of claims of right or of legal entitlement.[42] Rosenberg thinks of a lawyer arguing his conclusion that X is entitled to Y by the exclusion of all alternatives but one. Bubner suggests that transcendental arguments occupy a position "between the level of facticity and that of coercive principles," while Rosenberg enriches this approach by treating them as pieces of practical reasoning that state not a matter of fact but a matter of right with factual application. He explains:

> It is, in other words, to say that something may be done. It articulates a principle of permission. The conclusion of a transcendental deduction is thus to be a normative conclusion. And this, in turn, suggests that the judgment supporting it will belong to that species of argument, whatever it is, which is tailored to the establishing of normative conclusions. It suggests, in fact, that a transcendental deduction must be a piece of practical reasoning.[43]

The function of Husserl's transcendental reduction must be to establish a difference between "worldly" or positive and transcendental analysis at the same time that it keeps reflection tethered to the facticity of knowledge, as Bubner calls it. This tie to facticity is lost in principle in Husserl's Cartesian way but preserved in his various other ways through regional ontologies. Keeping the reduction tethered to the ways through mediating material ontologies means that the reduction always involves an account of essential structures that have internal connections to factual domains. But is Bubner correct in claiming that for Kant "the legitimization of such [transcendental] knowledge without the aid of absolute principles is only possible as a demonstration of the *lack of alternatives* to that knowledge?"[44] He is certainly correct to reject recourse to metaphysically higher insight. Phenomenology, in an effort to move beyond Husserl's first programmatic formulations, would reject this as well, especially if this refers to a type of intuition that is disconnected from proofs in the form of rational argumentation leading up to conclusions. But appealing to a lack of alternatives alone, as Bubner wants it, would entail that transcendental proofs be only indirect. As Rosenberg points out, transcendental proofs for Kant can never be indirect, as they do not have the form of a *reductio ad absurdum.*[45] They are always "ostensive."[46] Genova also argues that indirect proofs are at best refutations and not sufficient on their own, as they presuppose previously established transcendental deductions.[47]

The insistence upon intuition at the transcendental level, understood properly, requires that transcendental knowledge be a reconstruction of the self-referential features of factual knowledge. The advantage of phenomenology's procedure becomes clear if we think that there might be a number of different conceptual schemes that could account for a given region. The plurality of schemes means that an element of undecidability enters because, in theory, a second transcendental construction is always possible. Speaking of intuition in addition to argumentation, once freed of its Cartesian formulation, is a way of requiring the conceptual scheme to be the one that is actually employed in cognition and thus known by the subject. At the same time expanding phenomenology into a genetic method opens a mode of analysis in which synchronic questions of structural difference and conditions are returned to diachronic questions of origination. Husserl hoped that he could settle this issue of alternative conceptual cores by reformulating what Kant would reject as an "empirical reduction." Kant describes the empirical deduction as what "shows the manner in which a concept is acquired through experience and through reflection upon experience, and which therefore concerns, not its legitimacy, but only its *de facto* mode of origination."[48] For Husserl, however, the issue of mode of origination is treated by genetic analysis in a transcendental register. Genetic analysis allows for two different types of accounts. On the one hand, it permits Husserl to speak about the relationship between different regions with their correspondingly different transcendental categories and to understand their interrelationship not just synchronically but also diachronically. On the other hand, it also recognizes that categories are found only as parts of conceptual schemes that can themselves undergo historical transformation. Neither is a piece of psychological analysis but an account of transformation that attempts to understand the temporal development of one conceptual core into another or the possible derivation of one of the alternative schemes from the other.

E. TELEOLOGY AND TRANSCENDENTAL ARGUMENTS

Even if, as we just argued, a transcendental argument must refer back to the experience in which conceptual schemes with their categorial cores are deployed, we still have the problem of epistemological types, introduced in chapter 3, another issue that Husserl came to confront in a way that Kant did not. Having established the internal link between the categories constitutive of experience and my experiential acquaintance with these categories, and having suggested that any subsequent philosophical account of them necessarily refers back to the facticity of knowledge, there is the possibility that we could have incommensurate categorial frameworks that are rooted in different types of cognition, even if the same set of objects are covered by each. An appeal to actual experience will not be sufficient to decide between all schemes if it turns out that there are two different types of actual experience of the same domain and if one has categories that the other does not.[49]

To get at the issue we first need to sort out a few things. Rosenberg suggests in this context that the primary function of a transcendental deduction is to "legitimize the application in experience of a certain conceptual core as a replacement for and instead of some possible other, predecessor, core." He expands:

> In any experience, we conceive the world we experience through the medium of a particular conceptual core. What Kant taught us to do is to be aware of this as a conceptual practice, a piece of cognitive conduct, which stands in need of legitimization. A transcendental deduction is to be an argument that legitimizes such a practice, that gives us license and title to engage it.[50]

But Rosenberg may confuse a conceptual scheme with the categories that form its core. The rejection of a Cartesian way and the turn to the way through the world means that reflection alone is not adequate to free intentional life and experience of historically configured accretions of significance that always belong to conceptual schemes. As a first defense against the problem of theory succession we can readily admit historically defined changes in conceptual schemes, with one replacing the other; but this still leaves open the question of whether their cores are the same or not. If not, a Kantian might retort, this entails only that we have two different regions, not two incommensurate conceptual cores related to the same region. We end up in the final analysis with a relativity of phenomena or regions but not categorial cores. And certainly Husserl, if not Kant, would argue that we cannot reduce the specification of the cores to scientific descriptions or some direct derivation from the most recently accepted views of one of the positive, natural sciences. Thus there is always the possibility of describing a minimal core that remains the same across paradigmatically different reconceptualizations. Husserl, to continue this line of thought, would be in a much better position to articulate that core because of his emphasis upon description, thus solving Rosenberg's lack of clarity as to how its analysis is to be constructed. Furthermore, if we have the full scope of Husserl's method in view, we can dispense with Rosenberg's completely unnecessary hypothesis of "evolutionary naturalism" to support the idea that there can be a succession of reconceptualizations of the experienced world. All that is required is a notion of historicity whose analysis belongs to a genetic phenomenology.

Having argued this, however, transcendental theory cannot exclude at the outset the possibility of alternative categorial cores for the simple reason that it cannot exclude the possibility of epistemological type differences, i.e., the possibility that in reflection upon experience we discover experiences of a given field of objects that are paradigmatically different for another group of subjects or for the same group at another time without there being a change in regions. Both would have categorial cores but they would not be the same. For Kant this outcome would seem to undermine his transcendental deduction. But how does transcendental phenomenology come to grips with this issue?

The fact that our deduction above is self-referential gives us a crucial link to one aspect of Husserl's theory that I have deliberately kept to the side until now. Husserl is convinced that phenomenological analysis both discovers and requires a form of reasoning that is teleological in nature. In the *Crisis* he tells us:

> Our task is to make comprehensible the *teleology* in the historical becoming of philosophy, especially modern philosophy, and at the same time to achieve clarity about ourselves, who are the bearers of this teleology, who take part in carrying it out through our personal intentions.[51]

We are now in a position to understand how this fits into the project of transcendental analysis. In order for an argument with a self-referential structure to provide justification, as Rosenberg argues,[52] some larger epistemic end in view must be better served by reconceptualizing the world according to one categorial core as opposed to another. This is the link to practical reasoning. There is an interest that guides reconstructions and allows for a decision between competing reconstructions. Husserl's own transcendental descriptions and discourse are pieces of practical reasoning in the sense that they have an implicit reference to a certain end upon which they depend and which provides the descriptions of experience with a criterion of legitimization. As practical reasoning that is self-referential in the sense defined above, it also exercises a crucial control upon the way that phenomenology can employ transcendental arguments. The a priori is "worldbound," as we argued in chapter 3.[53] When used in transcendental arguments, it is further bound to the course of (possibly) actual cognition. It will never do, for example, to construct alternative conceptualizations of cognition at the level of mere thought experiments and to use them as binding counter-examples to a descriptive account of how it is structured. The tie to experience means that only alternative frameworks that arise from a reflection upon cognition and that introduce categories capable of being actually employed or deployed in experience, however broadly construed, can become contenders.

With these constraints in view, we can proceed to ask the question concerning the epistemic end by asking what features a conceptual core must have to achieve the end and then whether a new conceptual core has those features. This strategy can be used as an argument to replace one conceptual core with another when the newer better fulfills the criteria. But it also opens the possibility of there being more than one conceptual core that adequately meets the criteria. In this case, however, the assumption that the a priori is worldbound suggests either (a) that the difference in legitimate conceptual cores entails a difference, perhaps unrecognized to that point, in types of objects within a region or a difference splitting the region; or (b) that we can give a genetic account of the relationship between conceptual cores should they be constitutive of the same region.

What is the end that allows us to assess the legitimacy of a single and then of possibly different conceptual cores? A realist approach would treat the conceptual core as part of the given, existing independently of our experience. Our descriptions and, correspondingly, our experience approach and approximate what is already there. A conceptual approach would appeal to a fit or coincidence between a conceptual core (mental) and the structure of objects (physical). Neither will do at this level of analysis because the conceptual cores are themselves constitutive of objects only by being constitutive of our experience of objects, as our deduction above just showed. Rosenberg, following Kant, suggests that the end in view is "a unity of synthesis," the idea that our experience coheres and is unified. What justifies the adoption and employment of a core is that it allows for previously disconnected regularities to appear connected and as features of a single world as known by a single ego. "It is integrative success, then, which justifies our conceptual practices."[54] These considerations, however, leave us with the vital issue of the derivation of this telos. Given the self-referential and foundational nature of transcendental analysis, this end must come not from the "outside" but from the "inside," as Husserl also emphasizes in the *Crisis*.[55] If it is a principle that is ad hoc and not itself derived from experience, it becomes merely dialectical in Kant's sense.

Husserlian analysis in general agrees with this Kantian emphasis upon integrative success but stresses the way in which this end itself emerges as a regulative ideal in and out of the very course of our experience, thus preserving the self-referential character of the analysis and, in principle, avoiding an appeal to an external verification principle. But how does Husserl establish this?

Husserl's genetic phenomenology looks to the interplay of identity and difference, concordance and strife, resonance and dissonance, harmony and disharmony as the source from which meanings and senses emerge as qualitatively differentiated and interconnected unities that, for their part, configure the ongoing course of experience. Repeated harmonious experiences progressively establish a realization of what is the same, of what belongs to the object typically, of what is "usual." Over time we become familiar not only with the qualities of things but also with how these qualities themselves arise by virtue of a thing's differential relationship to yet other things. If we think of these together as the *integrity* of objects, then we can say that the notion of the "usual" is bound to that of integrity.

One of Husserl's great insights, however, is that the integrity of objects arises not only because their emergent qualities are retained and preserved in memory but also because our experience involves an anticipation of what the object is "in itself."[56] This means that the integrity of objects can be understood not only in terms of their history but also in terms of a certain projection of what the object is optimally. Optimality moves us beyond "usual" to the "normal," supplementing the retentional with the protentional and extending a tracing of what has been the case into an anticipation of what should be the case. In that experience has both a retentional and a protentional structure, we may say that it is not only memorially but also teleologically organized. In this context present experiences become understood as "approximations" to an ideal. What is anticipated is not just a particular idea or a particular approximation but also a sense of the whole that allows us to sort out and distinguish what belongs to yet larger typical patterns and what does not. What we anticipate is a certain world in which the things we experience are marked by integrity. Integrity, then, is a telos that itself emerges in the very course of experience and yet provides it with an overarching teleological structure without which it would fly apart into a thousand scattered islands. When the notion of integrity is combined with the explicit thematization of the whole and the engaged critique of alternatives, we move from the "normal" to the "normative," from a descriptive to a regulative ideal that guides the legitimatization of particular conceptual cores and, as we will see, the progression from one to another.

In this section we have shifted from a static to a genetic account, yet the account of the telos that we have introduced here is still "solipsistic." I have not attempted to account for it once the notion of transcendental subjectivity becomes expanded by that of intersubjectivity and once Husserl realizes that this somewhat formal account must give way to an historical account. The turn to this analysis in Husserl's last text, the *Crisis*, is fairly well known. What is not known is that he had undertaken a full and rich genetic analysis of the interconnection between intersubjectivity, history, and teleology a full decade before he began composing those texts. It is to this study from 1922 and 1923 that we now turn in order to deal with the question of legitimacy in the context of the problem of history.

12

Husserl and the Japanese

Freedom is an expression for the capability and, above all, for the acquired habit of assuming a critical stance to whatever presents itself to consciousness, at first without reflection, as true, as valuable, as practically meritorious; such a stance is the basis for a free decision being achieved.[1]

Autonomous mankind, thus, wants to build *this new world.* In the final analysis this requires a critique of principles and, in addition, a final grounding of last principles, including the principles that make critique possible and, on the other side, make possible a true life of reason.[2]

Mankind is directed to its idea as an artist toward his. The idea becomes continually determined in [the process of] being completed.[3]

—Husserl (1923–1924)

We continue to be surprised that the only pieces of sustained philosophizing that Husserl published in the fifteen years between *Ideas I* (1913) and *Internal Time-Consciousness* (1928) were three articles that appeared in *Kaizo,* a Japanese periodical, in 1923 and 1924.[4] We also find well-written drafts of two other articles that were to follow in the series but were never completed and submitted.[5] We are even more intrigued as we realize that in these texts Husserl takes up themes never touched in publications before and not touched again in his published pieces until the very late work surrounding the *Crisis.* While we know that his manuscripts contain continuous and extensive analyses of the essential forms of social and cultural life and of ethical normativity, the *Kaizo* articles build the only slender bridge actually published on these topics between his attack on "the new *Weltanschauung* philosophy" in his 1911 *Logos* article[6] and the 1934 to 1937 texts surrounding the *Crisis;*[7] slender, indeed, when we think that the articles were published not in Germany but in Japan and that the second and third appeared only in Japanese translation! Yet our intrigue is coupled with anticipation, for we have long wondered what Husserl would say to the Japanese, to a society highly developed and yet not Western, to a culture that does not have its beginnings in the Greek conception of science and knowledge and clearly poses the question of cultural diversity and the problem of legitimizing a transcendental phenomenology. And we have wondered how he could define ethical life in this context, how the analysis would proceed, and how the human and social sciences could play a role in the account that he gives.

A. BROKEN FAITH

What moves these texts beyond earlier formulations, what animates and gives them an urgency not found in previous publications, is the fact that, written in the wake of the First World War, they resonate as they respond to the threat of a shattered and broken faith.

It is, of course, true that Husserl's earlier work can be understood as a response to skepticism which, suggestively, grants to it the reduction of perception to belief in order to effect then a restoration of *doxa*. His first phenomenological account of truth is one that not only describes the web of knowledge but also, in ordering its various strands in terms of relations of dependence and independence and in terms of the various transformations by which some strands support others, treats the perceptual world in all its relativity as an integral part of this web. Husserl connects fields of knowledge to fields of experience and then orders fields of experience in such a way that they rest upon our ordinary and everyday engagement with things, what he freely calls belief. This initial notion of belief, then, is not a notion of faith, which would carry us beyond the pale of what can be naturally known. It is actually a belief in the world, in the integrity of our everyday perceptual engagement with the world. His first writings effect an *epistemological* rehabilitation of belief, and it is this that provides him with a reply to the ever recurring threat of skepticism.

In the texts before us, however, Husserl understands the loss of faith not epistemologically but culturally, affecting not so much the edifice of knowledge as the very city in which that edifice stands. It is his "present full of suffering" that wrenches Husserl out of his earlier preoccupation with narrower cognitive issues and even out of his concurrent interest in Fichte's ethical theory.[8] For the first time he moves from a crisis in thought to a crisis in the entire domain of European culture.

He writes as if Western culture has been stripped, exposing a lack of redemptive powers:

> The war, which, since the year 1914, laid waste to [Europe] and, since 1918, found in place of military force the "more refined" force of psychological torture and economic need, itself morally depraving, has disclosed the inner lack of truth and the senselessness of this culture.[9]

And in two letters from 1920, one to William Hocking and a second to Winthrop Bell, both North Americans, we read:

> What the war disclosed is the unspeakable not only moral and religious but also philosophical poverty of mankind.[10]

> This war, the most universal and deepest sinful fall of mankind in all known history, has displayed all the guiding ideas in their impotence and inauthenticity.[11]

But we quickly discover that this "sinful fall" is itself reinscribed into rationality. Husserl resists the views of many of his contemporaries, for he does not find European culture itself to be an ephemeral if glossy surface beneath which dance the gods who determine our fate. Nor did he find it inherently impotent, a trickling stream lacking sufficient force to turn the heart of a people toward the path of peace and harmony. He is not even willing to view the powers of Western culture as mixed, as containing both wheat and tares, the seeds of both liberating ideals and of destructive impulses. The fall did not really reveal the limits or weaknesses of European culture per se but almost its opposite: what Husserl ultimately sees in the recent barbarism is "the enchainment of its true, progressive power [*Schwungkraft*]."[12] The liberating force of this culture was never released. The darkness surrounding us is not itself a power but rather a lack, a privation, an absence. Correspondingly, the fall was into blindness, into an inability to *see* the generative powers inherent in cultural life.

> A nation, a humanity lives and works in the fullness of power when it is borne by a belief, keeping it in motion, in itself and in the meaning, beautiful and good, of its cultural life.[13]

> This belief, which lifted us and our fathers and which was delivered to nations, which nations such as the Japanese first embraced in the more recent era of the work of European culture, we and ever so many people have lost.[14]

It is because of this reinscription that Husserl's notion of faith bespeaks not salvation, as it did for Karl Barth's groundbreaking 1919 commentary on the book of Romans,[15] nor revolution, as in Rosa Luxemburg's work up to her death in 1918,[16] but rather "reform"[17] or "renewal": making new, but without overturning, what has become old, finding what has been lost, recovering what has been buried. What has "collapsed," Husserl argues, is not Western culture but a vision of the potential inherent in Western rationality.

It is tempting to find in Husserl's comments here and in the texts surrounding the *Crisis* a straightforward affirmation of the integrity of Western civilization with its ideals. But what saves Husserl from a simplistic strategy of counterpoising is his argument that the "formal universal structures"[18] of culture must be set in contrast to the current state of European civilization,[19] presently in disarray and itself the object of his own critical analysis. Yet his is a complex analysis, for it recognizes the internal and dynamic relationship between such structures and the course of human action and insists that in this sphere the analysis of norms is necessarily mediated by an analysis of the forms of such action. We must proceed carefully.

> For Husserl, culture is society viewed as an interrelated cluster of values. Animals live under mere instincts, mankind also under norms. Throughout all the types of acts of consciousness there runs a normative consciousness interwoven with them.[20]

Culture, then,

> is not [just] a general multiplicity of social activities and achievements, coalescing into a general type and fusing into unities of developing cultural forms, but rather a unified norm guides all these formations, mints for them rules and laws. And this norm is alive in the social consciousness itself, is itself progressively and historically shaped and objectivated as culture. . . . [21]

The notion of culture yields one of the most creative tensions we find in Husserl's writings. The phenomenology of the formal structure of culture will find its center in the analysis of the values and the normative ideal constitutive of a society. And if these values and this norm can be rationally justified, we can speak of true culture. Yet culture is an historical, human complex, which means that the existing actions and interactions of a people create the norm that defines its essence. It is this dynamic quality that leads Husserl to see values and the social norm as open:

> Should we wait to see if the culture does not become healthy by itself in its accidental interplay of value-productive and value-destructive forces? Should we let "the decline of the Occident" billow over us as a [finished] fact? This fact *exists* only if we act as passive observers. . . . [22]
>
> Mankind is directed toward its idea as an artist toward his. The idea is continually determined in [the process of] being completed.[23]

The very essence of culture involves the struggle by active, free subjects to realize a norm guiding and justifying their actions, yet this norm is found only in those actions that, in turn, "create" it.[24]

This tension cannot be resolved by arguing that human action is human striving, that in its course we can find certain transcendent ideals leading the process, and that among the multiplicity of available ideals we find "the possibility of continuous ethical progress under the guidance of ideals of reason."[25] Husserl could not simply present this as one among several options from which we can choose at will, for this would undercut its binding, normative status. The ideal of an ethical life guided by "a true practical rationality"[26] must itself take on the character of absolute ethical requirement.[27] Without this, Husserl is convinced, there could be no "rational reform of culture,"[28] no "rational science of human being and human society that would ground rationality in the areas of social and political practice and that would ground rational political technique."[29]

But how are we to move from ethical values as cultural facts to values as binding cultural norms? Or to cast the issue in terms of the question of phenomenological method, which is the focus of this book: how can Husserl give a phenomenological account of normativity that incorporates the historical development of values into the account without making the mistake of appealing to a particular, factual historical configuration as normative?

B. CONSTITUTIVE PHENOMENOLOGY AND CULTURAL LIFE

Husserl approaches his task by taking a step backwards. Before we can speak of cultural life we need to describe the nature of the human spirit in general and we must do so in rigorous fashion. At first we find Husserl using familiar contrasts. Phenomenology is not an inductive science that produces, as do physical and biological studies of nature, empirical laws that are only probable. Induction will never yield the essential laws necessary for a grounded and rational account of phenomena in terms of values. Phenomenology is not an empirical human science but rather an "a priori" discipline that treats the individual and society "in pure formal universality."[30]

At this juncture a shift to a deeper level of analysis intervenes, something often found after *Ideas I:* he treats these stark contrasts between fact and essence, the contingent and the a priori, the relative and the absolute, only as a first introduction, almost as a heuristic device, enabling him to "place" his account in opposition to the tradition, before he then reframes the analysis and provides a description of how one effects a *transition* from fact to essence, from the contingent to the a priori, from the relative to the absolute. We want to follow him here as his account sheds much light on the working method of a constitutive phenomenology once freed of Cartesian restraints.

For the first time in his published writings,[31] Husserl presents something more than an inexplicable *Wesensschau* to account for our apprehension of essences. He speaks of a twofold process of *Besinnung,* of "drafting" the concept under consideration as clearly and precisely as possible,[32] and, then, of "free variation,"[33] even calling it "abstraction,"[34] which discovers an invariant structure throughout the course of changing exemplars, thereby enriching and determining the provisional concept under consideration. In this way we turn our attention away from the accidental "empirical content" of the concepts in play to focus on what is general or universal. All empirical and factual differences, all "concrete circumstances of earthly life" become thereby "indeterminate," "freely variable."[35]

This expanded constitutive phenomenology actually incorporates three moments, what we might call "possibilizing," "essentializing," and "normalizing."

Step One. "We orient our concept of the a priori on mathematics."[36] Mathematics may "use" empirical bodies or shapes, but as it gains insight into mathematical concepts, such things serve as mere examples. "In principle the mathematician refrains from any judgment about empirical realities. They count for him only as contingent examples that can be manipulated at will in free phantasy."[37] In fact, purely imaginary examples could serve equally well, for "the thematic sphere of pure mathematical thought is not real nature but possible nature in general."[38] Real objects or complexes, then, are treated not as actual but as *possible,* real objects.

Step Two. Pure phantasy is not interested in "singular possibilities," which result from step one, but in *essential* possibilities, in "the pure 'idea' or 'essence' and 'essential laws.'"[39] It thinks not the thing but its condition; such thinking Husserl calls the "intuition of the essence,"[40] which he now explains as the terminal point of the process of variation.

> Through free variation . . . we are aware of an open infinity of possible bodies. That which is fixed as identical in such variations, in running through and overviewing the open infinity of variations, is fixed in evidence *as a pervading identity,* as their general 'essence,' their 'idea,' . . . their 'pure concept'. . . .[41]

Step Three. On the basis of such concepts general laws or rules (in mathematics, axioms) are produced. Rational knowledge is knowledge "out of principles," "knowledge of realities out of laws of their pure possibility." Yet the comparison with mathematics is used not to prescribe the form of explanation that is appropriate to a science of human culture but rather to describe the kind of *insight* that is involved and to substantiate the *contrast* between the purely factual and the purely conceptual. Depending on the starting point and what Husserl will begin to call the "interest"[42] undergirding the study, we can have, as in the case of the natural and human sciences, different regional analyses with paradigmatically different models of explanation: "the particular method and the whole type of the a priori theory must and can be quite different."[43]

To this "epistemic" account of the construction of concepts Husserl proposes an "ontological" counterpart; the application of essential laws "to factual reality rests on the fact that each reality evidentially contains in itself pure possibilities."[44] Indeed, each natural complex contains countless possibilities in itself. To this Husserl adds an even stronger thesis, drawing from his belief that manifolds achieve unity only in that they approach a *single* limit, that within a single discursive field "each reality has its pure 'essence' as its rational content, each makes possible and demands its rational ('exact') knowledge."[45] In prescribing a rule for the unity of an endless manifold and "the ideal possibility of its completeness" within a defined field, the essence simultaneously prescribes a rule for the "course" of the possible comprehension of that manifold in ideas.[46]

This breakthrough, this introduction of the notion of eidetic variation, we must hasten to add, does not overturn but certainly goes beyond the notion of constitutive phenomenology that Husserl first proposed in *Ideas I.* No doubt Husserl thought of it as supplementing his first articulation of transcendental theory there. Yet its application to questions of culture and ethical norms does make visible certain tensions in that method.

Husserl clearly recognizes that the "starting point" of the process of eidetic variation will produce different ideas and different essential relationships.[47] The same natural complex can be apprehended as physical or lived-body, as a social or a political unity depending on our point of orientation. The evidence or the intuition raising the analysis to the level of rigorous science, however, does not itself enclose the starting point. It remains a surd, something in excess, necessary for the process but not itself covered by the notion of absolute evidence. The perspectival nature of Husserl's analysis draws us to a theory of *interests* articulating the context in which a given regional discipline arises. This stands in tension with Husserl's insistence on Cartesian closure and the *absolute* character of his analysis.

There is another aspect of this first difficulty. Husserl recognizes that the process of variation must be "bound"[48] if it is to produce a true "differentiation" of an idea or essence. This means that variation is guided by insight into the essence for which it strives. But how can we have such insight binding the process of variation *before* the "object" to be seen is produced? How can insight into the essence guide the process of variation which first produces the essence? Recourse to something like a notion of adduction is quite plausible, but to the extent that the provisional concepts do not merely enumerate their extensions and are themselves constitutive of the field under consideration, to that extent the absolute character of the analysis is rendered uncertain.

Furthermore, culture itself presents special problems for Husserl, for we are dealing with a kind of complexity quite different from that suggested by his standard characterization of appearances. Unlike a perceptual object, culture as phenomenon is itself self-evolving and changing on the basis of principles internal to what it is in such a way that the theoretical representations of it become part of what appears and what it is. This suggests that perhaps culture cannot be comprehended by a structural phenomenological analysis based on the correlational model of acts and profiles presenting an object precisely because culture is an intervening field of normalizing praxis that produces a development of both consciousness, on the one hand, and the world, on the other. This development cannot be gleaned by a study of the correlational features of subjectivity.

Additionally, this first notion of eidetic variation actually excludes the social sciences from Husserl's account for the simple reason that he views them as "empirical" studies and thus as incapable of providing apodictic evidence. Except for psychology, he did not envision the movement beyond empirical inductive studies to structural studies that may utilize an analogue of his notion of constitution and thereby present phenomenology with analyses that call for incorporation. In place of a path through the social sciences into phenomenological analysis, Husserl gives raw, almost trivial pieces of conceptual analysis. Applying free variation to human beings, for example, we derive the general idea of a "bodily-soulish being." He claims that this notion is derived from "the freest variation of all moments capable of variation in the individual humans functioning as examples."[49] A process of "differentiation" further breaks down the concept into, for example, occupational life, leisure life, and so on. This process, we are told, works "exactly analogously" to the way the idea of a figure can be used to generate the ideas of closed figure, straight-lined figure, etc. And somehow all of this, without a single anthropological, psychological, or sociological investigation, rests not on "empty word thoughts" but "insightful knowledge of essences."[50]

C. GENETIC PHENOMENOLOGY AND ETHICAL NORMATIVITY

It would be possible to construct, as Husserl did, an ethical theory on the basis of the constitutive phenomenological method that we have described thus far. Roughly put, such an ethic would identify the values exhibited in social acts and actions, categorize them on the basis of their conceptual content, and organize them into an axiological system, placing lower in relation to higher, limited in relation to unlimited, and dependent in relation to independent values.[51] But then the problems we have just raised would still come to haunt such a system.

What almost eludes us but then catches us by surprise and places the *Kaizo* articles at the threshold of a new breakthrough for Husserl is the fact that, beginning with the third article, the entire analysis is positioned on a different plane. We know from the manuscript "Static and Genetic Phenomenological Methods," written in 1921, just one year before he began to compose these essays, that Husserl came to see the transcendental phenomenology of *Ideas I* as a piece of static phenomenological method.[52] The first two articles explicitly tell us that this method provides the framework and shapes his approach there to the study of cultural values.[53] But what we find in the third article is not a labor of "descriptive" but of "explanatory" phenomenology, not a piece of static but of "genetic" phenomenology; and it is named as such for the first time in Husserl's published writings.[54]

> Let us attempt to develop genetically the ethical form of life as an a priori and essential formation of possible human life, i.e., out of the motivation leading for essential reasons to the ethical form of life.[55]

Thus Husserl shifts his focus to the "genesis of renewal,"[56] to the question of not only what a human society is but of how its essence can be understood only "through development, through a becoming."[57] This method prevails in the unpublished fourth and fifth *Kaizo* articles as well:

> Thereby we note right away that all of this is not to be understood statically but dynamically and genetically. Strict science is not the objective being but the becoming of an ideal objectivity; if it is such only in the process of becoming, then also the idea of true humanity and its method of giving shape to itself is such only in the process of becoming.[58]

There is little doubt, then, that the third to fifth articles carry out a task first projected in the 1921 manuscript on static and genetic method. In his words there:

> With all of this there is bound up the questions of the sense in which the genesis of a monad can reach into the genesis of another, and in which sense the unity of genesis can lawfully bind a multiplicity of monads: on the one hand, there is the question of passive genesis, which, in the case of the constitution of an anthropological (or animalistic) world, points to constitutive physiological processes and the way in which they condition the unity of a physical world with a counterpoised lived body; on the other hand, there is active genesis in the form of the motivation of my thinking, valuing, willing through the other. Thus the consideration of the individuality of the monad leads to the question of the individuality of a multiplicity of coexisting monads, genetically bound with one another.[59]

We have already seen that our texts define static analysis in terms of the interrelated processes of *Besinnung* and eidetic variation. Both work on something that they are not, on phenomena from which the ego performing the analysis has been methodically excluded, as it then extracts essential forms. But a genetic phenomenology of society, which restores the tie between the activity of analysis and history, works on something which it itself is, for it is a process that is part of the human activity and its development submitted to analysis. As social activity it does not just reflectively view the social world but reflexively structures that world it views. What it becomes articulates what it is. To the extent that this activity sets itself in opposition to an existing social state with a view toward other possibilities, a genetic account of society transforms *Besinnung* into *critique.* Critique is the process of explicating as it itself embodies and exhibits the essential values latent in the actual and possible movement from one cultural complex to another.

The notion of critique combines with a second powerful thesis in these texts. In a move equally surprising, Husserl's application of genetic analysis to cultures (a) treats the essential traits of our human existence as "forms of life," (b) finds in one of those forms a "protoform" of ethical life, and (c) discovers in the *transformation* of the protoform to ethical life traits that establish its normative status. This analysis, which moves developmentally, bridges in praxis what *Ideas I* treats antithetically, for here the essence is one of the facts in the process of becoming.[60] The genetic account of ethical life is concerned not so much with a categorization of interrelated values but with the very *process* of *becoming* responsible ethical individuals.

We can only briefly touch upon the way in which the notions of critique and of forms of life interlace in his genetic account. Among the many essential features of human existence, ranging from different kinds of reflective awareness (self-consciousness, self-inspection, and self-evaluation) to reflective action (free action, striving for goals, etc.), Husserl isolates and then describes the form of self-regulation. We can overview our current life, both its actualities and possibilities, can set goals for ourselves, and can bring them under the control of a norm or a value that we have freely set.[61] Such a value takes on the character of a general goal, and we feel that without attaining it we will not be satisfied.

Certainly, life forms based on self-regulation (e.g., vocational goals) are a step beyond "animal naiveté" in that we freely choose and actively follow such goals. But it is possible to be caught in a second naiveté in which a "critique of the goals and the paths we choose to reach them"[62] is missing. At first critique may be concerned only with individual cases and may be simply preoccupied with questions of avoiding further pain or maximizing future pleasure. But there is also the possibility that we will reach beyond particular goals and that critique will become part of a general striving for a full and complete life, a life that can order and justify all its activities.[63] As humans we have the ability to "overview" our whole life, our possible activities and their consequences. As a result

> there arises in the progress of individual development not only the multiplicity and the complexity of practical projects and the activities executing them but also, in increasing measure, the inner lack of certainty of the person, the pressing care for authentic and abiding goods, for satisfaction that can be secured from all critique and exposure to devaluation.[64]

Notice also that the notion of critique is *internal* to the very notion of human life and that it is this "view from here" that provides the crucial transition to ethical life. But in order to reach this transition several other conditions must be described, for we are still not at the level of "ethical man." Husserl does propose two laws of "formal pragmatics,"[65] which will show that all values are interconnected; but they are immediately connected to what I will call three transformation laws, which attempt to present the life-form of ethical life as normative by accounting for and thus grounding the transformation of self-regulation into ethical life.

1. When multiple values offer themselves but their collective realization at the same time is impossible, the good of the lesser values is absorbed by the good of the higher values. This has the consequence of making the choice of the lesser value "practically bad" when competing for a higher practical good. Husserl calls this the "law of absorption."[66]

2. Values chosen and realized are necessarily conjoined to other values chosen and realized to produce a larger good than any one of the particular values. Furthermore, this larger good is of "higher value" than the particular goods contributing to it. This is the "law of summation."

3. The realization of particular limited or finite values will not produce "an enduring satisfaction," for "satisfaction arises not from particular satisfactions (even though they be pure and related to true values) but is grounded in the certainty of the largest possible, perduring satisfaction in the whole of life in general."[67] We can call this the law of maximal value. The values appropriate to the *whole* of life will not be those guiding the limited goals of life but those that have survived the critique of the limited and belong to the realm of the unlimited, of "what is without end."[68]

4. The activity of submitting limited goals to criticism and of transcending them in favor of higher or larger goals "creates the awareness of responsibility," what Husserl also calls the "ethical conscience."[69] Let us call this the law of responsibility. In the process of critique we become aware of ourselves as creatures of reason and therewith as responsible for what is correct and incorrect in our activities. We are unsatisfied when our activities lack correctness or reasonableness. And this brings with it a general interest:

> Out of this there arises, as a possible motivation that can be understood, a wish and will to rational self-regulation . . . namely, a wish and will to shape anew the *whole* of our life with *all* of its personal activities according to reason.[70]

5. Still, we are not yet clear as to just what these larger goals or values are, ones larger than, say, our choice of a career. Husserl argues that out of the above there arises the "possibility, not yet completely determined as to its content," of acting to the best of one's ability.[71] From this there comes "the form of life" of the rational person and the idea of true and authentic humanity. But to make this work Husserl needs what we can call a "law of completeness." The key to this is found in the special form of self-reflection that occurs

for persons in a community. Operative in our forms of life and practice we discover a "limit," an "ideal border" that "rises above the relative ideal of completeness, an absolute ideal of completeness."[72] And this extends beyond the individual; for in critical self-valuation and determination "there arises the authentic and essential graduality of the completeness of mankind as such, from which all justifiable construction of ideals must draw."[73]

> This is the ideal of a person *as* subject *of all* personal capabilities crowned by absolute reason, . . . of a person that would have, were we to think of it also as omnipotent and 'all powerful,' all the divine attributes.[74]

A limit that is itself a "difference," the idea of God establishes the "absolute limit" beyond all finitude that is the pole of all true human striving, however frail and limited that might be.[75] This provides the telos: the absolute idea of completeness, the idea of the autonomous individual. And it transforms this one form into a universal norm.

With this Husserl effects self-referentiality. On the one hand, "the absolutely rational person is *causa sui* in reference to its rationality."[76] Essence is defined by existence. On the other hand, it is the ideal of rationality that brings us as persons into the condition of being rational persons, that serves as the ideal of a process of *becoming* rational. Existence is defined by essence. Husserl's ethical theory culminates in a self-referential ideal of autonomy: "He is subject and, at the same time, object of his [ethical] striving, the work, becoming into infinity, whose workmaster he himself is."[77]

D. CRITIQUE AND CULTURE

The last section applied critique to the generation of ethical normativity, universal in scope and detached from the concrete development of given societies. Genetic analysis is still *abstract* in that it operates independently of the notion of culture. When Husserl takes up the question of culture, however, we find a significant reframing of both the nature and the scope of genetic analysis: the developments that it traces are historical; its analyses are fashioned as historical critique.[78] Genetic analysis becomes *historical* in that culture is treated not as a "factor" but as a "field" of development; the possibilities it begins with are bound, real historical configurations. At the same time we recognize that it is only with the expansion of phenomenology by genetic analysis that the scope of phenomenology can cover the field of culture.

At each step along the way we continually meet surprises. The first set of genetic analyses treated the person as a subject, as an individual "in general" that comes to ethical life on the basis of the structural development of certain forms of personal life. But now this study is supplemented by another, which recognizes that each person is drawn into and enveloped by a society:

> The circumstance that his life is ordered into the life of a society has [logical] consequences that determine ethical conduct from the outset and give more precise formal characteristics to the required categories.[79]

In this account the treatment of society as a field of values is what provides the definition of culture.[80] It is suggestive that Husserl does not take his Cartesian way into the analysis of the other, with its machinery of empathy and introjective perception,[81] but simply takes up the person *in* social relations, in a culture. His starting point is not consciousness but life. In the *Kaizo* articles he does not attempt a *reconstruction* of the pure evidence of other subjects but, rather, a description of the social and cultural ties that exist *before* we even come to raise the issue of evidence and justification. To use a distinction that cannot be maintained very long: the bond is not epistemic but ethical. At least we can say that it is a bond not of theoretical perception but of "practical will," a bond not of pure reason but of "true human life."[82] This is how Husserl describes it:

> In the social relationship he sees that the other, in so far as he is a good, is also for him a value, not merely a use-value but a value in himself: he, accordingly, has a pure interest in the ethical self-work of the other. . . . the best possible being and willing and realizing of the other also belongs to my own being and willing and realizing, and so vice versa.[83]

"Zu meinem eigenen Sein," to what will be called "die Eigenheitssphäre," the sphere of ownness in the *Cartesian Meditations*,[84] there already belongs the other as *value in himself* and as ethically developing. In a way that completely reverses the priorities of his Cartesian way, Husserl speaks of the individual or, more accurately, the ethical form of individual life as having an absolute but yet only a "limited" or "relative value"[85] compared to the "higher" value that falls to a good society. "The entire plateau of value of the individual [achievement] depends on that of the other."[86] The priority of the individual or of the ego required by a constitutive phenomenology of intentional cognition is here displaced by the priority of the other in a genetic phenomenology of social praxis. The "abstraction" from "all cultural predicates"[87] stipulated by Husserl's Cartesian way is replaced by an emphasis on the irreducibility of the process of communication, of "willfully coming to an understanding,"[88] which, in turn, is internally linked to the definition of the ethical individual: "wherever practical clashes result in social practice in the same environment, then a process of coming to ethical understanding intervenes."[89]

E. GENETIC ANALYSIS AND NORMATIVE INQUIRY

The account of culture allows Husserl to draw together the analysis of ethical norms and the account of science (*Wissenschaft*). Coming to ethical understanding is a cultural process of bringing issues under the jurisdiction of critical, normative inquiry, under the domain of "rigorous science." Husserl's genetic analysis of cultural normativity, as we will now try to show, is one that combines a thesis concerning the structural historicity of science with one concerning the historical priority of science in order to derive the normative priority of science. One of the most powerful results of this effort is that science is defined not as a body of knowledge but as a kind of human and cultural activity, as a mode of inquiry.

The Structural Historicity of Scientific Inquiry. Scientific inquiry plays an "ethical role" in discovering the normative principles operative in all forms of individual and social activity and "therewith handles the possible regions of culture and their normative forms."[90] At the same time it also treats itself as one of those activities and in so doing "first creates the practical possibilities of realizing the form of strict science."[91] Science as activity, culminating in philosophy, thereby has an essential historicity:

> The development of the universal theory of science (theory of reason and logic) is an organ and itself a consequence [*Zug*] of mankind's development, as mankind brings itself to higher self-realization. On the other side, the theory of science and the strict science coming about through this development is itself a basic component of higher culture in the objective sense, in the sense of the objective, spiritual world of value building itself up as the correlate of the development of the reason of mankind.[92]

Husserl thinks of the sciences as cumulative and progressive, as in a process of change but one that moves closer to a fuller disclosure of the truth. But here he seems to tie the *norm* of a rational society to the *process* by which it is achieved and even to allow the content of such a norm to arise in the context of this process. Here again is what he says about the "form" and norm of being a true human:

> Thereby we note right away that all of this is not to be understood statically but dynamically and genetically. Strict science is not [an] objective being but the becoming of an ideal objectivity; if it is such only in the process of becoming, then also the idea of true humanity and its method of giving shape to itself is such only in the process of becoming.[93]

The crucial issue will be, then, how Husserl understands this process of becoming.

The Historical Priority of Scientific Inquiry. The actual development of Western culture comes from historical transformations both in the realm of religion and of scientific inquiry. Husserl, like many contemporaries, thinks of culture as arising with mythic religions. But he resists the older positivist approach of devaluing this sphere and of viewing science as the triumph of reason over "fables." Rather, there is an internal development toward religious awareness itself that runs alongside and even contributes to the shape of science. For example, in the movement from the lower to the "higher level of mythic culture" in which forces become transcendent gods who, in turn, are understood as the prescribers of absolute norms, we find a remarkable form of development "which has in itself a unified idea serving as a goal that is objectively constituted in the consciousness of a society and that actively guides its development."[94] These ideas or goals are not present in random fashion for we, "led by an axiological point of view, observe a progressive development of values [*Werterhöhung*] and a culmination in a [certain] value-gestalt."[95] Only when we come to the person of Jesus Christ do we find more of an eruption than steady development in the course of history, a fundamental paradigm shift that shows deeper discontinuity than continuity with what came before;[96] for in Him we find an "individualized idea," a concrete universal unique in the course of our history,[97] to which we are related through a "fundamental religious experience,"[98] through "belief."[99] The Reformation, in turn, he understands not just as a reaction to the "hierarchical culture" of the Middle Ages but also as a "recovery" or a "restoration" of primary sources and of an originary religious experience[100] whose viability endures. Yet even in the discussion of religion Husserl transposes and finds "a concealed rationality" and higher ideals than came before.[101]

While belief undergirds religion, and while we find nascent rationality there, it is a different attitude that gives rise to science in the ancient Greeks. The "theoretical interest"[102] that spawns Greek philosophy comes from curiosity or wonder, "which has its original place in natural life as an intrusion into the course of 'serious living.'"[103] Husserl tells us a fairly standard, if one-sided story about the development of rigorous science in which Plato, but not Aristotle, is discussed.[104] "The tendency to universalization [*der universalistische Zug*], running through mathematics and natural science from the beginning on, designates the general character of modern philosophy and science."[105] It is this tendency combined with the role of critique that finally draws religion under its domain:

> The Reformation placed final authority, to which all norms are bound, in belief. For philosophy, however, belief is, at best, one of the sources of knowledge and, like all sources of knowledge, comes under free critique.[106]

The Normative Priority of Scientific Inquiry. The essential historicity of science combined with its emergence historically as the crowning form of knowledge is what enables Husserl to argue for its normative priority:

> This means nothing less than that we grant to European culture—whose type of development we have described precisely as realizing [the transformation of itself and its world by pure autonomous reason, by scientific reason]—not just the highest position relative to all historical cultures but

> rather we see in it the first realization of an *absolute* norm of development, one that is called to the task of revolutionizing all other cultures in the process of development.[107]

For Husserl this entails critical distance from the bodies of knowledge of other cultures, a distance he seems quite willing to take without arguments based on any detailed historical investigations:

> If one takes the concept of science and the concept of philosophy that originally coincided with it, then the Ancient Greeks are the creators of philosophy, i.e., science. What one calls sciences among the Babylonians, Egyptians, Chinese and even Indians may contain [elements of] knowledge that strict science can confirm, whose content it can take over, whose kind of method and attitude it can draw in, but basically we make with legitimacy a radical divide between the two and finally we must call the [very] same [elements of] knowledge and [attempts at] self-grounding prescientific or unscientific, on the one side, and scientific, on the other.[108]

This passage is very close to one that we find in Husserl's Vienna lecture of 1935. Once again, Husserl distances himself from the sciences of other cultures, only a little more sympathetically:

> It is understandable that this mythical-practical world-view and world-knowledge can give rise to much knowledge of the factual world, the world as known through scientific experience, that can later be used scientifically. But within their own framework of meaning this world-view and world-knowledge are and remain mythical and practical, and it is a mistake, a falsification of their sense, for those raised in the scientific ways of thinking created in Greece and developed in the modern period to speak of Indian and Chinese philosophy and science (astronomy, mathematics), i.e., to interpret India, Babylon, China in a European way.[109]

F. GENETIC PHENOMENOLOGY AND THE PRIORITY OF CRITIQUE

It is always tempting, at this point, to bemoan the devaluing of other cultural traditions and what seems to be a program of cultural imperialism. Husserl's *Kaizo* articles might be treated as mere tracts, encouraging the Japanese to "join in the work of European culture."[110] Even more damning, they seem to devalue indigenous cultural and religious traditions and to be overt efforts to colonize the intelligentsia of a nation whose commercial sector was well advanced in the process of adopting Western commercial and manufacturing technologies.

Yet we know from his short review of Neumann's translation of the sayings of the Buddha, published only two years (1925) after these articles, that this was not Husserl's attitude. We find in these sayings, Husserl recognizes, a way of seeing the world "fully opposite" our European way.[111] Yet Buddhism can be "paralleled" with the "highest formations of the philosophical and religious spirit of our European culture."[112] He even senses that this text contributes to the ethical, religious, and philosophical "renewal of our culture."[113] As is always the case with a thinker as powerful as Husserl, we must look deeper if we are to find both the richness and the poverty of his approach.

What Husserl deals with for the first time in these articles is the fact that systems of knowledge are wedded to culture, that they can even have a social consensus as to what counts as veridical, but that they can be mistaken, they can enchain rather than liberate. Keep in mind that Husserl clearly distinguished between European scientific culture and European civilization, and that science opens to scrutiny not just mythic-religious societies but the "imperialism"[114] and the accepted ideas of his own society. What he means by scientific inquiry, to put it negatively, is a strategy for dismantling an *edifice* of beliefs. In these texts Husserl realizes, perhaps for the first time, that the problem is not with particular claims or judgments but with the *context* of knowledge:

> The intersubjective solidity and objectivity of such a science rests not on the fact that its confirmations are rooted in individually changing material or emotional motives but on the fact that they are rooted in general, deeply entrenched convictions coming from old, well-worked traditions. In particular, mythological and religious motives are determining and, in a given culture, are generally the decisive force.[115]

The "absolute certainty" possessed by a particular system of knowledge he opposes to "evidence," to a confirmation that overturns the appeal to traditions and requires the "original givenness of facts and factual interconnections."[116] Thus, authentic science is much more than the "systematization" of judgments, for we find this already in prescientific systems of belief. "True knowledge is the fulfillment of a striving not for certainty in general but for certainty arising from and motivated by intuitive and self-given truth."[117] And this joins the notion of critique to that of intersubjectivity:

> Factually motivated judgments are objectively valid, i.e., intersubjectively shared validities, insofar as what I see others can see. Over and above all differences between individuals, nations and . . . traditions, stands things that are had in common, . . . [stands] the common factual world, which is constituted in the exchange of experiences so that each can understand the other and each take recourse to what we all see.[118]

Thus science is not the dominion of certainty but

> the kingdom of truth, which each can bring into view, which each can intuitively realize in himself, each from every circumscribed culture, friend and

> enemy, Greek or barbarian, child of God's people or child of the god of a hostile people.[119]

The genuine strength of Husserl's account is found in his view of science or philosophy not as a set of results that others must purchase but rather as a style of inquiry, as a *procedure* of coming to the truth. Whatever the limitations of his actual view of how this is achieved, the focus seems legitimate, for it is only in a process of critical investigation that we can move beyond our traditions and blind convictions and attempt to settle conflicting accounts. Yet it is also true that the attack on treasured ideas can be deeply disruptive.

> So the upheaval of national culture can proliferate, first of all when the advancing universal science becomes the common property of nations that were formerly alien to one another and the unity of a scientific community and the community of the educated spreads throughout the multiplicity of nations.[120]

The diversity of beliefs, the plurality of the gods, then, is not celebrated but overcome. "In the concept of God the singular is essential."[121]

But has Husserl really tied critique to a procedure of coming to the truth rather than a specific content, a specific conception of truth?

His account of critique assumes that historically similar values converge on a single norm, that diversity is necessarily subordinate to identity. The multiplicity of values, we saw above, is under a law of completeness, itself generated in the course of reflection. It is this that orders and then justifies the ideals we construct. However, there are not different ideals for different individuals or different societies but rather there is a *single* "absolute ideal," an absolute limit normative for all. The essence of the person is clarified by the telos of rational autonomy, or, to put it metaphorically, by the ideal of *becoming* God. To return to the analysis of the last chapter, the possibility of different categorial cores is controlled by a telos of rational integration. And when Husserl blends this account with that of history, we find that this general norm is none other than what is specifically and uniquely embodied by Western science and uniquely projected by transcendental phenomenology. The crucial flaw in all this is that Husserl's law of completeness might be mistaken even on his own grounds.

Completeness means (a) convergence of factual examples and gradations upon ideal types, (b) the convergence of types upon ideal limits, (c) the transvaluation of one of the ideal limits into an absolute norm, established by showing its ability to recursively enumerate and order in a closed system all other limits. Note that with (c) difference is controlled by identity, the relative is overcome by the absolute, and, with the addition of the essential historicity of science, many cultures are subordinated to the one culture forming their telos: the many cultural worlds converge on a single world framed as a *totality* rendering their diversity rationally intelligible.

I want to argue, working with a tension that can be found in Husserl's own thought, that the conception of the world as totality is a notion that in principle could function, if at all, only for the positive sciences and that it stands in opposition to a phenomenological characterization of the world. What brings this tension to the fore is the fact that the *Crisis* recognizes that the conception of the world as totality, making possible the notion of a single telos toward which history tends, is itself a product of historical transformations. We must briefly trace this.

As we have seen, Husserl views perceptual experience as teleological in a limited sense. Changes in perceived objects occur in an ordered fashion, i.e., changes are uniform for all things of the same type. In the midst of changes a certain (repeatable) order produces an optimal presentation of the object. The optimal presentation is, given a certain interest, what the experience tends toward, and thus it is privileged or normative.[122] From this analysis of ordinary perception and ordered environments Husserl moves to an account of the objects of science and their one world. What are the changes that give rise to the world of physical and thus scientifically determinable objects?

The process of variation, just traced, is transformed by the process of "idealization."[123] To stay with the treatment of the "shape" or the spatial form of objects, "typical" things that appear are "like" or "the same as" other things. We can think about their shapes abstractly and compare various samples, asking how each compares to the abstract shape. "This gradualness can be characterized as that of greater or less perfection."[124] But we can also press beyond the typical.

> . . . out of the praxis of perfecting, of freely pressing toward the horizons of *conceivable* perfecting [in the] "again and again," *limit-shapes* emerge toward which the particular series of perfectings tend, as toward invariant and never attainable poles. . . . Through a method of idealization . . . these limit-shapes have become acquired tools that can be used habitually and can always be applied to something new—an infinite and yet self-enclosed world of ideal objects as a field for study.[125]

This is more than a redescription of the everyday world. The very idealization of objects as spatio-temporal shapes, i.e., as mathematizable objects, entails a construction of the world as "an infinite *totality* of ideal objects that are determinable univocally, methodically, and quite universally for everyone."[126] Thereby "nature itself is idealized under the guidance of the new mathematics; nature becomes—to express it in a modern way—a mathematical manifold."[127]

But Husserl's last studies recognize that the conception of the world as totality is, at best, an ontological characterization[128] appropriate to the sciences:

> What is new, unprecedented, is the conceiving of this ideal of a rational infinite totality of being with a rational science systematically mastering it. An infinite world, here a world of idealities, is conceived not as one whose objects become accessible to our knowledge singly, imperfectly, and as it were accidentally, but as one which is attained by a rational, systematically coherent method. In the infinite progression of this method, every object is ultimately attained according to its full being-in-itself.[129]

But this only raises the question of whether a guiding ideal for the sciences is not uncritically adopted as the guiding ideal for phenomenological analysis. If, indeed, the life-world is the "forgotten meaning-fundament of natural science,"[130] then applying the notion of totality to it immediately runs the risk of an unjustifiable transposition. Why should we assume that it, too, is a totality, especially when any rigorous notion of totality would require our treating the world as a mathematical manifold?

It was always the case that Husserl worked with a basic distinction, not that far from Dilthey's, between the methods of the natural sciences and those of the human sciences. We can use this contrast to deepen the questions we are raising. In a 1934 text that he sent to the Eighth International Congress of Philosophy in Prague, Husserl cautions against a reduction of "spirit" to "nature," of the human sciences to the natural sciences, of the human world to the natural world. He seems to anticipate our questions. If nature and spirit are placed in the same world, he warns, the result is a mathematization of the spirit.[131] We must maintain a contrast between the world of the natural sciences and the "prescientific world." While the natural scientist takes bodies as "indexes" of an ideal that is mathematically rendered, the human scientist cannot view his/her concrete descriptive work in the same terms.[132] The notion of objectivity we find in the natural sciences cannot be generalized to all domains. "One can no longer compose the world from nature and spirit and thereby bring the sciences on either side into a single dimension."[133] His conclusion accents the question we are raising:

> The world-problem in philosophy becomes questionable, for the sense of the world has become problematic. One cannot bring the intuitive world—"in" which a human being "lives" as ego, as active and suffering subject, as person—under mathematical-objective nature. One cannot treat the being of the person and of personal societies in this world . . . as natural facts in universal, objective-exact nature.[134]

In fact what Husserl proposes is just the opposite. Having rejected the reduction of the human world to "mathematical, objective nature," he pulls the natural sciences into the domain of what he takes to be the "subjective," into the prescientific world. "This merely subjective being is, thus, the a priori for the being of nature in the exact sense."[135] Its totality is relativized to the totality of the cultural world. The fatal difficulty, however, is that this characterization of the prescientific world is *not* a piece of transcendental phenomenology. Immediately Husserl recognizes that it belongs to psychology[136] or anthropology.[137] Thus, the difference between the scientific and the prescientific worlds—both framed as totalities—clearly lies within the province of the "positive sciences."[138]

We know that Husserl handles this difference between the natural and the human worlds not by placing one in the other but by placing the achievements, intentional and historical, by which the natural world is substructed in the life-world.[139] But if we are to avoid confusing phenomenological analysis with positive science, a different characterization of the world is required, one that carries us beyond the "painful oppositions of nature and spirit."[140] At one point in the Prague text he urges us to recognize the special nature of the world understood phenomenologically as *horizon,* defined not in the order of referents but in the order of meaning:

> This is not a collective Allness, not beings externally bound with one another and to one another, but an All whose unity is inseparable from their ties of meaning [*Sinnbezügen*]. The universe is, however, for us a standing, endless open horizon of the pre-validity of beings, a horizon of the certainty of possible appropriation through experience and knowledge. . . . [141]

What I am suggesting, then, is that the characterization of the world as totality is not a phenomenological but an ontological characterization. The treatment of the world as totality is *required* once the mathematization of the world, initiated in the hands of Galileo and completed by modern physics, brought together a notion of infinity with that of a finite and closed system of rules or laws that definitively characterize the endless number of true facts in the universe, and once the human world was construed positively as its "counter-concept,"[142] as yet a more encompassing totality.[143] The phenomenological characterization of the world, however, attempts to articulate neither the whole of things nor the whole of culture but rather that order of significance that gives rise to the difference between nature and spirit.

The world is the life-world, i.e., the nexus of meaning in and through which things have presence. Presence, however, is not given but *achieved.* In the interplay of intending and fulfillment, the profiles through which objects become present implicate as they resonate other profiles not yet given. The very act of fulfillment sets up protentions that follow several lines of significance, often "contradictory," at the same time. As nexus of significance the world is woven with strands of referential implications that cross different orders and thus cannot be reduced to a single set or to a set of all sets. There can well be families of significance, even different orders of significance, without a rule-governed means of assimilating one to the other or of hierarchically ordering one under the other. The world is thereby described as horizon. What Husserl did not fully realize is that the horizon is such that it is always multiple, that it functions in cognitive syntheses not by a principle of unity but by an operation of deflection, that the necessary interplay of presence and absence that it makes possible means that it can never be captured as "phenomenon."[144] The world as horizon is a nexus of meaning that itself lacks synthetic unity. The very notion of completeness and closure, then, cannot be applied to this notion of the world. And with this goes the possibility of overcoming in theory the plurality and diversity of the various cultural worlds by positing one of their operative ideals as the *single* rational norm for all cultures.

The genetic analysis of the world is precisely what shifts the analysis in the direction of a theory of interests and, thus, places not a single telos, not a single goal of autonomy before us, but rather the possibility of a process of norm-guided transformations that, lacking sufficient conditions, are nevertheless open to rational argumentation. The justification of values lacking a single guiding norm requires critique. In his last writings Husserl thought of critique as situated *between* the "natural attitude," serving the natural interest of life, and the "theoretical attitude," necessarily constitutive of the positive sciences.[145] Thus he speaks of it as a new form of praxis, as

> the universal critique of all life and all life-goals, all cultural products and systems that have arisen out of the life of man; and thus it also becomes a critique of mankind itself and of the values which guide it explicitly or implicitly.[146]

Critique, precisely because it lacks completeness at the level of theory, strives for revaluation at the level of praxis by opening to view the rational interests that make renewal possible.

PART THREE

Constructions: Toward a Phenomenological Theory of Contexts

Husserl (left) and Martin Heidegger. St. Märgen. 1921. Courtesy of Husserl-Archief te Leuven.

13

World as Horizon

> Does not the 'infinity' of the world mean rather an 'openness' instead of a transfinite infinity (as if the world were fixed and self-existing, an all-encompassing thing, or a closed collection of things . . .). What can be meant by this?
>
> —Husserl (ca. 1917)[1]

> The world as it is for us becomes understandable as a structure of meaning [*Sinngebilde*] formed out of elementary intentionalities. The being of these intentionalities themselves is nothing but one meaning-formation [*Sinnbildung*] operating together with another, "constituting" new meaning [*Sinn*] through synthesis.
>
> —Husserl (1934–1936)[2]

LET US REGATHER those strands of our analysis in Part 1 that now allow us to confront the question of the world. I hope to find terms that do not overwhelm but facilitate a proper investigation of its structure.

What objects are is either internally linked to their actual and possible *appearance* to us as conscious, cognizing subjects, or it is not. Phenomenology wagers that it is. If not, it argues, what things are is in principle unknowable.

Thus phenomenology takes its starting point in our everyday experience of things, what Husserl calls appearances. Appearances, however, are complex. An object of experience is always present through multiple *modes of givenness*, each of which forms a *profile* of the object. The interplay of object and profile transpires according to the *sense* (*Sinn*) of the whole both determining and being determined by the sense of the profiles. Without senses the object would lack its experiential *qualities*. But senses exist not in the object or its profiles but in the *relationship* between them and the one to whom they appear.

Profiles are also *perspectives*, which means that an object is always present as spatially and temporally *situated*. Initially, we can say that neither the spatial *place* of the object nor its temporal *presence* exist *in* the object or its profiles. Rather, they exist in the relationship between them and the one to whom they appear.

The internal connection between profiles and objects is a clue to the nature of the conscious events in or through which they are experienced. Since these events are always directed to the object *through* its modes of givenness, they are *acts* that have an *ecstatic* structure; since sense is constitutive of that transcendence, they have intentionality. This means that they are not directed to themselves as events or achievements. Inasmuch as these acts are "objectively" directed, the fact that the interplay of profiles and object is "subjectively relational" is "forgotten."

The experience of profiles and objects in a given situation transpires in such a way that the coming profile is already anticipated and prefigured in our relationship to the profile in focus. Profiles, by virtue of their sense, point to or *indicate* other profiles in such a way that we find things situated in a field of possible appearances, i.e., in a determinate *horizon.* The horizon is not itself an appearance but is always "pregiven," i.e., it mediates the relationship between what is given and the anticipations that it solicits. The horizon is a *complex of senses,* themselves connected by what we can call differential implications, that structures the indications in play with any given profile. *Indication* is the horizon at play in the relationship between profiles and then between profile and object. *Differential implication* is the horizon at play within itself. Bringing these two strands together, we can describe the horizon as a *nexus of indications* (*Verweisungszusammenhang*).

Horizons are also tied to yet other horizons by differential implication. The nexus of these interconnected horizons is what constitutes the *world.* In Husserl's terminology the world is the horizon of all horizons.

In that horizons are constitutive of not just acts that experience objects but also of actions and activities that appropriate those things for practical and theoretical ends, the world can be understood as the *life-world.* Because the world does not appear but forms a *background* of significance concealed by the profiles and things that do appear, it too is "forgotten."

The *natural attitude* consists of a double forgetting of a double relativity: on the one hand, forgetting that objects are manifest *as* something only *for* conscious acts and that things are usable *as* something only *for* hands at work; on the other hand, forgetting the world *in* which this internal connection between the as- and the for-structure is rooted. In this third part we will begin by unraveling some of the complexities surrounding what is, in my estimation, the most difficult yet productive of phenomenology's theories, that of the world. Pioneer that he was, Husserl struggled to place the notion on its proper footing. In this chapter I will trace both the critical thrust that the notion affords his mature theory and the tensions in the concept that his last work, the *Crisis,* seeks to resolve. This will allow us to look in chapter 14 at some of the key differences between Husserl and Heidegger and also to discover a tacit reductionism in *Being and Time,* one that threatens to unravel its contribution to our understanding of the notion of the world. Still, the goal of these two chapters is not a detailed historical study of these two figures but the creation of a critical space in which to introduce two concepts, background and context, that will allow me to develop a theory of the world as horizon that stands on its own. Chapter 15 will explore the relationship between background and context by looking at both perceptual and discursive domains. I will be especially concerned to introduce a theory that allows us to see how both background and context are at play in acts of perception.

A. THE WORLD OF MODERN SCIENCE

The best and, perhaps, most fruitful way to understand Husserl's developed notion of the life-world is to isolate his characterization of it as horizon from his other characterizations and then to examine how it figures in his assessment of modern natural science, i.e., the science of medium-sized objects begun in the seventeenth century and running up to recent developments in quantum and astrophysical theory. (Other studies of his relate mathematics, logic, and the human sciences to the life-world, but we will leave their treatment to others.) He undertakes both a *critical* account—in which science precipitates a crisis for Western thought by valorizing the "objectivistic" image of the world, setting it in opposition to the life-world and then devaluing the latter as a folk world of mere belief—and a *genetic* account, in which science regains its moorings as we come to understand the scope of its legitimacy by seeing how it does arise from the life-world and how it can be connected to essential, human interests.

Let me pause to reintroduce the notion of totality, as it will become important shortly. In our "natural life" we are only tacitly acquainted with the world. Lost in its role of presencing things, it is not thematic; its own peculiar structure remains concealed. Yet our marginal awareness of the world can become the guiding thread for an objectivating theoretical reflection that attempts to characterize it from *within* the natural attitude in terms of different "objective" combinations of elements into classes and of "objective," rule-governed relations between those classes. If these groups and their relations are understood as self-sufficient and comprehensive, as occurs in modern science and those philosophies wedded to it, the world is construed as either an empirical or an eidetic whole, as either a totality of all that has (real) existence or as a totality of all that is the case. Here we might recall Wittgenstein's analysis and our treatment of it in chapter 3.

In his effort to overthrow the positivistic or objectivistic self-understanding of modern science, in the hope of then repositioning it on its proper philosophical ground and bringing it under the direction of rationally justifiable human ends, Husserl directly challenged the characterization of the world that modern science projects—roughly, the mathematized world of Newtonian physics consisting only of quantitative determinations—as the only true world-in-itself. The world in which we live and with which we are most familiar, day in and day out, is not the one projected by scientific thought. Rather, the things we "first" see belong to the world of what Husserl calls *Anschauung,* intuition, a term he uses to describe our direct perceptual and experiential acquaintance with the *everyday things* of our environment "before" they, wrapped in interpretation, stand forth as *data.* Here we find the lush green of a field in an early morning haze, not light waves 512 nanometers in length, refracted by vaporized H2O as the axis of the earth turns, etc.

The intuitive world should be defined not as a core of pre-cultural, primitive perceptions but as the world in which things appear in terms of their experiential qualities, values, and uses, and are integrated into our larger concerns on the basis of their integrity. This is the world that stands over against the quantified world of modern science.

Husserl offers not just a *separation* of the experiential world from the world (re)constructed through natural science, he offers an account of how the world projected in the natural sciences *arises from* the world of ordinary experience. He does this by showing that the world under a scientific description is a *construction* that takes its starting point from, and arises through, methodologically guided transformations of the life-world. As he first put it in lectures as early as 1919, "the objects of the immediately intuited world that lie before all theoretical thought . . . already have a sense-content that functions as substrate for scientific work."[3] The intuition of an object or event involves the interlocking of perception and apperception, of presentation and appresentation. As an intentional experience of the whole object, it is drawn beyond what analysis would describe as the directly given, for each profile is situated in a series of anticipated, possible profiles, predelineated by the horizon in play, and each intuition transcends the profile in its apprehension of the whole. The interplay between actual profile and anticipated profiles is not a random but a structured series, as within stable backgrounds the profiles tend to converge on an optimum that ongoing experience exhibits as it approaches the object. Through the "and so on" of profiles and an attending subordination of profiles to the wholes they indicate, senses become stable *types* and objects take up their familiar presence for us. The natural attitude relies on this constitution of a familiar world, yet without being able to thematize it as such.

Born of wonder, philosophy and science, not yet distinguished in ancient Greece, were efforts to discover and articulate the *logos* of this unthematized world.[4] They broke with, but not through, the natural attitude in the sense that they transcended the endless iteration produced by the horizon in order to grasp segments of it as wholes. They employed a reflection that temporally suspended the interests that sustain the functioning of differential implications, deliberately varied the appearances of a given field in such a way that their optima were allowed to exhibit a limiting ideal or point of unity (ideation), and, finally, articulated the rules that govern the series of phenomena that subsequently show themselves as instances of or approximations to the eidos (idealization). The value of this eidetic method is that it produces a *theoretical* or *critical* mastery of the objectifiable features or properties of a given region, a mastery that yields in its turn a *practical* or *technical* mastery allowing us to build and rebuild our environments.

Various disciplines arose as the Greeks concentrated on different regions of the world and submitted them to a process of classification and explanation. While breaking with it, they were originally *rooted in* the life-world, in the sense that they depended upon a wider, pregiven yet unthematized horizon distributing the different regions: in that the processes of ideation and idealization were continuous with the project of rendering the type-bound perceptual optima we experience exact, in that the sciences were largely practical arts whose explanatory schemes were designed to produce changes in the world, and in that their theoretical component, at least up to Aristotle, belonged to the same universe of discourse as ordinary language.

But the introduction of modern natural science brought about a fundamental paradigm shift. By transforming idealization into mathematization, by identifying the world as a totality covering all that exists, and then by characterizing it in terms of a mathematized notion of infinity, modern science interpreted the world and the things in it as mathematizable manifolds, i.e., reduced them to the intersection of sets of features that can be measured, plotted, and submitted to statistical description and verification. Its method is designed to eliminate *background* and establish the theoretical field of quantifiable predicates and causally linked relations as the sole *context* in which things, facts, or events can show themselves. While this yields even greater theoretical understanding and technical mastery over the things of nature, it results in science losing any recognizable bond to the life-world.[5]

Building on the double forgetting constitutive of the natural attitude, modern science is twice free yet twice blind: free from the relativity of subjectivity, and free from the relativity of the life-world; blind to those epistemic practices by means of which it is produced, and blind to its own transformations of background that allow phenomena to stand forth only as data.

The deperspectivalization of the world by modern science, however, can never be complete for two reasons: first, because its *content* comes forth from a field that, while universal, is constituted by theoretically sustained practices it must acknowledge as such when there is a breakdown or paradox generated in a given field of study (e.g., particle vs. wave theory); and, second, because its *method* relies on activities that involve ordinary intuitions and experimental operations that require non-formalizable acts of interpretation (e.g., reading marks on instruments). Since even the science that has rid the world of subjectivity can only be understood as the "correlate" of subjectivity, the phenomenological critique of science already points the way to an understanding of how science can be established; the developing theoretical and practical knowledge that allows for a mastery of nature must be blended into a broader range of human interests and the larger project of human emancipation.

B. FROM WORLD TO LIFE-WORLD

Thus far we have run with Husserl's characterization of the world as horizon and used it to critique objectivism. In order to understand the tensions in his theory, however, we need to pinpoint in this section where the concept of the world enters his thought and when it becomes reformulated as the notion of life-world.

As we saw in chapter 4, it was only in the period between the *Logical Investigations* (1900–1901) and *Ideas I* (1913) that Husserl realized that his phenomenological investigations into intentional experience and knowledge were not yet philosophy. His innocent naming of them, following Brentano, as "descriptive psychology" eventually enabled him to see both that the method was limited in scope and that the field it covered is not basic but derived. He had not moved beyond the natural attitude to the transcendental phenomenological attitude. This was "first explicitly presented," he reported to Misch,[6] in the lecture course of 1907, now published as *The Idea of Phenomenology,* refined in *Ideas I,* and then constantly developed over the next two decades.

The natural attitude, as we saw in chapter 2, is constitutive not only of prescientific and scientific life but also of any phenomenological discipline that covers a single field or region of experience, as does descriptive psychology. All regional ontologies remain wedded to the natural attitude in that they are able to unfold the constitution of essentially different regions only on the basis of a tacit belief, itself unanalyzable within the scope of those ontologies, in the existence of the world of which they are parts. Not fully free of the movement of objectivation necessary for any positive discipline, this belief involves the assumption that regions are situated on the ground of the totality of beings.

The totality of beings can itself become the topic of a universal ontology. This discipline also remains in the natural attitude, for it is undergirded by a belief in the existence of the totality of beings. As a consequence the totality is necessarily treated as an object or a being (of a higher, ideal order). Commensurate with the universal scope of universal ontology, we can clarify the totality of what is, but only according to certain formal "objective" requirements that bind all regions. We have failed to cover the underlying connection between what is and the manner in which it can be apprehended as such.

To understand this connection, the world, first identified within the natural attitude as the totality of beings,[7] must be resituated at the level of the to-be of all beings, thus securing its *difference* from beings and its transcendental status, and then phenomenologically characterized as the correlate of a "discoverable universality of synthetically connected accomplishments,"[8] thus securing its character as horizon and clarifying the sense in which the being of beings is internally connected to their disclosure.

Yet in *Ideas I* it seems that the world is introduced only to be excluded. When, in its opening pages, Husserl tentatively identifies the world with the totality of beings, the work gains a guiding thread that would provide a universal scope to the phenomenological analyses following in the later sections. In those sections he argues that the ground constitutive of the "straight out" posture of our natural life is a tacit belief in the existence of the world and, conjoined with it, an encompassing operation of "objectivation," running from naive sentience through sophisticated science and philosophy, in which experience and thought are "lost" to themselves as they are fixed on the given. As a consequence, the way the determinacy of things depends upon "subjectivity" is marginalized. What Husserl calls "bracketing" the existence of the world in *Ideas I* neutralizes the grip of the world and introduces a movement of reflection whereby we can study the different types of "subjective" cognitive achievements that undergird different regions of phenomena. The phenomenological reduction there consists of this combination of bracketing and reflection. At the same time that it frees philosophical analysis of the covert assumption of a world-in-itself, the reduction keeps the scope of the world (universality) as it reframes it, in a way we have yet to specify, as a "pregiven" structure that is the condition of the possibility of whatever is given in experience. In short, the reduction transposes our first "naive" account of the *existence* of the world and its *construction* into a "critical" account of the *presence* of the world and its *constitution.*

This transposition not only secures the transcendental character of Husserl's own phenomenological analysis but also provokes a phenomenological reinterpretation of the transcendental analyses of others. It calls for the transformation of the results of transcendental categorial analyses, be they in the style of Aristotle's *Metaphysics* or Hegel's *Logic,* into a phenomenological register, and for the overcoming of the tacit objectivism of Kant's analysis by a proper phenomenology of subjectivity. This, however, is another study.

These first excursions, which brought the notion of the world into the domain of phenomenology, required no more than a *regressive* phenomenological procedure that began with the structural differences between the appearances of different regions of beings and then "built backwards" to their general conditions. But they tended to be undercut by the strong epistemological requirements that Husserl tied to his notion of evidence. In an effort to avoid the speculative constructions of categorial analysis and the hypothetical deductive procedure of Kant, Husserl's account of transcendental constitution in *Ideas I* was supported by a Cartesian notion of reflection combined with a requirement of intuitive immediacy and adequacy for all elements admitted as secure into the system. That combination, however, drove a wedge, as it did for Descartes, between the immediacy and indubitability that attend the self-presencing of consciousness and the lack of such for the presence of the world. It resulted in transcendental subjectivity, or what Husserl in *Ideas I* calls "absolute consciousness," being characterized as a "residue" that is left over after the reduction methodologically "annihilates" the world.[9] The internal requirements of his theory of evidence also mean that he cannot rely on his first notion of totality and thus needs a method of securing the universal scope of the account that belongs to the domain of phenomenology proper. Building on the structural difference between the appearance of consciousness and that of the world, radical Cartesian doubt encompasses the totality of what exists in a single act of exclusion at the same time that it reframes all things as phenomena for consciousness, i.e., it secures the for-structure as a whole. The difficulty is that in principle it is incapable of covering the in-structure or, worse, that it loses the in-structure in the for-structure. Because *Ideas I* operates with dyadic oppositions (inner and outer, subject and object, immanence and transcendence), Husserl has no choice in this work but to treat the world itself as a phenomenon *for* absolute consciousness, thereby casting it back into being a totality.

Further studies, undertaken after *Ideas I,* into the constitution of the difference between the natural and the cultural worlds, the expansion of static into genetic phenomenology, and the discovery of alternative ways into transcendental analysis, all necessitated basic changes in the phenomenological approach to the world. First, the world bracketed and excluded in *Ideas I* can be understood concretely as an "objectified" world that is the result of historical development. This means that it can be set in contrast to a "preobjectified" world upon which it depends and to which it relates, a world whose presence may escape the reduction precisely because it does not have the type of existence that the reduction of positivity can capture. But this makes sense only if the world is phenomenologically characterized not as an object for consciousness (totality) but as a structure equiprimordial with consciousness, and only if it is understood as a nexus of meaning, having a complexity that Husserl had not previously recognized, on the basis of which all particular worlds are constituted. When he gradually fades his initial account of the world into a theory of the life-world during the 1920s, it signals his attempt to employ his developing genetic phenomenological method to effect a positive integration of the world into a transcendental account.

While one can trace connections to such thinkers as Wilhelm Dilthey,[10] Richard Avenarius,[11] and even the dramatist Hugo von Hofmannsthal,[12] it is Husserl who places the concept of the life-world at the very center of philosophical theory. Its impact on the broader philosophical and scientific community came through his last book manuscript, which was composed between 1934 and 1937, partially published (Parts I and II) in 1936, and then completely published (with Part III and the supplemental texts) in 1954. The groundwork for this concept, however, reaches back to a Göttingen lecture course given in 1910/11, which analyzes "the natural concept of the world" and clearly distinguishes the "naturalistic world" from the "socio-cultural [*geistige*] world,"[13] and to certain sections of *Ideas II,* first drafted in 1912, which deal with the constitution of "nature" and what he variously called the "personal world," the "cultural world," or the "world of [human] spirit." In a lecture course first given in 1919 in Freiburg and titled "Nature and Spirit," these ideas were developed and consolidated by a theory that understood "nature" and "spirit" as various "strata" or "levels" of the "environing world" (*Umwelt*) or "everyday world" (*Alltagswelt*). To my knowledge the term "life-world" finds its first public appearance in this course.[14] It is introduced there when his structural account of the "pre-given" *Umwelt* is brought together with a new interest in the "growth" or "reconfiguration" of one type of *Umwelt* into another.

C. WORLD AS EXPERIENTIAL MATRIX AND CONCRETE UNIVERSAL

With this term in hand Husserl struggled to further develop and clarify his theory of the life-world. While this idea was clearly introduced and its basic elements developed before Husserl became familiar with the content of Heidegger's *Being and Time,* a story told in chapter 5 (Section D), and while his intense work on the issue during his last period from 1932 to 1936 shows no direct appropriation of Heidegger's concept of the world and is certainly not an attempt to "incorporate Heidegger's insights into a more traditional framework,"[15] there is little doubt that Heidegger's ideas stimulated and provoked him to begin publishing his own theory. Yet he wrestled with the problem of giving a proper transcendental characterization of the life-world. What precisely is this "fundament" *on* which the world of science rests? Is not science also *in* the life-world and very much a part of it? If so, how can the life-world be its ground? To do justice to his theory, if only in an introductory way, we must catch the issue as it unfolds systematically.

The world projected in the modern sciences of nature arose, we saw, from specific transformations of a prior world. Initially Husserl envisioned this world not as the "cultural world" in which we are all situated but as a "natural world" which we experience "before" its refashioning in the hands of science. This first notion of the life-world treats it as the correlate of "prescientific" and "pretheoretical," unencumbered experience. But where would we find such experience and such a world, free of the multiple layers resulting from the interpretations of theoretical disciplines, not to mention everyday chatter?

The priority of the perceptual world over the theoretically constructed world should not be understood temporally, nor does its description require recourse to anthropology:

> It is not as though we are undertaking an historical-anthropological investigation, and are attempting to fix how humans envisioned [*vorstellen*] the world before the arrival of science or how different peoples envision the world who, even today, are without science and whose apprehension of the world is unaffected by science. The prescientific consciousness that we mean here, the only one that can come into question for us, can be constantly exhibited or, at least, produced in evidence through a methodological exclusion of all the apperceptions originating from [previous] theoretical acts.[16]

The life-world, characterized as a pre-scientific experiential world, is open to study by means of an *abstraction* or, to give this term its proper import, a process of *eidetic variation* that systematically factors out the interpretative overlay of science. This is not an artificial or speculative procedure because our reflection upon it follows a "guiding thread" at play even in encumbered perception, and because the life-world it frees up is itself "given," i.e., is the correlate of a mode of experience, nonepistemic in nature, that forms the background to the interpretative, epistemic perceptions of the empirical sciences.

But how can we speak of an experience of the world without reducing it to an intentional object and thus losing the difference between objects and the world in which they are situated? For this we must extend our opening account of Husserl's theory of perception.

In viewing the front side of the house I see the house as a whole. At the same time, the side directly facing me invites me to view other aspects, other profiles that are already prefigured for me by virtue of the senses already in play. In every perception I am given *more* than what is directly facing me. I can broaden my circle of experience by walking around the house, seeing its backside, but this only sets up yet other "inner" and "outer" anticipations. By entering the house I follow the inner indications and further explore, each room pointing me to yet others. Or I can follow the outer indications, for in "perceiving" the house I also "apperceive" the lush green field in which it is situated, which, in turn, points me to the valley in which it is located, the hills on either side, even the backside of those hills. The experiential world phenomenologically characterized is just the *inner* and *outer* horizons that make coherent perceptions of situated objects possible and is itself "pregiven" in and with each experience.

Expanding while transforming a notion central to Kant, Husserl calls the phenomenological discipline that explicitly reflects upon this pregiven world, and then analyzes its "standing, perduring structure," *transcendental aesthetics.* As we suggested in chapters 7 to 9, some of Husserl's richest studies are in this area. They cover such issues as lived space, lived time, perceptual fields, sense concatenations and anticipations, passive syntheses and perceptual modalizations, and, as the locus of perceptual experience, the lived-body and its unique constitution. We even find some later speculative texts in which Husserl begins to entertain a difference between world and earth.[17]

It is important to note that this first contrast between the life-world, understood as the world of unencumbered perception, and the world projected by modern natural science arises at the level of vision and its interpretation. The reason why the life-world is said to found the world of scientific observation hinges not just on the fact that we are acquainted with things and relations before we turn them into objects of scientific investigation, but also on the fact that such a qualified mode of observation can be understood as the result of specific noetic and noematic transformations of primary observation.

While this first contrast is sufficient to undercut the absoluteness of the modern scientific concept of nature, as I argued in the last section, and serves Husserl well in his efforts to preserve an internal link between "objective" nature and "subjectivity," it becomes quite problematic when we look at science not just as a theoretical discipline that frames a concept of nature *over against* the life-world but as an historical and cultural enterprise *within* the life-world. Here in the *Crisis* Husserl recognizes that the theory is in a bind:

> The concrete life-world . . . is the grounding soil of the "scientifically true" world and, at the same time, in its own universal concretion, encompasses it. How is that to be understood? And how are we to do justice systematically—that is, with appropriate scientific discipline—to the all-encompassing, so paradoxically demanding, manner of being of the life-world?[18]

Furthermore, science provides us not just with a way of seeing the world but also with a way of effecting its restructuring in practice. The transformations to which it gives rise are not just interpretative and projective but also, through the technologies it spawns, material and sensuous.[19] When coupled with a system of political economy, they transform the very things we see, the very course of our actions, even the places we dwell. Even when we look at originary perception itself we discover that our perception with the life-world is not only circumscribed by but also interwoven with the practical relationship we have to things. Thus when in the *Crisis* Husserl speaks of the accomplishments of technology "flowing into" the life-world, his first contrast between the life-world and the world of science seems to collapse. Nature, the universe that would be the correlate of originary perception, and not only the sociocultural world undergoes physical modification and development. Even if one could still claim unadulterated sight, there would be all too few pure objects to behold. They seem forever lost beneath the "sedimentation" of not just interpretative, theoretical but also material, technological transformations. Thus the problem of recovering the life-world as first defined returns with a vengeance.

In fact our difficulties are intensified when Husserl comes to treat the scientific world as but one of a number of different "particular worlds" (*Sonderwelten*),[20] each of which is constituted by a different regulative ideal or guiding end, be it practical or theoretical, and each of which "flows" into and changes the life-world. Husserl still maintains that whether it be the world of financial exchange, furniture making, or ultimate Frisbee, all operate against a background of intersubjective, sensible experience and can be understood in terms of the actions and interests, themselves susceptible of critical analysis, that effect the transformation of the experiential world. But he expressly recognizes that this idea produces a second bind in his theory:

> Here is again something confusing: every practical world, every science, presupposes the life-world; as purposeful structures they are *contrasted* with the life-world, which was always and continues to be "of its own accord." Yet, on the other hand, everything developing and developed by mankind (individually and in community) is itself a piece of the life-world; thus the contrast is suspended.[21]

This twofold bind carries us in the direction of a second concept of the life-world. To use terms that I will introduce shortly, Husserl's deconstruction of modern science argued, in essence, that the specific *context* of this science, the theoretical method of mathematizing nature, must be placed in relation to a particular abstractable *background,* our pretheoretical acquaintance with nature. But the notion of "particular worlds" introduces other contexts and the idea that these can transform background. Accordingly, we must enrich our account of background. This can take place not only by overturning the "ocular" restriction of the first description of the world of "primary sensibility," by extending it to include our practical engagement with things, but also by supplementing the results of a structural account with the genetic notions of sedimentation and transformation. This would be an account of how context becomes background, of how we develop a "secondary sensibility," of how culture acquires flesh. For the concrete world in which we actually live is the one that is already shot through with the results of practical and theoretical achievements. This implies that not only the logico-theoretical praxis of the empirical sciences, but also the multiplicity of particular worlds, and even the life-world in the narrow sense—the world of primary experience—all belong to "the full concretion of the life-world."[22] Husserl characterizes the life-world in this wider sense at one level as "the universe of life-world objects,"[23] at another as "the universal field of all actual and possible praxis, as horizon."[24]

While this second notion of the life-world covers both "nature" and "culture" and thus gains both a concreteness and a scope commensurate with the totality of beings, it may do so at the expense of the role that it was to serve in the first place. In the light of this second notion, Husserl's claim that the life-world is the ground of the empirical sciences is problematic precisely because this might mean only that the praxis of the sciences (now included in the notion of the life-world) is the basis for the theory of the sciences, not that there is a necessary connection between the world of originary perception and the world projected in natural science. Furthermore, if we allow praxis to specify what we mean by the life-world, then we might have a diversity of worlds correlative to the different styles of acting in or upon the world, be they individual or social. In gaining concreteness, we lose unity.

These tensions in Husserl's theory arise, I would suggest, because while he was the first to bring the characterization of the world as horizon into philosophical parlance, he tends to superimpose upon it features that arise if we think of it as totality. Only his last work breaks with that tendency, in principle if not always in practice.

> In opposition to all previously designed objective sciences, which are sciences on the ground of the world, this would be a science of the universal *how* of the pregivenness of the world, i.e., of what makes it a universal ground for any sort of objectivity.[25]

The world is treated both as the experiential world of intuition that *underlies* and grounds the worlds guided by practical and theoretical goals, and as a concrete whole which, due to the "flowing in" and "sedimentation" of practical and cultural achievements, *encompasses* the multiplicity of particular worlds. These two notions of life-world, world as experiential ground and world as concrete universal, are easier to place together if we consistently treat the world as horizon and supplement the notion of background with that of context. Let me supply a few suggestions in this direction.

Particular worlds are forged through intersubjective, social achievements and thus necessarily rely on different types of discursive interaction for the construction of their domains and the tacit norms within them. Language comes into play and, along with it, conceptual networks without which we would not have particular spheres. These networks are *contexts.* In contrast to backgrounds, which are complexes of senses deployed across our embodied relationship to things, contexts can be described as socially constructed and inscribed *matrices of meaning* (*Bedeutung*). The relationship between elements in a matrix is one of *differential entailment.* The relationship between facts and affairs-complexes constituted in contexts can be characterized as *referential entailment.*

We gain purchase on the notion of the life-world, I am suggesting, if we characterize the horizon in terms of the interplay of context and background. In that all regions are situated *within* differential blends of context and background, which they also (re)structure through sedimentation, the horizon is a concrete universal. In that all contexts presuppose and thus rest *upon* a (back)ground of embodied perceptual experiences (intuition) and practical involvement (know-how), the horizon is an experiential matrix.

Restricting the characterization of the life-world to the notion of horizon and elaborating upon it in terms of the interplay of background and context allows us to avoid three difficulties, two that Husserl struggled with on different occasions and one that touches my modification of his theory.

1. The life-world is not a certain *region* of objects or experience, be it "nature" (originarily given) as opposed to "scientific nature," as his critique of objectivism would lead us to believe; or "culture" that has a certain "ontological priority" over "nature," as he puts it in the second book of *Ideas.*[26] While we can still contrast the structure of the world projected by, say, Newtonian science—which sets the context for our recognition and characterization of scientific objects and relations—with the structure of the life-world in terms of the background constitutive of the experience of everyday things by embodied conscious subjects, that particular background does not exhaust what is meant by the life-world.

2. Because we understand the concept of the life-world as transcendental, it can be part of our account only if it can be experienced or, in Husserl's scheme, only if it is the correlate of experience. The notion of experience or intuition, however, should not be reduced to that of sensuous perception, for this is but one mode of our embodied experience of things. Experience involves not just our senses but also our hands, our movements, and our "tryings." As Heidegger will instruct us shortly, I can "directly" experience the object on the workbench as a hammer without having to interpret this experience as a complex act in which the thing is first perceived in terms of its sensuous qualities and then, using this as a substrate, subsequently interpreted as a hammer. I directly experience those movements as a dance, even though dances exist only in a social and cultural context. Intuition, if we are to retain the word in a transcendental characterization of horizons, must not be understood restrictively as the noetic correlate of prescientific nature but more

broadly as the noetic correlate of affective complexes "passively" present. The qualities intuited are the result not just of unencumbered perceptions and bodily actions upon things but also of the sedimentation of what were the products of prior active achievements, be they sonatas or sonograms, cultural or scientific. In short, to define the life-world as the correlate of intuition, once we avoid the temptation of then seeking an "object" of this noetic mode, may do no more than emphasize the fact that background and context are always "pregiven" and that they have a structure that must always be fleshed out in terms of conditions of experience.

3. Even if we conclude that the life-world is not a totality, we still have not resolved the question of whether it is a universal structure, nor have we indicated what makes this different from a totality. My tendency in chapter 4 was to characterize the life-world as a "concrete universal" and to argue for its universality on the basis of the general structure of indication and anticipation that allows divergent experience in different regions and even different worlds to be integrated into one concrete world.[27] But here again we must ask whether I am introducing requirements that are tethered to the characterization of the world as totality.

In the *Cartesian Meditations* Husserl models his theory of the transcendence and unity of the world after the Cartesian ideal of the adequate givenness of an object. While all empirical givens are arrested in inadequate presentations, they always point beyond themselves to their true nature:

> Actually existing object indicates a particular system within this multiplicity [of actual and possible experience], the system of evidences relating to the object and belonging together in such a manner that they combine to make up one (though perhaps an infinite) total evidence. This would be an absolutely perfect evidence, which would finally present the object itself in respect of all it is—an evidence in whose synthesis everything that is still unfulfilled expectant intention, in the particular evidences founding the synthesis, would attain adequate fulfillment.[28]

The relationship between profiles and the object, possessing a transcendence whose totality could be given only if we could recapitulate all of its perspectives, provides the operative model for his Cartesian understanding of the relationship between object and world:

> The reference to harmonious infinities of further possible experience . . . manifestly signifies that an actual object belonging to a world or, all the more so, a world itself is an infinite idea, related to infinities of harmoniously combinable experiences, an idea that is the correlate of a perfect experiential evidence, a complete synthesis of possible experience.[29]

This jump from the unity of an object to the unity of the world introduces a fatal mistake: in that the presence of the world is modeled on that of the complete givenness of an object through its profiles, the world itself becomes the "correlate" of an experience and necessarily an "object." What keeps my account from this mistaken objectification of the world is that I reject the Cartesian characterization in which the world is grasped as an "infinite idea" belonging to the order of referents and argue that, as nexus of implications and entailments, as the horizon of horizons, it belongs to the order of meaning. For without this difference, the in-structure collapses into the for-structure. We can see this in Husserl's own effort toward a "critique of experience" that "follows Descartes a piece"[30] as it uncovers a notion of subjectivity "in such a way that it is impossible to take it as *in* the world, as humanly existing."[31] Indeed, the in-structure is *reversed,* for now subjectivity transcendentally characterized is not in the world, but rather the world is discoverable only "in its immanence."[32] As a consequence the world I am in is the world that is in me: "I can *enter* no world other than the one that gets its sense and validity in and *from* me, myself."[33] By contrast, I would argue, characterizing the world as horizon does not require a single intuition that encloses it, nor must the world possess the singularity of an object. Rather, it is found not as an object of a higher or different order but in the difference between objects and then between different orders. Its ideality is based on its cross-referentiality. We have the world not as a single whole but as nexus of significance, and our approach to it is always from *within.* This allows for the possibility of a *multiplicity* of finite horizons, themselves lacking a single point of identity and thus closure.

14

Horizon and Discourse

The phenomenon of *indication* [*Anzeige*] is something which can be exhibited from the point of view of phenomenology. This insight, worked out as early as the *Logical Investigations*, already constitutes there the nucleus of genetic phenomenology.

—Husserl (1920s)[1]

Explication can draw the conceptuality belonging to the being to be unfolded from the being itself, or can force it into concepts to which that being, according to its manner of being, is opposed.

—Heidegger (1927)[2]

HEIDEGGER'S EFFORTS TO replace the concept of transcendental subjectivity with his notion of *Dasein* set Husserl's and Heidegger's analyses of subjectivity at odds with each other. Commentators have followed suit. But this approach quickly obscured deeper connections between their respective concepts of the world. This chapter is an effort to reclaim some of these basic affinities.

After a preliminary remark on a surprising though general parallel in their phenomenological methods, I will use the question of whether Heidegger thinks of all perception as interpretation as our point of access to his theory of the world and to the relationship between horizon and discourse. Toward the end of the chapter I will also attempt to locate the significant differences between Husserl and Heidegger, with a view to developing our theory of contexts.

Our analysis, in the first part of this study, of the difference between categorial, constitutive, and genetic phenomenology, allows us to see how deeply Heidegger's working method in *Sein und Zeit*, for all the striking differences in content resulting from its application, is indebted to Husserl's framework. While it does not actually attempt to carry them out, *Sein und Zeit* establishes a place for regional ontologies. Though the theoretical side of regional ontologies is sometimes labeled "ontological," he generally reserves the use of "ontological" for his transcendental account of Dasein, using the term "ontic" to characterize what Husserl calls regional ontologies. With that to the side, in Division I he undertakes extensive *structural* descriptions of the various moments of Dasein as being-in-the-world, as well as accounts of the "origins" of the present-at-hand, on the one hand, and assertions, on the other. He clearly works with the resources of a constitutive phenomenology, with one important qualification: Heidegger avoids treating any one constitutive level as absolutely basic, stressing in its stead the sense in which founding relations are relative and in which each level is yet another dependent "moment" of the whole structure of Dasein. In Division II, he then attempts to reframe the results of this account in terms of *temporality,* which is precisely what Husserl's notion of genetic phenomenology calls for. However different the content of their theories, there is a surprising coincidence between the architectonics of their systematic phenomenological methods. One might even wager that this proximity is what finally shocked Heidegger and spurred his turn to a different style of philosophizing after *Being and Time.* This similarity needs to be stressed because it frames their respective approaches to the analysis of the world. Both approaches begin with a synchronic account that is concerned with articulating the structure of the world, and both deepen this analysis by connecting their account to their respective theories of temporality and historicity.

While the standard view of Husserl's theory of perception takes it as a type of interpretation theory, the standard approach to Heidegger's theory views it as overcoming whatever hesitations Husserl had in this direction and as cementing the treatment of all experience as interpretation. Does not Heidegger insist that the as-structure essential to perception is a hermeneutic "as"? Does he not treat speech or discourse (*Rede*) as one of the "primordial" features of Dasein as a whole? For both Husserl and Heidegger, the story goes, all apprehension (Husserl: *Auffassung;* Heidegger: *Erfassung*) and thereby all perception (Husserl: *Wahrnehmung*) and/or circumspection (Heidegger: *Umsicht*) is interpretation. I call this the interpretation thesis.[3] I would suggest that this thesis rests on two claims, each of which, as I hope to show, is mistaken. Neither Husserl nor Heidegger would accept either.

1. All interpretation is interpretation. There is a slippery slide that runs from our usual understanding of interpretation as language-based to the belief that since perception is also "interpretation," the usual translation of *Auslegung,* its "determinacy" or articulate as-structure depends upon language. The conclusion found in some deconstructive theories that "there is no perception" is a fall-out of this assimilation.

2. All meaning is meaning. The as-structure essential to the articulate presence of things constitutes their significance. In that this structure is not found but arises only through our interaction with things, and in that this in-

teraction is undergirded by speech, it seems plausible to argue that all seeing (*Sicht*) is interpretation.

Over against the interpretation thesis, I want to suggest that characterizing Heidegger's notion of experience through the notion of interpretation is misleading because it fails to do justice to the richness and multidimensionality of his account. I am using this as a point of access to our analysis of horizon and discourse because it allows us to raise the broader issues of whether (a) experience is so language-bound that it always involves interpretation, and (b) whether the horizon can be reduced to differences inscribed in language. This is to say that, while I begin with an interpretative issue that will hopefully contribute to Heidegger scholarship, I am actually using a critique of what to me is a surface reading of Heidegger on the question of meaning to get at several systematic ideas that feed our efforts at constructing a viable theory of the world.

A. APPREHENSION AND INTERPRETATION

In *Being and Time* Heidegger observes that our basic sense of things comes from our practical involvement with them as implements or equipment (*Zeug*), not as items of disinterested perceptual cognition. In his terms, the objects that we are related to "proximally and for the most part" should not be characterized as *present-at-hand* (*vorhanden*), not as the sheer things we look *at* and cognitively register (*Sicht*), but as *ready-to-hand* (*zuhanden*), as objects that, in our looking *around,* we view as appropriate for certain practical tasks (*Umsicht*). This means that equipment, as what we use to reach a certain end, is defined by its functional *involvement in* (*Bewandtnis*) or relevance to a task or context in which we are also caught up. This entails that the basic sense that we have of ourselves is not as a cognizing subject that is related *to* things but as an engaged agent that is involved *with* them and that finds what it *is* in what it *does.* Because the dyads of inner and outer, passive and active, subject and object are inadequate to cover the reciprocal determination and circulation we find between actions, systems of involvement, and objects, Heidegger replaced Husserl's notion of subjectivity with the concept of *Dasein* (human existence).

While in use, equipment is not thematic as such. It is lost in the goal or the task at hand; i.e., it indicates or points not to itself but the nail to be struck, the board to be sawed, the shed to be built. But if the hammer or saw breaks, if it is not suitable for the task at hand, or if it is just plain missing, we are immediately redirected back to the item in terms of its instrumentality and its relation to other equipment. "When indication is disturbed . . . then indication becomes explicit."[4] *What* the object is becomes understood solely in terms of its *differential* relationship to other items within a region. Thereby, the region with its totality of equipment comes into view. "The nexus of equipment is lit up not as something never seen before, but as a whole constantly sighted before hand in circumspection. With this whole, however, the world announces itself."[5]

This preliminary "ontic" presencing of the world as environing world (*Umwelt*) becomes the guiding thread to Heidegger's "ontological" characterization of the "worldhood" of the world, i.e., the world as it belongs to the transcendental structure of Dasein. Each instrument points to a whole of equipment in which what is ready-to-hand shows itself as such. That whole, however, is a system of relevant involvement that can exist only by virtue of an internal relation to what *allows* for such involvement. Involvements are established for the sake of Dasein and its projects. But this happens in such a way that Dasein is necessarily referred to the nexus of involvement as that in which it comes to realize and understand itself. Heidegger's study of instrumental objects and practical settings allows him to uncover a structure that applies to all regions and thus belongs to Dasein itself: the world, to which all human action is referred, and in which it is situated, is the *nexus of differential indications* (*Verweisungszusammenhang*) that is constitutive of the involvement of self, objects, and others in various situations. In short, the world is background.

After this description of the things we "first" encounter as ready-to-hand and this initial characterization of the world belonging to Dasein's structure of being-in-the-world as a nexus of indications, *Being and Time* introduces *Befindlichkeit* (affectivity)[6] and *Verstehen* (understanding) as two basic modes of the in-structure of *Dasein*. Neither mode, it must be emphasized, is "thetic," and thus they factor in the account not of Dasein's encounter with beings, but of Dasein's disclosure of its basic structure *as a whole,* a point that we cannot develop here.[7] Affectivity opens Dasein to us in terms of contingency, "thrownness," facticity; understanding brings us before Dasein in terms of possibility, potentiality, "projecting," transcendence. Since it is Dasein as understanding that provides the key to the notion of meaning, we should briefly unpack this difference.

Affectivity is what roots Dasein and undergirds its relation to situations. Dasein always senses itself as "thrown," as caught up in the world in such a way that it is delivered over to the world. Yet a second mode is essential to Dasein, equally basic, in which it is "beyond" the situation in which it finds itself. If affectivity clarifies the sense in which Dasein is bound, understanding gives us the sense in which Dasein is free. Dasein as can-be, as being-possible, is disclosed in understanding. "Dasein *is* ever what it *can* be and is the manner [*Wie*] in which it is its possibility."[8] When we place the account of affectivity together with the account of understanding, each qualifies the other: as understanding, the style of Dasein's thrownness, but not thrownness itself, is open, is a possible thrownness; but as thrown, Dasein as possibility is bound, is situated, is ever "thrown possibility through and through."[9]

The tie to meaning, interestingly enough, moves not through the notion of thrownness but through understanding. In grasping its in-structure as can-be (*Seinkönnen*), *Dasein* necessarily understands the world of its being-in-the-world in terms of possibility. This delivers up the world not in terms of things, or even various ontic relationships between things, but in terms of *Bedeutsamkeit,* of significance. In addition, "not only is the world *qua* world disclosed as possible significance, but the freeing up of that which is within the world frees this being in terms of *its* possibilities."[10] In the case of the ready-to-hand, for example, what the hammer *is* can be seen only if it is apprehended in terms of what it *can* be used for, its service*ability,* its us*ability.*[11]

This yields the crucial link to *Auslegung,* to what is usually translated "interpretation." As projecting, understanding dwells in its possibilities. These possibilities, in turn, have a recursive effect (*Rückschlag*) on Dasein itself and determine its can-be.[12] In working out (*ausbilden*) possibilities, it develops (*ausbilden*) its own possibilities of being. "This working-out of understanding we call *Auslegung.*"[13]

Auslegung, to play with its components, means something like "laying out," "unfolding" and is clearly used in everyday contexts that have nothing to do with interpretation.[14] Because of the ease of moving to cognates like "explicate" and "the explicated," I will use "explication" and sometimes "unfolding" to render it, not "interpretation."[15] A provisional justification is found in the fact that Heidegger clarified it not only with the notion of *ausbilden* (to work out, develop, even educate) but also with the term *auseinanderlegen* (to take apart, lay out one from another). The combination of "ex-" and "plicate" (to fold) captures these connections better than "interpretation." It may turn out that *Auslegung is* interpretation, in a way yet to be defined. But let's begin with at least a terminological difference so as not to beg the question. Obviously, I am belaboring this point because I will argue that the usual and nearly universally accepted characterization of Heidegger's notion of apprehension or, more broadly, experience as interpretation is mistaken. I will also suggest that calling *Auslegung* interpretation at the outset does not allow us to isolate what actually is or might be the interpretative *element* in the process of unfolding or explication.

The process of "taking" an item in a particular way is internally linked to the qualities that the object so taken comes to display. Those qualities that "first" engage us are just the instrumental values operative in our practical use of an item. For this reason Heidegger thinks of the *actions* of preparing something for use, squaring things, repairing, improving, rounding out (his examples)[16] as all involving a type of seeing (*Sicht*), what he calls circumspection

(*Umsicht*), that allows just these types of qualities to stand forth. It operates by *ex-plicating* the item. Explication or unfolding is the process that allows the features of the ready-to-hand to become manifest. In unfolding, *Auslegung,*

> we take apart in its 'in-order-to' that which is circumspectively ready-to-hand, and we concern ourselves with it in accordance with what becomes visible through the process. That which has been circumspectively taken apart . . . has the structure of *something as something.*[17]

We see the item *as* a table, a door, a carriage, a bridge (his examples).[18] The "as" makes up the "explicitness" (*Ausdrücklichkeit*) of things, which is what allows Heidegger to treat circumspection as grounded in understanding, which discloses the field of significance or *possible* explicitness supporting the focal explicitness of the item.

What first clarifies the process of explication and the nature of this explicitness is the fact that an occurrence of explication does not depend upon my formulating a description or making an assertion (*Aussage*), nor does it seem to depend upon a *possible* assertion for either the "as" in focus or the web of possible explicitness to be in play. All of this takes place in circumspection alone.[19] In this sense it is clearly *prelinguistic.* Yet we still have the nesting of seeing in understanding, of the seen in a background. "Any mere pre-predicative seeing of the ready-to-hand is, in itself, already explicative understanding." Seeing would still "hide in itself the explicitness of the indicating relations (the in-order-to) that belong to the whole of involvement."[20] But this would suggest that whatever we mean by understanding (as in play in circumspection) and explication is not tied to the assertions we make or the set of assertions we could make about what is ready-to-hand. To argue that it is runs the risk of reducing the ready-to-hand to thematic objects, to what is present-at-hand, and of reducing circumspection (*Umsicht*) to thematic viewing (*Anschauen*). If interpretation proper cannot take place without actual or possible assertions, then we have a precise difference between interpretation proper and *Auslegung,* and a very strong argument that seeing is not interpretation and that the "context" of indications is not itself constituted by assertive discourse. We clearly have a process of articulation that comes "before" we make "thematic assertions."[21] Assertion is basically the task of rendering *conceptual* what is articulated in circumspection. The way the object is "conceived" can be "drawn" from the entity itself, Heidegger argues, or the interpretation can "force" the entity into concepts which are "opposed" to its manner of being.[22] This claim makes sense only if the "as" is not *formed* but only *expressed* by the assertion. This suggests, in contrast to circumspection, a level of conceptuality that is special to assertions and that is clearly bound to language. The fact that what "lies before us" is "something expressible" in assertions does not entail that its potential for expression in (propositional) concepts configures its explicitness, or that its significance coincides with the conceptuality carried by assertions.

Were we to stop our account here, Heidegger's and Husserl's accounts would have some surprising parallels. Both would set the level of experience or apprehension in opposition to the level of judgment or assertions. To be sure, Heidegger argues for a fundamental change both in the type of activity (concern) and in the corresponding item (ready-to-hand) that we find at the most basic level, and one can hardly emphasize how radical that difference is. Yet even here both accounts speak of the interplay of background and focal object, argue for the as-structure as basic to the difference between the entity and its qualities, and, as we will see, rely on the notion of *Sinn* to capture the intelligible structure of the "prepredicative" and on the notion of *Bedeutung* to get at the conceptuality inherent in assertions. Thus both Husserl and Heidegger might agree that if we call the activity of asserting an activity of interpretation, then perception (Husserl), apprehension (*Auffassung* in Husserl, *Erfassung* in Heidegger), and circumspection (Heidegger) are not interpretative acts.

We will follow up on the question of meaning shortly. But I should immediately state that our superficial comparison of Husserl and Heidegger, as well as the entire line of argument thus far, holds out little hope of understanding the rich relationship between language and experience, for the simple reason that placing propositional discourse next to circumspection completely misses the way in which language could play a role in the constitution of circumspection. This should become evident in the next section. From our present discussion I would extract only the point that propositional discourse clearly is a form of interpretation proper and, in a broad sense, a type of explication; yet Heidegger denies it any role in the explication that accounts for the explicitness that is in play in circumspection. Were it in play the ready-to-hand would collapse into the present-at-hand.

With this clarification of the as-structure, we can make one final point about the difference between *Auslegung* and interpretation. Having suggested that the *Auslegung* at play in circumspection does not require or assume interpretation proper, we must also note that Heidegger uses *Auslegung* very broadly. The scope extends well beyond any meaningful use of the notion of interpretation. If one insists on "interpretation," *all* of the following, each of which technically involves *Auslegung,* qualify as interpretative activities:

Specifying what is meant by light waves
Measuring light waves
Differentiating colors by light waves
Constructing a color chart
Using a color chart to figure out the shade of white in the living room

Looking at the color of the wall before using the chart
Sending your helper to fetch another brush
Dipping the brush in the paint bucket
Painting the wall
Picking paint from the brush with your little finger

The practical insertion of "hands" that use things, the discursive intervention of assertions that conceptually sort and characterize things, and even the theoretical intervention of propositions that specify and determine the properties of things are, in Heidegger's broad use, all forms of *Auslegung.* This creates few problems if we treat explication as a neutral term that isolates a general, structural feature of Dasein, uncovering the articulate structure special to each of these different domains. But the term interpretation simply begs the question as to what that is, all the more so since Heidegger begins by setting explication in opposition to asserting and describes the latter as what clearly does count as interpretation, namely, determining something through concepts or, better, allowing something to stand forth (or not) in terms of the conceptual determinations expressed in language.

B. MAKING MEANING OUT OF SENSE

The description of understanding as the disclosure of the significance grounding circumspection is the key to a Heideggerian theory of background, to use the term I introduced in the last chapter. But we have yet to account for why this is the case.

We suggested that actions dealing with what is to-hand are also a process of articulating the item. Items are used "in view of" a certain purpose that organizes the relationship between the action, making it one type as opposed to another, and the item, letting it stand forth in contrast to others in a setting. While the tool is what allows movements to become actions, the action is constitutive of the *manner* in which the object stands forth, the way it is "interspersed" (*gegliedert*) and "articulated" (*artikuliert*).[23] It unfolds the item one way or another. The manner in which the item is unfolded is its *as-structure.* Since it is not the actual but the *potential* use that is constitutive of the as-structure, and since the tool's articulate structure exists only in relationship to a whole of equipment, the presence of the tool is itself established by the way the object is or can be unfolded in circumspection. Unfolding does not make a preexisting "fold" visible, though it does depend upon a certain "pregiven" nexus of indications in terms of which items stand forth. Rather, unfolding is itself constitutive of the fold, for it establishes "that 'toward which' of projection from which something is understandable as something";[24] it establishes its *sense.*

Let us stay in Heidegger's workshop for now. Heidegger is careful to model senses neither as moments in things nor as psychological entities that "stand between" beings and Dasein,[25] probably an oblique reference to Husserl's theory of the noema. They function almost teleologically in that they are that toward which circumspection is projected, and which thereby allows a particular item to stand forth as articulated. Yet clearly senses are not concepts; in the shop, they are found not in the relationship between thoughts and things, or between assertions and referents, or even between thinking and action, but in a "preconceptual" interdependence between actions and the articulate structure of items-in-use. Expanding upon Husserl's later theory of perception, I would suggest that senses are schemata of our embodied actions upon, or interactions with, the ready-to-hand, by virtue of which it acquires its articulate *difference* from other items in a certain whole nexus of involvement. The sense in the process of being unfolded in circumspection is simultaneously the schema of our involvement *constitutive* of the as-structure.

Heidegger's account of the ready-to-hand should not be construed as a piece of regional ontology, giving us one domain among others. "We maintain that the specific world of concern is the one by which the world as a whole is encountered. . . . The worldhood of the world is grounded rather in the specific work-world."[26] Ontically, the domain of practical objects is found alongside other domains, but ontologically it is "fundamental," not in the sense that it is a stratum underlying all the others, but in the sense that it models for us the operation of implication that allows for the constitution of whole backgrounds as interconnected. At the same time, the difference between scenes of action and scenes of speaking, and then between practical and reflective settings, should attune us to the fact that an account of the sense operative in circumspective settings and acts of appropriation will not coincide with an account of significance as a feature of the world as a whole.

Heidegger finds it difficult to capture this larger significance in words. In his 1925 lectures, delivered as he was in the throes of writing *Being and Time,* he complains of "a certain embarrassment in the choice of the right expression for the complex phenomenon that we want to call meaningfulness [*Bedeutsamkeit*]."[27] He chooses the term *Bedeutung* to characterize the nexus of indications belonging to the world. This does preserve, Heidegger suggests, an important connection to language, but "I frankly admit that this expression is not the best, but for years I have found nothing better. . . . "[28] He is careful to use the notion of indication to clarify what he means by *Bedeutung.* One of the problems seems to be that *Bedeutung* is too closely linked to language, and it forces Heidegger to distinguish his present use from "another sense," from "the *Bedeutung* of a word, *Bedeutung* as something which word-combinations can have."[29] In *Being and Time* it seems that he responds to his embarrassment by shifting his nomenclature somewhat. While the characterization of the world as a whole still employs the notion of *Bedeutsamkeit,* he now picks out the term *Sinn* as its companion to describe the nexus of indications and "the formal existential framework of understanding"[30] as a whole.

If this is the case, then Heidegger sees a striking and important difference between the type of significance ingredient in the ready-to-hand, *Sinn,* and that type which is expressed through and tethered to assertions, *Bedeutung.* In order to keep this difference in play, to facilitate comparisons with Husserl, which Heidegger himself made in this connection,[31] and to locate what is radically new in Heidegger's approach, I will translate *Bedeutung* as meaning rather than significance[32] or signification.[33] *Sinn* will be rendered as sense.

Being and Time does not give us a developed theory of the type of significance we find in propositional discourse. Heidegger is convinced that all "assertion involves an articulation of what is pointed out, and this articulation is in accordance with meaning."[34] The meaning of assertions is itself clarified in terms of concepts: each "operates with a definite conceptuality."[35] The fact that our assertions can "force" an item into "concepts" that are "opposed to its manner of being"[36] is possible, I want to argue, only because those items have an articulated presence that is independent of the assertion.

However, Heidegger's distinction between sense and meaning is further clarified when he gives us an account of assertions as a "derivative mode" of explication and dwells on the transformation of the as-structure of the ready-to-hand that the process of predication introduces. Heidegger distinguishes between what we can call an exhibitive, or indexical, and a determinative function of all descriptive statements. As exhibitive they function simply to "point out" or "show" (*aufzeigen*) us a being. What is in focus does not belong to the order of significance but to that of reference: "a being in the way that it is ready-to-hand" is seen "from itself."[37] But assertions also introduce functions of their own. Asserting is a process of determining, of attributing a predicate to a subject, and, accordingly, of contrasting subject and predicate as it characterizes the object in terms of its determinate property. This involves a "narrowing of content" and a "narrowing of view" so that what is "already manifest" is open to us "expressly in its determinacy." Unlike Husserl, who often uses the notion of determinations to characterize the qualities of objects that are first given experientially, Heidegger thinks of determinations as properties specified in and by assertions. The reason assertions do not really exhibit the ready-to-hand is because in propositions, the ready-to-hand is "dimmed down" to a thematic object and, thus, to an item present-at-hand having a "determinable determinacy,"[38] having "properties."[39] "The assertion that determines the present-at-hand *as* [a certain] What draws that What *out of* the being present-at-hand."[40] The as-structure is fundamentally modified, for it "no longer reaches out into a nexus of involvement," and it is "cut off" from that type of significance "which, as such, constitutes environmentality."

Thus, whatever meaning comes to expression in assertions, it is necessarily different in kind from the sense that is constitutive of the ready-to-hand. Heidegger concludes:

> The "as" gets pushed back into the uniform plane of what is only present-at-hand. It dwindles to the structure of only-letting-one-see-in-determinations what is present-at-hand. This leveling of the basic "as" of circumspective explication to the "as" of the determination of the present-at-hand is the prerogative of assertion.[41]

We can pull these remarks together in this way. When first introduced in *Being and Time,* nothing is made of the difference between sense and meaning, as both are understood by the larger notion of significance. On the one hand, the relational whole of the various acts and activities engaged with the ready-to-hand is called "significance" or "meaningfulness" (*Bedeutsamkeit*).[42] On the other, *Bedeutsamkeit* is used to describe an ontological *condition* of the possibility of disclosing something like the "meanings" (*Bedeutungen*) that "found the possible being of words and of language."[43] But if we go on to restrict the notion of meaning to assertions, as Heidegger's later comments imply, then we have a basic difference, I would argue, between the type of significance and its organization that is constitutive of propositions, meaning, and the type that is involved in circumspection, sense. This becomes the basis for the contrast we drew earlier in this chapter between circumspective explication and predicational explication, and for suggesting that calling the first interpretation begs the question. While significance is the general term under which the notions of both sense and meaning fall, and while it may turn out that for other reasons we can assimilate sense to meaning, Heidegger's own contrasts require us to hold them apart at the outset.

Once again, though, this line of argument does not move us very far. To be sure, it does establish that not all meaning is meaning, i.e., that there is at least a type of significance, propositional meaning, that is not identical to sense. Its real value is just that it allows us to put our question precisely: is the account of assertions as a "derivative" mode of explication sufficient to establish a lasting difference between the explication of circumspective concern and interpretation, between a prelinguistic sense operative in circumspection and a linguistic meaning that attaches to our discourse about things, and, as a result, a difference between background and context?

C. MAKING SENSE OUT OF MEANING

At first it seems that sense controls meaning, that our involvement with the ready-to-hand establishes the qualities of things that are then exhibited through assertions. This would suggest that the "existential" as-structure as unfolded in circumspection would be "prepredicatively" unfolded. The assertion would only "exhibit," would itself be effaced by the weight of what it bears. Yet Heidegger also argues that in assertion what shows itself comes forth in terms that have been laid down by the proposition. The as-structure constitutive of the disclosure of the object, accordingly, would be "apophantic"; it would be predicatively determined. Assertions, to use his images, work on, constrain, sometimes force, narrow, and determine by means of their own conceptuality. The articulate structure of what is exhibited could only be the result of the conceptual schemes carried by language.

The solution to this dilemma will give us the key to a Heideggerian theory of background. The exhibitive function of assertions that Heidegger isolates is actually a placeholder for deeper analyses. What displaces the contrast between the ready-to-hand and assertions, and moves to the core of the issue of interpretation, is the fact that Heidegger discovers not just those features of propositional discourse that securely anchor it in the world, but also a whole new type of discourse, which he calls everyday talk (*Rede*), that is part of the horizon in terms of which the ready-to-hand shows itself. The movement from the circumspective "as" to the predicative "as," from the level of sense-constitution to meaning-constitution, also involves a transformation of talk into assertions, of reports into claims, as was described in chapters 1 and 7. What we have been calling the "prepredicative," as a result, is not the "prelinguistic," for now it seems that we find language already at play *within* the fields of sense constitutive of the ready-to-hand. But how are we to understand this?

The ready-to-hand, we have seen, stands forth from a certain setting. What brings it forth is its sense, which is defined in terms of a system of involvements. In being indicated by the item, this system places the ready-to-hand in a system of usage and thus gives the item its specific quality. This system of involvements, Heidegger suggests, forms the background and, as such, is always ours "in advance" of what becomes thematic through any particular action that unfolds the as-structure. Heidegger then suggests that explication as it operates in circumspection is actually grounded in a threefold "fore-structure."

1. A particular concernful action involves circumspection (*Umsicht*), that "sight" (*Sicht*) that belongs to our practical appropriation of items. The essential connection between a "pregiven" nexus of involvements and the articulate structure of the item unfolded in circumspection means that circumspection is grounded in what it *has in advance,* in a *Vorhabe.* What is held in advance in *fore-having* must be the nexus of indications which, as understood, can be described in terms of interconnected senses. Fore-having places us in relation to a back-ground.

2. Circumspection, however, operates within what is a "first cut" of this

background. It is always part of a larger task of appropriation guided by a "projective view" (*Hinsicht*) that brings what we are seeking to understand into a disclosive clearing. *Fore-sight, Vorsicht,* it seems, is what secures the internal relation between fore-having and the third moment, fore-grasping.

3. The *fore-grasp, Vorgriff,* is understood by Heidegger as a *fore-conception* that allows anything "held in our fore-having" and "envisioned in our fore-sight" to become "expressly grasped," *begriffen,* "conceptualized."[44] As a result, a certain "conceptuality," a certain way of conceiving of the item is already at play in circumspection.

How are we to understand this "certain conceptuality" which is part of the nexus of indications held in advance of any particular explication? The only way we have accounted for something like conceptuality thus far is in terms of assertions. In fact, when Heidegger goes on to discuss a third feature of assertions, their communicative function, he attributes a fore-structure to them as well. Its description sounds much like the fore-grasp of circumspective concern:

> To assertion as communication that *determines* there always belongs an articulation of what is pointed out that belongs to the *order of meaning* (*bedeutungsmässig*); it moves within a *certain conceptuality:* [e.g.,] the hammer is heavy, heaviness belongs to the hammer, the hammer has the property of heaviness. The fore-grasp always adjoining the assertion remains, for the most part, inconspicuous because language always hides in itself a developed conceptuality.[45]

Is the "certain conceptuality" at play in circumspective concern identical to the "certain conceptuality" adjoining assertions, now treated as "talk"? If so, we have settled our question by finding a coincidence between their respective fore-conceptions. But clearly this cannot be the case, for it would destroy the whole treatment of assertions as derivative as well as Heidegger's basic contrast between the two types of as-structures:

> The circumspective explication dealing with what is environmentally ready-to-hand, which "sees" it *as* table, door, carriage, bridge, does not require that what is unfolded in circumspection also already be taken apart in an assertion that determines it. Any mere, prepredicative seeing of the ready-to-hand is, in itself, already seeing that understands and unfolds.[46]

Indeed, assertions "level out" the basic "as" of the ready-to-hand to the "as" of what is present-at-hand, as we saw above. Only in this way do circumspective differences become concentrated properties. In fact, this leveling out and concentration is part of the very fore-grasp operative in propositional acts. So we cannot look to the fore-conception of propositions to explain the "conceptuality" within the nexus of involvements. Where are we to look?

Notice that even within circumspection fore-sight only narrows down the nexus of possible involvements to a certain situated set of possibilities in terms of which the ready-to-hand can possibly be conceived. On the one hand, fore-conception makes possible the explication of the ready-to-hand in terms of its articulate structure. Yet on the other hand, it seems that the conceptuality in play here cannot be the same structurally as the articulate structure of the ready-to-hand, for the simple reason that, *as generated in the process of explication,* the as-structure can either *encourage* or *resist* a particular way of conceiving it. We quote again:

> The explication can draw [*schöpfen*] the conceptuality belonging to the being to be unfolded from the being itself or can force it into concepts to which that being, according to its manner of being, is opposed.[47]

If this "prepredicative" conceptuality is part of the fore-structure of circumspective concern, its source must be found in a dimension more basic than those we have uncovered thus far. Heidegger breaks open a third fundamental feature of the in-structure, one that is "equiprimordial" with affectivity and understanding. He simply calls it "talk" (*Rede*) or "discourse."[48]

Recall that we have consistently contrasted the circumspective "as" with the assertoric "as" and have described the first in terms of the "articulate" differences of the ready-to-hand, in contrast with the "determinations" or "properties" of items referred to in propositions. Understanding, ontologically described, discloses the world as the nexus of our involvement with things; things consist of just these differences. Understanding, Heidegger tells us, is "always already articulated."[49] But with the notion of talk, he reaches for what amounts to a way of sustaining that nexus of differences commensurate with his understanding of Dasein as *Mitsein,* as co-being with others, and with his treatment of understanding as fundamental to being-in. "Talk," he adds, "is the articulation of understandability,"[50] or, as he puts it in another place, the "self-articulation of in-being and being-with."[51] He then joins this notion to the characterization of sense we discussed above. It literally reads:

> The articulatable in the explication—even more originally there already in talk—we called the "sense."[52]

We can paraphrase it this way:

> That which can be articulated in circumspective explication, and comes to articulation even more basically and originally in talk, since it undergirds our practical involvement with others, is what we earlier characterized in terms of "sense."

By "talk" Heidegger has in mind our everyday discourse with others as we go about the work of the day. But it serves primarily not to represent but to direct. It seems to be "more original" than nondiscursive circumspection, for it already places us in a broader field of interaction with what is ready-to-hand: "The understanding of communication is the *participation in what is manifest,*" the 1925 lectures tell us.[53] They further clarify:

> ... *discoursing about* ... does not stand primarily in the service of an investigative knowledge. Rather, making manifest through discourse first and foremost has the sense of interpretive [i.e., an explicative] appresentation of the environment under concern; to begin with, it is not at all tailored to knowledge, research, theoretical propositions, and propositional contexts.[54]

We are situated, then, not in the classroom but in the workshop, not in the laboratory but in the kitchen, not alone but with others. Our words are so many pointers, directors, instructions, and, often, songs whose tempo and rhythm modulate the work to be done.

This allows us to reformulate our main question: is the nexus of indications, whose internal organization Heidegger defines as a nexus of (possible) "articulate" differences of sense, *constituted* by discourse, in the sense that those differences are produced by the semantic oppositions in play in the different discursive fields organizing our everyday talk? Or, alternatively, is it *unfolded* by talk, in the sense that its own internal semantic organization establishes the fore-grasp that only circumscribes, but does not produce, the difference that can be articulated in our action upon and with the ready-to-hand? Does what is articulated in talk exhaust what Heidegger means by sense, or does it somehow work in coordination with sense?

I want to suggest that, in his effort to find an internal connection between talk and sense, Heidegger does not collapse one into the other; he thus decides in favor of the second option. But he also shows us how the first is itself *one* of the possibilities open to Dasein, perhaps the one in which it first finds itself. Let me suggest three clusters of ideas in favor of the approach I am taking.

1. The first set of considerations revolves around a subtle contrast we find in the notion of articulation, which will lead us into an account of the process by which signs become meaningful.

We saw that, when Heidegger distinguishes between prepredicative explication and assertion, he uses the term "sense" generally to cover the potential and actual differences uncovered by circumspective concern, in contrast to "meaning," which is what is carried by language. In that context he explains sense as follows:

> The articulated [*Gegliederte*] as such in the explication and what is sketched out beforehand in understanding in general as the articulatable [*Gliederbares*] is the sense.[55]

But once he introduces in Section 34 a distinction between everyday discourse and assertions, he seems to play with this contrast between the articulatable and the articulated in order to develop further his first notion of sense. The contrast we want to capture can be seen by placing the sentence cited above next to the one that follows it:

> The articulatable [*Artikulierbare*] in explication—even more originally there already in talk—we called the "sense."[56]
>
> The articulated [*Gegliederte*] as such in discursive articulation we call the whole of meaning.[57]

What *can* be articulated, sketched out beforehand in understanding, the explicatable as such, he views as a nexus of sense. What *has been* and *is* articulated in the process of talking (*redende Artikulation*) forms a nexus of meaning. The system of differences which we find *in* discursive articulation as such is a whole of meanings, thus linking talk, the linguistic, and meaning. If we collapse meaning and sense we miss their essential interplay. Immediately Heidegger adds that "the whole of meaning can be broken up into meanings. Meanings, as the articulated of the articulatable, always carry sense [*sinnhaft*]."[58] I think there is an interplay between that which is potentially articulatable through actions with and upon the ready-to-hand, which is where our citations want to put sense, and the articulated in talk, which is where they seem to put meaning. If there is no difference, then Heidegger's comment that meanings always carry sense, are always arrested in sense, is pointless. But what, then, does this mean? I would suggest that it opens up an account of the way signs *acquire* meaning.

In *Being and Time* itself Heidegger only drops one further hint with no explanation: "only from the temporality of talk—that means of Dasein as a whole—can we understand ontologically the 'origins' of 'meaning' and the possibility of a formation of concepts."[59] The 1925 lectures, however, add much to our understanding of how Heidegger wants to connect his notion of significance with the signs of everyday talk. There he links his analysis to a contrast that Husserl introduced in his First Investigation between expressions and indicators (*Anzeigen* here), the very notion that Husserl came to characterize as the "germinating seed" of his genetic phenomenology.[60] This allows Heidegger to avoid viewing signs as items present-at-hand that carry another item, meaning, and to draw from his account of equipment and involvement in order to get at the "origins" of their significance. Signs, like tools, are, for the most part, ready-to-hand and are called forth in the context of our involvement with things. Using as his model the red arrows that functioned as turn signals on early automobiles, Heidegger shows that the arrow serves as a signal because it is grounded in that very same "in order to" structure constitutive of the presence of tools. It functions, accordingly, not to identify something or to assimilate it under a concept but to provide direction and to invite a certain comportment on my part. "Primarily, the sign conveys no information [*Kenntnis*] but gives an *instruction* [*Anweisung*]."[61] In so doing it "appresents the environing world for concerned commerce."[62] He explains:

> This explicit concern in encountering the environing world is not focused on information [*Kenntnis*] but on the being-in-the-world which at first does not know thematically [*thematisch erkennende*]. It is the concerned being-in-the-world and not, say, the propensity of an isolated knowing [*Erkennen*], which *institutes signs,* simply because world is inexplicitly encountered in indications.[63]

Thus it is the world as an "indicative structure" that is the *basis* for signs being "on hand and handy."[64] In the terminology we have employed, it is only as signs function within a larger nexus of sense that they, in the very course of facilitating our involvement with things, acquire a stable significance. Here the signs themselves function like tools.

Heidegger also likens them to fetishes, not in the sense that a sign is an object that is somehow confused with its reference, but in the sense that the sign as ready-to-hand "has not yet become free from what it refers to [*Bezeichneten*]; and this is because such a preoccupation and such an elementary life with signs and in signs is still totally absorbed in what is pointed out. . . . "[65] "Concern still lives totally in the tool-as-pointing and draws what is pointed out into the sign."[66] For these reasons I would argue that what carries meaningfulness here in this instituting of signs are the interconnected senses of what is pointed out.[67]

Gradually signs cease being fetishes. As soon as our fascination with things is broken, or as soon as we "trip" over what is reported, or, perhaps, just as a result of sheer repetition and habitual use, a difference between (a) stable relationships between the signs and (b) the many things we do with them crystallizes, and a distance develops between what they convey and what they point out. Dwelling in sense, they "accrete" meanings. At first signs are controlled by sense, in that they only serve, they only facilitate our actions upon the ready-to-hand. But when we move to the level of discursive interaction over the ready-to-hand, signs begin to take on a life of their own. Senses are located in differences-in-use as articulated actionally; meanings arise as differences-in-use are articulated discursively. As such the nexus of sense is what is potentially articulatable in a nexus of meaning.

What seems to me to require a difference between meaning and sense, though, is the fact that talk is fundamentally communication: "Talk is the articulation in meaning that belongs to our being-with others and that carries being-with-one-another in the mode of concern."[68] Talk is not only "talking with" but "talking about."[69] It operates to make manifest, to disclose: " . . .

making manifest through discourse first and foremost has the sense of explicative appresentation of the environment under concern."[70] Because it is communication, we can separate two structural moments. It is discourse *about* something. The *about-which* becomes manifest in the discourse, yet in such a way that it is "always already there from the start, having the character of world of in-being."[71] Discourse also contains the *said* as such. When I say "The hammer is heavy," the hammer is that about which we are talking, manifest in a given chat as a function of our discourse about it, and its being heavy is the said as such. Talk provides for a mutual "participation in what is manifest."[72] The "co-affectivity and the understanding of being-with" gets "shared" through what is articulated.[73]

Heidegger will not need his notion of meaning to explain how I apperceive your mental states, nor how we exchange experiences back and forth, for the simple reason that circumspective discourse functions not to *express* mental entities but to allow for mutual involvement in what we are occupied with.[74] Heidegger recognizes that your talking about something often moves to our talking-something-through, to questions and answers, to settling what, as a result of this changed attitude, becomes an assertion. It seems that this is the level at which the *said as such,* and thereby the meaning of the string, becomes thematic.[75]

As long as considering something as something—"the function of explication"[76]—does not require or involve communication, we have a form of significance in play, namely sense, that cannot be identified with the said as such and thus with expressed meaning. If we reserve the term manifestation (*Offenbarung*) for what language does,[77] then we cannot directly identify explication with manifestation. No doubt talk "cultivates" and "renders explicit," and no doubt it is primary in pointing out what is manifest in intersubjective involvement. But it does not *produce* the articulate structure of the ready-to-hand as much as *open* it or bring it into view.

We can find yet another reason for distinguishing sense and meaning when we survey the transformation of talk (*Rede*) into idle talk or chatter (*Gerede*). If talk can open the world to view, chatter can close it down. In chatter we have a case where speech does *construct* the world that is experienced. It does this because a certain *approach* to the world is inscribed into its form of meaningful speech and, more deeply, because the dominance of its terms of interpretation does not allow for that form of authentic discourse in which the world stands forth according to its own sense.

> In language, as the way things have been expressed or spoken out, there is hidden a way in which the understanding of Dasein has been explicated. . . . Dasein is constantly delivered over to this explication, which controls and distributes the possibilities of average understanding and the affectivity belonging to it.[78]

This is explained by recourse to meaning:

> The way things have been expressed or spoken out is such that the whole of its articulated nexuses of meaning preserves an understanding of the disclosed world. . . .[79]

We can best understand this by returning to the fore-structure of involvement. In chatter the fore-grasping in play is structured by nexuses of meaning constructed by an impersonal, average They (*das Man*). Heidegger's account of idle talk allows us to see that the *reduction* of the significance composing the entire nexus of involvements to a certain "average" understanding is one end of a spectrum, one possibility in which the interpretation of talk "controls" and "cuts up" the world. The dominance of chatter is precisely a case where conceptuality "forces" things and "opposes" their manner of being. *Gerede* in a sense "closes down" the world by drawing its possibilities into its own circuit and dimming down the space of its disclosure. "One understands not so much the beings being discussed but one listens only to what is being said as such."[80] The "primary relationship of being to the beings being talked about has been lost, or else has never been achieved."[81]

"Idle talk loses its ground,"[82] i.e., this is not just a problem of one *type* of talk prevailing but is also structural, for it arises as a consequence of context "distributing" (*verteilen*) background. *Auslegung* becomes dominated by *Bedeutung,* i.e., we lose the difference between sense and meaning. In chatter, meaning functions not just at the level of the fore-conception of our involvement in relation to our fore-having of our world but also in such a way that our fore-having is leveled and overwhelmed by fore-conception. In this situation, circumspection is indeed always interpretation.

We can pull these ideas together by suggesting that the leveling of significance to meaning is, indeed, a possibility. But it is itself based on the fact that the fore-structure of involvement consists of two "poles" or structural moments that are always involved, in varying degrees, in establishing the nexus of involvement. The one, which we just described, isolates the role of discourse. The limits of the field of disclosive possibilities are established by semantic distinctions that are inscribed in discourse itself. This is what we have been calling *context.* The second moment we isolate by looking at the relationship between action, involvement, and indication. Explication, the unfolding of items according to their uses, opens systems of significance that form the necessary *background* in terms of which an item is articulated. Here explication involves (actual and possible) actional and circumspective schemata; the qualities of the ready-to-hand are rooted in possible types of actions with and upon them. If context accounts for what Heidegger means by fore-grasp or fore-conception, then we can understand his notion of fore-having as background.

We can see the mutual interdependence of context and background by looking at the sense in which each can, under certain circumstances, dominate the other. The prevalence of chatter, which we just described, obtains in a situation where an "average" understanding of the world prevails and, as a consequence, its conceptuality, sedimented into the meaning of its discourse, overtakes the construction of significance. Background recedes and context dominates, i.e., allows background to come into play only to the extent that actions already conform to acceptable types. The explication of circumspection collapses into the interpretation of idle talk. I see with their eyes; I speak with their voice. Yet there are opposite situations, harder to find, where significance is constituted almost entirely by sense and where my discourse echoes its indications. My hand moves the jack plane from place to place on the wooden board as the light, reflecting off its surface, shows other areas where the board is uneven. When it is time to finish the board I reach for the smaller finishing plane that stands next to it in my tool chest. Context recedes and background dominates. The field of significance is controlled by senses, and explication is outside the constraints of established speech. However, the two are only extremes between which most situations are found; normally both context and background configure the concrete presence of what we apprehend. The problem of their relationship is solved when we see that both are involved in circumspection.

Heidegger's argument that discourse is equiprimordial with affectivity and understanding is his way, far more developed that Husserl's, of building context into the essential account of the world and securing it as co-constitutive, with background, of horizons. Language in Husserl is always "after the fact." In Heidegger it comes before. But it may also be the case that Heidegger has the opposite problem from Husserl in that his account of the fore-grasping or fore-conception of involvement seems to rely upon discourse to establish that fore-conception. When we place Heidegger beside Husserl we are struck by the fact that he, unlike Husserl, does not attempt to locate sense-constitution within the domain of what Husserl, modifying Kant, labeled transcendental aesthetics. This can be see by the fact that, in general, the notion of sense is introduced not by his account of affectivity, but by his account of understanding. It seems that Heidegger does not want two fundamental types of nexuses, one that operates at the level of understanding and another that operates at the level of *Befindlichkeit.* Since he restricts the nexus to understanding, the drift into language is unavoidable. But why cannot *Befindlichkeit,* like understanding, be a way of anchoring the nexus of sense? In fact it plays this role in Heidegger's account of space and some aspects of his analysis of directionality. But in general affectivity seems to function only as, so to speak, a principle of restriction upon the (open) possibilities disclosed in understanding, and thus is not internal to Heidegger's characterization of sense. Furthermore, if *touch* is the way Heidegger understands the movement of affectivity, then Heidegger's failure to locate sense in *Befindlichkeit* might be yet another version of the dominance of vision he finds time and again in Western philosophy.

D. DIFFERENTIAL INDICATION

Clearly Husserl had developed, in course lectures and manuscripts, basic elements of his theory of the life-world before the publication of *Sein und Zeit.* There are strong indications that Heidegger was familiar with some of those texts.[83] Still, Heidegger's approach to the world through a study of instrumental backgrounds is original and sparkles with a precision missing even from Husserl's later accounts in the *Crisis.* We might set his account of the world over against Husserl's in roughly three ways:

1. Though Husserl came to broaden his notion of intuition, the mode in which the world is disclosed, it still yields only a derivative notion of objects and, as a consequence, of world, not the one that is in fact operative in the natural attitude, which is originally praxical in nature. Because looking-at or looking-onto (*An-schauen*) already effects a separation between the look and the use of things, Husserl gives at best a phenomenological account of the background constitutive of what is present-at-hand. At worst, he makes the mistake of attempting to derive the ready-to-hand (the world of practical objects) from the present-at-hand (the world of intuited objects).

Still, this point should be understood correctly. It is certainly not the case that Husserl gave priority to the perceptual, as opposed to the instrumental, qualities of the object in the factual sequencing of our experiences. For both Husserl and Heidegger what I "first" see is the hammer. But Husserl insists that I could also "first" see the object in terms of its perceptual qualities alone. It all depends upon the "interest" in place. The crucial difference for Husserl is the analysis of the constitution of the experiential object: he conceives of the constitutive syntheses and senses that give us the practical object as consisting of a "basic layer" (*Grundschicht*)[84] of sensible perception upon which the other syntheses accounting for its instrumentality are based. "The [experiential] world is, according to [its] basic layer, at least nature, universe of the *res extensa.*" Tools, Husserl argues, are founded in sensible perceptions.[85] Heidegger would respond that while a tool, when it breaks, can change into a sheer thing present-to-hand, and we can give an account of its perceptual constitution as such, we have not thereby isolated a "stratum" that is ingredient in our experience of it as ready-to-hand. Noetically, there are, among other things, different basic types of vision in play, circumspection (*Umsicht*) as opposed to looking-at (*An-schauen*). Noematically, we find modes of "in order to" that link our actions and the objects (Heidegger mentions, e.g., serviceability, conduciveness, usability, and manipulability).[86] Both are structurally different from what we find in sensible perception. The movement between them is not from upper to lower but lateral.

2. The tension that we find between Husserl's characterizations of the world as universe of intuition and concrete universal is clearly resolved by Heidegger's rejection of the first characterization and his modification of the second. While he does think of world as covering all regions of existence, both in the sense that as concrete it is "modifiable" to the structural wholes of whatever particular worlds we have at the time, and in the sense that its a priori structure is operative in each of them,[87] he institutes a mode of analysis that does not require turning the world into an object and thus preserves its integrity as a structure of meaning. The difference between the present-at-hand and the ready-to-hand not only describes a contrast that allows us to understand practical objects and to see that our "first" relationship is to them, but also works in a transcendental register to allow a characterization of the world that does not run it through Husserl's correlational scheme of description. At one point Husserl suggests that the "Vorhandenheit der Welt," the world as present-to-hand, is a "naturally naive concept" of its being and is "naturally first" only within the natural attitude.[88] But he does not so much attempt to replace it with another notion as to critique its "positivity" and recast it as a "sense-construct [*Sinnbildung*] of transcendental subjectivity,"[89] thereby reaffirming it as ground. Against Husserl's argument, itself directed against Kant,[90] that the world is an object, Heidegger sides with Kant. In Heidegger's account there are transcendental categories and structures, but no transcendental spheres or objects. The problem is that, in his effort to articulate the "subjective achievements" in and through which the world as world is constituted, Husserl's first Cartesian *Leitfaden* in the *Vorhandenheit* of the world leaves him no choice but to construe it as a world *for* consciousness and thus as "relative" to its being. Because Heidegger understands achievements as based in our practical interaction with things, which is itself caught in a nexus of involvement, he develops a hermeneutics of world that moves to it as a whole from within. As a result, he can do justice to Dasein's facticity (*Faktizität*), the sense in which Dasein is *in* the world and not just related *to* the world. Perhaps this is the reason why Division I of *Being and Time* does not directly employ Husserl's notion of horizon in its characterization of the world. Heidegger worries that even with the broader notion of life-world that covers all regions of existence, not just the intuitive, Husserl's account is still mixed and still bound to a "pre-ontological *existentiell* meaning."[91]

3. While both Husserl and Heidegger use the notion of indication as the key to the notion of world, there are important and subtle differences. For Husserl, indication (*Anzeige*)[92] operates by a movement of "one [item] point-

ing [*hinweisen*] to yet another"[93] in such a way that an item that is lifted out or prominent establishes anticipations of what is *similar.* Identity is primary; difference is derived: "the unlike comes to prominence on the basis of the common."[94] As a result, horizons are built up by "unifying syntheses" and should be described as webs with nodes having an identifiable sense-content that establishes relations of opposition and difference to other nodes, i.e., as nexuses of *identificational* schemata. For Heidegger, indication (*Verweisung*) is a constant movement of deferring, such that the similarity between objects, and then the identity of an object, results from its place in a web of functional oppositions and contrasts. Accordingly, the horizons are nexuses of *differential* schemata.

Husserl's theory of constitution worked with the image of layers or strata of meaning and with the thesis that objects could be ordered by a relation of founding-founded according to both the relative complexity of their strata and whether a given object has strata that, were they to stand alone, would be sufficient to account for the presence of a simpler object. A state-of-affairs, for example, has nested in it, among other things, a reference to an individual. An object of value is "built up" from a perceptual object; "strip" it of those value-qualities and we would be left with strata that are sufficient to account for our experience of objects "before" they are the correlates of valuing acts.

At no point did Husserl argue that these relations of before and after are temporal, or that the difference between lower and higher results from a temporal sequencing of two different acts. Before and after are contained within the present; even complex objects are the correlates of single acts. This account of constitution follows the order of sense implication. The crucial question is whether the nested levels of constitution are dependent or independent moments of the whole. While Husserl argues that levels within the most basic type of object, those of sensuous experience, require the presence of the others in order to subsist and, thus, are dependent moments of the whole, it seems that more complex objects would necessarily contain strata that could subsist without the others. While they are necessary for the constitution of an object of a certain complexity, and in that sense dependent moments, they also form a "core" that not only would perdure across different acts of valuation (the X that is loved, hated, treasured, etc.) but also exist independently of all such acts (the X that I simply see). This difference, no doubt, is what tempted Husserl to distinguish between life-world as universe of what is directly intuited and life-world as concrete historical complex.

At the center of the difference between Husserl and Heidegger is the fact that Heidegger rejects Husserl's thesis that complex objects have certain levels of sense that are independent. Heidegger envisioned constitution not in terms of strata of sense, some more basic than others; rather, he replaced the image of core with overlying strata by an emphasis upon function and therefore transformation.[95] The priority of the world of work comes about because concern is what allows us to encounter the world as a nexus of relational nodes tied together by use-values. Thus, the senses schematize not ways of representing, but ways of handling, and even transforming, the world.[96] As a consequence, the structural *differences* between the constitution of various types of objects do not entail the *dependence* of the more complex on the simpler. To put it in terms that correspond with Husserl's theory, the movement from one type to another (perception to valuing) so reorganizes the first type that it no longer functions in its original terms. The effect of this is to replace Husserl's image of stratification (*Sichtung*) with a notion of *lateral* relations that allows for a shift from one to the other without having to treat the first as the foundation or the core of the second.

But did Heidegger struggle with the limits of his own analysis as well? From the perspective of his later work, the developed ontological notion of world (and *Dasein* itself) in *Being and Time* was but a preliminary study which opened the way to the question of Being. In a lecture from 1951 it seems that the in-structure of Dasein, which was first understood in terms (*Befindlichkeit* and *Verstehen*) that somewhat parallel the traditional Kantian concepts of sensibility and understanding, is reinterpreted in terms of the notion of dwelling (*Wohnen*). Dwelling allows objects and others the type of involvement they have as it serves as the basis for building (*Bauen*), the primary activity of those who dwell and, we can add, the activity which framed the whole account of the ready-to-hand in *Being and Time.* However, involvement is defined here not by the notion of world but by the "fourfold" (*das Geviert*), by dwelling being on the *earth,* under the *heavens,* beckoned by the *Godhead,* in relation to *mortals.*[97] If dwelling is the basis of building, the project of founding and joining lived spaces, and building is essential to the worldhood of the world in which we dwell, as *Being and Time* might lead us to believe, then we can see the late Heidegger reaching for a notion, the fourfold, on which the world is based and from which it is derived.

However this is resolved, *Being and Time* provides us with a notion of background much richer than Husserl's, for it is derived from an analysis of our practical involvement with things, as well as fruitful hints as to how one can characterize the generation of meaning from sense. We also have an emphasis on intersubjective discourse that both stabilizes the notion of meaning and provides us with the key to those dimensions of the horizon that we are calling context. The task that remains for us is to undertake a concrete study of how these two notions of background and context function.

15

The Margins of the World

> Thus the particular object of our active consciousness, and correlatively the active, conscious having of it, being directed toward it, and dealing with it—all this is forever surrounded by an atmosphere of mute, concealed, but cofunctioning validities, a *vital horizon* into which the active ego can also direct itself voluntarily, reactivating old acquisitions, consciously grasping new apperceptive ideas, transforming them into intuitions. Because of this constantly flowing *horizonal character,* then, every straightforwardly performed validity in natural world-life always presupposes validities extending back, immediately or mediately, into a necessary subsoil of obscure but occasionally available reactivatable validities, all of which together, including the present acts, make up a single indivisible interrelated complex of life.
>
> —Husserl (1936)[1]

The deliberations of the last two chapters have introduced us to what I take to be the most revolutionary part of phenomenological theory, the concept of horizon. We begin this chapter by attempting to pull our discussion into a systematic summary of this notion.

A. CHARACTERIZING THE HORIZON

What makes the notion of horizon especially difficult to understand is that both Husserl and Heidegger travel between what I want to call a phenomenological *epistemic* and a phenomenological *ontic* characterization of the notion of world without fully realizing the difference. On the one hand, this range accounts for the fruitfulness of the notion; on the other, the mixed characterization often leads to the fusion of conditions of significance with conditions of being.

Getting at this difference is itself problematic, as the terminology here becomes strained. In chapter 3 we discussed Husserl's distinction between ontology and phenomenology, suggesting that the former is framed by the natural attitude, while the latter requires the phenomenological reduction. There we discovered an ontological characterization of the world—roughly, as totality of all that is the case—which we set in contrast to its phenomenological characterization as horizon. We then saw that the notion of world was developed into that of life-world with the introduction of the genetic method during the early 1920s (chapters 9 and 12), with the result that the later Husserl began to speak of the world in two different registers. On the one hand there is a concept of the world that does not belong to transcendental phenomenology proper, as it could be

> the subject matter of a science of its own, an ontology of the life-world purely as experiential world (i.e., as the world which is coherently, consistently, harmoniously intuitable in actual and possible experiencing intuitions).[2]

But, on the other hand, we also find the life-world being characterized in a transcendental phenomenological register.[3] A Cartesian could insist on a strict difference between them, but once we take the "regressive" way to transcendental analysis, these two become complementary stages of a single analysis, and we are finally free of the threat of a two-world theory. What is actually going on, I am suggesting, is that Husserl's earlier phenomenological characterization of world as horizon was basically an epistemic account; it is now being extended, and then prefaced, by phenomenological analysis that is ontic. In the *Crisis,* Husserl does use the term "ontic," and he speaks of the "ontic sense" of the world and sometimes of the "ontic universe" or "universal field" pregiven us.[4] Thus we read:

> In order to prepare the way for this new subject of investigation, which also essentially concerns the life-world but is not ontological, we shall undertake a general reflection. . . .
>
> This general reflection will at the same time have the function of making evident an essential distinction among the possible ways in which the pregiven world, the ontic universe [*das ontische Universum*] can become thematic for us. . . . The world is pregiven to us, the waking, always somehow practically interested subjects, not occasionally but always and necessarily as the universal field of all actual and possible praxis, as horizon.[5]

An ontic world, in this sense, is a *field* of action and thinking and thus belongs to the order of what is pregiven, not just what is preintended. The ontic world is that which becomes "pluralized" into different spheres of life, different particular worlds, as we described in chapter 13, and thus it is concrete. Husserl's term life-world emphasizes this. I will say more on this in a moment.

When Heidegger takes up the notion of the world in *Being and Time,* he also distinguishes between an ontic and an ontological account but uses that contrast rather differently. In his effort to move beyond the traditional mistake of viewing the world as a type of object, Heidegger presses for a phenomenological account that will do justice to the worldhood of the world.

What he provides is a characterization of its being as nexus of differential implication with the argument that this is its true being and this accounts for the way that it is manifest. The world as nexus of differential implications is labeled a phenomenological ontological notion; the world in its concrete presencing through particular worlds he thinks of as ontic. In short, Heidegger identifies what I have above called the epistemic characterization as ontological, treating this as fully phenomenological. While Heidegger is suspicious that Husserl's account of the life-world is fixed on the ontic and thus remains preontological (in his sense), he thinks of the ontic realm as internally tied to the ontological. The result is that Heidegger's *Being and Time* give us a theory of the world but not the life-world.

The advance that Heidegger makes over Husserl is that he calls for a further deobjectification of the notion of world. But the advantage of Husserl over Heidegger is that he requires a clarification of the ontic concept of world, which Heidegger does not spell out clearly, and its relationship to the ontological (in Heidegger's sense).

Rather than getting lost in this thicket of terminology, let me stipulate definitions of my own and then combine Husserl's and Heidegger's related characterizations of the horizon, discussed in the last two chapters, into a coherent scheme. The world is understood in terms of the phenomenological notion of the horizon. An *epistemic* characterization of the horizon attempts to clarify the constitution of significance or meaningfulness itself. An *ontic* characterization attempts to describe the constitution of regionally configured spheres or fields in which particular types of experience and discourse are situated. They are internally related in at least three ways:

1. The epistemic characterization accounts for the structure of significance on the basis of which we can have a world. The ontic characterization treats the world we do have in terms of the transformations of significance that constitute it.

2. An epistemic account describes spheres of existing significance; an ontic analysis describes spheres having significant existence. The spheres of significance articulate spheres of existence; spheres of existence deploy spheres of significance.

3. The epistemic characterization accounts for the pregiven horizon of our embodied and discursive involvement with objects of the world. The ontic characterization gives us the pregiven horizon of the world's involvement with us.

When we combine this difference with the contrast we began to develop between background and context, we get a rich typology of how the horizon itself is to be characterized. Echoing our account above, we understand *backgrounds* as complexes of senses, themselves connected by *differential implications*, that structure the *indications* configuring the situated objects with which we are concretely involved. Epistemically characterized, backgrounds are *nexuses of senses* internally tied by differential implications; ontically characterized, backgrounds are *webs of indications*, which themselves arise from, as they structure, the interplay of profiles and objects. Bringing these together, we can speak of background as the horizon of our embodied experiential and praxical involvement with environments.

However, we are not only people who labor with skilled hands, but also people who sometimes talk to, and sometimes sing with, others as we work. We live in our tasks but we dwell with others. We change things not only with the saw and the plane but also with the word and the pen. The interplay of embodied actions and discourse requires us to think of the horizon in terms of not only background but also context. Contexts consist of *fields of meanings* encoded in families of signs that are used in communication with others to "sort out" and "collect" the world. Epistemically considered, contexts consist of meanings encoded in signs related by *differential entailment*. Ontically considered, meanings encoded in signs are tied by *referential entailment*. Accordingly, we may speak of contexts as consisting of *frames of entailment* that control the concepts forming semantic fields.

This concluding chapter can be little more than an invitation to a systematic account of the concepts of background and context. Our discussion will be limited to an attempt to situate these notions as they function for phenomenological theory and to tracing one of the ways in which background and context reciprocally determine each other. Our effort to undergird the transcendental characterization just given will proceed by introducing the concept of margins, in contrast to fields, and by exploring its role in a theory of background (section B). We will then turn to semantic field theory in an effort to link our theory of contexts to the structure and status of what are called frames (section C). The last section will apply our distinction between background and context to the question of meaning as we introduced it in chapters 1 and 7.

B. PERCEPTUAL FIELDS AND MARGINS

I will use Gurwitsch's effort to distinguish between fields and margins to get at the nature of what I call background. Gurwitsch's account is all the more suggestive for us because he keeps it tethered to an analysis of consciousness. That restriction, however, produces a problem of its own.

As I am engaged in replacing the axle of my bicycle, to use a simple example, there is an object in focus, what Gurwitsch calls the "theme" of my actions. The bottom bracket has captured my attention. It has its determinacy not only in relation to the other experienced parts of the frame (the chain stays, the head bracket, the down tubes, etc.), and to other components in the gruppo (brakes, cranks, etc.) but also in relation to the tools required to work on it and even to those tools I do not need. Each theme is surrounded by a "thematic field," not just in the sense of an environment, the tool shed in this case, but also in the sense in which it belongs to different groups of materially related parts, components, and tools. This is then clarified phenomenologically by recourse to the notion of horizon, in this case a nexus of indicators that are related by differential indication. While the field itself is not in focus and thus not thematized, it is nevertheless constitutive of the determinacy of the theme. It can then be clarified phenomenologically in terms of the notion of horizon. Gurwitsch puts it this way:

> The noematic inner horizon, if we use this term, does not *surround* what appears in genuine sense experience but rather *pervades* and *permeates it.* What is given in genuine sense experience presents itself as a member of a system, becoming what it phenomenally is by its relatedness to the system, by the role which it plays in it, by its significance for it.[6]

Gurwitsch argues that at the same time that we are directly aware of the theme and, because of its material relevancy, indirectly aware of the thematic field in which we find the theme, we also have an awareness, even more oblique, of certain general dimensions of experience that are not themselves fields, though they accompany all fields. In Gurwitsch's language these dimensions are called "margins," i.e., they constitute the margins of all fields. The distinction between thematic field and margin, he tells us, "was never made by Husserl."[7] While the difference between theme and horizon is prevalent in Husserl, his notion of horizon itself tends to treat margins as if they were fields, i.e., more general fields, fields of fields.

Gurwitsch is best at maintaining the distinction between fields and margins when he argues for the difference between fields and our tacit awareness of consciousness itself, which he understands as the first and, perhaps, primary margin. He does this by finding a difference between acts and particular themes. While each object that appears brings with it a reflexive (not reflective) awareness of the act or of the mental state in and through which it appears, that act or state does not contribute to the material determinacy of the theme as such.

> In an exhaustive description of the theme, the inner awareness of the act through which the theme is given does not appear as an ingredient of that which is given. . . . Being experienced and the inner awareness of being experienced are not of material concern and relevancy to the theme as it stands before the experiencing subject's mind.[8]

Since themes entail an awareness of their fields, the contrast just introduced also entails a difference between (a) the "straightforward" awareness of the unfocused features (e.g., the backside) of objects that are our themes, and (b) the reflexive awareness of that span of our consciousness perceiving the theme: "... at every moment of conscious life we have a marginal awareness of a certain segment, more or less extended, of this very life."[9] It is this reflexive awareness, so different from the peripheral awareness of fields, that is the guiding thread for a reflection upon consciousness understood as a margin. Here Gurwitsch also recognizes clear limits. The margin reflected upon is never actually experienced in its entirety. Only the idealizing work of philosophical reflection seems able to encompass the whole, which it does not by experiencing the stream of consciousness in its entirety but by apprehending the *essence* or the "idea" of consciousness:

> To be sure, reflection does not apprehend the stream in its entirety all at once, but only that segment which culminates in the present. Through reflection in memory it is possible to extend the apprehended segment and to ascend to past experiences more and more remote from the phase experienced at present. However far we go in this direction, it is impossible ever to apprehend the stream in its entirety at a single glance. We may extend the part of the stream which we have apprehended and, therefore, objectivated more and more, but there is no limit to and, consequently, no termination of this progress. The stream of consciousness can be apprehended in its entire extension only "after the fashion of an Idea in the Kantian sense," i.e., through a process which involves infinity. The general type and direction of this process is well determined, but the process can never be completed in any finite number of steps. Each stage in this progressing process [of reflection] is an approximation to a limit which is ideal in that it can only be approximated [in experience] but never attained.[10]

We also clearly see how the idea of margins is applied to our bodily existence. Singular bodily experiences bring the body to the fore without it necessarily being unfolded and articulated as a whole:

> Owing to its pointing references beyond itself and especially to the mentioned horizon [of embodied existence], every particular bodily experience appears as belonging together with other experiences and therefore as pertaining to a wider range of facts. The particular bodily experience preannounces the horizon under discussion through pointing references and by the same token presents itself as incorporated into this horizon [of embodied existence].[11]

The body as a whole is not "actually given" but "announced." "What is actually given in the case of both the somatic and the psychic Ego is the marginal awareness of certain specific facts with their pointing references beyond themselves."[12] In that this awareness is reflexive yet prereflective, it involves a break, a qualitative difference, from the type of awareness that attends fields. Reflexive awareness becomes the "the points of departure of the explicit [reflective] apprehension of the Ego, both psychic and somatic."[13] Thus the contrast between margins and fields is secured.[14]

Only when Gurwitsch turns to his account of our awareness of the perceptual world as a whole, what he takes as the third type of marginal phenomenon, does he run into difficulties. He is tempted to base his argument on the independence of particular thematic fields from their larger surrounding environment. I can be occupied with recollecting the last time I replaced the axle in the bike while being completely oblivious to the world outside the tool shed, or I can be absorbed in the solution of a mathematical problem and unconcerned with this same world. Yet it is always there. Though it is not part of what is currently thematic, it is nevertheless persistently present. Since the world is different from the thematic field itself, Gurwitsch attempts to cover it theoretically by the notion of margins.[15]

However, the crucial difference between this third type of marginal awareness and those of the ego and the body is that the awareness of perceptual surroundings extends, rather than breaks with, our awareness of a perceptual field. What we really have, I want to argue, is a difference between *two* different fields, one narrow and one broad, not an opposition between field and margin. As a result, Gurwitch fails to describe the sense in which the world is margin.

If we refocus our attention on the perceptual field outside the shed, what was merely on the "horizon" comes into view. This is the case even when there is no material relevancy between thematic field and environment. For example, while being absorbed in the solution of a mathematical problem engages the thematic field of mathematical theory, different from the perceptual surroundings outside my door, this difference can be traversed if I turn my attention to this environment. Thus another field, not margin, comes into view. Gurwitsch himself thinks that "the horizon is experienced as an extension of the perceived sector. . . . "[16] Here we have a "continuity of context based upon relevancy."[17] But this is to confuse unfocused surroundings, or perhaps something like the Gestaltist notion of ground (vs. figure), with horizon (and our two phenomenologically characterized concepts of background and context). No matter how far our interest extends into an environment, the horizon is constantly receding. For Gurwitsch there is no break in kind between perceptual field and horizon, and thus the only differences consist of degrees of proximity, clarity, distinctness, and material relevancy. Because the dyad of thematic and unthematic controls Gurwitsch's account, and because our awareness of the perceptual world is not reflexive and, thus, cannot be used to secure the difference between margin and field, the world is treated strictly as "the wider environment,"[18] and thus as a larger field. The in-structure dominates and the world as margin is lost.

This account entails that, no matter how far I extend my experience of environments, I never encounter margins as margins, only broader environments. Put phenomenologically, no matter how far I extend my reflection upon fields, I only encounter other fields, not the margins of fields. When it comes to an account of the perceptual world, Gurwitsch conflates his characterizations of field and margins. This occurs because he depends upon an account of conscious awareness alone to decide the difference between theme, field, and margins. Margins, not as fields but margins of fields, are yet to be understood. The phenomenological theory of backgrounds that we are using is designed to be an account of margins.

C. SEMANTIC FIELDS AND FRAMES

While we correctly think of semantic field (*Bedeutungsfeld*) theory as traceable back to the lectures of Ferdinand de Saussure originally published in 1916,[19] there is little doubt that Roman Jakobson's groundbreaking work in phonetics provided linguists with their paradigm of the notions of contrast and opposition. Through him and others in the Moscow and then the Prague Circle, Husserl's logic of parts and wholes (his Third Investigation) and his pure grammar of meanings (his Fourth Investigation) exerted considerable influence as well.[20] Interestingly, Husserl's student Gustav Spet was a member of the Moscow Linguistics Circle that Jakobson helped found as a graduate student in 1915. No doubt this interest accounts for the fact that the first translation of the *Logical Investigations* was into Russian; it was published in 1909.[21] We find early essays in which Jakobson appropriated parts of the *Investigations,* as well as *Ideas I,* for his own use. In a seminar in Moscow in 1915/16 he handled Husserl's doctrine of apperception from *Ideas I.*[22] Commenting on this connection, Elmar Holenstein tells us that

> It was in Husserl's work that Jakobson found the first systematic formulations of the general laws that operate for a structural unit. . . . This very investigation [the Third Investigation], which found hardly an echo among Husserl's own students, was seized upon by the Prague linguists without his knowledge and proclaimed a kind of "fundamental view of structuralism" by Jakobson. . . . [T]here is hardly a basic theoretical or methodological concept of structural linguistics and poetics that does not undergo an explicit or implicit phenomenological determination and elaboration by Jakobson.[23]

This reference is of not only historical, but also strategic, importance. While Husserl used the Third and Fourth Investigations to spring into a phenomenological account of acts and cognition in his Fifth and Sixth Investigations, as did Jakobson himself, Saussure in particular and semantic field theory in general have been reluctant to take that turn. In this section we will follow Husserl's approach. In a way familiar to us by now, phenomenology will look to the gaps and tensions we find in semantic field theory as an invitation to undertake a further set of reflections that ground that domain in our cognitive involvement with the world. Using the results of linguistic analysis is doubly important because the analysis of language, as we have emphasized, situates us at a level that crosses any number of regions.

My analysis in this section will be spartan, as this is not the place to begin what could be another book. It begins by simply reproducing five central tenets of semantic field theory, giving a few examples and citing references in place of supplying sustained argumentation.[24] I take these as basic features of what I will in the next section call "natural meaning." As I proceed, I will attempt to locate unresolved tensions within this approach in order to suggest a distinction between semantic fields and frames, parallel to the contrast just developed between fields and margins, as a way of deepening the analysis. This brief account of semantic field theory will also allow us to enrich greatly our account of horizon.

1. Words or lexemes[25] that belong to a particular region or content domain are themselves organized within a semantic field by relations of affinity and contrast.[26] A semantic field, then, consists of two interdependent elements: (a) a set of lexemes, and (b) the paradigmatic and syntagmatic relationships between members of that set, which form the meaning or meanings of those lexemes.

The notion of lexemes "belonging to" or "applying to" a content domain contains an ambiguity that opens two different options for semantic field theory. The ambiguity is whether a meaning consists only of relations of affinity and contrast or whether there is a concept or conceptual "stuff," to use Husserl's rather quaint term, that subsists in addition to such ties. This raises the issue of whether relations of affinity and contrast holding between lexemes are constitutive or (only) regulative of their meaning. This ambiguity is connected to another: how do we understand the "content domain" to which lexemes apply? Granted that lexemes label concepts "supplied" by the content domain, the content domain can be understood either as a function of the meaning of the lexemes or as the referent of the lexemes, in both cases leaving open the status of the referent. Roughly put, the two options open to semantic field theory are illustrated in Figure 15.1.

To the extent that semantic field theory abstracts from issues of intentionality and restricts itself to the study of language, it can think of reference only from the "inside" of language, thus as semantic reference consisting of exemplars. It generally chooses Option 1 with the qualification that some theorists would want to adopt the notion of meaning we list under Option 2. But to the extent that one wants to relate lexemes to what is not linguistic, one must rely on systems of discursive usage and upon systems of experiential appropriation, both of which are a function of our involvement with the world and neither of which is directly available if we restrict ourselves to semantic

	Option 1	Option 2
Meaning of Lexemes	Concepts = relations of contrast and affinity	Concepts + relations of contrast and affinity
Reference of Lexemes	Linguistic exemplars	Extra-linguistic: objects, events, etc., as prototypes

Fig. 15.1

fields. Option 2 (with the provision that we could adapt the notion of meaning in Option 1 to it) is necessary if we are ever to say anything about the relationships among experience, discourse, and reality. Phenomenological theory argues for this option. The tendency in semantic field theory to characterize this relationship from the side of language as "encoding" is simply a way of hiding, not solving, the problem.

2. The characterization of meaning in terms of relationships of affinity and contrast is designed as an alternative to the theory that a sign is an external expression of an ideal, mental concept in the mind of the speaker, and that such concepts contain certain features, internal to them, on the basis of which we can account for their relationship to other concepts. Identity of the concept in that theory is the condition of its relationships, a notion that we find in part in the early Husserl. Semantic field theory reverses the order: the relationships of affinity and contrast are what give the lexeme its identity. In addition, these relationships are themselves defined strictly in terms of linguistic musters. The meaning of the term *washed* can be characterized in terms of its paradigmatic relationship of similarity and contrast to other terms that can be substituted for it, such as *scrubbed, rinsed, laundered, oiled, dried,* and *cleaned,* in the sentence *John washed the dog,* and in terms of its syntagmatic relationship to other terms in different grammatical positions in the same sentence, such as *John washed the engine parts, John washed the money, John washed his words,* and *John washed his conscience.* The theory of these different types of affinity and contrast is well developed and revolves around such notions as synonymy, hyponymy, antonymy, metonymy, inclusion, etc. In some semantic field theory, the meaning of a lexeme is just these patterns of substitution. Machines, therefore, can be said to "comprehend" meaning if they can replicate these substitutions. In most semantic field theory, relationships of affinity and contrast derived from lexemes replacing lexemes in musters are thought of in terms of

human comprehension of signs, and thus computer simulations cannot be identified with that process.

If we proceed by a comparison of words apart from their function in sentences, or if we assume that sentences can be reduced to the combination of their elements, we can easily fall into the theory that the meaning of a word is the particular content it designates (be it a concept or a real item). The value of semantic field theory is to argue that we cannot account for the meaning of words by correlating them to what they designate but must turn to the understanding of lexemes in sentential musters. To complete the momentum of this idea, however, a stronger distinction between meaning and reference is required. This allows us to show that what a word refers to (what fulfills a word) is not a condition of the word having meaning. *The large blowfish is sleeping in the chair* is perfectly meaningful even if no one had ever seen a blowfish or even if we know that blowfish cannot live out of water or sleep in chairs. It also allows us to integrate the full scope of syntagmatic relationships in accounting for the fluid and shifting nature of the meaning that terms do have. At the same time, the distinction requires us to go beyond the limits of semantic fields, for words are not just attached to a certain domain but are also used by us to grasp or to take what they refer to. A certain activity or act on the part of the speaker is involved: the meaning is the path or the direction constitutive of that activity. To throw this back upon Saussure, we are asking that the link between *langue* (language) and *parole* (speech) be reestablished or, better, that we not allow it to be severed in the first place. For without this we lack any internal connection between meaning and reference. The result of reintroducing speech-acts, as Husserl did in his *Logical Investigations*, was to replace a theory of representations with a theory of presentations.

3. The most recent work in semantic field theory has argued that a proper representation of linguistic categories cannot be achieved by a list of features but requires the use of frame analysis. A representation of a frame requires us to distinguish between attributes and values, i.e., a semantic field consists of "a co-occurring set of abstract attributes that adopt different values across exemplars."[27]

For example, the representation of a beach stone according to feature list analysis would consist of a list of properties such as: round, white, hand-sized, light, etc. For the sake of simplicity, I represent only four features (see Fig. 15.2).

For semantic field analysis, by contrast, a beach stone would be represented by the specification of a single value (the same four) on each of the attributes such as shape, color, size, weight, etc. (Fig. 15.3). (Again, for the sake of simplicity I greatly reduce the number of attributes and features that would be relevant.)

The terms *value* and *attribute* are relative: while *round* is a value of the

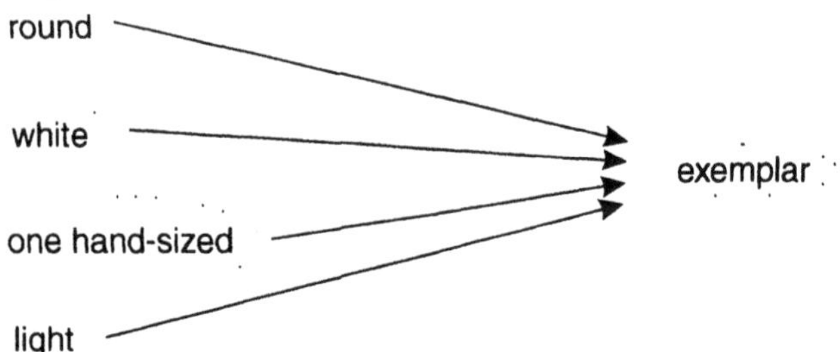

Fig. 15.2

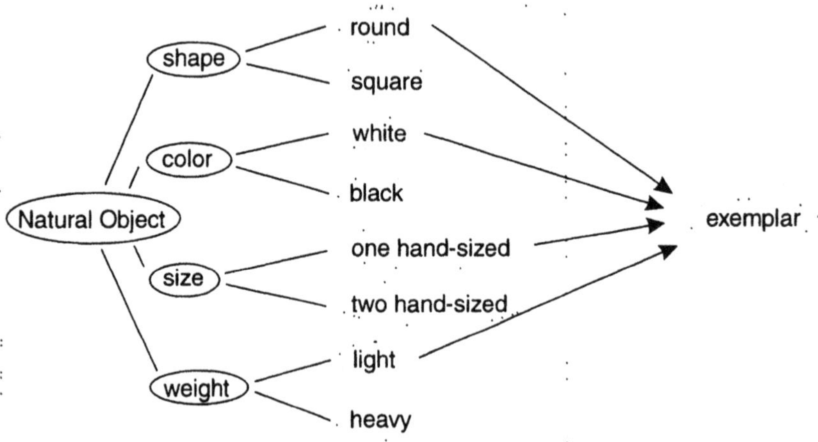

Fig. 15.3

attribute *shape, shape* is a value of the attribute *natural object.* Both values and attributes are concepts. On the one hand, values inherit information contained in the attributes to which they are subordinate; on the other, values contain additional information not in their respective attributes. The frame is in the box with the dotted lines.[28] Barsalou has argued convincingly that in addition to having value-attribute sets, frames possess structural invariants between attributes, due to the internal conceptual relations that hold across most prototypes or exemplars, as well as various constraint relations between attributes that account for the systematic variability in attribute values.[29] In short, structural invariants between attributes give us norms and normativity; constraint relations give us systematic variation. Frame is understood as a "finite generative mechanism." Barsalou explains:

> A modest amount of explicit frame information in memory enables the computation of a tremendously large number of concepts. By combining attribute values in new ways, people construct new concepts implicit within existing frame knowledge.[30]

The crucial question for us is what determines which groups of attributes are active in a frame. This is dependent upon two factors: the surrounding context and the specific prototypes in play.[31] The specificity of a given speech-act is suspended between the larger context of differing frames and alternative conceptual maps, on the one hand, and fields of experiential significance, on the other. But if neither of these can be directly captured through a structural analysis of the conceptual content of a given speech-act, then we must move beyond a frame in order to account for that frame (and thereby move beyond what will submit itself to computational models of concept construction and generation). We must move into an account of the "margins" of the frame.

4. There is considerable uncertainty as to what to include under the notion of a frame, with the options ranging from a narrower model consisting of attributes, values, and internal constraints, such as we just described, to something as broad as "a structured background of experience, belief, or practices, constituting a kind of conceptual prerequisite for understanding the meaning."[32] This has led Charles Fillmore and Beryl Atkins to suggest that semantic field theory is mainly concerned with paradigmatic and syntagmatic relationships between lexical items and with cataloguing "the kind of interitem relations that can be defined for the elements of a lexicon." By contrast, frame analysis according to them is founded on the "notion of *cognitive frames* or *knowledge schemata.*"[33] Fillmore and Atkins explain:

> Within such an approach, words or word senses are not related to each other directly, word to word, but only by way of their links to common background frames and indications of the manner in which their meanings highlight particular elements of such frames.[34]

Is there a way of sorting out this difference?

Let me suggest a contrast between a semantic field and the margins of a field, analogous to the distinction in the last section between a (perceptual) field and the margins of that field. A semantic field contains the concepts in a given domain. If we know only the attributes and values for the *beach stone* field given above, the domain would have 16 concepts, each composed of the combination of one value from each of the four attributes (2 shapes × 2 colors × 2 sizes × 2 weights = 16 combinations). If we allow for a situation in which any three attributes are used to identify a beach stone, in addition to ones where all four are factored, the combinations rise to 48. In addition, the frame for *natural object* would also include relations and constraints. So the value *white* might be constrained as a relation between *shape* and *color.*[35] As a result of these factors and others as well (recursivity, for example), the number of potential concepts is extremely large even for the simplest of frames.

These factors, which operate "within" a semantic field and can be isolated through standard semantic field analysis, are complemented by others that operate "outside" that field and define its "margins." This is what theorists like Fillmore call its frame. Capturing them requires us to attend not simply to the "inner" but also to the "outer" horizon of a semantic field. Frames are margins of fields and should be understood in terms of those schemata that are constitutive of their meaning. At least three factors, all related to the activity of using lexemes, are crucial.

a. In order for them to become part of a shared semantic field, and in order for a speaker to use them, the mass of concepts that could be in play in a given semantic field must become lexicalized. The "lexical concepts in a semantic field only capture a small fragment of the concepts in the conceptual field."[36] With few exceptions, we know far fewer concepts than could be generated in a given field. In addition, the acquisition of a name often generates the relevant concept.

b. Amateurs become experts. In the case of a rich frame (say, 10 attributes) in contrast to a cruder frame (say, 4 attributes) that apply to the same domain, there is a greater number of exemplars possible. The richer frame greatly enhances our ability to distinguish one exemplar from another, be it types of dogs or dances.

c. But even experts are governed by natural cycles, conventions of measurement and exchange, and the practical goals that must be reached by a system of classification. We settled on the number of attributes by what we are attempting to achieve. Frames are not only archeologically constructed but also teleologically regulated.

These ideas now allow us to sort out an internal connection between context and background. Semantic fields provide us with the context for a given well-formed string of utterances. Frames also integrate background and, with it, multiple, dynamic ties to perceptual fields and cultural practices. Much of the uncertainty in semantic field theory is due to the confusion of context with background.

5. The need for a notion like frame or background, one that requires us to turn "outside" language as a way of situating it, can be seen against the backdrop of two mistakes found in semantic field theory, especially following the work of Saussure, and that continue to haunt a number of deconstructive accounts. Calling the referent of the *beach stone* field above an *exemplar* is consistent with what can be proposed on the basis of an internal analysis of a semantic field. We have, in short, a semantic referent, one whose being is strictly the result of intersecting conceptual vectors.[37] Experience figures into

the account only as a contingent selection principle for the number of values and attributes that are linked to a semantic field.[38] For semantic referents, language is indeed the house of their being. However, the beach stones upon which we walk and which we sometimes throw are not exemplars. They are real objects that might be construed as instances of the exemplar but are not themselves exemplars. Even when gathered by language, and thereby moved from being objects in their typicality to being *prototypes,* they exhibit perceptual and experiential determinations and patterns that should not be directly identified with the content of linguistic concepts. If semantic fields are interpretative devices by which we understand a term's deployment, then we can set them in contrast to the experiential fields of involvement constitutive of the articulate structure of prototypes.

This distinction leads us to the question of whether semantic fields can be used as *explanatory* devices. The tendency in earlier structuralist theories was to assume that an analysis of the relational nature of meaning *accounts for* the deployment of lexemes. But perhaps semantic fields are "observable outcomes" that themselves need to be explained.[39] If so, then another level of analysis is required. This is what is behind our effort to distinguish semantic fields from frames and then to understand frames in terms of background and a correlational account of intentional acts and actions. This issue is brought home by James Ross, who argues for two explanatory dimensions or principles: semantic contagion (the adoption of the meaning of words to their verbal contexts) and pragmatic traction (the engagements of talk with action).[40] The first principle would attempt to account for the way the meaning of a term is dependent upon dynamic transformations found especially in syntagmatic ties between terms. I have called it *differential entailment.* One could even envision an expanded epistemic account in which questions of imagination and conceptual insight are considered. The second principle would bring Ross's account into Husserl's vicinity and advance recourse to intersubjective, communicative acts and actions as necessary for an adequate account. Once we avoid treating the relations of affinity and contrast that the fields display as if they explain semantic fields, we can raise the question of their margins and their origins.

D. MARGINS, FRAMES, AND NATURAL MEANING

To complete our account of world, we need to return, keeping in mind this discussion of context and background, to the question of meaning left hanging in chapter 7. Having distinguished everyday talk from propositional discourse, I only suggested a few implications of this distinction for a theory of meaning, and I did not give these hints a proper grounding. Now we can see why. At that point we lacked the concept of semantic fields, the key to an analysis of everyday discourse. The danger in such a discussion is that we will buy into an alliance of two errors, pervasive in the literature, that make the question of the relationship between language and reality close to insoluble. The first is the treatment of meaning as either literal or metaphorical. The second is the idea that, since we are limited by language, we can never get outside our representations. If we set claims in contrast to everyday talk or reports, as we did in chapter 7, we would rightly align the notion of literal meaning with the former notion. But that leaves us with no choice but to treat everyday talk—"folk" talk with its "folk" theories—as metaphorical. Whatever genuine cognitive content can be found there is gleaned only if we isolate the literal statements that are at the basis of its metaphors and analogies.

We are now in a position to account for the meaning of everyday talk in contrast to propositional discourse and to move beyond the dyad of literal and metaphorical meaning, a contrast that controls the discussion even of those who reject the primacy of propositional discourse. I will turn to Charles Taylor as a (rare) example of the latter and attempt to argue my case with reference to him.

When semantic field theory is applied to everyday talk it gives us an account of what I want to call "natural meaning." My suggestion is that the difference between literal and metaphorical meaning is derived from natural meaning, i.e., is the result of certain transformations in the way that terms function semantically and the way in which their meanings are configured. To put this differently, as a rule there is not a clean difference between literal and metaphorical meaning in everyday talk. Truth-conditional accounts of meaning have been blind to this fact, because they tend to focus on substantive terms and then treat their meanings in terms of extensional conditions. But if we treat labels as part of a semantic field, we can see a shifting center to their meanings that depends upon their paradigmatic relationships to other terms. Take the term *large* in the field of *large, extra-large, family sized,* and *jumbo* in contrast to the field of *tiny, small, medium,* and *large,* or think about the meaning of the term *car* in a field with only the terms *car* and *bicycle* in contrast to a field with *lawn mower, car, motorcycle,* and *lorry.* If we shift our attention to syntagmatic relationships we can see other ways in which meaning changes. Think about the meaning of the term *car* in the strings: *he drove the car, he walked through the car,* and *he loaded coal into the car.* It is only because of our tendency to treat the meaning of *car* in terms of truth conditions that we say that we have three different literal meanings here and do not treat the natural meaning of *car* as one that is fluid and itself controlled by such action terms as *drive, walk through,* and *load.* This is even more striking when we look at verbs or adverbs. Can we say that one of the following strings captures the literal meaning of *looked for* better than another?

She looked for her money
She looked for help
She looked for victory
She looked for the way home

Or which of the following would best exhibit the metaphoric meaning of *caught*?

He caught the fish
He caught the ball
He caught the last train
He caught a cold
He caught the wind

In each case the meaning is dynamically related to the other terms in the string (as well as to yet others that could replace it). What we come to call the literal meaning is the result either of one of the many uses becoming dominant, or of a process in which the term is "mentioned" and its meaning stipulated (perhaps by giving truth conditions).

In "Theories of Meaning"[41] Charles Taylor attempts to present an alternative conception to contemporary theories of meaning, especially Davidson-type truth-conditional theories, which takes its inspiration from thinkers like Herder, Humboldt, and Heidegger. After discussing certain key functions of language difficult to contain in a truth-conditional account—bringing what is unbounded to articulation, putting things in public space, and opening us to human concerns—he attempts to specify those dimensions of language that will have a direct bearing on a theory of meaning. He emphasizes that there is an expressive (in contrast to a representative) dimension of signs in which they function like gestures that bring us into rapport with others, a dimension that creates a public space between us.[42] We also find a constitutive dimension in which language does not depict as much as partially constitute the phenomena to which it refers.[43] Self-descriptions, for example, help to configure the feelings they describe; public norms and interpersonal relations are also dependent upon and realized in language.[44]

The expressive and the constitutive dimensions of language, however, may not really provide an alternative to truth-conditional approaches in that we can think of both dimensions as different from, and perhaps complementary to, the representational function. They would belong to rhetoric, and thus we should not confuse them with issues of truth. In essence, Taylor's reply—this now moves us to the difficulty I have—is not to reject the idea of literal meaning but to reject the truth-conditional account of it. He correctly argues that the central problem with such accounts is that "we cannot grasp what some of the truth-conditions are without some grasp of the language."[45] We cannot use truth- or satisfaction-conditions to explain meaning for the simple reason that, in order to grasp these conditions, we already have to understand them.[46] While truth-conditional theories, I would add, might give us a plausible reconstruction of how meaningful sentences can be true, they tell us nothing about how they are meaningful in the first place. Taylor, however, does not really use this point to dismantle the dyad of literal and metaphorical, or literal and mythical, but rather argues only that the literal is not primary.[47] In attempting to find an alternative to the primacy of the literal, he relies on the invocative function of speech in general (e.g., the invocation of the presence of the gods in a religious ceremony) and cases where descriptions can figure invocatively in particular (e.g., Henry the Navigator ordering that the name for the southern tip of Africa be changed from "Cape of Storms" to "Cape of Good Hope").[48] But surely this is a rather marginal use of descriptions for us, and so Taylor has to go to some length to construct a story about a primitive society in which the invocative function prevails and where descriptions are always part of "myth" (e.g., where a bull could not be described independently of its meaning in a religio-mythical context).[49] But this leads to unwelcome results. Taylor not only rejects the thesis that truth-conditional accounts are the best way of understanding meaning; he also rejects the thesis that our understanding of metaphoric and mythic language depends upon an understanding of ordinary, descriptive discourse. This is a result of his confusing the question of whether truth-conditional theories give an adequate account of literal meaning with the question of whether "ordinary" meaning is primary. He has to answer that it is not because he assumes that literal meaning is identical to what I am calling natural meaning and that it covers "ordinary, descriptive meaning." Since the only category he has as an alternative to literal meaning is myth, this forces him to deny that "there must be some acquaintance with these terms in their ordinary, descriptive meaning for the myth to be comprehensible" and then look to the "invocative context" as primary.[50]

No doubt, invocation is primary for *some* religious language in *certain* religions or religious contexts, and no doubt the idea of literal language, as Taylor discusses it, is quite alien to a small and diminishing number of cultures that have not been shaped by the rise of either a Western or an Eastern "objectivist" philosophical and scientific tradition. But, as Taylor recognizes, this is certainly not the case in our culture. Apart from a few Chicago Bulls or Oxford United fans, for whom their team's emblem assumes iconic, religious proportions and controls their construction of reality, it is precisely the everyday, "ordinary" meaning of bull that gives us access to its symbolic or mythical meaning. But this is not to claim that the literal meaning—understood according to truth-conditions—is primary; for I am suggesting that both literal and symbolic meaning or, better, the *contrast* between them, is derived from natural meaning. Unlike Taylor, I have no trouble affirming the thesis that we must be acquainted with terms in their "ordinary, descriptive meaning" in order for symbols or myths to be comprehensible, for the simple reason that this meaning can be understood as "natural" and need not be cast into the mold of "literal meaning." Nor would I be too quick to reject the notion of truth conditions as part of the description of literal meaning, as we saw in chapter 7. If, as Taylor would recognize, literal terms arise with critical reflection and analysis, then we have a key to the difference in characterization. Because a certain type of "mentioning" subtends the way in which we employ literal discourse and a certain interest in "correctness" pulls that discourse back from our involvement with things in order to represent them, we can come to think of the meaning of literal discourse in terms of certain satisfaction rules that must be adhered to in order for such terms to be admitted into the context of objective discourse. These rules, however, should never be confused with the schematizations that make possible the use of lexemes in ordinary discourse, governed, as it is, by different interests.

This discussion now allows us to ground the difference between reports and claims used throughout this work. Reports are pieces of ordinary discourse that have natural meanings; claims belong to rigorous, objective discourse and employ literal meanings. While claims serve to *represent* facts and can be said to provide depictions of them, reports serve to *present* matters by uncovering them in the course of our involvement with them. Claims sort and attribute; reports articulate and delineate. Claims consist of rules that regulate what they represent; reports consist of schemes that are partially constitutive of what they present. At the level of analysis we also find differences. For the account of natural meaning, the perspective of the participant is primary and its schematization must also map dialogical features of discourse. In the case of literal meaning, Husserl's insight that an account of meaning need rely only on the monologue may be correct, for it arises from the perspective of a detached observer.

The contrast between natural and literal meaning spares us from having to argue that, in the relationship between ordinary and mythical, invocative contexts, "the metaphorical is primary here," a statement that is rather at odds with the claim that we are looking for "two-way traffic."[51] Taylor seems uncertain of just how to put this, but at one point he introduces a perspective close to the one I am suggesting:

> It would be best to say that the whole distinction "literal sense/metaphorical sense" cannot apply to a case like this. There are not two senses of the term here, one of which deserves to be called literal. It serves no purpose to talk of a "literal sense" here; and will not until a more rationalizing culture develops with a concern for objective description, which descriptions in turn make a range of more "subjective" uses stand out as mere tropes.[52]

This points to where we want to go, but Taylor restricts his analysis to a tribal "stage of culture,"[53] which produces two significant difficulties. First, tribal cultures are rather distant from ours, and thus he does not give us insight into how we also have meaning at play in our culture in a way that "antedates" the opposition between the literal and the metaphorical. If it is just a matter of being at a different stage of development, then the problem with truth-functional accounts can be no more than the fact that they are "parochial, culture-centric," or "anachronistic."[54] This would imply that for our culture they are perfectly accurate, and thus we have gained little. I am sure that Taylor would be surprised that his approach feeds directly into Husserl's own account of the primacy of Western rationality, as we discussed it in chapter 12. All one needs is Husserl's additional argument for the way in which representational accounts are part of not just a different but also a "more rational" or "higher" stage of culture. My account of natural meaning, however, might suggest a way in which truth-functional accounts are highly inaccurate, with regard to not just mythic discourse, but also the way in which ordinary language with natural meaning functions even for our own culture. At the same time, we establish a place for these accounts by thinking of them as derivative and thus grounding them in certain transformations located in the life-world.

But there is also a second problem. Once we accept the dyad of literal and mythical language and restrict the notion of truth-conditions to the first, we are left with the unwelcome consequence that there is no connection between issues of truth conditions and the vast majority of things that matter to us. Taylor attempts to replace this notion of truth with the Heideggerian notion of *Erschlossenheit,* disclosure;[55] but the identification of literal with ordinary, descriptive discourse means that it is not this type, but only mythic discourse, that discloses. When we add to this the idea that mythic discourse works mainly by its "invocative/constitutive role,"[56] we come close to the notion that such discourse creates the realities it talks about. Even for religious discourse, especially that found in the Judeo-Christian biblical texts, this split is unwelcome. It employs the older Bultmann-Heidegger distinction between *Historie* (factual history) and *Geschichte* (story-history) and argues, as did they, that such texts give us only the latter. But these texts themselves make a distinction between straightforward, descriptive discourse and metaphorical discourse and generally assume that the ordinary descriptive meanings provide a semantic field from which we can then understand their parables, stories, and aphorisms. In addition, they often make historical claims and invite us to consider the truthfulness of these claims. If we take our starting point in fields of natural meaning and think of the difference between literal and metaphorical discourse as the result of transformations of those fields, we can see how the disclosive function of ordinary descriptions can be connected to the truth-conditions of literal discourse. At the same time we can argue for different types of truth relative to different semantic fields. We can also understand how the disclosive function of ordinary language enables, and even empowers, our understanding of metaphorical language, at the same time that such language models what escapes mundane existence and begins to open up the realm of mystery. Without this understanding and without modifying it so that it also applies to other crucial spheres such as political and ethical discourse, we are left with the language that matters most not having a point of reference beyond what it itself creates.

On the basis of these ideas and the ones developed in the last two sections, I am suggesting that it is the failure to understand the relationship between semantic fields and frames, and the subsequent reduction of background to context, that leads to the mistaken notion that the limits of language are the limits of the world. I have rejected this notion, one shared in different ways by many post-Wittgensteinian analytic and post-Heideggerian deconstructive thinkers, by arguing for the following sequence of ideas:

1. The principle of semantic fields. What a sign means can be defined only by considering its relationship to other signs. Signs are related by affinity and contrast, and are organized into semantic fields. The identity of the meaning of a lexeme depends upon its difference from other lexemes to which it is related.

2. The principle of contextual determinacy. This principle can be traced back to Frege's crucial insights, in contrast to the Lockean tradition, that sentences are not simply combinations of names, that names and sentences behave in very different ways, and that terms acquire their meaning only in the unity of a sentence. While great stress has been laid upon paradigmatic substitutions in a single sentence type, the fluidity of meaning and the range of its dynamic transformations is generally understood best by attending to syntagmatic relationships. In fact, recourse to paradigmatic and syntagmatic relationships also entails recourse to extended discourse or texts and to their role in the account of meaning.

3. The principle of margins. Semantic fields are not themselves explanatory structures but are based on conceptual networks that arise in connection with cognitive achievements and speech-acts. More accurately, there is a relationship of co-dependency. Sets of lexical *contrasts* rest upon differences in *the manner in which things are conceived,* just as they often make it possible for us to think of something in a new way. Systems of *relations* are rooted in systems of *usage,* just as those relations often introduce a new way of using language. Semantic *fields* depend upon the rules of language *games,* yet those games can be played only in those fields. Especially in practical discourse, "craft talk," and ritualized talk, "discourse is symbiotic with the activity it modified."[57] The notion of margins requires us to take *context* as the correlate of intersubjective discourse.

4. The principle of background dependency. Speaking and knowing-that are themselves circumscribed by experience and knowing-how. We have a type of involvement with things that does not require the mediation of language; things have a sense or significance that is not reducible to a function of meaning. In fact, any number of language games draw their meaning from this sense. Understood in this way, the notion of background carries us beyond the limits of language.

Once we understand the notion of horizon in terms of the interplay of context and background, we can see that the limits of the world are much broader than the limits of language. With this the hermeneutical circle is broken once and for all.

Appendix: The Standard Interpretation

Given the very different conceptions of philosophical discourse, the lack of a shared methodology, and the divergence of what counts as a philosophical problem or issue, one is puzzled to find a concurrence in the way that Husserl is interpreted by analytic philosophers, deconstructive writers, and thinkers inspired by critical theory. There are significant differences, but the agreement is deep and broad enough to speak of a standard picture. My goal in this appendix is to briefly review the literature and to sketch the basic elements of this picture. The alternative to the standard interpretation is what will be developed in Part 1 of this study.

A. ANALYTIC APPROACHES TO HUSSERL

The work on Husserl by analytic interpreters is insightful, precise, and strong in its application to issues in current intentionality theory, cognitive science, and analytical epistemology. Its development in the 1970s and into the 1980s forced Husserl studies beyond its earlier phase of exegesis and appropriation into one of detailed critical engagement, especially with his theories of meaning, perception, and judgment. In Germany there were groundbreaking studies by Ernst Tugendhat that used Husserl to mediate between the analytic and the German phenomenological and hermeneutic traditions.[1] Centering on the problem of intersubjectivity and communication, Theunissen's important study of Husserl also had clear implications for this project.[2] At the same time, English-speaking studies of Husserl by Føllesdal, Mohanty, and McIntyre and Smith[3] appeared that looked more to Frege[4] than Brentano[5] as their point of entry into Husserl's theory of intentionality. These works centered on his notion of the noema and argued, roughly, that Husserl identified intentional content with propositional content. This then allowed Dreyfus to show that Gurwitsch's effort to extend such a notion to perception leads to an infinite regress because it does not allow for any internal connection between meaning understood as an ideal entity (form) and sensorial matter (hyletic content). If we treat perception as "prelinguistic" and its determinacy as the basis for the way it is represented or "taken" in speech-acts, then perceptual matter itself would have to be structured in some way other than through "meaning-bestowing acts." But Husserl restricts his explanation of perceptual determinacy to a notion of meaning characterized in the same way as logical meaning, as an atemporal, eternal entity. Since hyletic matter is concrete and temporal, we are left with an infinite regress of perceptual content being constituted by a form to which it has no internal tie.[6] In an earlier work I concentrated on two related difficulties with this interpretation: first, the restriction of noematic content to Fregian-type propositions, and second, Dreyfus's argument that Husserl employed such a characterization of the perceptual noema to account for the intentional content (sense) of perceptual acts. I argued that Husserl not only has a terminological distinction but a difference in type between linguistic meaning (*Bedeutung*) and perceptual sense (*Sinn*). I also showed that his lecture manuscripts of the 1920s devote countless pages to developing just such a characterization of perceptual significance and to working out a proper phenomenology of perception. This development is complemented by another in yet later works in which he became increasingly concerned with how one can characterize the meaning of propositional discourse in view of its historical and temporal genesis.[7]

This first set of studies by analytical interpreters has been followed by a second, which places Husserl in relation to the newly developing disciplines of cognitive psychology and artificial intelligence (AI). Dreyfus extends his earlier critique of Husserl by suggesting that since he understands meanings as *rules* and since he analyzes meanings "solely in terms of the structures of contents of intentional states,"[8] he is committed to the same theoretical approach as proponents of AI.[9] As a result neither Husserl nor cognitive scientists are able to account for vast domains of meaningful experience in which rules are not constitutive, such as perception, our practical involvement with tools, and most forms of human action.[10] Interestingly, McIntyre shows considerable reluctance to follow Dreyfus in his "computationalist reading of Husserl" and attempts to bring this home by discovering important differences between Husserl and Fodor in both their conceptions of mental representations and of the role of meaning in mental life.[11]

In all of this, however, there is still no monograph by analytic interpreters that deals directly with Husserl's method as a whole on the basis of both his published and unpublished texts. Without arguing for this directly in a study on its own, they assume that what Husserl came to call his Cartesian way and its formulations are the final articulation of his method and exhaust the scope of his transcendental phenomenology. Only one thinker who is heavily engaged with the interface between analytic and phenomenological epistemological issues, J. N. Mohanty, understands that this is not the case. Still, he has concentrated on the conditions of framing a transcendental constitutive phenomenology, as we will see in chapters 4 and 7, and to my knowledge has not attempted to bridge that study with an account of genetic analysis.[12]

B. DECONSTRUCTING HUSSERL

By contrast, deconstructive thinkers have been concerned with little but Husserl's method, though they too have failed to read deeply in Husserl's manuscripts, especially the texts of the 1920s. The deconstructive approach to Husserl is based almost entirely on the work of Derrida who, beginning with an image first introduced by Levinas[13] and Berger,[14] and then established by Sartre[15] and, to some extent, Ricoeur,[16] wrote one long manuscript and published two books (1962 and 1967) on Husserl, and then used these studies as the point of departure for his own philosophical journey.[17] Bernhard Waldenfels claims that a reading of the manuscript—now published as *Le problème de la genèse dans la philosophie de Husserl*—clears up suspicions about insufficient knowledge of Husserl's works;[18] but while this text was published in 1990 it was composed between 1953 and 1954, at a time when only the first six volumes of the *Husserliana* and none of the lecture and manuscript materials from the 1920s were in print, precisely those texts that treat the problem of genesis. Not even the discussion of the various ways into the reduction that we find in *Erste Philosophy I and II,* published as *Husserliana,* Vols. 7 and 8, is mentioned. In France in the 1950s, as Françoise Dastur reports, "Husserlian philosophy appeared to be a new form of Cartesianism";[19] Derrida understands the way in which the phenomenological thrust of Husserl's texts carry us beyond its limitations, yet sees him as inescapably caught in the Modernist framework. In spite of Husserl's deliberate procedure of excluding all naturalistic and philosophical precommitments, Derrida, following Heidegger,[20] finds yet deeper metaphysical notions at play in Husserl's descriptive analyses, notions that represent the culmination of a development that began with Descartes, even dating back to the Greeks. These notions are ones Derrida is interested in bringing to light, thereby circumscribing and placing them in a tradition whose resources are spent. But Derrida's reading is based on a selection of Husserl's texts, those designed as "introductions" to phenomenology, and he does not handle the rich and powerful studies Husserl devoted in the 1920s to the problem of method in general and to genetic phenomenology in particular. Waldenfels, commenting on this limitation, also provides systemic insight for this neglect: "The fact that Derrida disregards genetic phenomenology so adamantly may be due to the fact that initially he expected all too much, or just about everything, from genesis."[21]

Rather than summarizing what is familiar territory to many readers, let me rather point to the way this concern with the question of Husserl's method is reflected in five recent studies that deal with or touch upon Derrida's relationship to Husserl.

In his *Delimitations,* John Sallis[22] correctly stresses the fact that for Derrida it is Husserl's theory of temporal constitution that can be turned against a notion of impressional presence and, finally, against that notion of closure "which for [Cartesian] phenomenology would be primordial."[23] Sallis does see this turn as occurring within Husserl's own work but does not attempt to sort this out and describe its implications for the question of Husserl's method.

John Caputo's *Radical Hermeneutics*[24] provides us with an extended section on Derrida's analysis of Husserl. But it is surprising to see his sensible handling of Husserl in this text overwhelmed by earlier comments casting Husserl in the mold of Cartesianism, "a foreign import."[25] The methodological prejudice of Cartesianism, Caputo claims, misled Husserl in his theory of intentional objects, "for it can hardly be denied that on the level of his descriptive analysis Husserl failed to give the hermeneutic element in his thought full play";[26] i.e., Husserl did not treat perception as interpretation. Even worse, Husserl's description of intentionality in effect "asks us to believe in two selves: one situated in the world and the other, its transcendental double."[27] While this problem is certainly inherent in a Cartesian approach that attaches ontological claims to its epistemological findings,[28] the notion of transcendental reflection, even in *Ideas I,* contains a clear distinction between the empirical ego and the transcendental structure of that ego and, thus, might avoid the difficulty.

The account of Husserl's method by Rodolphe Gasché in his *The Tain of the Mirror*[29] is greatly enhanced by his recognition that the "later Husserl" embodies "a type of philosophy that cannot comfortably be placed within the usual philosophical classification."[30] Because he stresses the systematic nature of Derrida's thought, Gasché finds more continuity with Husserl than with others who write on their relationship.[31] All of these writers, however, are mainly interested in Derrida and thus, while we find suggestive and provocative insights, none undertakes a systematic account of Husserl's method.

Claude Evans in his *Strategies of Deconstruction*[32] attempts not an appropriation of deconstruction, as in the works above, but a line-for-line critique of Derrida's texts on Husserl. I only point out that he engages Derrida's interpretation at a level rather different from my account. My wager is that the philosophically interesting response to Derrida requires a critical account of Husserl's method as a whole and asks whether it, properly reconstructed, does not itself dismantle precisely those implicit metaphysical elements that, according to Derrida, would be its undoing. Evans touches upon this issue at several points but his focus is upon Derrida's readings and misreadings in *Speech and Phenomena* and *Of Grammatology*[33] of individual doctrines of Husserl.

While Derrida's manuscript on Husserl was written (1953–1954) and his two works on Husserl were published (1962 and 1967) at a time when a number of key manuscript texts—such as *Erste Philosophie,* the three volumes of *Intersubjectivität,* and *Analysis of Passive Synthesis*—were just coming to press, and a number of substantial studies attuned to the range of his thought were yet to be published,[34] the same cannot be said for the essays collected in *Derrida's Interpretation of Husserl* (1994). Of the main essays that directly assess Derrida's interpretation of Husserl—and not all of them do—most concentrate on the *Logical Investigations* and *Ideas I,* with passing references to the *Crisis.* Only the piece by Waldenfels is informed by a broad and systematic reading of Husserl's corpus and by familiarity with the better secondary literature.

Though this is surprising, if not alarming, for a style of philosophical reflection that has inherited the rich historical focus of the Continental tradition, what I conclude from this is that the texts treated by deconstructive studies are as limited in range as the studies by analytic commentators. Perhaps this is the main reason we find a convergence in their readings. But how are we to characterize this convergence? How can we move beyond these elementary and superficial points about the selection of texts to the philosophically interesting features of their shared view of Husserl?

C. CONVERGENCE

According to both analytic and deconstructive accounts, Husserl's final formulation of phenomenology commits us to at least three theses concerning the structure of intentionality, yet another three on the nature of true philosophical method, and, as a consequence, three fatal philosophical mistakes. We begin with the analysis of intentionality.

1. All acts are intentional in nature, and this means that their structure is such that they are necessarily related to an object (absent or present) that is their theme. This relationship is made possible by an abstract, structural component or entity (present) which Husserl labels *Sinn* (sense) or *Bedeutung* (meaning). While it is the interpretation of acts as form that supplies his notion of the noesis, the characterization of the meaning as the content of an act provides the essential feature of Husserl's notion of the noema. At the same time the noema is taken as form relative to the sensible content of any appearance it configures. The correlation of noesis and noema defines the irreducible and universal structure of consciousness.

2. While Husserl goes on to make a *terminological* distinction between *Sinn* and *Bedeutung* paralleling a *structural* distinction between acts of perception and understanding (judging), he *characterizes* the meaning component of the noemata of both in terms that make it propositional, roughly in

Frege's sense, only then further to confuse this picture by insisting that perceptual *Sinne* are prelinguistic. We find, accordingly, the prevalence of a certain logistic or logo-centric characterization of intentional life in Husserl's theory into which his theory of perception does not fit. His efforts to characterize perception with such a model lead to problems that cannot be solved: either (1) we are confronted with an unbridgeable gap between formless matter (sense-data) and form (ideal meaning); or (2) taking at face value the terminological distinction that treats *Sinne* as prelinguistic, he holds the untenable position that senses are independent of language and that no perception is interpretation; or (3) privileging the logistic characterization of the noema, he is driven, contrary to his expressed theory, to the theory that perception can only be interpretation, i.e., that "'the look' cannot 'abide.'"[35]

3. The relationship between meaning, reference, and language is defined through a principle of expressibility: signs are physical tokens (real entities) that stand as proxy for and thus express meanings (ideal entities) by virtue of which those signs (now called expressions) refer to objects (real or ideal entities). Signs are, thus, externally related to both their meanings and their referents. They are no more necessary for the shape and existence of such meanings than they are for the configuration and presence of objects. In addition, meanings have both a subsistence (ideal) and a content (conceptual) that are independent of anything belonging to the realm of real existence. This also entails that the process of intersubjective communication, bound as it is to signs, is external to the content communicated, whether it be meaning or reference, as well as to the history of the communicative community. And this leads Husserl to the theory that justification or verification can be reduced to a question of evidence defined by the twin notions of (a) a direct or intuitive insight into the coincidence between intended meaning and fulfilling meaning, between "taking as" and "given as" and (b) the optimal presence of referents.

These ideas are then reflected in as they are founded upon three interdependent features of Husserl's method:

4. The characterization of meanings as an ideal structural component of acts entails that they are given in a way distinct from real entities, i.e., when the act-meaning correlation through which reference takes place becomes itself a referent, its givenness in reflection is fundamentally different from the "straightforward" givenness of real objects. The analysis of the "pure essences" of real objects and facts understands them as rules for the *possible* givenness of real instances in *possible* acts (without the actuality of the instances being necessary), while the insistence that such essences are interconnected in a field that can be given or presented to eidetic insight opens a gap between the sphere in which such essential correlations are displayed and the sphere of

real existence. Thereby the *epistemic* contrast between modes of presentation becomes an *ontic* distinction between the transcendental and the real spheres. And this entails that naturalistic or, as we prefer today, causal explanations are excluded from our understanding of intentional content.

5. To this phenomenological program Husserl adds the Cartesian project of closure, i.e., the requirement of an absolute starting point or ground for the *totality* of being that can itself be given in absolute knowledge. The real world is a transcendent field present to consciousness only perspectivally, and thus our understanding of it is necessarily open to correction by the ongoing course of experience. All empirical knowledge is dubitable and so does not provide a starting point for philosophy. But Husserl argues that the real world *as a whole* is the correlate of an underlying belief in its existence. The act of suspending the thesis of existence opens to intuitive inspection a second field, the field of immanence, with a mode of presence that permits secure evidence. For here there is an adequate coincidence between being and being given, which entails that our direct intuition of its presence is sufficient to secure its existence. The *ontic* difference between transcendental and real spheres is thereby transformed into an *ontological* difference between (absolute) consciousness and world. Since the reduction is said to give us consciousness as "an openly endless and yet self-contained sphere of being,"[36] absolute consciousness becomes the irreducible starting point for the thematization of the whole of being. In contrast to the sphere of transcendence, it is both immanent and transcendental, i.e., this second field is understood as the absolute consciousness of the one performing the reflection.

6. Husserl counters the threat of subjective idealism with the argument that, as displayed in the sphere of immanence, consciousness is structured in such a way that it always includes a *relation* to transcendence. The starting point is not a psychological event or a field of psychological events but the basic relation between the modes of the *cogito* and the appearances of the *cogitatum.* Husserl's famous procedure of "bracketing" the world does not mean that the world is lost but rather that it is thematized as "correlate," as the irreducible field of appearances. It is the transcendental explication of this relation between acts and appearances, in all of its diversity, that gives us the *ground* for the multiplicity of *all* the various regions of the transcendent. This difference, however, is secured at the expense of a unified theory of the ego, for now it appears that it is split between a transcendental and an empirical ego. The transcendental ego is the agent of constitution and the subject matter of a special discipline called transcendental phenomenology. The empirical ego would necessarily be one of the items constituted by the transcendental ego and would be the subject matter of a different discipline called phenomenological psychology.

With this account of intentionality and method taken as the irreducible core of Husserl's program, it is almost inevitable that critical assessments revolve about three clusters of problems, each of which develops critical strands we can find in even earlier thinkers.

7. The understanding of transcendental subjectivity as consciousness, and then of consciousness as having both its own inner form of being and of temporal self-presence, has the result of undercutting, at the deepest level, the adequacy of the self-presencing of consciousness to itself. Indeed, it is Husserl's own account of temporality that shows that presence is but a limit, even an "abstract" limit, between two irreducible forms of absence, between the past that is ever receding and the future that gives us, at best, only open paths. Attempts to bolster the notion of presence either by postulating the apodictic nature of recollection or by reestablishing identity as the condition of difference only betray how serious the problem is. And without the self-presencing of consciousness, Husserl's entire program loses its immovable starting point. It becomes only further entangled when we consider the sense of privileged, even private possession that attends this characterization of (transcendental) subjectivity in terms of a notion of consciousness, and when we attempt to place it in relation to yet other sentient creatures, i.e., when we raise the question of intersubjective temporality.

8. Husserl's foundationalist program places the world, the totality of entities and regions of entities, in relation to its ground at the same time that it works with a radical split between its empirical and a transcendental clarification. This introduces simultaneously a *constriction* of the way in which the world can come to givenness and an *exclusion* of our physical and human sciences from contributing anything philosophically essential to our understanding of that ground. Once transcendental subjectivity is positioned as that ground and once it is construed as consciousness, the world can come to givenness only as a dependent moment of conscious life. Since the sciences, whether natural or social, necessarily work within a region of the world, they do not and cannot articulate its structure as a whole, even though they all operate with a tacit assumption of its existence in play. In principle, then, the sciences cannot articulate the world's being as ground because they are founded upon the a priori correlation of subjectivity and world and receive their legitimacy and meaning by virtue of it. And this means that not only the physical sciences in which inanimate nature is studied but also the biological sciences in which the rhythms and dances of life are brought to representation, and even the human sciences that articulate our various spheres of historical existence, are excluded from that sphere in which the basic structure of consciousness is found and in which philosophy labors to finds its logos. Does not Husserl's equation of the difference between the transcendental and the real with the

opposition between consciousness (immanence) and the world (transcendence) commit us to an unbridgeable chasm between consciousness and concrete existence, and then between the science of the essential structures of intentional life and the empirical sciences, both natural and human?

9. Husserl's suspension of indication, what we now speak of as indexicality, is a necessary step on his way to isolating and then privileging the expressive dimension of signs and to solidifying the opposition between meaning and reference and, eventually, between consciousness and world. Since the phenomenon of expressive acts gave the *Logical Investigations* their point of access to the nature of subjectivity, Husserl was necessarily led to a representational theory of mind in which any consideration of real causal relations to the world was specifically excluded from the essential nature of mental acts and their content. Husserl's methodological solipsism is the counterpart to this approach. But this double exclusion—of expression from indication and of intentional consciousness from any modes of involvement with the world that might not consist of conceptual representations—is one that his own system cannot sustain. If signs cannot be fully extricated from their indicative ties, as he later realized, not only are our conceptual systems caught up in a "surplus" that we can only approach without ever encompassing, they are also related to an alterity, an otherness, a different order of being that cannot be captured through an account of "meaning-bestowing" acts. Whether it be the otherness of the text (Derrida), of various dimensions of sensibility (Dreyfus), or of the intersubjective community (Theunissen, Tugendhat, Waldenfels), Husserl's restriction to the field of expressions necessarily excludes them from any domain but that of phenomena, i.e., of what is constituted by the ego and its intentions. But does not Husserl's own notion of horizon require us to move beyond these limitations?

Undergirding this general approach to Husserl is a shared understanding of the relationship between Husserl and Heidegger. Having restricted Husserlian phenomenology to what this study will call its Cartesian formulation, the standard interpretation finds only distance between these two thinkers. While analytic interpreters find particular Husserlian doctrines they want to appropriate, deconstructive writers almost none, the tendency is to turn to *Being and Time*[37] and then beyond to overcome the methodological inadequacies of Husserl's approach. Dreyfus informs us that Heidegger "forced" Husserl to face the fact that "there are other ways of 'encountering' objects than relating to them as objects of perception or predication."[38] And when Dreyfus suggests that Føllesdal's interpretation of Husserl's theory of the noema is shared by Derrida,[39] this entails not only that we should see complementarity between the deconstructive and the analytic readings but also that we should recognize that a turn to Heidegger is the key to transcending Husserlian phenomenology for both Dreyfus and Derrida. The result, as I will suggest in Part 3, is that one misses both the deep continuity between the methods as well as what is genuinely different in the content of their phenomenologies.

Though it is anything but enthralled with Heidegger,[40] it is striking that the general representation of Husserl sketched above is also shared by Critical Theory, at least by Adorno and Apel. Both of these thinkers recognize a difference between the early and late Husserl, yet his entire program is treated as little more than a Cartesian radicalization of the transcendental question and, ultimately, is wedded to an untenable theory of a prehistorical or a prelinguistic pure consciousness. Allow me to expand briefly, because these thinkers engage Husserl with larger systematic methods of their own in hand.

Placing Husserl in opposition to Hegel, who was skeptical about absolute beginnings in the sense of a point of departure for thought that is certain and indubitable, Adorno argues that Husserl represents a reactionary philosophical force:

> Over against Hegel Husserl remained wedded to the end, under the rubric of his tightly interwoven and complete presentation of phenomenology, to that Cartesianism that takes an absolute foundation of philosophy as a valid ideal.[41]

Husserl's emphatic rejection of dialectics and a notion of mediation led, ultimately, to an "inhibiting of thought in the middle of thinking."[42] As is typical of those who define Husserl's final position as Cartesian, the late work in general and the unpublished material in particular is disregarded, and the *Cartesian Meditations* is taken as the definitive formulation of Husserl's method. Adorno tells us:

> My analysis is confined to what Husserl himself published and privileges thereby the true phenomenological writings, on which the restoration of ontology was based, over the late texts, in which Husserl's phenomenology betrayed itself and reverted into a subtly modified neo-Kantianism. . . . All the pre-phenomenological writings have been ignored . . . as well as the posthumous writings.[43]

Significantly, Husserl's last work, *Crisis*, was published only two years before Adorno's main work on Husserl appeared in print and several years after the bulk of its text was written. He does not cite it once. Of course, key texts such as *Erste Philosophie* and *Analysen zur passiven Synthesis* were not available to him.

Apel is convinced that the early Husserl has a thoroughly Platonic conception of meaning. Ideal meanings are a "transtemporal heaven of fixed stars," which Apel sets in contrast to "meanings realized in the flow of historical languages."[44] Apel finds this reinforced by Husserl's privileging meaning, monologically characterized, over intersubjective discourse:

> It is precisely changes in the content of meaning that Husserl, because of his conception, cannot recognize since, over against psychologistic and sociologistic relativism, he preserves the identity of meaning as the foundation of all intersubjectively valid propositional truth.[45]

While Apel does recognize a difference between the early and the late Husserl, he is not clear as to what it is. The few suggestions we do find tell us that Husserl was involved in a "Cartesian radicalization of the transcendental question" but that his "methodological solipsism" aligns itself with the approach of Neopositivism in the logic of science.[46] In Apel's analysis, Husserl believes that "everything I can intend [*meinen*] is simply and solely in my consciousness";[47] thus, Husserl's position is the antithesis of Apel's own privileging of an intersubjective linguistic community as the transcendental field from which analysis proceeds. Since even the concept "simply and solely in my consciousness" presupposes a "public language game," we are driven outside the borders of monological consciousness in search of a proper ground for analysis. Apel brings his point home with force:

> The consequence . . . appears to be that a *reflective* justification or critique of intentional achievements [*Leistungen*] is simply not possible. It is obvious that one cannot, as Husserl wants it, step behind language by means of a reflection upon the "intentional achievements of a pure consciousness." The intentional capacity is itself conditioned a priori through the "inner form" or the "deep grammar" of language whose use is "acquired" (Wittgenstein) with the rules of significant action and with the rules of understanding a world, including self-understanding. An objective structural analysis of language-games, or of more encompassing systems of symbols and understanding, takes over the place of a reflective understanding of oneself and, through analogy, of the other.[48]

Jürgen Habermas, however, has a much more subtle and sophisticated approach to Husserl. While earlier work does criticize Husserl for an insufficient understanding of the limits of his theory of constitution,[49] Habermas, having a good command of the later work, is able to think of Husserl beyond the constraints of a Cartesian program. In fact, I think it is fair to say that Habermas clearly appropriates Husserl's notion of a correlational a priori in his theory of communicative action. The first volume of his *Theorie des kommunikativen Handelns* could be construed as a piece of "noetic" analysis that has severed the notion of subjectivity from that of consciousness and translates Husserl's concept of *Leistung* into a theory of speech-acts; the second volume introduces the notion of the world as the correlation to communicative interaction and thus gives a "noematic" account. It is the correlation of linguistic interaction and world that constitutes the transcendental field of communicative action.[50]

Of course, the shared picture of Husserl should not blur the very different interests of these various approaches. Even though they detract from certain doctrines and the idea that methodological solipsism will provide us with an adequate method for the whole of philosophy, analytic commentators argue the importance and relevance of particular theories of Husserl for a host of current issues in analytic epistemology and cognitive science, using him often to correct some of their shortcomings. At the same time there is a tendency to take many of Husserl's late texts that collide with this picture of his method as marginal and inconsistent, even though none of the analysts have an interest in arguing for the viability of such a method and would be happy to find alternatives. The deconstructive and Critical Theory approaches keep the theory and the method as a whole tightly connected in order to then place them (along with analytic philosophy as well) within a tradition whose resources are now spent. Husserl's later texts, at best, are but inconclusive and inconsequential signposts, showing us the way beyond his own framework. Thus it is precisely Husserl's theory of intentionality, a version of which most analytic commentators want to embrace, that postmodern and Critical Theory studies want to deconstruct or submit to a form of ideology critique, i.e., not "refute" and "reject" but circumscribe by exploring the limits of its discourse. Still, all these groups, with such radically different starting points, interests, and even methods, provide us with a fairly uniform "reading" of Husserl. Or at least the *outcome* of their readings is such that we can speak of a standard picture of Husserl's program.

What I am calling the standard picture draws from earlier work, in particular the previously mentioned studies of Levinas, Berger, and Ricoeur in France and, unfortunately, to a far lesser extent, from Eugen Fink[51] and Oskar Becker[52] in Germany; but it took its present form and was established during the 1970s and 1980s. With few exceptions it has continued to define the parameters of more recent studies of Husserl's phenomenology. In particular it is the placing in these various studies of what he called genetic phenomenology that demonstrates this. Either it is not even mentioned, as in Dummett's otherwise insightful account of Husserl,[53] or it is viewed as an afterthought, perhaps as an effort to recuperate areas missing or marginalized by his transcendental method, or it is integrated by restricting it to an explication of implicated meanings and, thus, to what Husserl calls constitutive analysis, as in Ströker's study.[54] Even Kockelman's extensive study devoted to Husserl's method gives it only a few pages.[55] Among the more recent works only Bell[56] recognizes its importance but understandably struggles to place it in relation to the program of *Ideas I*.

Notes

INTRODUCTION

1. *Krisis*, 366; Eng. trans., 355.

Unless otherwise noted, all page reference to Husserl's German texts will be from the *Husserliana*. The reader should be aware, however, that the *Husserliana* volumes include material over and above any originally published text of Husserl. For example, *Formale und transzendentale Logik* contains not only the text *Formale und transzendentale Logik: Versuch einer Kritik der logischen Vernunft*, which originally appeared in *Jahrbuch für Philosophie und phänomenologische Forschung*, Vol. 10 (Halle a.d. Saale: Max Niemeyer, 1929), v–xiii, 1–298, but also several manuscripts from that period that were not published by Husserl himself. When in doubt, consult the list of abbreviated titles and the bibliography of Husserl's work in this volume.

2. Letter to Paul Natorp, February 1, 1922, *Briefwechsel*, 3/5, 151–152. The volumes of Husserl's correspondence are as follows: Vol. 3/1, *Die Brentanoschule;* Vol. 3/2, *Die Münchener Phänomenologen;* Vol. 3/3, *Die Göttinger Schule;* Vol. 3/4, *Die Freiburger Schule;* Vol. 3/5, *Die Neukantianer;* Vol. 3/6, *Philosophische Briefe;* Vol. 3/7, *Wissenschaftler Korrespondenz;* Vol. 3/8, *Institutionelle Schreiben;* Vol. 3/9, *Familienbriefe;* Vol. 3/10, *Einführung und Register.*

3. See "Appendix: The Standard Interpretation," pp. 393–404 below.

4. Yet even here I am dealing primarily with Husserl's descriptive or explanatory strategies and using this to understand his many "ways" into phenomenological analysis. While I must wait until chapter 6 to discuss this, I am convinced that the contrast between static and genetic analysis is more basic in that it gives us a deepening of method that then allows us to return to the question of "starting points." For an important study of Husserl's ways into transcendental analysis, see Iso Kern, *Husserl und Kant: Eine Untersuchung über Husserls Verhältnis zu Kant und zum Neukantianismus, Phaenomenologica*, Vol. 16 (The Hague: Martinus Nijhoff, 1964), 192–245; a slightly edited version of this chapter appeared as "Die drei Wege zur transzendentalen phänomenologischen Reduktion in der Philosophie Edmund Husserls," *Tijdschrift voor Filosofie* 24 (1962): 303–349; "The Three Ways to the Transcendental Phenomenological Reduction in the Philosophy of Edmund Husserl," *Husserl: Expositions and Appraisals*, ed. F. Elliston and P. McCormick (Notre Dame: University of Notre Dame Press, 1977), 126–149.

5. Ludwig Landgrebe's "Husserl's Departure from Cartesianism" was the first to show the movement beyond the Cartesian program of *Ideas I* from within

Husserl's own texts. See his "Husserls Abschied vom Cartesianismus," *Philosophische Rundschau* 9 (1962): 133–177; reprinted in his *Der Weg der Phänomenologie* (Gütersloh: Gerd Mohn, 1967), 163–206; also in "Husserl's Departure from Cartesianism," *The Phenomenology of Edmund Husserl: Six Essays,* ed. Donn Welton (Ithaca, N.Y.: Cornell University Press, 1981), 66–121.

6. Klaus Held, *Lebendige Gegenwart: Die Frage nach der Seinsweise des transzendentalen Ich bei Edmund Husserl, entwickelt am Leitfaden der Zeitproblematik, Phaenomenologica,* Vol. 23 (The Hague: Martinus Nijhoff, 1966).

7. Elmar Holenstein, *Phänomenologie der Assoziation: Zu Struktur und Funktion eines Grundprinzips der passiven Genesis bei E. Husserl, Phaenomenologica,* Vol. 44 (The Hague: Martinus Nijhoff, 1972).

8. Paul Janssen, *Geschichte und Lebenswelt: Ein Beitrag zur Diskussion von Husserls Spätwerk, Phaenomenologica,* Vol. 35 (The Hague: Martinus Nijhoff, 1970); David Carr, *Phenomenology and the Problem of History* (Evanston, Ill.: Northwestern University Press, 1974).

9. Vásquez Hoyos, *Intentionalität als Verantwortung, Phaenomenologica,* Vol. 67 (The Hague: Martinus Nijhoff, 1976).

10. Guido Antonio de Almeida, *Sinn und Inhalt in der genetischen Phänomenologie E. Husserls, Phaenomenologica,* Vol. 47 (The Hague: Martinus Nijhoff, 1972).

11. John Drummond, *Husserlian Intentionality and Non-foundational Realism: Noema and Object* (Dordrecht: Kluwer Academic Publishers, 1990).

12. See Robert Sokolowski, *Husserl's Concept of Constitution, Phaenomenologica,* Vol. 18 (The Hague: Martinus Nijhoff, 1964), and *Husserlian Meditations: How Words Present Things* (Evanston, Ill.: Northwestern University Press, 1974).

13. Antonio Aguirre, *Genetische Phänomenologie und Reduktion, Phaenomenologica,* Vol. 38 (The Hague: Martinus Nijhoff, 1970).

14. Carr, "Genetic Phenomenology," *Phenomenology and the Problem of History,* chapter 3.

15. Klaus Held, "Einleitung [I]," to Edmund Husserl, *Die phänomenologische Methode: Ausgewählte Texte I,* ed. Klaus Held (Stuttgart: Phillip Reclam, 1985), 5–51; "Einleitung [II]" to Edmund Husserl, *Phänomenologie der Lebenswelt: Ausgewählte Texte II,* ed. Klaus Held (Stuttgart: Phillip Reclam, 1986), 5–53.

16. Rudolf Bernet, Iso Kern, and Eduard Marbach, *Edmund Husserl: Darstellung seines Denkens* (Hamburg: Felix Meiner Verlag, 1989); *An Introduction to Husserlian Phenomenology* (Evanston, Ill.: Northwestern University Press, 1993). The seventh chapter, on the relationship between static and genetic method, was written by Kern.

17. Anthony Steinbock, *Home and Beyond* (Evanston, Ill.: Northwestern University Press, 1996).

18. They are found as Iso Kern's long introductions to the three volumes of Husserl's texts he edited on the issue of intersubjectivty: "Einleitung [I] des Herausgebers," in *Intersubjektivität I,* xvii–xlviii; "Einleitung [II] des Herausgebers," in *Intersubjektivität II,* xvii–xxxv; "Einleitung [III] der Herausgebers," in *Intersubjektivitat III,* xv–lxx. In chapters 5, 6, and 8 we will draw heavily from his materials. An earlier study of his, in addition to being the best book on the subject, is also especially helpful in its discussion of manuscript materials. See Kern, *Husserl und Kant.*

19. Karl Schuhmann, *Husserl-Chronik: Denk- und Lebensweg Husserls, Husserliana Dokumente,* Vol. 1 (The Hague: Martinus Nijhoff, 1977).

20. Cairns, *Conversations.*

21. Eugen Fink, *VI. Cartesianische Meditation,* Part I, *Die Idee einer transzendentalen Methodenlehre;* Part II, *Ergänzungsband, Husserliana Dokumente,* Vols. 2/1 and 2/2 (Dordrecht: Kluwer Academic Publishers, 1988). Ron Bruzina, "Translator's Introduction," Eugen Fink, *Sixth Cartesian Meditation: The Idea of a Transcendental Theory of Method,* trans. Ronald Bruzina (Bloomington: Indiana University Press, 1994), vii–xcii. See also Ronald Bruzina, "Die Notizen Eugen Finks zur Umarbeitung von Edmund Husserls Cartesianischen Meditationen," *Husserl Studies* 6 (1989): 97–128; Ronald Bruzina, "Solitude and Community in the Work of Philosophy: Husserl and Fink, 1928–1938," *Man and World* 22 (1989): 287–314.

22. The various editions of the *Logical Investigations* are as follows: *Logische Untersuchungen,* 2 vols. (Halle a.d. Saale: Max Niemeyer, 1900 and 1901); *Logische Untersuchungen* [2nd rev. ed.]; *Logische Untersuchungen,* Vol. 1: *Prolegomena zur reinen Logik,* ed. Elmar Holenstein, *Husserliana,* Vol. 18 (The Hague: Martinus Nijhoff, 1975); Vol. 2: *Untersuchungen zur Phänomenologie und Theorie der Erkenntnis,* Part I, ed. Ursula Panzer, *Husserliana,* Vol. 19 (The Hague: Martinus Nijhoff, 1984); Part II, ed. Ursula Panzer, *Husserliana,* Vol. 20 (The Hague: Martinus Nijhoff, 1984). Because of accessibility and convention, all citations from the *Logische Untersuchungen* will be according to the pages in the second edition published by Niemeyer. These page numbers can be found in the margins of the *Husserliana* volumes.

23. The various editions of *Ideas I* are as follows. It was first published as *Ideen zu einer reinen Phänomenologie und phänomenologischen Philosophie,* Vol. 1: *Allgemeine Einführung in die reine Phänomenologie,* in *Jahrbuch für Philosophie und phänomenologische Forschung* (Halle a.d. Saale: Max Niemeyer, 1913), 1–323. The first *Husserliana* edition was *Ideen zu einer reinen Phänomenologie und phänomenologischen Philosophie,* Vol. 1: *Allgemeine Einführung in die reine Phänomenologie,* ed. Walter Biemel, *Husserliana,* Vol. 3 (The Hague: Martinus Nijhoff, 1950). This has been superseded by *Ideen zu einer reinen Phänomenologie und phänomenologischen Philosophie,* Vol. 1: *Allgemeine Einführung in die reine Phänomenologie,* Vol. 2: *Ergänzende Texte* (1912–1929), ed. Karl Schuhmann, *Husserliana,* Vols. 3/a and 3/b (The Hague: Martinus Nijhoff, 1976). The best English translation is *Ideas Pertaining to a Pure Phenomenology and to a Phenomenological Philosophy,* Vol. 1: *General Introduction to a Pure Phenomenology,* trans. F. Kersten, *Collected Works,* Vol. 2 (The Hague: Martinus Nijhoff, 1983). Because of the different *Husserliana* editions, we will always cite the original pages of *Ideen I.* The first English translation is Edmund Husserl, *Ideas: General Introduction to Pure Phenomenology,* trans. W. R. Boyce Gibson (London: George Allen & Unwin, 1931). The Kersten translation is far superior and so will be cited as Eng. trans.

24. See note 1 above.

25. In the title, which reads *Formale und transzendentale Logik: Versuch einer Kritik der logischen Vernunft.*

26. *Zeitbewusstsein;* Eng. trans. *Ding und Raum.*

27. They are known as the Bernauer manuscripts on time and are presently being prepared for publication. For a comparison of Husserl and Heidegger on the

issue of temporality, see Rudolf Bernet, *Zeit und Zeitlichkeit bei Husserl und Heidegger, Phänomenologische Forschungen,* Vol. 14 (Freiburg: Verlag Karl Alber, 1983).

28. See my "Intentionality and Language in Husserl's Phenomenology," *Review of Metaphysics* 27 (1973): 261–297.

29. This text, known as the "Sixth Meditation," was one that he worked on extensively with Eugen Fink. For this and the documents surrounding it, see Fink, *VI. Cartesianische Meditation; Sixth Cartesian Meditation.*

30. Cairns reports as follows after asking Husserl how he wrote his books: "When it comes to a matter of writing a book he brushes aside all these manuscripts and writes freely and uninterruptedly, in a sort of trance. Thus the *Ideen* [I] and the *Formale und transzendentale Logik* were each written in six weeks. Certain additions to the *Ideen* [I] were made in proof, and Husserl can see today that these additions are inferior to the main text" (*Conversations,* 61).

31. Ingarden studied with Husserl in Gottingen from the Summer Semester of 1912 to the Summer Semester of 1914 and then again in the Summer Semester of 1915; he was also with him in the Summer Semester of 1916 and the final months of the Winter Semester of 1916/17. See Schuhmann's note in *Briefwechsel,* 3/3, 175.

32. Letter to Roman Ingarden, December 24, 1921, *Briefwechsel,* 3/3, 215.

33. See Rudolf Boehm, "Einleitung," Husserl, *Zeitbewusstsein,* xxxii–xxxiii.

34. Rudolf Bernet, "Einleitung" and "Editorischer Bericht," Edmund Husserl, *Texte zur Phänomenologie des inneren Zeitbewusstseins (1893–1917),* ed. Rudolf Bernet (Hamburg: Felix Meiner Verlag, 1985), xi–lxvii, lxix–lxxiii.

35. Cairns, *Conversations,* August 17, 1931, 16.

36. Cairns, *Conversations,* August 28, 1931, 28.

37. See Ludwig Landgrebe, "Vorwort," *Erfahrung und Urteil,* v–xii; "Editor's Foreword," Eng. trans., 3–8, and also Kern, "Einleitung [III] des Herausgebers," xvi. Cairns has this interesting exchange to report: "Upon my arrival Husserl asked me what I had been doing, and I replied that I had been working on the first part of the Logic [i.e., *Formale und transzendentale Logik*]. He asked if I had difficulties there, and I told him no. Then you are quite advanced, he said. He proceeded to say that he no longer remembered what was there, that he always had to have Fink tell him what was in his books." *Conversations,* September 17, 1931, 32. This was only three years after the *Logik* was published.

38. Letter to Alexander Pfänder, January 6, 1931, *Briefwechsel,* 3/2, 180.

39. Letter to Natorp, February 1, 1922, *Briefwechsel,* 3/5, 151–152.

40. Letter to Adolphe Grimme, March 5, 1931, *Briefwechsel,* 3/3, 90.

41. See his *Briefwechsel* and see note 2 above and bibliography for a complete listing of the volumes in it.

42. For a historical reconstruction of the decisive phases in Husserl's thought that complements the analysis here, see my "The Development of Husserl's Phenomenology," the introduction to *The Essential Husserl: Basic Writings in Transcendental Phenomenology,* ed. Donn Welton (Bloomington: Indiana University Press, 1999).

43. Michael Dummett, *The Origins of Analytical Philosophy* (Cambridge, Mass.: Harvard University Press, 1994), 2.

1. THE PHENOMENOLOGICAL TURN

1. "... ich kann nicht anders, als ehrlicherweise sagen (wenn ich nicht durch angelernte Theorien schon verwirrt bin): ich sehe jetzt Dinge, diese Dinge hier, sie selbst, ich sehe nicht Bilder von ihnen, nicht bloße Zeichen. Ich kann mich freilich auch täuschen. Aber woran erweist sich die Täuschung? An einem sich immer weider erprobenden Sehen als Sehen wirklicher Sachen selbst. Daß alles Sehen eine Täuschung ist [= wäre], hebt den Sinn der Reden von Täuschung auf." Manuscript, "Einleitung in die Philosophie," F I 29 (1922/23), 3a; transcription, 33.

2. *Analysen zur passiven Synthesis,* 3.

3. *Conversations,* November 12, 1931, 39.

4. Because our analysis here is introductory and provisional, we are blurring somewhat the important differences between profile, determination, and real property.

5. See Welton, "Verbindende Namen/Verbundene Gegenstände," Sections III and IV, for an elaboration of Frege's theory of predicates.

6. *Erste Philosophie II,* 45. Notice that this text was composed (1923/24) before Husserl had even the manuscript of Heidegger's *Being and Time* in hand. We will deal with this in detail in chapter 5.

7. *Krisis,* 163; after Eng. trans., 160.

8. Normally *Bedeutung* is translated as "meaning" while *Sinn* is rendered as "sense." Kersten gives *Bedeutung* as "signification." Macquarrie and Robinson also translate *Bedeutung* as "signification" but then use both "sense" and "meaning" for *Sinn.* In Husserl, *Bedeutung* is restricted to the linguistic sphere while *Sinn* is broader in application in that it applies to the experiential field as a whole, to the "prelinguistic" as well. See *Ideen I,* 256f.; Eng. trans., 294f. Heidegger shares this distinction but then characterizes *Sinn* as that which belongs to the framework of understanding and thus treats perception as itself a type of interpretation. "The 'as' makes up the structure of the explicitness of something that is understood. It constitutes the interpretation." See *Sein und Zeit,* 149; after Eng. trans., 189. See also 151ff.; Eng. trans., 192f. We will deal with Heidegger at length in chapters 5 and 14.

9. See *Vorlesungen über Bedeutungslehre: Sommersemester 1908,* ed. Ursula Panzer, *Husserliana,* Vol. 26 (Dordrecht: Kluwer Academic Publishers, 1989), especially chapters 1 and 2.

10. My descriptions here echo Robert Sokolowski's analysis of this phenomenon. See his *Presence and Absence: A Philosophical Investigation of Language and Being* (Bloomington: Indiana University Press, 1978), chapters 1 and 6 to 8. I am appropriating, with some modifications, his distinction between reports and claims (propositions) throughout this section. A first formulation of this distinction can be found in Husserl's *Formal and Transcendental Logic* (Section 89). As we will see in chapter 14, it is absolutely central to Heidegger's account in *Being and Time.*

11. See J. L. Austin, *How to Do Things with Words,* 2nd ed. (Cambridge, Mass.: Harvard University Press, [1962], 1975); John Searle, *Speech Acts: An Essay in the Philosophy of Language* (Cambridge: Cambridge University Press, 1969), and *Ex-*

pression and Meaning: Studies in the Theory of Speech Acts (Cambridge: Cambridge University Press, 1979).

12. The implications of Husserl's elimination of indication will be discussed in chapter 8 below. For our purposes now we need to stress only the fact that even the First Investigation gives us an analysis of the indicating and the expressing function of signs in communication (Sections 1 to 7) before it introduces its treatment of expressions in the monologue (Section 8).

13. We will take this up in the next chapter.

14. Both Husserl and Heidegger shared this view of the fourfold structure of phenomena, just as both attempted to see each of the levels as derived from yet deeper-lying transformations. Held, whose analysis I am following here, emphasized its importance in seminars given at Stony Brook during the Spring Semester of 1991.

15. Cf. *Ideen I,* 270; Eng. trans., 312.

16. *Sein und Zeit,* 151, 158; Eng. trans., 192f., 200. Cf. 83; Eng. trans., 114f.

17. Cf. *Ideen I,* 209; Eng. trans., 244.

18. Cf. *Sein und Zeit,* 84; Eng. trans., 116.

19. As Husserl gives it final formulation in the *Crisis,* it is the struggle between "objectivism" and "transcendentalism" that defines the meaning of the history of modern intellectual life. See Section 14. Thus the possibility that Husserl falls back into the former goes to the heart of his own philosophical enterprise.

20. This warning is repeatedly found throughout Heidegger's writings in the 1920s. See *Sein und Zeit,* 63ff., 130; Eng. trans., 92ff., 168; *Die Grundprobleme der Phänomenologie,* ed. Friedrich-Wilhelm von Herrmann, Gesamtausgabe, Vol. 24 (Frankfurt am Main: Vittorio Klostermann, 1989), 233–242; *The Basic Problems of Phenomenology,* trans. Albert Hofstadter (Bloomington: Indiana University Press, 1982), 164–170. We will return to this point in the latter part of this work.

2. DESCRIPTIVE EIDETICS

1. *Phänomenologische Psychologie,* 27–28; after Eng. trans., 19–20, 21.

2. Letter to Ingarden, November 13, 1931, *Briefwechsel,* 3/3, 278–281.

3. Immanuel Kant, *Kritik der reinen Vernunft* [1st ed. 1781; 2nd ed. 1787], ed. Raymund Schmidt (Hamburg: Felix Meiner Verlag, 1952); *Critique of Pure Reason,* trans. Norman Kemp Smith (London: Macmillan Press, 1933).

4. Ibid., B221–224; Eng. trans., 210–212.

5. *Krisis,* 103; Eng. trans., 100.

6. Ibid., 106; Eng. trans., 104.

7. Ibid., 102; after Eng. trans., 99.

8. Ibid., 118; after Eng. trans., 115–116. Kant, of course, cannot be dispatched so easily, and even this text worries about how it can really set its method of "questioning back" in contrast to Kant's regressive procedure. Once the notion of intuition undergoes "considerable expansion," as it will in a moment and then time and again throughout this work, an element of construction becomes inescapable.

9. *Ideen I,* second part.

10. *Ideen III,* 101; Eng. trans., 87.

11. On the difference between clarification and explication, see ibid., 94–105; Eng. trans., 80–90.

12. See chapters 3 and 4 of the third part of *Ideen I.*

13. Cf. *Krisis,* 169, 154; Eng. trans., 166, 151–152. See *Ideen I,* 187–189; Eng. trans., 220–222.

14. *Ideen I,* 287, 294; Eng. trans., 332, 339.

15. Almost all the standard accounts would take what we have just outlined as a sketch of the parameters of Husserl's phenomenology. We will see, however, that a full analysis of its depth requires more than what can be provided by an account of the interdependence of the as- and for-structure.

16. Husserl, *Phänomenologische Psychologie,* 27; after Eng. trans., 21.

17. Jürgen Habermas, *Vorstudien und Ergänzungen zur Theorie des kommunikativen Handelns* (Frankfurt am Main: Suhrkamp, 1984), 37.

18. Ms. B III 10 (1921), 22–30a, published in *Analysen zur passiven Synthesis,* 336–345.

19. We should pause to deal with a terminological problem here. We just employed the distinction *Ideas III* introduces between *Verdeutlichung,* making vague and nebulous terms transparent, and *Klärung,* making things clear by recourse to optimal perceptual experience. It is tempting to translate *"erklärende Phänomenologie"* as "clarificatory phenomenology." The difficulty, however, is that the original notion of "clarification" belongs to static analysis or what Husserl here calls "descriptive phenomenology"; and thus it would be unwise to use the same term to characterize genetic analysis, as Husserl does with "erklärende Phänomenologie." The term "explication" will not do either, as Husserl himself on different occasions uses *Explikation* to interpret both *Verdeutlichung* and *Klärung.* For the first, see "Vom Ursprung der Geometrie," *Krisis,* 374; "The Origin of Geometry," *Crisis,* 364. For the second, see *Erfahrung und Urteil,* 124ff.; Eng. trans., 112ff. Above we restricted "explication" to translating *Verdeutlichung.* The term "explanation" is used with some misgivings. This is "explanation" in the context of an account of "origins," a phenomenological notion, not "beginnings," a natural scientific concept. It is not a question of causal explanation but of structural interdependence. Husserl, as Kant before him, draws an emphatic contrast between *Anfang* and *Ursprung.* Cf. *Analysen zur passiven Synthesis,* 338f.

20. Ibid., 340.

21. Ibid.

22. Ibid.

23. Letter to Boyce Gibson, January 7, 1932, *Briefwechsel,* 3/6, 142. There is a parallel extension of the term ontology, as when Husserl speaks of phenomenology as a "truly universal ontology" in contrast to "ontology in positivity." See "Der Encyclopaedia Britannica Artikel," *Phänomenologische Psychologie,* 297; "Phenomenology" [Encyclopedia Britannica article], *Shorter Works,* 32.

24. *Analysen zur passiven Synthesis,* 345.

25. Ibid., 340.

26. Ibid.

27. *Krisis,* 173f.; Eng. trans., 170f.

28. In the first edition of the *Investigations* the term is used to speak of (a) "the constitution of the species," (b) a part belonging to a whole, as in "the parts

that constitute" the sensible object, and (c) the way in which categorial objectivities, such as states-of-affairs, have an "interpretative form" whose constitution points to founding objectivities and acts. For (a) see *Logische Untersuchungen* (1st ed.), I, 117–121; (2nd ed.), I, 117–121; Eng. trans., I, 140–143. For (b) and (c) see (1st ed.), II, 624–625; (2nd ed.), II/2, 152–153; Eng. trans., II, 792–793. While this anticipates one aspect of its use in *Ideas I,* it is little more than a general term for the relationship between wholes and parts: the whole is constituted or composed of its elements or constituent parts. Still, the reference to "sensibility" and "understanding" at the end of Section 47 [(1st ed.), II, 624; (2nd ed.), II/2, 152; Eng. trans., II, 792] echoes Kant's first *Critique,* and so we may assume that this is one of the rare places in the six investigations proper where his presence is felt.

29. *Logische Untersuchungen,* I, 234; II/1, 1–3; Eng. trans., I, 230, 249–250; *Ideen I,* 136–141; Eng. trans., 164–170.

30. See *Ideen I,* 138; Eng. trans., 166. Because the following is a general account and because we are not concerned to lay out the role of (linguistically formed) judgments in the formation of essences, I allow Husserl's notions of concept and essence to slide into each other here. For an excellent discussion of their difference see Sokolowski, *Husserlian Meditations,* Section 23.

31. For this reason alone, Dreyfus's attempt to park Husserl in the camp of computational models of cognition, by arguing that he, too, uses rules to clarify concepts, is misguided. See Hubert Dreyfus, "Introduction," *Husserl, Intentionality, and Cognitive Science,* ed. Hubert Dreyfus (Cambridge, Mass.: MIT Press, 1982), 9–14.

32. One could speak with good reason of a phenomenological reduction even though, strictly speaking, we do not yet have a transcendental account. Husserl was convinced that the *Logical Investigations* employed it before the transcendental turn of *Ideas I.* Even after that turn, we find lectures given in 1925 using the notion of phenomenological reduction in a way that spans the difference between transcendental phenomenology and phenomenological psychology even though they view the latter as framed by the "natural attitude." See *Phänomenologische Psychologie,* 48, 188; Eng. trans., 34, 144. These issues will occupy us in chapter 6.

33. *Ideen I,* 10f.; Eng. trans., 9. Cf. *Logische Untersuchungen,* II/1, 109; Eng. trans., I, 339f.

34. *Ideen I,* 40; Eng. trans., 41.

35. Ibid.

36. *Logische Untersuchungen,* II/1, 114f.; Eng. trans., I, 344.

37. *Ideen I,* 10–11; Eng. trans., 9. Italics removed.

38. Cf. *Logische Untersuchungen,* I, 101; Eng. trans., I, 128.

39. For example, ibid., II/1, 102–103; Eng. trans., I, 331–332.

40. Ibid., II/1, 103; Eng. trans., I, 331–332.

3. CATEGORIAL PHENOMENOLOGY AND ONTOLOGY

1. *Logische Untersuchungen,* II/1, 102; Eng. trans., I, 331.

2. *Krisis,* 360–361; after Eng. trans., 347.

3. A note on terms is required. We will distinguish between empirical, pure, and exact essences. The contrast between empirical and pure essences is described

by Husserl as a difference between universals (*Allgemeinen*) or empirical universals and eidos (*Eidos*) or pure universals in *Phänomenologische Psychologie,* 79; Eng. trans., 59, and *Erfahrung und Urteil,* 385, 409; Eng. trans., 321, 339.

4. In the opening sections of *Ideas II,* for example, we find Husserl referring to the necessity of "varying freely" as we construct regional ontologies. See *Ideen II,* 34; Eng. trans., 37.

5. *Logische Untersuchungen,* II/1, 109; Eng. trans., I, 340.

6. Ibid., II/1, 113; Eng. trans., I, 343.

7. *Erfahrung und Urteil,* 422, 429; Eng. trans., 349, 354.

8. Ibid., 431; Eng. trans., 356.

9. Ibid., 409; Eng. trans., 339. Cf. *Formale und transzendentale Logik,* 380ff.

10. *Ideen I,* 140; Eng. trans., 168, altered.

11. Ibid., 138; after Eng. trans., 166.

12. Cf. ibid., 141f.; Eng. trans., 169f.

13. Ibid., 140; Eng. trans., 168, altered.

14. Ibid.

15. *Phänomenologische Psychologie,* 75; after Eng. trans., 56.

16. Cf. ibid.

17. In Section 9 of *Phänomenologische Psychologie,* Husserl concentrates only on the intuition of pure essences and generally calls this process "ideation." But pp. 78f. (Eng. trans., 58f.) contrasts the intuition of universals and of pure essences in such a way that we should think of the latter as a further modification of the process already in play with the former. Thus I take the liberty of using the terms "empirical" and "pure ideation" rather than "empirical generalization" and "ideation." I also assume, contrary to the impression given in *Experience and Judgment,* that eidetic variation is in play in both, the difference being between bound and free variation.

It may be that the first edition of the *Logical Investigations* (1900–1901) already had the contrast between ideation and what *Ideas I* (1913) speaks of as idealization. When Husserl published the second edition of the first five investigations in 1913, he changed a passage in the Third Investigation (II/1, 245; Eng. trans., II, 450f., altered) to reflect this:

> Plainly the essential forms of all intuitive data are not in principle to be brought under "exact" or "ideal" notions, such as we have in mathematics. The spatial shape of the perceived tree, taken precisely as a "moment" found in the perceived tree as such in the relevant perception, is no geometric shape, no ideal or exact shape in the sense of exact geometry. Just so a seen color as such is no ideal color, whose Species occupies an ideal point in the color-pyramid. The essences which direct ideation elicits from intuitive data are "inexact" essences; they should not be confused with the "exact" essences, which are Ideas in the Kantian sense and which (like an "ideal point," an ideal surface or solid, or ideal Species of color in the ideal color-pyramid) arise through a peculiar "idealization."

For the parallel passage in *Ideas I,* see pp. 138–139; Eng. trans., 166–167.

18. *Phänomenologische Psychologie,* 77–78; after Eng. trans., 58.

19. Ibid., 73; after Eng. trans., 54.

20. Ibid., 78; after Eng. trans., 58.

21. Ibid., 80; after Eng. trans., 60.
22. *Logische Untersuchungen,* I, xiv; Eng. trans., I, 48.
23. *Phänomenologische Psychologie,* 74; after Eng. trans., 55.
24. Ibid., 77; after Eng. trans., 57.
25. Ibid.
26. *Erfahrung und Urteil,* 431; Eng. trans., 356.
27. Ibid.
28. Cf. *Phänomenologische Psychologie,* 79; Eng. trans., 59, and *Erfahrung und Urteil,* 425; Eng. trans., 351.
29. Cf. *Ideen I,* 140; Eng. trans., 168.
30. *Phänomenologische Psychologie,* 79; Eng. trans., 59.
31. Ibid. Eng. trans., altered. Cf. *Erfahrung und Urteil,* 422; Eng. trans., 349.
32. *Erfahrung und Urteil,* 409; Eng. trans., 339.
33. Ibid. Eng. trans., altered.
34. Ibid., 410; Eng. trans., 340, altered.
35. Ibid., 423f.; Eng. trans., 350, altered. Italics altered.
36. Ibid.
37. Ibid., 410; Eng. trans., 340.
38. Alan Plantinga, "Transworld Identity or Worldbound Individuals," in Stephen Schwartz, ed., *Naming, Necessity, and Natural Kinds* (Ithaca, N.Y.: Cornell University Press, 1977), 245–266; J. N. Mohanty, *The Possibility of Transcendental Philosophy, Phaenomenologica,* Vol. 98 (The Hague: Martinus Nijhoff, 1985), 35–39.
39. *Ideen I,* 90; Eng. trans., 108.
40. Ibid., 88; Eng. trans., 106.
41. Mohanty, *The Possibility of a Transcendental Philosophy,* 37–39.
42. *Erfahrung und Urteil,* 423f.; Eng. trans., 350f., altered. The effort by McIntyre and Smith to explicate Husserl's notion of meaning (and noema) in terms of possible worlds runs into two problems: (a) meaning and noema are in play in our apprehension of empirical universals, which Husserl construes as universals of the given world in contrast to possible worlds; and (b) possible worlds can be introduced apart from the phenomenological reflection upon intentionality. Drummond is correct when he argues that the admission of possible objects should not be confused with admission of possible worlds. The difference between actual and possible objects can be accommodated within the actual world, as this addition to the theory of empirical essences shows. See Ronald McIntyre and David Smith, *Husserl and Intentionality: A Study of Mind, Meaning, and Language* (Dordrecht: D. Reidel, 1982), 296ff., and Drummond, *Husserlian Intentionality and Non-Foundational Realism,* 218.
43. *Erfahrung und Urteil,* 389; Eng. trans., 324.
44. Ibid., 390; after Eng. trans., 325.
45. *Ideen I,* 27; Eng. trans., 27.
46. *Erfahrung und Urteil,* 411; Eng. trans., 341.
47. Ibid., 425; Eng. trans., 351f.
48. Ibid., 426; after Eng. trans., 352. Italics removed.
49. *Ideen I,* 135; Eng. trans., 163.

50. See the very suggestive article by Tamara Horowitz, "A Priori Truth," *Journal of Philosophy* 82/5 (May 1985): 229.

51. Ibid., 231.

52. After ibid., 231.

53. Ibid.

54. *Ideen I*, 29; Eng. trans., 29.

55. Ibid.

56. *Erfahrung und Urteil*, 435; after Eng. trans., 359.

57. *Ideen I*, 30; Eng. trans., 31.

58. Ibid., 31, 297–299; Eng. trans., 31, 342–344. On the diverse and manifold uses of the notion of *a priori* in Husserl, see Mohanty, *The Possibility of a Transcendental Philosophy*, esp. 104–106.

59. *Erfahrung und Urteil*, 432; Eng. trans., 356.

60. Cf. *Formale und transzendentale Logic*, 90–93; Eng. trans., 86–89. However, cf. p. 111; Eng. trans., p. 105.

61. Cf. ibid., 110–135; Eng. trans., 105–129.

62. Ibid., 76–77, 113; Eng. trans., 72, 107.

63. Ibid., 111–113, 119–120; Eng. trans., 106–108, 114. Husserl gives examples of such formal categories: object, property, relationship, plurality, etc.

64. Ibid., 58–60, 142; Eng. trans., 53–55, 137.

65. Ibid.

66. Ibid., 133; Eng. trans., 127.

67. See Susanne Bachelard, *A Study of Husserl's Formal and Transcendental Logic*, trans. Lester Embree (Evanston, Ill.: Northwestern University Press, 1968), and Sokolowski, *Husserlian Meditations*, 9–17, 271–289. See also Rudolf Bernet's first chapter in Bernet et al., *Edmund Husserl;* Eng. trans., *An Introduction to Husserlian Phenomenology*. And see Barry Smith, "Logic and Formal Ontology" as well as Gilbert T. Null, "Husserl's Doctrine of Essence," *Husserl's Phenomenology: A Textbook*, ed. J. N. Mohanty and William McKenna (Washington, D.C.: University Press of America, 1989), 29–67, 69–105.

68. *Formale und transzendentale Logic*, 94; Eng. trans., 90.

69. Ibid.

70. Ibid., 94–95; Eng. trans., 90–91.

71. Ibid. He speaks of the manifold as the totality of what would be referred to by any and all scientific theories. Quoting the *Prolegomena*, Husserl explains it in this way: "The objective correlate of the concept of a possible theory, determined only in its form, is the concept of *any possible province of cognition that would be governed by a theory having such a form*. Such a province, however, the mathematician (in his sphere) calls a *multiplicity*." Ibid., 94; after Eng. trans., 91.

72. *Ideen I*, 21–22; after Eng. trans., 21.

73. Bernet et al., *Edmund Husserl;* Eng. trans., *An Introduction to Husserlian Phenomenology*, 48–49.

74. *Phänomenologische Psychologie*, 28; after Eng. trans., 19–20.

75. *Logische Untersuchungen*, II/1, 12; Eng. trans., I, 257. Cf. Sections 4 and 5 of the Introduction to the *Investigations* for a full account of what he means by "analytic." This term will help us situate static analysis in relation to Husserl's

genetic phenomenology, first opened by a turn to an account of passive synthesis, a discipline that he called a "transcendental aesthetic." See chapter 8 below.

76. The discipline of formal ontology extends the logic of parts and whole introduced in the Third Investigation, while formal apophantics develops the analysis of pure grammar in the Fourth Investigation. Material ontologies, though they were not developed in the *Investigations,* follow from the discovery of part-whole relations in a determinate field of inquiry.

77. See *Formale und transzendentale Logic,* 93–97; Eng. trans., 90–93.

78. *Ideen II,* 27; Eng. trans., 29, calls these fields of sense "predicates."

79. Ibid., 186; Eng. trans., 195f.

80. Ibid., 2; Eng. trans., 4.

81. Ibid., 132, 186; Eng. trans., 139f., 195f.

82. Ibid., 187; Eng. trans., 197.

83. Ibid., 90, 142f.; Eng. trans., 96, 151f.

84. Ibid., 25, 186; Eng. trans., 27, 196.

85. Ibid., 187; Eng. trans., 196.

86. Ibid., 173–184; Eng. trans., 183–194.

87. Ibid., 25; Eng. trans., 27.

88. Ibid., 188; Eng. trans., 197f.

89. Ibid., 139, 142f.; Eng. trans., 146, 149f.

90. Ibid., 172–175; Eng. trans., 181–184.

91. On the difference between soul and person, see ibid., 139–140; Eng. trans., 146–147.

92. Ibid., 200, 242; Eng. trans., 210, 254. The concept of a "social act," which Husserl develops in contrast to the sociology of his day, is given extensive treatment in texts 9 and 10 in *Intersubjektivität II.*

93. Husserl speaks of social collectives as "comprehensive unities" and "personal" unities "of a higher order" in *Ideen II,* 242; Eng. trans., 254.

94. Ibid., 377f.; Eng. trans., 386f.

95. Ibid., 143; Eng. trans., 150.

96. *Ideen I,* 43–44; Eng. trans., 44. Italics removed.

97. These contrasts are found as early as the first section of *Ideas I* and are fully developed in the early parts of *Formal and Transcendental Logic.*

98. *Ideen I,* 139; Eng. trans., 167.

99. *Phänomenologische Psychologie,* 28; after Eng. trans., 21.

100. *Logische Untersuchungen,* II/1, 100; after Eng. trans., I, 329–330.

101. Ibid., II/1, 103; after Eng. trans., I, 332.

102. Ibid., I, 101; Eng. trans., I, 128.

103. Ibid., I, 159; Eng. trans., I, 172. I have found Bernet's analysis in Bernet et al., *Edmund Husserl;* Eng. trans., *An Introduction to Husserlian Phenomenology,* 37–38, especially helpful on this third point.

104. *Logische Untersuchungen,* I, 161; Eng. trans., I, 173.

105. Ibid., I, 159; Eng. trans., I, 171.

106. Ibid., I, 160–164; Eng. trans., I, 172–174.

107. Ibid., I, 173; Eng. trans., I, 181.

108. Ibid., I, 173; Eng. trans., I, 181–182.

109. See ibid., II/1, First Investigation, Section 18.

110. See Austin, *How to Do Things with Words,* and Searle, *Speech Acts.*

111. *Logische Untersuchungen,* II/1, 413; Eng. trans., II, 587. Italics removed.

112. In fact, he is not consistent here and also speaks not just of how the act is directed but also how the object is presented: "they present the same object, although 'in a different manner.'" Ibid., II/1, 414; Eng. trans., II, 588. The tension between the two descriptions will be resolved or at least built into the account of intentionality as Husserl introduces his theory of the noema in *Ideas I.* The *Investigations* does not yet have this, and its analyses remain one-sided, noetic.

113. *Logische Untersuchungen,* II/1, 415; Eng. trans., II, 589.

114. I will discuss the question of the matter or content of the act in the context of the problem of psychologism in sections B and C of chapter 10.

115. *Logische Untersuchungen,* II/1, 417; Eng. trans., II, 590.

116. Ibid., II/1, 411; Eng. trans., II, 586.

117. Ibid., II/1, 417; Eng. trans., II, 590.

118. Ibid., II/1, 418; Eng. trans., II, 591.

119. Ibid., II/1, 100–101; Eng. trans., I, 330.

120. Ibid., II/1, 312; Eng. trans., II, 506.

121. Ibid., II/1, 102; Eng. trans., I, 331.

122. See John Searle, *Minds, Brains, and Science* (Cambridge, Mass.: Harvard University Press, 1984).

123. *Logische Untersuchungen,* II/1, 97; Eng. trans., I, 327, altered.

124. Ibid., II/1, 98; after Eng. trans., I, 328.

125. Ibid., II/1, Section 6 of the "Introduction."

126. For a fuller analysis of this, see my *The Origins of Meaning: A Critical Study of the Thresholds of Husserlian Phenomenology, Phaenomenologica,* Vol. 88 (The Hague: Martinus Nijhoff, 1983), Part 3.

127. See Thomas Nenon, "Epistemological or Ontological Primacy: The Notion of Foundation in the *Logical Investigations,*" *Husserl in the Contemporary Context,* ed. Burt Hopkin (Dordrecht: Kluwer Academic Publishers, 1997).

128. Compare the changes Husserl made between the first and second edition to Section 6 of the "Introduction" to the second volume of the *Investigations.* See *Logische Untersuchungen* (1st ed.), II, 17–18, and *Logische Untersuchungen,* II/1, 16–19 in *Husserliana,* Vol. 19, 22–24; Eng. trans., I, 260–263.

129. Cf. *Logische Untersuchungen,* I, 169; Eng. trans., I, 179.

130. See chapter 10 for a detailed analysis of the question of psychologism.

131. See Karl Schuhmann, "Die Entwicklung der Sprechakttheorie in der Münchener Phänomenologie," *Sprache, Wirklichkeit, Bewußtsein,* ed. E. Orth (Freiburg: Verlag Karl Alber, 1988), 133–166. On Daubert, see Karl Schuhmann and Barry Smith, "Questions: An Essay in Daubertian Phenomenology," *Philosophy and Phenomenological Research* 47 (1986): 353–384. On Reinach, see *Speech Act and Sachverhalt: Reinach and the Foundations of Realist Phenomenology,* ed. K. Mulligan, *Primary Sources in Phenomenology,* Vol. 1 (Dordrecht: Martinus Nijhoff, 1987). Barry Smith himself agrees with them on this issue and speaks of the transcendental turn of *Ideas I* as a "great mystery." See "Logic and Formal Ontology," 29. For a criticism of Husserl's theory of the noema and arguments in favor of the position of the *Investigations,* see his "Husserl, Language, and the Ontology of the Act," *Speculative Grammar, Universal Grammar,*

Philosophical Analysis, ed. D. Buzzetti and M. Ferriane (Amsterdam: Benjamins, 1987), 143–165.

132. *Analysen zur passiven Synthesis,* 339f.

4. THE TRANSCENDENTAL IN TRANSCENDENCE

1. *Ideen I,* 49; Eng. trans., I, 52.
2. *Krisis,* 169; Eng. trans., 166, altered.
3. Letter to Ingarden, December 24, 1921, *Briefwechsel,* 3/3, 215.
4. *Krisis,* 173; Eng. trans., 170.
5. *Logische Untersuchungen,* I, 254; Eng. trans., I, 245.
6. *Ideen I,* 137; Eng. trans., 165.
7. Ibid.
8. See ibid., 140; Eng. trans., 169.
9. Ibid., 140; Eng. trans., 168.
10. *Ideen II,* 364; Eng. trans., 374.
11. Thomas Seebohm, "Transcendental Phenomenology," *Husserl's Phenomenology,* ed. Mohanty and McKenna, 356.
12. Aristotle, *The Metaphysics,* trans. Hugh Tredennich (Cambridge, Mass.: Harvard University Press, 1933), IV, 1003a. The translation is the one proposed by W. D. Ross, *Aristotle's Metaphysics* (Oxford: Clarendon Press, 1924), I, 252.
13. *Metaphysics,* IV, 1003a.
14. Ibid., III, 998b.
15. Heidegger also understands Husserl's notion of world in this fashion. See Martin Heidegger, *Prolegomena zur Geschichte des Zeitbegriffs,* Vol. 20, Gesamtausgabe (Frankfurt am Main: Vittorio Klostermann, 1979), 212–213; *History of the Concept of Time,* trans. Theodore Kisiel (Bloomington: Indiana University Press, 1985), 158.
16. *Ideen I,* 8; Eng. trans., 6.
17. Held has argued this point with precision and lucidity in his "Einleitung [I]," 30.
18. *Logische Untersuchungen,* I, 148; after Eng. trans., I, 163.
19. *Logische Untersuchungen* (1st ed.), II, 18f.; Eng. trans., I, 262f.; and *Logische Untersuchungen,* II/1, 397; Eng. trans., II, 576. Cf. *Phänomenologische Psychologie,* 34; Eng. trans., 24.
20. Its best articulation is in ibid., 1–234, and in "Der Encyclopaedia Britannica Artikel," ibid., 277–301; "'Phenomenology,' Edmund Husserl's Article for the *Encyclopaedia Britannica* (1927)," revised translation by Richard Palmer, in *Shorter Works,* 21–35.
21. *Erste Philosophie II,* 21–22. This function of skepticism has been forcefully demonstrated by Aguirre, *Genetische Phänomenologie und Reduktion,* 94–97.
22. *Die Idee der Phänomenologie,* passim; Eng. trans., passim.
23. *Ideen I,* 50; Eng. trans., 53. Italics removed.
24. "Kant und die Idee der Transzendentalphilosophie (1924)," *Erste Philosophie I,* 230–287; "Kant and the Idea of Transcendental Philosophy," *Southwest Journal of Philosophy* 5 (Fall 1974): 9–56.
25. *Phänomenologische Psychologie,* 62; after Eng. trans., 46.

26. *Ideen I,* 50f.; Eng. trans., 54.
27. Cf. ibid.
28. Ibid., 48ff.; Eng. trans., 49ff.
29. Ibid., 7; Eng. trans., 5. Italics removed.
30. Ibid., 51; Eng. trans., 54. Italics removed.
31. Cf. ibid., 53; Eng. trans., 57.
32. Gottlob Frege, "Begriff und Gegenstand," *Kleine Schriften,* ed. Ignacio Angelelli (Hildesheim: Georg Olms, 1967), 175f.; "On Concept and Object," *Translations from the Philosophical Writings of Gottlob Frege,* ed. Peter Geach and Max Black (Oxford: Basil Blackwell, 1966), 51f.; "Funktion und Begriff," *Kleine Schriften,* 136f.; "Function and Concept," *Writings,* 34f.; Husserl, *Logische Untersuchungen,* II/2, 137–157; Eng. trans., II, 780–795. On Husserl's notion of being and its impact on the thought of Heidegger, see Jacques Taminiaux, "Remarques sur Heidegger et les *Recherches Logiques* de Husserl," *Le regard et l'excédent, Phaenomenologica,* Vol. 75 (The Hague: Martinus Nijhoff, 1977), 156–182; "Heidegger and Husserl's *Logical Investigations,*" *Dialectic and Difference,* ed. and trans. Robert Crease and James Decker (Atlantic Highlands, N.J.: Humanities Press, 1985), 91–114.
33. *Plato's Republic,* 164–166 [509d–511d].
34. When Husserl says that the "general thesis of the natural attitude" operates with the belief that the world is ever and always there and that the goal of the empirical sciences or what he calls "the sciences of the natural attitude" is to grasp it in ever more comprehensive and dependable ways, he is speaking of the world in terms of what the natural attitude itself assumes it to be (i.e., as something that the sciences depict), not in terms of what a phenomenological analysis would discover as its proper being. These sciences as a whole he characterizes as "positive sciences, sciences of natural positivity." Addition to Husserl's copy A of *Ideen I,* 53; Eng. trans., 57, note 21. *Formale und transzendentale Logik,* 232; Eng. trans., 225, label the presupposition of the world by the positive sciences "naive."
35. Ibid., 231–232; Eng. trans., 223–225.
36. All of this is made even more complicated by the fact that we cannot assume that the two philosophical theories leading to these two characterizations would agree as to what the pregiven world is. What one means by the pregiven world is itself going to be shaped by the "style" and requirements of a theory that allows for a transcendental characterization as well as the type of statements that one allows as descriptions of phenomena. If those statements are not those of ordinary discourse but only those of established science, we end up with two very different notions of phenomena as well as what could count as pregiven. Even calling it pregiven and not given, as we have suggested in this account, is already dependent upon what we have labeled phenomenological disclosure. The wager, however, is that beginning here will allow us to eventually account for that notion of the world that is definitive for science, as I will argue in chapter 13.
37. Ibid., 415.
38. Ibid., 437–438.
39. *Ideen I,* 7; after Eng. trans., 5.
40. Ibid., 8; Eng. trans., 6.
41. *Formale und transzendentale Logik,* 442.

42. This had radical consequences for philosophy, ones that opened up a chasm between phenomenology and early analytic philosophy. The following discussion of Wittgenstein is also an attempt to get at one of the deeper issues that divided these two in the three quarters of a century of thought since his *Tractatus.*

43. There is one reference to the analysis of tautologies in the *Tractatus* found in an appendix to *Formal and Transcendental Logic,* but it was written by Oskar Becker. See *Formale und transzendentale Logik,* 334; Eng. trans., 337. While Husserl was not familiar with Wittgenstein, there is strong evidence that Wittgenstein became familiar with Husserl at least by 1929. Both his *Philosophische Bemerkungen,* ed. Rush Rhees, *Schriften,* Vol. 2 (Frankfurt am Main: Suhrkamp, 1964); *Philosophical Remarks,* trans. Raymond Hargreaves and Ryan White (Oxford: Basil Blackwell, 1964), and his *Preliminary Studies for the Philosophical Investigations: The Blue and Brown Books* (Oxford: Basil Blackwell, 1960) have references to phenomenology. There was a brief period when Wittgenstein entertained the idea of a phenomenological language. On this issue see Herbert Spiegelberg, *The Phenomenological Movement, Phaenomenologica* (The Hague: Martinus Nijhoff, 1965), II, 669–670, 762–763.

44. Ludwig Wittgenstein, *Tractatus logico-philosophicus* [1921], *Werkausgabe,* Vol. I (Frankfurt am Main: Suhrkamp, 1984); *Tractatus Logico-Philosophicus,* trans. D. Pears and B. McGuinness (London: Routledge & Kegan Paul, 1961).

45. Ibid., 1.1; 2.04. All references are to Wittgenstein's numbered sentences or paragraphs.

46. Ibid., 2.1; 2.13.

47. Ibid., 2.063.

48. Ibid., 2.171.

49. Ibid., 5.6.

50. Ibid., 4.121; 4.1212.

51. Ibid., 5.524; 2.0124.

52. Ibid., 4.023; 4.024; 4.25; 4.26.

53. Ibid., 5.4711.

54. Ibid., 5.61.

55. Ibid., 4.11.

56. Ibid., 6.13; 6.41.

57. Ibid., 6.45.

58. Ibid., 7.

59. Ibid., 6.53.

60. *Formale und transzendentale Logik,* Part 1.

61. For the following, see *Ideen I,* 80f.; Eng. trans., 94f., and Klaus Held, "Edmund Husserl," *Klassiker der Philosophie,* ed. Otfried Höffe (Munich: Verlag C. H. Beck), II, 289f.

62. Thus when Husserl speaks of the world as environment, as *Umwelt* (e.g., *Ideen I,* 50; Eng. trans., 53), he tends to undercut his own characterization. But then he may be giving us no more than the equivalent notion in the positive sciences. Cf. 53; Eng. trans., 57.

63. Ibid., 49; Eng. trans., 52. Italics removed. This section is the first place where the term "horizon" appears in *Ideen I.*

64. Ibid., 107; Eng. trans., 129.
65. *Krisis,* 171; Eng. trans., 168, altered.
66. *Ideen I,* 80; Eng. trans., 94, altered.
67. *Cartesianische Meditationen,* 82–83; Eng. trans., 45.
68. Ibid., 82; Eng. trans., 45.
69. Ibid., 82; Eng. trans., 44.
70. *Erste Philosophie II,* 79. Italics mine.
71. Husserl paraphrases Kant on this. See *Logische Untersuchungen,* II/2, 137; Eng. trans., II, 780.
72. *Logische Untersuchungen,* II/1, 477–499; Eng. trans., II, 636–651.
73. Actually *Experience and Judgment* speak of both *S is p* and *S has p* as basic, but it is only the first that has a predicate with an adjectival form. On this issue, see my *Origins of Meaning,* 109.
74. *Logische Untersuchungen,* II/2, 137; after Eng. trans., II, 780.
75. Ibid., II, 140; Eng. trans., II, 782–783.
76. *Ideen I,* 52–57; Eng. trans., 55–62.
77. *Ideen I,* 107; Eng. trans., 129.
78. We will return to this in detail in Part 3.
79. Held, "Edmund Husserl," 290.
80. *Cartesianische Meditationen,* 82; Eng. trans., 45.
81. *Ideen I,* 107; Eng. trans., 129.
82. This is precisely the point that Fink makes to Kaufmann in 1932 when he sent to Husserl for comment two reviews he had prepared. At the same time, Kaufmann's misunderstandings show just how much the Cartesian way dominates even a sympathetic reading of the reduction in *Ideas I.* See Bruzina's discussion of this in his "Translator's Introduction," *Sixth Cartesian Meditation,* xli.
83. *Die Idee der Phänomenologie,* 13; Eng. trans., 10.
84. *Einleitung in die Logik,* 427. My thanks to Bernet et al., *Edmund Husserl;* Eng. trans., *An Introduction to Husserlian Phenomenology,* 56–57, for this and the last reference.
85. This phrase is one that Husserl uses in contrast to the essential possibilities of transcendental consciousness in general. In "Kant und die Idee der Transzendentalphilosophie," *Erste Philosophie I,* 256–257; "Kant and the Idea of Transcendental Philosophy," 30–31, he calls this level "transcendental facticity" in contrast to "transcendental essence-research." This seems to echo *Ideas I,* where Husserl refers to the sphere opened by the reduction as a "region of individual being." *Ideen I,* 58; Eng. trans., 64. See note for copy A on p. 64 of Eng. trans. On the difference between the eidetic and the transcendental reduction see *Cartesianische Meditationen,* Section 34.

5. CARTESIAN ENCLOSURES

1. "Nachwort," *Ideen III,* 142; Eng. trans. ("Epilogue," *Ideen II*), 409.
2. "Nachwort," *Ideen III,* 147–148; Eng. trans., ("Epilogue," *Ideen II*), 415.
3. See Landgrebe, "Husserls Abschied vom Cartesianismus."
4. In this paragraph and the next I am following an analysis offered by

Manfred Frank, "Selbstbewußtsein und Rationalität," *Grenzbestimmungen der Vernunft,* ed. Petra Kolmer and Harald Korten (Freiburg: Verlag Karl Alber, 1994), 392–393.

5. Cf. *Analysen zur passiven Synthesis,* 19.

6. Frank, "Selbstbewußtsein und Rationalität," 394. Frank is citing Heinrich Jacobi, *Über die Lehre des Spinoza in Briefen an Herrn Moses Mendelssohn* (Breslau, 1789), 423f.

7. *Cartesianische Meditationen,* 66; Eng. trans., 27.

8. René Descartes, *Meditations on First Philosophy* [1641], trans. John Cottingham, *The Philosophical Writings of Descartes,* ed. and trans. John Cottingham, Robert Stoothalf, and Dugald Murdock (Cambridge: Cambridge University Press, 1985), II, 3–62.

9. *Logische Untersuchungen,* II/2, 225; Eng. trans., II, 854f.

10. The materials now published as *The Idea of Phenomenology* were lectures given in 1907 and clearly show Husserl's first appropriation of the Cartesian program was epistemological, not ontological.

11. *Ideen I,* 58; after Eng. trans., 63f.

12. Ibid., Section 44.

13. Ibid., Section 46.

14. *Ideen I,* 91–92; after Eng. trans., 110. Italics removed.

15. *Ideen I,* 93; after Eng. trans., 111.

16. *Ideen I,* 90; Eng. trans., 108.

17. *Ideen I,* 57; after Eng. trans., 61: " . . . I am not negating this 'world' as though I were a sophist; I am not doubting its factual being [Dasein] as though I were a skeptic; rather I am exercising the 'phenomenological epoché' which also completely shuts me off from any judgment about spatiotemporal factual being." Italics removed.

18. "Nachwort," *Ideen III,* 145; after Eng. trans. ("Epilogue," *Ideas II*), 413.

19. See *Ideen I,* 85; Eng. trans., 100.

20. *Cartesianische Meditationen,* 121; Eng. trans., 89. But Husserl believes that this means that his theory is not just a private affair: " . . . what is cognizable by one [changed to "my" in Copy D] Ego must of *essential necessity* be cognizable by *any* Ego." *Ideen I,* 90; Eng. trans., 108.

21. *Phänomenologische Psychologie,* 490.

22. *Ideen I,* Section 131, 270–273; Eng. trans., 313–316.

23. Ibid., 275; Eng. trans., 318.

24. Ibid., 109, 160–161; Eng. trans., 132, 190–192.

25. The problem of defining the noesis and the noema in Husserl has spawned significant controversy. I will not engage the issues here but refer the reader to my attempt to come to grips with these notions in my *Origins of Meaning,* especially Part 2.

26. *Ideen II,* 2; Eng. trans., 4.

27. Ibid., 7; Eng. trans., 9.

28. *Tractatus,* 5.632.

29. *Formale und transzendentale Logik,* 243; Eng. trans., 237.

30. *Ideen I,* 110; Eng. trans., 133.

31. *Logische Untersuchungen,* I, 238; Eng. trans., I, 233.

32. *Ideen I,* 109; Eng. trans., 132.
33. Ibid.
34. Ibid.; Eng. trans., 133.
35. *Ideen II,* 97–98; Eng. trans., 103–104.
36. Kant uses "function" strictly in relation to the unity of an act of understanding that brings the sensible manifold of experience under categories and does not extend, as Husserl wants it, to the domain of affection or what Husserl would call passive synthesis. See Kant, *Kritik der reinen Vernunft,* B93, A108, and B143; Eng. trans., 105, 136–137, 160.
37. *Ideen II,* 99; Eng. trans., 105.
38. Ibid., 105; Eng. trans., 111. Italics removed.
39. *Ideen I,* 93; Eng. trans., 111.
40. *Ideen II,* 106; Eng. trans., 113.
41. Ibid., 107; Eng. trans., 113.
42. Ibid., 108; Eng. trans., 115. Italics removed.
43. Manuscript B I 37, 26b. Pagination is according to original manuscript pages.
44. "Erkennen ist eine Funktion des Lebens. Aber Ichleben ist, wird man sagen, nicht nur erkennendes Leben." B I 37, 29a. Because this manuscript is not yet published and is in the public domain, I am including the German text in the notes.
45. "Aber in anderen Lebensformen ist das Streben auf anderes gerichtet, auf Schönes, auf wirtschaftlich Nützliches u. dgl. Das handelnde Subjekt erzeugt Wahrheitswerke, wie Theorien, es erzeugt Werke schöner Kunst, bearbeitet wirtschaftliche Güter. . . . " B I 37, 29a.
46. "Hatten wir nun früher, in der engeren Vernunftsregion, der der Erkenntnis, fordern müssen, daß die Subjektivität, und hier als erkennende, in reiner Reflexion zum universalen Thema gemacht wird und zunächst sogar vor allen Fragen nach Evidenz oder Nichtevidenz, Vernunft oder Unvernunft: so wird das gleiche auch für die totale Vernunftlehre gelten müssen. Also wird gefordert sein das universale Studium der vollen und ganzen Subjektivität, soweit sie irgend[wie] unter möglichen Vernunftnormen steht. Erst in der höheren Forschungsstufe müßte sie das Spezifische der Vernunft selbst und aller Vernunftarten und sowohl nach Seiten der spezifischen Vernunfttätigkeiten wie nach Seiten der Vernunftgebilde (Theorien, Kunstwerke usw.) zum Thema machen. Damit hätten wir also eine viel umfassendere Philosophie, die, wenn wir sie nur als Wissenschaft der letzten, der prinzipiellen Allgemeinheiten fassen, sich bezogen zeigt auf die Idee des Menschen überhaupt und die Idee einer echt humanen Kultur überhaupt." B I 37, 30b. We will return to the question of an authentic culture in chapter 12.
47. "die universale philosophische Vernunftlehre." B I 37, 31b.
48. "Da Subjektivität wesentlich Gemeinschaftssubjektivität oder in Gemeinschaftsform lebende ist, da das einzelne Leben nur ein Faden im Gewebe eines universalen, allumspannenden Gemeinschaftsleben ist, so bezieht sich diese Wissenschaft von vorneherein auf die universale Gemeinschaftssubjektivität und das universale Gemeinschaftsleben." B I 37, 31b. Husserl still thinks of this analysis as controlled by the "spiritual attitude" (*geistige Einstellung*) which, as we know from *Ideas II,* is the theoretical attitude that allows us to do regional ontologies of social

and cultural regions. But we can already see this attitude spilling beyond its first framework. Eventually this movement will carry Husserl into a full notion of intersubjectivity in a transcendental register, as we will trace in the next chapter.

49. *Ideen II,* 107; Eng. trans., 114.

50. *Ideen I,* 93; Eng. trans., 112.

51. It may be that in *Ideas I* Husserl underestimated the difficulties involved with taking the world as an object and did not realize the limitations of his analysis. We have to leave to another discussion the question of whether Kant's analysis of the antinomies of pure reason can be understood as a sustained argument against moving from a transcendental characterization of the ego and its appearances to the world as a whole. See Kant, *Kritik der reinen Vernunft,* B 432ff.; Eng. trans., 384ff.

52. *Ideen II,* 109; Eng. trans., 116.

53. Ibid., 257; Eng. trans., 269.

54. Ibid., 372–373; Eng. trans., 382. Italics removed.

55. Ibid., 375; Eng. trans., 384.

56. Ibid.; Eng. trans., 384–385.

57. *Formale und transzendentale Logik,* 239; Eng. trans., 232.

58. Ibid., 437.

59. Ibid., 241; Eng. trans., 234.

60. Ibid., 243; Eng. trans., 236.

61. Ibid., 440.

62. Ibid.

63. Ibid., 243; Eng. trans., 236.

64. "Husserls Abschied vom Cartesianismus"; "Husserl's Departure from Cartesianism."

65. See Manfred Sommer, "Husserls Göttinger Lebenswelt," Edmund Husserl, *Die Konstitution der geistigen Welt,* ed. Manfred Sommer (Hamburg: Felix Meiner, 1984), ix–xlii. The task of an analysis of the life-world, accordingly, consists of showing its compatibility with Husserl's Cartesian framework: "The theory of the life-world belongs to Cartesianism as its complement." P. x.

66. *Krisis,* 157–158; after Eng. trans., 155.

67. *Phänomenologische Psychologie,* 30; after Eng. trans., 21.

68. See Held "Einleitung [I]," 43.

69. Note to *Ideen I,* 57; Eng. trans., 63. The note is found in the Schuhmann edition of *Ideen I.* See *Ideen I* (Hua), 484. Cited after *Ideen I,* Eng. trans., 63.

70. "Nachwort," *Ideen III,* 152; after Eng. trans. ("Epilogue," *Ideen II*), 420.

71. *Erste Philosophie II,* 432–439.

72. Ibid., 432.

73. Husserl added this comment in the margins.

74. This lecture course, titled "Grundprobleme der Phänomenologie" (Winter Semester 1910/11) has now been edited and printed in *Intersubjektivität I,* 111–194.

75. *Erste Philosophie II,* 434. First italics mine.

76. "Nachwort," *Ideen III,* 149; Eng. trans. ("Epilogue," *Ideen II*), 417.

77. Ibid., 149; Eng. trans. ("Epilogue," *Ideen II*), 416.

78. Ibid., 153; after Eng. trans. ("Epilogue," *Ideen II*), 421.

79. *Erste Philosophie II*, 480.
80. Ibid.
81. Ibid., 481.
82. Ibid., 482.
83. Cf. ibid., 494ff.
84. We find this in various passages in ibid. as well as in *Analysen zur passiven Synthesis* and *Phänomenologische Psychologie*. The reason why this is misleading, however, is that even the *Logical Investigations* (1900–1901) and *Ideas II* take paths to phenomenological analysis that are not Cartesian. In his lecture course "Grundprobleme der Phänomenologie," from the Winter Semester of 1910/11, Husserl already attempts to move from the "natural concept of the world" to a transcendental phenomenology.
85. Relevant selections of this text are published in *Intersubjektivität I*, especially 188–191.
86. As used in the body of my text, there are three editions that I will cover with the italicized title *Cartesian Meditations*, to which we will also affix Husserl's label "the French Meditations":

a. The 1931 translation by Gabrielle Pfeiffer and Emmanuel Levinas, *Méditations cartésiennes*. This was made from the version sent to the translators on May 17, 1929, itself a revision and expansion of his Paris lectures given February 23 and 25, 1929.

b. The text that we are citing as *Cartesianische Meditationen* and that was published as *Husserliana*, Vol. 1. For our purposes this is the same text, with only minor variations, as the one sent to Pfeiffer and Levinas.

c. The *Cartesian Meditations*, translated by Dorion Cairns and published in 1960. Cairns used a copy of the original German text that varies some from (b) and is closer to (a).

When used in footnotes, *Cartesianische Meditationen* will continue to refer to (b), i.e., *Husserliana*, Vol. 1, with Eng. trans. standing for the Cairns translation, (c). I should stress that the German text sent to the translators appeared with minor differences in the first volume of the *Husserliana* in 1950 and was then published with only slight modifications in English translation by Dorion Cairns in 1960. For our purposes these can be treated as the same. On this point see Bruzina, "Translator's Introduction," *Sixth Cartesian Meditation*, lxix–lxx, note 8. The term "Cartesian Meditations" (in quotes) will attempt to do justice to the fact that Husserl quickly viewed the version that was published in French translation only as a first draft, much in need of revision. It names the project that he continued to labor on for the next few years. He also referred to this as the "German Meditations" not because the original version of the "French Meditations" was not German but because this new version was to be aimed at a German audience. More on this below.

87. Kern, "Einleitung [III] des Herausgebers," xvii–lxx; Schuhmann, *Husserl-Chronik*, Vol. 1; Bruzina, "Translator's Introduction," *Sixth Cartesian Meditation*, vii–lix, and an unpublished chapter in a forthcoming book on the relationship between Husserl, Heidegger, and Fink, which he was kind enough to let me see.
88. The text is now published as "Die Pariser Vorträge" in *Cartesianische*

Meditationen, 3–39; *The Paris Lectures,* trans. P. Koestenbaum (The Hague: Martinus Nijhoff, 1967).

89. Letter to Ingarden, May 26, 1929, *Briefwechsel,* 3/3, 248. See Kern, "Einleitung [III] des Herausgebers," xvii.

90. "I've had to sacrifice my holidays, since Husserl's *Phenomenology* gives me much trouble in the later sections, and I don't want to be accused of misunderstanding, as Messer and Cohn recently were." Letter to Engelbert Krebs, July 19, 1914, as cited in Hugo Ott, *Martin Heidegger* (Frankfurt am Main: Campus Verlag, 1988), 83; *Martin Heidegger,* trans. Allan Blunden (London: Fontana Press, 1994), 81.

91. At that time Heidegger was technically not in the same department as Husserl as he belonged to the Department of Christian Philosophy (Philosophy II) and not the regular Philosophy Department (Philosophy I). He changed over in 1918 or 1919.

92. Ott, *Martin Heidegger,* 102; Eng. trans., 102–103.

93. Letter to Ingarden, July 18, 1920, *Briefwechsel,* 3/3, 204.

94. Letter to Bell, August 11, 1920, *Briefwechsel,* 3/3, 21.

95. See letter to Ingarden, December 30, 1920, *Briefwechsel,* 3/3, 208.

96. Letter to Bell, August 11, 1920, *Briefwechsel,* 3/3, 14.

97. See his letter to Natorp, February 1, 1922, *Briefwechsel,* 3/5, 150–151.

98. Cited in Ott, *Martin Heidegger,* 125.

99. Ibid.

100. Letter to Jaensch, June 26 [or 30], 1925, *Briefwechsel,* 3/3, 334.

101. *Erste Philosophie I,* passim.

102. The London lectures, based on MS F I 29, are catalogued as M II 3a and 3b.

103. The text reads: "mit Ihnen belehren zu lassen."

104. Letter from Malvine Husserl to Heidegger, December 30, 1927, *Briefwechsel,* 3/4, 150.

105. The text reads: "Fortsetzer meiner Forschung zu sein."

106. Letter to Pfänder, January 6, 1931, *Briefwechsel,* 3/2, 181–182. This letter contains Husserl's most candid attempt to understand his falling-out with Heidegger. See 180–184.

107. The first two drafts of the article are preserved and reproduced in *Phänomenologische Psychologie,* 237–277. The fourth was the final draft published in the *Britannica.* See *Phänomenologische Psychologie,* 277–301; "Phenomenology," *Shorter Works,* 22–35. On this attempted collaboration, see Walter Biemel, "Husserls Encyclopaedia-Britannica Artikel und Heideggers Anmerkungen dazu," *Tijdschrift voor Filosofie* 12 (1950): 246–280; "Husserl's *Encyclopaedia Britannica* Article and Heidegger's Remarks Thereon," *Husserl: Expositions and Appraisals,* ed. Peter McCormick and Frederick Elliston (Notre Dame, Ind.: University of Notre Dame Press, 1977), 286–303; and Steven Crowell, "Husserl, Heidegger and Transcendental Philosophy: Another Look at the Encyclopaedia Britannica Article," *Philosophy and Phenomenological Research* 50 (March 1990): 501–518.

108. He actually began his teaching in the Winter Semester of 1923/24, i.e., at the end of 1923.

109. Kern, "Einleitung [III] des Herausgebers," xxiii.

110. Heidegger turned his attention to this task just after he finished *Being and Time* in 1926. The editing, however, was not that difficult, as he worked from a handwritten copy produced after long labor by Edith Stein in 1917. She was the one who tackled the difficult task of putting Husserl's manuscripts into coherent order. See Rudolf Boehm, "Einleitung," to Husserl, *Zeitbewusstsein*, xxxii–xxxiii. Husserl does come to regret giving the task to him. See letter to Pfänder, January 6, 1931, *Briefwechsel*, 3/2, 182.

111. *Conversations*, August 13, 1931, 9.

112. Letter to Pfänder, January 6, 1931, *Briefwechsel*, 3/2, 181.

113. Cf. Kern, "Einleitung [III] des Herausgebers," xxiii.

114. Ibid., xxii. Cf. the letter to Misch, June 27, 1929, *Briefwechsel*, 3/6, 275, and letter from Malvine Husserl to Ingarden, December 2, 1929, *Briefwechsel*, 3/3, 254. The brief text *On the Essence of Reasons*, written in 1928, appeared in a Festschrift published in 1929 dedicated to Husserl. Martin Heidegger, "Vom Wesen des Grundes," *Festschrift: Edmund Husserl zum 70. Geburtstag Gewidmet*, supplementary volume to *Jahrbuch für Philosophie und Phänomenologische Forschung* (Halle a.d. Saale: Max Niemeyer Verlag, 1929), 71–110; *The Essence of Reasons*, bilingual edition, trans. Terrence Malick (Evanston, Ill.: Northwestern University Press, 1969).

115. Published with a "Nachwort" as Martin Heidegger, "Was ist Metaphysik?" [1929] (Frankfurt am Main: Vittorio Klostermann, 1943). We will usually cite Martin Heidegger, "Was ist Metaphysik?" [1929], *Wegmarken* (Frankfurt am Main: Vittorio Klostermann, 1967), 1–19; "What Is Metaphysics?" *Basic Writings*, ed. David Krell (New York: Harper, 1993), 89–110. Heidegger explains the relationship between this lecture and his *The Essence of Reasons* in this way: "The treatise 'The Essence of Reasons' was written in 1928 at the same time as the lecture 'What is Metaphysics?' The latter considers the problem of Nothingness, while the former defines the Ontological Difference." Preface to third edition of "Vom Wesen des Grundes," 21; after Eng. trans., 2–3.

116. Cf. Kern, "Einleitung [III] des Herausgebers," xxiii.

117. "Was ist Metaphysik?" 6; Eng. trans., 97.

118. Ibid., 6; Eng. trans., 98.

119. Ibid., 8; Eng. trans., 100.

120. Ibid.

121. Ibid., 17–18; after Eng. trans., 109.

122. For Heidegger's own misgivings about this lecture, see his "Nachwort zu: 'Was ist Metaphysik?'" [1943], *Wegmarken*, 99–108.

123. The German is difficult here and reads as follows: " . . . daß er in der Ausbildung einer Systemphilosophie begriffen sei von jener Art, die für immer unmöglich zu machen ich zu meiner Lebensaufgabe stets gerechnet habe."

124. Letter to Pfänder, January 6, 1931, *Briefwechsel*, 3/2, 184.

125. In a marginal remark that Husserl made on page 16 of his copy of Heidegger's *Sein und Zeit*, he says: "In my sense that is the way to an intentional psychology of personality in the broadest sense, moving out from personal life in the world. . . . " Edmund Husserl, "Randbemerkungen Husserls zu Heideggers *Sein und Zeit* und *Kant und das Problem der Metaphysik*," ed. Roland Breeur, *Husserl Studies* 11 (1994): 14.

126. In another marginal remark, to page 13 of his copy of *Sein und Zeit,* his comments are even more biting: "Heidegger transposes or transvests the constitutive, phenomenological clarification of all regions of beings [*Seiende*] and universals, of the total region, world, into the anthropological. The entire problematic is a transference; Dasein corresponds to the ego, etc. Thereby everything becomes profoundly unclear and philosophically it loses its value." "Randbemerkungen," 13.

127. "Nachwort," *Ideen III,* 138; Eng. trans. ("Epilogue," *Ideen II*), 405; Kern, "Einleitung [III] des Herausgebers," xxv.

128. *Formale und transzendentale Logik,* 11; Eng. trans., 7. Cf. Bruzina, "Translator's Introduction," *Sixth Cartesian Meditation,* xi.

129. This is found on page 30 in the "Author's Preface to the English Edition" in the 1931 translation of *Ideas I* translated by Boyce Gibson. Boyce Gibson received the text in 1929. In the German version published in 1930 in the *Jahrbuch,* the paragraph was dropped. See Kern, "Einleitung [III] des Herausgebers," xxv–xxvi.

130. *Briefwechsel,* 3/3, 254; "Einleitung [III] des Herausgebers," xxvii.

131. Schuhmann identifies this work as *Being and Time.* See *Briefwechsel,* 3/3, 254, note 175.

132. The German reads, "Ausgestaltung der deutschen Ausgabe der *Cartesianischen Meditationen* zu meinem systematischen 'Hauptwerk.'" *Briefwechsel,* 3/3, 254.

133. This biting review, an interesting mixture of insightful, caustic criticism and respectful awe, appeared in *Mind* 38 (1929): 355–370.

134. Letter to Hicks, March 15, 1930, *Briefwechsel,* 3/6, 180–181.

135. "Einleitung [III] des Herausgebers," xxvii–xxviii.

136. Published in *Phänomenologische Psychologie,* 302–349.

137. Reproduced in Kern, "Einleitung [III] des Herausgebers," xxviii, note 1.

138. Letter to Ingarden, March 19, 1930, *Briefwechsel,* 3/3, 262. Just four days earlier he wrote Hicks, his host from Cambridge University during the lectures Husserl gave in London in 1922, that the German version of the *Meditations* would be a "very expanded reworking [*Bearbeitung*]" that will present "a complete outline [*Grundriß*] of my phenomenological philosophy in easy, accessible form." Letter to Hicks, March 15, 1930, *Briefwechsel,* 3/6, 180.

139. Kern, "Einleitung [III] des Herausgebers," xlii–xlv.

140. Fink, *VI. Cartesianische Meditation,* Part 2, 3–9.

141. Bruzina, "Translator's Introduction," *Sixth Cartesian Meditation,* xiv.

142. Letter to Pfänder, December 6, 1930, *Briefwechsel,* 3/2, 177.

143. Letter to Misch, November 16, 1930, *Briefwechsel,* 3/6, 282–283.

144. "Phänomenologie und Anthropologie," *Aufsätze und Vorträge (1922–1937),* 164–181.

145. Kern, "Einleitung [III] des Herausgebers," lii–liii.

146. *Briefwechsel,* 3/3, 273; after translation by Bruzina, "Translator's Introduction," *Sixth Cartesian Meditation,* xv.

147. Bruzina, "Translator's Introduction," *Sixth Cartesian Meditation,* xv.

148. Letter to Ingarden, May 15, 1931, *Briefwechsel,* 3/3, 294.

149. *Conversations,* July 11, 1931, 4.

150. Ibid., August 28, 1931, 27.

151. Ibid., September 1, 1931, 30.
152. Ibid., entry from November 9, 1931, 37–38.
153. *Briefwechsel,* 3/6, 142.
154. *Conversations,* May 4, 1932, 71.
155. At this point we can turn to the analysis of the complex relationship between Husserl and Fink by Bruzina. See "Translator's Introduction," *Sixth Cartesian Meditation,* xxiii–xxxii.
156. Letter to Ingarden, August 19, 1932, *Briefwechsel,* 3/3, 288.
157. The most important texts surrounding this project are found both in the supplemental texts and appendices of the *Krisis* and, more recently, in Edmund Husserl, *Ergänzungsband zur "Krisis,"* ed. Reinhold Smid, *Husserliana,* Vol. 29 (Dordrecht: Kluwer Academic Publishers, 1993).

6. TRANSCENDENTAL DISCLOSURES

1. *Krisis,* 114; after Eng. trans., 111–112.
2. "Nachwort," *Ideen III,* 148; Eng. trans. ("Epilogue," *Ideas II*), 416, altered.
3. *Intersubjektivität III,* 109.
4. Eugen Fink, MS Z-IV, 26a (1928–1929), as cited in Ronald Bruzina, "Solitude and Community in the Work of Philosophy: Husserl and Fink 1928–1938," *Man and World* 22 (1989):, 310, note 19.
5. *Conversations,* August 28, 1931, 27.
6. "Phänomenologische Methode und Phänomenologische Philosophie." The draft of the lectures is catalogued as F II 3, Landgrebe's transcription as M II 3. For an historical account of these lectures, see Herbert Spiegelberg, "Husserl in England: Facts and Lessons," *Journal of the British Society for Phenomenology* 1 (1970): 4–15.
7. Kern, "Einleitung [II] des Herausgebers," xviii–xvix.
8. The lecture course "Einleitung in die Philosophie" consists of a compilation from the following manuscripts, all from 1922–1923: B I 37, F I 29, M I 3b, F II 3, and B IV 2.
9. There are some thirty-nine manuscript pages (B I 37, 2–34, and F I 29, 3–7) added at the beginning, indicating that the issue of a starting point is problematic (the first point we will cover below). After the Cartesian reduction is carried out and Husserl begins to worry about the problem of memory and possible deception, roughly in the middle of the second London lecture (M II 3a, 49), Husserl adds some 113 pages (F I 29, 12–125) qualifying what he just did. We will use parts of this text in the second and third points below and then return to the question of memory in chapter 11.
10. F I 29, 12b.
11. *Cartesianische Meditationen,* 48; Eng. trans., 7.
12. Ibid., 51; Eng. trans., 10.
13. See his remarks at the end of ibid., 205–206.
14. *Ideen I,* 54; Eng. trans., 58.
15. Ibid., 53; Eng. trans., 57.
16. *Cartesianische Meditationen,* Sections 7 to 9.
17. *Conversations,* June 6, 1932, 80–81. Cf. May 11, 1932, 75.

18. "absolut zu rechtfertigen."

19. "ein notwendiges Fundament."

20. "was für <eine> Vollkommenheit ich unter dem Titel 'absoluter Rechtfertigung' für meine künftigen Erkenntnisse eigentlich meine und fordere." F II 3, 15a.

21. "exemplarisches Material für die Klärung dieses Ideals." Ibid.

22. "reine Möglichkeiten."

23. "bloß um daran Begriffe zu bilden." Ibid.

24. "einem Sehen oder Einsehen, derart, daß das Geglaubte nicht bloß geglaubt, sondern selbst gesehen oder eingesehen, selbst erfaßt, selbst ergriffen ist. Ein solcher nach 'evident' Gegebenem sich richtender Glaube heißt selbst ein evidenter oder evident begründeter." F II 3, 15b.

25. "allem voran." Ibid.

26. "vollkommene Evidenz."

27. "ein adäquates Sehen oder Einsehen."

28. "Selbsterfassen des geglaubten Gegenstandes."

29. "von einem antizipierenden Meinen." Ibid.

30. "Nur das pure Erleben als Tatsache, das was unangefochten bleibt, auch wenn ich annehme, es sei keine Welt, ist das apodiktische, das transzendentale 'Phänomen' der Phänomenologie." F II 3, 25a.

31. "Denn das Nichtsein der Welt berührt ja nicht das Sein dieser reinen Erlebnisse." F II 3, 26a.

32. "Es gibt verschiedene Wege in die Phänomenologie. Ich will für diese Vorlesungen den prinzipiellsten wählen." F II 3, 12a.

33. "Alles Bisherige war ein bloßes Vorspiel und gehört nicht zum Spiel selbst, das nun erst beginnen soll." F I 29, 3a.

34. "Und doch bezieht sich die Philosophie auf das Weltall in seiner vollen Universalität und auf das All des Seienden überhaupt in beliebig zu erweiterndem Sinne und bezieht sich damit auf alle Wissenschaften zurück; sie behandelt Probleme, die sie alle sehr ernst angehen, erfüllt Bedürfnisse oder will Bedürfnisse erfüllen, die sie alle und in allen Stufen ihrer Allgemeinheit nicht erfüllen und die doch in ihnen allen mitleben." B I 37, 3a.

35. " . . . seinen Blick rückwärts wendet, nämlich auf die tiefsten Grundlagen, auf Grundbegriffe und Grundsätze und nicht über die Technik, sondern über die Praxis seiner Methodik, und ähnlich verhält es sich, wenn es gilt, über das Mathematisch-Technische hinaus den tiefsten Sinn und die Grenzen des Rechts der ganzen mathematischen Leistung verständlich zu machen." B I 37, 3b–4a.

36. "Wenn der positive Forscher in seiner Arbeit ist, also konkret sachlich eingestellt beobachtet, experimentiert, theoretisiert, so gewinnt er in weitem Maß Theoreme und Theorien, die ihre Rationalität in sich haben, in ihrer notwendigen Geltung jeden Sachverständigen und ebenso Eingestellten überzeugen und sich weiterhin auch in der Erfahrung bewähren. Und doch, die Grundbegriffe, das begriffliche Urmaterial, aus dem alle wei • ren Begriffe, also alle Theoreme einer Wissenschaft ihren Sinn ableiten, hat einerseits zwar eine ursprüngliche klare Selbstverständlichkeit und anderseits doch eine rätselhafte Unbestimmtheit, ein rätselhaftes Schwanken des Sinnes, das sich darin zeigt, daß, wenn man evident eingesehene allgemeine Sätze frei anwenden, frei ihre Konsequenzen entfalten

lassen will, sich Unstimmigkeiten, ja Widersprüche ergeben, deren Grund unklar ist." B I 37, 4a.

37. "Für alle diese Begriffe gilt . . . : Sie sind zugleich selbstverständlich und voll Rätsel. Also sie dürfen nicht mehr die Rolle vorgegebener Selbstverständlichkeiten in den Wissenschaften spielen. . . . [Eine neue Wissenschaft ist erforderlich, die] ausschließlich das Selbstverständliche zum Problem macht. Und in der Tat, es ist nicht zuviel gesagt, daß all das, was für den natürlichen Menschen (und auch den natürlich eingestellt bleibenden Wissenschaftler) das Selbstverständliche ist, sich in der Reflexion als mit den tiefsten Rätseln behaftet zeigt, und es ist paradox, aber wahr, wenn man die Philosophie geradezu die Wissenschaft von dem Selbstverständlichen nennt." B I 37, 5a.

38. "Es zeigt sich dabei, daß es sich bei diesem Philosophischen nicht um bloße Reflexionen handelt, die getrennt den einzelnen positiven Wissenschaften anzuhängen sind. Vielmehr bedarf es, unter der Leitung jener weiten Gruppe von Begriffen, die ein notwendiges *Gemeingut* aller Wissenschaften ausmachen, zunächst einer *allgemeinen Wissenschaftslehre,* welche überhaupt alle Probleme behandelt, die mit der Idee einer Wissenschaft als Wissenschaft untrennbar verbunden sind. Das muß aber gelten in zwei korrelativen Richtungen, die wir als erkenntnismäßige Subjektivität und erkannte Objektivität gegenüberstellen, von welchen die letztere sich aber spaltet, so daß wir auch sprechen können von *drei korrelativen Richtungen:* 1. der Richtung auf *wissenschaftliches Erkennen,* der Richtung auf 2. die sich im Erkennen notwendig gestaltenden *Sinnesgehalte,* also Begriffe und Sätze bzw. Wahrheit und endlich 3. auf die durch diesen Sinnesgehalt sich bestimmende (und zwar in richtiger Erkenntnis sich in Wahrheit bestimmende) *Gegenständlichkeit.* Nur wenn die Wissenschaftslehre das Korrelative, also das untrennbar Zusammengehörige in seiner Korrelation erforscht, nur wenn sie die wechselseitigen Wesensbezüge im Auge behält, nur dann kann sie zu einer philosophischen Disziplin werden, zu wirklich allerletzter Wissenschaft, Wissenschaft letzter Klärung." B I 37, 5a–5b.

39. "In solchen Überlegungen waren wir also selbst schon auf dem höheren Standpunkt, der, die Positivität unter sich lassend, sie überschaute, einer gewissen Kritik unterwarf und dabei gegenüber den positiven Fragestellungen zu höheren vordrang und damit zu einem Feld höherer Erkenntnis." B I 37, 18b.

40. B I 37, 24a.

41. "die Urmethode aller philosophischer Methoden." F I 29, 3b.

42. Husserl, *Krisis,* Section 9.

43. Ibid., Section 43.

44. "The apodicticity of the transcendental consciousness is not the same as mundane apodicticity," Cairns records Husserl informing him. *Conversations,* November 20, 1931, 43.

45. *Erste Philosophie II,* 33.

46. *Ideen I,* 285–288; Eng. trans., 329–333.

47. Ibid., 288; Eng. trans., 333.

48. Ibid., 285; Eng. trans., 329.

49. Ibid., 287; Eng. trans., 332.

50. Ibid., 296; Eng. trans., 341.

51. Ibid.

52. Ibid., 296–297; Eng. trans., 341.
53. Ibid., 297; Eng. trans., 342.
54. Ibid., 285; Eng. trans., 330.
55. Ibid.
56. Ibid., 15; Eng. trans., 14.
57. Ibid., 300; Eng. trans., 345.
58. Ibid., 67; Eng. trans., 78.
59. Ibid.
60. Ibid., 68; Eng. trans., 79.
61. Ibid., 81; Eng. trans., 95. Husserl adds to his D copy: "in its present in each point of its Now." See the Schuhmann edition, *Ideen I* (Hua), 494; this note is translated in the Eng. trans. of *Ideen I*, 95.
62. Ibid., 81; Eng. trans., 95.
63. " . . . und bleibt das gesehene Ding ein Gemisch von eigentlich Gesehenem und nicht Gesehenem, also immer bleibt es offen, daß sich <im> Fortgang weiteren Wahrnehmens herausstelle, daß das Gesehene nicht so sei, als wie es vordem vermeintlich gesehen war, oder gar, daß es überhaupt nicht sei, daß sich das Gesehene in Illusion oder Traum auflöse." F II 3, 18b.
64. *Ideen I,* 81; Eng. trans., 96.
65. *Die Idee der Phänomenologie,* 32; Eng. trans., 24.
66. Ibid., 31; Eng. trans., 24.
67. Ibid., 35; Eng. trans., 28.
68. *Logische Untersuchungen,* II/1, 355; Eng. trans., II, 542. Translation altered. Husserl significantly altered this passage (published in 1913) over the original (published in 1901).
69. Note to *Ideen* I, 82, in the Schuhmann edition, *Ideen I* (Hua), 495. Not included in Eng. trans.
70. "satt erfüllte." F II 3, 15b.
71. *Ideen I,* 85; Eng. trans., 100.
72. "während etwas adäquat gegeben ist, kann es nicht negiert und nicht bezweifelt werden. Das bezeichnet sich auch mit den Worten: das adäquat Evidente ist in apodiktischer Gewissenheit gegeben." F II 3, 16a.
73. *Ideen I,* 87; Eng. trans., 103.
74. Ibid., 86; after Eng. trans., 103.
75. Ibid., 82; Eng. trans., 97, altered.
76. Ibid., 83; Eng. trans., 98.
77. Ibid.
78. Ibid., 85; Eng. trans., 100–101.
79. Ibid.; Eng. trans., 101, altered. In copy D Husserl qualified "my consciousness" with the phrase "as streaming present." The note is found in the Schuhmann edition, *Ideen I* (Hua), 495, and is translated on p. 101 of the Eng. trans.
80. Note to *Ideen I,* 85; Eng. trans., 101. The note is found in the Schuhmann edition, *Ideen I* (Hua), 496, and is translated on p. 101 of the Eng. trans.
81. *Ideen I,* 165; Eng. trans., 196.
82. Ibid., 166; Eng. trans., 197.
83. Ibid., 166–167; Eng. trans., 197–198.
84. "Statt der Wirklichkeiten betrachten wir die egologischen Möglich-

keiten. . . . Nicht eine Tatsachenwissenschaft von meinem Ego and seinen cogitationes, so wie es faktisch ist, gewinnen wir als erste, sondern eine eidetische Wissenschaft. Genauer, wir gewinnen zunächst ein unendliches Feld systematisch eidetischer Deskription unmittelbar adäquat erschaubarer und objektiv feststellbarer Wesenseigenheiten einer transzendentalen Subjektivität überhaupt, ihres möglichen Bewußtseins, ihrer möglichen intentionalen Leistungen." F II 3, 35b, 37a.

85. *Cartesianische Meditationen,* 62; Eng. trans., 22.

86. Ibid., 56; Eng. trans., 16.

87. Ibid.

88. Ibid.; Eng. trans., 15.

89. Ibid., 62; Eng. trans., 22–23. Curiously, Husserl uses the phrase "adäquat Erfahrene" and not "adäquat Erlebte," perhaps by mistake. Even for *Ideas I, Erfahrung* is always experience of a transcendent object and is never adequate. This seems to be the only passage where the *Meditations* does speak of the Now as adequately experienced.

90. Reading *als* in place of *nach.*

91. Ibid., 59; Eng. trans., 19.

92. Ibid., 131–132; Eng. trans., 101.

93. F I 29 as printed in *Analysen zur passiven Synthesis,* 366. Cf. *Ideen I,* 69; Eng. trans., 90.

94. F I 29 as printed in *Analysen zur passiven Synthesis,* 366.

95. We will return to this problem in chapter 11.

96. " . . . die Apodiktizität ist die Kehrseite der Adäquation, das Gemeinte ist unmittelbar und ohne jede Antizipation, deren Bestätigung noch in Frage bleibt, selbst gegeben." F I 29, 28a.

97. "Aber wir müssen nun anerkennen, daß originale Selbsterfassung eine notwendige Struktur hat und in sich wieder Gradualitäten hat, ohne die sie gar nicht denkbar ist, und gerade hier in der Kritik der immanenten Wahrnehmung ist die Stelle, es ursprünglich zu lernen. . . . Dabei aber hat gewiß das jeweilige aktuelle Jetzt den Vorzug einer *höchsten und vollkommensten* Phase der Selbstgegebenheit. Nur in ihr ist der Ton, als das betreffende Tonmoment, in absoluter Selbstheit nach Sein und Sosein erfaßt, im Erfassen in gewisser Weise reell enthalten. Und doch ist das nur eine abstrakte Rede und ist eigentlich von Sein und Sosein sinnvoll nur zu sprechen, weil diese Tonphase fungierende Phase ist in einer Synthesis des Abströmens. Der Ton selbst ist die Einheit, die sich in der strömenden Synthesis der kontinuierlichen Intentionalität des sich selbst abstufenden Selbsterscheinens als eines und identifizierbares gibt und ohne diese Abstufung gar nicht denkbar ist. . . . Und nun gar, wenn ich eine Melodie höre, so ist die in absoluter Originalität gehörte Melodie nicht der eine just erklingende und dauernde Ton, sondern eben die Melodie, die sich so und so gestaltende Wahrnehmungseinheit, sich gestaltend im Durchgang durch die Form des Jetzt, aber auch die Formen der Vergangenheit und die Form der offenen Zukunft. . . . " F I 29, 28a–28b.

98. *Cartesianische Meditationen,* Section 53.

99. *Conversations,* December 12, 1931, 55.

100. Ibid., March 11, 1932, 70. Fink also tells Cairns: "The *Ideen* analyzes acts

in the realm of the *Urmodus* <primitive mode> of givenness: presence." Ibid., August 24, 1931, 25.

101. This development has been traced in the classic article by John Brough, "The Emergence of an Absolute Consciousness in Husserl's Early Writings on Time-Consciousness," *Man and World* 5 (1972): 298–326.

102. For the best study on the issue of intersubjectivity, see Dan Zahavi, *Husserl und die transzendentale Intersubjektivität: Eine Antwort auf die sprachpragmatische Kritik, Phaenomenologica,* Vol. 135 (Dordrecht: Kluwer Academic Publishers, 1996); "Husserl's Intersubjective Transformation of Transcendental Philosophy," *Journal of the British Society for Phenomenology* 27 (October 1996): 228–245.

103. *Intersubjektivität III,* 50–52.

104. Ibid., 51.

105. Ibid.

106. Ibid., 46.

107. Ibid., 43.

108. Ibid., 51. Italics removed.

109. Ibid.

110. Ibid.

111. Ibid., 46. He adds the precaution that this should not be understood as a "genetic succession."

112. Ibid., 52. Italics mine.

113. Ibid.

114. *Cartesianische Meditationen,* 69; Eng. trans., 30.

115. Ibid.; Eng. trans., 30–31.

116. Kern suggests this in his "Einleitung [III] des Herausgebers," xxxiii.

117. *Intersubjektivität III,* 52.

118. We find it introduced in the Fourth Meditation, *Cartesianische Meditationen,* 100, 103, 109–114; Eng. trans., 66, 69, 75–81.

119. *Intersubjektivität III,* 51.

120. Ibid., 65.

121. Ibid., 65–66.

122. Ibid., 67–68.

123. Ibid., 69.

124. Reading *oder* in place of *und.*

125. Ibid., 74.

126. See *Intersubjektivität I,* especially 159–191.

127. "Die Einfühlung ist ihrer wesenseigentümlichen Seite nach eine Form der Vergegenwärtigung, insofern ähnlich der Erinnerung und Erwartung. Aber mit Unterschieden: Die Wiedererinnerung geht auf Vergangenheit und zwar meine Vergangenheit und, in transzendentaler Betrachtung, auf meine transzendentale Vergangenheit, mein vergangenes cogito, die ursprüngliche Erwartung ebenso auf meine Zukunft. Die Einfühlung aber geht auf die Gegenwart, aber nun nicht auf meine, sondern eine fremde Gegenwart und durch sie hindurch mittelbar auf fremde Vergangenheit und Zukunft. Auf mein gegenwärtiges Erleben geht ja mein Selbstwahrnehmen. Fremdes Erleben aber kann ich nicht eigentlich

wahrnehmen, sondern nur uneigentlich, durch Einfühlung mitwahrnehmen." F I 29, 19b.

128. "Hier würde der Rückgang zu dem Bewußtsein, die Reflexion in dieser Vergegenwärtigung zu einer real und hypothetisch möglichen Wahrnehmung führen, des Inhalts: Hätte ich soeben getastet, so würde ich das und das aktuell wahrnehmen, hätte ich den Blick in bestimmter Weise anders gewendet, so hätte ich jetzt das und das Bild, hätte ich mich auf den und den Standort gestellt, so wären meine Erscheinungen die und die usw." F I 29, 20a.

129. "Wenn wir nun die auf die physische Erfahrung des fremden Leibes aufgestufte einfühlende Erfahrung nicht als Basis eines objektiven Urteilens über den fremden Menschen als Glied der Welt verwerten, sondern ebenfalls phänomenologisch wenden, so erweitert sie den in sich geschlossenen Zusammenhang meiner wirklichen und motiviert möglichen Erlebnisse (meiner gegenwärtigen, vergangenen, künftig zu erwartenden oder bei meinem willkürlichen Eingreifen zu erwartenden Erlebnisse) um einen zweiten ebensolchen Zusammenhang, nämlich um eine ganze zweite Subjektivität. Durch Mienenspiel etc. werden nur einzelne Erlebniszusammenhänge zu spezieller Erfahrung kommen, aber sie sind dann umgeben von einem unbestimmten Horizont nicht näher bekannter Erlebnisse. Schließlich ist es ein ganzes Subjekt, das als ganzes schon durch den Gesamttypus des Leibes unbestimmt allgemein indiziert ist. Genauso wie mein eigener rein egologischer Erlebniszusammenhang, mit seinen wirklichen und für mich möglichen Erlebnissen, ein erfahrungsmäßig gegebener ist und diese Gegebenheit natürlich-naiven Rechtsgrund für Urteile abgibt, so ist der Zusammenhang zwischen meinem ganzen transzendentalen Leben und dem eines anderen als Erfahrungszusammenhang gegeben und kann empirisch transzendental beurteilt werden." F I 29, 20a.

130. "Ebenso aber reicht in meine Erlebnisgegenwart auch eine *fremde Erlebnisgegenwart* hinein, durch eine vergegenwärtigende Erfahrungsart, die Einfühlung. Und wenn ich nun die objektive Welt ausschalte und somit auch meinen Nebenmenschen als objektive Realität, so verbleibt mir doch der transzendentale Zusammenhang meines Bewußtseinsstroms mit dem seinen und dieser selbst als transzendental erfahrener im Zusammenhang mit dem meinen." F I 29, 20a–21b. The reference to the "empirical" is curious but there is one hint that suggests that he means that there are *traces* of the other that I find in myself, contingent in that they are due to the presence of the other, and I can employ these in my transcendental judgment leading to the givenness of the nexus of experience I share with the other. I suggest this because he goes on to argue that after the reduction and the bracketing of the experience of the "soul-life" of the other, I have "remaining" not only my own transcendental being but also "in me, in certain lines of my immanent 'empire' there is indexed the other transcendental subject." Ibid.

131. "die transzendental-soziale Subjektivität mir nicht so ursprünglich gegeben ist wie mein ego." F I 29, 22b.

132. "Das System der einfühlenden Vergegenwärtigung, das dem innengewendeten System der Wahrnehmungen und Wahrnehmungsmöglichkeiten vom fremden Leib entspricht und ihm überlagert ist, ist ein System transzendental reiner Erfahrungen vom Typus der Vergegenwärtigungen. Also wäre es falsch zu sagen,

daß die transzendental Reduktion mich auf mein eigenes Innensein und Innenleben, auf meine eigene transzendentale Subjektivität reduziert. Sie reduziert mich, wo immer ich in meiner Erfahrung fremde Subjektivität dieses und jenes oder eine Mehrheit von alter ego habe, auf eine sozusagen vielköpfige transzendentale Subjektivität, die mit meiner eigenen all diese alter ego, mit all ihrem Leben, mit all ihren Erscheinungen und intentionalen Korrelaten umspannt." F I 29, 22a–22b.

133. "ein universaler Zusammenhang." F I 29, 23a.

134. "Ich habe wirklich nur in meinem Einfühlungsfeld wenige alter egos, aber einen offenen Horizont immer neuer real möglicher Einfühlungen, die mir die weiteren alter egos ergeben würden." Ibid.

135. " . . . eine transzendental-soziale Zeit als die allgemeinsame Zeit, in der all die Zeiten der einzelnen ego sich decken und in der alle Bewußtseinsströme der einzelnen ego sich zu einem verbundenen transzendental-sozialen Bewußtseinsstrom einigen." F I 29, 23b.

136. Letter to Ingarden, March 19, 1930, *Briefwechsel,* 3/3, 262.

137. Let me emphasize that in what follows I am not discussing the way to phenomenological analysis, as we sketched it in chapter 1, but the way to a transcendental analysis in phenomenological terms. Aguirre suggests that because the Cartesian way presupposes and is built upon a "critique of experience," it too is "indirect." See Aguirre, *Genetische Phänomenologie und Reduktion,* 39. To the extent that the modified version of the Cartesian way abandons adequacy and relies upon critique, we lose any direct grounding of it. The sense in which it still remains direct will be explained presently.

138. *Krisis,* 158; after Eng. trans., 155.

139. "Kant und die Idee der Transzendentalphilosophie (1924)," *Erste Philosophie I,* 230–287; "Kant and the Idea of Transcendental Philosophy," *Southwest Journal of Philosophy* 5 (Fall 1974): 9–56.

140. Kant, *Kritik der reinen Vernunft,* B95–B106; Eng. trans., 106–114.

141. This is an "indirect way" ("Amsterdamer Vorträge," *Phänomenologische Psychologie,* 347) that moves from phenomenological psychology to transcendental philosophy. It can be found in *Erste Philosophie,* 132–163; in *Phänomenologische Psychologie* as a whole; and in *Krisis,* 194–276; Eng. trans., 191–265. *Erste Philosophie* treats this as the way through a critique of experience, a description that seems much more appropriate. To my knowledge Husserl does not include other ways under this general approach but it seems that in principle any of the social sciences dealing with interacting subjects, such as anthropology, social psychology, and sociology—phenomenologically constructed, of course—might also serve as a "clue." We label it the approach through intentional psychology by default, as Husserl did not consider other ways under this approach.

142. Especially important are lectures 47–51, 132–163. My analysis here is provisional, as I will take up his treatment in *Phenomenological Psychology* and the question of transcendental psychologism in some detail in chapter 10. I have found Aguirre's account of this section most helpful and my analysis overlaps his at several points. See *Genetische Phänomenologie und Reduktion,* 44–49.

143. *Erste Philosophie II,* 126.

144. Ibid., 143.

145. Ibid., 142.

146. Ibid.
147. Ibid., 153.
148. Ibid., 145.
149. Ibid., 153.
150. Ibid., 317.
151. This is the approach of *Formale und transzendentale Logik.*
152. Cf. *Erste Philosophie II,* 229–274.
153. This will be discussed presently.
154. *Krisis,* 175; after Eng. trans., 172.
155. Ibid., 70–71; Eng. trans., 68–70.
156. Ibid., 175; after Eng. trans., 172.
157. "Kant und die Idee einer Transzendentalphilosophie," *Erste Philosophie I,* 244; after Eng. trans., 20.
158. Ibid.
159. Ibid.
160. Ibid.
161. Ibid., 244–245; Eng. trans., 20–21.
162. Ibid., 245–246; after Eng. trans., 21.
163. Ibid., 246; Eng. trans., 21.
164. Ibid., 245; Eng. trans., 21.
165. Ibid., 248; after Eng. trans., 23.
166. Ibid., 247; after Eng. trans., 23.
167. Ibid., 248; after Eng. trans., 24.
168. Cf. ibid.
169. Ibid., 257–258; after Eng. trans., 31.
170. Ibid., 254; after Eng. trans., 28.
171. Ibid., 256–257; after Eng. trans., 30–31. Translation modified and italics removed. Thus he still speaks of "pure consciousness" as "the *absolutely self-contained realm of purely subjective being,*" though this is cashed out epistemologically, not metaphysically, for it is "the realm of a unique science in contrast to all 'positive' sciences." Ibid., 254; after Eng. trans., 29.
172. Ibid., 272; after Eng. trans., 44.

7. FROM CATEGORIAL TO CONSTITUTIVE PHENOMENOLOGY

1. *Ideen I,* 163; Eng. trans., 193–194, altered.
2. On the treatment of meaning as a species in the *Investigations,* see chapter 2 above.
3. At this time Husserl was in the throes of drafting his Bernauer manuscripts on time.
4. Letter to Ingarden, April 5, 1918, *Briefwechsel,* 3/3, 182.
5. *Conversations,* August 28, 1931, 27–28.
6. Husserl, *Phänomenologische Psychologie,* 30; after Eng. trans., 21.
7. For an account of the various texts used in *Experience and Judgment,* see Dieter Lohmar, "Zu der Entstehung und den Ausgangsmaterialien von Edmund Husserls Werk *Erfahrung und Urteil,*" *Husserl Studies* 13 (1996): 31–71.
8. For a full account of this, see Dan Zahavi, *Self-Awareness and Alterity: A*

Phenomenological Investigation (Evanston, Ill.: Northwestern University Press, 1999).

9. *Analysen zur passiven Synthesis,* 340.

10. In *Erfahrung und Urteil* the categorial and the constitutive are usually treated together. See pp. 50, 269f., 328; Eng. trans., 50, 226f., 274. In some other passages the constitutive and the genetic are taken as one. Cf. ibid., 78f.; Eng. trans., 74f. This distinction is not carried through *Ideen I,* probably because the problem of time was excluded from its considerations. Cf. pp. 197f.; Eng. trans., 193f. At the end of the 1921 text Husserl recalls this deficiency of *Ideen I* when he says: "Sometime I must go through the *Ideas* in order to become clearer as to what still distinguishes the doctrine of the structures of consciousness from constitutive considerations, if I also consider everything immanent 'constitutively.'" *Analysen zur passiven Synthesis,* 345.

11. One of the best arguments for a distinction between categorial and constitutive phenomenology is historical: the Munich school took up the phenomenology of the *Logical Investigations* with enthusiasm but emphatically rejected the constitutional problematic, and the method of reduction linked to it, as they were developed in *Ideas I.* Husserl himself understood that this was the decisive difference. We have already noted that he wrote to Ingarden in 1921 that "Even Pfänder's phenomenology is, in fact, something essentially different from mine. Because the problems of constitution never fully surface he, who is otherwise basically reliable and solid, lands in a dogmatic metaphysics." To Pfänder himself he wrote in 1931: "I have lost the belief, which I had in earlier years, that you would recognize the revolutionary meaning of the phenomenological reduction and the transcendental constitutive phenomenology springing from it and that you with your students would share [*sich beteiligen an*] the colossal problem of its meaning." Letter to Pfänder, January 6, 1931, *Briefwechsel,* 3/2, 183. On this point, see Karl Schuhmann, *Die Dialektik der Phänomenologie I: Husserl über Pfänder, Phaenomenologica,* Vol. 56 (The Hague: Martinus Nijhoff, 1973), 3.

12. *Analysen zur passiven Synthesis,* 340.

13. See W. Hogrebe, "Konstitution," *Historisches Wörterbuch der Philosophie,* ed. J. Ritter and K. Gründer (Darmstadt: Wissenschaftliche Buchgesellschaft, 1976), IV, 992ff.

14. *Analysen zur passiven Synthesis,* 340.

15. Cf. ibid., 25–191.

16. Ibid., 111, claims that transformations like retention (and, by extension, protention and all passive syntheses belonging to a complete act of perception, I would suggest) are not themselves intentional and thus cannot be modalized. The notion of modalization applies to whole intentional acts. With this said we will take the liberty of speaking of modes of passive synthesis and modalizations of active synthesis.

17. Ibid., 303.

18. *Intersubjektivität II,* 38. This will be discussed in the next chapter.

19. *Analysen zur passiven Synthesis,* 340.

20. Ibid.

21. Ibid., 344, 347.

22. *Intersubjektivität II,* 41.

23. *Analysen zur passiven Synthesis,* 40.

24. *Intersubjektivität II,* 41.

25. The use of the term "constitution" in *Logische Untersuchungen,* I, 116–121, 149; Eng. trans., I, 140–143, 163, is either biological or anthropological. Still, we can find clear anticipations of the notion as Sokolowski has shown in his *The Formation of Husserl's Concept of Constitution, Phaenomenologica,* Vol. 18 (The Hague: Martinus Nijhoff, 1964).

26. *Analysen zur passiven Synthesis,* 340.

27. We can see this in one passage from F I 29 where Husserl reaches into and corrects his original London lectures, which we were tracing in the last chapter. "Through empathy each can set themselves in the place of each other and recognize that his system of experience experiences what the other does. Each can also come to an understanding with each other and each can experience mediately the experiences of the other as confirmations and possibly as adjudication of his own experiences." (Durch Einfühlung kann sich jeder in jeden versetzen und erkennen, daß sein Erfahrungssystem dasselbe erfährt was das andere. Jeder kann sich auch mit jedem verständigen und jeder die Erfahrungen des anderen mittelbar erfahren als Bestätigungen seiner eigenen Erfahrungen, evtl. aber auch als Berichtigungen.) F I 37, 80a. A "kommunikative Ichallheit" is produced through empathy. Ibid.

28. See my *Origins of Meaning,* Parts 2 and 3, and "Verbindende Namen/Verbundene Gegenstände: Frege und Husserl über Bedeutung," *Phänomenologie im Widerstreit,* ed. Christoph Jamme and Otto Pöggeler (Frankfurt am Main: Suhrkamp, 1989), 141–191.

29. Jacques Derrida, *Speech and Phenomena,* trans. David B. Allison (Evanston, Ill.: Northwestern University Press, 1973), 64–66.

30. Cf. *Ideen I,* 103–105, 162; Eng. trans., 125–127, 192.

31. *Analysen zur passiven Synthesis,* 337.

32. Ibid., 338.

33. *Briefwechsel,* 3/3, 184–185. This is a draft of a letter sent by Ingarden to Husserl. It has this note by Ingarden: "Letter to Husserl about the 6th Investigation and Idealism." Ibid., 569. This note also refers to a complete rereading of the Sixth Investigation (Husserl had planned a full revision for a second edition, as we saw in chapter 5) and the important sections from *Ideas I* on the problem of idealism. The letter to Husserl continues: "There would have to be carried out more precisely the noetic differences between intuition . . . and signitive intention as well as a pure noematic (respectively, in a certain sense 'ontically') directed consideration of the 'meaning.'"

34. *Ideen I,* 29; Eng. trans., 29.

35. For a fuller account of this development, see Welton, *Origins of Meaning,* Part 2.

36. "Es wäre beispielsweise ein ganz verkehrtes Vorgehen bei der äußeren Wahrnehmungsanalyse, wenn man geleitet durch sensualistische Traditionen damit anfangen wollte zu sagen: wahrgenommen sind Komplexe von Sinnesdaten. Sinnesdaten sind in der Regel sogar falsche Produkte einer theoretischen Analyse in psychologischer Einstellung. Aber der notwendige Anfang jeder phänomenologischen Beschreibung ist das konkret volle Phänomen; genau so wie es in der un-

mittelbaren Anschauung sich darbietet. Direkt muß nach unserer Methode jede Aussage aus der reinen Anschauung geschöpft werden. In dieser Hinsicht ist es klar, daß das Erste nicht ist; 'ich sehe Empfindungsdaten', sondern ich sehe Häuser, Bäume usw. ich höre von ferne her Glocken, einen Wagen rasseln etc." F II 3, 29a.

37. See editor's dating in *Analysen zur passiven Synthesis,* xvii, 363.

38. *Analysen zur passiven Synthesis,* 363.

39. *Zeitbewusstsein,* 325; after Eng. trans., 338. Italics removed.

40. Ibid., 326; after Eng. trans., 338.

41. Letter to Ingarden, April 5, 1918, *Briefwechsel,* 3/3, 182.

42. *Erfahrung und Urteil,* 79; Eng. trans., 76. Here the ego does not act but "yields." See 81; Eng. trans., 77.

43. For Husserl's account of the body, see *Ideen II,* 55–90, 143–161; Eng. trans., 60–95, 151–169.

44. For a fuller account, see Welton, *Origins of Meaning,* chapters 6 and 7.

45. *Analysen zur passiven Synthesis,* 319.

46. See ibid., 25–64, on the varieties of perceptual modalizations.

47. See ibid., 341f. As we will see this does not exhaust genetic analysis but merely introduces it.

48. Searle, *Speech Acts,* 19–21.

49. We will consider the texts from Husserl's later writings that support the following analysis in chapter 9. For a fuller account of this as well as textual arguments concerning its development in Husserl's thought, see Welton, *Origins of Meaning,* chapters 7 to 9, and "Verbindende Namen/Verbundene Gegenstände," Section 13. Again, I am indebted to the way Robert Sokolowski in his *Presence and Absence* handles certain sections of *Formal and Transcendental Logic* for the distinction between reports and claims. See Sokolowski, *Presence and Absence,* especially chapter 8. I freely use his distinction, yet my analysis takes this contrast in a different direction than his. In particular, I maintain that reports have a meaning whose specification cannot be limited to the intentional content of claims.

50. *De Interpretatione, The Basic Works of Aristotle,* ed. Richard McKeon (New York: Random House, 1941), 42 (= 17a).

51. *De Poetica, Basic Works,* 1474 (= 1456b).

52. *Presence and Absence,* 99, 146.

53. *Analysen zur passiven Synthesis,* 27.

54. Ibid., 38.

55. Ibid., 39.

56. Ibid., 59.

57. Ibid., 60.

58. Ibid., 62.

59. Ibid., 62.

60. We will take up these distinctions in chapter 14.

61. *Ideen I,* 217; Eng. trans., 252–253.

62. *Formale und transzendentale Logik,* 129; Eng. trans., 124.

63. We cannot even begin to engage the full range of issues surrounding Husserl's theory of the noema and meaning. For an earlier attempt, see my *Origins of Meaning,* Parts 2 and 3. Since then Bernet has provided a masterful study of the

historical development of the concept of meaning and the noema between the *Logical Investigations* and *Ideas I* by looking at two lecture courses that Husserl gave, the first on logic and epistemology in the Winter Semester of 1906/07, the second on theory of meaning in the Summer Semester of 1908. I draw from his analysis of the latter below. See Rudolf Bernet, "Husserls Begriff des Noema," *Husserl-Ausgabe und Husserl-Forschung* (Dordrecht: Kluwer Academic Publishers, 1990), 61–80. The text of Husserl's two lecture courses are published as *Einleitung in die Logik* and *Vorlesungen über Bedeutungslehre.*

64. Husserl, *Vorlesungen über Bedeutungslehre,* 28, 38.

65. Ibid., 81–85.

66. Ibid., 85. I am following Bernet's analysis in this paragraph; see "Husserls Begriff des Noema," 72–73.

67. *Origins of Meaning,* Part 3.

68. Cf. Husserl, *Krisis,* 52, 371–372; Eng. trans., 52, 361.

69. To note a difference between epistemic and nonepistemic is already to speak in ideal types. Concrete perception and discourse will show variations and mixtures of the two.

70. Cf. McIntyre and Smith, *Husserl and Intentionality,* 200–204.

71. Dieter Henrich, "Ding an sich: ein Prolegomenon zur Metaphysik des Endlichen," *Vernunft des Glaubens,* ed. J. Rohls and G. Wenz (Göttingen: Vandenhoeck & Ruprecht, 1989), 42–92.

72. *Formale und transzendentale Logik,* 297; Eng. trans., 292; and *Analysen zur passiven Synthesis,* 295, 361, 362. This notion is defined in a way different from that of Kant: "For this transcendental theory of the senses researches precisely all the occurrences of aesthetic, perceptual and, in general, intuitive apperception." *Analysen zur passiven Synthesis,* 361.

73. *Logische Untersuchungen,* II/2, 128ff.; Eng. trans., 773ff.

8. THE TURN TO GENETIC ANALYSIS

1. Letter to Natorp, June 29, 1918, *Briefwechsel,* 3/5, 137.
2. *Intersubjektivität II,* 41.
3. Letter to Grimme, September 1, 1922, *Briefwechsel,* 3/3, 85.
4. *Phänomenologische Psychologie,* 30; after Eng. trans., 21.
5. *Ideen I,* 163; Eng. trans., 193.
6. Husserl, *Aufsätze und Vorträge (1922–1937),* 29, 55.
7. *Analysen zur passiven Synthesis,* 342.
8. These are known as the *Kaizo* articles, published in *Aufsätze und Vorträge (1922–1937),* 3–94. They will be discussed in detail in chapter 12 below.
9. See my "Verbindende Namen/Verbundene Gegenstände," passim.
10. See the first chapter of the Sixth Investigation in his *Logische Untersuchungen.*
11. See Section 124 of *Ideen I.*
12. Cf. *Ideen I,* 163; Eng. trans., 193–194.
13. As reported in Kern, "Einleitung [II] des Herausgebers," xvii.
14. Letter to Ingarden, November 25, 1921, *Briefwechsel,* 3/3, 213.
15. Letter to Ingarden, December 24, 1921, *Briefwechsel,* 3/3, 215.

16. Letter to Husserl, March 21, 1921, *Briefwechsel,* 3/2, 165.
17. Letter to Husserl, January 1, 1921, *Briefwechsel,* 3/2, 239.
18. Letter to Bell, September 22, 1920, *Briefwechsel,* 3/3, 20.
19. Letter to Ingarden, December 12, 1920, *Briefwechsel,* 3/3, 206.
20. Letter to Mahnke, February 21, 1926, *Briefwechsel,* 3/3, 453.
21. A course with this title had been offered several times before; but this time it is the London lectures, and then his interventions into them, as we traced in chapter 6, that formed his text.
22. Letter to Bell, December 13, 1922, *Briefwechsel,* 3/3, 43.
23. Letter to Bell, December 13, 1922, *Briefwechsel,* 3/3, 43–44.
24. Published as *Erste Philosophie I* and *II.*
25. See "Textkritische Anmerkungen," *Analysen zur passiven Synthesis,* 445.
26. See "Textkritische Anmerkungen," *Analysen zur passiven Synthesis,* for p. 411, line 4, on p. 524. This *Beilage* is from D 19.
27. What is now published as *Analysen zur passiven Synthesis* contains a lecture course as preserved in manuscripts with the signatures F I 37, F I 38, and F I 39. Husserl gave this course on three different occasions: the original version during the Winter Semester of 1920/21; a revised and shortened version, omitting F I 39, during the Summer Semester of 1923; and yet a further revised version, also omitting F I 39, during the Winter Semester of 1925/26. Pages 3–32 of F I 37 were incorporated into the "Introduction" and "Preparatory Considerations" of *Formale und transzendentale Logik* (written at the end of 1928 into 1929 and published in 1929). Pages 3–7 of the manuscript are reproduced on pages 1–3 and 14–15 (original pagination) of that work, as Husserl both places the subject matter of the manuscript there and then excludes it from any direct consideration. According to Husserl's original design, an account of the way in which the meaning of logical expressions "points back to their origination from experience" and arises from a "deeper lying genesis" is presupposed by the whole of *Formale und transzendentale Logik* (185; Eng. trans., 208). Another indication of this connection is found in the fact that F I 39, which in the original lectures of 1920/21 followed F I 37 and F I 38 and carried the title "Activity, Theme, Thematic Action," was used by Landgrebe in his edition of *Erfahrung und Urteil,* the work especially concerned with "Investigations into the Genealogy of Logic," as the subtitle reads. Cf. "Textkritische Anmerkungen," *Analysen zur passiven Synthesis,* 443. The forthcoming English translation of *Analysen zur passiven Synthesis* by Anthony Steinbock will reconstruct the *Husserliana* text, bringing it into conformity with Husserl's original lecture course.
28. Husserl often uses the term "transcendental aesthetic" in order to set his account of passive synthesis in contrast to "transcendental logic," a description of the sphere of predicative thought built upon it. See *Analysen zur passiven Synthesis,* 295, 361f., and especially 498.
29. Reprinted in *Philosophie der Arithmetik,* 1–283.
30. Ibid., 14, 71–76, 91–93.
31. Ibid., 32.
32. Ibid., 289–339.
33. *Logische Untersuchungen* (1st ed.), II, 4, 8; contrast *Logische Untersuchungen,* II/1, 3, 6; Eng. trans., I, 249, 252. Findlay's translation is of the second

edition but often includes translations of important sections of the first edition. If there is a corresponding translation I will give the page references to the translation.

34. *Logische Untersuchungen* (1st ed.), II, 335; contrast *Logische Untersuchungen,* II/1, 357; Eng. trans., II, 544.

35. *Logische Untersuchungen* (1st ed.), II, 335–336; contrast *Logische Untersuchungen,* II/1, 357–358; Eng. trans., II, 544–545.

36. *Logische Untersuchungen* (1st ed.), II, 336.

37. Ibid. By the second edition Husserl claims that what he has really done in Section 6 is isolate the "phenomenological content" of "the empirical ego in the sense of the soulish subject" and to "broaden out" the notion of experience "from what is inwardly perceived to the notion of the 'phenomenological ego,' by which the empirical ego is intentionally constituted," a claim that makes almost no sense at all. *Logische Untersuchungen,* II/1, 358–359; Eng. trans., II, 545.

38. *Logische Untersuchungen* (1st ed.), 336; after Eng. trans., II, 545f. For the background on the contrast between static and genetic analysis one should probably look to the work of Paul Natorp. Husserl mentions Natorp's *Allgemeine Psychologie* on p. xvi (Eng. trans., I, 49) of the Foreword to the second edition and so there is no doubt that he read his work. Paul Natorp, *Allgemeine Psychologie nach kritischer Methode,* First Book: *Objekt und Methode der Psychologie* [1912] (Amsterdam: E. J. Bonset, 1965). Also notice that he mentions Natorp just before he informs the reader that he has eliminated Section 7 of the Fifth Investigation, from which this quotation is taken. This influence is also suggested by the fact that Section 8 extensively quotes and criticizes Natorp's *Einleitung in die Psychologie nach kritischer Methode* (Freiburg im Breisgau: J. C. B. Mohr, 1888). For a fuller discussion of Natorp's role in the development of genetic method in Husserl, see my "The Systematicity of Husserl's Transcendental Philosophy: From Static to Genetic Method, *Husserl: A Critical Reader,* ed. Donn Welton (forthcoming).

39. *Logische Untersuchungen* (1st ed.), II, 342; Eng. trans., II, 549.

40. Of course, this usage can also be found on occasion in late texts: "The psychology of the [modern] era is psychology as natural sciences; its problems of origins are thus problems of causal genesis, whereby this causality is characterized more precisely as natural causality." "Über Ursprung [1930]," *Aufsätze und Vorträge (1922–1937),* 132.

41. Now published as *Die Idee der Phänomenologie.*

42. See *Logische Untersuchungen,* I, xiv; Eng. trans., I, 48.

43. *Logische Untersuchungen* (1st ed.), II, 339; Eng. trans., II, 548. Italics removed.

44. *Phänomenologische Psychologie,* 40; after Eng. trans., 28.

45. Ibid.

46. Ibid., 34; after Eng. trans., 24. See ibid., 36; Eng. trans., 25, for his elaboration of this point.

47. Ibid., 42–43; after Eng. trans., 30–31.

48. Ibid., 42; after Eng. trans., 30.

49. *Logische Untersuchungen,* II/2, 34; after Eng. trans., II, 695.

50. Ibid., II/2, 42; Eng. trans., II, 701.

51. Ibid., II/2, 34; Eng. trans., II, 696.

52. Ibid., II/2, 46; after Eng. trans., II, 704.

53. *Ideen III*, 125–126; Eng. trans., 113, altered.

54. Ibid., 129; Eng. trans., 117, altered.

55. There is an especially lucid account of this passage in Bernet et al., *Edmund Husserl;* Eng. trans., *An Introduction to Husserlian Phenomenology*, 197:

> According to Husserl's later conception, however, the analysis of this "system of manifestation and authentication," a system directed teleologically toward the primordial givenness of an object or toward the fulfillment of the corresponding intentions, is not yet genetic in the proper sense. To be sure, these systems are rules for the temporal courses of the multiplicities of consciousness, but such courses are only the subjective correlates of a stable identity, that is to say, they are the subjective correlates of the object that attains to givenness within them. In a properly genetic phenomenology, the concern will no longer be with analyzing these finished systems of correlation, but rather with inquiring into their genesis.

56. As far as I know, the term "genetic" does not occur in the texts gathered in *Zeitbewusstsein.*

57. *Intersubjektivität II*, 221.

58. *Cartesianische Meditationen*, 114; Eng. trans., 81.

59. Ibid., 169; Eng. trans., 142.

60. Brough, "Emergence of an Absolute Consciousness in Husserl's Early Writings on Time-Consciousness," 298–326; and "Translator's Introduction," *On the Phenomenology of the Consciousness of Internal Time (1893–1917)*, xi–lvii.

61. Husserl, *Analysen zur passiven Synthesis*, 340.

62. Ibid., 111.

63. Ibid., 128.

64. Ibid., 387. Text dated between 1920 and 1926.

65. Cf. ibid., 409.

66. Ibid., 128.

67. See letter to Natorp, June 29, 1918, *Briefwechsel*, 3/5, 137, cited as a caption to this chapter. The claim that this shift to the idea of transcendental genesis had been underway for over a decade is clearly overstated, probably provoked by the use of the term "genesis" in Natorp's own work. Still, it points to the way that Husserl thought of his newer genetic analysis as a development of the static framework of *Ideas I.* See Kern, *Husserl und Kant*, 346f.; and Bernet et al., *Edmund Husserl;* Eng. trans., *An Introduction to Husserlian Phenomenology*, 196–197.

68. *Ideen II*, 198, 215, 251, 316, 349, 357; Eng. trans., 209, 226, 263, 329, 360, 368.

69. See "Einleitung des Herausgebers," *Ideen II*, xvi.

70. *Aufsätze und Vorträge (1922–1937)*, 29. We will undertake a further study of these articles in chapter 12.

9. GENETIC PHENOMENOLOGY

1. *Intersubjektivität II*, 221.

2. Letter to Natorp, February 1, 1922, *Briefwechsel*, 3/5, 151–152. See Kern, "Einleitung [II] des Herausgebers," xix.

3. What are known as the *Kaizo* articles, written in 1923–1924, are the only

possible exception. They bear the title "Fünf Aufsätze über Erneuerung," *Aufsätze und Vorträge (1922–1937)*, 3–94. See chapter 12 for an analysis of them.

4. Kern, "Einleitung [II] des Herausgebers," xx.

5. Letter to Ingarden, August 31, 1923, *Briefwechsel*, 3/3, 218.

6. Letter to Daubert, December 22, 1923, *Briefwechsel*, 3/2, 80.

7. Letter to Misch, November 16, 1930, *Briefwechsel*, 3/6, 282–283.

8. Letter to Ingarden, December 21, 1930, *Briefwechsel*, 3/3, 270.

9. See Kern, "Einleitung [III] des Herausgebers," xl–xlii.

10. The German reads "zur egologischen Bewußtseinslehre" and thus has the connotation of "toward a doctrine of consciousness approached egologically."

11. The manuscript text breaks off here; the rest is Fink's typed copy of it.

12. This text has been preserved in a typed copy by Fink, but Kern has located the original stenographic text up to the beginning of "Volume IV" (manuscript F IV 1, 11). See "Einleitung [III] des Herausgebers," xxxv, note 2, on the question of the text and p. xxxvi for the text itself.

13. See Steinbock, *Home and Beyond*, for an analysis of generative phenomenology.

14. Text printed in Kern, "Einleitung [III] des Herausgebers," xxxvii–xl.

15. Letter to Ingarden, December 21, 1930, *Briefwechsel*, 3/3, 270; Kern, "Einleitung [III] des Herausgebers," xli.

16. Text printed in Kern, "Einleitung [III] des Herausgebers," xxxix.

17. Text printed in ibid.

18. "The progress of the planned work sketched by Husserl corresponds rather precisely to the four sections of Fink's disposition of the 'first book.'" Ibid., xli.

19. "Progressive phenomenology asks about the origin of space itself and not the representation of space." The section after the one on progressive phenomenology is called "Basic Features of Phenomenological Metaphysics." Text is printed in ibid., xxxix.

20. See letter to Misch, *Briefwechsel*, 3/6, 274.

21. In his letter to Misch of August 3, 1929, *Briefwechsel*, 3/6, 277, Husserl says that he has read them both in detail (*genau*); but Kern claims that an intensive study did not take place until April or May of 1930. They were published in *Der philosophische Anzeiger* III/3 (1929): 267–368, and III/3–4 (1929): 405–475. The third and final installment appeared in Volume IV/3–4 (1930): 181–330. If the third installment was not part of Husserl's study in April or May of 1930, not having appeared by then, Husserl had certainly read it by the time he wrote Misch in November of that year. See letter to Misch, November 27, 1930, *Briefwechsel*, 3/6, 283. The three installments were then published as a book titled *Lebensphilosophie und Phänomenologie: Eine Auseinandersetzung der Dilthey'schen Richtung mit Heidegger und Husserl* (Bonn: 1930; Darmstadt: Wissenschaftliche Buchgesellschaft, 1975).

22. After Kern, "Einleitung [III] des Herausgebers," xliii.

23. Surprised at how quickly he had responded, Husserl tells Misch that his will be the first review of the work. See letter to Misch, November 16, 1930, *Briefwechsel*, 3/6, 282.

24. Letter to Misch, November 27, 1930, *Briefwechsel*, 3/6, 283. See the only

surviving exchange of letters between Dilthey and Husserl from 1911, the year of Dilthey's death, in *Briefwechsel,* 3/6, 43–53. See also Kern, "Einleitung [I] des Herausgebers," xxxii–xxxiii, and "Einleitung [III] des Herausgebers," xlvii–xlviii, on Husserl's and Dilthey's relationship.

25. Letter to Misch, November 27, 1930, *Briefwechsel,* 3/6, 283.

26. See the discussion of the *Kaizo* articles in chapter 12.

27. *Logische Untersuchungen* (1st ed.), II, 331. Contrast *Logische Untersuchungen,* II/1, 353; Eng. trans., II, 541.

28. *Logische Untersuchungen* (1st ed.), II, 331.

29. *Logische Untersuchungen* (1st ed.), II, 336. Cf. *Logische Untersuchungen,* II/1, 358; Eng. trans., II, 545.

30. *Logische Untersuchungen* (1st ed.), II, 336. Contrast *Logische Untersuchungen,* II/1, 358; Eng. trans., II, 545.

31. It is no wonder that we see the second edition scrambling to set all this right, though with little success. After granting that the analysis gives us "the phenomenological content of the ego, of the empirical ego in the sense of the psychic [soulish] subject," Husserl adds: "The notion of experience has widened out from what is inwardly perceived, and that is in *this* sense conscious, to the notion of the 'phenomenological ego,' by which the empirical ego is intentionally constituted"! Ibid., II/1, 358–359; after Eng. trans., II, 545.

32. Ibid., I/1, 361; after Eng. trans., II, 549.

33. As a point about the method, not the content, of Kant's theory, it could be plausibly argued that in principle the approach taken in the First Critique yields only "static" analysis. This is due in the final analysis to his characterization of the "I" as "empty," i.e., the transcendental unity of apperception is strictly a "formal" unity. As a result, the movement between various "strata" (e.g., sensibility and understanding) or from judgments to categories can be defined only in terms of "conditions" that can be read off the content of what appears to understanding and thus is restricted to relations of founding and founded that follow the course of conceptual implications or, better, entailment.

34. "Nachwort," *Ideen III,* 159; after Eng. trans. ("Epilogue," *Ideas II*), 426.

35. *Ideen II,* 121; Eng. trans., 128, 413; "Nachwort," *Ideen III,* 145; Eng. trans. ("Epilogue," *Ideas II*), 412.

36. Bernet et al., *Edmund Husserl;* Eng. trans., *An Introduction to Husserlian Phenomenology,* 211.

37. A VI 30, 38b as cited and translated in Bernet et al., *Edmund Husserl;* Eng. trans., *An Introduction to Husserlian Phenomenology,* 213.

38. *Cartesianısche Meditationen,* 101; Eng. trans., 67.

39. *Ideen II,* 299–300; after Eng. trans., 313.

40. *Cartesianische Meditationen,* 109–110; Eng. trans., 75–76, altered. Italics removed.

41. *Erfahrung und Urteil,* 138; Eng. trans., 122–123, altered.

42. Strictly translated this sentence reads: "And on the basis of this appresentation—just as I in relation to my self meet practically an I-I determination—I can meet an I-Thou determination in relation to the Thou; the appresented I, likewise, can want to determine me; through the medium of empathy I can and must experience this determination as a real determination."

43. *Intersubjectivität II*, 276.
44. As found in *Sein und Zeit* [1928] (Tübingen: Max Niemeyer, 1967); *Being and Time*, trans. John Macquarrie and Edward Robinson (New York: Harper and Row, 1962), Part 1, chapter 5.
45. *Ideen III*, 128; Eng. trans., 116.
46. *Analysen zur passiven Synthesis*, 338.
47. Ibid., 339.
48. Ibid.
49. *Cartesianische Meditationen*, 109; Eng. trans., 75.
50. On this point see Manfred Frank, *Selbstbewußtsein und Selbsterkenntnis* (Stuttgart: Phillip Reclam, 1991), 18–19.
51. *Analysen zur passiven Synthesis*, 342.
52. Ibid., 343.
53. *Erfahrung und Urteil*, 78; Eng. trans., 75.
54. Sections 42 to 46 are especially suggestive.
55. *Formale und transzendentale Logik*, Sections 80 and 85. The following is taken from my "Verbindende Namen/Verbundene Gegenstände," Section 13.
56. In *Formale und transzendentale Logik*, 437–446, written between 1922 and 1926.
57. Ibid., 440.
58. Ibid.
59. Ibid., 25; Eng. trans., 21.
60. Ibid., 27; Eng. trans., 23.
61. Ibid., 31; Eng. trans., 27.
62. Cf. ibid., 192; Eng. trans., 185.
63. Ibid., 215; Eng. trans., 207.
64. Ibid.; Eng. trans., 208.
65. Ibid., 216; Eng. trans., 208.
66. Ibid., 207; Eng. trans., 199.
67. Ibid., 207; Eng. trans., 199–200.
68. For example, see his "Ursprung der Geometrie," *Krisis*, 365–386; Eng. trans., 353–378.
69. *Formale und transzendentale Logik*, 449.
70. Ibid., 344.
71. Ibid., 350. Italics mine.
72. *Erfahrung und Urteil*, 336; Eng. trans., 279.
73. *Cartesianische Meditationen*, 113; after Eng. trans., 80. Italics removed.
74. *Analysen zur passiven Synthesis*, 117.
75. *Cartesianische Meditationen*, 114; Eng. trans., 81.
76. "Natur und Geist," F I 32, 162a, as cited and translated in Bernet et al., *Edmund Husserl*; Eng. trans., *An Introduction to Husserlian Phenomenology*, 202–203. Kern dates this text as Summer Semester 1927. In this paragraph I am following his very incisive analysis on page 202.
77. *Ideen II*, 98; Eng. trans., 104.
78. *Analysen zur passiven Synthesis*, 342.
79. Ibid., 154.
80. Ibid., 187.

81. Cf. ibid., 190.
82. Ibid., 428.
83. Ibid., 73.
84. Ibid., 74.
85. Ibid., 77.
86. Ibid., 428.
87. Ibid.
88. Jean Piaget, *The Mechanisms of Perception,* trans. G. N. Seagrim (New York: Basic Books, 1969), passim.
89. *Formale und transzendentale Logik,* 316; Eng. trans., 316. Italics altered.
90. Manuscript B IV 12, p. 8/9, as cited in Kern, *Husserl und Kant,* 268.
91. *Analysen zur passiven Synthesis,* 345.
92. Ibid., 339.
93. *Formale und transzendentale Logik,* 318; Eng. trans., 318.
94. In this paragraph we are following Held's excellent analysis in "Einleitung [II]," 30. See also his *Lebendige Gegenwart,* passim.
95. Held, "Einleitung [II]," 30.
96. Ibid.
97. On this topic see Steinbock, *Home and Beyond.*
98. *Analysen zur passiven Synthesis,* 344.
99. *Intersubjectivität II,* 221.
100. "Nachwort," *Ideen III,* 141; after Eng. trans. ("Epilogue," *Ideas II*), 408–409.
101. *Ideen I,* 93; Eng. trans., 112.
102. *Intersubjektivität II,* 41.
103. *Ideen III,* 93–105; Eng. trans., 80–90.
104. *Formale und transzendentale Logik,* 191; Eng. trans., 184. This is also called "constitutive origins-research," "evidence-critique," and simply "transcendental critique." Ibid., 185, 209, 283; Eng. trans., 177, 202, 245.
105. *Analysen zur passiven Synthesis,* 340. See also ibid., 340–345.
106. *Krisis,* 59; Eng. trans., 58. See also ibid., 58–60, especially 365; Eng. trans., 57–59, 353–354.
107. *Intersubjectivitat II,* 221.

10. TRANSCENDENTAL PSYCHOLOGISM

1. "Nachwort," *Ideen III,* 146–147; Eng. trans. ("Epilogue," *Ideas II*), 414, altered.
2. *Logische Untersuchungen,* I, 93; Eng. trans., I, 122.
3. See Dieter Henrich, "Selbstbewußtsein—Kritische Einleitung in eine Theorie," *Hermeneutik und Dialektik,* ed. R. Bubner et al. (Tübingen: J. C. B. Mohr [Siebeck], 1970), I, 257–284; and see especially Manfred Frank, *Die Unhintergehbarkeit von Individualität* (Frankfurt am Main: Suhrkamp, 1986), and *Selbstbewußtsein und Selbsterkenntnis.*
4. *Phänomenologische Psychologie,* 257. This passage is quoted from the second draft of the *Encyclopaedia Britannica* article and was probably penned by

Heidegger. See Husserl's title to this section in the critical remarks to page 256 on page 597.

5. J. N. Mohanty, *Husserl and Frege* (Bloomington: Indiana University Press, 1982), 18–42.

6. Ibid.

7. Husserl, *Briefwechsel,* VI, 107–117; Eng. trans. in Mohanty, *Husserl and Frege* 117–126.

8. See the analysis in chapter 8 above.

9. Two older works that deal with these texts are Biemel, "Husserls Encyclopaedia-Britannica Artikel und Heideggers Anmerkungen dazu," 246–280 and, on psychologism, Bachelard, *A Study of Husserl's Formal and Transcendental Logic,* trans. Embree, 93–113.

10. *Logische Untersuchungen,* I, chapter 2.

11. Ibid., I, 12–14, 110–112; Eng. trans., I, 60–62, 135–137.

12. Ibid., I, 66; Eng. trans., I, 102.

13. Ibid., I, 119; Eng. trans., I, 142.

14. Ibid., I, 169–173; Eng. trans., I, 179–181.

15. Ibid., I, 119; Eng. trans., I, 141.

16. Ibid., I, 68; Eng. trans., I, 103.

17. Ibid., I, 83; Eng. trans., I, 114.

18. Ibid., I, 90–92; Eng. trans., I, 120–121.

19. Ibid., II/1, 101; Eng. trans., I, 330.

20. Ibid., II/1, 415; Eng. trans., II, 589.

21. Ibid., II/1, 411; Eng. trans., II, 586.

22. Ibid., II/1, 413; Eng. trans., II, 587.

23. See ibid., II/1, 397; Eng. trans., II, 576.

24. Frege to Husserl, October 30 to November 1, 1906, *Briefwechsel,* VI, 113; after translation by Mohanty in *Husserl and Frege,* 122.

25. Martin Heidegger, "My Way to Phenomenology," *On Time and Being,* trans. Joan Stambaugh (New York: Harper and Row, 1972), 76–77. Italics mine.

26. *Ideen I,* 177–178; Eng. trans., 209. Italics removed.

27. All of these texts are collected in Husserl, *Phänomenologische Psychologie.*

28. Ibid., 188; Eng. trans., 144.

29. Ibid., 188; Eng. trans., 144. Italics mine.

30. Ibid., 471.

31. Ibid. Cf. p. 467.

32. Ibid., 455, 470.

33. Ibid., 474.

34. Ibid., 452. Cf. p. 455.

35. Ibid., 450.

36. Ibid.

37. Ibid., 451.

38. Ibid., 457. Italics mine.

39. Ibid., 46–47, 49, 130; Eng. trans., 33–34, 99.

40. Ibid., 245, 274.

41. Ibid., 335. At one point Husserl does seem to say that transcendental analysis grounds the world as a whole "logically" (see comment ibid., 622, on p. 337; see also ibid., 344), whereas the sciences can only assume its existence and then study it in its determinate being. This would suggest a rather important contrast at the level of the givens, one that is identical to Husserl's characterization of phenomenology in *Ideas I.* Its unique theme would be "the totality of being" or, put phenomenologically, "how the world for us is 'the' world in this consciousness" (*Phänomenologische Psychologie,* 332). There are two reasons for not pursuing this line here. The direct reason is that Husserl comes close to suggesting that phenomenological psychology might have the same range. See pp. 347, 341–342. The indirect reason is that this is, indeed, a much more promising approach but it is one that outstrips the capacity of a Cartesian approach. Both Kant and Heidegger would remind us that there are difficulties involved in the idea that an essentially Cartesian phenomenology can have the world in its totality as phenomena. See p. 274 and Heidegger's remarks reproduced in footnotes 1 and 2. We will take this up in the third part of this study.

42. Ibid., 339.

43. Ibid. Cf., *Ideen I,* 142–143; Eng. trans., 172–173.

44. *Phänomenologische Psychologie,* 340.

45. Ibid., 342.

46. See ibid., 467, 469.

47. Ibid., 237ff.

48. Ibid., 302ff.

49. Ibid., 290–295, 336–246.

50. Ibid., 327–328.

51. *Logische Untersuchungen,* I, 93; Eng. trans., I, 122.

52. *Phänomenologische Psychologie,* 294.

53. *Intersubjektivität III,* 385, 403.

54. Cf. *Phänomenologische Psychologie,* 452.

55. In chapter 6 I suggested that this is relative since immanent perception also has a certain inadequacy that results from the fact that the fleeting, flowing *Erlebnis* cannot be grasped "completely." See *Ideen I,* 82; Eng. trans., 97. We will return to this point momentarily.

56. *Ideen I,* 81; Eng. trans., 95–96. Italics removed.

57. *Ideen I,* 81; after Eng. trans., 95–96. Italics removed. The changes, found in Husserl's Copy D, are reproduced in *Ideen I* (Hua), Vol. 3/b, 494.

58. *Ideen I,* 81; after Eng. trans., 95–96. Italics removed. The changes, found in Husserl's Copy D, are reproduced in *Ideen I* (Hua), Vol. 3/b, 495.

59. *Ideen I,* 149–150; Eng. trans., 179–180.

60. Husserl, *Zeitbewusstsein,* 29–32; Eng. trans., 30–33.

61. See Brough, "The Emergence of an Absolute Consciousness in Husserl's Early Writings on Time-Consciousness," 83–100; and Brough, "Translator's Introduction," *On the Phenomenology of the Consciousness of Internal Time (1893–1917);* and see Bernet "Die ungegenwärtige Gegenwart," 16–57. On the development of Husserl's theory of time see Klaus Held, *Lebendige Gegenwart.*

62. *Ideen I,* 282; Eng. trans., 326.

63. Ibid., 294; Eng. trans., 339. Italics removed.
64. Ibid., 283; Eng. trans., 327.
65. This is found in his *Zeitbewusstsein,* passim.
66. Cf. *Ideen I,* 145; Eng. trans., 175.
67. Ibid., 150; Eng. trans., 180.
68. Ibid., 150; Eng. trans., 181.
69. *Analysen zur passiven Synthesis,* 111.
70. Ibid.
71. Though published in 1928, his *Vorlesungen zur Phänomenologie des inneren Zeitbewusstseins,* ed. Martin Heidegger, *Jahrbuch für Philosophie und phänomenologische Forschung,* Vol. 9 (Halle a.d. Saale: Max Niemeyer, 1928), viii–ix, 367–498, consisted mostly of lecture materials and manuscripts that date between 1905 and 1910.
72. *Analysen zur passiven Synthesis,* 111–112.
73. Ibid., 113–114.
74. Ibid., 113. Notice that this footnote is taken from another manuscript (D 19) and does not belong to the main text (F I 38).
75. *Analysen zur passiven Synthesis,* 113.
76. Reading *Wiedererinnerung* in place of *Erinnerung.*
77. Reading *Wiedererinnerung* in place of *Erinnerung.*
78. Ibid., 384. Italics mine.
79. Ibid., 385.
80. "[Die Apodiktizität der Wiedererinnerung]," *Analysen zur passiven Synthesis,* 365–383; an English translation is found in Edmund Husserl, "The Apodicticity of Recollection," trans. Deborah Chaffin, *Husserl Studies* 2 (1985): 10–32.
81. Reading *ego cogito* in place of "*ego cogito.*"
82. Reading *ego cogito* in place of "*ego cogito.*"
83. Ibid., 366; Eng. trans., 10.
84. Ibid.; Eng. trans., 10–11, altered.
85. Ibid., 370; Eng. trans., 15–16.
86. See the whole of Ibid., 365–383; Eng. trans., 10–32.
87. Ibid., 382; Eng. trans., 30.
88. Ibid.
89. Ibid., 383; Eng. trans., 31.
90. *Ideen I,* 282; after Eng. trans., 326.
91. "[Die Apodiktizität der Wiedererinnerung]," *Analysen zur passiven Synthesis,* 372; Eng. trans., 18. Cf. ibid., 371, 374; Eng. trans., 17, 20.
92. Ibid., 373; Eng. trans., 19.
93. See ibid.
94. Cf. *Phänomenologische Psychologie,* 208; Eng. trans., 159.
95. It is not surprising that Husserl's first attempt, to my knowledge, to thematize this encloses history within Cartesian egology. We find this in a text written the year before *Ideas I* was published. See Beilage 1, *Ideen III,* 125–126. By the time of the texts from the 1920s that we have been considering, it is Husserl's systematic distinction between static and genetic analysis that circumscribes Cartesian egology.

96. *Phänomenologische Psychologie,* 455.
97. Ibid., 216; Eng. trans., 165.
98. *Ideen II,* 83, 86; Eng. trans., 88, 91.
99. Ibid., 133; Eng. trans., 141.
100. Ibid., 375; Eng. trans., 384–385.
101. *Phänomenologische Psychologie,* 294–295.
102. Ibid., 217; Eng. trans., 166.
103. Martin Heidegger, *Sein und Zeit* [1928] (Tübingen: Max Niemeyer, 1967), 115; *Being and Time,* trans. Macquarrie and Robinson, 151.

11. TRANSCENDENTAL PHENOMENOLOGY AND THE QUESTION OF ITS LEGITIMACY

1. *Krisis,* 117–118; after Eng. trans., 115–116.
2. Immanual Kant, *Prolegomena zu einer jeden künftigen Metaphysik die als Wissenschaft wird auftreten können* [1st ed. 1783], *Werke in zehn Bänden,* Vol. 5, *Schriften zur Metaphysik und Logik* (Darmstadt: Wissenschaftliche Buchgesellschaft, 1968), A 42; *Prolegomena to Any Future Metaphysics,* trans. Lewis White Beck (Indianapolis: Bobbs-Merrill, 1950), 23.
3. Ibid., A 40; Eng. trans., 22. I am following the analysis in Karl Mertens, *Zwischen Letztbegründung und Skepsis: Kritische Untersuchungen zum Selbstverständnis der transzendentalen Phänomenologie Edmund Husserls, Orbis Phaenomenologicus,* Section VI, Vol. 1 (Freiburg: Verlag Karl Alber, 1996), 94.
4. For an excellent overview of works on the question of transcendental analysis in English, see A. C. Genova, "Good Transcendental Arguments," *Kant-Studien* 75 (1984): 469–495. For a discussion of recent developments in the German literature, see Wolfgang Becker, "Kritik und Begründung in transzendentaler Argumentation," *Kant-Studien* 76 (1986): 170–195.
5. See Fink, *VI. Cartesianische Meditation,* Part 1, *Die Idee einer transzendentalen Methodenlehre,* Part 2, *Ergänzungsband, Husserliana Dokumente,* Vol. 2/1 and 2/2; *Sixth Cartesian Meditation,* trans. Bruzina, and Bruzina, "Translator's Introduction," *Sixth Cartesian Meditation,* for an overview.
6. See chapter 7, section D.
7. *Analysen zur passiven Synthesis,* 60.
8. Ibid., 59.
9. Ibid., 60.
10. Ibid., 61.
11. Ibid., 62.
12. Ibid.
13. To each of these steps there is a rough progression of phenomenological disciplines. The numbering follows the steps of the deduction:

> 1. The specification of these cores as necessary and general "conditions of the possibility" of X being an object of a certain type is the work of regional ontologies.
> 2. and 3. The analysis of the categories as constitutive is the labor of categorial phenomenology.

4. The account of the legitimization of the categories as a procedure falls to the theory of the method of categorial phenomenology.

14. I am applying Rosenberg's analysis to Husserl here. See Jay Rosenberg, "Transcendental Arguments Revisited," *Journal of Philosophy* 72/18 (October 1975): 619.

15. "I am conscious" and "ego cogito" are not the same, as there are states of consciousness that are not intentional acts.

16. See the analysis in chapter 1 for a richer account of these structures.

17. Of course, it would be possible to turn this another way and argue that the only notion of consciousness we do glean directly from this proof is one that treats it in terms of intentional experiences; its scope is restricted to being a quality of their field. But even here I would be reluctant to then speak of it as transcendental for the simple reason that transcendental analysis always involves an eidetic reduction.

18. See, for example, *Ideen II,* 29–53; Eng. trans., 31–56.

19. Cf. ibid., 35–41; Eng. trans., 38–44, for a first step in this direction.

20. Kant, *Kritik der reinen Vernunft,* ed. Schmidt, A737 = B765; Eng. trans., 592.

21. Charles Taylor, "The Validity of Transcendental Arguments," *Aristotelian Society,* New Series, 79 (1978/79): 159, 163.

22. See ibid., 160–161, for this suggestion.

23. Ibid., 161.

24. *Krisis,* 118; after Eng. trans., 116.

25. See Taylor "Transcendental Arguments," 162, for this point.

26. *Sein und Zeit,* 66–76; Eng. trans., 95–107.

27. Taylor, "Transcendental Arguments," 162.

28. Ibid.

29. Kant also provides a transcendental analysis of other regions but this involves a shift to other types of reason, for example, practical reason in the case of moral maxims.

30. See Rosenberg, "Transcendental Arguments Revisited," 614–615, for what follows.

31. Ibid., 615.

32. Ibid.

33. I leave open the question of whether Kant himself has a similar position that results from placing his first in relation to the second and third *Critique.* The reason we need not treat this here is that Husserl is claiming a plurality of ontologies within the scope of Kant's first *Critique.*

34. There might be a way of reconciling Kant and Husserl on the issue of core invariance for physical objects. Rosenberg suggests that we separate the notion of a conceptual core from the plurality of different object concepts that we find in physics (moving from a Newtonian object to that of a molecule or submicroscopic object to that of an elementary particle or quantum object) and think of a generic notion of an object. This generic notion would then be the core "upon which particular empirical descriptive systems are erected" (Rosenberg, "Transcendental Arguments," 615). As first framed, Husserl's material ontology of physical objects

was designed to describe such a core and could be distinguished from its treatment in one of the physical sciences because it was an experiential invariant. From the perspective of his later analysis, however, such a core may be no more than an abstraction. We will come back to this question in chapter 13.

35. Rosenberg, "Transcendental Arguments," 619.

36. Ibid.

37. Ibid.

38. Letter to Ingarden, April 5, 1918, *Briefwechsel*, 3/3, 182.

39. See chapter 7, section C.

40. Rüdiger Bubner, "Kant, Transcendental Arguments and the Problem of Deduction," *Review of Metaphysics* 28 (1975): 463.

41. Ibid.

42. Rosenberg, "Transcendental Arguments," 612.

43. Ibid.

44. Bubner, "Kant, Transcendental Arguments and the Problem of Deduction," 463.

45. Rosenberg, "Transcendental Arguments," 620.

46. *Kritik der reinen Vernunft,* A789 = B817, 716; Eng. trans., 625.

47. Genova, "Good Transcendental Arguments," 494.

48. *Kritik der reinen Vernunft,* A85 = B117; after Eng. trans., 121. Cf. Rosenberg, "Transcendental Arguments," 613.

49. Formulating the problem is actually much more difficult than this but I grant that it can be so formulated in order to ask whether Husserlian analysis can handle the difficulty.

50. Rosenberg, "Transcendental Arguments," 620.

51. *Krisis,* 71; after Eng. trans., 70.

52. Rosenberg, "Transcendental Arguments," 620.

53. See chapter 7, section B.

54. Rosenberg, "Transcendental Arguments," 622.

55. *Krisis,* 72; after Eng. trans., 71.

56. See especially *Analysen zur passiven Synthesis,* 192–217.

12. HUSSERL AND THE JAPANESE

This chapter is a slightly revised version of an article that first appeared with the same title in *The Review of Metaphysics* 44 (March 1991): 575–606.

1. This text, difficult to translate, reads as follows: "*Freiheit* ist ein Ausdruck für das Vermögen und vor allem für den erworbenen Habitus kritischer Stellungnahme zu dem, was sich, zunächst reflexionslos, als wahr, als wertvoll, als praktisch seinsollend bewußtseinsmäßig gibt, und zwar als Grundlage für das daraushin sich vollziehende freie Entscheiden." Husserl, *Aufsätze und Vorträge (1922–1937),* 63.

2. Ibid., 107.

3. Ibid., 119.

4. Of the three, only the first was published in German and Japanese; the next two appeared only in a Japanese translation and thus were not even available

in German until Nenon's and Sepp's edition of Husserl's essays and lectures between 1922 and 1937. The three articles are in ibid., 3-43. Only the first has appeared in English translation: "Renewal: Its Problem and Method," trans. Jeffner Allen, *Shorter Works*, 326-331. For the sake of continuity all translations of the *Kaizo* articles in this essay are my own.

5. See the editors' comments in *Aufsätze und Vorträge (1922–1937)*, xivf.

6. "Philosophie als strenge Wissenschaft (1911)," *Aufsätze und Vorträge (1911–1921)*, ed. Thomas Nenon and Hans Sepp, *Husserliana*, Vol. 25 (Dordrecht: Martinus Nijhoff, 1987), 3-62; "Philosophy as Rigorous Science," *Phenomenology and the Crisis of Philosophy*, trans. Quentin Lauer (New York: Harper and Row, 1965), 71–147. This attack is taken up again, but much more indirectly, in the 1931 lecture he gave to three different audiences entitled "Phänomenologie und Anthropologie," *Aufsätze und Vorträge (1922–1937)*, 164–181.

7. See ibid., 184-244; and see the editor's introduction to Husserl, *Krisis;* Eng. trans., xivff., translator's introduction.

8. Three lectures held during the war in 1917 and 1918, published in *Aufsätze und Vorträge (1911–1921)*, 267–295.

9. *Aufsätze und Vorträge (1922–1937)*, 3.

10. Letter to William Hocking, July 3, 1920, *Briefwechsel*, 3/3, 163.

11. Letter to Winthrop Bell, August 11, 1920, *Briefwechsel*, 3/3, 12.

12. *Aufsätze und Vorträge (1922–1937)*, 3.

13. Ibid.

14. Ibid.

15. *The Epistle to the Romans*, trans. Edwyn Hoskyns (London: Oxford University Press, 1933).

16. *Selected Political Writings of Rosa Luxemburg*, ed. Dick Howard (New York: Monthly Review Press, 1971).

17. *Aufsätze und Vorträge (1922–1937)*, 6.

18. Ibid., 10.

19. Ibid., 111.

20. Ibid., 59. Husserl is convinced that while animals have societies they do not have cultures, for their actions are not guided by conscious values. See p. 97.

21. Ibid., 63.

22. Ibid., 4.

23. Ibid., 119.

24. Ibid., 4.

25. Ibid.

26. Ibid., 6.

27. Cf. ibid., 4.

28. Ibid., 5f.

29. Ibid.

30. Ibid., 10.

31. Already the Third Book of *Ideas*, written some ten years before but never published, contains the seeds of this new analysis. See *Ideen III*, 101–105; Eng. trans., 86-90. The closest Husserl comes to the notion of eidetic variation in his published work before 1922 is found in Part Four of *Ideas I*. See *Ideen I*, 365f.; Eng.

trans., 357ff. But the concept of "ideation," which we can also find in yet earlier works, did serve as a placeholder for what becomes the theory of eidetic variation.

32. *Aufsatze und Vorträge (1922–1937)*, 10.
33. Ibid., 11.
34. Ibid.
35. Ibid.
36. Ibid., 13.
37. Ibid., 14.
38. Ibid.
39. Ibid., 15.
40. Ibid.
41. Ibid.
42. Cf. ibid., 78.
43. Ibid., 18.
44. Ibid., 16.
45. Ibid.
46. *Ideen I*, 366f.; Eng. trans., 357ff.
47. *Aufsätze und Vorträge (1922–1937)*, 17.
48. Ibid., 19.
49. Ibid.
50. Ibid.
51. For Husserl's earlier work on ethical theory, see his *Vorlesungen über Ethik und Wertlehre, 1908–1914*, ed. Ullrich Melle, *Husserliana*, Vol. 28 (Dordrecht: Kluwer Academic Publishers, 1988).
52. The reference to *Ideas I* is on p. 345 of *Analysen zur passiven Synthesis.*
53. Note the reference to the transcendental phenomenology of *Ideas I* on p. 18 of *Aufsätze und Vorträge (1922–1937)*.
54. Ibid., 29. Cf. *Analysen zur passiven Synthesis*, 340.
55. *Aufsätze und Vorträge (1922–1937)*, 29.
56. Ibid.
57. Ibid., 44.
58. Ibid., 55.
59. *Analysen zur passiven Synthesis*, 342.
60. On the opposition between fact and essence, see *Ideen I*, 10ff.; Eng. trans., 5ff.
61. *Aufsätze und Vorträge (1922–1937)*, 26f.
62. Ibid., 30.
63. Ibid.
64. Ibid., 31. Notice that Husserl's account really is an analysis of the structure of human living, i.e., we are clearly beyond the account of consciousness and in the realm of what Heidegger will call *Dasein*. Heidegger will "break" the binding power of this striving for a full and complete life by his introduction of death at precisely that point where Husserl will place the ideal of Western Humanity. And Husserl, for his part, will view death in a very different light (see p. 98). Nevertheless they are dealing with the same phenomenological field.
65. Ibid., 31.
66. Ibid.

67. Ibid.
68. Ibid., 32.
69. Ibid.
70. Ibid.
71. Ibid.
72. Ibid., 33.
73. Ibid., 35.
74. Ibid., 33.
75. Ibid.
76. Ibid., 36.
77. Ibid., 37.
78. This point entails that Husserl's deeper response to Dilthey is found neither in the earlier, 1911 *Logos* article, "Philosophie als strenge Wissenschaft" (*Aufsätze und Vorträge [1911–1921]*, 3–62; Eng. trans., 71–147), nor in the later 1931 lecture, "Phänomenologie und Anthropologie" (*Aufsätze und Vorträge (1922–1937)*, 164–181, for the simple reason that both remain on the plane of "constitutive phenomenology." Cf. ibid., 164. Of all the published work it is only the *Kaizo* articles and the *Crisis* that provide a reply, using the resources of his genetic phenomenology, that appropriates and systematically integrates Dilthey's work into his phenomenology. I think this explains his open attitude toward Dilthey in a letter responding to one from Dilthey after the *Logos* article:

> Now I would like to refer to your attempt to point out, on the basis of the all too few suggestions in my article, those boundaries within which our philosophical views agree and in which they differ.
>
> All things considered, I would much prefer not to acknowledge these boundaries, and it truly seems to me that there are no serious differences whatsoever between us. I think a lengthy conversation would lead to our complete agreement.

Briefwechsel, 3/3, 48; after "The Dilthey-Husserl Correspondence," trans. Allen, *Shorter Works,* 205.
79. *Aufsätze und Vorträge (1922–1937),* 45.
80. Cf. ibid., 48f.
81. *Cartesianische Meditationen,* 121ff.; Eng. trans., 89ff.
82. Cf. *Aufsätze und Vorträge (1922–1937),* 46.
83. Ibid.
84. *Cartesianische Meditationen,* 124ff.; Eng. trans., 92ff.
85. *Aufsätze und Vorträge (1922–1937),* 47.
86. Ibid., 48.
87. *Cartesianische Meditationen,* 127; Eng. trans., 95.
88. *Aufsätze und Vorträge (1922–1937),* 46.
89. Ibid.
90. Ibid., 56.
91. Ibid.
92. Ibid.
93. Ibid., 55.
94. Ibid., 61.
95. Ibid., 62. In saying that this is "an external point of view" (p. 62) he frees

his analysis from the metaphysical presumption that there is a spirit operating in the minds or the collective unconscious of a people "pushing" or "drawing" them toward this inevitable end. Indeed, other forms of religious culture are possible where the priests rule by arbitrary will, not a "consciously constituted goal idea," and where the people are oppressed.

96. Ibid., 66, and especially Beilage IV, 100–103.

97. Ibid., 101.

98. Ibid., 66.

99. Ibid., 101.

100. Ibid., 72.

101. Ibid., 101.

102. Ibid., 78.

103. *Krisis,* 332; Eng. trans., 285.

104. *Aufsätze und Vorträge (1922–1937),* 80f. There are a few scattered references to Aristotle in a very late piece. See pp. 193ff.

105. Ibid., 93.

106. Ibid., 91. He explains further: "This 'modern' stance to belief does not mean overthrowing belief as religious experience, nor does it mean overthrowing its essential belief-content. But, obviously, the autonomy of reason does mean a rejection of all previous obligation to remove, on the basis of the authority of the church or the authority of belief itself, the content of belief from free critique" (p. 92).

107. Ibid., 73.

108. Ibid.

109. *Krisis,* 331; Eng. trans., 284f.

110. *Aufsätze und Vorträge (1922–1937),* 3.

111. Ibid., 125.

112. Ibid., 126.

113. Ibid.

114. Cf. ibid., 53, 90.

115. Ibid., 76.

116. Ibid.

117. Ibid.

118. Ibid., 77.

119. Ibid.

120. *Krisis,* 335; Eng. trans., 288.

121. Ibid.

122. *Ideen II,* 58–61; Eng. trans., 63–66.

123. *Krisis,* 22; Eng. trans., 25.

124. Ibid.

125. Ibid., 23; Eng. trans., 26.

126. Ibid., 30; Eng. trans., 32.

127. Ibid., 20; Eng. trans., 23.

128. Cf. especially Section 51 of ibid.

129. Ibid., 19; Eng. trans., 22.

130. Ibid., 48; Eng. trans., 48.

131. *Aufsatze und Vorträge (1922–1937),* 195.

132. Ibid., 212.
133. Ibid.
134. Ibid., 213.
135. Ibid.
136. Ibid.
137. Cf. ibid., 164, 180, 214.
138. Ibid., 208.
139. Ibid., 224.
140. Ibid., 219.
141. Ibid., 227.
142. Cf. ibid., 194.
143. Even here, even for an ontological analysis, one might be able to use Gödel's and Cantor's results to argue for a necessary incompleteness to any system that would attempt to include all possibly true facts or statements of facts and thus argue that the notion of totality is mistaken. All that is suggested here is that *if* the notion has application at all, then it will be only to the positive sciences. Our interest is simply in arguing, independent of theoretical problems with the notion of totality in an ontology of the world relevant to the positive sciences, that it is fundamentally different from the notion of the world as horizon. See the next three chapters on this.
144. Cf. ibid., 175.
145. *Krisis*, 329; Eng. trans., 283.
146. Ibid.

13. WORLD AS HORIZON

1. *Ideen II*, 299.
2. *Krisis*, 171; after Eng. trans., 168.
3. F I 35, 25a (transcription, p. 28), as cited in Guy van Kerckhoven, "Zur Genese des Begriffs 'Lebenswelt' bei Edmund Husserl," *Archiv für Begriffsgeschichte* 29 (1985): 193.
4. For a suggestive phenomenological study of the roots of philosophy, see Klaus Held, *Heraklit, Parmenides und der Anfang von Philosophie und Wissenschaft: Eine phänomenologische Besinnung* (Berlin: de Gruyter, 1980).
5. On this line of thought, see Klaus Held, "Lebenswelt," *Theologische Realenzyklopädie* 20: 595.
6. Letter to Misch, August 3, 1929, *Briefwechsel*, 3/6, 277. On this point see Guy van Kerckhoven, "Die Grundansätze von Husserls Konfrontation mit Dilthey im Lichte der geschichtlichen Selbstzeugnisse," *Dilthey und der Wandel des Philosophiebegriffs seit dem 19. Jahrhundert, Phänomenologische Forschungen* 16 (n.d): 155.
7. See the very first section of *Ideas I* and *Erste Philosophie*, II, 260, 262.
8. *Krisis*, 148; Eng. trans., 145.
9. See Section 49 of *Ideas I*.
10. See van Kerckhoven, "Die Grundansätze von Husserls Konfrontation mit Dilthey."
11. See Sommer, "Husserls Göttinger Lebenswelt," xviii–xx; Bernet et al.,

Edmund Husserl; Eng. trans., *An Introduction to Husserlian Phenomenology,* 217, 220.

12. Hans Blumenberg, "Parallelaktion einer Begriffsbildung: Husserl, Hofmannsthal und die Lebenswelt," *Neue Zürcher Zeitung,* December 12 and 13, 1987.

13. See *Intersubjektivität I,* 111–194, especially 122–125. On Husserl's concept of the world during this period, see Sommer, "Husserls Göttinger Lebenswelt."

14. F I 35, p. 26b (transcription, p. 29b). The lecture course was given three times: 1919, 1921/22, and 1927. I have also found the term in a similar passage from 1919 printed as Beilage 12 in *Aufsätze und Vortrage 1911–1921,* 327. For other early uses of the term, see *Ideen II,* Beilage 13, 374–376 (a text from the first half of the 1920s, perhaps earlier); Eng. trans., 384–386; and *Erste Philosophie II,* 272 (a text that Husserl dates with uncertainty as "1930?" but that Boehm, the editor, places sometime after 1924). On these references to the term "life-world" and insightful analyses into the first occurrences of the concept, see van Kerckhoven, "Zur Genese des Begriffs 'Lebenswelt' bei Edmund Husserl," 182–203. The problem of the life-world, under the heading "world of experience" (*Erfahrungswelt*), receives extensive treatment in his 1923/24 lecture course titled "First Philosophy" and his 1925 and 1928 lectures on phenomenological psychology. See *Erste Philosophie II,* 44–50, 69–81, but especially 259–274, and *Phänomenologische Psychologie,* 52–118; Eng. trans., 38–90. On the identification of *Erfahrungswelt* and *Lebenswelt* in the latter, see p. 111 (p. 84). All of these texts, as far as I can tell, were written before the publication of Heidegger's *Being and Time.*

15. Harrison Hall, "Intentionality and World: Division I of *Being and Time,*" *The Cambridge Companion to Heidegger* (Cambridge: Cambridge University Press, 1993), 122.

16. F I 35, p. 25a (transcription, p. 28), as cited in van Kerckhoven, "Zur Genese des Begriffs 'Lebenswelt' bei Edmund Husserl," 192–193.

17. For a rich exploration of this, see Steinbock, *Home and Beyond.*

18. *Krisis,* 134; Eng. trans., 131, altered.

19. For a fuller account of technology from a phenomenological perspective, see Don Ihde, *Technology and the Lifeworld: From Garden to Earth* (Bloomington: Indiana University Press, 1990).

20. See *Krisis,* Beilage 17, 459–462; Eng. trans., Appendix 7, 379–383.

21. Ibid., 462; after Eng. trans., 382–383.

22. Ibid., 132; Eng. trans., 129.

23. Ibid., 176; Eng. trans., 173.

24. Ibid., 145; Eng. trans., 142.

25. Ibid., 149; after Eng. trans., 146.

26. *Ideas II,* 281, 297–302; Eng. trans., 294, 311–316.

27. I share this understanding of Husserl's theory with Held. See his "Lebenswelt," 597.

28. *Cartesianische Meditationen,* 98; after Eng. trans., 63. Italics removed.

29. Ibid., 97; after Eng. trans., 62. Italics removed.

30. *Erste Philosophie II,* 260.

31. Ibid., 263.

32. Ibid., 264.

33. *Cartesianische Meditationen,* 60; Eng. trans., 21. Translation altered and italics added.

14. HORIZON AND DISCOURSE

1. *Erfahrung und Urteil,* 78; after Eng. trans., 74–75. Parentheses around second sentence removed. The dating of this text is uncertain but my guess is that it was probably written during the 1920s. The first chapter of Part I consists mostly of texts from around the time of those now collected in *Analysen zur passiven Synthesis.* On the question of the manuscripts used in *Erfahrung und Urteil,* which was edited by Landgrebe and first published in 1939 in Prague, see Dieter Lohmar, "Zu der Entstehung und den Ausgangsmaterialien von Edmund Husserls Werk *Erfahrung und Urteil,*" *Husserl Studies* 13 (1996): 31–71.
2. *Sein und Zeit,* 150; Eng. trans., 191.
3. A recent example of this is David Hoy, "Heidegger and the Hermeneutic Turn," *Cambridge Companion to Heidegger* (Cambridge: Cambridge University Press, 1993), 181–186.
4. *Sein und Zeit,* 74; Eng. trans., 105.
5. Ibid., 75; Eng. trans., 105.
6. *Befindlichkeit* simply will not go into English. Perhaps the only way to capture it is with a highly interpretative translation, which is what I propose with "affectivity." While it preserves the connection to *Stimmung* (even "mood" is not adequate here) in that moods are "passive" nonthetic states of Dasein and thus affective, it loses the play on *sich befinden,* of "finding oneself in," and runs the risk of being understood as "some sort of reflection upon itself" or an "inner lived experience." See *Prolegomena,* 352; Eng. trans., 255. *Befindlichkeit* stresses the fact that Dasein "has" its world in the sense that it always finds itself as *in* the world, always situated.
7. Cf. *Sein und Zeit,* 144; Eng. trans., 184.
8. Ibid., 143; Eng. trans., 183.
9. Ibid., 144; Eng. trans., 183.
10. Ibid., 144; Eng. trans., 184.
11. Ibid., 145; Eng. trans., 184.
12. Ibid., 148; Eng. trans., 188.
13. Ibid.
14. For example, *Geld auf Zinsen auslegen* means to lay out or loan money at interest.
15. Clearly there are times when "interpretation" is an acceptable translation. The phrase *eine Stelle falsch auslegen* means to misinterpret a passage. *Ein Ausleger* is an expositor of a text; *Auslegung* is an exposition. Yet *Auslegen* is much *broader* in scope than interpretation. In using "explication" I am depending upon the fact that even the expositor or the expounder is engaged in an activity of opening up, of laying open what is "closed," and of then setting what is together apart so as to allow it to come forth *as* what it is. Explication is *not yet* interpretation. The more restricted notion of interpretation belongs to the broader image of laying out or unfolding or explication and so should not be used to translate it. In fact Heidegger makes a point of treating *Textinterpretation* as a "particular concrete

kind" (*die besondere Konkretion*) of *Auslegung.* Ibid., 150; after Eng. trans., 192. The main objection to not retaining interpretation as the translation of *Auslegung* is the fact that Heidegger calls the as-structure of the ready-to-hand the "existential-*hermeneutical* 'as'" in contrast to the "apophantic 'as'" of propositional attribution. Ibid., 158; Eng. trans., 201. (More on the "as" structure presently.) While I use "explication" to translate *Auslegung,* I recognize that calling the "as" of the ready-to-hand hermeneutical clearly pushes *Auslegung* in the direction of interpretation. This is supported by Heidegger's general claim that "'*Sinn*' must be conceived as the formal-existential framework of the disclosedness which belongs to understanding." Ibid., 151; Eng. trans., 193. One can understand, then, why Macquarrie and Robinson treat *Auslegung* and *Interpretation* as "synonyms." See Eng. trans., 19, note 3. We will deal with this issue directly in section C, below.

16. Ibid., 148; Eng. trans., 189.
17. Ibid., 149; after Eng. trans., 189.
18. Ibid.
19. Ibid.
20. Ibid.
21. Ibid., 149; Eng. trans., 190.
22. Ibid., 150; Eng. trans., 191.
23. Cf. ibid., 153; Eng. trans., 195.
24. Ibid., 151; Eng. trans., 193.
25. Ibid.
26. *Prolegomena,* 263; after Eng. trans., 194.
27. Ibid., 275; after Eng. trans., 202.
28. Ibid.
29. Ibid. Italics removed.
30. *Sein und Zeit,* 151; Eng. trans., 193.
31. *Prolegomena,* 276; Eng. trans., 203; *Sein und Zeit,* 166; Eng. trans., 492, note x to p. 209.
32. As in Macquarrie and Robinson's translation of *Being and Time.* They are careful, though, to preserve in translation a difference between *Sinn,* rendered as either "sense" or "meaning," and *Bedeutung,* rendered as "significance." I will continue to render *Bedeutsamkeit,* which is a much more general term, as "significance."
33. As in Kersten's translation of *Ideas I.* Likewise the difference between *Sinn,* sense, and *Bedeutung,* signification, is maintained.
34. *Sein und Zeit,* 157; Eng. trans., 199, altered.
35. Ibid., 157; Eng. trans., 199.
36. Ibid., 150; Eng. trans., 191.
37. Ibid., 154; after Eng. trans., 196.
38. Ibid., 155; Eng. trans., 197.
39. Ibid., 158; Eng. trans., 200.
40. Ibid.
41. Ibid., 158; Eng. trans., 201.
42. Ibid., 87; Eng. trans., 120.
43. Ibid., 87; Eng. trans., 121.
44. Ibid., 150; Eng. trans., 191.

45. Ibid., 157; Eng. trans., 199. Italics mine.
46. Ibid., 149; Eng. trans., 189.
47. Ibid., 150; Eng. trans., 191.
48. What follows will be an attempt to unpack the very difficult and laconic Section 34 of *Being and Time.*
49. *Sein und Zeit,* 161; Eng. trans., 203.
50. Ibid., 161; Eng. trans., 203–204.
51. *Prolegomena,* 361; after Eng. trans., 262.
52. *Sein und Zeit,* 161; Eng. trans., 204.
53. *Prolegomena,* 362; after Eng. trans., 263.
54. Ibid., 361; after Eng. trans., 262.
55. *Sein und Zeit,* 153; Eng. trans., 195, altered.
56. Ibid., 161; Eng. trans., 204.
57. Ibid.
58. Ibid.
59. Ibid., 349; Eng. trans., 401.
60. *Erfahrung und Urteil,* 78; Eng. trans., 75.
61. *Prolegomena,* 280; after Eng. trans., 205–206.
62. Ibid., 281; after Eng. trans., 206.
63. Ibid., 281; Eng. trans., 206, altered.
64. Ibid., 281; Eng. trans., 206.
65. Ibid., 284; Eng. trans., 208, altered.
66. Ibid.
67. In these lectures Heidegger uses not "sense" but "meaning," to capture this: "The indications and nexus of indications are primarily meaning. The meanings are the structure of our being-in-the-world." Ibid., 286; Eng. trans., 209, altered. But he does set "linguistic meanings and nexuses of meaning in general" in opposition to "meaning in the primary sense." Ibid., 288; Eng. trans., 211, altered. In *Being and Time* Heidegger identifies his meaning in the primary sense as sense. See *Sein und Zeit,* 151; Eng. trans., 192–193. I think that the advantage of this change is that it allows him to account for the way talk, especially idle talk, with its established preconceptions woven into the fabric of meaning, comes to (re)configure not just our representations of things but "meaning in the primary sense," i.e., the nexus of sense constitutive of the very way things show themselves in our experience. This will be developed presently.
68. Ibid., 161; Eng. trans., 204.
69. Ibid.
70. *Prolegomena,* 361; Eng. trans., 262, altered.
71. Ibid., 362; after Eng. trans., 262.
72. Ibid., 362; Eng. trans., 263.
73. *Sein und Zeit,* 162; Eng. trans., 205.
74. Cf. *Prolegomena,* 363; Eng. trans., 263.
75. Cf. ibid., 359–360; Eng. trans., 261.
76. Ibid., 360; after Eng. trans., 261.
77. E.g., ibid., 361; Eng. trans., 262.
78. *Sein und Zeit,* 167–168; Eng. trans., 211, altered.
79. Ibid., 168; Eng. trans., 211.

80. Ibid., 168; Eng. trans., 212.

81. Ibid., 168; Eng. trans., 212, altered.

82. Ibid., 169; Eng. trans., 213.

83. In *Sein und Zeit* Heidegger himself cites what is now published as *Ideen II* and gives a brief outline of its contents. In addition he makes explicit reference to Husserl's further lectures in Freiburg on these issues. Ibid., 47; Eng. trans., 73 and note ii of Division 1, chapter 1 on p. 489.

84. *Erste Philosophie II,* 260.

85. Ibid.

86. *Sein und Zeit,* 68; Eng. trans., 97.

87. Ibid., 65; Eng. trans., 93.

88. *Erste Philosophie II,* 263.

89. Ibid., 263.

90. See *Phänomenologische Psychologie,* 95; Eng. trans., 71.

91. *Sein und Zeit,* 65; Eng. trans., 93.

92. Introduced in his published writings in Section 2 of the First Investigation, *Logische Untersuchungen,* II/1, 24–25; Eng. trans., I, 269–271. "This insight, worked out as early as the *Logical Investigations,* already constitutes there the nucleus of genetic phenomenology." *Erfahrung und Urteil,* 78; after Eng. trans., 75.

93. Ibid., 78; Eng. trans., 75.

94. Ibid., 79; Eng. trans., 75.

95. Heidegger, *Prolegomena,* 273; Eng. trans., 201.

96. See ibid., 264; Eng. trans., 194. For an example of how Heidegger would treat the transition from perceived environmental object to perceived, natural thing, see pp. 48–49; Eng. trans., 38.

97. See "Bauen Wohnen Denken," *Vortrage und Aufsàtze* (Pfullingen: Neske, 1967), II, 25–26; "Building Dwelling Thinking," *Basic Writings,* ed. David Krell (New York: Harper and Row, 1977), 327–328.

15. THE MARGINS OF THE WORLD

1. *Krisis,* 152; after Eng. trans., 149.

2. Ibid., 176; after Eng. trans., 173.

3. Ibid., 176–177; Eng. trans., 173–174.

4. Ibid., 145; after Eng. trans., 142.

5. Ibid.

6. Aron Gurwitsch, *Studies in Phenomenology and Psychology* (Evanston, Ill.: Northwestern University Press, 1966), 348.

7. Aron Gurwitsch, *Marginal Consciousness,* ed. Lester Embree (Athens: Ohio University Press, 1985), 22.

8. Ibid., 4.

9. Ibid., 22. Italics removed.

10. Ibid., 20–21.

11. Ibid., 35.

12. Ibid., 37.

13. Ibid.

14. While he does not grasp consciousness as a whole "in its entire extension"

in a single intuition, Gurwitsch, like Husserl, has a higher order act that constructs the ego as idea and adduces the rules governing it. In other words, having abandoned Husserl's idea of the ego as an experiential and experienced unity of acts, there is a higher order idealization of the ego (and the body) as the unity of all its profiles. In Gurwitsch we still have to worry that what he gives up at the level of experience, of the given, he attempts to recover at the level of thought. Still, our direct first-order experience of such is always partial, always broken, never complete, and it belongs to a different order than that of materially related fields. This is what comes to the fore by speaking of margins.

15. Ibid., 40.

16. Ibid., 42. Italics removed.

17. Ibid., 46.

18. Ibid.

19. *Cours de linguistique générale* [1916], trans. W. Brokin (New York: Philosophical Library, 1968).

20. See Roman Jakobson, *Selected Writings,* Vols. 1–7 (The Hague: Mouton, 1962–1986), especially Vol. 2, *Word and Language,* and the frequent references to Husserl there.

21. See Herbert Spiegelberg, *The Phenomenological Movement, Phaenomenologica,* 2 vols. (The Hague: Martinus Nijhoff, 1965), 666.

22. Elmar Holenstein, *Roman Jakobson's Approach to Language: Phenomenological Structuralism,* trans. Catherine Schelbert and Tarcisius Schelbert (Bloomington: Indiana University Press, 1976), 51.

23. Ibid., 2–3. See Jakobson, *Word and Language,* especially 280–284.

24. I will draw from essays published in Adrienne Lehrer and Eva Feder Kittay, eds., *Frames, Fields, and Contrasts: New Essays in Semantic and Lexical Organization* (Hillsdale, N.J.: Lawrence Erlbaum Associates, 1992).

25. A lexeme is, roughly put, a term that appears in the dictionary and has at least one meaning. Lehrer and Kittay offer a more technical definition: "A lexeme is a meaning-form unit which consists of at least one word, but which ignores allomorphy. Where a lexeme consists of more than one word, its meaning is noncompositional, as in idioms." Lehrer and Kittay, "Introduction," *Frames, Fields, and Contrasts,* 3.

26. After ibid., 3. My change in their wording is due to the need to keep open the question of reference and not assume that the "domains" to which lexemes "apply" can be immediately identified as concepts or conceptual. More on this presently.

27. Lawrence Barsalou, "Frames, Concepts, and Conceptual Fields," *Frames, Fields, and Contrasts,* ed. Lehrer and Kittay, 23.

28. After ibid., 22–25.

29. Ibid., 35–40.

30. Ibid., 64.

31. Ibid., 35.

32. Charles Fillmore and Beryl Atkins, "Toward a Frame-Based Lexicon: The Semantics of RISK and Its Neighbors," *Frames, Fields, and Contrasts,* ed. Lehrer and Kittay, 76–77.

33. Ibid., 76.

34. Ibid., 77.

35. See Barsalou, "Frames, Concepts and Conceptual Fields," 63, for a similar example.

36. Ibid.

37. This is brought home by Barsalou's claim that "one can view an exemplar in a frame system as an existential proposition: there exists an entity *x* in category *C* that has values *p, q,* and *r* for attributes *P, Q,* and *R.*" Ibid., 45. The referent, as in Husserl's theory in *Ideas I,* is viewed as an X bearing the properties attributed to it by its predicates. There is still an interesting question as to whether anything more than exemplars are required for the linguist to carry out his or her work. Richard Grandy seems to think not: ". . . it is not clear that any specific information about prototypes ought to be included in the linguists' account of the lexicon because it appears mainly relevant to psychological and referential issues." "Semantic Fields, Prototypes, and the Lexicon," *Frames, Fields, and Contrasts,* ed. Lehrer and Kittay, 120.

38. Cf. Barsalou, "Frames, Concepts and Conceptual Fields," 64.

39. James Ross, "Semantic Contagion," *Frames, Fields, and Contrasts,* ed. Lehrer and Kittay, 144.

40. Ibid., 143–169.

41. Charles Taylor, "Theories of Meaning," *Human Agency and Language,* Vol. 1, *Philosophical Papers* (Cambridge: Cambridge University Press, 1985), 248–292.

42. Ibid., 264–265.

43. Ibid., 270.

44. Ibid., 271.

45. Ibid., 275.

46. Ibid., 277.

47. Cf. ibid., 284.

48. Ibid., 285.

49. Ibid., 287.

50. Ibid.

51. Ibid., 289.

52. Ibid.

53. Ibid.

54. Ibid., 285, 289.

55. Ibid., 269–270.

56. Ibid., 290.

57. Ross, "Semantic Contagion," 146. Italics removed.

APPENDIX

1. See Ernst Tugendhat, *Der Wahrheitsbegriff bei Husserl und Heidegger* (Berlin: de Gruyter, 1967) and *Einführung in die sprachanalytische Philosophie* (Frankfurt am Main: Suhrkamp, 1976), especially 143–160; translated by P. A. Garner as *Traditional and Analytical Philosophy: Lectures on the Philosophy of Language* (Cambridge: Cambridge University Press, 1982). A recent collection of

Tugendhat's essays appeared under the title *Philosophische Aufsätze* (Frankfurt am Main: Suhrkamp, 1992).

2. Michael Theunissen, *Der Andere* (Berlin: de Gruyter, 1965); *The Other: Studies in the Social Ontology of Husserl, Heidegger, Sartre, and Buber* (Cambridge, Mass.: MIT Press, 1984).

3. See Dagfinn Føllesdal, "Husserl's Notion of Noema," *Journal of Philosophy* 66 (October 16, 1969): 680–687; Ronald McIntyre and David Smith, "Husserl's Identification of Meaning and Noema," *Monist* 59 (January 1975): 115–132; Ronald McIntyre and David Smith, "Intentionality via Intentions," *Journal of Philosophy* 68 (September 16, 1971): 541–561; *Husserl and Intentionality: A Study of Mind, Meaning, and Language* (Dordrecht: D. Reidel, 1982). For helpful studies of Husserl in the context of analytical philosophy, see Ronald McIntyre, "Searle on Intentionality," *Inquiry* 27 (1984): 468–483, and "Husserl and the Representational Theory of Mind," *Topoi* 5 (1986): 101–113.

4. Two excellent books have traced the relationship between Frege and Husserl. See Mohanty, *Husserl and Frege,* and, most recently, Michael Dummett, *The Origins of Analytical Philosophy* (Cambridge, Mass.: Harvard University Press, 1994). Also see Ronald McIntyre, "Husserl and Frege," *Journal of Philosophy* 84 (October 1987): 523–535.

5. Approaching Husserl through Frege is especially fruitful when attempting to critically assess the notion of meaning and, thereby, the concept of the noema in Husserl. At the same time Husserl himself looks not to Frege but to Brentano, Husserl's teacher, as the one who influenced him the most: "my entire development is determined by my starting point in [*durch den Ausgang von*] F. Brentano." Letter to Welch, June 17 and 21, 1933, *Briefwechsel,* 3/6, 460.

6. Hubert Dreyfus, "The Perceptual Noema: Gurwitsch's Crucial Contribution," *Life-World and Consciousness: Essays for Aron Gurwitsch,* ed. Lester Embree (Evanston, Ill.: Northwestern University Press, 1972), 135–170, reprinted in *Husserl, Intentionality, and Cognitive Science* ed. Hubert Dreyfus (Cambridge, Mass.: MIT Press, 1987), 97–123.

7. For a response to the theory of meaning proposed by these writers, see my *Origins of Meaning* and "Verbindende Namen/Verbundene Gegenstände," 141–191.

8. Dreyfus, "Introduction," *Husserl, Intentionality, and Cognitive Science,* 21.

9. Ibid.

10. In fact he suggests that Husserl "is beginning to emerge as the father of current research in cognitive psychology and artificial intelligence." Ibid., 2.

11. McIntyre, "Husserl and the Representational Theory of Mind."

12. J. N. Mohanty, *The Possibility of a Transcendental Philosophy, Phaenomenologica,* Vol. 98 (The Hague: Martinus Nijhoff, 1985).

13. Emmanuel Levinas, *La théorie de l'intuition dans la phénoménologie de Husserl* (Paris, 1930); *The Theory of Intuition in the Phenomenology of Husserl,* trans. André Orianne (Evanston, Ill.: Northwestern University Press, 1973). There is a provocative reference in one of Husserl's own letters to this study of his phenomenology. In the midst of complaining about those who have fallen back into "the old philosophical naivete" and misunderstood his phenomenology (Scheler,

Heidegger, Hering-Strassburg, and others), he mentions Levinas's recently published book and says that it "brings my phenomenology [down] to the same level as the Heideggerian and, thereby, robs it of its authentic sense." Letter to Welch, June 17 and 21, 1933, *Briefwechsel,* 3/6, 458. Given the overwhelming tendency among French interpreters to read Husserl through Heidegger, the complaint has an almost prophetic ring to it.

There is no doubt that Husserl's *Cartesian Meditations* had great impact upon the French reception of his phenomenology. While Husserl did not publish it in German and even came to abandon his revisions of it in order to begin work on what we now have as *The Crisis of European Science,* it quickly appeared in a French translation in 1931 by Emmanuel Levinas and Gabrielle Pilfer. See *Méditations cartésiennes* (Paris: A. Colin, 1931). The work was an elaboration and extension of two lectures, now called "The Paris Lectures," which Husserl gave at the Sorbonne on February 23 and 25, 1929. For the original German texts see Husserl, *Cartesianische Meditationen* and the English translation. We will deal extensively with its place in Husserl's thought in chapters 5 and 6.

14. Gaston Berger, *Le cogito dans la philosophie de Husserl* (Paris: Aubier, 1941); *The "Cogito" in Husserl's Philosophy,* trans. Kathleen McLaughlin (Evanston, Ill.: Northwestern University Press, 1972).

15. Jean Paul Sartre, *L'être et le néant* (Paris: Librairie Gallimard, 1943); *Being and Nothingness: An Essay on Phenomenological Ontology,* trans. Hazel Barnes (New York: Philosophical Library, 1956).

16. Paul Ricoeur, *Husserl: An Analysis of His Philosophy,* trans. Edward Ballard and Lester Embree (Evanston, Ill.: Northwestern University Press, 1967).

17. Jacques Derrida, *Le problème de la genèse dans la philosophie de Husserl* (Paris: Presses Universitaires de France, 1990); *Edmund Husserl's l'origin de la géométrie,* trans. and intro. by Jacques Derrida (Paris: Presses Universitaires de France, 1962); Jacques Derrida, *Edmund Husserl's Origin of Geometry: An Introduction,* trans. John Leavey (Atlantic Highlands, N.J.: Nicholas Hays, 1978); *La voix et le phénomène* (Paris: Presses Universitaires de France, 1967); *Speech and Phenomena,* trans. David B. Allison (Evanston, Ill.: Northwestern University Press, 1973).

18. Bernhard Waldenfels, "Hearing Oneself Speak: Derrida's Recording of the Phenomenological Voice," *Spindel Conference [1993]: Derrida's Interpretation of Husserl,* ed. Leonard Lawlor, *Southern Journal of Philosophy* 32, Supplement, 75.

19. Françoise Dastur, "Finitude and Repetition in Husserl and Derrida," *Spindel Conference [1993],* 113.

20. The relationship between Husserl and Heidegger will be covered in chapters 5 and 14.

21. Waldenfels, "Hearing Oneself Speak," 75.

22. John Sallis, *Delimitations: Phenomenology and the End of Metaphysics* (Bloomington: Indiana University Press, 1986).

23. *Delimitations,* 24; cf. 143.

24. John Caputo, *Radical Hermeneutics: Repetition, Deconstruction, and the Hermeneutic Project* (Bloomington: Indiana University Press, 1987), 120–147.

25. *Radical Hermeneutics*, 56.

26. Ibid.

27. Ibid., 57.

28. See chapter 10 below.

29. Rodolphe Gasché, *The Tain of the Mirror: Derrida and the Philosophy of Reflection* (Cambridge, Mass.: Harvard University Press, 1986).

30. Ibid., 80.

31. See, e.g., ibid., 110–112, 244–250.

32. Claude Evans, *Strategies of Deconstruction: Derrida and the Myth of the Voice* (Minneapolis: University of Minnesota Press, 1991).

33. Jacques Derrida, *De la grammatologie* (Paris: Les Editions de Minuit, 1967); *Of Grammatology*, trans. Gayatri Spivak (Baltimore: Johns Hopkins University Press, 1976).

34. See my discussion of them in the Introduction, 1–10.

35. Derrida, *Speech and Phenomena*, 104.

36. This is an insertion into Husserl's own personal copy of *Ideen I*. See Appendix 37 in the Schuhmann edition of *Ideen I* for the quote. It is also found in the Biemel edition of *Ideen I*, 72, where it is inserted into the original text. Quoted here after Eng. trans., 65. For additional material on the background and the construction of *Ideen I*, see Karl Schuhmann, *Die Dialektik der Phänomenologie II: Reine Phänomenologie und phänomenologische Philosophie* (The Hague: Martinus Nijhoff, 1973).

37. Martin Heidegger, *Sein und Zeit* (Tübingen: Max Niemeyer, [1928] 1967); *Being and Time*, trans. John Macquarrie and Edward Robinson (New York: Harper and Row, 1962).

38. Dreyfus, "Introduction," *Husserl, Intentionality, and Cognitive Science*, 20–21.

39. "Husserl's Perceptual Noema," 98, note 4.

40. Theodor Adorno, *Jargon der Eigentlichkeit, Gesammelte Schriften*, Vol. 6 (Frankfurt am Main: Suhrkamp, 1973), 413–526; *The Jargon of Authenticity*, trans. Knut Tarnowski and Frederic Will (London: Routledge & Kegan Paul, 1973).

41. Theodor Adorno, *Zur Metakritik der Erkenntnistheorie* (Frankfurt am Main: Suhrkamp, 1970), 13; *Against Epistemology: A Metacritique*, trans. Willis Domingo (Cambridge, Mass.: MIT Press, 1982), 4f.

42. Ibid.

43. Ibid., 10; Eng. trans., 2, altered; see also ibid., 60; Eng. trans., 53.

44. Karl-Otto Apel, *Transformation der Philosophie*, Vol. 1: *Sprachanalytik, Semiotik, Hermeneutik* (Frankfurt am Main: Suhrkamp, 1973), 88.

45. Ibid., 88.

46. Karl-Otto Apel, *Transformation der Philosophie*, Vol. 2: *Apriori der Kommunikationsgemeinschaft* (Frankfurt am Main: Suhrkamp, 1973), 221, 234; *Toward a Transformation of Philosophy*, trans. Glyn Adey and David Frisby (Boston: Routledge & Kegan Paul, 1980), 137, 147. (The English translation has only part of the two-volume *Transformation der Philosophie*.)

47. Ibid., II, 315.

48. Ibid.

49. In this earlier study Habermas is concerned mainly with the question of whether a theory of the production of society and of social structures can be based on Husserl's notion of the constituting achievements of consciousness. He recognizes the advances Husserl made over Kant's notion of constitution, finds the internal motivation for Husserl's introduction of the notion of life-world, and realizes its genius in the fact that it provides an internal connection between the constitution of society and the issue of truth. His critical remarks there revolve around the thesis that such a connection cannot be adequately contained in a theory of consciousness, as Husserl hoped. I will deal with some of these ideas in chapter 4. See Habermas, *Vorstudien und Ergänzungen zur Theorie des kommunikativen Handelns,* 35–59.

50. For an early draft of his theory, see Jürgen Habermas, "Erkenntnis und Interesse" *Technik und Wissenschaft als "Ideologie"* (Frankfurt am Main: Suhrkamp, 1968), 152; "Knowledge and Human Interest: A General Perspective," *Knowledge and Human Interests,* trans. Jeremy J. Shapiro (Boston: Beacon Press, 1971), 306. For a more recent systematic account, see his *Theorie des kommunikativen Handelns,* Vol. 1: *Handlungsrationalität und gesellschaftliche Rationalisierung;* Vol. 2: *Zur Kritik der funktionalistischen Vernunft* (Frankfurt am Main: Suhrkamp, 1981); *The Theory of Communicative Action,* Vol. 1: *Reason and the Rationalization of Society,* Vol. 2: *Lifeworld and System: A Critique of Functionalist Reason,* trans. Thomas McCarthy (Boston: Beacon Press, 1984, 1987).

51. Eugen Fink, "Die phänomenologische Philosophie Edmund Husserls in der gegenwärtigen Kritik," *Kantstudien* 38 (1933): 321–383; reprinted in Eugen Fink, *Studien zur Phänomenologie, 1930–1939, Phaenomenologica,* Vol. 21 (The Hague: Martinus Nijhoff, 1966), 79–156; "The Phenomenological Philosophy of Edmund Husserl and Contemporary Criticism," trans. R. O. Elveton, *The Phenomenology of Husserl,* ed. R. O. Elveton (Chicago: Quadrangle Books, 1970), 73–147.

On the relationship between Fink and Husserl, see the superb "Translator's Introduction" by Ron Bruzina to Fink, *Sixth Cartesian Meditation,* vii–xcii. This volume is a translation of Fink, *VI. Cartesianische Meditation,* Part I, *Die Idee einer transzendentalen Methodenlehre.* See also Fink, *VI. Cartesianische Meditation,* Part II, *Ergänzungsband.* While Husserl treated Fink's article "Die phänomenologische Philosophie Edmund Husserls in der gegenwärtigen Kritik" as an accurate presentation of his thought, even giving it his authorization, Fink did not accept Cartesian phenomenology as an adequate philosophical method. There is, therefore, an important question as to whether Fink thought he was going against Husserl or with Husserl beyond it. On this issue, see Bruzina's "Translator's Introduction," *Sixth Cartesian Meditation.*

52. Oskar Becker, "Die Philosophie von Edmund Husserl," *Kant Studien* 38 (1933): 319–383; "The Philosophy of Edmund Husserl," trans. Elveton, *The Phenomenology of Husserl,* ed. Elveton, 40–72.

53. Dummett, *The Origins of Analytical Philosophy.* Dummett registers uneasiness with Dreyfus's account and certainly heads in the right direction with his analysis of pre-propositional meanings or what he calls "proto-thoughts" in chapter 12; but it seems that he is not familiar with Husserl's development of a genetic method. Thus he falls back upon Dreyfus's interpretation and argues that Husserl

did not distinguish thoughts from proto-thoughts, "the fundamental weakness of his theory" (p. 125). For Husserl's analysis of what Dummett calls proto-thoughts, see my *Origins of Meaning*, Part 2.

54. Elizabeth Ströker, *Husserls transzendentale Phänomenologie* (Frankfurt am Main: Vittorio Klostermann, 1987); *Husserl's Transcendental Philosophy*, trans. Lee Hardy (Stanford: Stanford University Press, 1993).

55. Joseph Kockelman, *Edmund Husserl's Phenomenology* (West Lafayette, Ind.: Purdue University Press, 1994), 265–269. The value of Kockelman's study is that it gives us a precise and detailed study not only of the difference between phenomenological psychology and transcendental phenomenology but also of how the first forms a bridge to the second. In chapter 6 I will suggest that this approach, though the easiest to combine and confuse with Cartesian analysis, already takes us beyond its limits.

56. David Bell, *Husserl* (London: Routledge, 1990).

Bibliography

Except for the list of the volumes in Husserliana, *this bibliography is restricted to work cited in this volume.*

THE WORKS OF EDMUND HUSSERL

Original Publications of Books in Chronological Order

Philosophie der Arithmetik: Psychologische und logische Untersuchungen, Vol. 1. Halle a.d. Saale: C. E. M. Pfeffer, 1891.

Logische Untersuchungen. 2 vols. Halle a.d. Saale: Max Niemeyer, 1900 and 1901.

Logische Untersuchungen. 2nd rev. ed. 2 vols. Halle a.d. Saale: Max Niemeyer, 1913 and 1921. [All page references to the *Logische Untersuchungen* are to this edition.]

Ideen zu einer reinen Phänomenologie und phänomenologischen Philosophie. Vol. 1: *Allgemeine Einführung in die reine Phänomenologie. Jahrbuch für Philosophie und phänomenologische Forschung,* Vol. 1. Halle a.d. Saale: Max Niemeyer, 1913. Pp. 1–323. [All page references to *Ideen I* are to this edition.]

Vorlesungen zur Phänomenologie des inneren Zeitbewusstseins. Edited by Martin Heidegger. *Jahrbuch für Philosophie und phänomenologische Forschung,* Vol. 9. Halle a.d. Saale: Max Niemeyer, 1928. Pp. viii–ix, 367–498.

Formale und transzendentale Logik: Versuch einer Kritik der logischen Vernunft. Jahrbuch für Philosophie und phänomenologische Forschung, Vol. 10. Halle a.d. Saale: Max Niemeyer, 1929. Pp. v–xiii, 1–298.

Méditations cartésiennes. Translated by Emmanuel Levinas and Gabrielle Pilfer. Paris: A. Colin, 1931.

Erfahrung und Urteil: Untersuchungen zur Genealogie der Logik. Edited by L. Landgrebe. Prague: Academia-Verlag, 1938; Hamburg: Claasen, 1954.

Husserliana Edition

Cartesianische Meditationen und Pariser Vorträge. Edited by Stephen Strasser. *Husserliana,* Vol. 1. The Hague: Martinus Nijhoff, 1963.

Die Idee der Phänomenologie: Fünf Vorlesungen. 2nd. ed. Edited by Walter Biemel. *Husserliana,* Vol. 2. The Hague: Martinus Nijhoff, 1958.

Ideen zu einer reinen Phänomenologie und phänomenologischen Philosophie. Vol. 1: *Allgemeine Einführung in die reine Phänomenologie.* Edited by Walter Biemel. *Husserliana,* Vol. 3. The Hague: Martinus Nijhoff, 1950.

Ideen zu einer reinen Phänomenologie und phänomenologischen Philosophie. Vol. 1: *Allgemeine Einfuhrung in die reine Phänomenologie,* Vol. 2: *Ergänzende Texte (1912–1929).* Edited by Karl Schuhmann. *Husserliana,* Vol. 3/a and 3/b. The Hague: Martinus Nijhoff, 1976.

Ideen zu einer reinen Phänomenologie und phänomenologischen Philosophie. Vol. 2: *Phänomenologische Untersuchungen zur Konstitution.* Edited by Marly Biemel. *Husserliana,* Vol. 4. The Hague: Martinus Nijhoff, 1952.

Ideen zu einer reinen Phänomenologie und phänomenologischen Philosophie. Vol. 3: *Die Phänomenologie und die Fundamente der Wissenschaften.* Edited by Marly Biemel. *Husserliana,* Vol. 5. The Hague: Martinus Nijhoff, 1952.

Die Krisis der europaischen Wissenschaften und die transzendentale Phänomenologie: Eine Einleitung in die phänomenologische Philosophie. Edited by Walter Biemel. *Husserliana,* Vol. 6. The Hague: Martinus Nijhoff, 1954.

Erste Philosophie (1923/24). Part 1: *Kritische Ideengeschichte.* Edited by Rudolf Boehm. *Husserliana,* Vol. 7. The Hague: Martinus Nijhoff, 1956.

Erste Philosophie (1923/24). Part 2: *Theorie der phanomenologischen Reduktion.* Edited by Rudolf Boehm. *Husserliana,* Vol. 8. The Hague: Martinus Nijhoff, 1959.

Phänomenologische Psychologie: Vorlesungen Sommersemester 1925. Edited by Walter Biemel. *Husserliana,* Vol. 9. The Hague: Martinus Nijhoff, 1968.

Zur Phänomenologie des inneren Zeitbewusstseins (1893–1917). Edited by Rudolf Boehm. *Husserliana,* Vol. 10. The Hague: Martinus Nijhoff, 1966.

Analysen zur passiven Synthesis: Aus Vorlesungs- und Forschungsmanuskripten 1918–1926. Edited by Margot Fleischer. *Husserliana,* Vol. 11. The Hague: Martinus Nijhoff, 1966.

Philosophie der Arithmetik: Mit ergänzenden Texten (1890–1901). Edited by Lothar Eley. *Husserliana,* Vol. 12. The Hague: Martinus Nijhoff, 1970.

Zur Phänomenologie der Intersubjektivität. Erster Teil: 1905–1920. Edited by Iso Kern. *Husserliana,* Vol. 13. The Hague: Martinus Nijhoff, 1973.

Zur Phänomenologie der Intersubjektivität. Zweiter Teil: 1921–1928. Edited by Iso Kern. *Husserliana,* Vol. 14. The Hague: Martinus Nijhoff, 1973.

Zur Phänomenologie der Intersubjektivität. Dritter Teil: 1929–1935. Edited by Iso Kern. *Husserliana,* Vol. 15. The Hague: Martinus Nijhoff, 1973.

Ding und Raum: Vorlesungen 1907. Edited by Ulrich Claesges. *Husserliana,* Vol. 16. The Hague: Martinus Nijhoff, 1974.

Formale und transzendentale Logik: Versuch einer Kritik der logischen Vernunft. Edited by Paul Janssen. *Husserliana,* Vol. 17. The Hague: Martinus Nijhoff, 1974.

Logische Untersuchungen. Vol. 1: *Prolegomena zur reinen Logik.* Edited by Elmar Holenstein. *Husserliana,* Vol. 18. The Hague: Martinus Nijhoff, 1975.

Logische Untersuchungen. Vol. 2: *Untersuchungen zur Phänomenologie und Theorie der Erkenntnis,* Part 1. Edited by Ursula Panzer. *Husserliana,* Vol. 19. The Hague: Martinus Nijhoff, 1984.

Logische Untersuchungen. Vol. 2: *Untersuchungen zur Phänomenologie und Theorie der Erkenntnis,* Part 2. Edited by Ursula Panzer. *Husserliana,* Vol. 20. The Hague: Martinus Nijhoff, 1984.

Studien zur Arithmetik und Geometrie: Texte aus dem Nachlaß (1886–1901). Edited by Ingeborg Strohmeyer. *Husserliana,* Vol. 21. The Hague: Martinus Nijhoff, 1983.

Aufsätze und Rezensionen (1890–1910). Edited by Bernard Rang. *Husserliana,* Vol. 22. The Hague: Martinus Nijhoff, 1979.

Phantasie, Bildbewußtsein, Erinnerung: Zur Phänomenologie der anschaulichen Vergegenwärtigungen: Texte aus dem Nachlaß (1898–1925). Edited by Eduard Marbach. *Husserliana,* Vol. 23. The Hague: Martinus Nijhoff, 1980.

Einleitung in die Logik und Erkenntnistheorie: Vorlesungen 1906/1907. Edited by Ulrich Melle. *Husserliana,* Vol. 24. The Hague: Martinus Nijhoff, 1984.

Aufsätze und Vorträge (1911–1921). Edited by Thomas Nenon and Hans Sepp. *Husserliana,* Vol. 25. Dordrecht: Martinus Nijhoff, 1987.

Vorlesungen über Bedeutungslehre: Sommersemester 1908. Edited by Ursula Panzer. *Husserliana,* Vol. 26. Dordrecht: Martinus Nijhoff, 1987.

Aufsätze und Vorträge (1922–1937). Edited by Thomas Nenon and Hans Rainer Sepp. *Husserliana,* Vol. 27. Dordrecht: Kluwer Academic Publishers, 1989.

Vorlesungen über Ethik und Wertlehre, 1908–1914. Edited by Ullrich Melle. *Husserliana,* Vol. 28. Dordrecht: Kluwer Academic Publishers, 1988.

Die Krisis der europäischen Wissenschaften und die transzendentale Phänomenologie: Ergänzungsband. Texte aus dem Nachlaß 1934–1937. Edited by Reinhold Smid. *Husserliana,* Vol. 29. Dordrecht: Kluwer Academic Publishers, 1993.

HUSSERL MANUSCRIPTS

"Einleitung in die Philosophie (1922/23)," B I 37, F I 29, M II 36, F II 3, and B IV 2.

[No title]. F IV 1 (various dates).

"Phänomenologische Methode und Phänomenologische Philosophie," F II 3 (1922), M II 3 (Landgrebe's transcription).

"Transzendentale 'Logik,' Vorlesungen WS 1920/21, Urkonstitution. 2. Teil." F I 38 (1920–1926).

"Vorlesung, Transzendentale Logik 1920/21. 1. Teil." F I 37 (1920–1926).

"Vorlesungen über transzendentale Logik 1920/21. 3. Teil." F I 39 (1920–1926).

Other Editions of Husserl's Works

Grundprobleme der Phänomenologie, 1910/1911. Edited by Iso Kern. Hamburg, 1977. [Texts from *Husserliana,* Vol. 13.]

Die Idee der Phänomenologie. Edited by Paul Janssen. Hamburg, 1986. [Text from *Husserliana,* Vol. 2.]

Die Konstitution der geistigen Welt. Edited by Manfred Sommers. Hamburg, 1984. [Text from *Husserliana,* Vol. 4.]

Phänomenologie der Lebenswelt: Ausgewählte Texte II. Edited by Klaus Held. Stuttgart: Phillip Reclam, 1986.

Die Phänomenologie und die Fundamente der Wissenschaften. Edited by Karl Heinz Lembeck. Hamburg, 1986. [Text from *Husserliana,* Vol. 5.]

Die phänomenologische Methode: Ausgewählte Texte I. Edited by Klaus Held. Stuttgart: Phillip Reclam, 1985.

Studienausgabe by the Felix Meiner Verlag

Gesammelte Schriften. Edited by Elizabeth Ströker. 8 vols. Hamburg, 1992. [Texts from *Husserliana,* Vols. 1, 3, 6, 7, 8, 12, 17, 18, and 19.]

Texte zur Phänomenologie des inneren Zeitbewusstseins (1893–1917). Edited by Rudolf Bernet. Hamburg, 1985. [Text from *Husserliana,* Vol. 10.]

Husserl's Correspondence

Briefwechsel. Edited by Karl Schuhmann in connection with Elisabeth Schuhmann. *Husserliana Dokumente,* Vol. 3. Dordrecht: Kluwer Academic Publishers, 1994.

Vol. 3/1. *Die Brentanoschule.*
Vol. 3/2. *Die Münchener Phänomenologen.*
Vol. 3/3. *Die Göttinger Schule.*
Vol. 3/4. *Die Freiburger Schule.*
Vol. 3/5. *Die Neukantianer.*
Vol. 3/6. *Philosophische Briefe.*
Vol. 3/7. *Wissenschaftler Korrespondenz.*
Vol. 3/8. *Institutionelle Schreiben.*
Vol. 3/9. *Familienbriefe.*
Vol. 3/10. *Einfuhrung und Register.*

Briefe an Roman Ingarden. The Hague: Martinus Nijhoff, 1968.

Additional Husserliana Documents

Fink, Eugen. *VI. Cartesianische Meditation.* Part 1, *Die Idee einer transzendentalen Methodenlehre.* Part 2, *Ergänzungsband. Husserliana Dokumente,* Vol. 2/1 and 2/2. Dordrecht: Kluwer Academic Publishers, 1988.

Fink, Eugen. *Sixth Cartesian Meditation: The Idea of a Transcendental Theory of Method.* Translated by Ronald Bruzina. Bloomington: Indiana University Press, 1994.

Schuhmann, Karl. *Husserl-Chronik: Denk- und Lebensweg Husserls. Husserliana Dokumente,* Vol. 1. The Hague: Martinus Nijhoff, 1977.

Other Works of Husserl

"Randbemerkungen Husserls zu Heideggers *Sein und Zeit* und *Kant und das Problem der Metaphysik.*" Edited by Roland Breeur. *Husserl Studies* 11 (1994): 3–63.

English Translations of Works by Husserl

"The Apodicticity of Recollection." Translated by Deborah Chaffin. *Husserl Studies* 2 (1985): 10–32.

Cartesian Meditations: An Introduction to Phenomenology. Translated by Dorion Cairns. The Hague: Martinus Nijhoff, 1960.

The Crisis of European Sciences and Transcendental Phenomenology: An Introduction to Phenomenological Philosophy. Translated by David Carr. Evanston, Ill.: Northwestern University Press, 1970.

Experience and Judgment: Investigations in a Genealogy of Logic. Translated by James Churchill and Karl Ameriks. Evanston, Ill.: Northwestern University Press, 1973.

Formal and Transcendental Logic. Translated by Dorion Cairns. The Hague: Martinus Nijhoff, 1969.

Husserl: Shorter Works. Edited by Peter McCormick and Frederick Elliston. Notre Dame, Ind.: University of Notre Dame Press, 1981.

The Idea of Phenomenology. Translated by William Alston and George Nakhnikian. The Hague: Martinus Nijhoff, 1964.
Ideas: General Introduction to Pure Phenomenology. Translated by W. R. Boyce Gibson. London: George Allen & Unwin, 1931.
Ideas Pertaining to a Pure Phenomenology and to a Phenomenological Philosophy. Book 1: *General Introduction to a Pure Phenomenology.* Translated by F. Kersten. *Collected Works,* Vol. 2. The Hague: Martinus Nijhoff, 1983.
Ideas Pertaining to a Pure Phenomenology and to a Phenomenological Philosophy. Book 2: *Studies in the Phenomenology of Constitution.* Translated by Richard Rojcewicz and André Schuwer. *Collected Works,* Vol. 3. Dordrecht: Kluwer Academic Publishers, 1989.
Ideas Pertaining to a Pure Phenomenology and to a Phenomenological Philosophy. Book 3: *Phenomenology and the Foundations of the Sciences.* Translated by Ted Klein and William Pohl. *Collected Works,* Vol. 1. The Hague: Martinus Nijhoff, 1980.
"Kant and the Idea of Transcendental Philosophy." *Southwestern Journal of Philosophy* 5 (Fall 1974): 9-56.
Logical Investigations. Translated by J. N. Findlay. 2 vols. New York: Humanities Press, 1970.
On the Phenomenology of the Consciousness of Internal Time (1893-1917). Translated by John Brough. *Collected Works,* Vol. 4. Dordrecht: Kluwer Academic Publishers, 1991.
The Paris Lectures. Translated by P. Koestenbaum. The Hague: Martinus Nijhoff, 1967.
Phenomenological Psychology: Lectures, Summer Semester, 1925. Translated by John Scanlon. The Hague: Martinus Nijhoff, 1977.
The Phenomenology of Internal Time Consciousness. Translated by James Churchill. Bloomington: Indiana University Press, 1964.
"Philosophy as Rigorous Science." *Phenomenology and the Crisis of Philosophy.* Translated by Quentin Lauer. New York: Harper and Row, 1965. Pp. 71-147.

WORKS BY OTHER PHILOSOPHERS

Adorno, Theodor. *Gesammelte Schriften.* Vol. 6: *Jargon der Eigentlichkeit,* 413-526. Frankfurt am Main: Suhrkamp, 1973. *The Jargon of Authenticity.* Translated by Knut Tarnowski and Frederic Will. London: Routledge & Kegan Paul, 1973.
——. *Zur Metakritik der Erkenntnistheorie.* Frankfurt am Main: Suhrkamp, 1970. *Against Epistemology: A Metacritique.* Translated by Willis Domingo. Cambridge, Mass.: MIT Press, 1982.
Aguirre, Antonio. *Genetische Phanomenologie und Reduktion. Phaenomenologica,* Vol. 38. The Hague: Martinus Nijhoff, 1970.
Apel, Karl-Otto. *Transformation der Philosophie.* Vol. 1: *Sprachanalytik, Semiotik, Hermeneutik.* Vol. 2: *Apriori der Kommunikationsgemeinschaft.* Frankfurt am Main: Suhrkamp, 1973. *Towards a Transformation of Philosophy.* Translated by Glyn Adey and David Frisby. Boston: Routledge & Kegan Paul, 1980.
Aristotle. *De Interpretatione. The Basic Works of Aristotle.* Edited by Richard McKeon. New York: Random House, 1941.
——. *The Metaphysics.* Translated by Hugh Tredennich. Cambridge, Mass.: Harvard University Press, 1933.
Aristotle's Metaphysics. Translated by W. D. Ross. Oxford: Clarendon Press, 1924.
Austin, J. L. *How to Do Things with Words.* 2nd ed. Cambridge, Mass.: Harvard University Press, [1962] 1975.

Bachelard, Susanne. *A Study of Husserl's Formal and Transcendental Logic.* Translated by Lester Embree. Evanston, Ill.: Northwestern University Press, 1968.

Bacon, Francis. *Novum Organum. The Works of Francis Bacon.* Edited by J. Spedding. London: Longman, 1857.

Barsalou, Lawrence. "Frames, Concepts and Conceptual Fields." *Frames, Fields, and Contrasts: New Essays in Semantic and Lexical Organization.* Hillsdale, N.J.: Lawrence Erlbaum Associates, 1992. Pp. 21–74.

Barth, Karl. *The Epistle to the Romans.* Translated by Edwyn Hoskyns. London: Oxford University Press, 1933.

Becker, Oskar. "Die Philosophie von Edmund Husserl." *Kant Studien* 38 (1933): 319–383. "The Philosophy of Edmund Husserl." Translated by R. O. Elveton. *The Phenomenology of Husserl.* Edited by R. O. Elveton. Chicago: Quadrangle Books, 1970. Pp. 40–72.

Becker, Wolfgang. "Kritik und Begründung in transzendentaler Argumentation." *Kant-Studien* 76 (1986): 170–195.

Bell, David. *Husserl.* London: Routledge, 1990.

Berger, Gaston. *Le cogito dans la philosophie de Husserl.* Paris: Aubier, 1941. *The "Cogito" in Husserl's Philosophy.* Translated by Kathleen McLaughlin. Evanston, Ill.: Northwestern University Press, 1972.

Bernet, Rudolf. "Einleitung" and "Editorischer Bericht." Edmund Husserl, *Texte zur Phänomenologie des inneren Zeitbewusstseins (1893–1917).* Edited by Rudolf Bernet. Hamburg: Felix Meiner Verlag, 1985. Pp. xi–lxvii, lxix–lxxiii.

———. "Husserls Begriff des Noema." *Husserl-Ausgabe und Husserl-Forschung.* Dordrecht: Kluwer Academic Publishers, 1990. Pp. 61–80.

———. "An Intentionality without Subject or Object?" *Man and World* 20 (1994): 231–255.

———. "Die ungegenwärtige Gegenwart: Anwesenheit und Abwesenheit in Husserls Analyse des Zeitbewußtseins." *Zeit und Zeitlichkeit bei Husserl und Heidegger. Phänomenologische Forschungen* 14 (1983): 16–57.

Bernet, Rudolf, Iso Kern, and Eduard Marbach. *Edmund Husserl: Darstellung seines Denkens.* Hamburg: Felix Meiner Verlag, 1989. *An Introduction to Husserlian Phenomenology.* Evanston, Ill.: Northwestern University Press, 1993.

Biemel, Walter. "Husserls Encyclopaedia-Britannica Artikel and Heideggers Anmerkungen dazu." *Tijdschrift voor Filosofie* 12 (1950): 246–280. "Husserl's *Encyclopaedia Britannica* Article and Heidegger's Remarks Thereon." *Husserl: Expositions and Appraisals.* Edited by Peter McCormick and Frederick Elliston. Notre Dame, Ind.: University of Notre Dame Press, 1977. Pp. 286–303.

Blumenberg, Hans. "Parallelaktion einer Begriffsbildung: Husserl, Hofmannsthal und die Lebenswelt." *Neue Zürcher Zeitung,* December 12 and 13, 1987.

Boehm, Rudolf. "Einleitung." *Zur Phänomenologie des inneren Zeitbewußtseins (1893–1917).* Edited by Rudolf Boehm. *Husserliana,* Vol. 10. The Hague: Martinus Nijhoff, 1966. Pp. xiii–xliii.

Brough, John. "The Emergence of an Absolute Consciousness in Husserl's Early Writings on Time-Consciousness." *Man and World* 5 (1972): 298–326. Reprinted in *Husserl: Expositions and Appraisals.* Edited by Frederick Elliston and Peter McCormick. Notre Dame, Ind.: University of Notre Dame Press, 1977. Pp. 83–100.

———. "Translator's Introduction." *On the Phenomenology of the Consciousness of Internal Time (1893–1917).* Translated by John Brough. *Collected Works,* Vol. 4. Dordrecht: Kluwer Academic Publishers, 1991. Pp. xi–lvii.

Bruzina, Ronald. "Introduction." Eugen Fink, *Sixth Cartesian Meditation: The Idea of a Transcendental Theory of Method.* Translated by Ronald Bruzina. Bloomington: Indiana University Press, 1994. Pp. vii–xcii.

———. "Die Notizen Eugen Finks zur Umarbeitung von Edmund Husserls Cartesianischen Meditationen." *Husserl Studies* 6 (1989): 97–128.

———. "Solitude and Community in the Work of Philosophy: Husserl and Fink 1928–1938." *Man and World* 22 (1989): 287–314.

Bubner, Rüdiger. "Kant, Transcendental Arguments and the Problem of Deduction." *Review of Metaphysics* 28 (1975): 453–467.

Cairns, Dorion. *Conversations with Husserl and Fink.* Edited by Richard Zaner. *Phaenomenologica,* Vol. 66. The Hague: Martinus Nijhoff, 1976.

Caputo, John. *Radical Hermeneutics: Repetition, Deconstruction, and the Hermeneutic Project.* Bloomington: Indiana University Press, 1987.

Carr, David. *Phenomenology and the Problem of History.* Evanston, Ill.: Northwestern University Press, 1974.

Crowell, Steven. "Husserl, Heidegger and Transcendental Philosophy: Another Look at the Encyclopaedia Britannica Article." *Philosophy and Phenomenological Research* 50 (March 1990): 501–518.

Dastur, Françoise. "Finitude and Repetition in Husserl and Derrida." *Spindel Conference 1993: Derrida's Interpretation of Husserl.* Edited by Leonard Lawlor. *Southern Journal of Philosophy* 32, Supplement (1994): 113–130.

De Almeida, Guido Antonio. *Sinn und Inhalt in der genetischen Phanomenologie E. Husserls. Phaenomenologica,* Vol. 47. The Hague: Martinus Nijhoff, 1972.

Derrida, Jacques. *Edmund Husserl's l'origin de la géométrie.* Translated and with an introduction by Jacques Derrida. Paris: Presses Universitaires de France, 1974. *Edmund Husserl's Origin of Geometry: An Introduction.* Translated by John Leavey. Atlantic Highlands, N.J.: Nicholas Hays, 1977; reprinted University of Nebraska Press, 1989.

———. *De la grammatologie.* Paris: Les Editions de Minuit, 1967. *Of Grammatology.* Translated by Gayatri Spivak. Baltimore: Johns Hopkins University Press, 1976.

———. *Le problème de la genèse dans la philosophie de Husserl.* Paris: Presses Universitaires de France, 1990.

———. *La voix et le phénomène.* Paris: Presses Universitaires de France, 1967. *Speech and Phenomena.* Translated by David B. Allison. Evanston, Ill.: Northwestern University Press, 1973.

Descartes, René. *Meditations on First Philosophy* [1641]. Translated by John Cottingham. *The Philosophical Writings of Descartes.* Edited and translated by John Cottingham, Robert Stoothalf, and Dugald Murdock. Cambridge: Cambridge University Press, 1985. II, 3–62.

Dreyfus, Hubert. "Introduction." *Husserl, Intentionality, and Cognitive Science.* Edited by Hubert Dreyfus. Cambridge, Mass.: MIT Press, 1982. Pp. 1–27.

———. "The Perceptual Noema: Gurwitsch's Crucial Contribution." *Life-World and Consciousness: Essays for Aron Gurwitsch.* Edited by Lester Embree. Evanston, Ill.: Northwestern University Press, 1972. Pp. 135–170. Reprinted in *Husserl, Intentionality, and Cognitive Science.* Edited by Hubert Dreyfus. Cambridge, Mass.: MIT Press, 1982. Pp. 97–123.

Dreyfus, Hubert, ed. *Husserl, Intentionality, and Cognitive Science.* Cambridge, Mass.: MIT Press, 1982.

Drummond, John. *Husserlian Intentionality and Non-Foundational Realism: Noema and Object.* Dordrecht: Kluwer Academic Publishers, 1990.

Dummett, Michael. *The Origins of Analytical Philosophy.* Cambridge, Mass.: Harvard University Press, 1994.

Elveton, R. O., ed. *The Phenomenology of Husserl.* Chicago: Quadrangle Books, 1970.

Evans, Claude. *Strategies of Deconstruction: Derrida and the Myth of the Voice.* Minneapolis: University of Minnesota Press, 1991.

Fillmore, Charles, and Beryl Atkins. "Toward a Frame-Based Lexicon: The Semantics of RISK and Its Neighbors." *Frames, Fields and Contrasts: New Essays in Semantic and Lexical Organization.* Edited by Eva Feder Kittay and Adrienne Lehrer. Hillsdale, N.J.: Lawrence Erlbaum Associates, 1992. Pp. 75–102.

Fink, Eugen. "Die phänomenologische Philosophie Edmund Husserls in der gegenwärtigen Kritik." *Kantstudien* 38 (1933): 321–383. "The Phenomenological Philosophy of Edmund Husserl and Contemporary Criticism." Translated by R. O. Elveton. *The Phenomenology of Husserl.* Edited by R. O. Elveton. Chicago: Quadrangle Books, 1970. Pp. 73–147.

Føllesdal, Dagfinn. "Husserl's Notion of Noema." *Journal of Philosophy* 66 (October 16, 1969): 680–687. Reprinted in *Husserl, Intentionality, and Cognitive Science.* Edited by Hubert Dreyfus. Cambridge, Mass.: MIT Press, 1982. Pp. 73–80.

Frank, Manfred. "Selbstbewußtsein und Rationalität." *Grenzbestimmungen der Vernunft.* Edited by Petra Kolmer and Harald Korten. Freiburg: Verlag Karl Alber, 1994. Pp. 389–438.

———. *Selbstbewußtsein und Selbsterkenntnis.* Stuttgart: Phillip Reclam, 1991.

———. *Die Unhintergehbarkeit von Individualitat.* Frankfurt am Main: Suhrkamp, 1986.

Frege, Gottlob. *Kleine Schriften.* Edited by Ignacio Angelelli. Hildesheim: Georg Olms, 1967. *Translations from the Philosophical Writings of Gottlob Frege.* Edited by Peter Geach and Max Black. Oxford: Basil Blackwell, 1966.

Gasché, Rodolphe. *The Tain of the Mirror: Derrida and the Philosophy of Reflection.* Cambridge, Mass.: Harvard University Press, 1986.

Genova, A. C. "Good Transcendental Arguments." *Kant-Studien* 75 (1984): 469–495.

Gurwitsch, Aron. *Marginal Consciousness.* Edited by Lester Embree. Athens: Ohio University Press, 1985.

———. *Studies in Phenomenology and Psychology.* Evanston, Ill.: Northwestern University Press, 1966.

Habermas, Jurgen. "Erkenntnis und Interesse." *Technik und Wissenschaft als "Ideologie."* Frankfurt am Main: Suhrkamp, 1968. Pp. 146–168. "Knowledge and Human Interest: A General Perspective." *Knowledge and Human Interests.* Translated by Jeremy J. Shapiro. Boston: Beacon Press, 1971. Pp. 301–317.

———. *Theorie des kommunikativen Handelns.* Vol. 1: *Handlungsrationalität und gesellschaftliche Rationalisierung;* Vol. 2: *Zur Kritik der funktionalistischen Vernunft.* Frankfurt am Main: Suhrkamp, 1981. *The Theory of Communicative Action.* Vol. 1: *Reason and the Rationalization of Society;* Vol. 2: *Lifeworld and System: A Critique of Functionalist Reason.* Translated by Thomas McCarthy. Boston: Beacon Press, 1984, 1987.

———. *Vorstudien und Ergänzungen zur Theorie des kommunikativen Handelns.* Frankfurt am Main: Suhrkamp, 1984.

Hall, Harrison. "Intentionality and World: Division I of *Being and Time.*" *The Cambridge*

Companion to Heidegger. Edited by Charles Guignon. Cambridge: Cambridge University Press, 1993. Pp. 122–140.

Heidegger, Martin. *Basic Writings.* Edited by David Krell. Revised and expanded edition. New York: Harper and Row, 1993.

———. "Bauen Wohnen Denken." *Vorträge und Aufsätze.* Pfullingen: Neske, 1967. II, 19–36. "Building Dwelling Thinking." *Basic Writings.* Edited by David Krell. New York: Harper and Row, 1977. Pp. 319–339.

———. *Die Grundprobleme der Phänomenologie.* Edited by Friedrich-Wilhelm von Herrmann. Gesamtausgabe, Vol. 24. Frankfurt am Main: Vittorio Klostermann, 1989. *The Basic Problems of Phenomenology.* Translated by Albert Hofstadter. Bloomington: Indiana University Press, 1982.

———. "Nachwort zu: 'Was ist Metaphysik?'" [1943]. *Wegmarken.* Frankfurt am Main: Vittorio Klostermann, 1967. Pp. 99–108.

———. *On Time and Being.* Translated by Joan Stambaugh. New York: Harper and Row, 1972.

———. *Prolegomena zur Geschichte des Zeitbegriffs.* Frankfurt am Main: Vittorio Klostermann, 1979. *History of the Concept of Time.* Translated by Theodore Kisiel. Bloomington: Indiana University Press, 1985.

———. *Sein und Zeit* [1928]. Tübingen: Max Niemeyer, 1967. *Being and Time.* Translated by John Macquarrie and Edward Robinson. New York: Harper and Row, 1962.

———. "Vom Wesen des Grundes." *Festschrift: Edmund Husserl zum 70. Geburtstag gewidmet.* Ergänzungsband zum *Jahrbuch für Philosophie und Phänomenologische Forschung.* Halle a.d. Saale: Max Niemeyer, 1929. Pp. 71–110. "Vom Wesen des Grundes" [1929]. *Wegmarken.* Frankfurt am Main: Vittorio Klostermann, 1967. Pp. 21–71. *The Essence of Reasons.* Bilingual edition. Translated by Terrence Malick. Evanston, Ill.: Northwestern University Press, 1969.

———. *Was ist Metaphysik?* [1929]. *Wegmarken.* Frankfurt am Main: Vittorio Klostermann, 1967. Pp. 1–19.

Held, Klaus. "Edmund Husserl." *Klassiker der Philosophie.* Edited by Otfried Höffe. Munich: Verlag C. H. Beck. II, 274–297.

———. "Einleitung [I]." Edmund Husserl. *Die phänomenologische Methode: Ausgewählte Texte I.* Edited by Klaus Held. Stuttgart: Phillip Reclam, 1985. Pp. 5–51. Klaus Held. "The Phenomenological Reduction." Translated by Lanei Rodemeyer. *Husserl: A Critical Reader.* Edited by Donn Welton. Forthcoming. (Translation of "Einleitung [I].")

———. "Einleitung [II]." Edmund Husserl. *Phänomenologie der Lebenswelt. Ausgewählte Texte II.* Edited by Klaus Held. Stuttgart: Phillip Reclam, 1986. Pp. 5–53. Klaus Held. "Phenomenology of the Lifeworld." Translated by Lanei Rodemeyer. *Husserl: A Critical Reader.* Edited by Donn Welton. Forthcoming. (Translation of "Einleitung [II].")

———. *Heraklit, Parmenides und der Anfang von Philosophie und Wissenschaft: Eine phänomenologische Besinnung.* Berlin: de Gruyter, 1980.

———. *Lebendige Gegenwart: Die Frage nach der Seinsweise des transzendentalen Ich bei Edmund Husserl, entwickelt am Leitfaden der Zeitproblematik. Phaenomenologica,* Vol. 23. The Hague: Martinus Nijhoff, 1966.

———. "Lebenswelt." *Theologische Realenzyklopädie,* 20: 594–600.

Henrich, Dieter. "Ding an sich: Ein Prolegomenon zur Metaphysik des Endlichen." *Ver-*

nunft des Glaubens. Edited by J. Rohls and G. Wenz. Göttingen: Vandenhoeck & Ruprecht, 1989. Pp. 42–92.

———. "Selbstbewußtsein—Kritische Einleitung in eine Theorie." *Hermeneutik und Dialektik.* Edited by R. Bubner et al. Tübingen: J. C. B. Mohr [Siebeck], 1970. I, 257–284.

Hogrebe, W. "Konstitution." *Historisches Wörterbuch der Philosophie.* Edited by J. Ritter and K. Gründer. Darmstadt: Wissenschaftliche Buchgesellschaft, 1976. IV, 992ff.

Holenstein, Elmar. *Phänomenologie der Assoziation: Zu Struktur und Funktion eines Grundprinzips der passiven Genesis bei E. Husserl. Phaenomenologica,* Vol. 44. The Hague: Martinus Nijhoff, 1972.

———. *Roman Jakobson's Approach to Language: Phenomenological Structuralism.* Translated by Catherine Schelbert and Tarcisius Schelbert. Bloomington: Indiana University Press, 1976.

Horowitz, Tamara. "A Priori Truth." *Journal of Philosophy* 82/5 (May 1985): 225–239.

Hoy, David. "Heidegger and the Hermeneutic Turn." *The Cambridge Companion to Heidegger.* Edited by Charles Guignon. Cambridge: Cambridge University Press, 1993. Pp. 170–194.

Hoyos, Vásquez. *Intentionalität als Verantwortung. Phaenomenologica,* Vol. 67. The Hague: Martinus Nijhoff, 1976.

Ihde, Don. *Technology and the Lifeworld: From Garden to Earth.* Bloomington: Indiana University Press, 1990.

Jacobi, Heinrich. *Über die Lehre des Spinoza in Briefen an Herrn Moses Mendelssohn.* Breslau, 1789.

Jakobson, Roman. *Selected Writings.* Vols. 1–7. The Hague: Mouton, 1962–1986.

———. *Word and Language.* Vol. 2: *Selected Writings.* The Hague: Mouton, 1971.

Janssen, Paul. *Geschichte und Lebenswelt: Ein Beitrag zur Diskussion von Husserls Spätwerk. Phaenomenologica,* Vol. 35. The Hague: Martinus Nijhoff, 1970.

Kant, Immanuel. *Kritik der reinen Vernunft* [1st ed. 1781; 2nd ed. 1787]. Edited by Raymund Schmidt. Hamburg: Felix Meiner Verlag, 1952. *Critique of Pure Reason.* Translated by Norman Kemp Smith. London: Macmillan Press, 1933.

———. *Prolegomena zu einer jeden künftigen Metaphysik die als Wissenschaft wird auftreten können* [1st ed. 1783]. *Werke in zehn Bänden,* Vol. 5: *Schriften zur Metaphysik und Logik.* Darmstadt: Wissenschaftliche Buchgesellschaft, 1968. *Prolegomena to Any Future Metaphysics.* Translated by Lewis White Beck. Indianapolis: Bobbs-Merrill, 1950.

Kerckhoven, Guy van. "Die Grundansätze von Husserls Konfrontation mit Dilthey im Lichte der geschichtlichen Selbstzeugnisse." *Dilthey und der Wandel des Philosophiebegriffs seit dem 19. Jahrhundert. Phänomenologische Forschungen* 16 (1985): 134–160.

———. "Zur Genese des Begriffs 'Lebenswelt' bei Edmund Husserl." *Archiv für Begriffsgeschichte* 29 (1985): 182–203.

Kern, Iso. "Die drei Wege zur transzendentalen phänomenologischen Reduktion in der Philosophie Edmund Husserls." *Tijdschrift voor Filosofie* 24 (1962): 303–349. "The Three Ways to the Transcendental Phenomenological Reduction in the Philosophy of Edmund Husserl." *Husserl: Expositions and Appraisals.* Edited by F. Elliston and P. McCormick. Notre Dame, Ind.: University of Notre Dame Press, 1977. Pp. 126–149.

———. "Einleitung [I] des Herausgebers." Edmund Husserl, *Zur Phänomenologie der Intersubjektivität, Erster Teil: 1905–1920.* Edited by Iso Kern. *Husserliana,* Vol. 13. The Hague: Martinus Nijhoff, 1973. Pp. xvii–xlviii.

———. "Einleitung [II] des Herausgebers." Edmund Husserl, *Zur Phänomenologie der Intersubjektivität, Zweiter Teil: 1921–1928.* Edited by Iso Kern. *Husserliana,* Vol. 14. The Hague: Martinus Nijhoff, 1973. Pp. xvii–xxxv.

———. "Einleitung [III] des Herausgebers." Edmund Husserl, *Zur Phänomenologie der Intersubjektivität, Dritter Teil: 1929–1935.* Edited by Iso Kern. *Husserliana,* Vol. 15. The Hague: Martinus Nijhoff, 1973. Pp. xv–lxx.

———. *Husserl und Kant: Eine Untersuchung über Husserls Verhältnis zu Kant und zum Neukantianismus. Phaenomenologica,* Vol. 16. The Hague: Martinus Nijhoff, 1964.

Kittay, Eva Feder, and Adrienne Lehrer. "Introduction." *Frames, Fields, and Contrasts: New Essays in Semantic and Lexical Organization.* Edited by Eva Feder Kittay and Adrienne Lehrer. Hillsdale, N.J.: Lawrence Erlbaum Associates, 1992. Pp. 1–18.

Kittay, Eva Feder, and Adrienne Lehrer, eds. *Frames, Fields, and Contrasts: New Essays in Semantic and Lexical Organization.* Hillsdale, N.J.: Lawrence Erlbaum Associates, 1992.

Kockelman, Joseph. *Edmund Husserl's Phenomenology.* West Lafayette, Ind.: Purdue University Press, 1994.

Landgrebe, Ludwig. "Husserls Abschied vom Cartesianismus." *Philosophische Rundschau* 9 (1962): 133–177. Reprinted in Ludwig Landgrebe, *Der Weg der Phänomenologie.* Gütersloh: Gerd Mohn, 1967. Pp. 163–206. "Husserl's Departure from Cartesianism." *The Phenomenology of Edmund Husserl: Six Essays.* Edited by Donn Welton. Ithaca, N.Y.: Cornell University Press, 1981. Pp. 66–121.

———. *The Phenomenology of Edmund Husserl: Six Essays.* Edited by Donn Welton. Ithaca, N.Y.: Cornell University Press, 1981.

Lawlor, Leonard, ed. *Spindel Conference 1993: Derrida's Interpretation of Husserl. Southern Journal of Philosophy* 32, Supplement (1994).

Levinas, Emmanuel. *La théorie de l'intuition dans la phénoménologie de Husserl.* Paris: Alcon, 1930; Vrin, 1963. *The Theory of Intuition in the Phenomenology of Husserl.* Translated by André Orianne. Evanston, Ill.: Northwestern University Press, 1973.

Lohmar, Dieter. "Zu der Entstehung und den Ausgangsmaterialien von Edmund Husserls Werk *Erfahrung und Urteil.*" *Husserl Studies* 13 (1996): 31–71.

Luxemburg, Rosa. *Selected Political Writings of Rosa Luxemburg.* Edited by Dick Howard. New York: Monthly Review Press, 1971.

Malick, Terrence. "Translator's Introduction." *The Essence of Reasons.* Bilingual edition. Translated by Terrence Malick. Evanston, Ill.: Northwestern University Press, 1969. Pp. xi–xviii.

McIntyre, Ronald. "Husserl and Frege." *Journal of Philosophy* 84 (October 1987): 528–535.

———. "Husserl and the Representational Theory of Mind." *Topoi* 5 (1986): 101–113.

———. "Searle on Intentionality." *Inquiry* 27 (1984): 468–483.

McIntyre, Ronald, and David Smith. *Husserl and Intentionality: A Study of Mind, Meaning, and Language.* Dordrecht: D. Reidel, 1982.

———. "Husserl's Identification of Meaning and Noema." *Monist* 59 (January 1975): 115–132. Reprinted in *Husserl, Intentionality, and Cognitive Science.* Edited by Hubert Dreyfus. Cambridge, Mass.: MIT Press, 81–92.

———. "Intentionality via Intentions." *Journal of Philosophy* 68 (September 16, 1971): 541–561.

Merleau-Ponty, Maurice. *Phénoménologie de la perception.* Paris: Gallimard, 1945. *Phe-*

nomenology of Perception. Translated by Colin Smith. London: Routledge & Kegan Paul, 1962.

——. *Le visible et l'invisible.* Paris: Gallimard, 1964. *The Visible and the Invisible.* Translated by Alphonso Lingis. Evanston, Ill.: Northwestern University Press, 1964.

Mertens, Karl. *Zwischen Letztbegründung und Skepsis: Kritische Untersuchungen zum Selbstverständnis der transzendentalen Phänomenologie Edmund Husserls. Orbis Phaenomenologicus,* Section VI, Vol. 1. Freiburg: Verlag Karl Alber, 1996.

Misch, Georg. *Lebensphilosophie und Phänomenologie: Eine Auseinandersetzung der Dilthey'schen Richtung mit Heidegger und Husserl.* Bonn, 1930; Darmstadt: Wissenschaftliche Buchgesellschaft, 1975. Originally published in three installments in the *Philosophischer Anzeiger* 3/3 (1929): 267–368; 3/3–4 (1929): 405–475; 4/3–4 (1930): 181–330.

Mohanty, J. N. *Husserl and Frege.* Bloomington: Indiana University Press, 1982.

——. *The Possibility of a Transcendental Philosophy. Phaenomenologica,* Vol. 98. The Hague: Martinus Nijhoff, 1985.

Mohanty, J. N., and William McKenna, eds. *Husserl's Phenomenology: A Textbook.* Washington, D.C.: University Press of America, 1989.

Mulligan, K., ed. *Speech Act and Sachverhalt: Reinach and the Foundations of Realist Phenomenology. Primary Sources in Phenomenology,* Vol. 1. Dordrecht: Martinus Nijhoff, 1987.

Natorp, Paul. *Allgemeine Psychologie nach kritischer Methode.* First Book, *Objekt und Methode der Psychologie* [1912]. Amsterdam: E. J. Bonset, 1965.

——. *Einleitung in die Psychologie nach kritischer Methode.* Freiburg: J. C. B. Mohr, 1888.

——. *Philosophische Systematik.* Edited by Hans Natorp. Hamburg: Felix Meiner Verlag, 1958.

Nenon, Thomas. "Epistemological or Ontological Primacy: The Notion of Foundation in the *Logical Investigations.*" *Husserl in the Contemporary Context.* Edited by Burt Hopkin. Dordrecht: Kluwer Academic Publishers, 1997. Pp. 159–177.

Null, Gilbert. "Husserl's Doctrine of Essence." *Husserl's Phenomenology: A Textbook.* Edited by J. N. Mohanty and William McKenna. Washington, D.C.: University Press of America, 1989. Pp. 69–105.

Ott, Hugo. *Martin Heidegger.* Frankfurt am Main: Campus Verlag, 1988. *Martin Heidegger.* Translated by Allan Blunden. London: Fontana Press, 1994.

Piaget, Jean. *The Mechanisms of Perception.* Translated by G. N. Seagrim. New York: Basic Books, 1969.

Plantinga, Alan. "Transworld Identity or Worldbound Individuals." *Naming, Necessity and Natural Kinds.* Edited by Stephen Schwartz. Ithaca, N.Y.: Cornell University Press, 1977. Pp. 245–266.

Plato's Republic. Translated by G. M. A. Grube. Indianapolis: Hackett, 1974.

Ricoeur, Paul. *Husserl: An Analysis of His Philosophy.* Translated by Edward Ballard and Lester Embree. Evanston, Ill.: Northwestern University Press, 1967.

Rorty, Richard. "Verification and Transcendental Arguments." *Noûs* 5 (1971): 3–14.

Rosenberg, Jay. "Transcendental Arguments Revisited." *Journal of Philosophy* 72/18 (October 23, 1975): 611–624.

Ross, James. "Semantic Contagion." *Frames, Fields, and Contrasts: New Essays in Semantic and Lexical Organization.* Edited by Eva Feder Kittay and Adrienne Lehrer. Hillsdale, N.J.: Lawrence Erlbaum Associates, 1992. Pp. 143–169.

Sallis, John. *Delimitations: Phenomenology and the End of Metaphysics.* Bloomington: Indiana University Press, 1986.

Sartre, Jean Paul. *L'être et le néant.* Paris: Librairie Gallimard, 1943. *Being and Nothingness: An Essay on Phenomenological Ontology.* Translated by Hazel Barnes. New York: Philosophical Library, 1956.

Saussure, Ferdinand de. *Cours de linguistique générale* [1916]. Translated by W. Brokin. New York: Philosophical Library, 1968.

Schuhmann, Karl. *Die Dialektik der Phänomenologie I: Husserl über Pfänder. Phaenomenologica,* Vol. 56. The Hague: Martinus Nijhoff, 1973.

———. *Die Dialektik der Phänomenologie II: Reine Phänomenologie und phänomenologische Philosophie. Phaenomenologica,* Vol. 57. The Hague: Martinus Nijhoff, 1973.

———. "Die Entwicklung der Sprechakttheorie in der Münchener Phänomenologie." *Sprache, Wirklichkeit, Bewußtsein.* Edited by E. Orth. Freiburg: Verlag Karl Alber, 1988. Pp. 133–166.

Schuhmann, Karl, and Barry Smith. "Questions: An Essay in Daubertian Phenomenology." *Philosophy and Phenomenological Research* 47 (1986): 353–384.

Searle, John. *Expression and Meaning: Studies in the Theory of Speech Acts.* Cambridge: Cambridge University Press, 1979.

———. *Minds, Brains, and Science.* Cambridge, Mass.: Harvard University Press, 1984.

———. *Speech Acts: An Essay in the Philosophy of Language.* Cambridge: Cambridge University Press, 1969.

Seebohm, Thomas. "Transcendental Phenomenology." *Husserl's Phenomenology: A Textbook.* Edited by J. N. Mohanty and William McKenna. Washington, D.C.: University Press of America, 1989. Pp. 345–385.

Smith, Barry. "Husserl, Language, and the Ontology of the Act." *Speculative Grammar, Universal Grammar, Philosophical Analysis.* Edited by D. Buzzetti and M. Ferriane. Amsterdam: Benjamins, 1987. Pp. 143–165.

———. "Logic and Formal Ontology." *Husserl's Phenomenology: A Textbook.* Edited by J. N. Mohanty and William McKenna. Washington, D.C.: University Press of America, 1989. Pp. 29–67.

Sokolowski, Robert. *Husserlian Meditations: How Words Present Things.* Evanston, Ill.: Northwestern University Press, 1974.

———. *Husserl's Concept of Constitution. Phaenomenologica,* Vol. 18. The Hague: Martinus Nijhoff, 1964.

———. *Presence and Absence: A Philosophical Investigation of Language and Being.* Bloomington: Indiana University Press, 1978.

Sommer, Manfred. "Husserls Göttinger Lebenswelt." Edmund Husserl, *Die Konstitution der geisitigen Welt.* Edited by Manfred Sommer. Hamburg: Felix Meiner Verlag, 1984. Pp. ix–xlii.

Spiegelberg, Herbert. *The Phenomenological Movement. Phaenomenologica,* Vols. 5 and 6. Third revised and enlarged edition. The Hague: Martinus Nijhoff, 1965.

Steinbock, Anthony. *Home and Beyond.* Evanston, Ill.: Northwestern University Press, 1996.

Ströker, Elizabeth. *Husserls transzendentale Phänomenologie.* Frankfurt am Main: Vittorio Klostermann, 1987. *Husserl's Transcendental Philosophy.* Translated by Lee Hardy. Stanford: Stanford University Press, 1993.

Stroud, Barry. "Transcendental Arguments." *Journal of Philosophy* 65 (1968): 241–256.

Taminiaux, Jacques. "Remarques sur Heidegger et les *Recherches Logiques* de Husserl." *Le regard et l'excédent. Phaenomenologica,* Vol. 75. The Hague: Martinus Nijhoff, 1977. Pp. 156–182. "Heidegger and Husserl's *Logical Investigations.*" *Dialectic and Difference.* Edited and translated by Robert Crease and James Decker. Atlantic Highlands, N.J.: Humanities Press, 1985. Pp. 91–114.

Taylor, Charles. "Theories of Meaning." *Philosophical Papers.* Vol. 1, *Human Agency and Language.* Cambridge: Cambridge University Press, 1985. Pp. 248–292.

———. "The Validity of Transcendental Arguments." *Aristotelian Society,* New Series, 79 (1978/79): 151–165.

Theunissen, Michael. *Der Andere.* Berlin: de Gruyter, 1965. *The Other: Studies in the Social Ontology of Husserl, Heidegger, Sartre, and Buber.* Cambridge, Mass.: MIT Press, 1984.

Thompson, Judith. "Private Language." *American Philosophical Quarterly* 1 (1964): 20–31.

Tugendhat, Ernst. *Einführung in die sprachanalytische Philosophie.* Frankfurt am Main: Suhrkamp, 1976. *Traditional and Analytical Philosophy: Lectures on the Philosophy of Language.* Translated by P. A. Garner. Cambridge: Cambridge University Press, 1982.

———. *Philosophische Aufsätze.* Frankfurt am Main: Suhrkamp, 1992.

———. *Der Wahrheitsbegriff bei Husserl und Heidegger.* Berlin: de Gruyter, 1967.

Waldenfels, Bernhard. "Hearing Oneself Speak: Derrida's Recording of the Phenomenological Voice." *Spindel Conference 1993: Derrida's Interpretation of Husserl.* Edited by Leonard Lawlor. *Southern Journal of Philosophy* 32, Supplement, 65–77.

———. *In der Netzen der Lebenswelt.* Frankfurt am Main: Suhrkamp, 1985.

Welton, Donn. "The Development of Husserl's Phenomenology." *The Essential Husserl: Basic Writings in Transcendental Phenomenology.* Edited by Donn Welton. Bloomington: Indiana University Press, 1999. Pp. ix–xv.

———. "Husserl and the Japanese." *Review of Metaphysics* 44 (March 1991): 575–606.

———. "Intentionality and Language in Husserl's Phenomenology." *Review of Metaphysics* 27 (1973): 261–297.

———. *The Origins of Meaning: A Critical Study of the Thresholds of Husserlian Phenomenology. Phaenomenologica,* Vol. 88. The Hague: Martinus Nijhoff, 1983.

———. "The Systematicity of Husserl's Transcendental Philosophy: From Static to Genetic Method." *Husserl: A Critical Reader.* Edited by Donn Welton (forthcoming).

———. "Verbindende Namen/Verbundene Gegenstände: Frege und Husserl über Bedeutung." *Phänomenologie im Widerstreit.* Edited by Christoph Jamme and Otto Pöggeler. Frankfurt am Main: Suhrkamp, 1989. Pp. 141–191.

Wittgenstein, Ludwig. *Philosophische Bemerkungen* [1930]. Edited by Rush Rhees. Werkausgabe, Vol. 2. Frankfurt am Main: Suhrkamp, 1964. *Philosophical Remarks.* Translated by Raymond Hargreaves and Ryan White. Oxford: Basil Blackwell, 1964.

———. *Preliminary Studies for the Philosophical Investigations: The Blue and Brown Books* [1933–1935]. Edited by Rush Rhees. Oxford: Basil Blackwell, 1960. *Das Blaue Buch. Eine Philosophische Betrachtung (Das Braune Buch).* Translated from the English by Petre von Morstein. Werkausgabe, Vol. 5. Frankfurt am Main: Suhrkamp, 1989.

———. *Tractatus logico-philosophicus* [1921]. Werkausgabe, Vol. I. Frankfurt am Main: Suhrkamp, 1984. *Tractatus Logico-Philosophicus.* Translated by D. Pears and B. McGuinness. London: Routledge & Kegan Paul, 1961.

Zahavi, Dan. *Husserl und die transzendentale Intersubjektivität: Eine Antwort auf die sprachpragmatische Kritik. Phaenomenologica,* Vol. 135. Dordrecht: Kluwer Academic Publishers, 1996.

——. "Husserl's Intersubjective Transformation of Transcendental Philosophy." *Journal of the British Society for Phenomenology* 27 (October 1996): 228–245.

——. *Self-Awareness and Alterity: A Phenomenological Investigation.* Evanston, Ill.: Northwestern University Press, 1999.

Index

Donn Welton is Professor of Philosophy at the State University of New York, Stony Brook. He is author of *The Origins of Meaning: A Critical Study of the Thresholds of Husserlian Phenomenology* and editor of *The Essential Husserl: Basic Writings in Transcendental Phenomenology* as well as the forthcoming *Husserl: A Critical Reader.* He has also edited and contributed to two works on the concept of body, *Body and Flesh* and *The Body.*

9 780253 21558

www.ingramcontent.com/pod-product-compliance
Ingram Content Group UK Ltd.
Pitfield, Milton Keynes, MK11 3LW, UK
UKHW030807140325
456233UK00007B/90